BAKER & TAYLOR Books

a GRACE Distribution company

Somerville Service Center
50 Kirby Avenue
P.O. Box 734
Somerville, N.J. 08876-0734

(908) 722-8000

Dear Continuation Service Manager:

The publisher asserts that all volumes of the enclosed edition have been produced in the same manner. Though the quality of these volumes is below the standard of the material Baker & Taylor Continuation Service offers, we are supplying them to fulfill our commitment of providing our customers with a continual and timely flow of material.

Thank you.

The Continuation Service

PERSONAL GROWTH AND BEHAVIOR 95/96

Fifteenth Edition

Editor

Karen G. Duffy
SUNY College, Geneseo

Karen G. Duffy holds a doctorate in psychology from Michigan State University and is currently a professor of psychology at SUNY at Geneseo. She sits on the executive board of the New York State Employees Assistance Program and is a certified community and family mediator. She is a member of the American Psychological Society and the Eastern Psychological Association.

Annual Editions
A Library of Information from the Public Press

Cover illustration by Mike Eagle

The Dushkin Publishing Group, Inc.
Sluice Dock, Guilford, Connecticut 06437

The Annual Editions Series

Annual Editions is a series of over 65 volumes designed to provide the reader with convenient, low-cost access to a wide range of current, carefully selected articles from some of the most important magazines, newspapers, and journals published today. Annual Editions are updated on an annual basis through a continuous monitoring of over 300 periodical sources. All Annual Editions have a number of features designed to make them particularly useful, including topic guides, annotated tables of contents, unit overviews, and indexes. For the teacher using Annual Editions in the classroom, an Instructor's Resource Guide with test questions is available for each volume.

Printed on Recycled Paper

VOLUMES AVAILABLE

Africa
Aging
American Foreign Policy
American Government
American History, Pre-Civil War
American History, Post-Civil War
Anthropology
Archaeology
Biology
Biopsychology
Business Ethics
Canadian Politics
Child Growth and Development
China
Comparative Politics
Computers in Education
Computers in Business
Computers in Society
Criminal Justice
Developing World
Drugs, Society, and Behavior
Dying, Death, and Bereavement
Early Childhood Education
Economics
Educating Exceptional Children
Education
Educational Psychology
Environment
Geography
Global Issues
Health
Human Development
Human Resources
Human Sexuality
India and South Asia

International Business
Japan and the Pacific Rim
Latin America
Life Management
Macroeconomics
Management
Marketing
Marriage and Family
Mass Media
Microeconomics
Middle East and the Islamic World
Money and Banking
Multicultural Education
Nutrition
Personal Growth and Behavior
Physical Anthropology
Psychology
Public Administration
Race and Ethnic Relations
Russia, the Eurasian Republics, and
    Central/Eastern Europe
Social Problems
Sociology
State and Local Government
Urban Society
Violence and Terrorism
Western Civilization,
    Pre-Reformation
Western Civilization,
    Post-Reformation
Western Europe
World History, Pre-Modern
World History, Modern
World Politics

Cataloging in Publication Data
Main entry under title: Annual editions: Personal growth and behavior. 1995/96.
        1. Personality—Periodicals. 2. Adjustment (Psychology)—Periodicals. I. Duffy, Karen G.,
comp. II. Title: Personal growth and behavior.
155'.2'05   75–20757   ISBN 1–56134–366–8

Fifteenth Edition

Printed in the United States of America

Editors/ Advisory Board

To the Reader

In publishing ANNUAL EDITIONS we recognize the enormous role played by the magazines, newspapers, and journals of the *public press* in providing current, first-rate educational information in a broad spectrum of interest areas. Within the articles, the best scientists, practitioners, researchers, and commentators draw issues into new perspective as accepted theories and viewpoints are called into account by new events, recent discoveries change old facts, and fresh debate breaks out over important controversies.

Many of the articles resulting from this enormous editorial effort are appropriate for students, researchers, and professionals seeking accurate, current material to help bridge the gap between principles and theories and the real world. These articles, however, become more useful for study when those of lasting value are carefully *collected, organized, indexed,* and *reproduced* in a *low-cost format,* which provides easy and permanent access when the material is needed. That is the role played by *Annual Editions.* Under the direction of each volume's *Editor,* who is an expert in the subject area, and with the guidance of an *Advisory Board,* we seek each year to provide in each *ANNUAL EDITION* a current, well-balanced, carefully selected collection of the best of the public press for your study and enjoyment. We think you'll find this volume useful, and we hope you'll take a moment to let us know what you think.

Have you ever watched children on a playground? Some children are reticent; they sit demurely watching the other children play and shun becoming involved in the fun. Some children readily and happily interact with their playmates. They take turns, share their toys, and follow the rules of the playground. Others are bullies who brazenly taunt the playing children and take their possessions. What makes each child so different? Do childhood behaviors forecast adult behaviors? Can children's (or for that matter, adults') antisocial behaviors be changed?

These questions are not new. Lay persons and social scientists alike have been curious about human nature for thousands of years. The answers to our questions, though, are incomplete at present because attempts to address these issues are relatively new or just developing. Psychology, the science that can and should answer questions about individual differences, and which is the primary focus of this book, is just over one hundred years old. One hundred years may seem old to you, but it is young when other disciplines are considered. Mathematics, medicine, and philosophy are thousands of years old.

Via psychology and related sciences, this anthology will help you explore the issues of individual differences and their origins, as well as methods of coping, personality change, and other issues concerning human adjustment. The purpose of this anthology is to compile the newest, most complete, and readable articles that examine individual behavior and adjustment as well as the dynamics of personal growth and interpersonal relationships. The articles in this book offer interesting insights into both the everyday and scientific worlds, a blend welcomed by most of today's specialists in human adjustment.

This anthology is revised each year and reflects both traditional viewpoints as well as emerging perspectives about people's behavior. Thanks to the advisory board's valuable advice, the present edition has been completely revised. Those of you familiar with past editions will notice that there are more new articles included in the present edition than ever before.

Annual Editions: Personal Growth and Behavior 95/96 is comprised of six units, each of which serves a distinct purpose. The first unit is concerned with issues related to self-identity. For example, one theory addressed in this anthology, humanism, hypothesizes that self-concept, our feelings about who we are and how worthy we are, is the most valuable component of personality. This unit includes companion articles that are supplemental to the theoretical articles in that they provide applications of or offer alternate perspectives to popular theories about individual differences and human adjustment.

The second unit provides information on *how* and *why* a person develops in a particular way. In other words, what factors determine or direct individual growth: physiology, heredity, experience, or some combination.

The third unit pertains to problems commonly encountered in the different stages of development: infancy, childhood, adolescence, and adulthood.

The fourth and fifth units are similar in that they address problems of adjustment—problems that occur in interpersonal relationships and problems created for individuals by the prevailing social environment. For example, unit four contains articles on topics such as competition, love, and friendship while unit five houses articles on the pace of American life, racism, and social dilemmas. The final unit focuses on adjustment, or how most people cope with some of these and other problems.

This anthology will challenge you. It will provide you with many answers, but it will also stimulate many questions. Perhaps it will inspire you to continue your study of the burgeoning field of psychology that is responsible for exploring personal growth and behavior. As has been true in the past, your feedback on this edition would be particularly valuable for future revisions. Please take a moment to fill out and return the article rating form on the last page. Thank you.

Karen Grover Duffy

Karen Grover Duffy
Editor

Unit 1

Becoming a Person: Seeking Self-Identity

Six selections discuss the psychosocial development of an individual's personality. Attention is given to values, lifestyles, and self-concept.

To the Reader iv
Topic Guide 2

Overview 4

1. **The Last Interview of Abraham Maslow,** Edward Hoffman, *Psychology Today,* January/February 1992. 6
Although initially "sold on behaviorism," Abraham Maslow became one of the founders of a comprehensive human psychology or *humanistic psychology.* In an important last interview, Maslow shares his philosophy on the nature of human beings and of the potential for world peace and understanding.

2. **Self-Esteem: The Keystone to Happiness,** Ralph Hyatt, *USA Today Magazine (Society for the Advancement of Education),* March 1991. 10
Psychologists, educators, and even legislators are convinced of the value of high *self-esteem.* Some self-tests to measure reader esteem and some guidelines for raising high-esteem children are shared with the reader.

3. **The Assault on Freud,** Paul Gray, *Time,* November 29, 1993. 12
Sigmund Freud's *psychoanalytic theory* and his famous cases are dissected in a multiplicity of new books. While most authors criticize Freud, his theory, nonetheless, has left its mark on psychiatry and psychology.

4. **Clues to the Irrational Nature of Dreams,** Sandra Blakeslee, *New York Times,* July 12, 1994. 15
The bizarre nature of dreams is beginning to make sense to scientists. Physiological, as well as psychological, examination of *sleeping* and *dreaming* are helping us understand normal states as well as *mental illness.*

5. **Piecing Together Personality,** Bruce Bower, *Science News,* March 5, 1994. 19
Current psychological research on *personality* casts doubt on traditional psychiatric diagnoses. Contemporary researchers suggest that our personalities vary along five major dimensions; this includes the personalities of those individuals with psychological disorders.

6. **Personality: Major Traits Found Stable Through Life,** Daniel Goleman, *New York Times,* June 9, 1987. 22
There are at least three major stable *traits* that do not change over a lifetime, or so say recent researchers. Their evidence contradicts the conclusions of stage theorists such as Erik Erikson and Sigmund Freud.

The concepts in bold italics are developed in the article. For further expansion please refer to the Topic Guide, the Index, and the Glossary.

Unit 2

Determinants of Behavior: Motivation, Environment, and Physiology

Nine articles examine the effects of nutrition, culture, genes, and emotions on an individual's behavior.

Overview   24

7. **Nature or Nurture? Old Chestnut, New Thoughts,** *The Economist,* December 26, 1992–January 8, 1993.   26
   Are **criminals** born or made? The age-old question about the roles of **nature and nurture** in human behavior are examined with a special eye toward the controversies this issue raises.

8. **Sizing Up the Sexes,** Christine Gorman, *Time,* January 20, 1992.   29
   Most **gender differences,** if any, are statistically small. Scientists today are taking a good look at the influence of **biology** and the **environment** on the two sexes.

9. **Born Gay?** William A. Henry III, *Time,* July 26, 1993.   34
   The origins of **homosexuality** may never be fully understood because the phenomenon is complex and varied. William Henry explores the issue of **heredity** in studies of genes, family trees, and DNA.

10. **Mapping the Brain,** *Newsweek,* April 20, 1992.   37
    By describing modern techniques for **mapping the brain** and by providing fun and modern "brainteasers," this article divulges how the brain and its various parts function to comprehend **thoughts, emotions,** and **language.**

11. **The Return of Phineas Gage: Clues About the Brain from the Skull of a Famous Patient,** Hanna Damasio, Thomas Grabowski, Randall Frank, Albert M. Galaburda, and Antonio R. Damasio, *Science,* May 20, 1994.   42
    In 1848, while working on the construction of a railroad line, Phineas Gage suffered an amazing **brain injury** and survived. He remained able-bodied and intelligent, but his respect for social conventions vanished. Modern technology and similar cases have helped scientists pinpoint a region in the frontal lobes responsible for **social cognition** and **behavior.**

12. **Understanding the Genetics Age,** Jim H. Smith, *St. Raphael's Better Health,* May/June 1994.   46
    A succinct review of the history of **genetic** studies is provided. The explosion of modern genetics research is also discussed and includes the startling discovery of genetic "cures" for such afflictions as cystic fibrosis.

13. **The Sniff of Legend,** Karen Wright, *Discover,* April 1994.   49
    Is **chemical communication** possible in humans? Common among other animals, **pheromones** and receptors for them are now thought by scientists to exist in humans as well.

The concepts in bold italics are developed in the article. For further expansion please refer to the Topic Guide, the Index, and the Glossary.

Unit 3

Problems Influencing Personal Growth

Nine articles consider aging, development, self-image, depression, and social interaction and their influences on personal growth.

14. **On the Power of Positive Thinking: The Benefits of Being Optimistic,** Michael F. Scheier and Charles S. Carver, *Current Directions in Psychological Science,* February 1993.   **54**
Two psychologists discuss **optimism** and its relationship to **psychological and physical well-being** as well as to other psychological constructs such as **self-efficacy.**

15. **The Mind and the Body,** C. David Jenkins, *World Health,* March/April 1994.   **59**
Physical illness and pain affect how we feel psychologically. Research is now demonstrating that how we feel psychologically can affect our **physical health.**

Overview   **62**

16. **Clipped Wings,** Lucile F. Newman and Stephen L. Buka, *American Educator,* Spring 1991.   **64**
A recent report for the Education Commission of the States is excerpted in this article. Details of research compilations demonstrate that **prenatal exposure** to drugs, alcohol, and nicotine hampers **children's development,** especially their **learning.**

17. **How Kids Benefit from Child Care,** Vivian Cadden, *Working Mother,* April 1993.   **70**
When surveyed, **working mothers** nearly unanimously agree that children benefit from **early child care.** The mothers report enhanced **educational** and **social development.**

18. **Rush to Judgment,** *Newsweek,* April 19, 1993.   **74**
Americans are at fever pitch over **child sex abuse.** Nearly three million children were recently reported as suspected victims. Psychologists worry that the way children are questioned and interviewed distorts their **memories** of and **testimony** about the alleged events.

19. **Why Schools Must Tell Girls: "You're Smart, You Can Do It,"** Myra Sadker and David Sadker, *USA Weekend,* February 4–6, 1994.   **79**
Boys tend to capture teachers' attention no matter what grade in **school.** To the detriment of many **girls,** education has become a spectator sport for them.

The concepts in bold italics are developed in the article. For further expansion please refer to the Topic Guide, the Index, and the Glossary.

20. Teaching Young Children to Resist Bias: What Parents Can Do, Louise Derman-Sparks, María Gutiérrez, and Carol B. Phillips, *NAEYC,* Number 565, 1989.   82

Children who harbor *bias* and children against whom *prejudice* is held both are victims robbed of certain *developmental advantages* because of bigotry. This article reveals how parents and teachers can help children mature with open minds.

21. Adolescent Childbearing: Whose Problem? What Can We Do? Diane Scott-Jones, *Phi Delta Kappan,* November 1993.   87

Young people become biologically mature at very early ages, putting biological forces at odds with societal ones. *Teen pregnancy* is not just a minority youth or a female problem. This article addresses what *society* can do about the epidemic of children bearing children.

22. Critical Life Events and the Onset of Illness, Blair Justice, *Comprehensive Therapy,* Volume 20, Number 4, 1994.   97

Feeling a *sense of control* and having *social support* help us appraise life events less negatively. Control and support serve to reduce *stress* from both positive and negative life events.

23. The New Middle Age, Melinda Beck, *Newsweek,* December 7, 1992.   104

Middle age is the least studied developmental stage. However, research has demonstrated that few of us actually struggle with a *midlife crisis.* Rather, we need to cope with certain predictable *life transitions.*

24. The Mystery of Suicide, David Gelman, *Newsweek,* April 18, 1994.   109

Through analysis of suicidal singer Kurt Cobain, David Gelman helps the reader understand the frequency of, causes of, and interventions used with those individuals who commit *suicide.*

Overview   112

25. How Competitive Are You? Josh Halberstam, *Self,* October 1993.   114

The United States is among the most competitive countries in the world. Is all this *competition* harmful? Josh Halberstam resoundingly answers "yes." He helps us recognize and manage personal competitiveness.

26. The Secret World of Siblings, *U.S. News & World Report,* January 10, 1994.   117

The importance of *siblings* is being recognized by scientists because siblings are taking over parental roles. Why siblings are similar yet different and how and why siblings develop relationships in childhood and adulthood are being scrutinized.

Unit 4

Relating to Others

Six articles examine some of the dynamics involved in relating to others. Topics discussed include friendship, love, the importance of family ties, and self-esteem.

27. **What Friends Are For,** Phillip Lopate, *Utne Reader,* 123
September/October 1993.
Phillip Lopate explores what **friendship** is, what produces friendship (e.g., similarity), and why and how friendships last. Special
friendships like those among gays and lesbians are also discussed.

28. **When the Bond Breaks,** Caroline Knapp, *Utne Reader,* 128
September/October 1993.
Some **friendships** end in a loud bang; others just die out. The
reasons friends break up vary from lack of common ground to
betrayal.

29. **What Is Love?** Paul Gray, *Time,* February 15, 1993. 131
Is **love** merely a phony emotion our pop culture celebrates?
Although unpopular, some scientists are dissecting this complex
and often celebrated **emotion.** One important study indicates
that love is found in most societies.

30. **Patterns of Abuse,** *Newsweek,* July 4, 1994. 133
Two million women are beaten every year; they are **victims of
domestic violence.** The article focuses on who they are, who the
abusers are, why the women stay or leave, and where they can
get help.

Overview 138

31. **The Dynamics of Social Dilemmas,** Natalie S. Glance 140
and Bernardo A. Huberman, *Scientific American,* March
1994.
Social dilemmas often pit the common good against selfishness.
Scientific research and theories indicate that **cooperation** cannot
generally be sustained in certain groups. The dimensions of
groups and dilemmas that impact on cooperativeness and other
processes are examined.

32. **Trying to Decipher Those Inscrutable Signs of Our** 145
Times, Richard Wolkomir, *Smithsonian,* September 1993.
All of life may be a grand theater of **communication.** Richard
Wolkomir introduces the reader to **semiotics,** the science of
signs and symbols.

33. **Crossing the Divide,** Leonard Pitts Jr., *The Miami Herald,* 149
February 14, 1993.
Leonard Pitts says the answer to America's **race relations problem** is education in conjunction with other programs such as
school desegregation and **affirmative action.** Both blacks and
whites, as well as the media, need to be pro-active to reduce racial
tension.

34. **The Ruses of Racism,** Michel Wieviorka, *The UNESCO* 152
Courier, February 1993.
Violent racism is resurfacing around the world. Sociologist Michel Wieviorka attempts to offer a variety of explanations for its
development as well as thoughtful commentary on how it perpetuates itself.

Unit 5

Dynamics of Personal Adjustment: The Individual and Society

Six selections discuss some of the problems
experienced by individuals as they attempt to adjust to
society.

The concepts in bold italics are developed in the article. For further expansion please refer to the Topic Guide, the Index, and the Glossary.

Unit 6

Enhancing Human Adjustment: Learning to Cope Effectively

Eleven selections examine some of the ways an individual learns to cope successfully within today's society. Topics discussed include therapy, depression, stress, and interpersonal relations.

35. Flirting with Disaster, Joshua Halberstam, *Self,* March 1994.   **155**

As more women enter the traditional male **workplace,** the issue of sexual harassment looms. It has not been easy for managers and legal experts to outline and reinforce proper conduct. Personal understanding of what **sexual harassment** is may be even harder to come by.

36. Media, Violence, Youth, and Society, Ray Surette, *The World & I,* July 1994.   **158**

Violence is a cultural product. Years of research have linked violence on our streets to **mass media.** The article suggests other reasons for our epidemic of violence as well as solutions for decreasing violence.

Overview   **166**

37. What You Can Change and What You Cannot Change, Martin E. P. Seligman, *Psychology Today,* May/June 1994.   **168**

Americans seem to be on constant **self-improvement** kicks, many of which fail. Martin Seligman explains which attempts to change are a waste of time and which are worthwhile. He discusses **diets** and **psychological disorders** in particular.

38. A Buyer's Guide to Psychotherapy, Frank Pittman III, *Psychology Today,* January/February 1994.   **176**

Frank Pittman discusses what **psychotherapy** is and is not. More importantly, he discusses what kinds of **therapists** are good therapists. Not all therapy and therapists are created equal.

39. The Last Self-Help Article You'll Ever Need, Susan Baxter, *Psychology Today,* March/April 1993.   **183**

Susan Baxter offers an intense, albeit humorous, attack on **self-help groups** of all types that are typically unregulated by any watchdog agencies. These groups may even be detrimental to their members. She suggests instead that we learn to focus on our own strengths and potentials.

40. The Importance of Solitude, Rae André, *Bottom Line Personal,* October 30, 1993.   **187**

We tend to distrust solitary people; however, **solitude** provides opportunities for **self-discovery** and **growth.** Ways to find solitude and how to use it once it is discovered are highlighted by Rae André.

The concepts in bold italics are developed in the article. For further expansion please refer to the Topic Guide, the Index, and the Glossary.

41. **How to Master Your Moods,** Melvin Kinder, *Psychology Digest,* Summer 1994.   **189**
Each of us has a natural **temperament** that permeates everything we do. Melvin Kinder reviews four different **mood styles** and how each can be moderated.

42. **Unload Stress for '94,** John Butterfield, *USA Weekend,* December 31, 1993–January 2, 1994.   **195**
Stress is part of the 1990s lifestyle. How to recognize, avoid, and manage stress are important skills. This article covers these aspects and includes some quick self-assessors for stress.

43. **Defeating Depression,** Nancy Wartik, *American Health,* December 1993.   **205**
Millions are afflicted with **depression.** Scientists believe a combination of **genetics, personality structure,** and **life events** triggers major depression. A self-assessment quiz is included as well as a discussion of a variety of all-important interventions.

44. **Losing Weight: What Works, What Doesn't,** *Consumer Reports,* June 1993.   **212**
Genetics plays a large role in our body shape and weight, but Americans long to be svelte. Researchers have discovered that **losing weight** can sometimes be as detrimental to our health as gaining weight.

45. **Sexual Desire,** *U.S. News & World Report,* July 6, 1992.   **219**
Sexual-desire disorders seem "epidemic" today although perhaps no more frequent than yesteryear. Various **sexual-desire disorders and their treatments** are reviewed in this article.

46. **Alcohol in Perspective,** *University of California at Berkeley Wellness Letter,* February 1993.   **224**
Alcohol can kill either by itself or as a lubricant to accidents. **Alcoholism** is treatable, but the alcoholic and the family need assistance.

47. **High Anxiety,** *Consumer Reports,* January 1993.   **227**
There are many **drugs** for the treatment of **anxiety.** This article reviews many of these drugs with an emphasis on Xanax and its effects on **panic disorder.** The conclusion is that no pill can deliver peace of mind without a price.

Glossary   **233**
Index   **241**
Article Review Form   **244**
Article Rating Form   **245**

The concepts in bold italics are developed in the article. For further expansion please refer to the Topic Guide, the Index, and the Glossary.

Topic Guide

This topic guide suggests how the selections in this book relate to topics of traditional concern to students and professionals involved with the study of personal growth and behavior. It is useful for locating articles that relate to each other for reading and research. The guide is arranged alphabetically according to topic. Articles may, of course, treat topics that do not appear in the topic guide. In turn, entries in the topic guide do not necessarily constitute a comprehensive listing of all the contents of each selection.

TOPIC AREA	TREATED IN:	TOPIC AREA	TREATED IN:
Abuse	18. Rush to Judgment 30. Patterns of Abuse	Dreams	4. Clues to the Irrational Nature of Dreams
Adolescents	21. Adolescent Childbearing 23. New Middle Age	Drug Therapy	47. High Anxiety
Alcohol/ Alcoholism	46. Alcohol in Perspective	Environment	7. Nature or Nurture? 8. Sizing Up the Sexes
Anxiety	47. High Anxiety	Friends/ Friendship	27. What Friends Are For 28. When the Bond Breaks
Brain	10. Mapping the Brain 11. Return of Phineas Gage	Freud, Sigmund	3. Assault on Freud 6. Personality
Child Abuse	18. Rush to Judgment	Genetics	8. Sizing Up the Sexes 9. Born Gay? 12. Understanding the Genetics Age
Children	16. Clipped Wings 17. How Kids Benefit from Child Care 18. Rush to Judgment 19. Why Schools Must Tell Girls: "You're Smart, You Can Do It" 20. Teaching Young Children to Resist Bias	Homosexuality	9. Born Gay?
		Humanistic Psychology	1. Last Interview of Abraham Maslow
Communication	32. Trying to Decipher Those Inscrutable Signs	Immune System/ Health	15. Mind and the Body 22. Critical Life Events
Competition	25. How Competitive Are You?	Love	29. What Is Love?
Day Care	17. How Kids Benefit from Child Care	Maslow, Abraham	1. Last Interview of Abraham Maslow
Death	24. Mystery of Suicide	Middle Age	23. New Middle Age
Depression	43. Defeating Depression	Moods	41. How to Master Your Moods 43. Defeating Depression
Development	16. Clipped Wings 17. How Kids Benefit from Child Care 18. Rush to Judgment 20. Teaching Young Children to Resist Bias	Nature/Nurture	7. Nature or Nurture? 8. Sizing Up the Sexes 9. Born Gay?
		Optimism	14. On the Power of Positive Thinking
Diets	37. What You Can Change 44. Losing Weight	Personality	5. Piecing Together Personality 6. Personality

TOPIC AREA	TREATED IN:	TOPIC AREA	TREATED IN:
Prenatal Life	16. Clipped Wings	**Sexual Harassment**	35. Flirting with Disaster
Psychotherapy	38. Buyer's Guide to Psychotherapy	**Siblings**	26. Secret World of Siblings
Racism/Prejudice	20. Teaching Young Children to Resist Bias 33. Crossing the Divide	**Sleep**	4. Clues to the Irrational Nature of Dreams
Schools	19. Why Schools Must Tell Girls: "You're Smart, You Can Do It" 33. Crossing the Divide	**Smell**	13. Sniff of Legend
		Social Dilemmas	31. Dynamics of Social Dilemmas
Self-Esteem	2. Self-Esteem	**Stress**	42. Unload Stress for '94
Self-Help/Self-Improvement	37. What You Can Change 39. Last Self-Help Article You'll Ever Need 40. Importance of Solitude 41. How to Master Your Moods	**Suicide**	24. Mystery of Suicide
		Television/Media	36. Media, Violence, Youth, and Society
Sex Differences/ Gender	8. Sizing Up the Sexes 19. Why Schools Must Tell Girls: "You're Smart, You Can Do It"	**Traits**	5. Piecing Together Personality 6. Personality
Sexuality	45. Sexual Desire	**Violence**	36. Media, Violence, Youth, and Society

Becoming a Person: Seeking Self-Identity

A baby girl sits in front of a mirror and looks at herself. A chimpanzee sorts through photographs while its trainer watches carefully for the chimp's reaction. What do each of these events have in common? If your answer is "nothing," you are wrong. Both are examples of techniques utilized to investigate self-concept.

The baby has a red dot on her nose. The researchers watch to see if the child reaches for the dot in the mirror or touches her own nose. In recognition of the fact that the image she sees in the mirror is her own, the baby touches her real nose, not the nose in the mirror.

The chimpanzee has been trained to sort photographs into piles of human or animal pictures. If the chimp has been raised with humans, the researcher wants to know into which pile (animal or human) the chimp will place its own picture. Is the chimp's concept of itself animal or human? Or does the chimp have no concept of self at all?

These research projects are designed to investigate how self-concept develops. Most psychologists believe that people develop a personal identity or a sense of self that is a sense of who we are, our likes and dislikes, our characteristic feelings and thoughts, and an understanding of why we behave as we do. Self-concept is knowledge of gender, race, and age, as well as the sense of self-worth and more. Strong positive or negative feelings are usually attached to this identity. Psychologists are studying how and when this sense of self develops. Most psychologists do not believe that infants are born with a sense of self but rather that children slowly develop self-concept as a consequence of their experiences.

This section of the book delineates some of the popular viewpoints regarding how the sense of self and personality develop and how or whether they guide behavior. This knowledge of how self develops provides an important foundation for the rest of the units in this book. In this unit, we are going to explore three major theories or forces in psychology: self or humanistic psychology, psychoanalysis, and trait theory. For many theories, we will also examine related research, applications, or concepts in companion articles.

The first two articles are devoted to humanistic psychology. In the first article, "The Last Interview of Abraham Maslow," Maslow, a founder of humanistic psychology, discusses the evolution of his theory. In the interview he discusses his philosophy of human nature and its potential for peaceful living and other positive outcomes for humans. The second article is a companion article. In "Self-Esteem: The Keystone to Happiness," the author details what self-esteem is and its history as a concept in psychology. One conclusion is that self-esteem is an overworked concept in today's literature.

The next two articles relate to psychoanalysis, a theory and form of therapy to which humanism was a reaction. The main proponent of psychoanalysis was Sigmund Freud, who believed that individuals possess a dark, lurking unconscious that often motivates negative behaviors. The article, "The Assault on Freud," delineates and critiques Freud's psychoanalytic theory, and it also includes some of his famous cases. In the second, companion article, dreams are examined. Freud claimed that the unconscious expresses itself at night in our dreams. Thus, to know more about the unconscious all we need to do is to understand or interpret our dreams. The article, "Clues to the Irrational Nature of Dreams," will help you understand sleeping and dreaming.

The next unit article offers a contrasting viewpoint of human nature known as the trait or dispositional approach. Trait theories in general hold that our personalities are comprised of various traits, possibly tied together by our self-concept. In the fifth article, "Piecing Together Personality," the author discusses personality traits that vary across five dimensions. In the companion article, "Personality: Major Traits Found Stable Through Life," Daniel Goleman claims that most personality traits remain constant over time. This contradicts Maslow's growth theory and Freud's psychoanalytic stage theory.

Be aware that there are psychologists who are convinced that people do not possess a sense of self at all. Individuals can never really come to "know" themselves. Dreams do not have hidden meaning. Instead, actions at the moment are based either on past learning experiences or on immediate stimuli in our environments. There is no self-concept upon which people regularly rely or reflect. These psychologists are proponents of behaviorism.

Looking Ahead: Challenge Questions

Does the sense of self develop the same way in each individual? Are there various aspects of self, such as gender, that develop faster than other aspects?

How can we raise children with high esteem? What happens to children and adults with low esteem? Do you think that programs designed to raise self-esteem in

children work? How do effective programs differ from ineffective ones?

Is self-concept stable or does it seem to change regularly? What events create change? How could an individual change his or her self-concept?

Is self a uniquely human concept? Could animals develop a sense of self? How would you test animals for self-concept?

How and when do you think children develop a sense of self? How do people show others they have a sense of self?

Is self-concept the only guide for our behaviors? Do individuals have a number of selves and show different ones to different people? If so, is this normal, or does it signal some kind of maladjustment?

Suppose someone developed on a desert island with no human contact. What might this individual be like? How might the person appear to others who have been raised in civilization?

Do you believe in the unconscious? Can you give examples from your own life of its influence? What scientific evidence exists that demonstrates the potential of the unconscious? Do you think dreams reveal unconscious wishes? What do various dreams and dream symbols mean to you? To Freudians?

Do you think there is such a thing as a personality trait? Do you agree that there are five main traits that describe everyone?

Which theory of human personality (humanistic, psychoanlytic, or trait) do you think is best and why?

The Last Interview of
ABRAHAM MASLOW

Edward Hoffman, Ph.D.

About the author: Edward Hoffman received his doctorate from the University of Michigan. A clinical psychologist on New York's Long Island, he is the author of several books, including The Right to be Human: A Biography of Abraham Maslow *(Tarcher).*

When Abraham Maslow first shared his pioneering vision of a "comprehensive human psychology" in this magazine in early 1968, he stood at the pinnacle of his international acclaim and influence.

HIS ELECTION AS PRESIDENT OF THE AMERican Psychological Association some months before capped an illustrious academic career spanning more than 35 productive years, during which Maslow had steadily gained the high regard—even adulation—of countless numbers of colleagues and former students. His best-known books, *Motivation and Personality* and *Toward a Psychology of Being*, were not only being discussed avidly by psychologists, but also by professionals in fields ranging from management and marketing to education and counseling. Perhaps even more significantly, Maslow's iconoclastic concepts like peak experience, self-actualization, and synergy had even begun penetrating popular language.

Nevertheless, it was a very unsettling time for him: Recovering from a major heart attack, the temperamentally restless and ceaselessly active Maslow was finding forced convalescence at home to be almost painfully unbearable. Suddenly, his extensive plans for future research, travel, and lecturing had to be postponed. Although Maslow hoped for a speedy recovery, frequent chest pains induced a keen sense of his own mortality. As perhaps never before, he began to ponder his career's accomplishments and his unrealized goals.

In 1968 PSYCHOLOGY TODAY was a precocious one-year-old upstart, but such was its prestige that it was able to attract perhaps the country's most famous psychologist for an interview.

Maslow likely regarded the PT interview as a major opportunity to outline his "comprehensive human psychology" and the best way to actualize it. At 60, he knew that time permitted him only to plant seeds (in his own metaphor) of re-

search and theory—and hope that later generations would live to see the flowering of human betterment. Perhaps most prescient at a time of global unrest is Maslow's stirring vision of "building a psychology for the peace table." It was his hope that through psychological research, we might learn how to unify peoples of differing racial and ethnic origins, and thereby create a world of peace.

Although the complete audiotapes of the sessions, conducted over three days, disappeared long ago under mysterious circumstances, the written condensation that remains provides a fascinating and still-relevant portrait of a key thinker at the height of his prowess. Intellectually, Maslow was decades ahead of his time; today the wide-ranging ideas he offers here are far from outdated. Indeed, after some twenty-odd years, they're still on the cutting edge of American psychology and social science. Emotionally, this interview is significant for the rare—essentially unprecedented—glimpse it affords into Maslow's personal history and concerns: his ancestry and upbringing; his mentors and ambitions; his courtship, marriage, and fatherhood; and even a few of his peak experiences.

Maslow continued to be puzzled and intrigued by the more positive human phenomenon of self-actualization. He was well aware that his theory about the "best of humanity" suffered from methodological flaws. Yet he had become ever more convinced of its intuitive validity, that self-actualizers provide us with clues to our highest innate traits: love and compassion, creativity and aesthetics, ethics and spirituality. Maslow longed to empirically verify this lifelong hunch.

In the two years of his life that remained, this gifted psychologist never wrote an autobiography, nor did he ever again bare his soul in such a public and wide-ranging way. It may have been that Maslow regarded this unusually personal interview as a true legacy. More than 20 years later, it remains a fresh and important document for the field of psychology.

Mary Harrington Hall, for PSYCHOLOGY TODAY: A couple of William B. Yeats's lines keep running through my head: "And in my heart, the daemons and the gods wage an eternal battle and I feel the pain of wounds, the labor of the spear." How thin is the veneer of civilization, and how can we understand and deal with evil?

Abraham H. Maslow: It's a psychological puzzle I've been trying to solve for years. Why are people cruel and why are they nice? Evil people are rare, but you find evil behavior in the majority of people. The next thing I want to do with my life is to study evil and understand it.

PT: By evil here, I think we both mean destructive action without remorse. Racial prejudice is an evil in our society which we must deal with. And soon. Or we will go down as a racist society.

Maslow: You know, when I became A.P.A. president, the first thing I wanted to do was work for greater recognition for the Negro psychologists. Then I found that there were no Negroes in psychology, at least not many. They don't major in psychology.

PT: Why should they? Why would I think that psychology would solve social problems if I were a Negro living in the ghetto, surrounded by despair?

Maslow: Negroes have really had to take it. We've given them every possible blow. If I were a Negro, I'd be fighting, as Martin Luther King fought, for human recognition and justice. I'd rather go down with my flag flying. If you're weak or crippled, or you can't speak out or fight back in some way, then people don't hesitate to treat you badly.

PT: Could you look at evil behavior in two ways: evil from below and evil from above? Evil as a sickness and evil as understood compassionately?

Maslow: If you look at evil from above, you can be realistic. Evil exists. You don't give it quarter, and you're a better fighter if you can understand it. You're in the position of a psychotherapist. In the same way, you can look at neurosis. You can see neurosis from below—as a sickness—as most psychiatrists see it. Or you

can understand it as a compassionate man might: respecting the neurosis as a fumbling and inefficient effort toward good ends.

PT: You can understand race riots in the same way, can't you?

Maslow: If you can only be detached enough, you can feel that it's better to riot than to be hopeless, degraded, and defeated. Rioting is a childish way of trying to be a man, but it takes time to rise out of the hell of hatred and frustration and accept that to be a man you don't have to riot.

PT: In our society, we see all behavior as a demon we can vanquish and banish, don't we? And yet good people do evil things.

Maslow: Most people are nice people. Evil is caused by ignorance, thoughtlessness, fear, or even the desire for popularity with one's gang. We can cure many such causes of evil. Science is progressing, and I feel hope that psychology can solve many of these problems. I think that a good part of evil behavior bears on the behavior of the normal.

PT: How will you approach the study of evil?

Maslow: If you think only of evil, then you become pessimistic and hopeless like Freud. But if you think there is no evil, then you're just one more deluded Pollyanna. The thing is to try to understand and realize how it's possible for people who are capable of being angels, heroes, or saints to be bastards and killers. Sometimes, poor and miserable people are hopeless. Many revenge themselves upon life for what society has done to them. They enjoy hurting.

PT: Your study of evil will have to be subjective, won't it? How can we measure evil in the laboratory?

Maslow: All the goals of objectivity, repeatability, and preplanned experimentation are things we have to move toward. The more reliable you make knowledge, the better it is. If the salvation of man comes out of the advancement of knowledge—taken in the best sense—then these goals are part of the strategy of knowledge.

PT: What did you tell your own daughters, Ann and Ellen, when they were growing up?

Maslow: Learn to hate meanness. Watch out for anybody who is mean or cruel. Watch out for people who delight in destruction.

PT: How would you describe yourself? Not in personality, because you're one of

the warmest and sweetest men I've ever met. But who are you?

Maslow: I'm someone who likes plowing new ground, then walking away from it. I get bored easily. For me, the big thrill comes with the discovering.

PT: Psychologists all love Abe Maslow. How did you escape the crossfire?

Maslow: I just avoid most academic warfare. Besides, I had my first heart attack many years ago, and perhaps I've been unconsciously favoring my body. So I may have avoided real struggle. Besides, I only like fights I know I can win, and I'm not personally mean.

PT: Maybe you're just one of the lucky few who grew up through a happy childhood without malice.

Maslow: With my childhood, it's a wonder I'm not psychotic. I was the little Jewish boy in the non-Jewish neighborhood. It was a little like being the first Negro enrolled in the all-white school. I grew up in libraries and among books, without friends.

Both my mother and father were uneducated. My father wanted me to be a lawyer. He thumbed his way across the whole continent of Europe from Russia and got here at the age of 15. He wanted success for me. I tried law school for two weeks. Then I came home to my poor father one night after a class discussing "spite fences" and told him I couldn't be a lawyer. "Well, son," he said, "what do you want to study?" I answered: "Everything." He was uneducated and couldn't understand my passion for learning, but he was a nice man. He didn't understand either that at 16, I was in love.

PT: All 16-year-olds are in love.

Maslow: Mine was different. We're talking about my wife. I loved Bertha. You know her. Wasn't I right? I was extremely shy, and I tagged around after her. We were too young to get married. I tried to run away with her.

PT: Where did you run?

Maslow: I ran to Cornell for my sophomore year in college, then to Wisconsin. We were married there when I was 20 and Bertha was 19. Life didn't really start for me until I got married.

I went to Wisconsin because I had just discovered John B. Watson's work, and I was sold on behaviorism. It was an explosion of excitement for me. Bertha came to pick me up at New York's 42nd Street library, and I was dancing down Fifth Avenue with exuberance. I embarrassed her, but I was so excited about

Watson's behaviorist program. It was beautiful. I was confident that here was a real road to travel: solving one problem after another and changing the world.

PT: A clear lifetime with built-in progress guaranteed.

Maslow: That was it. I was off to Wisconsin to change the world. I went there to study with psychologist Kurt Koffka, biologist Hans Dreisch, and philosopher Alexander Meiklejohn. But when I showed up on the campus, they weren't there. They had just been visiting professors, but the lying catalog had included them anyway.

Oh, but I was so lucky, though. I was young Harry Harlow's first doctoral graduate. And they were angels, my professors. I've always had angels around. They helped me when I needed it, even fed me. Bill Sheldon taught me how to buy a suit. I didn't know anything of amenities. Clark Hull was an angel to me, and later, Edward L. Thorndike.

PT: You're an angelic man. I've heard too many stories to let you deny it. What kind of research were you doing at Wisconsin?

Maslow: I was a monkey man. By studying monkeys for my doctoral dissertation, I found that dominance was related to sex, and to maleness. It was a great discovery, but somebody had discovered it two months before me.

PT: Great ideas always go in different places and minds at the same time.

Maslow: Yes, I worked on it until the start of World War II. I thought that working on sex was the easiest way to help mankind. I felt if I could discover a way to improve the sexual life by even one percent, then I could improve the whole species.

One day, it suddenly dawned on me that I knew as much about sex as any man living—in the intellectual sense. I knew everything that had been written; I had made discoveries with which I was pleased; I had done therapeutic work. This was about 10 years before the Kinsey report came out. Then I suddenly burst into laughter. Here was I, the great sexologist, and I had never seen an erect penis except one, and that was from my own bird's-eye view. That humbled me considerably.

PT: I suppose you interviewed people the way Kinsey did?

Maslow: No, something was wrong with Kinsey. I really don't think he liked women, or men. In my research, I interviewed 120 women with a new form of interview. No notes. We just talked until I got some feeling for the individual's personality, then put sex against that background. Sex has to be considered in regard to love, otherwise it's useless. This is because behavior can be a defense—a way of hiding what you feel—particularly regarding sex.

I was fascinated with my research. But I gave up interviewing men. They were useless because they boasted and lied about sex. I also planned a big research project involving prostitutes. I thought we could learn a lot about men from them, but the research never came off.

PT: You gave up all your experimental research in these fields.

Maslow: Yes, around 1941 I felt I must try to save the world, and to prevent the horrible wars and the awful hatred and prejudice. It happened very suddenly. One day just after Pearl Harbor, I was driving home and my car was stopped by a poor, pathetic parade. Boy Scouts and old uniforms and a flag and someone playing a flute off-key.

As I watched, the tears began to run down my face. I felt we didn't understand—not Hitler, nor the Germans, nor Stalin, nor the Communists. We didn't understand any of them. I felt that if we could understand, then we could make progress. I had a vision of a peace table, with people sitting around it, talking about human nature and hatred, war and peace, and brotherhood.

I was too old to go into the army. It was at that moment I realized that the rest of my life must be devoted to discovering a psychology for the peace table. That moment changed my whole life. Since then, I've devoted myself to developing a theory of human nature that could be tested by experiment and research. I wanted to prove that humans are capable of something grander than war, prejudice, and hatred. I wanted to make science consider all the people: the best specimen of mankind I could find. I found that many of them reported having something like mystical experiences.

PT: Your work with "self-actualizing" people is famous. You have described some of these mystical experiences.

Maslow: Peak experiences come from love and sex, from aesthetic moments, from bursts of creativity, from moments of insight and discovery, or from fusion with nature.

I had one such experience in a faculty procession here at Brandeis University. I saw the line stretching off into a dim fu-

ture. At its head was Socrates. And in the line were the ones I love most. Thomas Jefferson was there. And Spinoza. And Alfred North Whitehead. I was in the same line. Behind me, that infinite line melted into the dimness. And there were all the people not yet born who were going to be in the same line.

I believe these experiences can be studied scientifically, and they will be.

PT: This is all part of your theory of metamotivation, isn't it?

Maslow: But not all people who are metamotivated report peak experiences. The "nonpeakers" are healthy, but they lack poetry and soaring flights of the imagination. Both peakers and nonpeakers can be self-actualized in that they're not motivated by basic needs, but by something higher.

PT: Real self-actualization must be rare. What percentage of us achieve it?

Maslow: I'd say only a fraction of one percent.

PT: People whose basic needs have been met, then, will pursue life's ultimate values?

Maslow: Yes, the ultimate happiness for man is the realization of pure beauty and truth, which are the ultimate values. What we need is a system of thought—you might even call it a religion—that can bind humans together. A system that would fit the Republic of Chad as well as the United States: a system that would supply our idealistic young people with something to believe in. They're searching for something they can pour all that emotion into, and the churches are not much help.

PT: This system must come.

Maslow: I'm not alone in trying to make it. There are plenty of others working toward the same end. Perhaps their efforts, aided by the hundreds of youngsters who are devoting their lives to this, will develop a new image of man that rejects the chemical and technological views. We've technologized everything.

PT: The technologist is the person who has fallen in love with a machine. I suppose that has also happened to those in psychology?

Maslow: They become fascinated with the machine. It's almost a neurotic love. They're like the man who spends Sundays polishing his car instead of stroking his wife.

PT: In several of your papers, you've said that you stopped being a behaviorist when your first child was born.

Maslow: My whole training at Wisconsin was behaviorist. I didn't question it until I began reading some other sources. Later, I began studying the Rorschach test.

At the same time, I stumbled into embryology and read Ludwig von Bertalanffy's *Modern Theories of Development*. I had already become disillusioned with Bertrand Russell and with English philosophy generally. Then, I fell in love with Alfred North Whitehead and Henri Bergson. Their writings destroyed behaviorism for me without my recognizing it.

When my first baby was born, that was the thunderclap that settled things. I looked at this tiny, mysterious thing and felt so stupid. I felt small, weak, and feeble. I'd say that anyone who's had a baby couldn't be a behaviorist.

PT: As you propose new ideas, and blaze new ground, you're bound to be criticized, aren't you?

Maslow: I have worked out a lot of good tricks for fending off professional attacks. We all have to do that. A good, controlled experiment is possible only when you already know a hell of a lot. If I'm a pioneer by choice and I go into the wilderness, how am I going to make careful experiments? If I tried to, I'd be a fool. I'm not against careful experiments. But rather, I've been working with what I call "growing tip" statistics.

With a tree, all the growth takes place at the growing tips. Humanity is exactly the same. All the growth takes place in the growing tip: among that one percent of the population. It's made up of pioneers, the beginners. That's where the action is.

PT: You were the one who helped publish Ruth Benedict's work on synergy. What's it about?

Maslow: That it's possible to set up social institutions that merge selfishness and unselfishness, so that you can't benefit yourself without benefiting others. And the reverse.

PT: How can psychology become a stronger force in our society?

Maslow: We all should look at the similarities within the various disciplines and think of enlarging psychology. To throw anything away is crazy. Good psychology should include all the methodological techniques, without having loyalty to one method, one idea, or one person.

PT: I see you as a catalyst and as a bridge between many disciplines, theories, and philosophies.

Maslow: My job is to put them all together. We shouldn't have "humanistic psychology." The adjective should be unnecessary. I'm not antibehaviorist. I'm antidoctrinaire.

PT: Abe, when you look back on your own education, what kind would you recommend for others?

Maslow: The great educational experiences of my life were those that taught me most. They taught me what kind of a person I was. These were experiences that drew me out and strengthened me. Psychoanalysis was a big thing for me. And getting married. Marriage is a school itself. Also, having children. Becoming a father changed my whole life. It taught me as if by revelation. And reading particular books. William Graham Sumner's *Folkways* was a Mount Everest in my life: It changed me.

My teachers were the best in the world. I sought them out: Erich Fromm, Karen Horney, Ruth Benedict, Max Wertheimer, Alfred Adler, David Levy, and Harry Harlow. I was there in New York City during the 1930s when the wave of distinguished émigrés arrived from Europe.

PT: Not everyone can have such an illustrious faculty.

Maslow: It's the teacher who's important. And if this is so, then what we are doing with our whole educational structure—with credits and the idea that one teacher is as good as another? You look at the college catalog and it says English

342. It doesn't even bother to tell you the instructor's name, and that's insane. The purpose of education—and of all social institutions—is the development of full humaneness. If you keep that in mind, all else follows. We've got to concentrate on goals.

PT: It's like the story about the test pilot who radioed back home: "I'm lost, but I'm making record time."

Maslow: If you forget the goal of education, then the whole thing is lost.

PT: If a rare, self-actualizing young psychologist came to you today and said, "What's the most important thing I can do in this time of crisis?", what advice would you give?

Maslow: I'd say: Get to work on aggression and hostility. We need the definitive book on aggression. And we need it now. Only the pieces exist: the animal stuff, the psychoanalytic stuff, the endocrine stuff. Time is running out. A key to understanding the evil which can destroy our society lies in this understanding.

There's another study that could be done. I'd like to test the whole, incoming freshman class at Brandeis University in various ways: psychiatric interviews, personality tests, everything. I want to follow them for four years of college. For a beginning, I want to test my theory that emotionally healthy people perceive better.

PT: You could make the college study only a preliminary, and follow them through their whole life span, the way Lewis Terman did with his gifted kids.

Maslow: Oh yes! I'd like to know: How good a father or mother does this student become? And what happens to his/her children? This kind of long-term study would take more time than I have left. But that ultimately doesn't make any difference. I like to be the first runner in the relay race. I like to pass on the baton to the next person.

SELF-ESTEEM:
THE KEYSTONE TO HAPPINESS

"There are few experiences in life that equal the wonderful feelings of self-satisfaction."

Ralph Hyatt

Dr. Hyatt, Psychology Editor of USA Today, is professor emeritus of psychology, Saint Joseph's University, Philadelphia, Pa.

UNDERSTANDING the human personality is fascinating, but difficult. Not only are there hundreds of personal characteristics to consider as they interplay with one another, but the creativity and stamina of researchers truly are tested in their attempts to study them scientifically. Just when one seems securely tied down, it slips and slides away. Yet, there's no doubt about its existence.

Self-esteem is one of those esoteric personality variables. Simply, it refers to the general value you place on who you are. When you don't like yourself very much, esteem is low. You hunch your back, you see the world as overwhelming, there's a tendency to grovel, and you're sensitive. With high esteem, your back is straight, you walk briskly, speech is confident, nothing seems too much, and negatives roll off your back.

How does your self-esteem measure up? The following selected thoughts, feelings, and behaviors, if they tend to recur, may hint at your esteem sensitivities:
- Choosing to sit in the last row of a classroom.
- Blaming yourself for almost everything.
- Self-consciousness when approaching a group of peers.
- Embarrassment at dressing improperly.
- Not sharing an idea in a group for fear of saying something stupid.
- Inner panic at being called upon at a meeting.
- Believing that you constantly are being taken advantage of by others.
- Feeling wimpy when someone quickly pulls into *your* parking space.
- Wondering why you frequently are misunderstood by friends.
- Being turned on by flashy clothing, jewelry, automobiles, and/or home furnishings.
- Bragging about your activities, successes, children, etc.
- Loudly expressing your ideas, attracting attention in crowds.
- Feeling ill after being told that you don't look well.

Those with adequate esteem ordinarily select any classroom seat that is comfortable, do not fret about their party dress the morning after, enjoy sharing ideas with a group, and feel sufficiently comfortable with themselves so as not to overreact to the statements and actions of others, especially strangers.

Self-esteem runs on a continuum from low to high. There are days and occasions when you'll feel a loss of confidence and somewhat insecure. Overwork, fatigue, failures, and tension tend to lower esteem. In the main, however, what you think of yourself is fairly constant. It influences how you act and react. Even though others may not use the term esteem—they may call you moody, sensitive, boisterous, or shy—it affects how you are perceived and accepted by family and friends.

Given the perennial popularity of self-help books, one easily could conclude that the esteem deficit outruns, by far, America's combined budget and trade deficits. Werner Erhardt, the wizard of EST, convinced us in the 1970's that our esteem needed a thorough overhaul. Now, he transmits the same message to baby-boomers. He probably can prove his thesis most convincingly by pointing to the vast numbers who flock to his seminars.

John Vasconcellos, a California legislator, attributes crime, drug abuse, and adolescent pregnancy to low self-esteem. He and a task force he formed recommend that teachers and welfare workers receive training in self-esteem to combat these and other social problems. Interestingly, Vasconcellos became a believer only after personally experiencing a variety of psychotherapeutic approaches, including encounter groups and individual counseling. His present level of self-esteem is great. What's good for him, he holds, should be of value to others.

There are those who differ, however. Journalist Charles Krauthammer, in an essay in *Time* magazine (Feb. 5, 1990), decries that American 13-year-olds, compared to similarly aged youth in Korea, Spain, Britain, Ireland, and Canada, came in last on a standardized math test. The real shocker is that they ranked *first* in their self-estimates—that is, how proficient they believe they are in mathematics. They feel good even about things they don't know. In other words, they have learned esteem, but not basic math! Krauthammer concludes: "The pursuit of good feeling in education is a dead end. The way to true self-esteem is through real achievement and real learning."

Labels and tattoos

From birth onward, perhaps even pre-natally, self-esteem is influenced by events around you. Parents often glibly "train" their children by calling them weird, odd, stupid, or clumsy. Being "good" or "bad" easily is inculcated. Verbal and non-verbal messages are "stamped in." When labels stick, they become tattoos. These are the basic rules for labels and tattoos:

● Labels can be positive or negative.
● The younger you are when labeled, the stronger the imprint.
● The more powerful the imprint, the greater the holding power.
● The more you are given the same label, the stickier it is.
● Parents can label their offspring more effectively than anyone else.
● The larger the number of people giving the same label—siblings, friends, teachers—the greater the stickiness.

● Life experiences—opportunities and stresses, successes and failures—print significant labels, with tattoo potential.

Depending on your health, intelligence, family patterns, physical attractiveness, social experiences, special talents and skills, and school achievement, self-esteem develops from the day you are born. With a reasonable number of pluses in many of these areas, esteem can withstand a fair amount of stress without faltering. With shaky developmental experiences, vulnerability to even minor stressors increase and self-esteem dips.

There are two additional considerations. It's fine to stretch for your goals and expect success. However, if expectations are too lofty, you're flirting with failure. Don't develop goals that are "a piece of cake" or unrealistically high. Establish objectives which you have to reach for, but are achievable.

Second, don't overlook your genetic makeup. You very well may be "built" to be quiet, introverted, and sensitive. Some personality traits associated with vulnerability—shyness, for example—can not be blamed universally on poor parenting skills, a rural background, sibling rivalry, economic deprivation, etc. Inborn temperament may be as influential as learning.

What can you do about it? First, admit that you tend to be highly vulnerable. Then, select stressors carefully whenever you have that luxury. Don't overreach. Make a point of objectively assessing your tender emotions, when they do blossom, giving enough power to the possibilities of hypersensitivity. Unless it is perfectly clear otherwise, give the other person the benefit of the doubt before you attack or shrink away. When similar situations occur in the future, attempt to pre-empt your touchiness by recalling past insights. Finally, evaluate how the behaviors of others may be changing, as you alter your sensitivity reactions to them.

No one is suggesting that it will be easy. After all, you are battling a basic social approach that has been going on and has been reinforced for years. In fact, you may not have been totally aware of the nuances of your behaviors and tender feelings. By taking small steps and not expecting too much of yourself all at once, your self-esteem eventually can be elevated.

The necessary exchanges between a child's biology and the environment bring into clear relief the exquisite skills necessary for parenting. No wonder that the "wisdom of Solomon" often is required. Self-esteem frequently is made or broken by parental interventions. Here are some tips:

Raise your child in an atmosphere of acceptance. However, not everything he or she does should be considered "correct" or "good." Differentiate between the behavior and the child. Psychologist Carl Rogers coined the term "unconditional positive regard." He urged that we do not

place conditions of worth on the child ("If you do this, I will not love you"). Confidence in your love usually equips your child with the strength and insights to understand why you can not accept some of his or her behaviors.

Give your children enough room to think for themselves. Allow your offspring opportunities for learning how to solve problems independently, barring a potential catastrophe. Afterwards, a calm, respectful conversation about the problem-solving process could be meaningful as you encourage another try, perhaps an alternate approach.

When necessary, be clear and firm about the rules. Children must be prohibited from injuring themselves or others. They must learn to eat, sleep, and do other things on time. There are occasions when a crisp command is required. Be sure, however, to explain the reasons for the rules and/or the limitations on their behavior. Children thrive on reasonable structure in their lives. When you correct them, describe more efficient ways of acting.

No matter how exasperated you become, do not belittle your children or label them negatively. Parents are not saints. There are times when we lose our cool. Explain to the child why you are annoyed. Step away a bit, cool off, then, together, formulate a constructive plan for dealing with the problem. Try not to yell—that places you in a weaker psychological position with the child. It also teaches him or her an ineffective way of dealing with annoyances. Yelling erodes esteem for both of you.

Don't forget to reinforce good things positively. We sometimes become so intense about teaching youngsters not to do wrong that we overlook the multiple occasions when they perform well. These are not necessarily restricted to academic achievements or exceptional accomplishments. They can include such everyday nice things as constructing an airplane model, playing cooperatively with friends, sitting quietly and enjoying television, interacting positively with a sibling, etc. Hug and kiss them, state how much you love them, and share your pride in them.

There are few experiences in life that equal the wonderful feelings of self-satisfaction. Genuine satisfaction can be derived only by meeting reasonable standards we have set for ourselves. As children, good feelings about self are largely a result of healthy home relationships. As adults, a positive self-image depends more on living consistently with our fundamental values and beliefs. A context of love helps considerably at all developmental levels.

Abraham Maslow, the noted humanistic psychologist, considered self-esteem as a core psychological need for humans—not a want, but a necessity, like food and oxygen. One might add that self-esteem is the keystone of happiness.

THE ASSAULT ON
FREUD

He invented psychoanalysis and revolutionized 20th century ideas about the life of the mind. And this is the thanks he gets?

PAUL GRAY

MANY ARE THE WAYS OF COPING WITH THE WORLD'S vicissitudes. Some people fear and propitiate evil spirits. Others order their schedules according to the display of the planets across the zodiac. There are those who assume that they carry, somewhere inside of them, a thing called the unconscious. It is mostly invisible, although it can furtively be glimpsed in dreams and heard in slips of the tongue. But the unconscious is not a passive stowaway on the voyage of life; it has the power to make its hosts feel very sad or behave in strange, self-destructive ways. When that happens, one recourse is to go to the office of a specially trained healer, lie down on a couch and start talking.

The first two beliefs can, except by those who hold them, easily be dismissed as superstitions. The third—a tenet of the classic theory of psychoanalysis devised by Sigmund Freud—has become this troubled century's dominant model for thinking and talking about human behavior. To a remarkable degree, Freud's ideas, conjectures, pronouncements have seeped well beyond the circle of his professional followers into the public mind and discourse. People who have never read a word of his work (a voluminous 24 volumes in the standard English translation) nonetheless "know" of things that can be traced, sometimes circuitously, back to Freud: penis envy; castration anxiety; phallic symbols; the ego, id and superego; repressed memories; Oedipal itches; sexual sublimation. This rich panoply of metaphors for the mental life has become, across wide swaths of the globe, something very close to common knowledge.

But what if Freud was wrong?

This question has been around ever since the publication of Freud's first overtly psychoanalytical papers in the late 1890s. Today it is being asked with unprecedented urgency, thanks to a coincidence of developments that raise doubts not only about Freud's methods, discoveries and proofs and the vast array of therapies derived from them, but also about the lasting importance of Freud's descriptions of the mind. The collapse of Marxism, the other grand unified theory that shaped and rattled the 20th century, is unleashing monsters. What inner horrors or fresh dreams might arise should the complex Freudian monument topple as well?

That may not happen, and it assuredly will not happen all at once. But new forces are undermining the Freudian foundations. Among them:

▶ The problematical proliferation, particularly in the U.S., of accusations of sexual abuse, satanic rituals, infant human sacrifices and the like from people, many of them guided by therapists, who suddenly remember what they allegedly years or decades ago repressed. . . . Although Freud almost certainly would have regarded most of these charges with withering skepticism, his theory of repression and the unconscious is being used—most Freudians would say misused—to assert their authenticity.

▶ The continuing success of drugs in the treatment or alleviation of mental disorders ranging from depression to schizophrenia. Roughly 10 million Americans are taking such medications. To his credit, Freud foresaw this development. In 1938, a year before his death, he wrote, "The future may teach us to exercise a direct influence, by means of particular chemical substances." Still, the recognition that some neuroses and psychoses respond favorably to drugs chips away at the domain originally claimed for psychoanalytic treatment.

▶ The Clinton health-care reform proposals, oddly enough, which are prompting cost-benefit analyses across the whole spectrum of U.S. medicine, including treatments for mental illness. Whatever package finally winds its way through Congress, many experts concede that insurance will not be provided for Freud's talking cure. (A 50-min. hour of psychoanalysis costs an average of $125.) Says Dr. Frederick K. Goodwin, director of the National Institute of Mental Health: "It's clear that classical psychoanalysis, which is four to five times a week for a four- to five-year duration, will not be covered. It won't be covered because there is no real evidence that it works." Goodwin, for the record, professes himself an admirer of Freud the theoretician.

▶ A spate of new books attacking Freud and his brainchild psychoanalysis for a generous array of errors, duplicities, fudged evidence and scientific howlers.

This last phenomenon is an intensification of an ongoing story. While Freud was winning cadres of acolytes and legions of notional recruits, he and his ideas regularly attracted sharp attacks, often from influential quarters. As early as 1909, philosopher

William James observed in a letter that Freud "made on me personally the impression of a man obsessed with fixed ideas." Vladimir Nabokov, whose novels trace the untrammeled and unpredictable play of individual imaginations, regularly tossed barbs at "the witch doctor Freud" and "the Viennese quack." For similar reasons, Ludwig Wittgenstein objected to the pigeonholing effects of psychoanalytic categories, even though he paid Freud a backhanded compliment in the process: "Freud's fanciful pseudo explanations (precisely because they are so brilliant) perform a disservice. Now any ass has these pictures to use in 'explaining' symptoms of illness."

The steady rain of anti-Freud arguments did little to discourage the parade of his theories or to dampen the zeal of his followers. In fact, Freud erected an apparently invulnerable umbrella against criticisms of psychoanalytical principles. He characterized such disagreements, from patients or anyone else, as "resistance" and then asserted that instances of such resistance amounted to "actual evidence in favor of the correctness" of his assertions. For a long time, this psychoanalytic Catch-22 worked wonders: those who opposed the methods put forth to heal them and others could be banished, perhaps with a friendly handshake and a knowing smile, as nuts.

That illogical defense has largely crumbled. The recent discovery of documents relating to Freud and his circle, plus the measured release of others by the Freud estate, has provided a steadily expanding body of evidence about the man and his works. Some of the initial reassessments are unsettling.

For one example, the 10-year collaboration between Freud and Carl Gustav Jung broke off abruptly in 1914, with profound consequences for the discipline they helped create. There would henceforth be Freudians and Jungians, connected chiefly by mutual animosities. Why did a warm, fruitful cooperation end in an icy schism? In *A Most Dangerous Method* (Knopf; $30), John Kerr, a clinical psychologist who has seen new diaries, letters and journals, argues that the growing philosophical disputes between Freud and Jung were exacerbated by a cat-and-mouse game of sexual suspicion and blackmail. Freud believed an ex-patient of Jung's named Sabina Spielrein had also been Jung's mistress; Jung in turn surmised that Freud had become involved with his sister-in-law, Minna Bernays. Both antagonists in this standoff held bombshells that could blow each other's reputation from Vienna to Zurich and back; both backed off, divided up the spoils of their joint investigations and retreated into opposing tents of theory.

Was this any way to found an objective science? Freud's defenders argue that his personal life is irrelevant to his contributions to learning—a rather odd contention, given Freud's statement that his development of the analytic method began with his pioneering analysis of himself. Nevertheless, Arnold Richards, editor of the American Psychoanalytic Association newsletter, dismisses any attention paid to Freud's private conduct: "It has no scientific practical consequence. It's not relevant to Freud's theory or practice."

What, then, about attacks on Freud's theory and practice? In *Father Knows Best: The Use and Abuse of Power in Freud's Case of 'Dora'* (Teachers College Press; $36), academicians Robin Tolmach Lakoff and James C. Coyne offer a fresh view of one of Freud's most famously botched analyses. When "Dora," 18, sought Freud's help at her father's insistence in 1901, she told him the following story: her father was having an affair with the wife of Herr "K," a family friend. Herr K had been paying unwanted sexual attentions to Dora since she

> Sigmund Freud's rich panoply of metaphors for the mental life has evolved into something closely resembling common knowlege

was 14 and was now being encouraged in this pursuit by her father, presumably as a way to deflect attention from the father's alliance with Frau K. After hearing this account, Freud, as feminists say, did not get it. He decided Dora really desired Herr K sexually, plus her father to boot, and he criticized her "hysterical" refusal to follow her true inclinations, embrace her circumstances and make everyone, including herself, satisfied and fulfilled. She left Freud's care after three months.

IF THIS SOUNDS DAMNING, MORE OF the same and then some can be found in Allen Esterson's *Seductive Mirage: An Exploration of the Work of Sigmund Freud* (Open Court; $52.95). As a mathematician, Esterson is vulnerable to charges from Freud loyalists that he is an amateur, unqualified to discuss the mysteries of psychoanalysis. Maybe so, but his relentless examinations of discrepancies, doctored evidence and apparent lies within Freud's own accounts of individual cases make for disturbing reading. Esterson's argument is often most effective when it quotes the analyst directly on his therapeutic techniques. Freud regularly sounds like a detective who solves a crime before interviewing the first witness: "The principle is that I should guess the secret and tell it to the patient straight out." Once Freud had made a diagnosis, the case, as far as he was concerned, was closed, although the treatment continued: "We must not be led astray by initial denials. If we keep firmly to what we have inferred, we shall in the end conquer every resistance by emphasizing the unshakable nature of our convictions."

Noting the fact that Freud's published case histories largely record inconclusive or lamentable results, some loyalists have adopted a fall-back position: Freud may not have been very good at practicing what he preached, but that lapse in no way invalidates his overarching theories.

These defenders must now confront *Validation in the Clinical Theory of Psychoanalysis* (International Universities Press; $50) by Adolf Grünbaum, a noted philosopher of science and a professor at the University of Pittsburgh. The book, which builds on Grünbaum's 1984 critique of psychoanalytic underpinnings, is a monograph (translation: no one without a Ph.D. need apply) and a quiet, sometimes maddeningly abstruse devastation of psychoanalysis' status as a science. Grünbaum dispassionately examines a number of key psychoanalytic premises: the theory of repression (which Freud called "the cornerstone on which the whole structure of psychoanalysis rests"), the investigative capabilities offered by free association, the diagnostic significance of dreams. Grünbaum does not claim that the idea of repressed memories, for instance, is false. He simply argues that neither Freud nor any of his successors has ever proved a cause-and-effect link between a repressed memory and a later neurosis or a retrieved memory and a subsequent cure.

Off the page, Grünbaum is able to make his critique a little more accessible to lay people. Of the presumed link between childhood molestation and adult neurosis, he remarks, "Just saying the first thing happened and the second thing happened, and therefore one caused the other, is not enough. You have to show more." Grünbaum finds similar flaws in the importance Freud attached to dreams and bungled actions, such as so-called Freudian slips: "All three of these tenets—the theory of neurosis, the theory of why we dream and the theory of slips—have the same problem. All are undermined by Freud's failure to prove a causal relationship between the repression and the pathology. That's why the foundation of psychoanalysis is very wobbly."

How wobbly? Interestingly, Grünbaum himself thinks all is not lost, although his verdict is not entirely cheering: "I categorically don't believe Freud is dead. The question is, Are they trustworthy explanations? Have the hypotheses been validated by cogent, solid evidence? My answer to that is no."

FRANK SULLOWAY, A VISITING scholar of science history at M.I.T. and a longtime critic of Freud's methods, takes a somewhat more apocalyptic view: "Psychoanalysis is built on quicksand. It's like a 10-story hotel sinking into an unsound foundation. And the analysts are in this building. You tell them it's sinking, and they say, 'It's O.K.; we're on the 10th floor.'"

Sure enough, the view from this imaginary elevation remains largely untroubled. Psychoanalysts like to point out that their treatment is gaining converts in Spain, Italy and Latin America, plus parts of the former Soviet Union, where it had formerly been banned. Some 14,000 tourists a year flock to the Freud Museum in London, where they walk through the Hampstead house Freud owned during the last year of his life. His daughter Anna, who carried on her father's work with dedication and skill, remained there until her death in 1982. Freud's library and study, the latter containing a couch covered with an Oriental rug, remain largely as he left them. Some visitors last week may have come fresh from seeing a Channel 4 TV documentary put together by Peter Swales, another persistent critic of Freud, titled *Bad Ideas of the 20th Century: Freudism*. If so, their interest in Freud memorabilia seemed undiminished. Michael Molnar, the Museum's research director and an editor of Freud's diaries, acknowledges that psychoanalysis is being challenged by new drug treatments and advances in genetic research. "But," he argues, "Freud is in better shape than Marx."

Across the English Channel, a play called *The Visitor*, by the young French dramatist Eric-Emmanuel Schmitt, has opened in Paris, featuring the octogenarian Freud and his daughter Anna as principal characters. Meanwhile, the Grand Palais is staging an exhibition called "The Soul in the Body," with objects that manifest the interplay between art and science. One of the major displays is the couch on which Freud's patients in Vienna reclined. In his leather-upholstered office a few blocks away, Serge Leclaire, 69, an ex-president of the French Society for Psychoanalysis, notes all this cultural hubbub in France and contrasts it with the assaults on Freud in the U.S. "What happened to Freudian psychoanalysis in America is the fault of American psychoanalysts," he says. "They froze things into a doctrine, almost a

religion, with its own dogma, instead of changing with the times."

For their part, U.S. psychoanalysts admit that Freud has been taking some pretty hard knocks lately but deny that his impact or importance has waned as a result. Says George H. Allison, a Seattle-based analyst: "I think Freud's influence in mental health as well as the humanities is much greater than it was 40 years ago. I hear much more being written and said about Freud." Allison points to the proliferation of therapies—there are now more than 200 talking cures competing in the U.S. mental health marketplace, and 10 to 15 million Americans doing some kind of talking—and he argues that "they really are based on Freudian principals, even though a lot of people who head these movements are anti-Freudian officially. But they are standing on the shoulders of a genius."

This image raises anew the quicksand question. If Freud's theories are truly as oozy as his critics maintain, then what is to

> # In the ultimate accounting, psychoanalysis and all its offshoots may turn out to be no more reliable than phrenology or mesmerism

keep all the therapies indebted to them from slowly sinking into oblivion as well? Hypothetically, nothing, though few expect or want that event to occur. Surprisingly, Peter Kramer, author of the current best seller *Listening to Prozac*, comes to the defense of talking cures and their founder: "Even Freudian analysts don't hold themselves 100% to Freud. Psychotherapy is like one of those branching trees, where each of the branches legitimately claims a common ancestry, namely Freud, but none of the branches are sitting at the root. We'd be very mistaken to jettison psychotherapy or Freud."

Frederick Crews, a professor of English at the University of California, Berkeley, and a well-known reviewer and critic, once enthusiastically applied Freudian concepts to literary works and taught his students to do likewise. Then he grew disillusioned and now ranks as one of Freud's harshest American debunkers. Even while arguing that Freud was a liar and that some of his ideas did not arise from clinical observa-

tions but instead were lifted from "folklore," Crews grows cautious about the prospect of a world suddenly without Freud or his methods: "Those of us who are concerned about pointing out Freud's intellectual failings are not, by and large, experts in the entire range of psychotherapy. I take no position on whether psychotherapy is a good thing or not."

Such prudence may be well advised. Freud was not the first to postulate the unconscious; the concept has a long intellectual ancestry. Nor did Freud ever prove, in empirical terms that scientists would accept, the existence of the unconscious. But Jonathan Winson, professor emeritus of neurosciences at Rockefeller University in New York City, who has done extensive research on the physiology of sleep and dreams, now claims Freud's intuition of its existence was correct, even if his conclusions were off the mark: "He's right that there is a coherent psychological structure beneath the level of the conscious. That's a marvelous insight for which he deserves credit. And he deserves credit too for sensing that dreams are the 'royal road' to the unconscious."

That, finally, may be the central problem with declaring Freud finished. For all of his log rolling and influence peddling, his running roughshod over colleagues and patients alike, for all the sins of omission and commission that critics past and present correctly lay on his couch, he still managed to create an intellectual edifice that *feels* closer to the experience of living, and therefore hurting, than any other system currently in play. What he bequeathed was not (despite his arguments to the contrary), nor has yet proved itself to be, a science. Psychoanalysis and all its offshoots may in the final analysis turn out to be no more reliable than phrenology or mesmerism or any of the countless other pseudosciences that once offered unsubstantiated answers or false solace. Still, the reassurances provided by Freud that our inner lives are rich with drama and hidden meanings would be missed if it disappeared, leaving nothing in its place.

Shortly after Freud actually died in 1939, W.H. Auden, one of the many 20th century writers who mined psychoanalysis for its ample supply of symbols and imagery, wrote an elegy that concluded:

> . . . *sad is Eros, builder of cities,*
> *and weeping anarchic Aphrodite.*

Auden's choice of figures from Greek mythology was intentional and appropriate. Perhaps Homer and Sophocles and the rest will prove, when all is said and done, better guides to the human condition than Freud. But he did not shy away from such competition. —*Reported by Ann Blackman/ Washington, Barry Hillenbrand/London, Janice M. Horowitz/ New York and Benjamin Ivry/Paris*

Clues to the Irrational Nature of Dreams

Sandra Blakeslee

First comes drowsiness and a sense that it's time to rest. Eyelids grow heavy. Stray thoughts flicker through the mind as sleep begins, often with a sudden twitch. And then the human brain falls into a state of profound madness filled with hallucinations, delusions and confabulations.

Dreams unfold. We walk, run, fly and float through strange landscapes. Characters appear and turn into different people. Objects are transformed. A rope becomes a snake. Uncle Harry turns into a Tibetan monk and it all makes sense in some screwy, dreamlike way.

The bizarre nature of dreams is beginning to make sense to scientists who study the biological and physiological changes that occur in the brain during sleep, wakefulness and the many related states, like dreamless sleep, daydreaming and, some say, the writing of poetry and other creative acts.

For example, researchers have found that during sleep the brain is bombarded by wild, erratic pulses from the brainstem and flooded with nervous system chemicals that induce the insanity of dreams. Areas that control sleep are near areas that control body movements, which explains why eyelids grow heavy with drowsiness and why dreams are full of fictive movements.

Finally, the research is shedding light on the biological basis of some forms of schizophrenia, and may also help explain why deep meditation or isolation tanks can induce hallucinations and offer insight into the nature of consciousness itself.

"We study sleeping to understand waking," said Dr. Allan Hobson, a neuroscientist at Harvard University who has helped develop some of the leading theories on the biology of dreams. "We study dreaming to understand madness."

We study sleeping to understand waking and dreaming to understand madness.

Dr. Hobson and his colleagues presented their latest findings at the annual meeting of the Society for Sleep Research in Boston last month.

Dream researchers disagree about many of the details, "but the Hobson model is the best thing we have going for us now," said Dr. Stanley Krippner, president of the Association for the Study of Dreams and a veteran dream psychologist. "It can tell us a lot about how memory is constructed and reconstructed and how people use personal myths" to define reality.

Machines like electroencephalograms that measure electrical brain activity and others that measure magnetic brain activity cannot distinguish the awake brain from the dreaming brain, Dr. Hobson said in a recent interview.

The awake brain receives copious amounts of information from the outside world, mainly in the form of light and sound frequencies, chemical signals and physical touch, Dr. Hobson said. It processes these signals in vast, oscillating networks of brain cells to form representations of the external world and combines these maps with memories, movements, emotions and forethought in a way that gives rise to self-awareness and an ability to navigate the world during waking hours.

The dreaming brain employs all of the same systems and networks, Dr. Hobson said, but with a few critical differences. Input from the outside world is screened out. Self-awareness ceases. The body is paralyzed. And everything that the dreaming brain sees, hears or feels is generated from within.

During sleep the nondreaming brain falls physiologically somewhere between these two states, Dr. Hobson said. New technology allows researchers to examine the chemical, electrical and physical properties of each state. "We can study each of these states to see what the differences are," he said.

The key to dreams is found in several tiny nodes within the brainstem that contain cells which squirt out different chemical transmitters, Dr. Hobson said. These cells have projections that carry the chemicals throughout the brain and modulate its activity. The projections also extend down to the spinal cord and help control movement.

The awake brain is dominated by

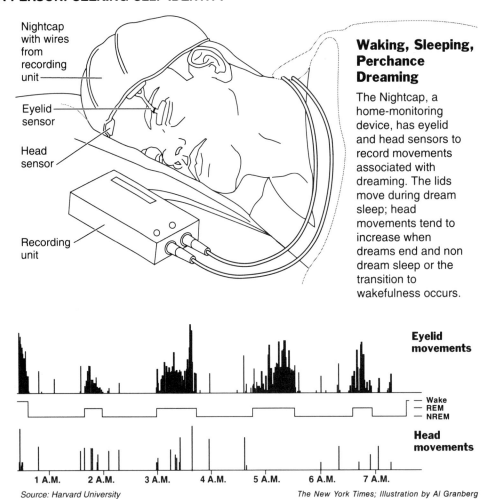

Waking, Sleeping, Perchance Dreaming

The Nightcap, a home-monitoring device, has eyelid and head sensors to record movements associated with dreaming. The lids move during dream sleep; head movements tend to increase when dreams end and non dream sleep or the transition to wakefulness occurs.

Nightcap with wires from recording unit

Eyelid sensor

Head sensor

Recording unit

Eyelid movements

Wake
REM
NREM

Head movements

1 A.M.　2 A.M.　3 A.M.　4 A.M.　5 A.M.　6 A.M.　7 A.M.

Source: Harvard University　　*The New York Times; Illustration by Al Granberg*

so-called adrenergic chemicals released from two of these nodes, Dr. Hobson said. The cells fire these chemicals in pacemaker fashion, keeping the brain alert, enhancing attention and priming motor activity. In the adrenergic state thought processes are generally stable and the brain is not easily dominated by stray images.

'Gimmick' to Induce Sleep

As the brain goes to sleep, the adrenergic system begins to shut down, Dr. Hobson said. Other nodes release so-called cholinergic chemicals which, although active in performing important brain functions during the day, begin to dominate the brain's chemistry. Self-awareness ceases and memory is lost. The brain enters a state of dreamless sleep featuring fuzzy images. It is not organized.

The cholinergic neurons are located one millimeter away from neurons that control muscles in the eyelids, Dr. Hobson said. This is why the eyelids get heavy when cholinergic signals take over. "It's the body's gimmick to get you to sleep," he said.

Soon, Dr. Hobson said, adrenergic neurons cease firing altogether. Cholinergic chemicals decouple the extensive networks used for cognition and behavior. In this state, the brain is ultrasensitive to stray thoughts and can jump from one class of images to another without realizing contradictions. In other words, it dreams.

The bifurcations of thought and the bizarre nature of dreams are also driven by cholinergic neurons, he said. Instead of firing steadily, as they do during the day, these cells begin bursting hundreds of times a second and sending erratic pulses into higher brain regions. These pulses, called PGO, or

pontine-geniculate-occipital, waves, occur only during dreams and have multiple effects.

First, they stimulate the body's motor centers, found in the brainstem. This would cause the dreamer to walk, run and carry out a vast repertoire of movements except that another signal is sent simultaneously to the spinal cord, resulting in total muscle paralysis except for the eyes. This increase in cholinergic activity is what makes many people twitch or startle when they are drifting off to sleep, Dr. Hobson said. And it explains why sleepwalking almost always occurs during nondream sleep, when the muscles are not paralyzed.

In dreams, Dr. Hobson continued, complex motor patterns are activated. "It's no accident that we are always in motion," he said. "We are practicing all sorts of movements in a kind of neural gymnastics."

The Sleep-Dream Cycle at the Brain-Cell Level

Two types of brain cells show different activity patterns in waking, non-dreaming sleep and dreaming sleep. The type called locus ceruleus neurons, controlling the adrenergic chemical system, are most active during waking hours, drop during non-rapid-eye-movement (NREM) sleep and are quiescent in REM, or dream, sleep. The type called giant pontine neurons, controlling the cholinergic chemical system, are least active in waking, progressively more active in NREM sleep and most active in dreaming.

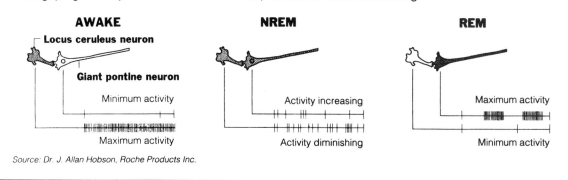

Source: Dr. J. Allan Hobson, Roche Products Inc.

The New York Times

The Stuff of Dreams

PGO waves also bombard the brain's emotional circuits and give rise to the strong feelings that often accompany dreams, Dr. Hobson said. One-third of all adult dreams involve anxiety and fear, he said, followed by joy, anger, sadness, guilt and eroticism.

Finally, the PGO waves shoot into the brain's higher regions where vast networks for processing information reside. Except now, Dr. Hobson said, every sight, sound and sensory input is generated internally by the brain itself. The higher networks, which are used to making representations of the world during the waking state, try to make sense of the internal images and feelings by concocting stories in the cholinergic brain, he said. The repertoire of possible combinations of images, memories and story lines on any given night is extremely large, and chance stimulation probably plays a large role in the content of our dreams.

People can enter a cholinergic state without going to sleep, said Dr. Edgar Garcia-Rill, a neuroscientist at the University of Arkansas in Little Rock, in an interview after the Boston meeting. He points out that such states exist during meditation, as well as sometimes when people are in sensory isolation tanks. Pilots occasionally experience these states when they stare at nothing but blue sky. Hallucinations, as in dreams, may result.

Many scientific insights have occurred in dreams, when the brain is open to unusual associations, Dr. Garcia-Rill said. He suggested that poets may be more naturally cholinergic. And, in work underway in his laboratory, Dr. Garcia-Rill has found that some schizophrenics have an abnormal number of cholinergic neurons in their brainstems, and that this defect may explain the hallucinations that mark the disorder.

To explore dreams in a more natural setting than the hospital-based sleep laboratory, Harvard researchers recently invented a device called the Nightcap. It is a cloth bandanna, worn pirate-style around the head, attached to a wallet sized instrument that tucks under the pillow. One lead goes to a tiny box stitched into the bandanna that registers each time a person's head moves. A second lead sticks to one eyelid and records lid movements all night long. The lids move during dream sleep, whereas head movements tend to occur when dreams end and nondream sleep or the transition to wakefulness occurs, said Robert Stickgold, a researcher in the laboratory.

The Nightcap can record up to 30 nights of sleep, Mr. Stickgold said. The device plugs into a computer so that any individual's sleep patterns can be analyzed in minutes, easily and relatively inexpensively, while he sleeps at home in his own bed. A Nightcap user can program the device to sound a signal during a dream episode to wake him up, so that he can recall the dreams.

Alcohol, Prozac and Exercise

Home dream reports are four times longer than dream reports taken in laboratories, Mr. Stickgold said.

In experiments described in the March issue of the journal Consciousness and Cognition, the Nightcap showed that alcohol use suppresses dream sleep, that Prozac intensifies it and that heavy exercise can result in no body movements throughout the night.

Mr. Stickgold said that researchers in Thailand plan to use the device to explore why many young men who live near the Laotian border die suddenly in their sleep. The current explanation is that the men are being visited by the widow ghost who punishes them for infidelity.

"We also hope to send the Nightcap into space," Mr. Stickgold said. Astronauts on the Mir space station could use it to study the effects of zero gravity on dreams: "Do you still shift your body after coming out of a dream? Are dream reports going to be different?" he said.

The Harvard laboratory is also studying the content of dreams for insights into changing brain states. Dreams are full of discontinuities, incongruities, uncertainties and jumps in plot, scene location, characters and objects. What do these say about dream mentation?

Using 453 dream reports from 45 volunteers, the Harvard researchers cut dream reports into segments at discontinuity points—as when a beach scene abruptly and nonsensically turns into an indoor scene. The segments were spliced together in novel ways, while other dreams were left intact. Independent observers were asked to pick out the spliced dreams. They did no better than chance.

The Nature of Consciousness

In a second experiment, the researchers studied character and object transformations in dreams. Can a teacher turn into a whale? Can a barn turn into a teacher? Apparently not, for when people were shown two columns of characters and objects and asked to pair those that made sense, they got it right 80 percent of the time.

"There are limits to the transformations that can occur at some deep category level," Dr. Hobson said.

Eventually, he added, research into sleep and dreaming may help explain the nature of consciousness. People cycle through different brain states every 24 hours, he said. If more can be learned about each state, it might be possible to subtract one from the other to learn how consciousness is engineered.

Piecing Together Personality

BRUCE BOWER

Psychological research presents a challenge to psychiatric diagnosis

Alice exhibited a bewildering array of problems when she entered psychotherapy. At least three separate conditions in the *Diagnostic and Statistical Manual of Mental Disorders* (DSM) — the bible of psychiatry — applied to the 24-year-old woman. Unfortunately, each diagnosis held different implications for how best to help her.

Frequent eating binges followed by induced vomiting qualified Alice for a diagnosis of bulimia. But she also heeded destructive urges to abuse a wide variety of drugs and to seek anonymous sexual encounters, felt intensely self-conscious, careened between anxiety and depression, and showed other signs of what DSM labels borderline personality disorder. And to complete the triple whammy, her extreme inhibition and timidity supported a diagnosis of avoidant personality disorder.

Faced with this morass of distress, Alice's therapist, psychologist Cynthia G. Ellis of the University of Kentucky in Lexington, took a heretical step: She abandoned DSM's guiding principles and instead evaluated her client's behavior, feelings, and motivations along five broad dimensions. This allowed the psychologist to characterize Alice as displaying a single personality disorder marked by introversion and excessive neuroticism — in Alice's case, primarily impulsive acts, emotional vulnerability, and depression.

Ellis then composed a treatment plan.

First, she dealt with Alice's immediate symptoms of bulimia. Then, over the next 2½ years, therapy sessions began carefully to explore Alice's longstanding fears of emotional intimacy and their reverberations in her life.

A minority of psychotherapists would take this dimensional approach to treating Alice or anyone else whose personality somehow goes seriously awry. But an increasingly vocal group of scientists is pushing for official recognition of dimensional techniques — particularly the five-factor model employed by Ellis.

"There may never be a consensus on how to define and measure personality," asserts University of Kentucky psychologist Thomas A. Widiger. "But there's enough support for the five-factor model to indicate that it provides a useful point of departure for understanding personality disorders."

In 1980, the DSM's authors elevated personality disorders to a status alongside so-called symptom disorders, such as depression and schizophrenia. In a single stroke, certain personality traits — enduring ways of behaving, perceiving, and thinking about oneself and others — coalesced into medical disorders that lay across a theoretical Rubicon from "normal" personalities.

Clinicians diagnose personality disorders alone or in combination with symptom disorders. However, the frequency with which personality disorders occur in the general population is unknown.

Widiger served on the task force that developed definitions of the 11 personality disorders in the current DSM and of the 10 that will be retained in the fourth edition, or DSM-IV, slated for publication by the American Psychiatric Association later this year. An appendix in DSM-IV will list two additional personality disorders deemed worthy of further study.

Although many DSM diagnoses have sparked debate, personality disorders quickly achieved the dubious distinction of arousing the most intense controversy. Psychiatrists and other mental health workers disagreed over which personality defects truly belonged in DSM, and tempers flared over proposed diagnoses that carried social and political overtones, such as the self-defeating and sadistic disorders (SN: 2/25/89, p.120).

Studies also found that clinicians often disagreed about which personality disorder to assign to a given individual. Some reports noted that people displaying severely disturbed personalities met DSM criteria for an average of four different personality disorders, a sure recipe for clinical confusion.

As psychiatrists grappled with these issues, psychologists undertook intensive studies of individual differences in personality traits for the first time in more than 20 years. This work had fallen out of favor during the 1960s and 1970s, which featured behaviorists' examinations of conditioned responses to various rewards and punishments and social psychologists' emphasis on how specific situations mold thoughts and behaviors.

Amid the current resurgence of personality research, some psychologists contend that attempts to chart unchanging traits fail to illuminate the ways in which the same personality changes from one social situation to another. Others argue that individuals construct multiple selves, a theory that questions the entire notion of stable, measurable personalities.

Nevertheless, trait theories of personality — exemplified by the five-factor model — enjoy considerable prominence. Their proponents treat personality disorders as instances in which traits that are present to some degree in all people reach inflexible and harmful extremes. DSM's partitioning of personality disturbances into medical conditions ignores the underlying links between well-functioning and disrupted personalities, these researchers hold.

The five-factor model focuses on the extent to which personality traits vary across five broad dimensions: neuroticism, or proneness to various forms of psychological distress and impulsive behavior; extroversion, the tendency to seek interactions with others and feel joy and optimism; openness to experience, a measure of curiosity, receptivity to new ideas, and the ability to experience emotions; agreeableness, which indicates the extent to which someone shows both compassion and antagonism toward others; and conscientiousness, the degree of organization and stick-to-itiveness regarding personal goals.

One set of questionnaires to measure these traits comes from studies of adjectives used to describe personality. Factor analyses, which mathematically divvy up such adjectives into as few coherent groups as possible, identified five independent personality dimensions as early as 1934. In the January 1993 AMERICAN PSYCHOLOGIST, Lewis R. Goldberg, a psychologist at the University of Oregon in Eugene, describes attempts to develop ratings scales for the five factors based on factor analysis.

Perhaps the bulk of research now focuses on one particular questionnaire inspired by the five-factor model. Paul T. Costa Jr. and Robert R. McCrae, both psychologists at the National Institute on Aging's Gerontology Research Center in Baltimore, devised this instrument to elicit self-reports as well as observations by spouses, peers, and clinicians. It consists of 181 statements that describe personality attributes; those who complete the questionnaire rate their level of agreement with each statement on a scale of 0 to 4.

Costa and McCrae's questionnaire breaks down each of the five factors into a number of component parts, or facets. An overall neuroticism score, for instance, consists of items that provide separate measures for anxiety, hostility, depression, self-consciousness, impulsiveness, and emotional vulnerability.

Studies of large groups administered this questionnaire indicate that numerous personality traits and factors proposed by other scientists — which have often created a sense of disarray in personality research — fall within the bounds of the five-factor model, Costa and McCrae argue.

On the heels of these findings comes a book in which researchers and clinicians apply the five-factor model to personality disorders. Costa and Widiger edited the volume, titled *Personality Disorders and the Five-Factor Model of Personality* (1994, American Psychological Association).

One chapter describes research supporting the view that the five-factor model accounts for both broken-down and finely tuned personalities. Directed by Lee Anna Clark, a psychologist at the University of Iowa in Iowa City, this work finds that people diagnosed with various personality disorders stretch one or more of the five basic traits to maladaptive extremes.

Clark's group administered trait questionnaires developed by Goldberg, Costa and McCrae, and her own scales derived from DSM criteria for personality disorders to groups of college students and psychiatric patients. All three inventories, particularly the one informed by DSM symptoms, accurately identified people in each population who suffered from personality disorders, Clark contends.

More specifically, in cases of borderline personality disorder, data on the five factors gleaned from Costa and McCrae's questionnaire offer valuable insight to clinicians, according to Cynthia Sanderson and John F. Clarkin, both of Cornell University Medical College in New York City. In a study of 64 women assigned this diagnosis, Sanderson and Clarkin find extremely high levels of neuroticism, as evidenced by anxiety, depression, self-consciousness, and a wide range of impulsive behaviors.

The same women also display low conscientiousness, reflected in aimlessness and a lack of clear goals, and low agreeableness, marked by cynicism, vengefulness, and constant attempts to manipulate others. Not surprisingly, psychotherapists encounter many difficulties in treating borderline personalities and need to monitor their problem traits from the start, the researchers maintain.

Widiger, Costa, and their colleagues propose five-factor profiles of each DSM personality disorder. Their profile of paranoid personality disorder, for instance, stresses excessively low agreeableness, characterized most strongly by suspiciousness and antagonism. Hostility, one facet of neuroticism, also shows up consistently in people diagnosed with this disorder, they contend.

Agreeableness also plummets in both narcissistic and antisocial personality disorders, the researchers note. The exorbitant self-importance and arrogance typical of the former condition translate into low scores on the agreeableness facets of modesty, altruism, and empathy, they assert. The latter disorder, marked by repeated criminal, aggressive, and irresponsible acts, features low altruism and a copious supply of extroversion, particularly as measured by items that signal a constant need for excitement and sensory stimulation.

Five-factor descriptions of paranoid personality disorder and other diagnoses that involve odd or eccentric behavior may be improved by rewording the openness-to-experience items to address such peculiarities directly, Widiger says. Auke Tellegen, a psychologist at the University of Minnesota in Minneapolis, has completed such a revision and changed the name of the dimension from "openness-to-experience" to "unconventionality."

Unlike its predecessor, Tellegen's unconventionality scale assesses, for instance, the tendency to read hidden and threatening meanings into others' remarks, one symptom of a paranoid personality. This scale also considers the magical thinking and perceptual illusions that often characterize schizotypal personality disorder.

Tellegen also proposes adding two new factors to the five-factor model; these tap into highly negative and positive qualities attributed to the self, such as a propensity for evil, treachery, excellence, and superiority.

A more far-reaching challenge to the five-factor model comes from research directed by C. Robert Cloninger, a psychiatrist at Washington University School of Medicine in St. Louis. In the December 1993 ARCHIVES OF GENERAL PSYCHIATRY, Cloninger and his coworkers describe the seven dimensions that they deem crucial to understanding healthy and disordered personalities.

Four dimensions account for temperament: novelty seeking, harm avoidance, reward dependence, and persistence. Individuals largely inherit their temperamental styles, which are triggered by perceptions of their surroundings, Cloninger's group theorizes. Temperament orchestrates the habitual behaviors that a person carries out unthinkingly throughout the day, they suggest.

The St. Louis scientists also devised three character dimensions: self-directedness (a measure of commitment to goals and purposes), cooperativeness, and self-transcendence (associated with deeply held spiritual beliefs and feelings of connection with nature or the universe). Character development leans heavily on a conscious sorting out of one's memories and experiences, the investigators argue. This process picks up steam during adulthood as misfortunes and death more frequently intrude on people's lives, they note.

Cloninger and his colleagues administered a true-false questionnaire consisting of 107 temperament items and 119 character items to 300 psychologically healthy adults. Volunteers ranged in age from 18 to 91. The seven personality dimensions clearly emerged in the sample, they contend. Character dimensions assumed increasing importance and complexity in older age groups.

The researchers also obtained questionnaire responses from 66 psychiatric patients who ran the gamut of DSM personality disorders. Low self-directedness and low cooperativeness emerge as core features of all personality disorders, they report. Moreover, each personality disorder displays a unique pattern of temperament and character scores, the investigators contend.

Most clinicians, and particularly psychiatrists, who deal with people suffering from personality disorders remain skeptical of the five-factor model and other dimensional measures of personality.

Theodore Millon, a psychiatrist at Harvard Medical School in Boston, considers it best to view the symptoms that make up each DSM category as a prototype, or most typical example, of that personality disorder. Individuals assigned the same diagnosis usually differ to some degree from the prototype, Millon asserts.

So, for example, a diagnosis of borderline personality disorder may apply to someone exhibiting five of the eight required symptoms listed in the current DSM. Other cases of borderline personality disorder may include more than five symptoms and may feature shifting mixes and different intensities of the various symptoms.

In this approach, the personality disorders shade into one another as they veer farther away from their prototypes. Clinicians must determine the degree to which a person's symptoms match prototypes of relevant personality disorders in order to come up with a primary diagnosis, Millon argues.

Dimensional models deal with surface characteristics that may only illuminate the few personality disorders that create moderate problems, adds John G. Gunderson, a psychiatrist at McLean Hospital in Belmont, Mass. Severe personality disorders, including borderline and antisocial disorders, occur most frequently and involve complex underlying problems that elude trait questionnaires, Gunderson asserts.

Other psychiatrists harbor more practical concerns. Although the dimensional approach holds much promise for analyzing personality disturbances, its acceptance and sophisticated use by clinicians "will require a monumental educational effort," according to Allen J. Frances of Duke University Medical Center in Durham, N.C. Frances directed work on DSM-IV.

What's more, notes five-factor proponent Thomas Widiger, many clinicians fear that discarding DSM categories for a dimensional focus on normal traits gone bad will result in denial of insurance coverage for treatment of serious personality disturbances.

Ongoing research aims to establish cutoff points at which scores on five-factor questionnaires signify major personality problems, Widiger says. Some psychologists have proposed that the American Psychological Association issue a rival DSM that takes this approach. Widiger, however, hopes that the next edition of DSM will include the five-factor model as a supplement to traditional personality disorder categories.

DSM-IV includes a statement acknowledging the existence of several dimensional models of personality but fails to recommend any of them for clinical use, Widiger says.

Michael H. Stone, a psychiatrist at Columbia University, would welcome a hybrid approach to treating personality disturbances.

"Sophisticated clinicians use both categories and dimensions all the time in thinking about their patients," Stone asserts. "But psychiatrists have largely ignored the research of personality psychologists."

In a book titled *Abnormalities of Personality* (1993, W.W. Norton), Stone lists 500 negative and 100 positive personality adjectives that he considers components of the five-factor model. He often administers to his patients questionnaires that inquire about these qualities; the results greatly assist in diagnosis and treatment planning, he says.

For the most part, though, psychiatrists prefer that personality dimensions take a backseat to DSM's personality disorders. "The general psychiatric public may not be ready for a sea change in diagnostic practice," Stone contends.

But true to form, personality disturbances continue to make waves.

Personality: Major Traits Found Stable Through Life

Daniel Goleman

Studies challenge theories that see transitions.

The largest and longest studies to carefully analyze personality throughout life reveal a core of traits that remain remarkably stable over the years and a number of other traits that can change drastically from age to age.

The new studies have shown that three basic aspects of personality change little throughout life: a person's anxiety level, friendliness and eagerness for novel experiences. But other traits, such as alienation, morale and feelings of satisfaction, can vary greatly as a person goes through life. These more changeable traits largely reflect such things as how a person sees himself and his life at a given point, rather than a basic underlying temperament.

One of the recently completed studies followed 10,000 people 25 to 74 years old for nine years. Another involved 300 couples first tested in 1935. The studies are joined by a new analysis of more than two dozen earlier studies of lifetime personality and a study of twins that looks at the genetic contribution.

The recent work poses a powerful challenge to theories of personality that have emphasized stages or passages—predictable points in adult life—in which people change significantly.

The new research is "a death knell" for the passage theories of adult personality, in the view of a researcher who conducted one of the new studies. "I see no evidence for specific changes in personality due to age," said the researcher, Paul T. Costa Jr. "What changes as you go through life are your roles and the issues that matter most to

you. People may think their personality has changed as they age, but it is their habits that change, their vigor and health, their responsibilities and circumstances—not their basic personality."

But the new work has not made converts of the theorists who see adult life through the framework of passages. Rather they assert that simple pencil and paper tests cannot discern the richness inherent in the maturing personality. A theory proposed by Daniel Levinson, a psychologist at Yale University, suggests a series of sometimes troubled transitions between psychological stages; Erik Erikson coined the term "identity crisis" for the difficulties some young people have in settling on a life course.

Proponents of the most recent studies say, however, that the notion of passages, built on clinical interviews, was never objectively tested.

Some of the strongest evidence for the stability of the core personality throughout adulthood comes from a study by Dr. Costa and Robert McCrae, psychologists at the National Institute on Aging in Baltimore. They interviewed thousands of people in 100 places throughout the United States in 1975, and again in 1984.

The researchers found virtually no change in the three key personality traits. Their report in a recent issue of the Journal of Gerontology asserts that a person who was calm and well-adjusted at 25 years of age would remain so at 65, while a person who was emotionally volatile at 25 would be about the same at 65. Their findings represented

averages, however, and could not reflect the changes in some individuals that might have been brought on by, for instance, psychotherapy or a personal catastrophe.

ONLY THE FORM CHANGES

"There is no evidence of any universal age-related crises; those people who have crises at one point or another in life tend to be those who are more emotional," said Dr. Costa. "Such people experience some degree of distress through most of life; only the form of the trouble seems to change."

A mellowing in midlife, found by other studies, has now been shown to relate more to a muting of some of a person's more extreme feelings than to any change in the overall pattern of personality.

The new studies find no increase in irritability with aging. "The stereotype that people become cranky and rigid as they age does not hold up," said Dr. Costa. "The calm, outgoing, adventurous young person is going to stay that way into old age, given good health. Those who are dogmatic and closed to experience early in life remain that way."

The greatest changes in core personality occur in childhood and from adolescence to early adulthood, according to Dr. Costa. "After 25, as William James said, character is set in plaster," he said. "What does change is one's role in life, and the situations that influence your temporary behavior one way or another."

Support for Dr. Costa's large study comes from a recent study of twins that found an important genetic influence on the three main traits. Early childhood experiences, the investigators concluded, are not the main influence in shaping the most persistent of personality traits, though they may shape them to some degree, as they do all personality.

In this study of 203 pairs of twins at Indiana University, the researchers, Michael Pogue-Geile and Richard Rose, administered a personality test when the subjects were 20, and again when they were 25. The researchers were looking to see whether fraternal twins changed in the same ways as identical twins in that time, which is one of the stages of turbulent transition proposed by some theorists. If a particular trait is genetically determined it will tend to change more similarly in identical twins than it will in fraternal twins.

There was evidence of significant genetic influence on the three main personality traits of anxiety or emotionality, friendliness and openness to new things.

Life experience also shaped these basic traits. But it had a far greater influence on other personality traits, including alienation, morale and feelings of satisfaction. These traits change so much over the course of adult life that there is virtually no relationship between their levels when a person is in his 20's and when he is in his 60's, according to James Conley, who studied 300 couples who were tested in 1935, 1955 and 1980, when the researchers were able to interview 388 of the original 600 men and women.

"If you try to predict how alienated or satisfied with life people will be in their later years from how they seem in college, you will fail abysmally," he said.

Dr. Conley is among those finding that the three basic traits change little over a lifetime. In addition to the study of couples, he has reviewed data from more than two dozen other long-term personality studies.

Some personality traits may make certain crises in life more probable. For instance, the study of couples suggests that specific combinations of personality in a marriage are explosive. Over the course of 45 years, the highest probability of divorce occurred in those marriages where both the husband and wife were emotionally volatile and the husband had little impulse control.

"The evaluations in 1935, by five friends, of the personalities of an engaged couple was highly predictive of which marriages would break up," Dr. Conley said, "If you have a couple with emotional hair triggers, and where the husband philanders, gambles, drinks, or loses jobs, a break-up is almost certain. Some marriages broke up right away: some took 45 years to end. Data from younger couples suggests that today the dangerous combination of personalities is the same, except now it can

Critics say the new studies lack necessary subtlety.

be either the wife or the husband whose impulsiveness triggers the trouble."

Walter Mischel, a psychologist at Columbia University, wrote an influential article in 1968 arguing that the variation in expression of a given trait from situation to situation is so great that the notion of personality traits itself was of little use in accounting for how people behave.

VARIATIONS WITH SITUATION

"There is lots of evidence for the stability of some traits, such as extroversion, over time," Dr. Mischel said in a recent interview. "But the same person may be quite outgoing in some circumstances, and not at all in others."

Kenneth Craik, a psychologist at the University of California at Berkeley, said, "The belief for 10 to 15 years after Mischel's critique was that the situation determined far more than personality

about how people behave." Now, within the last few years, he said, "personality and situation are seen by most researchers as having about equal influence."

Researchers are concluding that the influence of one situation or another on how a person acts may also create the impression that personality itself changes more than is the case; apparent changes in personality may actually reflect temporary circumstances.

"Any trait can vary with the moment," said Seymour Epstein, a personality psychologist at the University of Massachusetts at Amherst. "You need to look at the person in many situations to get a stable rating of that trait."

And people seem to differ in how much situations affect their actions, according to research by Mark Snyder, a psychologist at the University of Minnesota. In "Public Appearances, Private Reality," published recently by W.H. Freeman & Company, Dr. Snyder reviews evidence showing that some people are virtual chameleons, shaping themselves to blend into whatever social situation they find themselves, while others are almost oblivious to the special demands and expectations of differing situations, being more or less the same person regardless of where they are.

The situation-oriented, Dr. Snyder has found, are skilled at social roles: At a church service, they display just the right combination of seriousness and reserve; at a cocktail party they become the friendly and sociable extrovert.

Those less affected by situations are more consistent in their behavior, putting less effort into role-playing: They have a smaller wardrobe, wearing the same clothes in more situations, than do the situation-oriented.

It is as though each type were playing to a different audience, one inner, the other outer, says Dr. Snyder.

Those adept at situations flourish in jobs where they deal with a range of **different groups, Dr. Snyder reports.**

Determinants of Behavior: Motivation, Environment, and Physiology

On the front pages of every newspaper, in practically every televised newscast, and on many magazine covers the problems of substance abuse in America haunt us. Innocent children are killed when caught in the crossfire of the guns of drug lords. Prostitutes selling their bodies for drug money spread the deadly AIDS virus. The white-collar middle manager loses his job because he embezzled company money to support his cocaine habit.

Why do people turn to drugs? Why doesn't all of the publicity about the ruining of human lives diminish the drug problem? Why can some people consume two cocktails and stop while others feel helpless against the inebriating seduction of alcohol? Why do some people crave heroin as their drug of choice when others choose marijuana?

This section focuses on the causes of individual behavior. If physiology, either biochemistry or genes, is the determinant of our behavior, then solutions to such puzzles as alcoholism lie in the field of psychobiology (the study of behavior in relation to biological processes). However, if experience as a function of our environment and learning histories creates personality and causes subsequent behavior, normal or not, then researchers must take a different tack and explore features of the environment responsible for certain behaviors. A third explanation involves some complex interaction or interplay between experience and biology. If this interaction accounts for individual characteristics, scientists have a very complicated task ahead of them.

Conducting research designed to unravel the determinants of behavior is difficult. Scientists must call upon their best design skills to develop studies that will yield useful and replicable findings. A researcher hoping to examine the role of experience in personal growth and behavior needs to be able to isolate one or two stimuli or environmental features that seem to control a particular behavior. Imagine trying to sufficiently delimit the complexity of the world so that only one or two events stand out as the cause of an individual's alcoholism. Likewise, researchers interested in psychobiology also need refined, technical knowledge. Suppose a scientist hopes to show that a particular form of mental illness is inherited. One cannot merely examine family genetic histories, be-

cause family members can also learn maladaptive behaviors from one another. The researcher's ingenuity will be challenged; he or she must use intricate techniques such as comparing children to their adoptive as well as to their biological parents. Volunteer subjects might be difficult to find, and even then, the data may be hard to interpret.

The articles in this section are meant to familiarize you with a variety of hypothesized determinants of behavior. The first article, "Nature or Nurture? Old Chestnut, New Thoughts," discusses the age-old issue of biology vs. environment as contributors to our psychological makeup. In other words, the article examines the nature-nurture controversy. Thus, the article provides an overview for the rest of this unit.

The next two articles collectively examine the nature-nurture controversy with specific examples. In "Sizing Up the Sexes," Christine Gorman raises the issue of sex differences and reviews theories and studies designed to determine whether genetics, hormones, or environment play the greatest role in shaping sex differences. In a similar article entitled, "Born Gay?" the author examines what the causes of homosexuality might be. Interesting new research suggests that preference for same-sex partners might be more biological than learned, contrary to what most researchers first thought. This issue, in particular, is examined by author William Henry.

We next turn to possible contributors of behavior and examine them individually and in more detail. The role of biological factors is explored in the next three articles. In "Mapping the Brain" you will learn about the parts of the nervous system and how they are responsible for influencing our behaviors. The article incorporates information about mapping the brain, fun brainteasers for the reader to try, and discussion of how various parts of the brain function to contribute to thought, language, and, most importantly for us, emotions. In a complementary article, a remarkable accident is described. In the 1800s, railroad worker Phineas Gage's brain was impaled by a large iron rod. He miraculously survived, and his case allowed researchers to study the effects of injury in a specific region of the brain. We learned from Gage's experience that one particular center in the brain controls moral reasoning and social behavior, which was sorely lacking in

Gage after his accident. In "Understanding the Genetics Age," Jim Smith provides a succinct review of the study of genetics. The article also describes certain cures for some severe, modern maladies. We turn our attention to sensory apparati in "The Sniff of Legend." Karen Wright raises an interesting issue, namely, whether humans communicate chemically. We know that certain animals communicate by means of pheromones, or chemical stimuli, and Wright queries whether this is possible in humans.

Two final articles speculate on whether our minds and bodies are connected; that is, whether what we think and feel influences our physical being. In "On the Power of Positive Thinking: The Results of Being Optimistic," Michael Scheier and Charles Carver review research on optimism. Optimism is important to both our psychological and our physical well-being. In the last article, "The Mind and the Body," C. David Jenkins concedes that physical health affects how we feel mentally, but he is less sure whether how we feel mentally affects our physical health. This controversy is investigated by Jenkins.

In summary, this unit covers factors that determine our behavior. The factors may be internal (as in genetics, physiology, and our own private thoughts) or external (such as our environment and those around us).

Looking Ahead: Challenge Questions

Based on your experience observing children, what would you say most contributes to their personal growth: physiological or environmental factors?

Name some bona fide sex differences. What perceived differences are due to stereotypes and therefore untrue? From where do sex differences originate? Do you think the sexes are more similar than they are different?

Where do you think homosexuality originates? Would knowing that genetics are responsible for homosexuality alter your opinion of homosexuality? How would you feel if the environment accounted for the preference for same-sex partners?

Besides sex differences and homosexuality, can you think of other psychological phenomena that would be interesting or worth examining to determine what factors contribute to them? What utility or practical application does searching for causes of behaviors have?

How can we map the brain? Do you know the various parts of the brain? Can you ascribe certain behaviors to certain parts of the brain? Do you have any brainteasers you can share with your class?

Do you know of anyone besides Phineas Gage who has had a brain injury? Describe how the injury altered their personalities or abilities and how the injury altered their lives. After reading about Gage, what, if anything, should we do about individuals like Gage whose antisocial behavior is beyond their control?

Why do you think that it is important to study genetics? If we knew that an illness, physical or mental, was inheritable, what could/should we do about it?

How do animals communicate chemically? Do you think that humans communicate chemically? Explain your answer.

How are optimists different from pessimists, both psychologically and physically? Does the mind control the body? Do you think there is a link between the mental state and bodily illness? Provide anecdotal evidence or research support.

NATURE OR NURTURE?

■

Old chestnut, new thoughts

Few questions of human behaviour are more controversial than this: are people programmed by their genes, or by their upbringing? There is no simple answer, but the academic world is starting to hear a lot more from the genes brigade—on both sides of the political spectrum

ARE criminals born or made? Is homosexuality a preference or a predisposition? Do IQ tests measure innate abilities or acquired skills?

For the past 50 years, respectable academic opinion, whenever it has deigned to deal with such layman's questions, has come down firmly for nurture over nature. Nazism discredited even the mildest attempts to produce genetic explanations of human affairs. And economic growth after the second world war encouraged most western governments to imagine that they could eliminate social problems by a mixture of enlightened planning and generous spending—that, in effect, they could steer (even change) human nature.

In this atmosphere, the social sciences flourished as never before. Sociologists made lucrative careers producing "nurture" explanations of everything from school failure to schizophrenia. Geneticists stuck to safe subjects such as fruit flies and honey bees, rather than risk being accused of a fondness for jackboots and martial music.

The fashion is beginning to change. The failure of liberal reforms to deliver the Great Society has cast doubt on the proposition that better nurture can deliver better nature. The failure of sociologists to find even a few of the purported (Freudian or social) causes of schizophrenia, homosexuality, sex differences in criminal tendencies and the like has undermined their credibility. And a better understanding of how genes work has made it possible for liberals who still believe in the perfectibility

of man to accept genetic explanations. In at least one case—homosexuality—it is now the liberals who espouse nature and their opponents who point to nurture.

The pro-nature people are still a minority in universities. But they are a productive and increasingly vocal minority—and one which is beginning to increase its influence in the media. Open the American newspapers and you can read left-inclined pundits like Micky Kaus arguing that income inequality is partly the result of genetic differences. Turn on the television and you can see intelligent, unbigoted people claiming that male homosexuals have a different brain structure from heterosexual men.

This is only the beginning. Richard Herrnstein, a professor of psychology at Harvard University, and Charles Murray, a controversial critic of the welfare state, are collaborating on a study of the implications of biological differences for public policy. The book will highlight the tension between America's egalitarian philosophy and the unequal distribution of innate abilities.

The reaction of orthodox opinion has been scathing. America's National Institutes of Health provoked such an angry response to its decision to finance a conference on genetics and crime that it decided to withdraw the money. Mr Murray lost the patronage of the Manhattan Institute, a New York-based think-tank, when he decided to study individual differences and social policy.

Even in these days of politically correct fetishes, on no other subject is the gulf be-

tween academics and ordinary people so wide. Even the most hopeful of parents know that the sentiment "all men are created equal" is a pious dream rather than a statement of fact. They know full well that, say, one of their sons is brighter, or more musical or more athletic than another; they see, despite their best attentions, that girls turn every toy into a doll and boys turn every toy into a weapon; they rarely persist in believing that each and all of these differences is the result of early encouragement or training. They know that even if full equality of opportunity could be guaranteed, equality of outcome could not. Ability is not evenly distributed.

But parents' opinions are unscientific. Not until 1979 did a few academics begin to catch up. In that year the Minnesota Centre for Twin and Adoption Research began to contact more than 100 sets of twins and triplets who had been separated at birth and reared apart, mostly in the United States and Britain.

The centre subjected each pair to thorough psychological and physiological tests. If two twins are identical (or "monozygotic"), any differences between them are due to the environment they were reared in; so a measure of heritability can be attached to various mental features. The study concluded that about 70% of the variance in IQ was explained by genetic factors. It also found that on a large number of measures of personality and temperament—notably personal interests and social attitudes—identical twins reared apart are about as similar as identical twins reared together.

The Minnesota study represents the respectable end of an academic spectrum that stretches all the way through to outright racists. If IQ is 70% inherited, then perhaps much of the IQ difference between races is also inherited. The logic does not necessarily follow, since the differences could all lie in the 30% that is nurture; but still it is a hypothesis worth testing—at least for those prepared to risk being called politically incorrect.

Unfortunately, because there are no black-white pairs of identical twins, nobody has yet found a way to test whether racial differences in IQ are genetic. It would require getting 100 pairs of black parents and 100 pairs of white parents to rear their children on identical incomes in an identical suburb and send the children of 50 of each to the same good school and 50 of each to a bad one. Impossible.

This means that racial differences in IQ tend to attract scientists with dubious motives and methods. With increasing enthusiasm over the past decade, some psychologists have disinterred a technique already consigned to the attic by their Victorian predecessors: using physiological data to measure intellectual skill.

Arthur Jensen, a professor of educational psychology at the University of California, Berkeley, has assembled a large body of results purportedly demonstrating that IQ is closely correlated with speed of reaction, a theory abandoned around 1900. He claims that intelligence is correlated with the rate at which glucose is consumed in the brain, the speed of neural transmission and a large number of anatomical variables such as height, brain size and even head size.

Jean Philippe Rushton, a professor of psychology at the University of Western Ontario, Canada, has revived craniometry, the Victorian attempt to correlate head size with brain power. (In "The Adventure of the Blue Carbuncle", one of Arthur Conan Doyle's most ingenious Christmas stories, Sherlock Holmes deduces that a man is an intellectual from the size of his hat: "It is a question of cubic capacity . . . a man with so large a brain must have something in it.")

Mr Rushton has studied data on the head sizes of thousands of American servicemen, gathered to make sure that army helmets fit. Adjusting the raw data for variables such as body size, he argues that men have bigger craniums than women, that the well-educated have bigger craniums than the less educated, and that orientals have bigger craniums than whites, who have bigger craniums than blacks.

Mr Rushton has done wonders for the protest industry. David Peterson, a former premier of Ontario, called for his dismissal. Protesters likened him to the Nazis and the Ku Klux Klan. The Ontario Provincial police even launched an investigation into his work. An embarrassed university establishment required Mr Rushton to give his lectures on videotape.

Even if you could conclude that blacks have lower IQs than whites after the same education, it is not clear what the policy prescription would be. Presumably, it would only add weight to the argument for positive discrimination in favour of blacks, so as to redress an innate inferiority with a better education. The "entitlement liberalism" that prevails in American social policy and finds its expression in employment quotas and affirmative-action programmes already assumes that blacks need preferential rather than equal treatment. Indeed, to this way of thinking, merit is less important than eliminating group differences and promoting social integration.

The gene of Cain

Compared with the study of racial differences, the study of the genetics of criminality is only slightly more respectable. Harvard's Mr Herrnstein teamed up in the early 1980s with James Wilson, a political scientist, to teach a class on crime. The result was "Crime and Human Nature" (1985), a bulky book which argues that the best explanation for a lot of predatory criminal behaviour—particularly assault and arson—may be biological rather than sociological.

Certainly, a Danish study of the children of criminals adopted into normal households lends some support to the idea that a recidivist criminal's son is more likely to be a criminal than other sons brought up in the same household. But Mr Herrnstein and Mr Wilson then spoil their case with another Victorian throwback to "criminal types"—people with low verbal intelligence and "mesomorphic" (short and muscular) bodies who, they believe, are more likely to be criminal.

One reason such work strikes horror into sociologists is that it suggests an obvious remedy: selective breeding. Mr Herrnstein has suggested that the greater fertility of stupid people means that the wrong kind of selective breeding is already at work and may be responsible for falling academic standards. "We ought to bear in mind", Mr Herrnstein ruminates gloomily about America, "that in not too many generations differential fertility could swamp the effects of anything else we may do about our economic standing in the world." Luckily for Mr Herrnstein, studies reveal that, despite teenage parents in the inner cities, people of high social status are still outbreeding those of low social status. Rich men have more surviving children—not least because they tend to have more wives—than poor men.

In one sense, it is plain that criminality is innate: men resort to it far more than women. Martin Daly and Margo Wilson, of McMaster University in Canada, have compared the homicide statistics of England and Wales with those of Chicago. In both cases, the graphs are identical in shape, with young men 30 times as likely as women of all ages to commit homicide. It is perverse to deny the connection between testosterone and innate male aggressiveness. But it is equally perverse to ignore the fact that the scales of the two graphs are utterly different: young men in Chicago are 30 times as likely to kill as young men in England and Wales—which has nothing to do with nature and much to do with nurture. The sexual difference is nature; the national difference is nurture.

The most successful assault on the nurturist orthodoxy, however, has come not over race, or intelligence, or crime, but over sex. In the 1970s the nurturists vigorously repulsed an attack on their cherished beliefs by the then fledgling discipline of sociobiology. Sociobiology is the study of how animal behaviour evolves to fit function in the same way that anatomy does.

When sociobiologists started to apply the same ideas to human beings, principally through Edward Wilson of Harvard University, a furore broke out. Most of them retreated, as geneticists had done, to study animals again. Anthropologists insisted that their subject, mankind, was basically different from animals because it was not born with its behaviour but learnt it.

In the past few years, however, a new assault from scientists calling themselves Darwinian psychologists has largely refuted that argument. Through a series of experiments and analyses, they have asserted that (a) much sophisticated behaviour is not taught, but develops autonomously; and (b) learning is not the opposite of instinct, but is itself a highly directed instinct.

The best example of this is language. In 1957 Noam Chomsky of the Massachusetts Institute of Technology (MIT) argued that all human languages bear a striking underlying similarity. He called this "deep structure", and argued it was innate and not learnt. In recent years Steven Pinker of MIT and Paul Bloom of the University of Arizona have taken this idea further. They argue that human beings have a "language organ", specially designed for learning grammatical language. It includes a series of highly specific inbuilt assumptions that enable them to learn grammar from examples, without ever being taught it.

Hence the tendency to learn grammatical language is human nature. But a child reared in isolation does not start to speak Hebrew unaided. Vocabulary, and accent, are obviously 100% nurture. In this combination of nature and nurture, argue the Darwinian psychologists, language is typical of most human traits. Learning is not the opposite of instinct; people have innate instincts to learn certain things and not others.

This is heresy to sociologists and anthropologists, who have been reared since Emile Durkheim to believe the human

27

mind is a *tabula rasa*—a blank slate upon which any culture can be written. To this, John Tooby and Leda Cosmides of the University of California at Santa Barbara, two leading thinkers on the subject, have replied: "The assertion that 'culture' explains human variation will be taken seriously when there are reports of women war parties raiding villages to capture men as husbands."

Nor will the Darwinian psychologists concede that to believe in nature is to be a Hobbesian fatalist and that to believe in nurture is to be a Rousseau-ist believer in the perfectibility of man. Many totalitarians are actually nurturists: they believe that rearing people to worship Stalin works. History suggests otherwise.

The making of macho

Physiologists have also begun to add weight to the nature side of the scale with their discovery of how the brain develops. The brain of a fetus is altered by the child's genes, by its and its mother's hormones and, after birth, by its learning. Many of the changes are permanent; so as far as the adult is concerned, they are all "nature", though many are not genetic. For example, the human brain is feminine unless acted upon by male hormones during two bursts—one in the womb and another at puberty. The hormone is nurture, in the sense that it can be altered by

injections or drugs taken by the mother. But it is nature in the sense that it is a product of the body's biology.

This discovery has gradually altered the views of many psychologists about sex and education. An increasing number recognise that the competitiveness, roughness, mathematical ability and spatial skills of boys are the product of their biology (genes and hormones) not their family, and that the character-reading, verbal, linguistic and emotional interest and skills of girls are also biological. Hence girls get a better early education when kept away from boys. This conclusion, anathema to most practising educational psychologists, is increasingly common among those who actually do research on it.

Indeed, radical feminism is increasingly having to recognize the biological theme that underlies its claims. Feminists demand equality of opportunity, but they also routinely argue that women bring different qualities to the world: consensus-seeking, uncompetitive, caring, gentle qualities that inherently domineering men lack. Women, they argue, should be in Parliament or Congress in representative numbers to "represent the woman's point of view", which assumes that men cannot.

Many homosexuals have already crossed the bridge to nature. When sociobiologists first suggested that homosexuality might be biological, they were called

Nazis and worse. But in the past few years things have turned around completely. The discovery that the identical twin of a homosexual man has an odds-on chance of being homosexual too, whereas a non-identical twin has only a one-in-five chance, implies that there are some influential genes involved. And the discovery that those parts of the brain that are measurably different in women and men are also different in heterosexuals and homosexuals adds further weight to the idea that homosexuality is as natural as left-handedness. That is anathema to pro-family-value conservatives, who believe that homosexuality is a (misguided) personal choice.

Assuming that the new hereditarians are right and that many human features can be related to genes (or, more likely, groups of genes), it might one day be possible to equip each member of the species with a compact disc telling him which version of each of the 50,000-100,000 human genes he has. He might then read whether he was likely to have a weight problem, or be any good at music, whether there was a risk of schizophrenia or a chance of genius, whether he might go manic-depressive or be devoutly religious. But he could never be sure. For beside every gene would be an asterisk referring to a footnote that read thus: "This prediction is only valid if you are brought up by two Protestant, middle-class, white parents in Peoria, Illinois."

Sizing Up The Sexes

Scientists are discovering that gender differences have as much to do with the biology of the brain as with the way we are raised

CHRISTINE GORMAN

What are little boys made of?
What are little boys made of?
Frogs and snails
And puppy dogs' tails,
That's what little boys are made of.

What are little girls made of?
What are little girls made of?
Sugar and spice
And all that's nice,
That's what little girls are made of.
　　—Anonymous

Many scientists rely on elaborately complex and costly equipment to probe the mysteries confronting humankind. Not Melissa Hines. The UCLA behavioral scientist is hoping to solve one of life's oldest riddles with a toybox full of police cars, Lincoln Logs and Barbie dolls. For the past two years, Hines and her colleagues have tried to determine the origins of gender differences by capturing on videotape the squeals of delight, furrows of concentration and myriad decisions that children from 2 1/2 to 8 make while playing. Although both sexes play with all the toys available in Hines' laboratory, her work confirms what most parents (and more than a few aunts, uncles and nursery-school teachers) already know. As a group, the boys favor sports cars, fire trucks and Lincoln Logs, while the girls are drawn more often to dolls and kitchen toys.

But one batch of girls defies expectations and consistently prefers the boy toys. These youngsters have a rare genetic abnormality that caused them to produce elevated levels of testosterone, among other hormones, during their embryonic development. On average, they play with the same toys as the boys in the same ways and just as often. Could it be that the high levels of testosterone present in their bodies before birth have left a permanent imprint on their brains, affecting their later behavior? Or did their parents, knowing of their disorder, somehow subtly influence their choices? If the first explanation is true and biology determines the choice, Hines wonders, "Why would you evolve to want to play with a truck?"

Not so long ago, any career-minded researcher would have hesitated to ask such questions. During the feminist revolution of the 1970s, talk of inborn differences in the behavior of men and women was distinctly unfashionable, even taboo. Men dominated fields like architecture and engineering, it was argued, because of social, not hormonal, pressures. Women did the vast majority of society's child rearing because few other options were available to them. Once sexism was abolished, so the argument ran, the world would become a perfectly equitable, androgynous place, aside from a few anatomical details.

But biology has a funny way of confounding expectations. Rather than disappear, the evidence for innate sexual differences only began to mount. In medicine, researchers documented that heart disease strikes men at a younger age than it does women and that women have a more moderate physiological response to stress. Researchers found subtle neurological differences between the sexes both in the brain's structure and in its functioning. In addition, another generation of parents discovered that, despite their best efforts to give baseballs to their daughters and sewing kits to their sons, girls still flocked to dollhouses while boys clambered into tree forts. Perhaps nature is more important than nurture after all.

Even professional skeptics have been converted. "When I was younger, I believed that 100% of sex differences were due to the environment," says Jerre Levy, professor of psychology at the University of Chicago. Her own toddler toppled that utopian notion. "My daughter was 15 months old, and I had just dressed her in her teeny little nightie. Some guests arrived, and she came into the room, knowing full well that she looked adorable. She came in with this saucy little walk, cocking her head, blinking her eyes, especially at the men. You never saw such flirtation in your life." After 20 years spent studying the brain, Levy is convinced: "I'm sure there are biologically based differences in our behavior."

Now that it is O.K. to admit the possibility, the search for sexual differences has expanded into nearly every branch of the life sciences. Anthropologists have debunked Margaret Mead's work on the extreme variability of gender roles in New Guinea. Psychologists are untangling the complex interplay between hormones and aggression. But the most provocative, if as yet inconclusive, discoveries of all stem from the pioneering exploration of a tiny 3-lb. universe: the human brain. In fact, some researchers predict that the confirmation of innate differences in behavior could lead to an unprecedented understanding of the mind.

Some of the findings seem merely curious. For example, more men than women are lefthanded, reflecting the dominance of the brain's right hemisphere. By contrast, more women listen equally with both ears while men favor the right one.

Other revelations are bound to provoke more controversy. Psychology tests, for instance, consistently support the notion that men and women perceive the world in subtly different ways. Males excel at rotating three-dimensional objects in their head. Females prove better at reading emotions of people in photographs. A growing number of scientists believe the discrepancies reflect functional differences in the brains of men and women. If true, then some misunderstandings between the sexes may have more to do with crossed wiring than cross-purposes.

Most of the gender differences that have been uncovered so far are, statistically speaking, quite small. "Even the largest differences in cognitive function are not as large as the difference in male and female height," Hines notes. "You still see a lot of overlap." Otherwise, women could never read maps and men would always be lefthanded. That kind of flexibility within

EMOTIONS
FEMALE INTUITION: THERE MAY BE SOMETHING TO IT
Do women really possess an ability to read other people's hidden motives and meanings? To some degree, they do. When shown pictures of actors portraying various feelings, women outscore men in identifying the correct emotion. They also surpass men in determining the emotional content of taped conversation in which the words have been garbled. This ability may result from society's emphasis on raising girls to be sensitive. But some researchers speculate that it has arisen to give women greater skill in interpreting the cues of toddlers before they are able to speak.

MALE INSENSITIVITY: IT'S A CULTURAL RELIC
If men seem less adept at deciphering emotions, it is a "trained incompetence," says Harvard psychologist Ronald Levant. Young boys are told to ignore pain and not to cry. Some anthropologists argue that this psychic wound is inflicted to separate boys from their mothers and prepare them for warfare. Many men, says Levant, can recognize their emotions only as a physical buzz or tightness in the throat—a situation that can be reversed, he insists, with training.

the sexes reveals just how complex a puzzle gender actually is, requiring pieces from biology, sociology and culture.

Ironically, researchers are not entirely sure how or even why humans produce two sexes in the first place. (Why not just one—or even three—as in some species?) What is clear is that the two sexes originate with two distinct chromosomes. Women bear a double dose of the large X chromosome, while men usually possess a single X and a short, stumpy Y chromosome. In 1990 British scientists reported they had identified a single gene on the Y chromosome that determines maleness. Like some kind of biomolecular Paul Revere, this master gene rouses a host of its compatriots to the complex task of turning a fetus into a boy. Without such a signal, all human embryos would develop into girls. "I have all the genes for being male except this one, and my husband has all the genes for being female," marvels evolutionary psychologist Leda Cosmides,

of the University of California at Santa Barbara. "The only difference is which genes got turned on."

Yet even this snippet of DNA is not enough to ensure a masculine result. An elevated level of the hormone testosterone is also required during the pregnancy. Where does it come from? The fetus' own undescended testes. In those rare cases in which the tiny body does not respond to the hormone, a genetically male fetus develops sex organs that look like a clitoris and vagina rather than a penis. Such people look and act female. The majority marry and adopt children.

The influence of the sex hormones extends into the nervous system. Both males and females produce androgens, such as testosterone, and estrogens—although in different amounts. (Men and women who make no testosterone generally lack a libido.) Researchers suspect that an excess of testosterone before birth enables the right hemisphere to dominate the brain, resulting in lefthandedness. Since testosterone levels are higher in boys than in girls, that would explain why more boys are southpaws.

Subtle sex-linked preferences have been detected as early as 52 hours after birth. In studies of 72 newborns, University of Chicago psychologist Martha McClintock and her students found that a toe-fanning reflex was stronger in the left foot for 60% of the males, while all the females favored their right. However, apart from such reflexes in the hands, legs and feet, the team could find no other differences in the babies' responses.

One obvious place to look for gender differences is in the hypothalamus, a lusty little organ perched over the brain stem that, when sufficiently provoked, consumes a person with rage, thirst, hunger or desire. In animals, a region at the front of the organ controls sexual function and is somewhat larger in males than in females. But its size need not remain constant. Studies of tropical fish by Stanford University neurobiologist Russell Fernald reveal that certain cells in this tiny region of the brain swell markedly in an individual male whenever he comes to dominate a school. Unfortunately for the piscine pasha, the cells will also shrink if he loses control of his harem to another male.

Many researchers suspect that, in humans too, sexual preferences are controlled by the hypothalamus. Based on a study of 41 autopsied brains, Simon LeVay of the Salk Institute for Biological Studies announced last summer that he had found a region in the hypothalamus that was on average twice as large in heterosexual men as in either women or homosexual men. LeVay's findings support the idea that varying hormone levels before birth may immutably stamp the developing brain in one erotic direction or another.

These prenatal fluctuations may also steer boys toward more rambunctious behavior than girls. June Reinisch, director of the Kinsey Institute for Research in Sex, Gender and Reproduction at Indiana University, in a pioneering study of eight pairs of brothers and 17 pairs of sisters ages 6 to 18 uncovered a complex interplay between hormones and aggression. As a group, the young males gave more belligerent answers than did the females on a multiple-choice test in which they had to imagine their response to stressful situations. But siblings who had been exposed in utero to synthetic antimiscarriage hormones that mimic testosterone were the most combative of all. The affected boys proved significantly more aggressive than their unaffected brothers, and the drug-exposed girls were much more contentious than their unexposed sisters. Reinisch could not determine, however, whether this childhood aggression would translate into greater ambition or competitiveness in the adult world.

While most of the gender differences uncovered so far seem to fall under the purview of the hypothalamus, researchers have begun noting discrepancies in other parts of the brain as well. For the past nine years, neuroscientists have debated whether the corpus callosum, a thick bundle of nerves that allows the right half of the brain to communicate with the left, is larger in women than in men. If it is, and if size corresponds to function, then the greater crosstalk between the hemispheres might explain enigmatic phenomena like female intuition, which is supposed to accord women greater ability to read emotional clues.

These conjectures about the corpus callosum have been hard to prove because the structure's girth varies dramatically with both age and health. Studies of autopsied material are of little use because brain tissue undergoes such dramatic changes in the hours after death. Neuroanatomist Laura Allen and neuroendocrinologist Roger Gorski of UCLA decided to try to circumvent some of these problems by obtaining brain scans from live, apparently healthy people. In their investigation of 146 subjects, published in April, they confirmed that parts of the corpus callosum were up to 23% wider in women than in men. They also measured thicker connections between the two hemispheres in other parts of women's brains.

Encouraged by the discovery of such structural differences, many researchers have begun looking for dichotomies of function as well. At the Bowman Gray Medical School in Winston-Salem, N.C., Cecile Naylor has determined that men and women enlist widely varying parts of their brain when asked to spell words. By monitoring increases in blood flow, the neuropsychologist found that women use both sides of their head when spelling

PERCEPTION

HE CAN READ A MAP BLINDFOLDED, BUT CAN HE FIND HIS SOCKS?

It's a classic scene of marital discord on the road. Husband: "Do I turn right?" Wife, madly rotating the map: "I'm not sure where we are." Whether men read maps better is unclear, but they do excel at thinking in three dimensions. This may be due to ancient evolutionary pressures related to hunting, which requires orienting oneself while pursuing prey.

IF LOST IN A FOREST, WOMEN WILL NOTICE THE TREES

Such prehistoric pursuits may have conferred a comparable advantage on women. In experiments in mock offices, women proved 70% better than men at remembering the location of items found on a desktop—perhaps reflecting evolutionary pressure on generations of women who foraged for their food. Foragers must recall complex patterns formed of apparently unconnected items.

while men use primarily their left side. Because the area activated on the right side is used in understanding emotions, the women apparently tap a wider range of experience for their task. Intriguingly, the effect occurred only with spelling and not during a memory test.

Researchers speculate that the greater communication between the two sides of the brain could impair a woman's performance of certain highly specialized visual-spatial tasks. For example, the ability to tell directions on a map without physically having to rotate it appears stronger in those individuals whose brains restrict the process to the right hemisphere. Any crosstalk between the two sides apparently distracts the brain from its job. Sure enough, several studies have shown that this mental-rotation skill is indeed more tightly focused in men's brains than in women's.

But how did it get to be that way? So far, none of the gender scientists have figured out whether nature or nurture is more important. "Nothing is ever equal, even in the beginning," observes Janice Juraska, a biopsychologist at the University of Illinois at Urbana-Champaign. She points out, for instance, that mother rats lick their male offspring more frequently than they do their daughters. However, Juraska has demonstrated that it is possible to reverse some inequities by manipulating environmental factors. Female rats have fewer nerve connections than males into the hippocampus, a brain region associated with spatial relations and memory. But when Juraska "enriched" the cages of the females with

stimulating toys, the females developed more of these neuronal connections. "Hormones do affect things—it's crazy to deny that," says the researcher. "But there's no telling which way sex differences might go if we completely changed the environment." For humans, educational enrichment could perhaps enhance a woman's ability to work in three dimensions and a man's ability to interpret emotions. Says Juraska: "There's nothing about human brains that is so stuck that a different way of doing things couldn't change it enormously."

Nowhere is this complex interaction between nature and nurture more apparent than in the unique human abilities of speaking, reading and writing. No one is born knowing French, for example; it must be learned, changing the brain forever. Even so, language skills are linked to specific cerebral centers. In a remarkable series of experiments, neurosurgeon George Ojemann of the University of Washington has produced scores of detailed maps of people's individual language centers.

First, Ojemann tested his patients' verbal intelligence using a written exam. Then, during neurosurgery—which was performed under a local anesthetic—he asked them to name aloud a series of objects found in a steady stream of black-and-white photos. Periodically, he touched different parts of the brain with an electrode that temporarily blocked the activity of that region. (This does not hurt because the brain has no sense of pain.) By noting when his patients made mistakes, the surgeon was able to determine which sites were essential to naming.

Several complex sexual differences emerged. Men with lower verbal IQs were more likely to have their language skills located toward the back of the brain. In a number of women, regardless of IQ, the naming ability was restricted to the frontal lobe. This disparity could help explain why strokes that affect the rear of the brain seem to be more devastating to men than to women.

Intriguingly, the sexual differences are far less significant in people with higher verbal IQs. Their language skills developed in a more intermediate part of the brain. And yet, no two patterns were ever identical. "That to me is the most important finding," Ojemann says. "Instead of these sites being laid down more or less the same in everyone, they're laid down in subtly different places." Language is scattered randomly across these cerebral centers, he hypothesizes, because the skills evolved so recently.

What no one knows for sure is just how hardwired the brain is. How far and at what stage can the brain's extraordinary flexibility be pushed? Several studies suggest that the junior high years are key. Girls show the same aptitudes for math as

LANGUAGE

IN CHOOSING HER WORDS, A WOMAN REALLY USES HER HEAD

For both sexes, the principal language centers of the brain are usually concentrated in the left hemisphere. But preliminary neurological studies show that women make use of both sides of their brain during even the simplest verbal tasks, like spelling. As a result, a woman's appreciation of everyday speech appears to be enhanced by input from various cerebral regions, including those that control vision and feelings. This greater access to the brain's imagery and depth may help explain why girls often begin speaking earlier than boys, enunciate more clearly as tots and develop a larger vocabulary.

IF JOHNNY CAN'T READ, IS IT BECAUSE HE IS A BOY?

Visit a typical remedial-reading class, and you'll find that the boys outnumber the girls 3 to 1. Stuttering affects four times as many boys as girls. Many researchers have used these and other lopsided ratios to support the argument that males, on average, are less verbally fluent than females. However, the discrepancy could also reflect less effort by teachers or parents to find reading-impaired girls. Whatever the case, boys often catch up with their female peers in high school. In the past few years, boys have even begun outscoring girls on the verbal portion of the Scholastic Aptitude Test.

Is Sex Really Necessary?

Birds do it. Bees do it. But dandelions don't. The prodigious spread of these winsome weeds underscores a little-appreciated biological fact. Contrary to human experience, sex is not essential to reproduction. "Quite the opposite," exclaims anthropologist John Tooby of the University of California at Santa Barbara. "From an engineer's standpoint, sexual reproduction is insane. It's like trying to build an automobile by randomly taking parts out of two older models and piecing them together to make a brand-new car." In the time that process takes, asexual organisms can often churn out multiple generations of clones, gaining a distinct edge in the evolutionary numbers game. And therein lies the puzzle: If sex is such an inefficient way to reproduce, why is it so widespread?

Sex almost certainly originated nearly 3.5 billion years ago as a mechanism for repairing the DNA of bacteria. Because ancient earth was such a violent place, the genes of these unicellular organisms would have been frequently damaged by intense heat and ultraviolet radiation. "Conjugation"—the intricate process in which one bacterium infuses genetic material into another—provided an ingenious, if cumbersome, solution to this problem, although bacteria continued to rely on asexual reproduction to increase their numbers.

Animal sex, however, is a more recent invention. Biologist Lynn Margulis of the University of Massachusetts at Amherst believes the evolutionary roots of egg and sperm cells can be traced back to a group of organisms known as protists that first appeared some 1.5 billion years ago. (Modern examples include protozoa, giant kelp and malaria parasites.) During periods of starvation, Margulis conjectures, one protist was driven to devour another. Sometimes this cannibalistic meal was incompletely digested, and the nuclei of prey and predator fused. By joining forces, the fused cells were better able to survive adversity, and because they survived, their penchant for union was passed on to their distant descendants.

From this vantage point, human sexuality seems little more than a wondrous accident, born of a kind of original sin among protozoa. Most population biologists, however, believe sex was maintained over evolutionary time because it somehow enhanced survival. The mixing and matching of parental genes, they argue, provide organisms with a novel mechanism for generating genetically different offspring, thereby increasing the odds that their progeny could exploit new niches in a changing environment and, by virtue of their diversity, have a better chance of surviving the assaults of bacteria and other tiny germs that rapidly evolve tricks for eluding their hosts' defenses.

However sex came about, it is clearly responsible for many of the most remarkable features of the world around us, from the curvaceousness of human females to the shimmering tails of peacocks to a lion's majestic mane. For the appearance of sex necessitated the evolution of a kaleidoscope of secondary characteristics that enabled males and females of each species to recognize one another and connect.

The influence of sex extends far beyond the realm of physical traits. For instance, the inescapable fact that women have eggs and men sperm has spurred the development of separate and often conflicting reproductive strategies. University of Michigan psychologist David Buss has found that men and women react very differently to questions about infidelity. Men tend to be far more upset by a lover's sexual infidelity than do women: just imagining their partner in bed with another man sends their heart rate soaring by almost five beats a minute. Says Buss: "That's the equivalent of drinking three cups of coffee at one time." Why is this so? Because, Buss explains, human egg fertilization occurs internally, and thus a man can never be certain that a child borne by his mate is really his. On the other hand, because women invest more time and energy in bearing and caring for children, they react more strongly to a threat of emotional infidelity. What women fear most is the loss of their mates' long-term commitment and support.

The celebrated war between the sexes, in other words, is not a figment of the imagination but derives from the evolutionary history of sex—from that magic moment long, long ago when our unicellular ancestors entwined in immortal embrace.

—*By J. Madeleine Nash/Chicago*

HOW OTHER SPECIES DO IT

Humans think there's nothing more natural than males and females in mutual pursuit of the urge to be fruitful and multiply. But nature follows more than one script. Not every species has two sexes, for example. And even when it does, neither their behavior nor their origin necessarily conforms to human notions of propriety. Some of the more bizarre cases in point:

TURTLES

Among most reptiles, males are literally made in the shade. The gender of a turtle hatchling, for instance, is determined not by sex chromosomes but by the temperature at which it was incubated. Eggs that develop in nests located in sunny areas, where it is warm and toasty, give rise to females. Eggs nestled in shady places, where it may be 5°C (10°F) cooler, will yield a crop of males.

WHIPTAIL LIZARDS

For some varieties of these lizards there's no such thing as a battle of the sexes. All of them are female. In a process known as parthenogenesis, they produce eggs that hatch without ever being fertilized. Yet, because they evolved from lizards that come in two sexes, pairs of these single-minded creatures will take turns imitating males and mount each other. The act apparently stimulates greater egg production.

JACANA BIRDS

Females usually rule the roost on every shore, marsh and rice field where these long-legged "lily trotters" abound. They are generally larger than the males, which are saddled with the duties of building the nest, incubating the eggs and raising the chicks. In fact in some varieties, female Casanovas regularly jilt their domestic-minded mates and search for more sexually available males.

CICHLIDS

These fish come in three sexes: brightly hued macho males, paler females, and male wimps that look and act like females. There are only a few sexually active males in a school. But the minute a piscine Lothario dies, an ambitious wimp rises to the occasion. His brain unleashes sex hormones that bring color to his scales and make him feisty, but he can revert to pallid impotence if challenged by a more macho fish.

boys until about the seventh grade, when more and more girls develop math phobia. Coincidentally, that is the age at which boys start to shine and catch up to girls in reading.

By one account, the gap between men and women for at least some mental skills has actually started to shrink. By looking at 25 years' worth of data from academic tests, Janet Hyde, professor of psychology and women's studies at the University of Wisconsin at Madison, discovered that overall gender differences for verbal and mathematical skills dramatically decreased after 1974. One possible explanation, Hyde notes, is that "Americans have changed their socialization and educational patterns over the past few decades. They are treating males and females with greater similarity."

Even so, women still have not caught up with men on the mental-rotation test. Fascinated by the persistence of that gap, psychologists Irwin Silverman and Marion Eals of York University in Ontario wondered if there were any spatial tasks at which women outperformed men. Looking at it from the point of view of human evolution, Silverman and Eals reasoned that while men may have developed strong spatial skills in response to evolutionary pressures to be successful hunters, women would have needed other types of visual skills to excel as gatherers and foragers of food.

The psychologists therefore designed a test focused on the ability to discern and later recall the location of objects in a complex, random pattern. In series of tests, student volunteers were given a minute to study a drawing that contained such unrelated objects as an elephant, a guitar and a cat. Then Silverman and Eals presented their subjects with a second drawing containing additional objects and told them to cross out those items that had been added

and circle any that had moved. Sure enough, the women consistently surpassed the men in giving correct answers.

What made the psychologists really sit up and take notice, however, was the fact that the women scored much better on the mental-rotation test while they were menstruating. Specifically, they improved their scores by 50% to 100% whenever their estrogen levels were at their lowest. It is not clear why this should be. However, Silverman and Eals are trying to find out if women exhibit a similar hormonal effect for any other visual tasks.

Oddly enough, men may possess a similar hormonal response, according to new research reported in November by Doreen Kimura, a psychologist at the University of Western Ontario. In her study of 138 adults, Kimura found that males perform better on mental-rotation tests in the spring, when their testosterone levels are low, rather than in the fall, when they are higher. Men are also subject to a daily cycle, with testosterone levels lowest around 8 p.m. and peaking around 4 a.m. Thus, says June Reinisch of the Kinsey Institute: "When people say women can't be trusted because they cycle every month, my response is that men cycle every day, so they should only be allowed to negotiate peace treaties in the evening."

Far from strengthening stereotypes about who women and men truly are or how they should behave, research into innate sexual differences only underscores humanity's awesome adaptability. "Gender is really a complex business," says Reinisch. "There's no question that hormones have an effect. But what does that have to do with the fact that I like to wear pink ribbons and you like to wear baseball gloves? Probably something, but we don't know what."

Even the concept of what an innate difference represents is changing. The physical and chemical differences between the brains of the two sexes may be malleable and subject to change by experience: certainly an event or act of learning can directly affect the brain's biochemistry and physiology. And so, in the final analysis, it may be impossible to say where nature ends and nurture begins because the two are so intimately linked.

—*Reported by*
J. Madeleine Nash/Los Angeles

BORN GAY?

Studies of family trees and DNA make the case that male homosexuality is in the genes

WILLIAM A. HENRY III

WHAT MAKES PEOPLE GAY? TO conservative moralists, homosexuality is a sin, a willful choice of godless evil. To many orthodox behaviorists, homosexuality is a result of a misguided upbringing, a detour from a straight path to marital adulthood; indeed, until 1974 the American Psychiatric Association listed it as a mental disorder. To gays themselves, homosexuality is neither a choice nor a disease but an identity, deeply felt for as far back as their memory can reach. To them, it is not just behavior, not merely what they do in lovemaking, but who they are as people, pervading every moment of their perception, every aspect of their character.

The origins of homosexuality may never be fully understood, and the phenomenon is so complex and varied—as is every other kind of love—that no single neat explanation is likely to suffice to explain any one man or woman, let alone multitudes. But the search for understanding advanced considerably last week with the release of new studies that make the most compelling case yet that homosexual orientation is at least partly genetic.

A team at the National Cancer Institute's Laboratory of Biochemistry reported in the journal *Science* that families of 76 gay men included a much higher proportion of homosexual male relatives than found in the general population. Intriguingly, almost all the disproportion was on the mother's side of the family. That prompted the researchers to look at the chromosomes that determine gender, known as X and Y. Men get an X from

their mother and a Y from their father; women get two X's, one from each parent. Inasmuch as the family trees suggested that male homosexuality may be inherited from mothers, the scientists zeroed in on the X chromosome.

Sure enough, a separate study of the DNA from 40 pairs of homosexual brothers found that 33 pairs shared five different patches of genetic material grouped around a particular area on the X chromosome. Why is that unusual? Because the genes on a son's X chromosome are a highly variable combination of the genes on the mother's two X's, and thus the sequence of genes varies greatly from one brother to another. Statistically, so much overlap between brothers who also share a sexual orientation is unlikely to be just coincidence. The fact that 33 out of 40 pairs of gay brothers were found to share the same sequences of DNA in a particular part of the chromosome suggests that at least one gene related to homosexuality is located in that region. Homosexuality was the only trait that all 33 pairs shared; the brothers didn't all share the same eye color or shoe size or any other obvious characteristic. Nor, according to the study's principal author, Dean Hamer, were they all identifiably effeminate or, for that matter, all macho. They were diverse except for sexual orientation. Says Hamer: "This is by far the strongest evidence to date that there is a genetic component to sexual orientation. We've identified a portion of the genome associated with it."

The link to mothers may help explain a conundrum: If homosexuality is hereditary, why doesn't the trait gradually disappear, as

gays and lesbians are probably less likely than others to have children? The answer suggested by the new research is that genes for male homosexuality can be carried and passed to children by heterosexual women, and those genes do not cause the women to be homosexual. A similar study of lesbians by Hamer's team is taking longer to complete because the existence and chromosomal location of responsible genes is not as obvious as it is in men. But preliminary results from the lesbian study do suggest that female sexual orientation is genetically influenced.

In a related, unpublished study, Hamer added to growing evidence that male homosexuality may be rarer than was long thought—about 2% of the population, vs. the 4% to 10% found by Kinsey and others. Hamer notes, however, that he defined homosexuality very narrowly. "People had to be exclusively or predominantly gay, and had to be out to family members and an outside investigator like me. If we had used a less stringent definition, we would probably have found more gay men."

BEFORE THE NCI, RESEARCH IS ACcepted as definitive, it will have to be validated by repetition. Moreover, the tight focus on pairs of openly homosexual brothers, who are only a subset of the total gay population, leaves many questions about other categories of gay men, lesbians and bisexuals. The NCI researchers concede that their discovery cannot account for all male homosexuality and may be just associated with gayness rather than be a direct cause.

But authors of other studies indicating a biological basis for homosexuality saluted it as a major advance.

Simon LeVay, who won wide publicity for an analysis of differences in brain anatomies between straight and gay men, acknowledges that the brains he studied were of AIDS victims, and thus he cannot be sure that what he saw was genetic rather than the result of disease or some aspect of gay life. Says LeVay: "This new work and the studies of twins are two lines of evidence pointing in the same direction. But the DNA evidence is much stronger than the twin studies." Dr. Richard Pillard, professor of psychiatry at Boston University School of Medicine and co-author of some twin studies—showing that identical twins of gay men have a 50% chance of being gay—is almost as laudatory. Says he: "If the new study holds up, it would be the first example of a higher-order behavior that has been found to be linked to a particular gene."

Whatever its ultimate scientific significance, however, the study's social and political impact is potentially even greater. If homosexuals are deemed to have a foreordained nature, many of the arguments now used to block equal rights would lose force. Opponents of such changes as ending the ban on gays in uniform argue that homosexuality is voluntary behavior, legitimately subject to regulation. Gays counter that they are acting as God or nature—in other words, their genes—intended. Says spokesman Gregory J. King of the Human Rights Campaign Fund, one of the largest gay-rights lobbying groups: "This is a landmark study that can be very helpful in increasing public support for civil rights for lesbian and gay Americans." Some legal scholars think that if gays can establish a genetic basis for sexual preference, like skin color or gender, they may persuade judges that discrimination is unconstitutional.

In addition, genetic evidence would probably affect many private relationships. Parents might be more relaxed about allowing children to have gay teachers, Boy Scout leaders and other role models, on the assumption that the child's future is written in his or her genetic makeup. Those parents whose offspring do turn out gay might be less apt to condemn themselves. Says Cherie Garland of Ashland, Oregon, mother of a 41-year-old gay son: "The first thing any parent of a gay child goes through is guilt. If homosexuality is shown to be genetic, maybe parents and children can get on with learning to accept it." Catherine Tuerk, a nurse psychotherapist who is Washington chapter president of Parents and Friends of Lesbians and Gays, regrets sending her son Joshua into therapy from ages eight to 12 for an "aggression problem"—preference for games involving

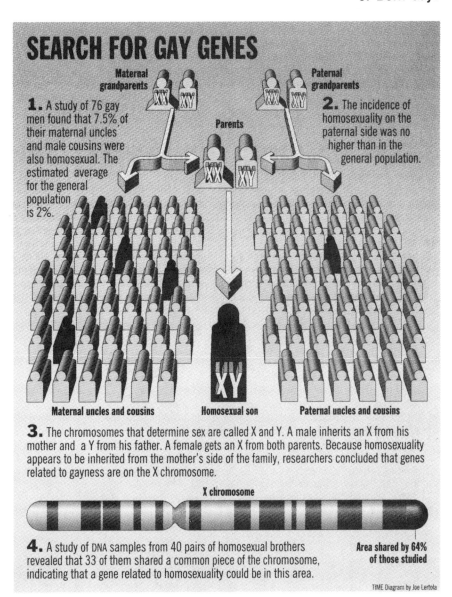

SEARCH FOR GAY GENES

1. A study of 76 gay men found that 7.5% of their maternal uncles and male cousins were also homosexual. The estimated average for the general population is 2%.

Maternal grandparents

Paternal grandparents

Parents

2. The incidence of homosexuality on the paternal side was no higher than in the general population.

Maternal uncles and cousins — Homosexual son — Paternal uncles and cousins

3. The chromosomes that determine sex are called X and Y. A male inherits an X from his mother and a Y from his father. A female gets an X from both parents. Because homosexuality appears to be inherited from the mother's side of the family, researchers concluded that genes related to gayness are on the X chromosome.

X chromosome

4. A study of DNA samples from 40 pairs of homosexual brothers revealed that 33 of them shared a common piece of the chromosome, indicating that a gene related to homosexuality could be in this area.

Area shared by 64% of those studied

TIME Diagram by Joe Lertola

relationships instead of macho play with, say, toy trucks. Says she: "We were trying to cure him of something that doesn't need to be cured. There was nothing wrong with him." On the other hand, mothers who used to blame themselves for faulty upbringing may start blaming themselves for passing on the wrong genes.

Gay brothers surveyed for the study welcome its findings. Rick and Randy Gordon, twins from Orlando, Florida, never felt being gay was a matter of free will. Rick, who works in a law firm, says, "I don't honestly think I chose to be gay." Randy, a supervisor at a bed-and-breakfast, agrees: "I always believed that homosexuality was something I was born with. If homosexuality is genetic, there is nothing you can do about it. If there is more research like this in years to come, hopefully homosexuality will be accepted rather than treated as an abnormality."

Ralph White, 36, an attorney with the General Accounting Office, says he was fired from a senatorial staff in 1982 after admitting he was gay. He foresees abiding significance in the study: "I don't expect people to suddenly change their minds. But the long-term impact will be profound. I can't imagine that rational people, presented with evidence that homosexuality is biological and not a choice, would continue to discriminate." His brother David, 32, a public relations officer, wishes he had had a basis for believing in a genetic cause during his turbulent adolescence: "I was defiant, and to this day I'm probably still that way, because when you're gay in this society you almost have to be."

While many gay leaders welcomed the study, some are queasy. Its very existence, they fret, implies that homosexuality is wrong and defective. Says Donald Suggs of the New York chapter of the Gay & Lesbian Alliance Against Defamation: "Homosexuality is not something to justify and explain, but something that should be accepted. Until people accept us, all the scientific evidence in the world will not do anything to change homophobia." Moreover, gays are worried that precise identification of a "gayness gene" might prompt efforts to tinker with the genetic code of gay adults or to test during pregnancy and abort potentially gay fetuses. Says Thomas Stoddard, director of the Campaign for Military Service: "One can imagine the science of the future manipulating information of this kind to reduce the number of gay people being born."

WARNS ERIC JUENGST OF THE National Center for Human Genome Research: "This is a two-edged sword. It can be used to benefit gays by allowing them to make the case that the trait for which they're being discriminated against is no worse than skin color. On the other hand, it could get interpreted to mean that different is pathological."

Anti-gay activists took up that cry immediately, saying that a genetic basis for homosexuality does not make it any more acceptable. They noted that genetic links are known or suspected for other traits that society judges "undesirable," such as mental and physical illness. Said the Rev. Louis Sheldon, chairman of the Traditional Values Coalition: "The fact that homosexuality may be genetically based will not make much difference for us from a public policy perspective." Reed Irvine, whose watchdog group, Accuracy in Media, increasingly criticizes favorable reportage about gays and gay rights, called for more coverage of studies that he claims show homosexuality can be "cured"—an assertion that both gays and health professionals widely dispute. Says Irvine: "It's a little more complicated than just saying you can prove there's a hereditary factor. The media have given zero attention to the many, many homosexuals who have gone straight. I think it's sending gays the wrong message to say you cannot change because it's something your genes have determined."

Even gays admit that Irvine is partly right. Homosexuality is not simply programmed but is a complex expression of values and personality. As researcher Hamer says, "Genes are part of the story, and this gene region is a part of the genetic story, but it's not all of the story." We may never know all of the story. But to have even part of it can bring light where of late there has been mostly a searing heat. —*Reported by Ellen Germain/Washington and Alice Park/New York*

MAPPING THE
BRAIN

With powerful new devices that peer through the skull and see the brain at work, neuroscientists seek the wellsprings of thoughts and emotions, the genesis of intelligence and language. They hope, in short, to read your mind.

If you have one of 1,000 test copies of this magazine, sometime while you read this article a specially embedded microchip will give you a mild electric shock. If you have an ordinary copy, there is no danger.

Deep inside your brain, a little knob-shaped organ no bigger than a chickpea is going like gangbusters right now (at least if you're the gullible type). The organ is called the amygdala, and when neuroscientists gave volunteers a version of this warning—that sometime during an experiment they might receive an electric shock—the nerve cells in the volunteers' amygdalae lit up like telephone lines during the World Series earthquake. How did the scientists know? They were reading their volunteers' minds—by mapping their brains.

It seems only fitting that, with 1492 in the air, one of the greatest uncharted territories in science is finally attracting its own cartographers. The terrain is the gelatinous three-pound world called the Brain, and the map makers' sextants are devices that stare right through the solid wall of the skull. The maps they are slowly piecing together will carry labels even more provocative than the 15th century's "Disappointment Islands." They will show, with the precision of the best atlas, the islands of emotion and the seas of semantics, the land of forethought and the peninsula of musical appreciation. They will show, in short, exactly where in the brain cognition, feelings, language and everything else that makes us human comes from.

It's called a functional map of the brain, and it is one of the grandest goals of what Congress and President George Bush have declared the "Decade of the Brain." The neuroscientists might actually achieve it, thanks to the technologies that open windows on the mind. With 100 billion cells—neurons—each sprouting about 1,000 sylphlike fingers to reach out and touch another, it's quite a view. "The brain is the last and greatest biological frontier," says James Watson, codiscoverer of the double helix that is DNA. In a book from the National Academy of Sciences released last month entitled "Discovering the Brain," Watson calls it "the most complex thing we have yet discovered in our universe."

To make sense of the jungle of neurons and swamps of gray matter, it won't be enough to take snapshots with, say, a CAT scanner. Computer-assisted tomography produces lovely pictures of brain structure, but can't distinguish between a live brain and a dead one. The challenge for brain cartography is to move beyond structure—all the cranial continents have been identified—to create a detailed diagram of which parts do what. For that, the map makers rely on an alphabet soup of technologies, from PETs to SQUIDs (page 39), that pinpoint neural activity in all its electrical, magnetic and chemical glory.

Each technique adds a different piece to the neural puzzle. Some magnetic imaging, for instance, is so spatially precise it can distinguish structures as small as a millimeter, but is much too slow to reveal the sequence in which different clumps of neurons blink on during a thought. But together, the technologies are yielding a map as detailed as that expected to be drawn for human DNA—though much more interesting. For instance, neuroscientists thought that the cerebellum was the patron saint of the clumsy, the region that controls balance and coordination and so keeps people from stumbling. New studies suggest that the cerebellum may also house the memory of rote movements: touch-typing or violin fingering may originate in the same place as the command not to trip over your own two feet. "Perhaps the brain can package a task very efficiently, even take it out of the conscious world [of the cortex] and just run the program unconsciously," speculates neurologist John Mazziotta of the University of California, Los Angeles. The mapping expeditions have also perked up philosophy. Once again, eminent thinkers are dueling over whether the mind is anything more than the brain.

The lofty abilities of the brain reside in the cortex, the quarter-inch-thick cap of grooved tissue that runs from the eyebrows to the ears. The cortex consists of two hemispheres, a left and a right, each composed of four distinct lobes (diagram, next page) and connected by a highway of fibers called the corpus callosum. Studies of patients with brain lesions, as well as electrical stimulation of conscious patients during brain surgery, have pinpointed scores of regions that seem to specialize in particular jobs. Some make sense of what the eyes see. Others distinguish irregular from regular verbs. But research on brain-damaged people always runs the risk that they aren't representative. The power of the new imaging techniques is that they peer inside the minds of the healthy. "They allow us to study how the living brain performs sophisticated mental functions," says neuroscientist Eric Kandel of Columbia University. "With them, we can address the most complicated questions in all science."

Some of the maps confirm what studies of brain-damaged patients had already shown. Last November, for instance, research-

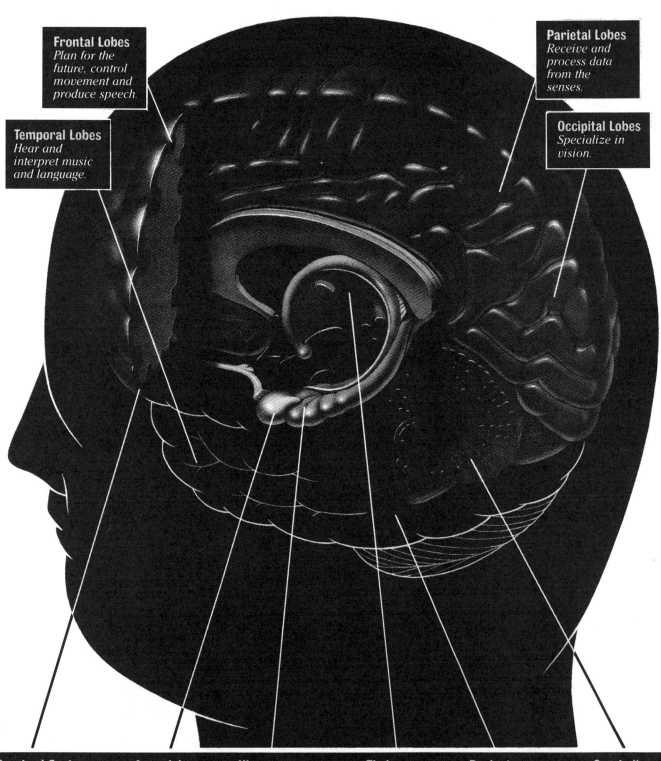

Frontal Lobes
Plan for the future, control movement and produce speech.

Parietal Lobes
Receive and process data from the senses.

Temporal Lobes
Hear and interpret music and language.

Occipital Lobes
Specialize in vision.

Cerebral Cortex
Covers the four lobes that make up the left and right hemispheres of the brain. It is just a few millimeters thick.

Amygdala
Generates emotions from perceptions and thoughts.

Hippocampus
Consolidates recently acquired information, somehow turning short-term memory into long term.

Thalamus
Takes sensory information and relays it to the cortex.

Brainstem
Controls automatic body functions like breathing. It is the junction between the brain and the spine.

Cerebellum
Governs muscle coordination and the learning of rote movements.

ers reported on a PET (positron emission tomography) study confirming that the hippocampus, a little sea-horse-shaped structure deep inside the brain, is necessary for forming and retrieving memories of facts and events (NEWSWEEK, Nov. 25, 1991). That's just what studies of amnesiacs had found. But while confirmation of old notions is nice, what the brain mappers really want is to stumble upon a Northwest Passage, connections that were totally unexpected, symphonies of neurons that had gone completely unheard. PET may do that. For a PET scan, volunteers are injected with radioactive glucose. Glucose, the body's fuel, mixes with the blood and wends its way to the brain. The more active a part of the brain is, the more glucose it uses. PET sensors arrayed around the head of a volunteer, who sits in a modified dentist's chair with his head behind black felt to keep out distractions, pinpoint the source of the radioactivity, and hence the heightened activity. They send the data to computers that produce two-dimensional drawings showing the neural hot spots.

brain thinks, lots of extraneous or inefficient neural circuits crackle. Intelligence, in this model, is a function not of effort but of efficiency. Intelligence "may involve learning what brain areas *not* to use," says Haier.

One key to intelligence may be "pruning." At birth, a baby's brain is a rat's nest of jumbled neurons. It uses up more and more glucose until the child is about 5, when it is roughly twice as active as an adult's. Then glucose use and the number of circuits plummet until the early teen years. This is called neural pruning, and Haier speculates it's the key to neural efficiency. More intelligent people may get that way by more pruning, which leaves remaining circuits much more efficient. Might pruning explain the link between genius and madness? "Overpruning may result in the high intelligence often associated with creativity, but hyperpruning may result in psychopathology," suggests Haier. No one has a clue as to why some brains prune their circuits like prize bonsai and others let them proliferate

PET is hardly the only technique to discover that the brain is organized in weird ways. Take music—as a team at New York University did. It has pioneered the use of the SQUID (superconducting quantum interference device), which senses tiny changes in magnetic fields. (When neurons fire, they create an electric current; electric fields induce magnetic fields, so magnetic changes indicate neural activity.) The device looks like a hair dryer from hell. When the NYU scientists aimed a SQUID at a brain listening to various notes, they found an eerie reflection of the black and white keys on a piano. NYU physicist Samuel Williamson and psychologist Lloyd Kaufman saw not only that the brain hears loud sounds in a totally different place from quieter sounds, but also that the areas that hear tones are laid out like a keyboard. "The distance between brain areas that hear low C and middle C is the same as the distance between areas that hear middle C and high C—just like on a piano," says Williamson.

In another unexpected find, brain systems that learn and remember faces turn out to reside in a completely different neighborhood from those that learn and recall man-made objects. The memory of a face activates a region in the right part of the brain that specializes in spatial configurations. The memory of a kitchen spatula, in contrast, activates areas that govern movement and touch. "What counts is how the brain acquires the knowledge," says neuroscientist Antonio Damasio of the University of Iowa College of Medicine. "The brain lays down knowledge in the very same systems that are engaged with the interactions"—in the case of a spatula, the memory resides in that part of the cortex that originally processed how the spatula felt and how the hands moved it.

Imagine four squares and form them into an "L." Now imagine two squares side by side. Fit the pieces into a smooth rectangle.

An area near the left side of the back of your head snapped to attention, especially if you're doing this without pencil and paper. It's one of the brain's centers for spatial reasoning—no surprise there. The astonishing thing is how hard it works. At the Brain Imaging Center at UC, Irvine, Richard Haier had volunteers play the computer game Tetris while in a PET scanner. In Tetris, players move and rotate squares, in various configurations such as an "I" or an "L," to create a solid block. This year, Haier found that people used lots of mental energy while learning Tetris, but after practicing for several weeks their brains burned much less energy—even though their scores had improved 700 percent. "Watching someone play Tetris at an advanced level, you might think, 'That person's brain must really be active'," says Haier. However, "[their] brains were actually not working as hard as when they played for the first time." Even more intriguing, the greater a volunteer's drop in the energy his brain used, the higher his IQ.

Intelligence, then, may be a matter of efficiency—neural efficiency. Smart brains may get away with less work because they use fewer neurons or circuits, or both. Conversely, when a less smart

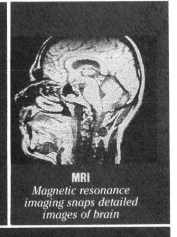

WINDOWS ON THE MIND?

Each scanning device has strengths and weaknesses. PET accurately tracks brain function, but can't resolve structures less than .5 inch apart. MRI can't detect function, but can distinguish structures even .05 inch apart.

MRI
Magnetic resonance imaging snaps detailed images of brain

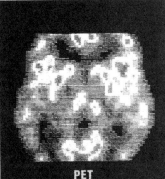

PET
Positron emission tomography tracks blood flow, a proxy for brain activity

SQUID
Superconducting quantum interference device picks up magnetic fields, a mark of brain action

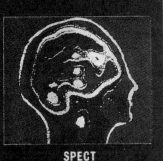

SPECT
Single-photon emission computerized tomography tracks blood flow, a sign of activity

EEG
Electroencephalogram, an early brain-monitoring technique, detects electrical activity

like out-of-control wisteria. Edward Scissorhands, call Dr. Frankenstein.

Decide whether any words in this sentence rhyme. Now name an animal with a very long neck.

Your vision center, at the back of your head right behind your eyes, has been buzzing with activity as you read. That's to be expected. But until recently, scientists thought that all language skills—reading, writing and rhyming—were contained within a single brain circuit. They were wrong. Naming and reading are governed from two different places. You can thank several clusters of neurons scattered across the cortex for coming up with "giraffe"; that's where naming comes from. But these clusters are not necessarily involved in reading. Similarly, regions that process spoken language, midway back on the left side of your head, told you that no words in the sentence rhymed. That spot had been basically dormant until then: contrary to psych texts, words do not have to be pronounced in the mind's ear in order for the brain to assign them a meaning. In the new model, the brain processes

PETTING THE BRAIN

LEARNING
The brain of a novice computer-game player (left) is very active; with practice, the brain uses less energy

MENTAL RETARDATION
The brain of a retarded patient (left) is much more active than that of a normal volunteer

DEPRESSION
The brain of a clinically depressed person shows less activity (right) than that of a healthy person

words by sight *or* sound. The result goes to the left frontal lobe, which imparts meaning to information received by either sense.

That finding undercuts psychologists' certainty that language is processed like a football play. Scholars had thought that to speak aloud a written word, the printed word had to pass from the visual cortex that saw it to the area that decoded it. From there, it was lateraled to the area in the frontal lobe that pronounces it. Touchdown! "The surprise is that when you see a word, and say it, it doesn't pass through the auditory part of the brain at all," says neuroscientist and PET pioneer Marcus Raichle of Washington University in St. Louis. "The old idea was that before you could say a word, the brain must change a visual code into a sound code. We don't see that at all." In fact, auditory areas of the brain are not active when one speaks, says Raichle: "You don't listen to what you say in the same way that you hear what others say."

Board. Tweal. Nlpfz.

Your visual cortex is still on the job, seeing words. But so are areas way outside the vision centers. To get at the great questions of language, Raichle and colleagues started small—with single words. As words flashed by on a computer screen, one per second, the PET volunteers' visual cortex lit up, as expected. But so did dime-size clusters of neurons way outside the vision centers, on the left side of the brain. Perhaps they hold the meanings of words. Call it Semantic Central. These same areas lit up when the volunteers saw nonwords that nevertheless obeyed rules of English— "tweal"—as if the brain were scrambling to assign a meaning to something that by all rights should have one. These semantic areas stayed dark when the volunteers saw consonant letter strings—*nlpfz*. Since babies aren't born knowing which letters form words and which don't, the brain has apparently learned what conforms to rules of English spelling and what does not. And it has carved out special zones that do nothing but analyze these rule-obeying strings of letters.

Supply a verb for each noun: pencil, oven, broom. And tell which animals in this list are dangerous: tapir, lion, lamb.

Two clusters in your cerebral cortex lit up. One, in the left frontal lobe, kicks in when the brain deals with meanings. But it gets bored easily. If you were asked to supply verbs for the same nouns, or analyze the same animals, over and over, the region wouldn't life a neuron: it seems to play a role only "in the acquisition of a new skill, in this case linguistic," says Raichle. Then it bows out. The brain can still provide "write" for "pencil," but seems to do so on automatic pilot. In addition, to focus on the word problems, the "anterior cingulate gyrus" turns on, as it does whenever "subjects are told to pay attention," says Raichle. It also shines with activity when researchers ask volunteers to read words for colors—red, orange, yellow—written in the "wrong" color ink, such as "red" written in blue. Some neural arbiter must choose which processing center, that for reading "red" or naming blue, to activate. As the brain tries to resolve the conflict, the front of something called the cingulate cortex, located an inch or so beneath the center line of the front of the scalp, positively glows.

Scans make it clear that the brain is a society of specialists. Different grape-size regions process proper but not common nouns, for instance. Not only that, separate zones also harbor tiny fragments of a larger idea, says Antonio Damasio. It can be an idea as lofty as Truth or as mundane as silver candlesticks. The Ph.D.s haven't figured out Truth yet, but they think they have a pretty good idea how your mind's eye sees the candlestick. PET scans show that these fragments come together in time but not in space, thanks to an as-yet-undiscovered maestro that takes the disparate tones and melds them into perfect harmony.

Fragments of knowledge are scattered around the brain, especially in the back of the cortex. Areas closer to the front contain what Damasio calls "combinatorial codes," which assemble information from the rear. Damasio has christened these "convergence zones"; their location varies from one person to the next. A convergence zone recalls where in the back office the different attributes of the candlestick are stored. When it's time to reconstruct the silver candlestick, the convergence zone activates all the relevant storage sites simultaneously. One bundle of nerves sends in a pulse that means "silver," another shoots out "cylinder shaped," another offers "burns." "Our sensory experiences happen in different places," says Damasio. "There must be an area where the facts converge."

PETs have seen clues to convergence zones in people who, because of brain lesions, cannot name famous faces. They register a flicker of recognition, but deny they know whose face it is. The knowledge exists, says Damasio, but is "unavailable to consciousness." The lesion has apparently disrupted the links between the memories for various parts of a face—the shapes of its features, the tone of its skin—tucked away in the right part of the cortex and the memory of the name in another back office. The fragments remain, but the convergence zone cannot bring them together.

Sing "Row, Row, Row Your Boat." Lift your finger when you come to a four-letter word.

If you're female, tiny spots on both sides of your brain light up. If you're male, only one side does. That's the kind of map Cecile Naylor of the Bowman Gray School of Medicine saw when she scanned brains of people who had been marked with a radioactive tracer that homes in on active areas. In one task, they listened to words and raised a finger when they heard one four letters long. Women's mental acrobatics were all over the brain; men's were compartmentalized. In women but not in men, some areas associated with vision lit up. "You wonder if females are using more of a visual strategy than males," says Naylor. Perhaps they see the spelled word in their mind's eye and then count letters.

New windows into the brain are ready to open. Robert Turner of the National Institutes of Health recalls "the awe-inspiring experience" of lying inside a colossal MRI (magnetic resonance imaging) magnet as images flashed on and off before his eyes. The machine recorded changes in his brain that came 50 milliseconds apart. "You can see different areas light up at different times," marvels Turner. NYU uses five SQUIDs to spy on the brain; the Japanese are hard at work on a 200-SQUID array. At Massachusetts General Hospital, researchers are putting the finishing touches on "ecoplanar MRI," which snaps a picture of the brain in just 45 milliseconds. The brain's cartographers are poised to glimpse thoughts, feelings and memories as they spring from one tiny clump of cells, ignite others and blossom into an idea or a passion, a creative leap or a unique insight. When they do, science may truly have read the mind.

SHARON BEGLEY *in St. Louis with* LYNDA WRIGHT *in Los Angeles,* VERNON CHURCH *in New York and* MARY HAGER *in Washington*

The Return of Phineas Gage: Clues About the Brain from the Skull of a Famous Patient

When the landmark patient Phineas Gage died in 1861, no autopsy was performed, but his skull was later recovered. The brain lesion that caused the profound personality changes for which his case became famous has been presumed to have involved the left frontal region, but questions have been raised about the involvement of other regions and about the exact placement of the lesion within the vast frontal territory. Measurements from Gage's skull and modern neuroimaging techniques were used to reconstitute the accident and determine the probable location of the lesion. The damage involved both left and right prefrontal cortices in a pattern that, as confirmed by Gage's modern counterparts, causes a defect in rational decision making and the processing of emotion.

Hanna Damasio, Thomas Grabowski, Randall Frank,
Albert M. Galaburda, Antonio R. Damasio*

H. Damasio and A. R. Damasio are in the Department of Neurology, University of Iowa Hospitals & Clinics, Iowa City, IA 52242, and the Salk Institute for Biological Research, San Diego, CA 92186–5800, USA. T. Grabowski and R. Frank are in the Department of Neurology, University of Iowa Hospitals & Clinics, Iowa City, IA 52242, USA. A. M. Galaburda is in the Department of Neurology, Harvard Medical School, Beth Israel Hospital, Boston, MA 02215, USA.

*To whom correspondence should be addressed.

On 13 September 1848, Phineas P. Gage, a 25-year-old construction foreman for the Rutland and Burlington Railroad in New England, became a victim of a bizarre accident. In order to lay new rail tracks across Vermont, it was necessary to level the uneven terrain by controlled blasting. Among other tasks, Gage was in charge of the detonations, which involved drilling holes in the stone, partially filling the holes with explosive powder, covering the powder with sand, and using a fuse and a tamping iron to trigger an explosion into the rock. On the fateful day, a momentary distraction let Gage begin tamping directly over the powder before his assistant had had a chance to cover it with sand. The result was a powerful explosion away from the rock and toward Gage. The fine-pointed, 3-cm-thick, 109-cm-long tamping iron was hurled, rocket-like, through his face, skull, brain, and then into the sky. Gage was momentarily stunned but regained full consciousness immediately thereafter. He was able to talk and even walk with the help of his men. The iron landed many yards away [1].

Phineas Gage not only survived the momentous injury, in itself enough to earn him a place in the annals of medicine, but he survived as a different man, and therein lies the greater significance of this case. Gage had been a responsible, intelligent, and socially well-adapted individual, a favorite with peers and elders. He had made progress and showed promise. The signs of a profound change in personality were already evident during the convalescence under the care of his physician, John Harlow. But as the months passed it became apparent that the transformation was not only radical but difficult to comprehend. In some respects, Gage was fully recovered. He remained as able-bodied and appeared to be as intelligent as before the accident; he had no impairment of movement or speech; new learning was intact, and neither memory nor intelligence in the conventional sense had been affected. On the other hand, he had become irreverent and capricious. His respect for the social conventions by which he once abided had vanished. His abundant profanity offended those around him. Perhaps most troubling, he had taken leave of his sense of responsibility. He could not be trusted to honor his commitments. His employers had deemed him "the most efficient and capable" man in their "employ" but now had to dismiss him. In the words of his physician, "the equilibrium or balance, so to speak, between his intellectual faculty and animal propensities" had been destroyed. In the words of his friends and acquaintances, "Gage was no longer Gage" [1]. Gage began a new life of wandering that ended a dozen years later, in San Francisco, under the custody of his family. Gage never returned to a fully independent existence, never again held a job comparable to the one he once had. His accident had made headlines but his death went unnoticed. No autopsy was obtained.

Twenty years after the accident, John Harlow, unaided by the tools of experimental neuropsychology available today, perceptively correlated Gage's cognitive and behavioral changes with a presumed area of focal damage in the frontal region [1]. Other cases of neurological damage were then revealing the brain's foundation for language, motor function, and perception, and now Gage's case indicated something even more surprising: Perhaps there were structures in the human brain dedicated to the planning and execution of personally and socially suitable behavior, to the aspect of reasoning known as rationality.

Given the power of this insight, Harlow's observation should have made the scientific impact that the comparable suggestions based on the patients of Broca and Wernicke made [2]. The suggestions, although surrounded by controversy, became the foundation for the understanding of the neural basis of language and were pursued actively, while Harlow's report on Gage did not inspire a search for the neural basis of reasoning, decision-making, or social behavior. One factor likely to have contributed to the indifferent reception accorded Harlow's work was that the intellectual atmosphere of the time made it somewhat more acceptable that there was a neural basis for processes such as movement or even language rather than for moral reasoning and social behavior [3]. But the principal explanation must rest with the substance of Harlow's report. Broca and Wernicke had autopsy results, Harlow did not. Unsupported by anatomical evidence, Harlow's observation was the more easily dismissed. Because the exact position of the lesion was not known, some critics could claim that the damage actually involved Broca's so-called language "center," and

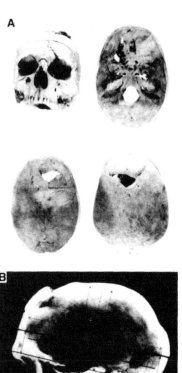

Fig. 1. Photographs of (**A**) several views of the skull of Phineas Gage and (**B**) the skull x-ray.

a particular type of cognitive and behavioral defect caused by damage to ventral and medial sectors of prefrontal cortex, rather than to the left dorsolateral sector as implicit in the traditional view. It then occurred to us that some of the image processing techniques now used to investigate Gage's counterparts could be used to test this idea by going back in time, reconstituting the accident, and determining the probable placement of his lesion. The following is the result of our neuroanthropological effort.

We began by having one of us (A.M.G.) photograph Gage's skull inside and out and obtain a skull x-ray (Fig. 1) as well as a set of precise measurements (6) relative to bone landmarks. Using these measurements, we proceeded to deform linearly the three-dimensional reconstruction of a standard human skull (7) so that its dimensions matched those of Phineas Gage's skull. We also constructed Talairach's stereotactic space for both this skull and Phineas Gage's real skull (8). On the basis of the skull photographs, the dimensions of the entry and exit holes were scaled and mapped into the deformed standard skull. Based on measurements of the iron rod and on the recorded descriptions of the accident, we determined the range of likely trajectories of the rod. Finally, we simulated those trajectories in three-

dimensional space using Brainvox (9). We modeled the rod's trajectory as a straight line connecting the center of the entry hole at orbital level to the center of the exit hole. This line was then carried downward to the level of the mandibular ramus. The skull anatomy allowed us to consider entry points within a 1.5-cm radius of this point (20 points in all) (Fig. 2).

Possible exit points were determined as follows: We decided to constrain the exit point to be at least 1.5 cm (half the diameter of the rod) from the lateral and posterior margins of the area of bone loss (Fig. 3) because there were no disruptions of the outer table of the calvarium in these directions (Fig. 1, lower right panel). However, we accepted that the rod might have passed up to 1.5 cm anterior to the area of bone loss because inspection of the bone in this region revealed that it must have been separated completely from the rest of the calvarium (Fig. 1). Furthermore, the wound was described as an inverted funnel (1). We tested 16 points within the rectangular-shaped exit area that we constructed (Fig. 3).

The trajectory connecting each of the entry and exit points was tested at multiple anatomical levels. The three-dimensional skull was resampled in planes perpendicular to the best a priori trajectory (C in Figs. 2 and 3). We were helped by several impor-

perhaps would also have involved the nearby "motor centers." And because the patient showed neither paralysis nor aphasia, some critics reached the conclusion that there were no specialized regions at all (4). The British physiologist David Ferrier was a rare dissenting voice. He thoughtfully ventured, in 1878, that the lesion spared both motor and language centers, that it had damaged the left prefrontal cortex, and that such damage probably explained Gage's behavioral defects, which he aptly described as a "mental degradation" (5).

Harlow only learned of Gage's death about 5 years after its occurrence. He proceeded to ask Gage's family to have the body exhumed so that the skull could be recovered and kept as a medical record. The strange request was granted, and Phineas Gage was once again the protagonist of a grim event. As a result, the skull and the tamping iron, alongside which Gage had been buried, have been part of the Warren Anatomical Medical Museum at Harvard University.

As new cases of frontal damage were described in this century, some of which did resemble that of Gage, and as the enigmas of frontal lobe function continued to resist elucidation, Gage gradually acquired landmark status. Our own interest in the case grew out of the idea that Gage exemplified

Fig. 2. View of the entry-level area with the a priori most likely first trajectory. (**A**) Skull with this first vector and the level (dotted line) at which entry points were marked. (**B**) View of a segment of section 1. On the left is the mandibular ramus, and on the right is the array of entry points. (**C**) Enlargement of the array of entry points. One additional point was added (L20) to ensure that every viable entry point was surrounded by nonviable points. Nonviable vectors are shown in black and viable vectors with labels identifying their exit points are shown in grey. Abbreviations: A, anterior; L, lateral; P, posterior; AM, anteromesial; AL, anterolateral; PL, posterolateral; C. central.

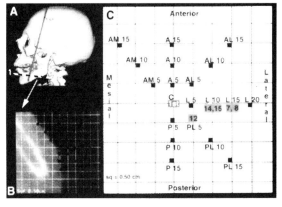

Fig. 3. (**A**) View from above the deformed skull with the exit hole and the anterior bone flap traced in black. The black circle represents the first vector tested, and the grey surface represents the area where exit points were tested. (**B**) Schematic enlargement of the exit hole and of the area tested for exit points. The letter C marks the first tested vector. The numbers 1 through 15 mark the other exit points tested. Black indicates nonviable vectors, grey indicates viable vectors, and the label identifies the entry point. Note that the a priori best fit C was not viable.

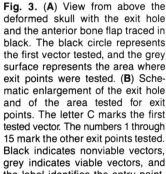
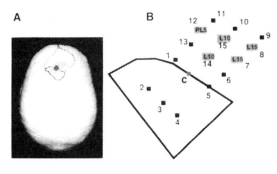

tant anatomical constraints. We knew that the left mandible was intact; that the zygomatic arch was mostly intact but had a chipped area, at its medial and superior edge, that suggested the rod had grazed it; and that the last superior molar socket was intact although the tooth was missing. Acceptable trajectories were those which, at each level, did not violate the following rules: The vectors representing the trajectories could not be closer than 1.5 cm from the mid-thickness of the zygomatic arch, 1 cm from the last superior molar, and 0.5 cm from the coronoid process of the mandible (10). Only seven trajectories satisfied these conditions (Fig. 4). Two of those seven invariably hit the anterior horn of the lateral ventricle and were therefore rejected as anatomically improbable because they would not have been compatible with survival (the resulting massive infection would not have been controllable in the preantibiotic era). When checked in our collection of normal brains, one of the remaining five trajectories behaved better than any other relative to the lower constraints and was thus chosen as the most likely trajectory. The final step was to model the five acceptable trajectories of the iron rod in a three-dimensional reconstruction of a human brain that closely fit Phineas Gage's assumed brain dimensions (11). Talairach's stereotactic warpings were used for this final step.

The modeling yielded the results shown in Fig. 5. In the left hemisphere, the lesion involved the anterior half of the orbital frontal cortex (Brodmann's cytoarchitectonic fields 11 and 12), the polar and anterior mesial frontal cortices (fields 8 to 10 and 32), and the anterior-most sector of the anterior cingulate gyrus (field 24). However, the lesion did not involve the mesial aspect of field 6 [the supplementary motor area (SMA)]. The frontal operculum, which contains Broca's area and includes fields 44, 45, and 47, was also spared, both cortically and in the underlying white matter. In the right hemisphere, the lesion involved part of the anterior and mesial orbital region (field 12), the mesial and polar frontal cortices (fields 8 to 10 and 32), and the anterior segment of the anterior cingulate gyrus (field 24). The SMA was spared. The white matter core of the frontal lobes was more extensively damaged in

the left hemisphere than in the right. There was no damage outside of the frontal lobes.

Even allowing for error and taking into consideration that additional white matter damage likely occurred in the surround of the iron's trajectory, we can conclude that the lesion did not involve Broca's area or the motor cortices and that it favored the ventromedial region of both frontal lobes while sparing the dorsolateral. Thus, Ferrier was correct, and Gage fits a neuroanatomical pattern that we have identified to date in 12 patients within a group of 28 individuals with frontal damage (12). Their ability to make rational decisions in personal and social matters is invariably compromised and so is their processing of emotion. On the contrary, their ability to tackle the logic of an abstract problem, to perform calculations, and to call up appropriate knowledge and attend to it remains intact. The establishment of such a pattern has led to the hypothesis that emotion and its underlying neural machinery participate in decision making within the social domain and has raised the possibility that the participation depends on the ventromedial frontal region (13). This region is reciprocally connected with subcortical nuclei that control basic biological regulation, emotional processing, and social cognition and behavior, for instance, in amygdala and hypothalamus (14). Moreover, this region shows a high concentration of serotonin S_2 receptors in monkeys whose behavior is socially adapted as well as a low concentration in aggressive, socially uncooperative animals (15). In contrast, structures in the dorsolateral region are involved in other domains of cognition concerning extrapersonal space, objects, language, and arithmetic (16). These structures are largely intact in Gage-like patients, thus accounting for the patients' normal performance in traditional neuropsychologic tests that are aimed at such domains.

The assignment of frontal regions to different cognitive domains is compatible with the idea that frontal neurons in any of those regions may be involved with attention, working memory, and the categorization of contingent relationships regardless of the domain (17). This assignment also agrees with the idea that in non–brain-damaged individuals the separate frontal regions are interconnected and act cooperatively to support reasoning and decision making. The mysteries of frontal lobe function are slowly being solved, and it is only fair to establish, on a more substantial footing, the roles that Gage and Harlow played in the solution.

REFERENCES AND NOTES

1. J. M. Harlow, *Pub. Mass. Med. Soc.* **2**, 327 (1868).
2. P. Broca, *Bull. Soc. Anthropol.* **6**, 337 (1865); C. Wernicke, *Der aphasische Symptomencomplex* (Cohn und Weigert, Breslau, Poland, 1874). A remarkable number of basic insights on the functional specialization of the human brain, from motor function to sensory perception and to spoken and written language, came from the description of such cases mostly during the second half of the 19th century. The cases usually acted as a springboard for further research, but on occasion their significance was overlooked, as in the case of Gage. Another such example is the description of color perception impairment (achromatopsia) caused by a ventral occipital lesion, by D. Verrey [*Arch. Ophthalmol. (Paris)* **8**, 289 (1888)]. His

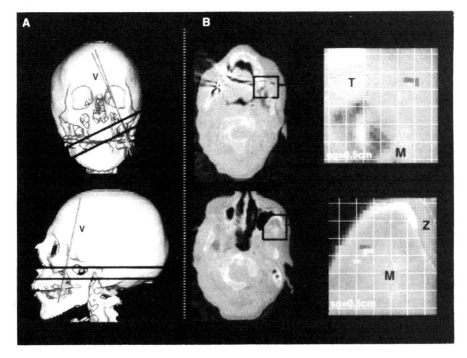

Fig. 4. (A) Front and lateral skull views with the projection of the five final vectors (V). The two black lines show the position of the two sections seen in **(B)**. **(B)** Skull sections 2 and 3: examples of two bottleneck levels at which the viability of vectors was checked. Next to each section is an enlargement of the critical area. Abbreviations: T, missing tooth; M, intact mandible; Z, intact zygoma with a chipped area (white).

astonishing finding was first denied and then ignored until the 1970s.

3. Reasoning and social behavior were deemed inextricable from ethics and religion and not amenable to biological explanation.

4. The reaction against claims for brain specialization was in fact a reaction against phrenological doctrines, the curious and often unacknowledged inspiration for many of the early case reports. The views of E. Dupuy exemplify the attitude [*Examen de Quelques Points de la Physiologie du Cerveau* (Delahaye, Paris, 1873); M. MacMillan, *Brain Cognit.* 5, 67 (1986)].

5. D. Ferrier, *Br. Med. J.* 1, 399 (1878).

6. The first measurements were those necessary to construct Gage's Talairach stereotactic space and deform a three-dimensional, computerized tomography skull: the maximum length of the skull, the maximum height of the skull above the inion-glabella line, the distance from this line to the floor of the middle fossa, the maximum width of the skull, and the position of the section contour of Gage's skull relative to the inion-glabella line. The second measurements were those necessary to construct the entry and exit areas: on the top external view, the measure of edges of the triangular exit hole; on the internal view the distances from its three corners to the mid-sagittal line and to the nasion; the distance from the borders of the hole to the fracture lines seen anteriorly and posteriorly to this hole; and the dimensions of the entry hole at the level of the orbit.

7. Thin-cut standard computerized tomography image of a cadaver head obtained at North Carolina Memorial Hospital.

8. We introduced the following changes to the method described by P. Fox, J. Perlmutter, and M. Raichle [*J. Comput. Assist. Tomogr.* 9, 141 (1985)]. We calculated the mean distance from the anterior commissure (AC) to the posterior commissure (PC) in a group of 27 normal brains and used that distance for Gage (26.0 mm). We also did not consider the AC-frontal pole and the PC-occipital pole distances as equal because our group of normals had a mean difference of 5 mm between the two measures, and Talairach himself did not give these two measurements as equal [J. Talairach and G. Szikla, *Atlas d'Anatomie Stereotaxique du Telencephale* (Masson, Paris, 1967); J. Talairach and P. Tournoux, *Co-Planar Stereotaxic Atlas of the Human Brain* (Thieme, New York, 1988)]. We introduced an anterior shift of 3% to the center of the AC-PC line and used that point as the center of the AC-PC segment. This shift meant that the anterior sector of Talairach's space was 47% of the total length and that the posterior was 53%. We had no means of calculating the difference between the right and left width of Gage's brain; therefore, we assumed them to be equal.

9. H. Damasio and R. Frank, *Arch. Neurol.* 49, 137 (1992).

10. There were two reasons to allow the vector this close to the mandible: (i) The zygomatic arch and the coronoid process were never more than 2 cm apart; (ii) we assumed that, in reality, this distance might have been larger if the mouth were open or if the mandible, a movable structure, had been pushed by the impact of the iron rod.

11. The final dimensions of Phineas Gage's Talairach space were as follows: total length, 171.6 mm; total height, 111.1 mm; and total width, 126.5 mm. Comparing these dimensions to a group of 27 normal subjects, we found that in seven cases at least two of the dimensions were close to those of Phineas Gage [mean length, 169.9 mm (SD, 4.1); mean height, 113.6 (SD, 2.3); mean width, 125 (SD, 3.9). The seven brains were fitted with the possible trajectories to determine which brain areas were involved. There were no significant differences in the areas of damage. The modeling we present here was performed on subject 1600LL (length, 169 mm; height, 115.2 mm; width, 125.6 mm).

12. Data from the Lesion Registry of the University of Iowa's Division of Cognitive Neuroscience as of 1993.

13. P. Eslinger and A. R. Damasio, *Neurology* 35, 1731 (1985); J. L. Saver and A. R. Damasio, *Neuropsychologia* 29, 1241 (1991); A. R. Damasio, D. Tranel, H. Damasio, in *Frontal Lobe Function and Dysfunction*, H. S. Levin, H. M. Eisenberg, A. L. Benton, Eds. (Oxford Univ. Press, New York, 1991), pp. 217–229; S. Dehaene and J. P. Changeux, *Cereb. Cortex* 1, 62 (1991).

14. P. S. Goldman-Rakic, in *Handbook of Physiology; The Nervous System*, F. Plum, Ed. (American Physiological Society, Bethesda, MD, 1987), vol. 5, pp. 373–401; D. N. Pandya and E. H. Yeterian, in *The Prefrontal Cortex: Its Structure, Function and Pathology*, H. B. M. Uylings, Ed. (Elsevier, Amsterdam, 1990); H. Barbas and D. N. Pandya, *J. Comp. Neurol.* 286, 253 (1989).

15. M. J. Raleigh and G. L. Brammer, *Soc. Neurosci. Abstr.* 19, 592 (1993).

16. M. Petrides and B. Milner, *Neuropsychologia* 20, 249 (1982); J. M. Fuster, *The Prefrontal Cortex* (Raven, New York, ed. 2, 1989); M. I. Posner and S. E. Petersen, *Annu. Rev. Neurosci.* 13, 25 (1990).

17. P. S. Goldman-Rakic, *Sci. Am.* 267, 110 (September 1992); A. Bechara, A. R. Damasio, H. Damasio, S. Anderson, *Cognition* 50, 7 (1994); A. R. Damasio, *Descartes' Error: Emotion, Reason and the Human Brain* (Putnam, New York, in press).

18. We thank A. Paul of the Warren Anatomical Museum for giving us access to Gage's skull. Supported by National Institute of Neurological Diseases and Stroke grant PO1 NS19632 and by the Mathers Foundation.

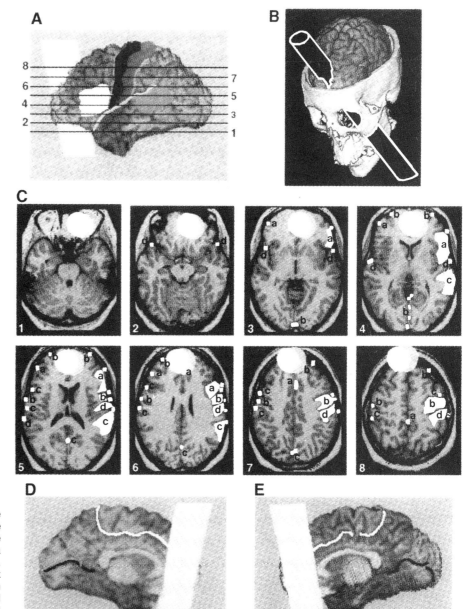

Fig. 5. Normal brain fitted with the five possible rods. The best rod is highlighted in solid white [except for (**B**), where it is shown in black]. The areas spared by the iron are highlighted: Broca (a); motor (b); somatosensory (c); Wernicke (d). (**A**) Lateral view of the brain. Numbered black lines correspond to levels of the brain section shown in (**C**). (**D** and **E**) Medical view of left and right hemispheres, respectively, with the rod shown in white.

Major breakthroughs in genetic research hold staggering implications for us.

UNDERSTANDING THE GENETICS AGE

Jim H. Smith

Jim Smith lives in Newington, Connecticut.

Within the nucleus of each human cell is the blueprint of life—the 23 pairs of chromosomes, made up of strands of deoxyribonucleic acid that can be divided into genes. These genes, in turn, are approximately 100,000 minuscule, but awesomely powerful, chromosomal segments that define every one of our physical characteristics.

One by one, we have discovered the secrets of these incredibly small elements. We have learned how they are shaped and how they telegraph their information. We have learned how they create organisms of dazzling beauty. And, we have learned the dark converse—what happens when they are flawed.

Through all the centuries of human history, behind the locked door of the living cell, the genes have performed their inscrutable magic. Even without being able to open that final door into the clockwork of the human cell, scientists from earlier centuries painstakingly deduced what was there.

Nonetheless, the door had remained locked. Last October, however, researchers at the Howard Hughes Medical Institute of the University of Iowa opened it.

Putting genes on a "ferry"

In tests on three people with cystic fibrosis (CF), America's most common fatal inherited disorder, researchers demonstrated they could use cold viruses that had been genetically altered to "ferry" healthy genes directly into the heart of the body's cells. Once inside the cells, the healthy genes replaced defective ones, rapidly reversing the genetic abnormality. Simply put, the researchers stunned the medical world by announcing they'd developed what amounted to a cure for cystic fibrosis.

Of course, at the time of the announcement, the researchers had not yet tried the new therapy on human lungs, the organ that inevitably fails in cystic fibrosis victims, causing their deaths. So, they were not entirely certain it would work. But the researchers were quick to note that the genetic abnormality that causes CF was exactly the same in every cell in the subjects' bodies. There was abundant reason to be optimistic.

The medical discovery is on a parallel with the development of open-heart surgery, or antibiotics. In the history of medical research, it was one of those watershed moments that occur when a therapeutic advance promises to change the face of medicine altogether.

Staggering implications

It was the bigger implications of the effective technology that made the announcement so important. Over the space of five years, researchers have also identified the genes for such disorders as multiple sclerosis, neurofibromatosis, Alzheimer's disease, alcoholism, and many others. Indeed, armed with computer-based technological advances that would have seemed like science fiction ten or fifteen years ago, researchers have been pinpointing gene after gene in their quest to unravel the last secrets of human life.

Now, 40 years after James Watson and Francis Crick broke the "code" of heredity with their discovery of DNA — the basic material of genes — we suddenly are there. We are opening that ancient door. And we were poised to learn the dazzling magic that has been waiting so long.

How did we get there so quickly? And what do these near miraculous advances mean for the future of health in America? To understand where we're going, we must take a look back at where we've come from.

Father Mendel's garden

In Austria, 130 years ago, there was an Augustinian monk named Gregor

Mendel. He aspired to a noble, but humble occupation — to teach natural science in secondary school.

But Mendel lacked the qualifications. Four times, he failed to pass the necessary teaching examinations. Undaunted, he enrolled in the University of Vienna, where he threw himself into intense research for four semesters, trying to make up for the educational deficiencies that stood between him and his chosen profession.

By the 1850s, when Mendel embarked upon his education, many of the prevailing ideas about science were changing. Thoroughly immersed in the rapidly evolving scientific studies of mid-19th century Europe, Mendel hungered for a direction to give richer meaning to his work. He found this focus in a radical departure from the naive assumptions of earlier generations. One of those was the so-called "homunculus theory," which argued that every human began, preformed, as homunculus, or "little person", perfectly proportioned within the womb of his or her mother. It held that each woman had, within her, a certain number of these homunculi, even as an infant.

In place of this thesis, mid-19th century revisionists were enthusiastically climbing on the bandwagon of a new theory which proposed that each part of the human body somehow contributed its special qualities to the "germ cells," the sperm and the egg. Offspring, these scientists concluded, were the consequence of a "blending" (which took place at the moment of conception) of the characteristics of their parents.

While this changing view of the nature of life made eminently more sense than the homunculus, it left many questions unanswered. And in those unanswered questions, Mendel found his focus.

What happens, Mendel wanted to know, when hybrids — living organisms whose "parents" have different characteristics — are themselves bred? How do the characteristics of the first generation replicate themselves in following generations? Is there a pattern? If so, is that pattern predictable? Why?

Lessons from the sweet peas

To aid him in answering these questions, Mendel used plants as his working model. In 1857, in a little garden behind the monastery where he lived,

Mendel planted sweet peas and contemplated the door of life. Eight years and 8,000 plants later, he published the results of his research and changed science forever.

Here are the three most important things he learned:

• Individuals receive their many characteristics in separate, independently transmitted units. Each trait is influenced by units transmitted by each parent. Mendel therefore proved that heredity is not a blending process.

• Each parent gives you an equal number of genes. All your physical characteristics come from the interaction between two genes.

• If the genes you inherit for a specific trait aren't identical, in most cases one will dominate the other.

Mendel's findings were profound. Most important, they explained how healthy parents can produce children with genetic disorders. Not all genetic disorders work the same way, but many, such as sickle cell anemia or Tay-Sachs disease, require two defective genes.

If an individual has one defective gene for disorders like these, and one normal gene, the normal gene will dominate. The individual will be perfectly healthy, but will be a "carrier" for the disorder. That means his or her offspring could inherit the disorder if his or her spouse also is a carrier and they both pass along the defective gene. What Mendel's research did not reveal was how the genes work, what they look like, or how to control them.

Breaking the DNA code

James Watson, from Chicago, just 23 years old in 1951, had a Ph.D. in biology and a passionate commitment to figuring out how genes work. He traveled to Cambridge University in England, and became a colleague with Francis Crick who, like himself, was a genius intrigued by the mysteries of the gene.

Together, they created models to clarify how DNA stores genetic information and how it can replicate itself quickly and accurately. Their first few models failed, but by 1953, Watson and Crick had broken the code. They had **discovered that DNA is a double helix, or two long strands of genetic information that intertwine each other. Between them, the strands are bound together by chemical bases that look**

like the rungs of a ladder. Whenever DNA wants to reproduce itself, the two strands unwind at incredible speed, and each strand then forms a new helix.

Without that information, scientists had known only that all of our traits are controlled by our genes. With Watson and Crick's discovery, they understood why—and they had the basic knowledge needed to move into the "Golden Age of Genetics."

That's the term Francis S. Collins of the University of Michigan used to describe today's age of accelerated genetic research. In September 1989, working in the thick of that research, Dr. Collins and Dr. Lap-Chee Tsui of the Hospital for Sick Children, Toronto, found the gene that causes cystic fibrosis. A mere four years after their discovery, researchers learned how to replace that defective gene.

Opening doors where none existed

Until very recently, breakthroughs like these were not merely rare; they did not exist. The primary force in genetics research is the Human Genome Project — the unprecedented worldwide collaboration inaugurated four years ago jointly by the National Institute of Health and the U.S. Energy Department. The project's goal is to map all the human genes. The project galvanized the scientific community globally and the result has been a torrent of genetic discoveries, with more coming. By the time the project is completed (it has a 15-year projected schedule), the way in which we think about medicine will have been changed entirely.

Genetic screening identifies risks

As new genes are discovered, researchers often can develop easy-to-administer blood tests to screen for genetic disorders. One of these is the blood test that has helped doctors detect phenylketonuria (PKU) in newborns for some two decades. PKU is a genetic disorder that makes it impossible for babies to metabolize milk protein appropriately. If the disorder is detected early, children can be fed a modified diet that allows them to develop normally. If it's not detected, severe and irrevocable mental retardation inevitably results.

The blood screen for PKU was one of the first examples of an effective way to intervene and prevent some of the horrible consequences of errant genes that our ancestors suffered for centuries. It's not likely to be the last such test, though. While one means of dealing with aberrant DNA might be to replace it, another might be to discover it and take steps to prevent what always has been its inevitable result.

Our Cholesterol Collector

Inside all of us there is a protein called apolipoprotein B. It flows in our blood and its job is to collect cholesterol before it can stick to the walls of our arteries. Apolipoprotein B carries cholesterol to the liver, where it is broken down and, ultimately, secreted from the body. Most of the time, apolipoprotein B does its job just fine, especially if we help it out by eating a low-fat diet.

But one person in every 500 has a problem. A defective gene causes the protein itself to be defective. As a result, the cholesterol remains in the arteries, where it becomes plaque and causes arteriosclerosis.

Thanks to early screening, however, people with this defect don't have to die as a consequence of their mutation. They can help themselves by exercising and eating a modified diet, to protect themselves from their elevated risk of coronary disease.

Those are just two examples of the kinds of medical breakthroughs. Now, more are just over the next hill. In fact, if you ask geneticists to estimate when the next breakthrough will come, they're often reticent to make a commitment. So many things have happened so quickly, even projections that were considered optimistic just a few years ago now seem overly conservative.

Mapping the human genome

Early last year, for instance, researchers worldwide were astonished when they learned that a French geneticist named Daniel Cohen was on the brink of completing the first map of the human genome. When the Human Genome project was launched in 1989, researchers hoped they'd complete the

job shortly after the turn of the century. Just before Christmas, Cohen's team announced completion of the first, rough genome map.

How did Cohen beat the clock so momentously? The human genome contains more than 3.5 billion "base pairs" — the sets of chemical constituents that make up each gene. Ultimately, researchers aim to understand those base pairs for every gene. But first they must analyze long fragments of tenetic material — an incredibly tedious and time-consuming process.

Cohen worked out a means to rapidly analyze much longer segments of the genome — a total of 500 pieces, each of which contains more than 7 million base pairs. His map won't provide fine detail about the base pairs, but it will, researchers acknowledge, be an invaluable aid that should move research ahead at an even more brisk clip.

In transgenics — the field of genetic research in which animals are used as research models— other breakthroughs might occur. By inserting foreign DNA into test subjects such as mice, researchers can determine what genes do, and they can create test animals with human diseases. This process has proven so useful that hundreds of research universities and biotech laboratories have developed transgenics programs in the past few years. Their discoveries are eagerly awaited by pharmaceutical firms, and their collective work is like a powerful engine, driving the rate of discovery forward.

Research is "explosive"

"Genetic research today is explosive," says Dr. Robert Greenstein, Director of the Division of Human Genetics at the University of Connecticut Health Center in Farmington. "In the next five to ten years, we're going to see extraordinary advances."

In health care, Greenstein predicts, these advances will follow three basic tracks — diagnosis (including prenatal diagnosis), treatments for genetic disorders and, ultimately, cures. An entire line of research rests on the working assumption that many genetic disorders result because of defective genes. For example, those that can cause coronary disease and emphysema fail to give the body the chemical cues it needs to cre-

ate appropriate protective chemicals. Once we know what those chemicals are, researchers are poised to synthesize them — the drugs of the future.

Effectively treating these disorders, though, is only one goal. Ultimately, the hope of genetic researchers is to cure them. Recent advances make both of these goals suddenly appear to be tantalizingly close.

Whether they are will depend in large part on the availability of research funding, says Greenstein. The pace of genetic research almost surely will be determined, at least in part, by willingness of taxpayers to fund it. And their willingness, in turn, will depend on how clearly they can see the potential benefits.

"I think it's absolutely essential that the public get better educated about research," Greenstein says. "We'll need to answer important questions about how we spend limited resources, and the public will be asked to provide some of those answers. We're on the verge of great discoveries, but research must continue if we're going to get there."

■ ■ ■

Last fall, in the *New York Times*, Dr. Phillip Sharp, professor of Biology at the Massachusetts Institute of Technology and the 1993 Nobel laureate in Physiology and Medicine, echoed Greenstein's sentiments when he made an impassioned argument for continuing basic genetic research. "Especially in biomedical science," he wrote, "we must resist the temptation to starve exploratory research to support research with tangible benefits. No matter how much money is made available to treat killers like cancer, AIDS and heart disease, we will probably not curb them significantly until we gain a more fundamental understanding of their basic biological mechanisms."

In hard times, people must establish priorities and make difficult choices, Sharp said. "But in our well-intentioned drive to improve treatment for diseases that consume millions of our citizens physically, emotionally and economically, let us not forget to encourage the exploration that seeks to understand their root causes."

THE SNIFF OF LEGEND

HUMAN PHEROMONES? CHEMICAL SEX ATTRACTANTS? AND A SIXTH SENSE ORGAN IN THE NOSE? WHAT ARE WE, ANIMALS?

Karen Wright

Karen Wright is a former visiting senior editor at Discover *and the recipient of the 1991 Evert Clark young science journalist award. Wright is at work on her first novel, about a naturalist's struggle to save an endangered species of desert fish.*

IT'S MONDAY MORNING, AND ONCE again Brad Murray finds himself in the position of research subject: lying flat on his back on a lab bench, flaring his nostrils for science.

Luis Monti-Bloch bends over the supine graduate student and, murmuring apologetically, sticks a stork-bill-shaped instrument called a nasal speculum into the left chamber of Murray's nose. The subject flinches but hangs tough as Monti-Bloch spreads the bifurcated beak of the speculum, thereby enlarging the aperture of Murray's own beak. The researcher trains the light from his headlamp into the orifice. He peers through his binocular loupes.

"I can see it right . . . there," says Monti-Bloch, pointing with a cotton swab. He adjusts the loupes, his gaze never straying from Murray's mucosa. He sighs. "It's really beautiful."

Monti-Bloch is one of half a dozen distinguished scientists who believe they've discovered a new sense organ half an inch or so inside the human nose. It's called the vomeronasal organ, or VNO, and if the hunches of these researchers are correct, it detects chemical signals passed unconsciously among human beings—signals that might be

about identity, arousal, or sexual receptivity and that go by the name of pheromones. Such chemical communication, common among other animals, was heretofore thought to be nonexistent in humans.

Using stalwart volunteers like Murray and equipment he designed himself, Monti-Bloch has been testing the effects of putative human pheromones on cells in the VNO. To do so, he has to locate the organ's opening, a pale, tiny pit near the bottom of the septal wall dividing the nose. Assuming that Murray is bilaterally symmetrical like the rest of us, a matching inlet lies on the other side of the septum, too. It's not the kind of thing you'd notice on casual inspection.

In fact, it's the kind of thing that anatomists have overlooked for centuries. Though the human vomeronasal organ was first described almost 300 years ago, the few investigators who bothered to look for it thereafter had trouble finding it. Consequently, even as pheromones and their corresponding sensory systems gained renown for their role in the social and mating behavior of other animals, researchers concluded that people got by (and down) without them. Modern medicine had declared the VNO to be mostly absent in humans, and where present, vestigial.

Still, several late-twentieth-century scientists were captivated by the notion that human beings might have a sixth sense. One was an electron microscopist in Boulder, Colorado, who scavenged the septal tissue of nose-job patients for VNO

specimens. Another was a neuroanatomist in Salt Lake City who insisted on including a VNO primer in his lectures to medical students. And then there was the physician-cum–venture capitalist in Menlo Park, California, who suspected he'd accidentally isolated human pheromones from extracts of sloughed-off skin.

Five years ago, united by the enthusiasm and lucre of David Berliner, the venture capitalist, these researchers and a few colleagues began to compare notes. With the help of Monti-Bloch, a physiologist at the University of Utah, they've now presented the first strong evidence that human beings do indeed possess a functioning vomeronasal organ. Even skeptical observers admit that the team's findings seem solid; Berliner, who is not so skeptical, has already spun off a pharmaceutical company to synthesize drugs that could be delivered via the VNO, and he's bottled his alleged human pheromones in a perfume called Realm, 50 milliliters of which retails for $79.99.

But all parties concerned stress that the evidence is as preliminary as it is provocative. Although recent surveys show that almost everybody has a VNO after all, researchers still aren't absolutely sure the organ works. Until he received patents for his pheromones last December, Berliner had refused to divulge their makeup, so investigators outside his sphere of influence—that is, those not vested in his company—are only now attempting to replicate his group's findings. For now, no one inside or outside the Berliner camp has

INSTEAD OF DISCRETE PERCEPTIONS, PHEROMONES COULD BE SAID TO MEDIATE IMPRESSIONS: BAD VIBES, WARM FUZZIES, INSTANT DISLIKES, IRRESISTIBLE ATTRACTIONS.

come close to answering the most provocative question of all: How might pheromones influence human beings?

Until recently, medical science claimed that they *don't*, period. Historical reports of the human VNO were as erratic and improbable as UFO sightings and were accorded as much credibility. A Dutch military surgeon first described the structure in 1703 in a soldier with a facial wound. In 1891 a French doctor reported seeing it in a quarter of the 200 people he examined. In 1934 one researcher wrote that the VNO "is almost constantly found in the human embryo and with diligence may occasionally be found in the adult." During the course of human development, this researcher noted, the VNO—like many a UFO—just seemed to disappear.

Finally, in the late 1930s, a widely respected neuroanatomist named Elizabeth Crosby dealt a seemingly decisive blow to the recurring rumors of the human VNO. The so-called sixth sense couldn't exist, she explained, because the place in the brain where other animals process neural impulses from the VNO—a structure known as the accessory olfactory bulb—doesn't persist past the first trimester of fetal development in humans. Even if the "end organ" was there, Crosby argued, it couldn't be functional.

UNLIKE HER PREDECESSORS, CROSBY never stooped to the level of actually searching for the VNO in embryos or adults. Instead she based her conclusion on her formidable knowledge of the olfactory processing center in the brain. Few medical researchers were qualified to challenge her; most took her word as gospel. And if the human VNO was kaput, they figured, there was no use looking for human pheromones either.

In the decades that followed, though, research amply demonstrated the importance of chemical signals to the sex lives of other animals. The vomeronasal organ was found in amphibians, reptiles,

and most mammals, and it was implicated in the most intimate details of vertebrate physiology. For example, researchers discovered that pheromones in the urine of male prairie voles make a female vole's hormones go haywire. Her ovaries swell, her uterus triples in size, and she ovulates within two days.

Pheromones were also found to exert profound effects on reproductive behavior. When a female pig gets a whiff of the pheromones in a male pig's breath, she humps her back, steels her haunches, and submits her posterior to the inevitable. Behaviorists call this a fixed-action response because free will doesn't enter into it: one blast of boar breath and she's gotta have it. Similarly, male mice whose VNOS are surgically removed lose all interest in the procreative act. They won't mount a female nor even sniff at her nether regions.

"If you want to lead a life that is dictated by chemistry, then have a vomeronasal organ," says Charles Wysocki, a neuroscientist at the Monell Chemical Senses Center in Philadelphia who's studied the rodent VNO for 15 years. To be a rodent, Wysocki says, is to live from one pheromonal fix to the next. In addition to their orchestration of sex, pheromones help animals identify relatives, mark territories, and communicate bad intentions.

The discovery of pheromones' potent effects on other animals seemed to confirm the prevailing assumption that the chemicals aren't acting on human beings: if they were, scientists reasoned, we'd know it—wouldn't we? Maybe not, says Wysocki. It's true that in humans socialization is shaped more by experience than it is in other animals, so our responses to chemical signals probably aren't as inflexible. But if they occurred, pheromonal exchanges among human beings couldn't be seen, felt, tasted, or heard—and probably not smelled, either. Unlike those conscious sensations, the messages conveyed via the VNO would bypass mental awareness and make a beeline for the primitive brain. Instead of distinct, discrete perceptions, like the taste of a cherry or the sight of a sunset, pheromones could be said to mediate impressions: bad vibes, warm fuzzies, instant dislikes, irresistible attractions.

It was a sudden change in vibes at his laboratory that led David Berliner to wonder whether such experiences could be ascribed, literally, to chemistry. Working at the University of Utah in the early 1960s, Berliner was trying to characterize the chemical components of human skin when, one

day, he and his co-workers were overcome with an inexplicable bonhomie.

Someone suggested that they learn bridge over lunch. It was an unprecedented notion.

"We all looked at her and said, 'Uh-oh. Either she's having an affair or she's going to get married,' " says Berliner. "And then we all said, 'Sure!' So now over lunch we're playing bridge. The ambience of the group became much friendlier, and I was feeling very good.

"Until we closed those flasks," he says—the flasks containing his skin extracts. "I put them away, and bridge stopped automatically. No more bridge." When Berliner brought out the extracts again several months later, camaraderie revived, as did the card game.

Berliner noticed the connection, but he was a busy man with a surfeit of good ideas. A chance investment in an oral-contraceptive manufacturer would soon land him a pile of money with which he would launch biotech companies marketing technology he himself often helped pioneer. Cetus, Alza, Advance Polymer Systems, and Biosource Genetics are among the corporations Berliner has had a hand in; his more notable (and lucrative) involvements include the development of the skin-patch technique for drug delivery. The skin patch has been used to administer estrogen to menopausal women, nitroglycerin to people at risk of a heart attack, and nicotine to smokers trying to kick the habit.

Berliner never lacked inspiration but was always short of time. Not until the mid-1980s—several decades, several millions, and several companies later—would he again thaw "those flasks" to find the secret ingredients that could compel earnest scientists to squander their lunch hour on frivolous pursuits.

At about the same time Berliner began thinking about thawing his flasks, David Moran and Bruce Jafek were conferring in a University of Colorado clinic in Denver. Moran, an electron microscopist in the university's medical school, had recently tired of studying balance sensors in the giant African cockroach and had become intrigued with the processing of sensory information in higher animals. He was particularly interested in describing the microscopic structure of human olfactory tissue, a feat that had never been achieved, owing in part to the tissue's inconvenient location in a cleft just a few hundredths of an inch wide and roughly three inches up the human nostril. One of Moran's graduate students had designed an evil-looking wire device that could collect material from the olfactory cleft, and Moran had begun taking specimens for electron microscope preparations.

Jafek, who'd recently been appointed chairman of the otolaryngology department, heard about Moran's research and asked to collaborate with him on the biopsy work. During a rambling discussion of things olfactory, Jafek happened to mention that one of his graduate students was doing some research on the VNO of the human fetus. The question arose: Whatever happened to the *adult* VNO?

"Bruce said, 'I'm going to start looking for this thing, and see what I can see,'" says Moran. As a practicing surgeon specializing in nose jobs, Jafek had access to plenty of proboscises. His grad student's work on the fetal VNO gave him an idea of where the organ's inlets might be located in the adult. "And once he learned the right place to look, he saw the VNO in everybody," says Moran. "He used a long-working-distance dissecting microscope, and he'd lay people on their backs, shine a light in there looking for this thing, and—there it was."

"So we took everyone in the lab and did an I'll-show-you-mine-if-you-show-me-yours thing. And sure enough, I had one on each side; a friend of mine had one on each side; everyone we looked at in the lab had a pair of vomeronasal pits. That," says Moran, "bent the nail over for me," confirming his belief in the existence of an adult VNO.

Moran and Jafek examined more than 200 people and found the pits in every last one of them. Eventually, surveys done by other investigators would confirm that the structures are present in more than 90 percent of noses. That these other surveys did not find the VNO in all subjects can be explained, says Moran, by the fact that the noses in question were about to undergo surgical procedures and probably had higher-than-average proportions of nasal anomalies that could obscure the organ's opening. Also, he points out, many surveyors didn't realize that the size range of vomeronasal pits straddles the line between the visible and the invisible.

"Sometimes you can see them with the naked eye and sometimes you can't," he says. "The big ones you see right away—the largest I've seen is almost a tenth of an inch across, which is a big hole. But some are as small as a hundredth of an inch. That's the human eye's limit of resolution, so you can't see the

IS THE HUMAN VOMERONASAL ORGAN OPERATIONAL? IS IT SENDING SIGNALS TO THE BRAIN? OR IS IT SIMPLY A BURNT-OUT VESTIGE OF A SCRATCH-AND-SNIFF PAST?

small ones without magnification." Moran says that other surveyors, having seen the largest cavities, assumed they didn't need a microscope to find the pits and wound up missing the smallest ones.

For Moran, the electron microscopist, seeing the VNO at 40X wasn't entirely gratifying either. Moran asked Jafek to call him into the operating room when patients were having the part of the septum near the pits surgically removed; he then took biopsies from those patients for viewing at magnifications hundreds of times higher.

His preparations showed that each pit led into a tiny duct a few tenths of an inch long and that some of the cells lining the duct looked like neurons, or nerve cells—to be exact, like receptor cells, which pick up sensory information and pass it on to the brain. But they did not look like olfactory receptors. And they did not look like nociceptors, cells that react to painful stimuli. "They didn't look like any other nerve cells I'd ever seen before in the human body," says Moran.

In 1985 he presented his micrographs in a poster session at the annual meeting of the Association for Chemoreception Sciences. "People just sort of walked by and went, 'Huh,' and walked away," says Moran. "The work was met with apathy of exciting proportions." Moran's peers wanted to know what, if anything, the neurons were doing. He didn't claim to know the answer—but several years later David Berliner would.

IT WAS 1989 WHEN BERLINER DECIDed to let his genies out of their bottles. "Let me ask you a question," he'd said to his friend Larry Stensaas, a neuroanatomist at the University of Utah. "If you thought you had some human pheromones, how would you go about finding out whether they worked?"

Stensaas had just finished debriefing Berliner on a research project he'd conducted for one of Berliner's biotech companies. He had been working with

Berliner for years, but the subject of pheromones had never come up before.

"I told him, 'In all other mammals, pheromones have to have a vomeronasal organ to work on,'" says Stensaas. "And nobody's seen the human vomeronasal organ for a long time. Berliner then said, 'Well, has anybody looked?'"

Stensaas didn't know the answer to that question, even though he himself was something of a fan of the organ. Year after year, over the protests of colleagues, he'd delivered to his medical students a detailed VNO lecture in which he candidly admitted that most experts believe the adult human version doesn't exist. He'd never had the time or the funding to pursue his interest, but it had persisted nonetheless.

"I found it fascinating that this stupid little organ could control sexual behavior in animals," Stensaas says. "And I liked the idea of the human vomeronasal organ, even if no one had seen one."

Actually, someone *had* seen the human VNO not long before. When Stensaas turned to the sensory literature, he found that in 1985 a group of Canadian investigators, working without magnification, had located at least one pit in 39 of the 100 people they examined. Discouraged by the numbers, the Canadians had abandoned their search; Stensaas took up the quest. His training as a neuroanatomist had taught him to look beyond surface phenomena, so he began to collect the brains and septal tissue from cadavers and aborted fetuses and dissect them. Unlike Elizabeth Crosby, Stensaas looked for the VNO as well as the nerve fibers associated with it, and he found the organ in most of his specimens. He also found that Crosby was right about the accessory olfactory bulb: it wasn't evident past the first trimester of fetal development. But Stensaas thought he knew why.

"Because the frontal lobes of the brain grow so big in human beings, the olfactory bulb is pulled away from its location near the brain stem," says Stensaas. As the cortex develops, the bulb becomes flattened, its nerve fibers stretched in order to maintain its connection with the frontal lobes and the brain stem; the result is that it becomes difficult to see. "Elizabeth Crosby couldn't find the accessory olfactory bulb, because it had been smeared out by this process. It isn't recognizable." But, Stensaas maintains, it's there.

The next step was to test whether or not the human VNO was operational. Is the organ sending signals to the brain? Or is it simply a burnt-out vestige of a scratch-and-sniff past? To help answer that question, Stensaas recommended Monti-Bloch, a longtime friend who'd spent decades studying the function of chemoreceptors. When the physiologist met Berliner early in 1990 he voiced some skepticism.

"I was not sure what could come out of this," says Monti-Bloch. "What I read was that in humans the organ was atrophic. And there wasn't any work we could refer to on studying the physiology of the VNO in mammals, let alone humans." He told Berliner he'd give the project six months. "'If it doesn't work by then,' I said, 'it doesn't work, period,'" says Monti-Bloch.

In the next few months Monti-Bloch designed a system for delivering chemical substances to the VNO and measuring any electrical impulses that might be generated at the organ's entrance. The trick was to contain the dispersal of the test substances so they would trigger only the cells in the VNO pits and not the smell sensors in the olfactory cleft or other nerve receptors in the nose. Monti-Bloch found that he could get the desired effect using a thin wire electrode surrounded by two concentric plastic shafts—the inner one to administer chemicals in a puff of air, and the outer one to suck away the puff like a vacuum cleaner. Placed in the VNO pit of a cooperative human subject, the rounded tip of the electrode, protruding slightly from the plastic sheaths, could detect any electrical activity that followed the chemical pulse.

Monti-Bloch connected the instrument with wires and tubes to a device that would both control the puffs of air and receive electric signals. He could inject one-second blasts of test chemicals into the airstream by depressing a pedal. A computer monitored the entire procedure, recording the chemical and electrical impulses on a chart called—what else?—an electrovomeronasogram (aka EVG).

Building the electrovomeronasometer itself required the machining of several novel parts and the extensive modification of off-the-shelf equipment. When Monti-Bloch had the system together, he tested it by positioning the electrode in some poor unfortunate's olfactory cleft and recording the responses of olfactory receptors to smelly substances such as mint and clove oil. The apparatus worked for olfactants, but the six months were nearly up.

"I am going to send you a little package with some things for you to try on the VNO," Berliner told Monti-Bloch when the physiologist phoned in from Utah.

"I asked him, 'What are these things?'" says Monti-Bloch. "And he said, 'I can't tell you that.' But the first thing I noticed when I got them was that they didn't smell. So I grabbed one of my collaborators and tried the substances in his olfactory cleft, and indeed, they didn't have any effect.

"Then I placed the electrode in the vomeronasal organ, put a puff of the substance into the airstream, and all of a sudden—" Monti-Bloch raises his eyebrows and becomes speechless. In short, the substances Berliner had shipped put spikes all over the EVG of Monti-Bloch's volunteer, suggesting that neurons in the VNO were discharging in response to those substances.

Monti-Bloch has now tested several dozen of the putative pheromones, all of which are derived from the 20 natural isolates Berliner discovered in his skin extracts. The tests have shown that the substances can evoke other physiological reactions, including changes in heart rate, respiration, pupil size, and skin temperature. Responses vary from person to person, and some of the compounds affect only men or only women—as would be expected, given the role of pheromones in the rest of the animal kingdom.

The possible behavioral effects of Berliner's compounds are still unproved. Though Monti-Bloch has yet to conduct a systematic appraisal of subjective reactions (that is, vibes), some volunteers have mentioned feeling less nervous and more confident during their exposure to Berliner's elixirs. Brad Murray, for example, claims to have experienced "a little bit of a relaxing effect from one or two of the substances." But he admits to being distracted by procedural details. "Mostly it just feels like somebody stuck a wire up my nose," he says.

In 1991 Stensaas heard about David Moran's work through a colleague and passed his phone number on to Berliner. Moran's micrographs of the human VNO provided visual support for the physiological evidence Monti-Bloch had been collecting. In Moran's pictures the cells lining the vomeronasal pits look like receptor cells; Monti-Bloch's work suggests they act like receptor cells too. In 1992 Berliner asked olfaction experts at the University of Kentucky to identify the cell types; the Kentucky team treated VNO tissue with chemical markers that bind to nerve cells. The markers indicate that the apparent receptors in the VNO are indeed neurons and "probably some kind of receptor cells," says Kentucky neuroscientist Marilyn Getchell. "But the question we still haven't answered is, are there nerve fibers coming out of this organ to the brain?"

That's what everyone in VNO research would like to know. From Moran's and Getchell's work, it's clear that the surface of the VNO is chockablock with receptor cells. From Stensaas's exploration of fetal and cadaver tissue, it's clear that the region surrounding the VNO is laden with neurons that make all kinds of interesting connections to the brain. Monti-Bloch's experiments demonstrate that stimulating the VNO receptors can effect significant changes in physiology. For most people, this assembly of evidence would be proof enough that the VNO is sending signals to the brain.

But neuroscientists are not most people. And so far no one has demonstrated exactly how VNO receptor cells hook up with their neighboring nerve complex.

"The wiring diagram hasn't been worked out yet," says Moran. "And that's because not many people are willing to have dyes that trace nerve cells injected into their brains, then have their heads cut off so you can take sections and look to see where the dyes went."

STENSAAS AND HIS COLLEAGUES, believers in a functioning human accessory olfactory bulb, already suspect the general direction. They think nerve fibers emanating from the vicinity of the vomeronasal organ head straight through the bulb to the hypothalamus, the command center for basic body functions such as sleeping, eating, and mating. Nerves from the VNO may also rendezvous with the limbic system, where emotions are thought to originate.

To the researchers, these neural pathways suggest that the human vomeronasal organ is linked inextricably, albeit subconsciously, with psyche and soma alike. If true, the organ would be an ideal target for pharmaceutical intervention—a point that has not been lost on Berliner. Drugs delivered via the VNO could in theory remedy both psychological and somatic disturbances without the side effects, such as nausea, that can be common with oral and intravenous medications. Berliner's team claims it has already identified certain substances that may decrease anxiety, diminish hunger, and relieve PMS.

But what about, you know, the boar-breath effect.

If Berliner has discovered an aphrodisiac, he isn't saying. The substances in his perfume, for example, are meant to enhance only the wearer's "positive feelings of romance, confidence, attractiveness, and self-assurance," according to Realm's infomercial. True, the perfume comes in male and female versions, reflecting the fact that each has a sex-specific formula. But Berliner says his women's scent contains a pheromone only women can detect, while the men's will only boost the "positive feelings" of men. He claims to have an ethical aversion to substances that would act on other people rather than the user. Of course, there's nothing to stop a scheming man from liberally dousing himself with the female scent, or a designing woman with the male. Berliner's stance may have less to do with ethics than

with the Food and Drug Administration's requirement that any product calling itself an aphrodisiac be sold as a prescription drug.

Whether or not Realm is *l'eau de lust*, the idea that chemicals can stimulate arousal in human beings is not farfetched. The presence of a vomeronasal organ could account for menstrual synchrony in women who are in frequent and close contact with one another, says Monell's Wysocki. It may also explain how mothers and infants can identify each other by what was thought to be smell alone. As for chemical communication between genders, Wysocki's colleague George Preti has shown that the timing of a woman's menstruation can be altered by smearing her upper lip with an extract of male underarm sweat.

Fortunately, there is a more palatable way to swap pheromones with your loved ones. "The kiss might play a very important role in the transference of chemical signals," says Wysocki. "In other species, physical contact is often necessary for the exchange of the substances that activate the vomeronasal organ.

"On the other hand, one could argue that in the course of evolution human beings are shedding control by pheromones and leading more of an independent life. If one takes that view, then the kiss is nothing more than a vestigial behavior for transmitting pheromones."

Of course, a kiss is nothing less, either. And for now, a sigh *is* still a sigh. But no doubt its role too will be clarified—as time goes by.

On the Power of Positive Thinking: The Benefits of Being Optimistic

Michael F. Scheier and Charles S. Carver

Michael F. Scheier is Professor of Psychology at Carnegie Mellon University. **Charles S. Carver** is Professor of Psychology at the University of Miami. Address correspondence to Michael F. Scheier, Department of Psychology, Carnegie Mellon University, Pittsburgh, PA 15213; e-mail: ms0a@andrew.cmu.edu.

If believing in something can make it so, then there really would be power in positive thinking. From the little train in the children's tale who said, "I think I can," to popular writers such as Norman Cousins and Norman Vincent Peale, to wise grandmothers everywhere—many people have espoused the benefits of positive thinking. But are these benefits real? Do people who think positively really fare better when facing challenge or adversity? Do they recover from illness more readily? If so, how and why do these things happen?

We and a number of other psychologists who are interested in issues surrounding stress, coping, and health have for several years focused our research attention on questions such as these. The primary purpose of this brief review is to provide a taste of the research conducted on this topic. We first document that positive thinking can be beneficial. We then consider why an optimistic orientation to life might confer benefits. After considering how individual differences in optimism might arise, we take up the question of whether optimism is always good and pessimism always bad. We close by discussing the similarities between our own approach and other related approaches.

CHARACTERIZING POSITIVE THINKING

Psychologists have approached the notion of positive thinking from a variety of perspectives. Common to most views, though, is the idea that positive thinking in some way involves holding positive expectancies for one's future. Such expectancies are thought to have built-in implications for behavior. That is, the actions that people take are thought to be greatly influenced by their expectations about the likely consequences of those actions. People who see desired outcomes as attainable continue to strive for those outcomes, even when progress is slow or difficult. When outcomes seem sufficiently unattainable, people withdraw their effort and disengage themselves from their goals. Thus, people's expectancies provide a basis for engaging in one of two very different classes of behavior: continued striving versus giving up.

People can hold expectancies at many levels of generality. Some theoretical views focus on expectancies that pertain to particular situations, or even to particular actions.[1] Such an approach allows for considerable variation in the positivity of one's thinking from one context to the next. Thus, a person who is quite optimistic about recovering successfully from a car accident may be far less optimistic about landing the big promotion that is up for grabs at work.

Our own research on positive and negative thinking began with a focus on situation-specific expectancies, but over the years we began to con-sider expectancies that are more general and diffuse. We believe that generalized expectancies constitute an important dimension of personality, that they are relatively stable across time and context. We refer to this dimension as optimism and construe it in terms of the belief that good, as opposed to bad, things will generally occur in one's life. We focus on this dimension for the rest of this article.

MEASURING OPTIMISM

We measure individual differences in optimism with the Life Orientation Test, or LOT.[2] The LOT consists of a series of items that assess the person's expectations regarding the favorability of future outcomes (e.g., "I hardly ever expect things to go my way," "In uncertain times, I usually expect the best"). LOT scores correlate positively with measures of internal control and self-esteem, correlate negatively with measures of depression and hopelessness, and are relatively unrelated to measures of social desirability.[2]

If dispositional optimism is in fact a personality characteristic, it should be relatively stable across time. We have reported a test–retest correlation of .79 across a 4-week period.[2] More recently, Karen Matthews has found a correlation of .69 between LOT scores assessed 3 years apart in a sample of 460 healthy, middle-aged women. Indeed, LOT scores seem to remain relatively stable even in the face of catastrophes. For example, Schulz, Tompkins, and

Rau[3] tracked LOT scores in a group of stroke patients and their primary caregivers across a 6-month period. Although the LOT scores of both the patients and the support persons dropped over time (significantly so for the latter), the absolute magnitude of the drop was exceedingly small (less than 1 point on a 32-point scale). Thus, optimism as measured by the LOT seems to be a relatively enduring characteristic that changes little with the vagaries of life.

Factor analyses of the LOT routinely yield two separate factors,[2,4] comprised of positively worded (optimistic) items and negatively worded (pessimistic) items, respectively. Identification of two factors raises the question of whether it is better to view optimism and pessimism as opposite poles of a single dimension or as constituting two separate but correlated dimensions.[4] Though this is an interesting question, we have thus far taken the former view.

PSYCHOLOGICAL WELL-BEING

A growing number of studies have examined the effects of dispositional optimism on psychological well-being.[5] These studies have produced a remarkably consistent pattern of findings: Optimists routinely maintain higher levels of subjective well-being during times of stress than do people who are less optimistic. Let us briefly describe two illustrative cases.

One study[6] examined the development of postpartum depression in a group of women having their first children. Women in this study completed the LOT and a standard measure of depression in the third trimester of pregnancy. They completed the same depression measure again 3 weeks postpartum. Initial optimism was inversely associated with depression 3 weeks postpartum, even when the initial level of depression was controlled statisti-

cally. In other words, optimism predicted changes in depression over time. Optimistic women were less likely to become depressed following childbirth.

Conceptually similar findings have recently been reported in a study of undergraduate students' adjustment to their first semester of college.[7] A variety of factors were assessed when the students first arrived on campus, including dispositional optimism. Several measures of psychological well-being were obtained 3 months later. Optimism had a substantial effect on future psychological well-being: Higher levels of optimism upon entering college were associated with lower distress levels 3 months later. Notably, the effects of optimism in this study were distinct from those of the other personality factors measured, including self-esteem, locus of control, and desire for control. Thus, an optimistic orientation to life seemed to provide a benefit over and above that provided by these other personality characteristics.

PHYSICAL WELL-BEING

If the effects of optimism were limited to making people feel better, perhaps such findings would not be very surprising. The effects of optimism seem to go beyond this, however. There is at least some evidence that optimism also confers benefits on physical well-being.

Consider, for example, a study conducted on a group of men undergoing coronary artery bypass graft surgery.[8] Each patient was interviewed on the day prior to surgery, 6 to 8 days postsurgery, and again 6 months later. Optimism was assessed on the day prior to surgery by the LOT. A variety of medical and recovery variables were measured at several times, beginning before surgery and continuing through surgery and several months thereafter.

The data showed a number of effects for dispositional optimism.

One notable finding concerns reactions to the surgery itself. Optimism was negatively related to physiological changes reflected in the patient's electrocardiogram and to the release of certain kinds of enzymes into the bloodstream. Both of these changes are widely taken as markers for myocardial infarction. The data thus suggest that optimists were less likely than pessimists to suffer heart attack during surgery.

Optimism was also a significant predictor of the rate of recovery during the immediate postoperative period. Optimists were faster to achieve selected behavioral milestones of recovery (e.g., sitting up in bed, walking around the room), and they were rated by medical staff as showing better physical recovery.

The advantages of an optimistic orientation were also apparent at the 6-month follow-up. Optimistic patients were more likely than pessimistic patients to have resumed vigorous physical exercise and to have returned to work full-time. Moreover, optimists returned to their activities more quickly than did pessimists. In sum, optimists were able to normalize their lifestyles more fully and more quickly than were pessimists. It is important to note that all of the findings just described were independent of the person's medical status at the outset of the study. Thus, it was not the case that optimists did better simply because they were less sick at the time of surgery.

HOW DOES OPTIMISM HELP?

If an understanding can be gained of why optimists do better than pessimists, then perhaps psychologists can begin to devise ways to help pessimists do better. One promising line of inquiry concerns differences between optimists and pessimists in how they cope with stress. Research from a variety of sources is beginning to suggest that optimists cope in more adaptive ways than do pessimists.[5] Optimists are more likely than pessimists to take direct action to solve their problems, are more planful in dealing with the adversity they confront, and are more focused in their coping efforts. Optimists are more likely to accept the reality of the stressful situations they encounter, and they also seem intent on growing personally from negative experiences and trying to make the best of bad situations. In contrast to these positive coping reactions, pessimists are more likely than optimists to react to stressful events by trying to deny that they exist or by trying to avoid dealing with problems. Pessimists are also more likely to quit trying when difficulties arise.

We now know that these coping differences are at least partly responsible for the differences in distress that optimists and pessimists experience in times of stress. When Aspinwall and Taylor[7] studied adjustment to college life, they collected information about the coping tactics the students were using to help themselves adjust to college, as well as measuring their optimism and eventual adjustment. Optimists were more likely than pessimists to rely on active coping techniques and less likely to engage in avoidance. These two general coping orientations were both related to later adjustment, in opposite directions. Avoidance coping was associated with poorer adjustment, whereas active coping was associated with better adjustment. Further analysis revealed that these two coping tendencies mediated the link between optimism and adjustment. Thus, optimists did better than pessimists at least partly because optimists used more effective ways of coping with problems.

A similar conclusion is suggested by a study of breast cancer patients that we and our colleagues recently completed. The women in this study reported on their distress and coping reactions before surgery, 10 days after surgery, and at 3-month, 6-month, and 12-month follow-ups. Throughout this period, optimism was associated with a coping pattern that involved accepting the reality of the situation, along with efforts to make the best of it. Optimism was inversely associated with attempts to act as though the problem was not real and with the tendency to give up on the life goals that were being threatened by the diagnosis of cancer. Further analyses suggested that these differences in coping served as paths by which the optimistic women remained less vulnerable to distress than the pessimistic women throughout the year.

ANTECEDENTS OF OPTIMISM

Where does optimism come from? Why do some people have it and others not? At present, not much is known about the origins of individual differences on this dimension. The determinants must necessarily fall in two broad categories, however: nature and nurture.

On the nature side, the available evidence suggests that individual differences in optimism-pessimism may be partly inherited. A translated version of the LOT was given to a sample of more than 500 same-sex pairs of middle-aged Swedish twins, and the heritability of optimism and pessimism was estimated to be about 25% using several different estimation procedures.[9] Thus, at least part of the variation in optimism and pessimism in the general population seems due to genetic influence.

On the environmental side, less is known. It is certainly reasonable to argue that optimism and pessimism are partly learned from prior experiences with success and failure. To the extent that one has been successful in the past, one should expect success in the future. Analogously, prior failure might breed the expectation of future failure. Children might also acquire a sense of optimism (or pessimism) from their parents, for example, through modeling. That is, parents who meet difficulties with positive expecta-tions and who use adaptive coping strategies are explicitly or implicitly modeling those qualities for their children. Pessimistic parents also provide models for their children, although the qualities modeled are very different. Thus, children might become optimistic or pessimistic by thinking and acting in ways their parents do.

Parents might also influence children more directly by instructing them in problem solving. Parents who teach adaptive coping skills will produce children who are better problem solvers than children of parents who do not. To the extent that acquiring adaptive coping skills leads to coping success, the basis for an optimistic orientation is provided. We have recently begun a program of research designed to examine how coping strategies are transmitted from parent to child, with particular emphasis on the manner in which parental characteristics affect the kinds of coping strategies that are taught.

IS OPTIMISM ALWAYS GOOD? IS PESSIMISM ALWAYS BAD?

Implicit in our discussion thus far is the view that optimism is good for people. Is this always true? There are at least two ways in which an optimistic orientation might lead to poorer outcomes. First, it may be possible to be too optimistic, or to be optimistic in unproductive ways. For example, unbridled optimism may cause people to sit and wait for good things to happen, thereby decreasing the chance of success. We have seen no evidence of such a tendency among people defined as optimistic on the basis of the LOT, however. Instead, optimistic people seem to view positive outcomes as partially contingent on their continued effort.

Second, optimism might also prove detrimental in situations that are not amenable to constructive action. Optimists are prone to face problems with efforts to resolve them, but perhaps this head-on approach is maladaptive in situations that are uncontrollable or that involve major loss or a violation of one's world view. Data on this question are lacking, yet it is worth noting that the coping arsenal of optimists is not limited to the problem-focused domain. Optimists also use a host of emotion-focused coping responses, including tendencies to accept the reality of the situation, to put the situation in the best possible light, and to grow personally from their hardships. Given these coping options, optimists may prove to have a coping advantage even in the most distressing situations.

What about the reverse question? Can pessimism ever work in one's favor? Cantor and Norem[10] recently coined the term *defensive pessimism* to reflect a coping style in which people expect outcomes that are more negative than their prior reward histories in a given domain would suggest. Defensive pessimism may be useful because it helps to buffer the person against future failure, should failure occur. In addition, defensive pessimism may help the person perform better because the worry over anticipated failure prompts remedial action in preparation for the event.

Defensive pessimism does seem to work. That is, the performance of defensive pessimists tends to be better than the performance of real pessimists, whose negative expectations are anchored in prior failure. On the other hand, defensive pessimism never works better than optimism. Moreover, this style apparently has some hidden costs: People who use defensive pessimism in the short run report more psychological symptoms and a lower quality of life in the long run than do optimists.[10] Such findings call into serious question the adaptive value of defensive pessimism.

RELATIONSHIP TO OTHER APPROACHES

The concept of optimism, as discussed here, does not stand apart from the rest of personality psychology. There are easily noted family resemblances to several other personality constructs and approaches that have arisen in response to the same questions that prompted our line of theorizing. Two well-known examples are attributional style[11] and self-efficacy.[1] It may be useful to briefly note some similarities and differences between our conceptualization and these other approaches.

Attributional Style

Work on attributional style derives from the cognitive model[11] that was proposed to account for the phenomenon of learned helplessness[12] in humans. In this model, people's causal explanations for past events influence their expectations for controlling future events. The explanations thus influence subsequent feelings and behavior. As the attributional theory developed, it evolved toward a consideration of individual differences and began to focus on the possibility that an individual may have a stable tendency toward using one or another type of attribution. A tendency to attribute negative outcomes to causes that are stable, global, and internal has come to be known as pessimistic. A tendency to attribute negative events to causes that are unstable, specific, and external has come to be known as optimistic.

There is a clear conceptual link between this theory and the approach that we have taken. Both theories rely on the assumption that the consequences of optimism versus pessimism derive from differences in people's expectancies (at least in part). This assumption has been focal in our theory, and it is also important—albeit less focal—in the attributional approach. More-

over, despite differences in the types of measures used to assess optimism and attributional style, research findings relating attributional style to psychological and physical well-being have tended to parallel findings obtained for dispositional optimism.[13] Thus, the data converge on the conclusion that optimism is beneficial for mental and physical functioning.

Self-Efficacy

Self-efficacy expectancies are people's expectations of being either able or unable to execute desired behaviors successfully. Although there are obvious similarities between self-efficacy and optimism-pessimism, there are also two salient differences. One difference involves the extent to which the sense of personal agency is seen as the critical variable underlying behavior. Our approach to dispositional optimism intentionally deemphasizes the role of personal efficacy. Statements on self-efficacy make personal agency paramount.[1]

The second difference concerns the breadth of the expectancy on which the theory focuses. Efficacy theory holds that people's behavior is best predicted by focalized, domain-specific (or even act-specific) expectancies. Dispositional optimism, in contrast, is thought to be a very generalized tendency that has an influence in a wide variety of settings. Interestingly, relevant research[8] suggests that both types of expectancies (specific and general) are useful in predicting behavior.

CONCLUDING COMMENT

Our purpose in writing this article (perhaps in line with its subject matter) was to put a positive foot forward in presenting work on the benefits of optimism. In so doing, we may have created a false sense that the important questions about positive thinking have all been answered. Such is not the case. Understanding of the nature and effects of optimism is still in its infancy, and there is much more to learn. For example, although the effects of optimism seem attributable in part to differences in the ways optimists and pessimists cope with stress, this cannot be the complete answer. It is impossible to account fully for differences between optimists and pessimists on the basis of this factor alone.

Similarly, more work is needed to tease apart the effects of optimism from the effects of related variables. As noted earlier, a number of personality dimensions bear a conceptual resemblance to optimism-pessimism. Some of these dimensions, such as personal coherence, hardiness, and learned resourcefulness, have appeared in the literature only recently. Other dimensions, such as neuroticism, self-esteem, and self-mastery, have a longer scientific past. Given the existence of these related constructs, it is reasonable to ask whether their effects are distinguishable. This question cannot be resolved easily on the basis of one or two studies alone. An answer must await the gradual accumulation of evidence from many studies using different methodologies and assessing different outcomes.

There does seem to be a power to positive thinking. It surely is not as simple and direct a process as believing in something making it so. But believing that the future holds good things in store clearly has an effect on the way people relate to many aspects of life.

Acknowledgments—Preparation of this article was facilitated by National Science Foundation Grants BNS-9010425 and BNS-9011653, by National Institutes of Health Grant 1R01HL44432-01A1, and by American Cancer Society Grant PBR-56.

Notes

1. A. Bandura, *Social Foundations of Thought and Action: A Social Cognitive Theory* (Prentice-Hall, Englewood Cliffs, NJ, 1986).

2. M.F. Scheier and C.S. Carver, Optimism, coping, and health: Assessment and implications of generalized outcome expectancies, *Health Psychology, 4,* 219–247 (1985).

3. R. Schulz, C.A. Tompkins, and M.T. Rau, A longitudinal study of the psychosocial impact of stroke on primary support persons, *Psychology and Aging, 3,* 131–141 (1988).

4. G.N. Marshall, C.B. Wortman, J.W. Kusulas, L.K. Hervig, and R.R. Vickers, Jr., Distinguishing optimism from pessimism: Relations to fundamental dimensions of mood and personality, *Journal of Personality and Social Psychology, 62,* 1067–1074 (1992).

5. See M.F. Scheier and C.S. Carver, Effects of optimism on psychological and physical well-being: Theoretical overview and empirical update, *Cognitive Therapy and Research, 16,* 201–228 (1992).

6. C.S. Carver and J.G. Gaines, Optimism, pessimism, and postpartum depression, *Cognitive Therapy and Research, 11,* 449–462 (1987).

7. L.G. Aspinwall and S.E. Taylor, Modeling cognitive adaptation: A longitudinal investigation of the impact of individual differences and coping on college adjustment and performance, *Journal of Personality and Social Psychology* (in press).

8. M.F. Scheier, K.A. Matthews, J.F. Owens, G.J. Magovern, Sr., R. Lefebvre, R.C. Abbott, and C.S. Carver, Dispositional optimism and recovery from coronary artery bypass surgery: The beneficial effects of optimism on physical and psychological well-being, *Journal of Personality and Social Psychology, 57,* 1024–1040 (1989).

9. R. Plomin, M.F. Scheier, C.S. Bergeman, N.L. Pedersen, J.R. Nesselroade, and G.E. McClearn, Optimism, pessimism and mental health: A twin/adoption analysis, *Personality and Individual Differences* (in press).

10. N. Cantor and J.K. Norem, Defensive pessimism and stress and coping, *Social Cognition, 7,* 92–112 (1989).

11. L.Y. Abramson, M.E.P. Seligman, and J.D. Teasdale, Learned helplessness in humans: Critique and reformulation, *Journal of Abnormal Psychology, 87,* 49–74 (1978).

12. M.E.P. Seligman, *Helplessness: On Depression, Development, and Death* (Freeman, San Francisco, 1975).

13. For a review, see C. Peterson and L.M. Bossio, *Health and Optimism: New Research on the Relationship Between Positive Thinking and Physical Well-Being* (Free Press, New York, 1991).

Recommended Reading

Scheier, M.F., and Carver, C.S. (1992). Effects of optimism on psychological and physical well-being: Theoretical overview and empirical update. *Cognitive Therapy and Research, 16,* 201–228.

Seligman, M.E.P. (1991). *Learned Optimism* (Knopf, New York).

Taylor, S.E. (1989). *Positive Illusions: Creative Self-Deception and the Healthy Mind* (Basic Books, New York).

The mind and the body

C. David Jenkins

Professor C. David Jenkins is Director of the WHO Collaborating Centre for Phychosocial Factors and Health, University of Texas Medical Branch, Galveston, TX 77555-1053, USA.

Psychological, social and behavioural forces make major contributions to the leading causes of disability and death in nations around the world, irrespective of their stage of economic development. It is very clear that smoking cigarettes, drinking too much alcohol, becoming obese and failing to get preventive health care, such as immunizations, are all easily observable behaviours that raise the risk of illness and premature death. It is also well known that the personal and social environments surrounding us either contribute to our well-being or increase our risks of illness.

A third channel through which psychosocial and behavioural factors can affect our physical health works entirely inside our bodies. Our personalities, behavioural patterns, kinds of emotions and their intensity, and the way we cope with them – all influence our bodies in complex ways. Our psychological nature develops from our past experiences and choices, and influences our central nervous system. Our nervous system interacts with the glands of our endocrine system and also with our immune system, which protects us

The competitive and aggressive attitudes that are expected of staff in modern businesses put employees at risk of cardiovascular disease.

from many diseases ranging from infections to cancers.

We all know how physical illness or pain affects the way we think and feel. Now science is making exciting discoveries about how the way we think and feel affects all the rest of our bodily systems.

Psychological mechanisms affect our bodies before, during and after physical illnesses. Here are some examples of recent research results which have implications that may help people everywhere to reduce the risk of some illnesses and perhaps even recover faster from others.

We all know how physical illness or pain affects the way we think and feel. Now science is making exciting discoveries about how the way we think and feel affects all the rest of our bodily systems.

Distress

Life-changes and problems often cause feelings of distress. When we measure how distressed people feel about what has been happening in their lives, we find a predictive relationship with future rates of mild and moderate illnesses. We measured work-related life-change distress in 400 air traffic controllers in the United States. Men with the highest scores had an average of 69% more illness episodes over the next 27 months than those in the lowest quartile. This study is typical of many that have been done throughout the world.

Distress also has a strong relationship to the recovery process.

We studied over 500 men and women undergoing coronary artery bypass or cardiac valve surgery. Before their operation we measured their level of life-change stress, their hopefulness and many other psychological and biomedical variables. Six months after their surgery, we interviewed them about the frequency with which they were experiencing heart symptoms, such as chest discomfort and shortness of breath. Of the patients with high life-change stress before their operation, only 42% were completely free of heart symptoms, whereas 70% of those with low life-change stress were free of symptoms. A similar pattern emerged for the personality characteristic of hopefulness. Of the patients who were generally hopeful about life (top 25% of scores), 66% were free of heart symptoms six months later, whereas from the group with the lowest scores on hopefulness only 37% were free from post-operative heart symptoms. This difference was so large that it could occur by chance only one time in a thousand.

The Type A behaviour pattern

People who are competitive, aggressive, easily angered, always in a hurry, and in a constant struggle against time and their environment are said to display the Type A behaviour pattern. This pattern was originally found to be associated with a doubled risk of developing ischaemic heart disease (IHD), particularly in men under the age of 60 years. The power of the Type A behaviour pattern to predict IHD has been shown in many countries, with the most recent data coming from Belgium, China, India, Japan and Lithuania. Even when account is taken of other IHD risk factors like cigarette smoking, high blood pressure and elevated serum cholesterol, the Type A pattern appears to contribute still further risks in many – but not all – subpopulations of people.

Now researchers are studying the relationship of Type A behaviour to other health outcomes. In the US study of air traffic controllers, Type A workers had 38% more mild and moderate illnesses from all causes than their colleagues. Furthermore, Type A men had three and a half times as high a frequency of injuries compared with those without that behaviour. It makes sense that aggressive, competitive, hurried, impulsive behaviour will lead to more accidents on the road, at home and during sports. The important thing, however, is that we can measure this risk quantitatively and recommend that changing one's behaviour pattern to a more average, easy-going, cooperative and friendly style might very well lower the risk of both heart attack and injury.

Hostility

Hostility is part of the Type A behaviour pattern, and it has often been studied independently for its effect on health. Hostile, angry, unfriendly people not only make life difficult for their families and co-workers, they also bring ill-health upon themselves. A number of large research studies – some with as long as 20 years of follow-up – have shown that hostility is a major risk factor for IHD. It also seems predictive of higher rates of future mortality from all causes. In the prospective study of US air traffic controllers, hostile attitudes towards management were predictive of future increased risks of both minor illnesses and injuries. In the study of recovery after major heart surgery, patients who scored highest on the hostility scale before their operations were twice as likely as the least hostile quarter of the group to be experiencing heart symptoms six months later.

Again we see this interesting continuity of effect. Some of the

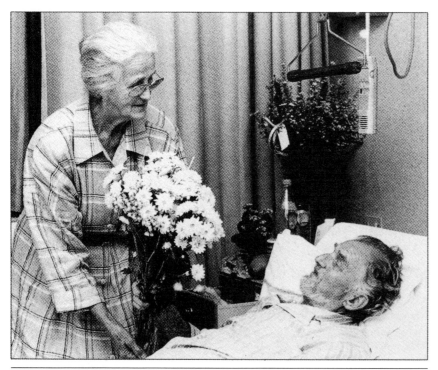

Positive inward feelings increase the chances of recovery among cardiovascular patients.

same psychological risk factors that increase a person's chances of suffering an illness or injury also seem to influence the rate of recovery after an acute medical or surgical crisis.

Steps you can take

What do these findings tell us about the influence of psychological factors on physical health? These few examples from a much larger body of research indicate that high levels of distress due to life crises, the Type A behaviour pattern, and hostility are important examples of psychological factors that influence both the chance of becoming ill or injured and the speed of one's recovery. It is possible – although difficult – to change our exposure to the kinds of events that cause stress, Type A reactions and hostility in us. What is easier is to try to see the world in a new way and reinterpret our life circumstances in a way that is more benign and less troubling to our feelings. Finally, there are certain relaxation and meditative techniques that seem to be able to change our physical responses to our experiences and feelings.

A number of excellent books and monographs have been written in recent years about approaches that can be used to change behaviours. Each of these techniques works for some persons but not for others. Through psychosocial and behavioural research we are learning more and more about the causes of physical illness, and we are also learning how psychological and behavioural techniques can help preserve and promote our own total health.

Problems Influencing Personal Growth

At each stage of development from infancy to old age, humans are faced with new challenges. The infant has the rudimentary sensory apparati for seeing, hearing, and touching but needs to begin coordinating stimuli into meaningful information. For example, early in life the baby begins to recognize familiar and unfamiliar people and usually becomes attached to those who are the primary caregivers. In toddlerhood, the same child must master the difficult skills of walking, talking, and toilet training. This energetic, mobile, and sociable child also needs to learn the limits on his or her behavior set by others. As the child matures, not only do physical changes continue to take place, but the child's family composition may change when siblings are added, parents divorce, or the mother decides to work outside the home. Playmates become more influential, and others in the community, such as day-care workers and teachers, have an increasing impact on the child. The child eventually may spend more time at school than at home. The demands in this new environment require that the child sit still, pay attention,

learn, and cooperate with others for long periods of time; behaviors perhaps never before required of the child.

In adolescence the child's body noticeably changes. Peers may pressure the individual to indulge in new behaviors such as using illegal drugs or engaging in premarital sex. Some youths are said to be faced with an identity crisis; the older teenager must often choose among career, education, and marriage. The pressures of work and family life exact a toll on less mature youths while others are satisfied with the workplace and home.

Adulthood and middle age may bring contentment or turmoil as individuals face career peaks, empty nests, advancing age, and perhaps the death of loved ones such as parents. Again some individuals cope more effectively with these events than do other individuals.

At any step in the developmental sequence, unexpected stressors challenge individuals. Stressors include major illnesses, accidents, natural disasters, economic recessions, and family or personal crises. It is important to remember, however, that an event need not be negative to be stressful. Any major life change may cause stress. As welcome as weddings, new babies, and job promotions may be, they too can be stressful because of the changes in daily life they require. Each challenge and each change must be met and adjusted to if the individual is going to move successfully to the next stage of development. Some individuals continue along their paths unscathed; others do not fare so well.

This section of the book examines major problems in various stages of life from childhood to old age. The first article begins with prenatal life. In "Clipped Wings," the results of a recent report on the deleterious effects of drugs, alcohol, and other substances on the fetus are shared with the reader. Even before life commences, problems exist that may impact on development.

Toddlerhood is the next stage of development. Many American parents need to decide whether both parents will work outside the home and, if so, whether the child will be placed in child care. In "How Kids Benefit from Child Care," Vivian Cadden reveals the results of a survey of working mothers whose children were in day care. They nearly unanimously agree that this early experience provided advantages for their children.

The life era called childhood is the next step in development. Child abuse is the topic of "Rush to Judgment." This article looks at the effects of a child's testimony in court about abuse.

Childhood problems also include inequality in the way girls and boys are treated in school. Myra and David Sadker's research clearly demonstrates that American schools are unfair to girls. Girls have become spectators in education compared to boys who are more actively engaged in learning by their teachers. The Sadkers point is made in "Why Schools Must Tell Girls: 'You're Smart, You Can Do It.' "

Yet another social problem is addressed in the article "Teaching Young Children to Resist Bias: What Parents Can Do." The article pertains to racial prejudice and discrimination. The issue of children learning to resist bias and prejudice is placed squarely on the shoulders of the adults surrounding the children.

Adolescence is the next life stage. A prevalent social problem in the United States is teen pregnancy. The United States has the highest teen pregnancy rate of any industrialized Western society. In "Adolescent Childbearing: Whose Problem? What Can We Do?" Diane Scott-Jones examines a myriad of relevant issues.

Even in adulthood, developmental crises continue to occur. The next article explores whether critical life events affect our physical health. The article is entitled "Critical Life Events and the Onset of Illness" by Blair Justice. Middle age is the developmental stage showcased in "The New Middle Age." Middle age is stereotyped as the adult stage at which crisis is most likely to occur. Middle age need not be a time of crisis, according to Melinda Beck. She maintains that few of us actually struggle with midlife crisis.

The ultimate developmental stage is death. Death is a topic that fascinates and frightens most of us. There are some individuals, however, who choose to die. In "The Mystery of Suicide," David Gelman discusses the serious topic of suicide.

Looking Ahead: Challenge Questions

Individuals face challenges at every stage of development. What are some challenges typical of each stage that have not been mentioned in this reader? Is any one stage more demanding than the others? Why?

If drugs and other addictive substances have detrimental effects on the fetus, should we hold addicted parents responsible for the care and treatment of their addicted and deformed infants? If you answered "yes," how should we hold them responsible? If you answered "no," defend your answer. What other factors besides drugs and alcohol influence prenatal life?

How can we enhance children's early development?

Many issues face American children. What are some of the effects of child care, child abuse, and sex and racial bias on American children? What are some other problems and their effects on children?

Some cultures rear their children quite differently from the way Americans do. Are there lessons to be learned from other cultures that might be incorporated into American childrearing methods? Are there strategies and techniques Americans could teach others?

What are the causes for such a high rate of adolescent pregnancy? Is this an issue just for the girls? Is it primarily minority adolescents who get pregnant? What are some other social problems affecting adolescents?

Do you think that American adults face more crises today than did earlier generations? What could we do to change society so that adulthood provides continual positive growth experiences? Do you think there is a link between critical life events in adulthood and propensity for illness?

What are some myths about middle and old age? How can social scientists and older adults change our attitudes and correct any misinformation? According to research, what positive changes come from aging? What negative changes occur as a result of aging?

CLIPPED WINGS

*The Fullest Look Yet at How
Prenatal Exposure to Drugs, Alcohol, and Nicotine
Hobbles Children's Learning*

LUCILE F. NEWMAN AND STEPHEN L. BUKA

*Lucile F. Newman is a professor of community health
and anthropology at Brown University and the director of the Preventable Causes of Learning Impairment
Project. Stephen L. Buka is an epidemiologist and
instructor at the Harvard Medical School and School of
Public Health.*

SOME FORTY thousand children a year are born with
learning impairments related to their mother's alcohol use. Drug abuse during pregnancy affects 11 percent
of newborns each year—more than 425,000 infants in
1988. Some 260,000 children each year are born at below
normal weights—often because they were prenatally
exposed to nicotine, alcohol, or illegal drugs.

What learning problems are being visited upon these
children? The existing evidence has heretofore been
scattered in many different fields of research—in pediatric medicine, epidemiology, public health, child development, and drug and alcohol abuse. Neither educators,
health professionals, nor policy makers could go to one
single place to receive a full picture of how widespread
or severe were these preventable causes of learning
impairment.

In our report for the Education Commission of the
States, excerpts of which follow, we combed these various fields to collect and synthesize the major studies that
relate prenatal exposure to nicotine, alcohol, and illegal
drugs* with various indexes of students' school performance.

The state of current research in this area is not always
as full and satisfying as we would wish. Most of what

exists is statistical and epidemiological data, which document the frequency of certain high-risk behaviors and
correlate those behaviors to student performance. Such
data are very interesting and useful, as they allow teachers and policy makers to calculate the probability that a
student with a certain family history will experience
school failure. But such data often cannot control for the
effects of other risk factors, many of which tend to cluster in similar populations. In other words, the same mother who drinks during her pregnancy may also use drugs,
suffer from malnutrition, be uneducated, a teenager, or
poor—all factors that might ultimately affect her child's
school performance. An epidemiological study generally can't tell you how much of a child's poor school performance is due exclusively to a single risk factor.

Moreover, the cumulative damage wrought by several
different postnatal exposures may be greater than the
damage caused by a single one operating in isolation. And
many of the learning problems that are caused by prenatal exposure to drugs can be compounded by such
social factors as poverty and parental disinterest and,
conversely, overcome if the child lives in a high-quality
postnatal environment.

All of these facts make it difficult to isolate and interpret the level and character of the damage that is caused
by a single factor. Further, until recently, there was little
interest among researchers in the effects of prenatal alcohol exposure because there was little awareness that it
was affecting a substantial number of children. The large
cohort of children affected by crack is just now entering
the schools, so research on their school performance
hasn't been extensive.

What does clearly emerge from the collected data is
that our classrooms now include many students whose
ability to pay attention, sit still, or fully develop their visual, auditory, and language skills was impaired even before
they walked through our schoolhouse doors. On the

---

*The full report for the ECS also addressed the effect on children's learn-
ing of fetal malnutrition, pre- and postnatal exposure to lead, and child
abuse and neglect.

Reprinted with permission from *American Educator,* the quarterly journal of the American Federation of Teachers, Spring
1991, pp. 27-33, 42. Adapted from "Every Child a Learner: Reducing Risks of Learning Impairment During Pregnancy and
Infancy," supported by the Exxon Educational Foundation, published by the Education Commission of the States.

brighter side, the evidence that many of these impairments can be overcome by improved environmental conditions suggests that postnatal treatment is possible; promising experiments in treatment are, in fact, under way and are outlined at the end of this article.

1. Low Birthweight

The collection of graphs begins with a set on low birthweight, which is strongly associated with lowered I.Q. and poor school performance. While low birthweight can be brought on by other factors, including maternal malnutrition and teenage pregnancy, significant causes are maternal smoking, drinking, and drug use.

Around 6.9 percent of babies born in the United States weigh less than 5.5 pounds (2,500 grams) at birth and are considered "low-birthweight" babies. In 1987, this accounted for some 269,100 infants. Low birthweight may result when babies are born prematurely (born too early) or from intrauterine growth retardation (born too small) as a result of maternal malnutrition or actions that restrict blood flow to the fetus, such as smoking or drug use.

In 1987, about 48,750 babies were born at very low birthweights (under 3.25 lbs. or 1,500 grams). Research estimates that 6 to 8 percent of these babies experience major handicaps such as severe mental retardation or cerebral palsy (Eilers et al., 1986; Hack and Breslau, 1986). Another 25 to 26 percent have borderline I.Q. scores, problems in understanding and expressing language, or other deficits (Hack and Breslau, 1986; Lefebvre et al., 1988; Nickel et al., 1982; Vohr et al., 1988). Although these children may enter the public school system, many of them show intellectual disabilities and require special educational assistance. Reading, spelling, handwriting, arts, crafts, and mathematics are difficult school subjects for them. Many are late in developing

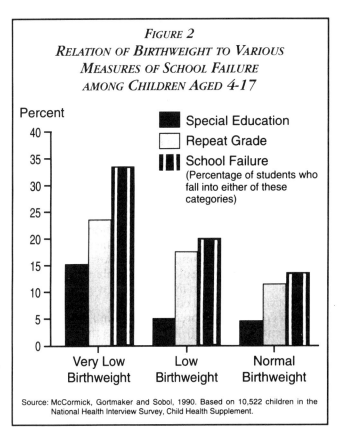

FIGURE 2
RELATION OF BIRTHWEIGHT TO VARIOUS
MEASURES OF SCHOOL FAILURE
AMONG CHILDREN AGED 4-17

Source: McCormick, Gortmaker and Sobol, 1990. Based on 10,522 children in the National Health Interview Survey, Child Health Supplement.

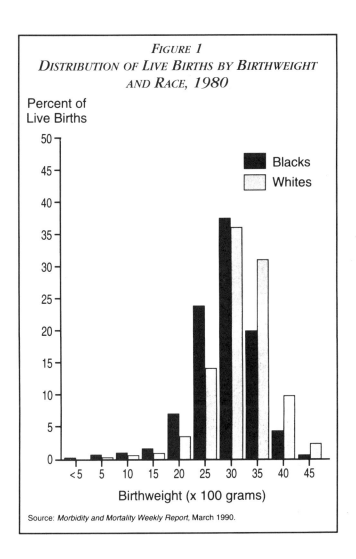

FIGURE 1
DISTRIBUTION OF LIVE BIRTHS BY BIRTHWEIGHT
AND RACE, 1980

Source: *Morbidity and Mortality Weekly Report*, March 1990.

their speech and language. Children born at very low birthweights are more likely than those born at normal weights to be inattentive, hyperactive, depressed, socially withdrawn, or aggressive (Breslau et al., 1988).

New technologies and the spread of neonatal intensive care over the past decade have improved survival rates of babies born at weights ranging from 3.25 pounds to 5.5 pounds. But, as Figures 2 and 3 show, those born at low birthweight still are at increased risk of school failure. The increased risk, however, is very much tied to the child's postnatal environment. When the data on which Figure 2 is based are controlled to account for socioeconomic circumstances, very low-birthweight babies are approximately twice, not three times, as likely to repeat a grade.

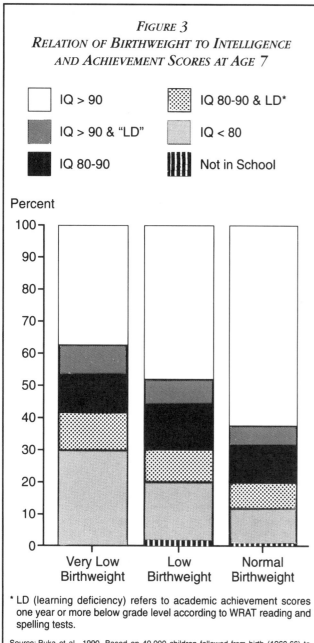

FIGURE 3
RELATION OF BIRTHWEIGHT TO INTELLIGENCE
AND ACHIEVEMENT SCORES AT AGE 7

IQ > 90

IQ > 90 & "LD"

IQ 80-90

IQ 80-90 & LD*

IQ < 80

Not in School

* LD (learning deficiency) refers to academic achievement scores one year or more below grade level according to WRAT reading and spelling tests.

Source: Buka et al., 1990. Based on 40,000 children followed from birth (1960-66) to age 7 in the National Collaborative Perinatal Project.

to, among other problems, frequent hospitalization and school absence (Streissguth, 1986). A growing number of new studies has shown that children of smokers are smaller in stature and lag behind other children in cognitive development and educational achievement. These children are particularly subject to hyperactivity and inattention (Rush and Callahan, 1989).

Data from the National Collaborative Perinatal Project on births from 1960 to 1966 measured, among other things, the amount pregnant women smoked at each prenatal visit and how their children functioned in school at age seven. Compared to offspring of nonsmokers, children of heavy smokers (more than two packs per day) were nearly twice as likely to experience school failure by age seven (see Figure 4). The impact of heavy smoking is apparently greater the earlier it occurs during pregnancy. Children of women who smoked heavily during the first trimester of pregnancy were more than twice as likely to fail than children whose mothers did not smoke during the first trimester. During the second and third trimesters, these risks decreased. In all of these analyses, it is difficult to differentiate the effects of exposure to smoking before birth and from either parent after birth; to distinguish between learning problems caused by low birthweight and those caused by other damaging effects of smoking; or, to disentangle the effects of smoke from the socioeconomic setting of the smoker. But it is worth noting that Figure 4 is based on children born in the early sixties, an era when smoking mothers were fairly well distributed across socioeconomic groups.

One study that attempted to divorce the effects of smoking from those of poverty examined middle-class children whose mothers smoked during pregnancy (Fried and Watkinson, 1990) and found that the infants showed differences in responsiveness beginning at one week of age. Later tests at 1, 2, 3, and 4 years of age showed that on verbal tests "the children of the heavy smokers had mean test scores that were lower than those born to lighter smokers, who in turn did not perform as well as those born to nonsmokers." The study also indicated that the effects of smoke exposure, whether in the womb or after birth, may not be identifiable until later ages when a child needs to perform complex cognitive functions, such as problem solving or reading and interpretation.

3. Prenatal Alcohol Exposure

Around forty thousand babies per year are born with fetal alcohol effect resulting from alcohol abuse during pregnancy (Fitzgerald, 1988). In 1984, an estimated 7,024 of these infants were diagnosed with fetal alcohol syndrome (FAS), an incidence of 2.2 per 1,000 births (Abel and Sokol, 1987). The three main features of FAS in its extreme form are facial malformation, intrauterine growth retardation, and dysfunctions of the central nervous system, including mental retardation.

There are, in addition, about 33,000 children each year who suffer from less-severe effects of maternal alcohol use. The more prominent among these learning impairments are problems in attention (attention-deficit disorders), speech and language, and hyperactivity. General

Indeed, follow-up studies of low-birthweight infants at school age have concluded that "the influence of the environment far outweighs most effects of nonoptimal prenatal or perinatal factors on outcome" (Aylward et al., 1989). This finding suggests that early assistance can improve the intellectual functioning of children at risk for learning delay or impairment (Richmond, 1990).

2. Maternal Smoking

Maternal smoking during pregnancy has long been known to be related to low birthweight (Abel, 1980), an increased risk for cancer in the offspring (Stjernfeldt et al., 1986), and early and persistent asthma, which leads

school failure also is connected to a history of fetal alcohol exposure (Abel and Sokol, 1987; Ernhart et al., 1985). Figure 5 shows the drinking habits of women of childbearing age by race and education.

When consumed in pregnancy, alcohol easily crosses the placenta, but exactly how it affects the fetus is not well known. The effects of alcohol vary according to how far along in the pregnancy the drinking occurs. The first trimester of pregnancy is a period of brain growth and organ and limb formation. The embryo is most susceptible to alcohol from week two to week eight of development, a point at which a woman may not even know she is pregnant (Hoyseth and Jones, 1989). Researchers have yet to determine how much alcohol it takes to cause problems in development and how alcohol affects each critical gestational period. It appears that the more alcohol consumed during pregnancy, the worse the effect.

And many of the effects do not appear until ages four to seven, when children enter school.

Nearly one in four (23 percent) white women, eighteen to twenty-nine, reported "binge" drinking (five

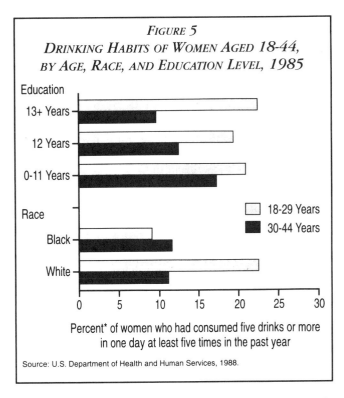

FIGURE 5
DRINKING HABITS OF WOMEN AGED 18-44, BY AGE, RACE, AND EDUCATION LEVEL, 1985

Percent* of women who had consumed five drinks or more in one day at least five times in the past year

Source: U.S. Department of Health and Human Services, 1988.

drinks or more a day at least five times in the past year). This was nearly three times the rate for black women of that age (about 8 percent). Fewer women (around 3 percent for both black and white) reported steady alcohol use (two drinks or more per day in the past two weeks).

4. Fetal Drug Exposure

The abuse of drugs of all kinds—marijuana, cocaine, crack, heroin, or amphetamines—by pregnant women affected about 11 percent of newborns in 1988—about 425,000 babies (Weston et al., 1989).

Cocaine and crack use during pregnancy are consistently associated with lower birthweight, premature birth, and smaller head circumference in comparison with babies whose mothers were free of these drugs (Chasnoff et al., 1989; Cherukuri et al., 1988; Doberczak et al., 1987; Keith et al., 1989; Zuckerman et al., 1989). In a study of 1,226 women attending a prenatal clinic, 27 percent tested positive for marijuana and 18 percent for cocaine. Infants of those who had used marijuana weighed an average of 2.8 ounces (79 grams) less at birth and were half a centimeter shorter in length. Infants of mothers who had used cocaine averaged 3.3 ounces (93 grams) less in weight and .7 of a centimeter less in length and also had a smaller head circumference than babies of nonusers (Zuckerman et al., 1989). The study concluded that "marijuana use and cocaine use during pregnancy are each independently associated with impaired fetal growth" (Zuckerman et al., 1989).

In addition, women who use these substances are like-

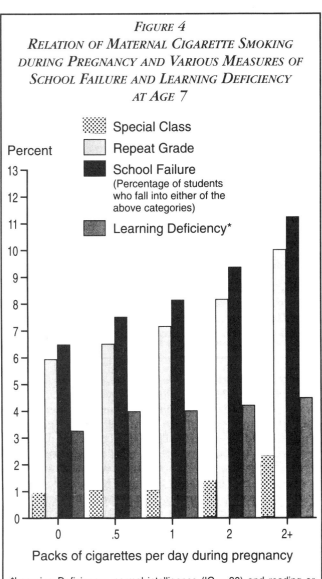

FIGURE 4
RELATION OF MATERNAL CIGARETTE SMOKING DURING PREGNANCY AND VARIOUS MEASURES OF SCHOOL FAILURE AND LEARNING DEFICIENCY AT AGE 7

Special Class
Repeat Grade
School Failure
(Percentage of students who fall into either of the above categories)
Learning Deficiency*

Packs of cigarettes per day during pregnancy

*Learning Deficiency= normal intelligence (IQ > 90) and reading or spelling scores one year or more below grade level on the WRAT.

Source: Duka et al., 1990. Based on 40,000 pregnancies with infants followed to age 7 in the National Collaborative Perinatal Project.

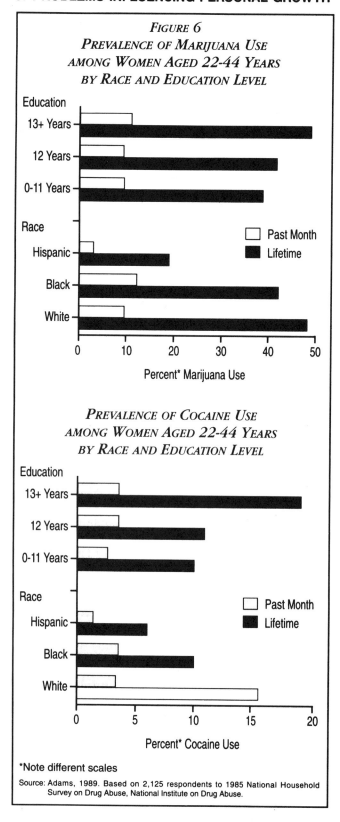

FIGURE 6
PREVALENCE OF MARIJUANA USE
AMONG WOMEN AGED 22-44 YEARS
BY RACE AND EDUCATION LEVEL

PREVALENCE OF COCAINE USE
AMONG WOMEN AGED 22-44 YEARS
BY RACE AND EDUCATION LEVEL

*Note different scales

Source: Adams, 1989. Based on 2,125 respondents to 1985 National Household Survey on Drug Abuse, National Institute on Drug Abuse.

aged nearly a pound (14.6 ounces or 416 grams) smaller than those born to women who had normal weight gain and did not use cigarettes, marijuana, and cocaine (see Table 1). The effect of these substances on size is more than the sum of the risk factors combined.

Like alcohol use, drug use has different effects at different points in fetal development. Use in very early pregnancy is more likely to cause birth defects affecting organ formation and the central nervous systems. Later use may

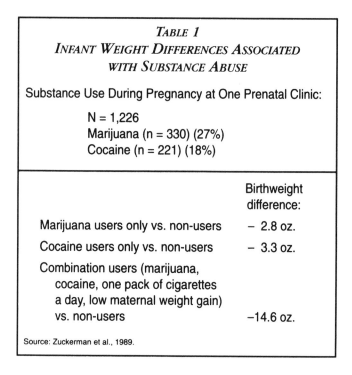

TABLE 1
INFANT WEIGHT DIFFERENCES ASSOCIATED
WITH SUBSTANCE ABUSE

Substance Use During Pregnancy at One Prenatal Clinic:

N = 1,226
Marijuana (n = 330) (27%)
Cocaine (n = 221) (18%)

	Birthweight difference:
Marijuana users only vs. non-users	− 2.8 oz.
Cocaine users only vs. non-users	− 3.3 oz.
Combination users (marijuana, cocaine, one pack of cigarettes a day, low maternal weight gain) vs. non-users	−14.6 oz.

Source: Zuckerman et al., 1989.

result in low birthweight due to either preterm birth or intrauterine growth retardation (Kaye et al., 1989; MacGregor et al., 1987; Petitti and Coleman, 1990). While some symptoms may be immediately visible, others may not be apparent until later childhood (Weston et al., 1989; Gray and Yaffe, 1986; Frank et al., 1988).

In infancy, damaged babies can experience problems in such taken-for-granted functions as sleeping and waking, resulting in exhaustion and poor development. In childhood, problems are found in vision, motor control, and in social interaction (Weston et al., 1989). Such problems may be caused not only by fetal drug exposure but also by insufficient prenatal care for the mother or by an unstimulating or difficult home environment for the infant (Lifschitz et al., 1985).

WHAT CAN be done to ameliorate the condition of children born with such damage? Quite a bit, based on the success of supportive prenatal care and the results of model projects that have provided intensive assistance to both baby and mother from the time of birth. These projects have successfully raised the I.Q. of low- and very-low birthweight babies an average of ten points or more—an increase that may lift a child with below-average intelligence into a higher I.Q. cate-

ly to smoke and to gain less weight during pregnancy, two factors associated with low birthweight. The cumulative effect of these risk factors is demonstrated by the finding that infants born to women who gained little weight, who had smoked one pack of cigarettes a day, and who tested positive for marijuana and cocaine aver-

gory (i.e., from retarded to low average or from low average to average). Generally known as either educational day care or infant day care, these programs provide a developmentally stimulating environment to high-risk babies and/or intensive parent support to prepare the parent to help her child.

In one such program based at the University of California/Los Angeles, weekly meetings were held among staff, parents, and infants over a period of four years. By the project's end, the low-birthweight babies had caught up in mental function to the control group of normal birthweight children (Rauh et al., 1988). The Infant Health and Development Project, which was conducted in eight cities and provided low-birthweight babies with pediatric follow-up and an educational curriculum with family support, on average increased their I.Q. scores by thirteen points and the scores of very-low birthweight children by more than six points. Another project tar-

geted poor single teenage mothers whose infants were at high risk for intellectual impairment (Martin, Ramey and Ramey, 1990). One group of children was enrolled in educational day care from six and one-half weeks of age to four and one-half years for five days a week, fifty weeks a year. By four and one-half years, the children's I.Q. scores were in the normal range and ten points higher than a control group. In addition, by the time their children were four and one-half, mothers in the experimental group were more likely to have graduated from high school and be self-supporting than were mothers in the control group.

These studies indicate that some disadvantages of poverty and low birthweight can be mitigated and intellectual impairment avoided. The key is attention to the cognitive development of young children, in conjunction with social support of their families.

HOW KIDS BENEFIT FROM CHILD CARE

In a breakthrough study, over 1,700 readers reveal that their children learn critical academic and social skills from being in day care

Vivian Cadden

Vivian Cadden, a WORKING MOTHER contributing editor, is a member of the board of the Child Care Action Campaign.

Attitudes among working women toward child care have changed profoundly. A solid three out of four mothers of infants, toddlers and preschoolers believe that their child is learning more in day care than he or she would staying home with Mom all day. This surprisingly positive view of the advantages of child care emerges from a survey of 1,762 readers of WORKING MOTHER.

"The recognition that a quality child care arrangement can actually be *educational* for children represents an entirely new perspective; as recently as fifteen years ago, child care was seen as just an unavoidable necessity for working families," says Barbara Reisman, executive director of the Child Care Action Campaign (CCAC), which coauthored the survey. (The results of the questionnaire will be presented at the CCAC conference, "Child Care and Education: The Critical Connection," taking place in New York City March 31st through April 2nd.)

In fact, so great is the acceptance of child care now, that working mothers are almost unanimously (97 percent) convinced that their child benefits from it because it is educational, contributes to personal development and builds social skills. The women also have decided opinions on how young children learn and why certain forms of care are more conducive to learning than others:

- Eighty-five percent say that because their youngster is in child care he or she is "more independent."
- Eighty percent believe that "children who have had good child care are readier for first grade than other children."
- Three quarters say their kids gain valuable social skills in child care.
- Signaling a new trend, a majority (56 percent) prefer center-based care as a learning environment.
- Women have a new respect for teachers as professionals who are experts on child development.
- Respondents believe that one-on-one care, whether by a nanny, a relative or the mother herself, is of lesser educational value than group care.

What Children Learn

Parents put an especially high premium on the social skills their child gains from a group experience. In answer to an open-ended question, "What is the most impor-

tant thing your youngster has learned from child care?", the most frequent responses were "learning to share" and "making friends." It is these perceptions that lead mothers to believe that their child is learning more from outside care than he would staying home with Mom.

"The most important thing my daughter has learned is how to interact with other children and adults. I don't think she would have received the stimulation and encouragement at home that she has received from her center's director, teachers and classmates," writes a woman from Waverly Hall, Georgia.

A San Ramon, California, mother says, "In addition to sharing and taking turns, my two-year-old has learned a wonderful quality—empathy. If Amanda sees another child cry, she asks what's wrong and tries to cheer him up."

A majority of women say that their youngster is "more outgoing" and "happier" because of being in child care; about half believe that he or she is "smarter," "less clingy" and "more cooperative."

Mothers of three- and four-year-olds are likely to talk about academic accomplishments that they believe contribute to their youngster's readiness for first grade: the growth of vocabulary and mastery of ABCs and numbers and color.

A Norfolk, Virginia, mother, for instance, is proud that her four-year-old "can count to twenty, knows her ABCs and can recognize letters."

Many mothers have such a strong belief in the benefits of group care that they would want their child to spend part of the day or several days a week in group care even if they didn't work. A Freeport, New York, woman writes, "Our center offers so much that I'm not trained to do. . . . I have often said that even if I didn't work I would want my son to attend this center a couple of days a week!"

Good Marks for Centers

One notable finding of the survey is a new enthusiasm for center-based care and a preference for it over every other type of care. This mirrors a trend in the country at large, but the preference is greater among WORKING MOTHER readers.

Overall, 57 percent of mothers in the survey have their youngster in a child care center, while 32 percent use a family day care home; 5 percent have in-home care, and 3 percent rely on a spouse or other relative. Even mothers of infants under two use center care about as often

The Educational Benefits

Here's how the mothers of children in each particular child care setting rate their youngsters' educational experiences.

	Child Care Center	Family Day Care Home	In-Home Caregiver	Spouse or Other Relative
Do you think your child is getting a learning experience in child care?	97% YES	86% YES	84% YES	79% YES
What grade would you give your caregiver as an educator?	65% A	52% A	48% A	48% A
Do you think your child would learn more if you were home with her?	12% YES	29% YES	37% YES	42% YES

ILLUSTRATED CHARTS BY STANFORD KAY/PARAGRAPHICS

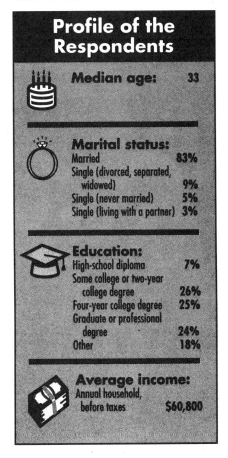

Profile of the Respondents

Median age: 33

Marital status:
Married	83%
Single (divorced, separated, widowed)	9%
Single (never married)	5%
Single (living with a partner)	3%

Education:
High-school diploma	7%
Some college or two-year college degree	26%
Four-year college degree	25%
Graduate or professional degree	24%
Other	18%

Average income:
Annual household, before taxes	$60,800

as they do family day care. And a whopping 72 percent of three- and four-year-olds are cared for in centers.

Even more striking is the degree of satisfaction mothers express with center care and their faith in its educational content. On practically every question dealing with the educational value of care, the center comes out on top. Mothers were asked, for example, "What grade would you give your caregiver for the job she is doing at providing learning experiences for your child?" Sixty-five percent of those whose child attends a center answered "A," compared to only 52 percent of those with a child in family care. And barely half—48 percent—were as pleased with the learning experience a child got from a nanny or relative. (See "The Educational Benefits.")

A Lowell, Massachusetts, respondent whose six-year-old and three-year-old

have been in centers since infancy writes, "Our children have gained insight into many facets of life, which I believe they would not have experienced if they had stayed home with me: exposure to many different types of adults and children; a wide variety of toys, games, books and activities; learning about cooperation and sharing; being able to giggle and act silly with lots of friends one day and being alone in a cozy corner with a book the next day; being in a physical environment that supports children's needs instead of placing limitations on them; being in a place where children are not pushed to learn but where they learn and discover because it's fun and they want to do it."

Anne Mitchell, senior consultant to CCAC on the New York City conference, marveled at the sophistication of readers' views as expressed in their replies. "Clearly, these women know the kind of environment in which children learn and flourish," she says.

The high regard for center care is all the more remarkable because over the years such care has so often come under attack. Mothers are aware of this, and many comment on it in their letters.

The Lowell, Massachusetts, mother says of her children's center, "This is the kind of day care center that should be featured when television journalists insist on 'exposing the care that children get in the day care centers of our nation.'"

"Many of us," a Brooklyn mother adds, "are disgusted by the negative media coverage of child care centers."

Teachers Are Pros

Readers also voice great respect for the people who care for their children. Likely to be well educated themselves (see "Profile of the Respondents"), these women value the training their children's caregivers have acquired.

A mother with a graduate degree who has a one-year-old daughter in a center says, "I don't have the experience nor do I know how and what to teach a kid!" Another writes, "I feel teachers are better geared to educate a small child. After all, that's what they went to college for."

Many women feel that if they were home all day they wouldn't be concentrating on educational activities for their child as teachers are able to do. A mother from Newnan, Georgia, puts it this way: "The day care center doesn't have to worry about washing clothes, cleaning house, running errands and getting distracted."

A Bloomington, Indiana, mother writes, "I am not as focused on creative ideas for children." As an example, she describes how her four-year-old learned to lace his shoes at his center by lacing a shoe box that had been made into a mock shoe. "I was so amazed," she says, "that I brought the teacher flowers!"

After citing some of the things her toddler has learned in child care, a Newark, Delaware, mother says, "I, too, have learned from child care, observing the teachers. I have learned how to talk to Jennifer in a positive and encouraging way. I have learned how much she is capable of doing. I have learned to give her choices whenever possible, to encourage her to make decisions."

Readers also understand that teaching young children is not a matter of formal indoctrination. "Learning is not shoved down my son's throat. He learns by playing and the thoughtful direction of his teachers" is how one mother puts it.

In fact, her enlightened view that "children learn through playing" is shared almost unanimously by the respondents: Ninety-eight percent agree.

One-on-One Care

The respondents' enthusiasm about the educational value of day care does not carry over to their assessment of one-on-one care provided by nannies or relatives.

Only 12 percent of mothers who use center care believe their child would learn more if they stayed home. But a hefty 42 percent of those who rely on a spouse or other relative think so. And 37 percent of moms with a nanny feel they could give their child a better learning experience if they stayed home.

The marked confidence in group care and more tepid enthusiasm for individual care represents a real turnabout in women's opinion. An affluent Arlington, Virginia, mother with an infant in center care says, "I am particularly interested in your

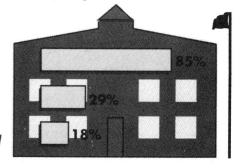

What Government Should Do

One of the most remarkable findings of the survey is how strongly women feel about the need for public schools to accommodate the changing needs of society. The vast majority, for instance, want before- and after-school care for elementary-age children. In fact, at a time when most people feel enormously burdened by taxes, 85 percent of the respondents not only think public schools should provide such care, but an amazing 74 percent would be willing to pay higher taxes for it.

There is less enthusiasm for schools getting involved in child care for the very young, however. Only 29 percent of the women support public-school programs for three-to-five-year-olds and a meager 18 percent want such programs for children from birth through three.

What should public schools provide?

Before- and after-school programs   85%

Child care for kids three and up   29%

Child care for kids from birth onward   18%

What would you pay more taxes for?

Better public schools   **79%**

Before- and after-school programs   **74%**

Child care for four-year-olds   **41%**

Child care for three-year-olds and up   **36%**

Child care for infants and toddlers   **34%**

survey because I have begun to believe that as social creatures, babies and children are meant to be around many more familiar people than is the norm in our culture. Many societies have a much broader, extended family network in which children are with many older children and adults throughout the day. It strikes me as odd that we see mother and child cloistered at home as the ideal."

The Income Factor

Across the board, no matter what their income, mothers believe almost unanimously that their child benefits from child care. But their answers to other questions suggest that income (with the consequent ability or inability to afford high-quality care) plays an important part in

determining the learning experience the youngster receives.

■ Asked "Would you change your child's arrangement if another affordable option were available?", about 32 percent of mothers with household incomes under $20,000 replied "yes." Only 17 percent with household incomes of $100,000 and over would make a change.

■ Twenty-eight percent of those in the lowest income group believe their child would learn more if Mom stayed home; only 18 percent of those with household incomes of $100,000 and over think so.

These findings are consistent with other studies, in which respondents with family incomes above $60,000 express high levels of general satisfaction with their child care arrangement, while respondents with incomes below $20,000 are less satisfied.

The outstanding impression that has emerged from the survey results and the readers' letters is that working mothers with children in quality child care believe their youngsters are getting the best of two worlds. As an Aurora, Colorado, woman with a two-year-old and a six-year-old puts it: "My children are growing up seeing Mom and Dad as their base, but also having the ability to branch out in relationships and experiences they would not have readily received staying at home with me all day."

Editor's note: Readers who need assistance finding child care in their area can call the National Association of Child Care Resource and Referral Agencies at this number: 1-800-424-2246.

Rush to Judgment

*America is now at war against child abuse. But some recent cases suggest
we may be pushing too hard, too fast.*

It had been a horrible eight months, and Ray and Shirley Souza needed a break. Their kids, even their grandchildren, were saying shocking things about them, and a Florida vacation sounded wonderful. On March 1, 1991, the Souzas returned to their small, gray house in Lowell, Mass., feeling a little better, and found a shambles. All the family pictures had been pulled off the wall, broken glass littered the floor and an angry note apparently written by one of their daughters waited for them. "Who are you? What are you? Don't try to contact us or we'll take legal action against you." Today the Souzas stand convicted of sexually abusing two of their grandchildren; they are waiting to learn whether they will spend the rest of their lives in prison. The evidence? Most of it comes from the confusing testimony of two small girls.

Shirley Ann dreamt her parents raped her. She begged Heather, 'Keep your children away from them'

Americans are at fever pitch over child sex abuse these days: we haven't done very well at preventing it, but we're frantic to root it out and stomp it to death no matter where it lurks–or doesn't. Woody Allen is accused, day-care teachers are jailed, women go on TV to describe their latest memories of childhood victimization. Earlier this month Ellie Nesler, 40, pulled out a gun in a Jamestown, Calif., courtroom and shot the man accused of abusing her son and three other boys. When she was arraigned on murder charges, dozens of demonstrators showed up waving FREE ELLIE bumper stickers. Sometimes, amid all the noise, real sex abusers are identified and convicted. But too often, critics charge, the evidence is flimsy and the pursuit maniacal. A far better way to fight child sex abuse is to

learn how to talk–and listen–to children. Unfortunately, they are the experts.

Like most of the notorious sex-abuse cases of the last decade, Ray and Shirley's story is haunted with ambiguities. Their troubles began with a recurrent bad dream in the spring of 1990. Their daughter Shirley Ann, then 24, kept dreaming she was being raped by her parents. In June she called her sister-in-law Heather, hysterical. "Please, please," Heather says Shirley Ann begged, "keep your children away from them." She meant Ray and Shirley.

The Souzas, both 61, have lived in Lowell all their lives, Ray working as a lineman at Massachusetts Electric Co. while Shirley worked as a nurse. Ray coached Little League, Shirley volunteered at the American Cancer Society; and piles of old photographs show the couple and their five children at weddings and barbecues and summer vacations. But few families really live up to their idyllic photos, and the Souzas are no exception. Family members who spoke to NEWS-WEEK–including Ray, Shirley, their daughter Sharon, and Heather–all agree that as adults, various of the Souza siblings have been plagued at times with depression, sexual dysfunction, heavy drinking and drug use. "All those kids have problems," says Heather, who is now divorced from David Souza. "You have to ask yourself why."

Sharon, 31, thinks she knows why. Like Shirley Ann, she has read "The Courage to Heal," by Ellen Bass and Laura Davis, a controversial self-help book for women who suffered sex abuse as children. "If you don't remember your abuse, you are not alone," runs a famous passage in the book. "Many women don't have memories, and some never get memories. This doesn't mean they weren't abused." Sharon testified that Ray and Shirley abused her as well as their granddaughters. Heather, who also read "The Courage to Heal," became increasingly concerned about what might have happened to her daughter, Cindy (not her real name), 5, so she went on to read more about child abuse. "When you know what to look for, it's so easy to see," she says. She says she found that Cindy had 18 of the 19 indicators of sex abuse listed in one book. These checklists normally contain such behaviors as bed-wetting, nightmares, sexualized play and frequent masturbation, all of which may indicate conditions other than sex abuse. Cindy's most genuinely alarming behavior, according to trial testimony, appears to have been a habit of sexually abusing her dolls and her little brother. Heather questioned Cindy herself, and then took her to a therapist some of whose notes have been entered into the court record. "[Cindy's] information was repetitive and somewhat confused," ran a notation in November 1990; that day the therapist added, "It seems that there might be mother's pressure . . ." Two months later Heather switched therapists. "I wanted someone who was a specialist in child sexual abuse," she testified, and she was happy with her new choice. At their very first session the second therapist was able to diagnose Cindy's problem as posttraumatic stress disorder – a classic symptom of sex abuse.

Sharon, too, had been telephoned by Shirley Ann, but at first she didn't believe her children were in any danger. "I was praying, I didn't want it to be my children," says Sharon. But that summer she began noticing that her daughter Nancy (not her real name), then 4, was behaving strangely. Sharon testified that Nancy had nightmares about scary figures she identified as her grandparents, and said she hated Ray and Shirley and didn't want to visit them. About six months after Shirley Ann's warning, Sharon said, Nancy started talking about how her grandparents were hurting her. Soon she was seeing the same therapist as her cousin Cindy.

By the time the case was tried last January, Cindy and Nancy had undergone some two and a half years of questioning on sexual matters from their parents, their therapists and court personnel. At first timid and uncertain, their responses grew more detailed – and more vivid. In court, Cindy testified that her grandparents had stuck their fingers into her vagina and her "bum," put her into a cage in the basement, taped her mouth shut and tied her to a bed. She also testified that her father, David Souza, abused her in all the same ways her grandparents did. When Nancy's turn came, she said her grandparents put "their whole hand" into her vagina, stuck "their head" into her as well and wiggled it around, and made her touch their penis and vagina. Nancy also said her grandparents pressed a button to operate a machine as big as a room with hands that hurt her. Asked if there was a cage in the basement, she said no.

The prosecuting attorneys (and, for that matter, the Souzas' defense team) believe that David Souza did abuse Cindy, just as she alleged – which could itself account for her sexualized behavior. (Family members

say David has suffered a breakdown; there are no plans to file charges against him.) But the prosecutors insist that David was not the sole abuser. As proof, they cite the girls' responses when asked how it felt to put their hands in their grandmother's vagina. "Slimy," said Nancy. That description, says Assistant District Attorney Sheila Calkins, "was from being sexually abused by a woman, and she identified that woman as her grandmother."

Heather and Sharon deny that they or anybody else questioning the girls planted ideas in their heads. But Richard Gardner, a Columbia University psychiatrist specializing in child sexual abuse, who testified for the defense, was highly critical of the interviewing. He singled out an exchange in which Cindy told an examiner from the D.A.'s office, "I would like to ask you a question . . . It is going to be very tough to ask . . . Mommy told me that Papa [her name for her grandfather] tied me up . . .
EXAMINER: . . . Did Papa do that?
CINDY: Uh huh.
EXAMINER: And what part of your body did he tie up?
CINDY (*mumbles*): I forget.

"[The examiner] ignores the most important thing that happens in the interview," Gardner testified.

To Judge Elizabeth Dolan, who ruled in the case after the Souzas waived their right to a jury trial, the children did not sound coerced, they sounded credible. She found the trial testimony sufficient to prove the Souzas guilty beyond a reasonable doubt. But Heather says there is still no justice. "Even jail isn't punishment enough for what they took from my kid," she says.

Gardner and other critics trace today's frantic attention to sex abuse back to 1974, when Congress passed the Child Abuse Prevention and Treatment Act. The act and its amendments funded long-overdue programs to fight child abuse, but in order to qualify for funds, states had to institute "mandated reporting." When teachers, health-care professionals and others suspect that a child is endangered – because they see injuries, or for any other reason – they are legally required to report the child to local authorities. The numbers have been skyrocketing ever since. A study by the National Committee for Prevention of Child Abuse shows that nearly 3 million children were reported as suspected victims last year. As in the past, however, fewer than half those reports were found to merit further investigation. Poor children are at the greatest risk, but owing to scarce public funds, only about two thirds of the families in which abuse or neglect was confirmed received help. "This is a system that overreaches and gets jammed up," says Elizabeth Vorenberg, president of the National Coalition for Child Protection Reform, a group of lawyers, academics and others who believe that the current system ends up hurting children. "Children get placed in foster care when it may not be necessary, cases of real abuse go undetected and people are wrongly reported as possible abusers. The system fails everybody."

Nobody knows for sure whether child-abuse numbers are inflated with spurious allegations, or vastly underrepresent a crime that is often kept secret. One of the most shocking and widely cited figures comes from a 1985 survey showing that one in four women has suffered childhood sexual abuse. In this survey, however, "childhood" was any time through age 18, and "abuse" included everything from a single glimpse of a flasher to forced intercourse. Studies limited to girls under 14, defining abuse as sexual contact with a man at least five years older, have shown a fairly consistent rate of 10 to 12 percent since the 1940s.

Just as the numbers have ballooned, so have the size and scope of the allegations. Right now jury selection is underway in the trial of Dale Akiki, 35, a former Sunday-school teacher charged with sexually abusing 10 children at Faith Chapel, outside San Diego. His case unfolded like many before it: a 3-year-old girl, who had been seen crying in Sunday school, was questioned by her mother. Had anyone hurt her? Yes, she said, Akiki and another teacher had spanked her. After hours of questioning, the child said that Akiki had "showed me him's [sic] penis." Word spread around the congregation, and soon more children began saying they had been abused. Over months of therapy, the accusations piled up. The children said Akiki stripped and assaulted them, sodomized them with a curling iron, put them in the shower and alternated hot and cold water until they vomited, stuck their heads into the toilet, forced them to ingest feces and urine, and made them drink blood. Nobody attending church services noticed anything amiss in Akiki's classroom, which was nearby. He maintains his innocence.

Lurid accusations like the ones leveled against Akiki seem to show up everywhere. "I am a survivor of cult ritual abuse," wrote the author of a recent Ms. magazine cover story. "I was forced to watch as they killed my baby sister by decapitation in a ritual sacrifice." A preliminary estimate in 1991 suggested that one third of local prosecutors around the country had handled such cases, known as satanic ritual abuse (SRA). Some professionals take the charges seriously. "It's hard to believe, but so were the reports about Nazi atrocities," says Bennett Braun, director of the Dissociative Disorders Program at Chicago's Rush-Presbyterian-St. Luke's Medical Center. "Then we found the concentration camps." Skeptics are still waiting for the equivalent to a concentration camp to be found. No investigation has ever turned up so much as a bloodstain that could be traced with certainty to these bizarre activities. What's indisputable is the existence of a busy network of therapists specializing

in SRA. "These allegations are produced by the unrelenting pressure of the therapist," says Richard Ofshe, a professor of sociology at the University of California, Berkeley, who studies cults and thought control. "You will eventually come up with bizarre stuff because you run out of all the ordinary stuff."

Today there's a handful of professionals in the field of child abuse who make up what's come to be known as the backlash. The vast majority of child-abuse allegations are valid, say backlashers; but sometimes—during bitter custody disputes or when day-care centers are suddenly swamped with rumors—it's too easy for zealotry and hysteria to replace impartial investigation. At the grass-roots level, too, revisionist thinking is gaining ground. Some of the better-known defendants have garnered support groups, including Akiki and the "Edenton Seven," defendants in the Little Rascals preschool case in Edenton, N.C. In Massachusetts, more than 600 people signed a petition in support of the Souzas directed to Judge Dolan and Gov. William Weld.

More dramatic signs that professional and popular opinion on child abuse may be swinging back toward a middle ground came late last month in two highly sensational cases. Woody Allen, who had been accused by his ex-lover Mia Farrow of abusing their daughter Dylan, 7, announced that an investigation by a team of specialists at the Yale-New Haven Child Abuse Evaluation Clinic found that no abuse had occurred. The Yale report did criticize the "sexualized overtone" of Allen's behavior with the girl, but the team apparently was not convinced by Farrow's chief evidence: her own videotape of Dylan allegedly making the accusations.

To prompt testimony, the judge held the children on his lap, coaxed, praised them

Next came the startling reversal of the Kelly Michaels case, one of the most disturbing day-care cases in the country. Children at the Wee Care preschool in Maplewood, N.J., alleged that Michaels, their teacher, would round them up at nap time, lead them through the church that housed Wee Care and into a choir room, and make them strip. They said they were forced to engage in sexual acts, to ingest feces and urine and to lick peanut butter off her genitals; they also accused Micheals of putting kitchen utensils and Lego toys into their vaginas and rectums. No staff members said they saw, heard, smelled or suspected any of these activities. "We did not believe the jury would actually convict me," says Michaels, 31, who had received an excellent evaluation and a promotion at Wee Care. "There was no way rational, intelligent-thinking people were going to sit and not be able to see through what truly happened. I would turn around and look at my family [as if to say], 'I don't believe this is happening'." On Aug. 2, 1988, she was sentenced to 47 years in prison.

But late last month the New Jersey court of appeals ruled that Michaels did not receive a fair trial, in part because the judge's questioning of the children was less than impartial. He questioned them in his chambers; while the jury watched on closed-circuit TV, he "played ball with the children, held them on his lap and knee at times, whispered in their ear and had them do the same, and encouraged and complimented them," stated the ruling. The state is appealing the decision, but Michaels is free on bail.

'It's not that hard to get people to construct false memories,' says one expert

---

Both these turnarounds represent a new willingness to look at children's testimony as just that—the word of children. While it's rare for children to invent tales of sex abuse, some experts are convinced that in many instances children describe fantasies generated during months of intense questioning. Michaels's attorneys appealed her conviction in part on the ground that "the children were abused by the investigators." This is an excerpt from an interview with Davey (not his real name), a Wee Care child.
INTERVIEWER: Did she put the fork in your butt? Yes or no?
DAVEY: I don't know. I forgot . . . I hate you.
INTERVIEWER: Aw, come on, Davey, if you just answer that, you can go. . . . Tell me now . . . what did Kelly do to your hiney?
DAVEY: I'll try to remember.
INTERVIEWER: What did she put in your hiney?
DAVEY: The fork?
Psychologists who study the way children remember and recount events are building up a huge body of research on how easily children can be swayed. In a series of experiments by Alison Clarke-Stewart, a psychologist at the University of California, Irvine, and her colleagues, interviewers questioned children about what a man posing as Chester, the janitor, had done while he was in a room with them. The more strongly the interviewer slanted the questions, the more readily the children agreed with them—no matter what they had actually seen happen. This is exactly what can occur, says Stephen Ceci, professor of developmental psychology at Cornell University, when parents or evaluators suspect child abuse. "A parent gets alarmed and starts pursuing one hunch with a child," he says.

"Or a child-protection worker has a hunch. His job is to get the goods and make the case."

Ceci, who with his colleagues staged a suggestibility experiment with results similar to Clarke-Stewart's, later showed child-abuse experts his videotapes of children describing what they had seen. The experts were unable to distinguish between the truthful children and the mistaken ones. One reason the children were so convincing, he believes, is that their memories of the event may have actually changed in the course of questioning; by the end of the experiment they were telling the truth as best they could.

It's not that hard to get people to construct false memories," says Elizabeth Loftus, a psychologist at the University of Washington who specializes in memory. Loftus once implanted in a 14-year-old boy an entirely fictitious memory of being lost in a shopping mall at age 5. His older brother described the episode to the boy; two days later the boy began talking about how scared he had been that day, and soon he was "remembering" the old man in the flannel shirt who found him.

For interviewers, the worst problems arise when they strongly suspect abuse but good interview techniques aren't getting them anywhere. "A little boy tells his teacher he saw his stepdad 'messing with' his sister, says Lucy Berliner, director of research at the Sexual Assault Center of Seattle's Harborview Medical Center. "When the child-protection worker interviews him, the child says nothing. The family has a history of drug use and violence. The kid says, 'I'm afraid I'll get into trouble if I talk.' What do you do? And maybe the kid is afraid, not because of abuse but because he knows his parents' drug use will get them into trouble. So you try in every way you can think of to help the child talk— without conveying what you think happened."

Solid interviews and impartial investigations can keep a community from descending into mania when abuse allegations are made. In the spring of 1989, the parents of 4-year-old Addie (not her real name) reported that she had been sexually abused by her teacher at the Breezy Point Day School in Holland, Pa. Addie said a teacher had touched her vagina "with cream." By summer two more children had made similar charges. But after local police investigators interviewed 30 Breezy Point children separately, they reported that no child claimed to have seen or experienced abuse of any sort. The accusations had largely emerged through the parents' questioning of the children. District Attorney Alan Rubenstein also learned that about a month before Addie made her accusation, her mother and grandmother had applied ointment to her vagina for a rash. "Originally, I thought this was the crime of the century," says Rubenstein. "Ultimately, I thought this was the hoax of the century." All the same, he believes that if he had decided to pursue the case, he would have had a good chance of convicting the teacher.

The stakes are very high, as thousands of children and adults now know. Carol (not her real name) is 13, and her mother says the girl still has "anniversary reactions": night terrors and agitation around the time she says Kelly Michaels began abusing her. Therapy has helped, but she is "panic-stricken," says her mother, that someone at her school will find out about her past.

Kelly Michaels has memories, too. She remembers the police knocking on the door. "At first, I thought it was because I was playing my music very loud," she says. "When they told me they were investigating an allegation of child abuse, that's when I remember not being able to breathe." Today, fully enjoying her freedom after five years in jail, she remains angry about what happened. "They took five years of my life. My name is now associated with this case forever. I can't get that back."

As for Ray and Shirley Souza, whose faces are lined with worry, they are waiting for their sentencing date next month. Again and again, they say they are innocent. "We didn't do *anything*," says Shirley in a trembling voice. Soon she may be back in court, for she faces further charges of abusing another granddaughter.

LAURA SHAPIRO *with* DEBRA ROSENBERG *and* JOHN F. LAUERMAN *in Boston and* ROBIN SPARKMAN *in New York*

How to Safeguard Your Own Children

When lurid tales from sex-abuse trials hit the news, parents get the jitters. They needn't—but they're right to be watchful. Most often, sex abuse leaves no physical signs, but parents may notice changes in a child's outlook and behavior. The National Committee for Prevention of Child Abuse lists such indicators as a sudden interest in sexual acts, a display of sexual knowledge beyond the child's years and sexualized play with toys or other kids. The usual symptoms of stress—clinginess, loss of appetite, a reversion to bed-wetting or thumb-sucking—may indicate abuse, but parents should be careful to rule out all other explanations first. For more information, call the NCPCA (312-663-3520) or a local child-abuse hot line.

Often, a parent first becomes suspicious when a child makes a chance remark: a teacher touched her, a janitor scared him. It's vital for parents to keep their heads as they try to find out what happened. If her parents get frantic, a small child may clam up. Or, if her answers don't seem to satisfy the grown-ups, she may try to produce details—true or not. "We don't ask suggestive questions, we let the material come from the child," says Ethel Amacher, clinical director of the National Children's Advocacy Center in Huntsville, Ala. "Children are remarkably able to tell the truth."

Too often, parents jump to conclusions, and the hysteria can spread quickly to other families. "As a parent, wondering whether your child has been abused, how do you live with the uncertainty?" says a psychologist familiar with several of the more notorious preschool cases. "It might be easier to decide it happened, because then there's a whole bunch of positive things you can do. Maybe living with the ambiguity is just too hard."

By far the best way to deal with sex abuse is to prevent it from occurring. In-school prevention programs abound, but there is little agreement on the most effective methods. "The best programs emphasize communication, teaching children to tell somebody," says Karen McCurdy of the NCPCA. "According to interviews with men who have committed sex abuse, that would be a big deterrent." Interviews with offenders also indicate that they tend to prey on children they consider vulnerable—lonely, or easily manipulated. Perhaps the best way for parents to help their children avoid victimization is to instill in them more than just the facts about danger. Parents can encourage self-confidence early on, and make sure their kids feel comfortable talking to them about anything. No child can be made invulnerable—but many can be made strong.

L. S.

Why schools must tell girls:
'YOU'RE SMART, YOU CAN DO IT'

Myra and David Sadker

Bias in education *is an issue that has stirred debate since 1954's Brown vs. Board of Education, the Supreme Court decision integrating public schools. In a new book,* Failing at Fairness: How America's Schools Cheat Girls *(Charles Scribner's Sons, $22), the focus is on girls. Authors Myra and David Sadker document how teachers and schools unwittingly shortchange girls up and down the educational ladder, from kindergarten through graduate school. Here the Sadkers, professors of education at The American University in Washington, D.C., and among the nation's leading experts in sex discrimination, describe the problem—and what educators and students are doing to combat it.*

Rachel Churner, 15, remembers seventh grade at her McKinney, Texas, middle school as the year she was scared silent. "You couldn't be too dumb because then you would be laughed at," she says. "But if you were too smart, you would be called a brain."

Rachel decided it was best for girls to be completely average. She stopped answering questions in class and tried to hide her intelligence. "If I got an A and people asked me how I did, I would say, 'I just got a B minus.' There were even times I wrote down the wrong answer to make a lower grade."

Reading from the same textbook, listening to the same teacher, sitting in the same classroom, girls and boys are getting very different educations. For 20 years, we've been watching girls in the classroom and studying their interactions with teachers. After thousands of hours of classroom observation, we remain amazed at the scope and stubborn persistence of gender bias.

These studies show that from grade school to grad school boys capture the lion's share of teachers' time and attention. Whether the class is science or social studies, English or math—and whether the teacher is female or male—girls are more likely to be invisible students, spectators to the educational process.

One reason that boys receive more teacher attention: They demand it. Boys call out eight times more often than girls—and get real feedback. But when girls call out, they're more likely to be reprimanded or to get the brushoff with responses like "OK."

'If you were too smart, you'd be called a brain.' —Rachel Churner

Girls not only are less visible in classrooms; they're missing from textbooks, too. Brand-new history textbooks still devote only 2 percent of their space to women. A simple test demonstrates the impact of this male curriculum. We've walked into classrooms—elementary, secondary, even college—and asked students to name 20 famous American women from history. We've given only one restriction: no athletes or entertainers. Few have met the challenge. Many couldn't name 10, or even five. One class of Maryland fifth-graders, embarrassed at coming up with so few, put "Mrs." in front of presidents' names, creating an instant list of famous-sounding women they knew nothing about. Other students wrote down names like Mrs. Fields, Betty Crocker and Aunt Jemima in a desperate attempt to find famous females.

Education is not a spectator sport. Over time, the lack of attention by teachers and the omission of women in textbooks takes its toll in lowered achievement, damaged self-esteem and limited career options. The proof:

• In the early grades, girls are equal to or even ahead of boys on almost every standardized test. By the time they leave high school or college, they have fallen behind.

• By high school, girls score lower on the SAT and ACT exams, crucial for college admission. The gender gap is greatest in math and science.

• On the College Board achievement exams, required by the most selective colleges, boys outscore girls on 11 of 14 tests by an average 30 points.

Girls are the only group who begin school scoring ahead and leave behind, a theft occurring so quietly that most people are unaware of its impact

---

Today, in small towns and large cities across the nation, parents and teachers, concerned about the future of America's daughters, have begun to take action. From college professors in Urbana, Ill., to elementary school teachers in Portland, Maine, educators are asking for help, signing up for workshops that we conduct on fighting gender bias in the classroom. Women's colleges such as Smith and Mount Holyoke have started sponsoring special summer sessions to help elementary and secondary school teachers battle bias against girls, especially in math and science.

And high on the agenda for change is renewed interest in girls-only education, until recently an endangered species.

Although not everyone agrees, most studies show that girls in single-sex schools achieve more, have higher self-esteem and are more interested in subjects like math and science.

Says Rachel Churner, now at Hockaday, a private all-girls school in Dallas: "Now I put my education first. I don't think that would have happened if I had stayed in my coed school."

Even coed schools are experimenting with single-sex classes. This includes some public schools, in one of the most surprising developments of the 1990s. After nine years of teaching coed high school math, Chris Mikles now teaches an all-girls Algebra II class at public Ventura (Calif.) High School. "The girls come in with such low self-esteem," she says. "I keep trying to get through to them: 'You're smart. You can do it.'"

This year, the Illinois Math and Science Academy in Aurora, a public coed residential school for 620 gifted students, is trying for the first time an experiment that tests a girls-only class. In the first part of the year, the school separated 13 girls for an all-girls calculus-based physics class. For the second half of the school year, the girls have rejoined coed classes. School officials will compare their performance with and without the boys, as well as against the girls and boys in coed classes.

Girls in the experimental class are feeling the results. In the girls-only class, Denab Bates, 17, says she was "more enthusiastic, more there than in my other classes"—asking and answering more questions, jumping "out of my seat to put a problem on the board. In my other classes, I sink back—'Oh, please, don't call on me.'" Kara Yokley, 15, also says she participated more, but she is not sure what will happen this semester as the class goes coed. "We need to make sure we don't lose our newfound physics freedom," she says.

Not every girl is as positive. "We took the same exams as the coed class, but the guys thought that girls weren't learning on the same level," worries 16-year-old Masum Momaya.

Legally, single-sex education in public schools is a sticky business. Laws like Title IX prohibit sex discrimination in public schools, including teaching girls and boys separately in most cases. In Illinois, educators say it works because IMSA is a laboratory school set up by the state to try innovations. In Ventura, Mikles says all-girls classes are permissible because they are open to male students, although not a single boy has yet enrolled.

Many educators have reservations that go beyond legal problems. They view single-sex education as a defeatist approach, one that gives up on girls and boys learning equally, side by side. Other critics say that the model focuses on "fixing up the girls" but leaves boys in the dust.

Where the Boys Are

It was not long ago that the focus was on boys—specifically, black boys, who some educators believed would benefit from separate schools. That movement has since lost steam. "Without a body of research to prove their effectiveness," Myra Sadker explains, boys-only schools "ran into legal problems."

AN UPDATE:

• **In Detroit,** the Malcom X Academy, an elementary and middle school with 500 students, and two other public schools were established in 1990 as all-boys schools. They were forced to admit girls after a judge ruled the same year that single-sex schools violated Title IX. Today, Malcolm X is 92 percent male.

• **The Milwaukee** school board wanted to create three boys-only schools in 1990, after evaluating the poor performance of many black males in public schools. School officials halted the project after the Detroit decision; instead, schools changed their curricula.

• **New York City's** Ujamaa Institute, intended for black and Hispanic boys, has yet to open since the proposal was challenged in court by the New York Civil Rights Coalition.

—Myron B. Pitts

Diane Ravitch of the Brookings Institution in Washington, D.C., is outspoken in her view that girls already are treated fairly in the educational system. Ravitch, assistant secretary of Education under President Bush, points to the fact that more women than men are enrolled in college, more women than men earn master's degrees, and the number of women graduating with law and medical degrees has increased dramatically since 1970. "The success of women in education has soared in the last 20 years," Ravitch says.

Despite such progress, women still tend to major in lower-paying fields, such as education and literature. Today, a woman with a college degree earns little more than a man with a high school diploma.

The remedy? Realistically, most schools remain committed to coeducation for philosophic, legal and economic reasons. Increasingly, though, educators are becoming convinced that changes need to be made. And when teachers change, so do their students. Our research suggests these key ways to make girls more active and assertive:

- Teachers and parents must encourage girls to speak up—both at home and in school.
- Textbooks need to be monitored to make sure that enough women are included.
- Seating arrangements in class need to be flexible, because students in the front or middle of the class get more attention.
- Comments to girls should encourage their academic progress. "You look so pretty today" and "Your handwriting is so neat"—standard comments to girls—are less helpful than "What a great test score" or "That was an insightful comment."

Parents, girls and even traditional women's organizations are beginning to join educators in making such simple but important changes. And groups nationwide are providing support and service. The National Women's History Project in California, for example, develops books and posters on multicultural women's history. The Girl Scouts has featured images of active girls in printed materials and highlighted badges in math and science. The Women's Educational Equity Act Publishing Center in Massachusetts says requests for materials have surged recently, especially in science and math. The American Association of University Women has sponsored research projects and roundtables. The Gender Equity in Education Act, currently before Congress, proposes programs to help pregnant teenagers, combat sexual harassment and provide gender-equity training for teachers.

Throughout the history of education in America, the angle of the school door has determined the direction girls travel to various adult destinies. Sometimes the door was locked and barred; at other times it was slightly ajar. Today girls face subtle inequities that have a powerful cumulative impact, chipping away at their achievement and self-esteem. But as a new generation of teachers and parents enters the school system, and an existing generation becomes increasingly open to reform, schools and educators appear ready to adapt—and girls will be the winners.

Teaching Young Children to Resist Bias

What Parents Can Do

Louise Derman-Sparks, María Gutiérrez, and Carol B. Phillips

Building self-identity and skills for social interaction are two major tasks in early childhood. Gradually, young children begin to figure out how they are the same and different from other people, and how they feel about the differences. What children learn in the preschool years greatly influences whether they will grow up to value, accept, and comfortably interact with diverse people or whether they will succumb to the biases that result in, or help to justify, unfair treatment of an individual because of her or his identity.

Research tells us that between ages 2 and 5, children become aware of gender, race, ethnicity, and disabilities. They also become sensitive to both the positive attitudes and negative biases attached to these four key aspects of identity, by their family and by society in general. Young children develop "pre-prejudice": misconceptions, discomfort, fear, and rejection of differences that may develop into real prejudice if parents and teachers do not intervene.

"Girls aren't strong." "Boys can't play house."
"You're a baby in that wheelchair; you can't walk."
"You can't play with us, only light-skinned kids can."

Many adults find it hard to accept that 2-, 3-, and 4-year-olds actually make these comments. They would prefer to believe that young children are blissfully unaware of the differences between people upon which prejudice and discrimination are based. But young children not only recognize differences, they also absorb values about which differences are positive and which are not. How we as parents and teachers react to the ideas that young children express will greatly affect the feelings they will form. If we want children to like themselves and to value diversity, then we must learn how to help them resist the biases and prejudice that are still far too prevalent in our society.

HOW BIAS INFLUENCES CHILDREN'S DEVELOPMENT

Bias based on gender, race, handicap, or social class creates serious obstacles to all young children's healthy development. When areas of experience are gender stereotyped and closed to children simply because of their sex, neither boys nor girls are fully prepared to deal intellectually or emotionally with the realities and demands of everyday life. "Handicapism" severely harms children with disabilities by limiting access to the educational experiences necessary for well-rounded development. It also prevents non-disabled children from knowing and comfortably interacting with different types of people and teaches a false and anxiety-inducing sense of superiority based on their not being disabled.

Racism attacks the very sense of self for children of color. It creates serious obstacles to their obtaining the best education, health care, and employment. Racism also teaches White children a false identity of superiority and distorts their perceptions of reality. Thus they are not equipped to fairly and productively interact with more than half of the world's humanity.

The "isms" interfere as well with our ability as adults to effectively teach children about themselves and others. All of us have learned the negative values attached to gender, race, class, and handicapping conditions. And, to varying degrees, they make us uncomfortable as they affect our personal attitudes and behavior. At times, we hide such negative feelings from ourselves by denying the reality or significance of differences. We may hope to sidestep the impact of prejudice by saying, "people are all the same," or teaching children it is impolite to notice or ask about differences. However, avoidance doesn't give children the information they need. By selectively ignoring children's natural curiosity, we actually teach them that some differences are not acceptable. And by failing to attach positive value to certain specific differences, children are left to absorb the biases of society. The more that we face our own prejudiced and discriminatory attitudes toward diversity and, where necessary, change them, the better prepared we will be to foster children's growth.

WHAT PARENTS AND TEACHERS CAN DO

Recognize that because we live in a racist and biased society, we must actively foster children's anti-bias development. Remember that in such an environment, we are all constantly and repeatedly exposed to messages that subtly reinforce biases. If we do nothing to counteract them, then we silently support these biases by virtue of our inaction.

Create an environment at home or at school that deliberately contrasts the prevailing biased messages of the wider society.

Provide books, dolls, toys, wall decorations (paintings, drawings, photographs), TV programs, and records, that reflect diverse images that children may not likely see elsewhere in

- Gender roles (including men and women in nontraditional roles)
- Racial and cultural backgrounds (e.g., people of color in leadership positions)
- Capabilities (people with disabilities doing activities familiar to children)
- Family lifestyles (varieties of family composition and activities)

Show that you value diversity in the friends you choose and in the people and firms you choose for various services (e.g., doctor, dentist, car mechanic, teachers, stores). Remember that what you do is as important as what you say.

Make it a firm rule that a person's identity is never an acceptable reason for teasing or rejecting them. Immediately step in if you hear or see your child engage in such behavior. Make it clear that you disapprove, but do not make your child feel rejected. Support the child who has been hurt. Try to find out what underlies the biased behavior. If the reason is a conflict about another issue, help your child understand the real reason for the conflict and find a way to resolve it. If the underlying reason is discomfort with or fear or ignorance about the other child's differences, plan to initiate activities to help overcome negative feelings.

Helping children to deal with bias

Lisa, Pete, and Elana are playing hospital when Lisa's dad hears an argument break out over who will be the doctor and who will be the patient. Lisa finally says, "I don't want to be your friend anymore, you stupid Mexican!" Lisa's dad intervenes, "Lisa, what you just said is mean and it hurts Elana." Putting his arm around Elana's shoulders, he says, "I am sorry Lisa said that to you." Turning to all three children, he asks, "What is the problem?" Each child explains her side. Dad says, "Sounds like the real problem is that you both want to be the doctor. That has nothing to do with Elana being Mexican. Elana, who you are is just fine, just like who you, Lisa, and you, Peter, are is also just fine. But you all have a problem with taking turns. How can you work that out?"

Another step would need to happen if the scenario were somewhat different. For instance: Elana and her family have just moved into the neighborhood, and Lisa's parents invite them over for a visit. When they arrive, Lisa refuses to play with Elana in her room. After the family leaves, Lisa says, "I don't like them. Mexicans are stupid!" "I wonder why you think that?" her mom asks. "That's what my friend Cindy says." To which Lisa's mom replies, "Lisa, Cindy is wrong! To say that Mexicans are stupid is unfair and hurtful. Mexican people are just as smart as everyone else. Tomorrow, let's go to the library and get some books about Mexican-Americans so that we can learn more about them.

We want you to get to know Elana and her family because they are our neighbors."

One evening, after watching his favorite TV show, Mark (age 4) says, "I wish I wasn't Black." "Why?" asks his mother. "Cause I want to be a paramedic."

"You think you have to be White to be a paramedic, because that's what you saw on TV, isn't it?" Seeing Mark nod yes, his mother says "Even though you saw only White paramedics on TV, there are many Black paramedics, Black firefighters, and Black police officers. You can be anything you want when you grow up. You know, there should be more Black people on many TV shows. Some people who write the stories and own TV stations are not being fair. They are allowing racism to exist. Let's write a letter to the TV station and say that they should show paramedics, firefighters, and all kinds of people of all colors on TV." (From: Derman-Sparks et al., 1980)

"Heather wouldn't let me play house with her at school today," complains 5-year-old Miriam. "She says I act like a boy because I like boy things." "I'm sorry that happened. How did you feel?" "It hurt my feelings and made me mad." "I would feel that way too. You know, Heather is wrong. You don't act like a boy. You act like a girl who likes to play with blocks and trucks and to play ball."

Initiate activities and discussions to build positive self-identity and to teach the value of differences among people. Educate yourself about common stereotypes in our society so that you can evaluate your selection of children's materials and experiences. Whenever possible, either remove those containing biased messages, or learn to use such material to teach children about the difference between "fair" and "true" images and those that are "unfair" and "untrue" and which hurt people's feelings.

Talk positively about each child's physical characteristics and cultural heritage. Tell stories about people from your ethnic group of whom you are especially proud. Include people who have stood up against bias and injustice. Encourage children to explore different kinds of materials and activities that go beyond traditional gender behaviors.

Help children learn the differences between feelings of superiority and feelings of self-esteem and pride in their heritage.

Provide opportunities for children to interact with other children who are racially/culturally different from themselves and with people who have various disabilities. If your neighborhood does not provide these opportunities, search for them in school, after-school activities, weekend programs, places of worship, and day camps.

Visit museums, concerts, and cultural events that reflect diverse heritages as well as your own.

Respectfully listen to and answer children's questions about themselves and others. Do not ignore questions, change the subject, sidestep, or admonish the child for asking a question. These responses suggest that what a child is asking is bad. However, do not *over-respond.* Answer all questions in a direct, matter-of-fact, and brief manner. Listen carefully to what children want to know *and* what they are feeling.

Teach children how to challenge biases about who they are. By the time children are 4 years old, they become aware of biases directed against aspects of their identity. This is especially true for children of color, children with disabilities, and children who don't fit stereotypic gender norms. Be sensitive to children's feelings about themselves and immediately respond when they indicate any signs of being affected by biases. Give your children tools to confront those who act biased against them.

Teach children to recognize stereotypes and caricatures of different groups. Young children can become adept at spotting "unfair" images of themselves and others if they are helped to think critically about what they see in books, TV, movies, greeting cards, and comics.

Use accurate and fair images in contrast to stereotypic

Common questions that parents and teachers ask

Q: "My child never asks questions about race, disability, or gender. If I raise it myself, will I introduce her to ideas she wouldn't have thought of on her own?"
A: Yes, you may, thereby expanding your child's awareness and knowledge. Your child may also have had questions for which she didn't have words or didn't feel comfortable raising until you brought up the subject. Remember that children do not learn prejudice from open, honest discussion of differences and the unfairness of bias. Rather, it is through these methods that children develop anti-bias sensitivity and behavior.

Q: "I don't feel competent to deal with these issues; I don't know enough. What if I say the wrong thing?"
A: Silence "speaks" louder than we realize, sending messages that are counter to the development of anti-bias attitudes. It is far better to respond, even if, upon hindsight, you wish you had handled the incident differently. You can always go back to your child and say "Yesterday, when you asked me about why Susie uses a wheelchair, I didn't give you enough of an answer. I've thought about your question some more, and today I want to tell you . . ." If you really do not have the information to answer a question, you can say, "That's a good question, but I don't know the answer

right now. Let me think about it a little and I will tell you later." Or, "Let's go find some books to help us answer your question." Then be sure to follow through.

Examine your own feelings about the subject raised by your child's questions or behaviors. Feelings of incompetence often come from discomfort rather than a lack of knowledge. Talk over your feelings with a sympathetic family member or friend in order to be better prepared the next time.

Q: "I don't want my children to know about prejudice and discrimination until they have to. Won't it upset them to know about injustices?"
A: It is natural to want to protect our children from painful subjects and situations. Moreover, adults may mask their own pain by choosing not to address issues of bias with their children. Avoiding issues that may be painful doesn't help children. Being unprepared to deal effectively with life's realities only leaves them more vulnerable and exposed to hurt. Silence about children's misconceptions and discriminatory behavior gives them permission to inflict pain on others. It is alright for children to sometimes feel sad or upset as long as they know that you are there to comfort and support them.

Common questions children ask and ways to respond

"Why is that girl in a wheelchair?"
Inappropriate
"Shh, it's not nice to ask." (admonishing)
"I'll tell you another time." (sidestepping)
Acting as if you didn't hear the question. (avoiding)
Appropriate
"She is using a wheelchair because her legs are not strong enough to walk. The wheelchair helps her move around.

"Why is Jamal's skin so dark?"
Inappropriate
"His skin color doesn't matter. We are all the same underneath."
This response denies the child's question, changing the subject to one of similarity when the child is asking about a difference.
Appropriate
"Jamal's skin is dark brown because his mom and dad have dark brown skin."
This is enough for 2- or 3-year-olds. As children get older, you can add an explanation of melanin:
"Everyone has a special chemical in our skin called melanin. If you have a lot of melanin, your skin is dark. If you only have a little, your skin is light. How much melanin you have in your skin depends on how much your parents have in theirs."

"Why am I called Black? I'm brown!"
Inappropriate
"You are *too* Black!"
This response is not enough. It doesn't address the child's confusion between actual skin color and the name of the racial and/or ethnic group.
Appropriate
"You're right; your skin color *is* brown. We use the name 'Black' to mean the group of people of whom our family is a part. Black people can have different skin colors. We are all one people because our great-great-grandparents once came from a place called Africa. That's why many people call themselves 'Afro-Americans.' "

"Will the brown wash off in the tub?"
This is a fairly common question because children are influenced by the racist equation of dirtiness and dark skin in our society.

Inappropriate
Taking this as an example of "kids say the darndest things" and treating it as not serious.
Appropriate
"The color of Jose's skin will never wash off. When he takes a bath, the dirt on his skin washes off, just like when you take a bath. Whether they have light or dark skin, everybody gets dirty, and everyone's skin stays the same color after it is washed. Everybody's skin is clean after they wash it, no matter what color their skin is."

"Why does Miyoko speak funny?
Inappropriate
"Miyoko can't help how she speaks. Let's not say anything about it."
This response implies agreement with the child's comment that Miyoko's speech is unacceptable, while also telling the child to "not notice," and be polite.
Appropriate
"Miyoko doesn't speak funny, she speaks *differently* than you do. She speaks Japanese because that's what her mom and dad speak. You speak English like your mom and dad. It is okay to ask questions about what Miyoko is saying, but it is *not* okay to say that her speech sounds funny because that can hurt her feelings."

"Why do I have to try out that dumb wheelchair? . . ."
. . . asks Julio who refuses to sit in a child-sized wheelchair in the children's museum.
Inappropriate
"It is not dumb. All the children are trying it and I want you to."
This response does not help uncover the feelings underlying Julio's resistance and demands that he do something that is clearly uncomfortable for him.
Appropriate
Putting his arm around Julio, his dad gently asks, "Why is it dumb?" Julio: "It will hurt my feet, just like Maria's feet." Dad: "Maria's feet can't walk because she was born with a condition called cerebral palsy. The wheelchair helps her move around. Nothing will happen to your legs if you try sitting and moving around in the wheelchair. It's OK if you don't want to, but if you do try it you'll find out that your legs will still be fine."

ones, and encourage children to talk about the differences. For example, at Thanksgiving time, greeting cards which show animals dressed up as "Indians" and a stereotypic image of an "Indian" child with buckskins and feather headdress abound. Talk about how it is hurtful to people's feelings to show them looking like animals, or to show them portrayed inaccurately. Read good children's books to show the reality and the variety of Native American peoples. As children get older, you can also help them learn about how stereotypes are used to justify injustice, such as lower wages, poor housing and education, etc.

Let children know that unjust things can be changed. Encourage children to challenge bias and give them skills appropriate to their age level. First set an example by your own actions. Intervene when children engage in discriminatory behavior, support your children when they challenge bias directed against themselves and others, encourage children to identify and think critically about stereotypic images, and challenge adult biased remarks and jokes—all methods of modeling anti-bias behavior.

Involve children in taking action on issues relevant to their lives.

- Talk to a toy store manager or owner about adding more toys that reflect diversity, such as dolls, books, and puzzles.
- Ask your local stationery store to sell greeting cards that show children of color.
- Take your child to a rally about getting more funding for child care centers.

As you involve children in this type of activity, be sure to discuss the issues with them, and talk about the reasons for taking action.

SUMMARY

Keep in mind that developing a healthy identity and understanding of others is a long-term process. While the early years lay an essential foundation, learning continues throughout childhood and into adulthood and will take many different forms. Children will change their thinking and feelings many times.

FOR FURTHER INFORMATION

Contact the Council On Interracial Books For Children, 1841 Broadway, New York, NY 10023. 212-757-5339.

BIBLIOGRAPHY

The Children's Foundation. (1990). *Helping children love themselves and others: A professional handbook for family day care.* Washington, DC: Author.

Council On Interracial Books For Children. *Selecting bias-free textbooks and storybooks.* New York: Author.

Derman-Sparks, L., & the A.B.C. Task Force. (1989). *Anti-bias curriculum: Tools for empowering young children.* Washington, DC: National Association for the Education of Young Children. (To order NAEYC #242, send $7 [includes postage and handling] to NAEYC, 1834 Connecticut Avenue, N.W., Washington, DC 20009.)

Derman-Sparks, L., Hilga, C. T., & Sparks, B. (1980). Children, race and racism: How race develops. *Interracial Books for Children Bulletin, 11* (3 & 4), 315.

Children *can* learn to become anti-biased!

We can all take heart from examples such as the following examples of 4- and 5-year-olds challenging racism: Kiyoshi, (age 4 1/2) sees a stereotypic "Indian warrior" figure in the toy store. "That toy hurts Indians' feeling," he points to his grandmother.

* * *

Casey (age 5), and another White friend, Tommy, are playing. Casey calls two other boys to join them. "You can't play with them, they're Black," Tommy says to him. Casey replies. "That's not right. Black and White kinds should play together. My Dad tells me civil rights stories."

* * *

After hearing the story of Rosa Parks and the Montgomery bus boycott, Tiffany (age 5 1/2), whose skin is light brown, ponders whether she would have had to sit in the back of the bus. Finally, she firmly asserts, "I'm Black, and anyway all this is stupid. I would just get off the bus and tell them to keep their old bus."

* * *

Kiyoshi, Casey, and Tiffany are learning to think critically and to speak up when they believe something is unfair. They are becoming "empowered": gaining the confidence and skills that will enable them to resist and challenge bias and to participate in the creation of a more just society.

Adolescent Childbearing

Whose Problem?
What Can We Do?

Diane Scott-Jones

DIANE SCOTT-JONES is an associate professor in the Department of Psychology, Temple University, Philadelphia.

ATTENTION to the phenomenon of adolescent childbearing typically focuses on its most sensational and titillating aspects. The image of an impoverished 13- or 14-year-old African American or Latino female with more than one baby becomes imprinted in the public mind as the symbol of the problem. Yet the issues surrounding adolescent childbearing are more complex than this stereotypical image suggests. Even the statistics are often presented in a dramatic and misleading fashion.

A careful examination of the data on adolescent childbearing yields the following statistical composite of the typical adolescent mother in the U.S.: she is white and in her late teen years. Childbearing among her peers is not an "epidemic." Indeed, the rate is lower than in the 1950s. However, she is more likely to bear children than are her counterparts in any other industrialized democracy in the world.

Our understanding of adolescent childbearing and our efforts to ameliorate its attendant problems are diminished by unexamined, emotionally charged beliefs regarding race/ethnicity, poverty, gender, and even the transitional nature of adolescence in the course of life. As is often true of issues about which we care deeply, the problem of adolescent childbearing is surrounded by myths that are perpetuated in the mass media and in everyday discussions of concerned and caring individuals. In order

> **Young people in our society become biologically mature at very early ages, putting biological forces at odds with social ones.**

to understand complex problems, we sometimes oversimplify our explanations and proposed solutions. We come to see such problems as limited only to certain groups, and we ignore the broader social contexts — thus allowing normal aspects of human behavior to be defined as problematic. Pregnancy and parenthood are, after all, highly valued in American society. Unlike other problems of adolescence, such as drug abuse or delinquency, pregnancy and parenthood are problematic only because of their early timing in the lifecourse.

As we explore adolescent childbearing and consider what we can do to prevent it, we must keep in mind the enormous changes adolescents experience. The dramatic physical changes of adolescence occur very rapidly; this rate of growth is unsurpassed at any point in life, with the exception of the prenatal period and infancy. To this great change within individuals, we must add the changes in social expectations for adolescents, changes in the structure and

content of formal education for middle and high school students, and the effect of difficult conditions in our society. Then one can imagine how tough the transition into adulthood can be for many adolescents. As a society, we must ask how we can establish more supportive contexts for adolescents' transition to adulthood. It is in that spirit that I ask "whose problem" adolescent childbearing is and what we can do about it.

WHOSE PROBLEM?

As is the case with any social phenomenon, we need to begin our analysis with an accurate and thorough description. Adolescent childbearing is embedded in pervasive societal problems and cannot be understood completely as a problem *within* individual adolescents. Adolescent childbearing affects many segments of society and is not limited to ethnic minority groups. Moreover, the behavior of males is an important factor. Finally, the problems are different for younger and older adolescents.

For the most part, *adolescence* is defined as ages 13 through 19, although some studies have used slightly different age ranges. For example, adolescent fertility is often reported as live births to females 15 to 19 years of age. The reason for this range is that relatively few births occur to females younger than 15. Age differences within the adolescent years are very important for any research or intervention program.

NOT JUST INDIVIDUAL ADOLESCENTS

Sometimes we mistakenly assume that adolescents' problems are *within* the adolescents themselves. Yet adolescents must make the transition from childhood to adulthood in a society that places many obstacles in their paths. For some adolescents, the prospects for adult life look bleak. For many families and communities the recession of the early 1990s might well be called a depression. And in these tough economic times, some individuals have created lucrative businesses from the manufacture and distribution of drugs in the communities that are least able to fight them. Our social climate is infected with racism, sexism, and class bias that we have not overcome despite valiant efforts.

Current social conditions make it generally difficult to become a responsible adult, and developing sexual responsibility is particularly difficult for those making the transition to adulthood. We are plagued with the mysterious and uncontrolled sexually transmitted disease AIDS. In spite of the life-threatening nature of AIDS, the mass media continue to bombard adolescents with sexual stimuli and sexual themes in all genres, from rock videos to product advertisements.[1] At the same time, sexual harassment too frequently invades the workplace. As a result, adolescents have few positive role models for adult sexual behavior and lack clear standards for accepting themselves as sexually mature and sexually responsible individuals.

In addition, two important changes have occurred in the *timing* of adolescence in the life span. First, girls today reach biological maturity at very early ages. The average age of menarche is 12.5 years, and for some girls the first menstrual period occurs as early as age 9. We can contrast this early age with the average for European populations in the 19th century: the average age for the first menstrual period in the mid-19th century was 16.5 to 17 years.[2]

Why does menarche occur so early today? Menarche is triggered by a girl's proportion of body fat. High-calorie diets and a relatively sedentary lifestyle have combined to lower the average age of menarche. The current average age of menarche may be the earliest possible for the human species. Boys are, on average, two years behind girls in attaining reproductive maturity.

But as young people in our society become biologically mature at very early ages, we have not responded by accepting them as adults at earlier ages. Instead, we have done just the opposite. We have delayed the time that adolescents can begin to function as adults.

We now expect girls and boys to complete many more years of education than was true in the past. Advanced education is now needed for adequate employment outside the home. Marriage is often delayed, and many women delay childbearing until they are close to the end of their reproductive years.[3] Thus, at the same time that young girls become biologically ready to have children at very early ages, we as a society expect them to wait until they are much older before they behave as adults. Biological forces and social forces are at odds.

The current trend toward later marriage and childbearing in our society, especially among affluent women, causes us to consider adolescent childbearing quite inappropriate. Yet, in the not too distant past, early childbearing was the norm in our society, just as adolescent childbearing remains the norm throughout most of the world. Biologically, optimal time for childbearing begins in the late adolescent years. In fact, in *Walden Two* B. F. Skinner advocated childbearing in late adolescence. In the United States in the 1950s, many young women in their late teens became pregnant, and the adolescent birthrate was higher than in recent years. For every 1,000 females between 15 and 19 years of age, there were 90 births in 1955, 68 births in 1970, and 51 births in 1986.[4] These facts are surprising to those who think that adolescent childbearing is a recent phenomenon and that it has become an epidemic.

Adolescent childbearing was not widely acknowledged as a problem in the 1950s because pregnant adolescents tended to get married, to remain in stable families, and to live relatively prosperous lives. Even men with little formal education could find good jobs in factories, steel mills, and so on. But those manufacturing jobs are no longer widely available, and young people with the same level of education today are faced with low-paying service jobs, such as those in the fast-food industry. Thus today's economy makes it very difficult for young people to form families as they did in the 1950s. Marriage is made still more unlikely by the current economic recession. Many young fathers are not able to find employment that would allow them to support a family. The situation today is vastly different from that of the 1950s.

The fact that adolescent childbearers tend to be unmarried must be placed in the context of the increase in nonmarital childbearing for older women in our society. A re-

> For every 1,000 females between the ages of 15 and 19, there were 90 births in 1955, 68 births in 1970, and 51 births in 1986. These facts are surprising to those who think that adolescent childbearing is a recent phenomenon and that it has become an epidemic.

cent Census Bureau report of data from June 1992 indicates that approximately 24% of single adult women had given birth.[5] The greatest increases in the rate of childbearing among single adult women occurred among women who were college-educated, employed, and white. Nonmarital childbearing actually declined slightly for African American women at the same time as it rose sharply, almost doubling, for white women. Although higher percentages of nonmarital childbearing still occur among African American women and women who have not completed high school, these figures indicate that nonmarital childbearing among adult women does not fit stereotypes and cuts across ethnic and socioeconomic lines.

It is in the current social and economic environment that we must try to understand the challenges facing adolescents and the opportunities we can provide them as they move into their adult lives. The current focus on adolescent childbearing as a social problem of enormous magnitude results at least partly from changed societal conditions. Thus we can conclude that adolescent childbearing is a socially constructed problem and not simply the result of individual pathology. In addition to interventions with individuals, social change is necessary to eliminate the problems associated with adolescent childbearing.

NOT JUST AFRICAN AMERICANS AND LATINOS

There is a bias among researchers and the mass media that shifts the focus of adolescent sexual behavior, pregnancy, and childbearing almost exclusively to African Ameri-

Adolescent birth rates declined from the 1970s to the 1980s, and the decrease was sharper for African Americans than for whites.

Photo by Kathy Sloane

cans and Latinos and ignores the same problems in white adolescents. Rates of sexual activity, pregnancy, and childbearing are higher for African American adolescents than for white adolescents. Yet many problems exist for white adolescents as well. In addition, statistical comparisons of racial and ethnic groups can be misleading, because a disproportionate number of members of ethnic minority groups are poor. Differences attributed to race or ethnicity often stem at least partly from socioeconomic differences. With that caveat, I will briefly review the data on sexual activity, pregnancy, and childbearing. (The comparisons are reported most frequently for African Americans and whites, and data are not as readily available for other American racial and ethnic groups.)

The largest increase in adolescent sexual activity over the past two decades has occurred for white adolescents. Consequently, the difference between African Americans and whites in rates of sexual activity has declined dramatically in the past two decades, almost to a point of convergence. In 1970, 27% of white adolescent females

and 46% of black adolescent females had become sexually active. In 1988, the figures were 51% for white and 59% for black adolescent females.[6] Furthermore, older (18- to 19-year-old) black adolescent females' rate of sexual activity actually declined, from 83% in 1985 to 77% in 1988. The rate of sexual activity for white 18- to 19-year-old females, in contrast, increased from 61% in 1985 to 73% in 1988.

Adolescent females of all racial and ethnic groups are becoming sexually active at earlier ages. In 1988, 25.6% of 15-year-old female adolescents reported having had sexual intercourse, compared to 4.6% in 1970.[7] Once they become sexually active, white adolescent females have sex more frequently and with more partners than do black adolescent females.[8]

The pregnancy rate for 15- to 19-year-old adolescents has been approximately 11% since 1982, which is an increase over the rate of 9.9% in 1974.[9] The overall increase in the pregnancy rate is the result of increases for white adolescents. The pregnancy rates for African American and white adolescents are not close to convergence,

however. In 1985 the adolescent pregnancy rate of 18.6% for African Americans was twice that of the 9.3% rate for white adolescents.[10]

However, white adolescents who become pregnant are more likely than pregnant African American adolescents to be married, and both groups are less likely to be married than were pregnant adolescents in the past. In the 1950s one-third of first births to adolescents were conceived out of wedlock; in the 1980s two-thirds of first births to white adolescents were conceived out of wedlock, and 97% of first births to African American adolescents were conceived out of wedlock. White adolescents who become pregnant are somewhat more likely to have abortions than are their African American counterparts. In 1985, 41% of 17- to 19-year-old pregnant African American adolescents had abortions, compared to 46% of white adolescents in this age group.[11]

Adolescent birthrates declined from the 1970s to the 1980s, and the decrease was sharper for African Americans than for whites. The birthrate for African American adolescents between the ages of 15 and 19 was 12.3% in 1973 and 9.5% in 1983. Corresponding rates for white adolescents were 4.9% in 1973 and 4.4% in 1983.[12] From 1986 to 1988, birthrates for both African American and white adolescents increased but remained below the 1973 rates. The birthrate for African American adolescents remains double that of white adolescents. Although adolescent birthrates are higher for African Americans, two-thirds of adolescent childbearers are white.[13]

The U.S. has the highest adolescent birthrate of all industrialized, democratic nations. Even if only white adolescents are considered, the U.S. rate remains higher than that in all other similar countries.[14] Included in this cross-national comparison were 37 countries selected on the basis of two criteria: a relatively low fertility rate for women overall and a relatively high per-capita income. Canada, England (including Wales), France, the Netherlands, and Sweden were chosen for more extensive analyses because of their similarity to the U.S. in cultural heritage and economic growth.

In addition to the higher birthrate, the adolescent pregnancy rate is higher in the U.S. than in any other Western country.[15] In addition, the adolescent abortion rate in the United States in 1983 was the highest of any country for which data were available.[16]

These comparisons with other developed countries strongly suggest that the common stereotypes regarding adolescent sexuality in this country cannot explain our higher adolescent childbearing rate. The U.S. rate is not higher because of African Americans, for the rate remains higher when only white adolescents in the U.S. are considered. In addition, other countries in the cross-national comparisons also include nonwhite minority groups. Moreover, U.S. adolescents do not have a higher rate of sexual activity than adolescents in the comparison countries. Nor does U.S. welfare assistance explain higher rates of pregnancies and births; the comparison countries have more generous welfare provisions.

One important difference, however, is that the comparison countries have a more equitable distribution of income and more extensive benefits in such areas as health and unemployment. A second pronounced difference is that sex education, contraceptives, and abortion services are more widely available in the comparison countries.[17] I should point out that the availability of abortion typically coincided with the availability of contraception in the comparison countries, so that the need for abortion

among adolescents in those countries was minimized. Another important difference is that the comparison countries have a more open and accepting attitude toward sexual activity among young people. The rate of sexual activity among adolescents is not greater in the comparison countries than in the U.S., but apparently adolescents in the comparison countries are more responsible when they become sexually active.

In addition to the notion that adolescent childbearing is almost exclusively a problem of ethnic minorities, another common stereotype is that children born to African American adolescent mothers will themselves become adolescent parents. It is assumed that a cycle of early parenting is repeated generation after generation. How-

---

> **Apparently adolescents in the comparison countries are more responsible when they become sexually active.**

---

ever, the majority of daughters of adolescent mothers delay their first birth beyond the adolescent years. In a 20-year follow-up of urban African American adolescent mothers, Frank Furstenberg, Judith Levine, and Jeanne Brooks-Gunn found that nearly two-thirds of the daughters had delayed their first birth until they were 19 years of age or older. The three researchers found the same result when they examined data for African Americans in the National Longitudinal Survey of Youth; two-thirds of the daughters of adolescent mothers delayed their first birth until age 19 or older.[18] This research clearly demonstrates that the cycle of adolescent childbearing is not repeated generation after generation in African American families.

NOT JUST FEMALES

The role of males in adolescent childbearing has received too little attention. Adolescent males who become fathers typically are not included in intervention programs for adolescent parents. However, the majority of fathers of babies born to adolescent females are not adolescents; they are men older than 20. This creates a serious problem in understanding early unplanned pregnancies as an *adolescent* issue. The interactions of an adolescent female and a young adult male may involve a compelling power

differential that is not acknowledged in research or in prevention and intervention programs. Thus the sexual encounters of adolescent females may involve some elements of coercion, whether psychological or physical.

Curbing the physical and psychological intimidation of females in schools is also important. The Educational Foundation of the American Association of University Women sponsored a national survey of eighth-through 11th-graders in 1993. The survey found that sexual harassment is widespread in our middle schools and high schools. Although males were also victims of sexual harassment, far more females than males had experienced and were disturbed by sexual harassment. Some females reported being afraid in school because of the sexual harassment they experienced.[19]

Males' attitudes toward females and sexuality are especially important, given that adolescents, when they do use contraception, rely heavily on a male contraceptive method—the condom.[20] Adolescent males, however, tend not to use contraceptives regularly. Estimates of contraceptive nonuse range from approximately one-half to two-thirds of adolescent males in research samples, including a study of black male inner-city junior and senior high school students and the 1988 National Survey of Adolescent Males.[21]

Although adolescent males do not use contraceptives regularly, most indicate that they are willing to share the responsibility for contraceptive use.[22] Joseph Pleck and his colleagues used a perceived costs-benefits model to test the importance of different motivations for condom use and found that adolescent males' belief in male responsibility for pregnancy prevention was related to condom use. However, the personal benefit that would result from preventing pregnancy was not a factor in their decision to use condoms. Other important factors were the perception that their female partners expected them to use condoms, and the perception of personal risk of acquiring AIDS. Perceptions of reduced sexual pleasure and of embarrassment were negatively related to condom use.[23]

Ethnic differences may exist in adolescent males' use of contraceptives, but current research is not consistent on this point. African American adolescents in the 1979 and 1988 national surveys conducted by Pleck and his colleagues reported the highest consistency of condom use, compared to white and Hispanic adolescents. However, in a small sample of 13- to 14-year-olds, of those who used contraception of any kind, African Americans tended to use withdrawal, which is not effective as a contraceptive, and whites tended to use condoms.[24] Age and the lower rates of sexual activity among younger adolescents may account for the inconsistencies between these studies.

Media warnings delivered by a highly regarded celebrity may have some limited impact on risky sexual behaviors, but adolescents may be influenced even less than young adults. The November 1991 announcement that basketball star Earvin "Magic" Johnson was infected with the human immunodeficiency virus (HIV) appears to have affected some but not all risky sexual behaviors of young patients in a suburban Maryland clinic.[25] The study was ongoing at the time of Johnson's announcement; comparisons were made of those interviewed prior to and after the announcement. The participants were 60% male and 73% African American; 85% had at least a high school diploma. Their average age was 25. No difference was found in reported condom use before and after Johnson's announcement. However, the number of sexual partners reported by participants was significantly lower for those interviewed after the announcement than for those interviewed prior to the announcement. Unfortunately, this reduction took effect for patients aged 25 and older but not for the younger patients (16 to 24 years of age).

YOUNGER AND OLDER ADOLESCENTS

The majority of births to adolescents are to older adolescents. Only 1% to 2% of all births to adolescents are to those younger than 15.[26] Childbearing and related issues are very different for older adolescents than for younger ones. With adolescent mothers who are at least 15 years of age, the medical risks of pregnancy could be normalized with adequate nutrition and adequate prenatal care.[27] Older adolescent childbearers face issues related to the transition to adulthood: completing school, finding employment, and forming stable adult relationships.

Although childbearing occurs less frequently in young adolescents, the potential negative outcomes are great. Adolescents younger than 15 face serious biomedical risks when they become pregnant. In addition, the younger the adolescent female is when she becomes sexually active, the more likely she is to experience little intimacy and some degree of coercion in her relationships. The transition from late childhood to early adolescence is often difficult, and early sexual relations, pregnancy, and childbearing greatly exacerbate the normal developmental challenges.

Although childbearing occurs less frequently in young adolescents, the potential negative outcomes are great.

WHAT CAN WE DO?

What can we do to help adolescents make good choices about sexual activity, pregnancy, and childbearing? Adolescents need guidance at many decision points. They need comprehensive sex education programs to prevent early sexual activity and unplanned pregnancies.

We also need to reframe the question of adolescents' motivation. Too frequently, researchers and practitioners assume that adolescent sexual activity is a problem behavior whose origins are the same as those for drug use and delinquency. The association of adolescent sexual activity with pathology needs to be replaced by an acknowledgment that becoming sexually active is a normal aspect of human development as adolescents make the transition into adulthood. In our present society, however, early sexual activity and early pregnancy greatly diminish the possibility of positive developmental outcomes for adolescents. We need to learn more about how to motivate adolescents to delay sexual activity and to avoid unplanned pregnancy.

In addition to sex education programs, adolescents need programs that indirectly help to reduce the risk of unplanned pregnancy by focusing on educational expectations, educational achievement, and career preparation. Although controversial, abortion and adoption are possible resolutions of unplanned pregnancy, and they need careful consideration, along with acknowledgment of and respect for differing values on these issues. When adolescents have children, they need to continue in school, and child-care programs are important ways of helping them do so. Prevention and intervention programs should target males as well as females. Finally, separate strategies are needed for younger and for older adolescents.

Claire Brindis offers some excellent practical information on preventing unplanned pregnancy among adolescents — drawing on and evaluating the efforts of a number of communities.[28] Although some general guidelines apply broadly, local communities will need to develop prevention plans that are suited to the particular issues and problems they face.

COMPREHENSIVE SEX EDUCATION

The sex education that adolescents receive may be too little, too late. In a study of African American adolescent females, Sherry Turner and I found that the majority had had sex education programs in school.[29] The majority also said that they had discussed sexual topics with their parents. But our analyses indicated that one-half to two-thirds of the adolescents became sexually active *before* they had had a sex education program. And many young adolescents in our study who were not sexually active had not yet had a sex education program. In addition, one-half of the adolescents found the information typically provided them to be inadequate. So, although most adolescents receive some form of sex education, the *quality* and *timing* of their programs and discussions of sexuality are crucial.

However, objections to sex education programs in the schools continue. Only 17 states and the District of Columbia include sex education as a mandated part of the school curriculum.[30] Moreover, many sex education programs promote abstinence without also providing information about contraception. U.S. policy regarding sex education stands in sharp contrast to that of other Western democracies, where sex education is far more extensive. Indeed, the only federal program for adolescent pregnancy prevention, the Adolescent Family Life Act, will not support programs that focus on contraception unless they are targeted toward the prevention of second pregnancies among adolescents who have experienced first pregnancies. The thinking represented in this federal legislation is that it is acceptable to talk about contraception with teens who have already had one baby but not acceptable to talk about contraception with teens who have yet to become pregnant!

Despite current sex education policies, some adolescents do use contraceptives. This is evidenced by the fact that adolescent pregnancies have not increased at the same rate as adolescent sexual activity has increased.[31]

In some communities, sex education is seen as the cause of adolescent pregnancy.

Many people believe that giving teens accurate information about sex and contraception will increase the numbers who are sexually active and become pregnant. There is no research to support this idea. In one small town in a rural area of California where only 25 girls were in the graduating class, more than half were pregnant or had

> ## Adolescents who have high expectations for their own attainment are less likely to become sexually active.

already had a baby at the time of graduation. The response of the community and school was to ban sex education programs in the school.

In many instances, sex education is a small part of a health course and is not given sufficient attention. But comprehensive sex education programs that give adolescents accurate information about reproduction and contraception are needed, and they are needed before adolescents become sexually active.

Technical information about sexuality should be augmented with discussions of the close personal relationships in which the responsible expression of sexuality occurs. The current trend in our society is toward delayed marriage. And we don't have clear age norms for the appropriate time for the initiation of sexual activity. Moreover, some early sexual encounters may occur in the context of sexual harassment. Thus attention to the *relationship* in which sexual expression occurs is critical in sex education programs.

Most adolescents who attend sex education programs do so in schools. In our research, Turner and I found that very few adolescents had sex education programs in community centers or churches. The resources of these organizations could be used in a comprehensive sex education program and might be very important to adolescents' understanding of community values related to sexuality, pregnancy, and the relationships in which pregnancy occurs.

EDUCATION AND CAREER PROGRAMS

Comprehensive sex education programs are necessary but not sufficient to prevent unplanned pregnancies. In addition to programs that focus directly on sexuality and pregnancy prevention, we need programs that focus on educational expectations and educational achievement. These programs reduce the risk of unplanned pregnancy indirectly by giving adolescents a positive focus for their lives. Anne White and I found that adolescents who have high expectations for their own educational attainment are less likely than others to become sexually active and more likely to use contraceptives when they do become sexually active. Adolescents who see formal education as a viable route to adult success have a *reason* to delay sexual activity and childbearing.[32] As the Children's Defense Fund puts it, "The best contraceptive is a real future." Programs for adolescents need to emphasize the good things they can do with their lives and not just the negative possibilities that we want to prevent. If pregnancy pre-

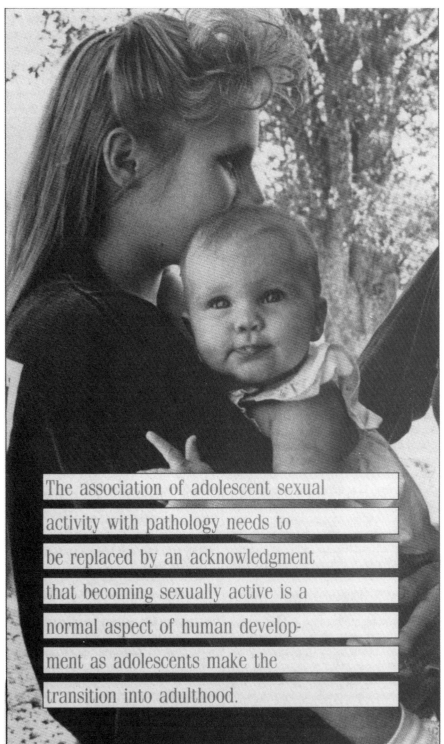

The association of adolescent sexual activity with pathology needs to be replaced by an acknowledgment that becoming sexually active is a normal aspect of human development as adolescents make the transition into adulthood.

Photo by Kathy Sloane

vention programs focusing on abstinence can be characterized by the slogan "Just say no," then the programs I am advocating here could be characterized by the slogan "Just say yes." Adolescents need to be shown positive options that they can embrace.

Many adolescent childbearers were not performing well in school prior to their pregnancy.[33] The developmental trajectory that leads to poor outcomes for adolescent childbearers appears to be set in motion before the pregnancy and includes low achievement, low engagement in school, and even dropping out of school. Thus having a child usually does not deflect an adolescent from a positive developmental trajectory; many adolescents who bear children were already moving in a negative direction.

Therefore, we must consider the meaning and value of schools for adolescents. Schools today may not be educating and socializing adolescents appropriately for the transition to adulthood. At a time in their lives when they need more guidance from caring adults, adolescents may get less attention from them. For many adolescents, school becomes less and less meaningful. Few high school students, especially those who are not college-bound, believe that they will use the material they are expected to learn in school. Some are already working part-time jobs similar to the kinds of jobs that await them upon graduation. From their own experience, they may know that what they are expected to learn in school is not related to the employment available to them.

An apprenticeship system for adolescents, similar to that in Germany, has been proposed for the U.S.[34] In programs of this type, adolescents would be socialized to perform well not only on academic tasks but also in a real job setting.

Some current efforts to make high schools more meaningful for adolescents include a Public Service Academy, located in a high school in a very poor area of Washington, D.C. This program orients students toward careers in government — the largest employer in their community — and provides them appropriate internships and part-time government jobs. Public schools, private companies and foundations, and universities collaborated to create the Pubic Service Academy. A second example is Houston's High School for Health Professions, which has been operated as a partnership of the public school district and a Houston medical school since 1972. The majority of students in these high school programs will go

on to college. However, similar programs could provide an avenue toward employment for those who do not attend college.

Overall, the educational attainment of adolescent childbearers has increased from the 1950s, and the educational attainment of African American adolescent childbearers has increased more than that of whites. Dawn Upchurch and James McCarthy investigated educational attainment among three cohorts of women who were 21 to 29 years of age in 1958, in 1975, and in 1986. Although women who delayed childbearing were more likely to have graduated from high school than adolescent childbearers, adolescent mothers in 1986 were more likely to have graduated than their 1975 or 1958 counterparts. For black adolescents who were 17 years of age or younger when their first child was born, only 16.6% had graduated in 1958, compared to 60.6% in 1986. The corresponding rates for their

---

Child rearing places enormous demands on adolescents, who must also complete their schooling and enter the workplace.

---

white counterparts were 19.6% in 1958 and 53.7% in 1986.[35]

African American adolescent mothers appear to fare better educationally than both their white and their Hispanic counterparts. The National Longitudinal Survey of Youth revealed that, among adolescent mothers whose children were in elementary school, African American mothers had achieved higher educational levels than whites or Hispanics.[36] In addition, in a study of the birth records of one midwestern state, African American childbearers deviated less from expected educational attainment than did Hispanic or white childbearers.[37]

ABORTION: A CONTROVERSIAL OPTION

Perhaps no issue involved in adolescent childbearing is more controversial than abortion. Adolescents' minor status means that their right to obtain abortions is more restricted than that of adult females.

More than 30 states have laws that require the involvement of a parent or a third party in a minor's decision regarding abortion. The "third party" requirement exists so that

adolescents have the option of attempting to convince a third party — typically a judge — that they are competent to make the decision independently or that the abortion is in the adolescent's best interest. This "third party" mechanism is a way of bypassing the parental consent requirement for adolescent abortion. Data from actual court hearings indicate that adolescent minors' requests to bypass parental consent are almost always granted. Judges may find the determination of maturity or best interest difficult and may therefore grant all requests. Anita Pliner and Suzanne Yates question whether the consent legislation meets the goals of encouraging communication between parents and adolescents and protecting the rights of minor adolescents.[38] They found that health professionals working with adolescents before and after passage of the legislation indicated that psychological and medical counseling were needed more than pro forma legal procedures. Time spent on the legal proceedings might have been better spent on psychological and medical counseling.

Pliner and Yates recommend that states follow the example of Maryland, where a physician or mental health provider, instead of a judge, makes the determination of maturity and best interest. A second option they suggest is to include mandatory counseling in the legislation, as is done in Maine and Connecticut. Finally, Pliner and Yates recommend that the parental notification and consent laws be limited to adolescents 15 years of age and younger.

Although legal constraints may prevent some adolescents from seeking an abortion, many adolescents do not choose abortion in any case. We might wonder why more adolescents do not seek abortion. Laurie Zabin and Sarah Hayward found that attitudes toward abortion were not different between adolescents who chose abortion and those who carried their babies to term. The difference was that those who chose abortion were very unhappy — unequivocally so — about the pregnancy. Although other adolescents did not indicate that they had wanted or planned to become pregnant, many were ambivalent rather than completely negative about having a child. Zabin and Hayward concluded that, unless there is an "overriding reason to avoid childbearing" — a bright future that will be damaged by early childbearing — the adolescent will have the child rather than choose abortion.[39]

Despite strong feelings on all sides of the abortion controversy, little research exists to help determine the effect on an adoles-

93

Affordable, high-quality care for children younger than school age is not widely available. A number of high schools across the country have responded by providing child-care programs in the school building.

Photo by Kathy Sloane

cent of having an abortion compared to completing a pregnancy. More research and monitoring of outcomes of legislation should lead to appropriate policy in this area. More research is also needed on adolescents' capabilities to make various decisions about health care.[40] It may not be possible to reach consensus on the issue of abortion, but those who work to create pregnancy prevention programs must find ways to acknowledge differing values and beliefs in this area.

ADOPTION: AN INFREQUENTLY USED OPTION

When adolescents have babies, they very rarely place them for adoption.[41] The overwhelming majority — approximately 97% — of all adolescent childbearers keep their babies. Because of private adoptions and confidential records, however, statistics on adoption may not be entirely accurate. White adolescents are more likely to give their babies up for adoption than are ethnic minority adolescents. But over the past two decades the adoption rate for white adolescent parents has declined sharply, from 19% to 3%, whereas the adoption rate for African American adolescents has re-

mained relatively constant at 1%. It has been suggested that, for African American adolescent parents, an informal type of adoption may occur, with members of the extended family helping to care for the baby.

Research on factors that contribute to adolescents' decision not to place their babies for adoption suggests that adolescents feel emotionally attached to their babies and are thus unable to give them to someone outside their families. In addition, the mothers, peers, and partners of pregnant adolescents may not encourage adoption. Finally, the current organization of adoption procedures may mean that a pregnant adolescent is not given accurate information about adoption as an alternative, may feel pressured into adoption, or may be frightened by the requirement of a complete severing of ties with the baby. Together, these factors may lead adolescent parents to equate adoption with abandonment of the child.

Research on adoption outcomes is sparse. The small number of studies on mothers' responses following adoption often use clinical samples and inadequate research design. However, these studies suggest that mothers experience a long-term sense of loss following adoption and have no accept-

able outlets for expressing their emotions. Michael Sobol and Kerry Daly recommend increasing the involvement of birth parents in the adoption plan as a means of alleviating adolescent parents' belief that placing a baby for adoption is irresponsible.[42] Programs encouraging pregnant adolescents to choose adoption are funded by the federal Adolescent Family Life Act.

CHILD-CARE PROGRAMS

Although child rearing places enormous demands on adolescents, who must also complete their schooling and find a place in the work world, some adolescents are able to manage these developmental tasks. Continued education becomes a key factor in the resilience of adolescent parents. Sherry Turner and I studied three groups of African American women aged 20-24, 25-34, and 35-44 who were part of the National Survey of Family Growth. We found that women who had their first birth during adolescence generally completed fewer years of school and earned lower incomes than women who delayed childbearing.[43] Some of those who had been adolescent mothers, however, had stayed in school longer, and, when we controlled for educational attainment, we found that adolescent childbearing was not a significant predictor of adult income. The number of years of education completed was a stronger predictor of women's income than was the experience of adolescent childbearing.

Social and material support from the family, the community, and the school are essential if the adolescent mother is to remain in school. Adequate child care is especially important for adolescent parents who are enrolled in school. Affordable, high-quality care for children younger than school age is not widely available. But the provision of child care may allow adolescent mothers to resume their schooling more quickly and more easily than would otherwise be possible.

A number of high schools across the country have responded to this situation by providing child-care programs in the school building. We are in the process of studying child-care programs for the children of adolescent mothers as part of our research at the National Center on Families, Communities, Schools, and Children's Learning.

One of our study sites is Orr Community Academy, a public high school in Chicago that maintains an impressive child-care facility. Before the child-care facility was opened, the high school had already established a rich array of programs linking the school to the community and to families. The child-care center was planned in the context of an active umbrella program that connected the high school with surrounding elementary schools and with the community. In June 1989 this urban high school, 13 elementary feeder schools in the area, and a local bank initiated the Orr School Network. This network connects the schools to one another and to the city's educational, cultural, and social service resources. Network principals meet each month to plan and implement programs revolving around three major initiatives: intervening in early childhood, enriching the school years and removing academic deficits, and increasing family and community support for children. One component of the early childhood initiative is the child-care center in the high school.

The high school also contains a comprehensive health clinic for students and a prekindergarten program. The health clinic provides a broad range of health services, including contraception, to adolescents whose parents give written consent. The prekindergarten program operates four days a week in two half-day shifts; 20 children are enrolled in each shift. The high school is also a site for the Women, Infants,

Sexual restraint and pregnancy prevention should be presented as necessary prerequisites for a bright future.

and Children program, a federally funded supplemental program that provides food packages and nutritional counseling to eligible mothers. Another special program that operates out of the high school building is Enrichment for Latinas Leading to Advancement, a comprehensive career program for Latina students that emphasizes nontraditional areas of work for females, such as real estate, banking, medicine, and engineering.

The Orr Infant and Family Development Center, which is operated by Jane Addams Hull House, a Chicago social service agency, is licensed to serve 24 adolescent parents and their children from 6 weeks to 3 years of age. The center has an exemplary physical layout for the care and education of young children. It has its own separate entrance and an outdoor playground separated by a wall from the rest of the school grounds. A bus provides transportation exclusively for the adolescent parents and their children.

To use the center, the adolescent parent must be enrolled in school, must work in the child-care facility for one hour a day, and must take a parenting class. Adolescent parents and *their* parents must sign a contract agreeing that the adolescent will attend and pass all classes. Adolescent parents also complete a plan detailing goals that they wish to accomplish with their children. The Orr Infant and Family Development Center provides much-needed assistance to adolescent parents, but it also encourages responsibility and achievement on the part of the young parents.

PROGRAMS FOR YOUNG FATHERS

Most programs focus on adolescent females. Because the majority of fathers of babies born to adolescent mothers are young adult males, programs that seek to reach young fathers may be more effective if they are based in the community rather than in the school. One example of such a community-based program is the Responsible Fathers Program, run by the Philadelphia Children's Network. This program, which in 1992 served 57 young unwed fathers between the ages of 16 and 25, focuses on

parenting skills and encourages the men to be actively involved in their children's lives. The young men are also linked to educational resources, employment opportunities, and social services. The program promotes communication and cooperation between fathers and mothers as they raise their children. Claire Brindis provides some examples of other programs for males.[44]

SEPARATE STRATEGIES FOR DIFFERENT AGE GROUPS

The developmental needs of early adolescence, which involves the transition from late childhood, are very different from the developmental needs of late adolescence, which involves the transition to adulthood. Thus programs for older adolescents need to address such matters as completing formal schooling, entering the labor force, and maintaining responsible relationships.

Young adolescents, on the other hand, need sex education programs that begin before they become sexually active. Open discussions with parents, teachers, and counselors are also important. In these discussions, the adults should listen to adolescents, in addition to conveying adult beliefs and values. Young adolescents need accurate information about sexuality and contraception, and they need the opportunity to discuss with adults the close personal relationships in which responsible sexual expression occurs. Sexual restraint and pregnancy prevention should not be presented in negative terms but as necessary prerequisites for a bright future that would be tarnished by an unplanned pregnancy.

When young adolescents do become pregnant, they are more likely than older adolescents to face medical risks that need attention. In addition, the number of years of school remaining for young adolescent parents affects program strategies. For example, in school-based child-care programs for adolescent parents, the children served are usually under age 3. This age range is appropriate for the needs of older adolescents and would allow them to have child care until they completed high school. Children born to younger adolescents, however, would be older than 3 before the adolescent parent completed high school and would need care through a different program.

 N SPITE of the difficulties adolescents face as they grow into adulthood, we must remain optimistic. Adolescents encounter many problems as they become adults in the imperfect world we have created. Gary Melton has written about the importance of recognizing adolescents as *persons*.[45] We must respect them as such in the programs we plan for them. They are not children, even though we do not yet recognize them as adults. Adolescents' views need to be incorporated into the design and evaluation of pregnancy prevention programs. Through the dreams and aspirations of our adolescents and through the opportunities we provide them to grow into productive adults, we might truly change our society.

1. Issues of the newsletter of the National Coalition on Television Violence, June-August 1991.

2. Phyllis B. Eveleth, "Timing of Menarche: Secular Trends and Population Differences," in Jane B. Lancaster and Beatrix A. Hamburg, eds., *School-Age Pregnancy and Parenthood* (New York: Aldine, 1986), pp. 39-52.

3. Linda H. Holt, "Medical Perspectives on Pregnancy and Birth: Biological Risks and Technological Advances," in Gerald Y. Michaels and Wendy A. Goldberg, eds., *The Transition to Parenthood: Current Theory and Research* (New York: Cambridge University Press, 1988), pp. 157-75.

4. Wendy H. Baldwin, *Adolescent Pregnancy and Childbearing — Rates, Trends, and Research Findings from the Center for Population Research* (Washington, D.C.: National Institute of Child Health and Human Development, 1984); and Tom Luster and Mary Mittelstaedt, "Adolescent Mothers," in Tom Luster and Lynn Okagaki, eds., *Parenting: An Ecological Perspective* (Hillsdale, N.J.: Erlbaum, 1993), pp. 69-100.

5. *Fertility of American Women: June 1992* (Washington, D.C.: U.S. Bureau of the Census, Current Population Reports, Series P-20, No. 470, 1993).

6. "Sexual Risk Behaviors of STD Clinic Patients Before and After Earvin 'Magic' Johnson's HIV-Infection Announcement — Maryland, 1991-1992," *Morbidity and Mortality Weekly Report*, Centers for Disease Control, 29 January 1993, pp. 45-48.

7. Ibid.

8. Laurie S. Zabin and Sarah C. Hayward, *Adolescent Sexual Behavior and Childbearing* (Newbury Park, Calif.: Sage, 1993).

9. Stanley Henshaw et al., *Teenage Pregnancy in the United States: The Scope of the Problem and State Responses* (New York: Alan Guttmacher Institute, 1989); and Select Committee on Children, Youth, and Families, U.S. House of Representatives, *Teen Pregnancy: What Is Being Done?* (Washington, D.C.: U.S. Government Printing Office, 1986).

10. Henshaw et al., op. cit.

11. Ibid.

12. Luster and Mittelstaedt, p. 69.

13. Claire D. Brindis et al., *Adolescent Pregnancy Prevention: A Guidebook for Communities* (Palo Alto, Calif.: Stanford Center for Research in Disease Prevention, 1991).

14. Elise Jones et al., *Teenage Pregnancy in Industrialized Countries* (New Haven, Conn.: Yale University Press, 1986).

15. Charles F. Westoff, "Unintended Pregnancy in America and Abroad," *Family Planning Perspectives*, vol. 20, 1988, pp. 254-61.

16. Henshaw et al., op. cit.

17. Jones et al., op. cit.

18. Frank Furstenberg, Judith Levine, and Jeanne Brooks-Gunn, "The Daughters of Teenage Mothers: Patterns of Early Childbearing in Two Generations," *Family Planning Perspectives*, vol. 22, 1990, pp. 54-61.

19. *Hostile Hallways: Survey on Sexual Harassment in American Schools* (Washington, D.C.: American Association of University Women, 1993).

20. Leo Hendricks, *Unmarried Adolescent Fathers: Problems They Face and the Ways They Cope with Them* (Washington, D.C.: Institute for Urban Affairs and Research, 1979); Diane Scott-Jones and Anne B. White, "Correlates of Sexual Activity in Early Adolescence," *Journal of Early Adolescence*, vol. 10, 1990, pp. 221-38; and Freya Sonenstein, "Risking Paternity: Sex and Contraception Among Adolescent Males," in Arthur B. Elster and Michael E. Lamb, eds., *Adolescent Fatherhood* (Hillsdale, N.J.: Erlbaum, 1986), pp. 31-54.

21. Loretta S. Jemmott and John B. Jemmott, "Sexual Knowledge, Attitudes, and Risky Sexual Behavior Among Inner-City Black Male Adolescents," *Journal of Adolescent Research*, vol. 5, 1990, pp. 346-69; and Joseph H. Pleck, Freya L. Sonenstein, and Leighton C. Ku, "Adolescent Males' Condom Use: Relationships Between Perceived Cost-Benefits and Consistency," *Journal of Marriage and the Family*, vol. 53, 1991, pp. 733-45.

22. Hendricks, op. cit.

23. Joseph H. Pleck, Freya L. Sonenstein, and Scott O. Swain, "Adolescent Males' Sexual Behavior and Contraceptive Use: Implications for Male Responsibility," *Journal of Adolescent Research*, vol. 3, 1988, pp. 275-84; and Pleck, Sonenstein, and Ku, op. cit.

24. Scott-Jones and White, op. cit.

25. "Sexual Risk Behaviors."

26. Zabin and Hayward, op. cit.

27. Joy D. Osofsky, Howard J. Osofsky, and Martha O. Diamond, "The Transition to Parenthood: Special Tasks and Risk Factors for Adolescent Parents," in Gerald Y. Michaels and Wendy A. Goldberg, eds., *The Transition to Parenthood: Current Theory and Research* (New York: Cambridge University Press, 1988), pp. 209-34.

28. Brindis, op. cit.

29. Diane Scott-Jones and Sherry L. Turner, "Sex Education, Contraceptive and Reproductive Knowledge, and Contraceptive Use Among Black Adolescent Females," *Journal of Adolescent Research*, vol. 3, 1988, p. 171-87.

30. Brindis, op. cit.

31. Janet Gans et al., *America's Adolescents: How Healthy Are They?* (Chicago: American Medical Association, 1990); and Luster and Mittelstaedt, op. cit.

32. Scott-Jones and White, op. cit.

33. Dawn M. Upchurch and James McCarthy, "The Timing of a First Birth and High School Completion," *American Sociological Review*, vol. 25, 1990, pp. 224-34.

34. Stephen F. Hamilton, *Apprenticeship for Adulthood: Preparing Youth for the Future* (New York: Free Press, 1990).

35. Upchurch and McCarthy, op. cit.

36. Tom Luster and Eric Dubow, "Predictors for the Quality of the Home Environment That Adolescent Mothers Provide for Their School-Aged Children," *Journal of Youth and Adolescence*, vol. 19, 1990, pp. 475-94.

37. Diane Scott-Jones, "Adolescent Childbearing: Risks and Resilience," *American Journal of Education*, vol. 24, 1991, pp. 53-64.

38. Anita J. Pliner and Suzanne Yates, "Psychological and Legal Issues in Minors' Rights to Abortion," *Journal of Social Issues*, vol. 48, 1992, pp. 203-16.

39. Zabin and Hayward, p. 80.

40. *Adolescent Health — Vol. I: Summary and Policy Options* (Washington, D.C.: U.S. Congress Office of Technology Assessment, OTA-H-468, April 1991).

41. Michael P. Sobol and Kerry J. Daly, "The Adoption Alternative for Pregnant Adolescents: Decision Making, Consequences, and Policy Implications," *Journal of Social Issues*, vol. 48, 1992, pp. 143-61.

42. Ibid.

43. Diane Scott-Jones and Sherry L. Turner, "The Impact of Adolescent Childbearing on Educational Attainment and Income of Black Females," *Youth and Society*, vol. 22, 1990, pp. 35-53.

44. Brindis, op. cit.

45. Gary B. Melton, "Are Adolescents People? Problems of Liberty, Entitlement, and Responsibility," in Judith Worell and Fred Danner, eds., *The Adolescent as Decision-Maker: Applications to Development and Education* (San Diego: Academic Press, 1989), pp. 281-306.

Selected Resources

REPORTS

☑ *Adolescent Health — Vol. I: Summary and Policy Options*. Washington, D.C.: U.S. Congress Office of Technology Assessment, OTA-H-468, April 1991.

☑ Hayes, Cheryl D., ed. *Risking the Future: Adolescent Sexuality, Pregnancy, and Childbearing, Vol. I*. Washington, D.C.: National Academy Press, 1987.

☑ Hofferth, Sandra L., and Cheryl D. Hayes, eds. *Risking the Future: Adolescent Sexuality, Pregnancy, and Childbearing, Vol. II: Working Papers and Statistical Appendices*. Washington, D.C.: National Academy Press, 1987.

☑ Ooms, Theodora, and Lisa Henrendeen. *Teenage Pregnancy Prevention Programs: What Have We Learned?* Washington, D.C.: Family Impact Seminar, 1990.

☑ *Teenage Drug Use: Uncertain Linkages with Either Pregnancy or School Drop-Out*. Gaithersburg, Md.: U.S. General Accounting Office, GAO/PEMD-91-3, January 1991.

INFORMATION RESOURCES

☑ Brindis, Claire D., et al. *Adolescent Pregnancy Prevention: A Guidebook for Communities*. Palo Alto, Calif.: Stanford Center for Research in Disease Prevention, 1991.

☑ Creighton-Zollar, Ann. *Adolescent Pregnancy and Parenthood: An Annotated Guide*. New York: Garland, 1990.

☑ Data Archives on Adolescent Pregnancy and Pregnancy Prevention, Sociometrics, Los Altos, Calif.

☑ *Family Planning Perspectives* (journal published by the Alan Guttmacher Institute).

☑ "Special Issue: Adolescence in the 1990s: Risk and Opportunity." *Teachers College Record*, Spring 1993.

ORGANIZATIONS AND CLEARINGHOUSES

Alan Guttmacher Institute
2010 Massachusetts Ave. N.W.
Washington, DC 20036

Center for Population Options
1025 Vermont Ave. N.W.
Washington, DC 20005

Children's Defense Fund
122 C St. N.W.
Washington, DC 20001

Girls Clubs of America
205 Lexington Ave.
New York, NY 10016

National Urban League
500 E. 62nd St.
New York, NY 10021

Share Resource Center on Teen Pregnancy Prevention
P.O. Box 2309
Rockville, MD 20852

CRITICAL LIFE EVENTS AND THE ONSET OF ILLNESS

Blair Justice, PhD

Professor of Psychology University of Texas School of Public Health, Houston, Texas

■ In 1925, when Hans Selye was a medical student at the ancient German University of Prague and observing his first clinical cases, he asked a question that was considered so naive or pointless that his professor dismissed it as unworthy of reply. The question was: What is the "general syndrome of just being sick?"[1] What young Selye—who over the next 50 years became the world's leading authority on stress and disease—wanted to know was, why do all sick people have certain signs and symptoms in common: fatigue, loss of appetite, aches, pains, and other shared features.

After migrating to Canada and joining the biochemistry department at McGill University in Montreal, Selye began the research that eventually answered, at least in part, his original question. People get sick from "diverse noxious agents,"[2] and the resultant stress on the body produces certain nonspecific effects that sick people share in common. Selye learned that these "noxious" influences may come not only from harmful physical agents (such as viruses, bacteria, excessive cholesterol), but from an individual's appraisal of "noxious" or painful stimuli—how one looks at events in life and the meaning one attaches to them.[3]

After many years of studying the physiological effects on the body of stressors of all kinds—from chemical to emotional—Selye formulated a philosophy of life that he considered essential to health and happiness. Since unfavorable events—failures, rejections, losses—occur in everyone's life avoiding such stressors is impossible. What is important physiologically. Selye noted, is not the event but the person's reaction to it. "It's not what happens that counts; it is how you take it,"[4] he was fond of saying.

Although Selye's own work did not establish this finding, other research, both during his time and since, supports his ideas. These studies carefully document that the level and duration of potentially damaging neurochemicals in the body—such as epinephrine, norephrinephrine and cortisol—are a function of how we appraise life events and circumstances.[5,6] If we interpret a "noxious" experience as meaning it is the end of the world, the heart and immune system, as well as the gastrointestinal system, are placed at increased risk of impairment or compromise.[7,8] If, instead, we view an event as being bad, but not something so bad that we "can't stand it," then the body reacts less intensely. Neurochemicals are elevated just enough to prod us into effective action rather than helpless floundering.

How we react to an event—whether it is an illness, a divorce, a nuclear power plant accident, a pregnancy or childbirth—is strongly influenced by our perceived sense of acceptance and affirmation by others, by our interpersonal relationships and by social circumstances. The emerging science of psychoneuroimmunology (PNI) recognizes the association of such psychosocial factors with changes in biological functioning.

Almost a century and a half ago, Rudolph Virchow recognized that our very resistance to disease is affected by social conditions.[9] This perceptive German pathologist and physician char-

*Reprint requests to Blair Justice, PhD, University of Texas School of Public Health, 1200 Herman Pressler, Houston, TX 77030.

From *Comprehensive Therapy,* Vol. 20, No. 4, 1994, pp. 232-238. Reprinted with permission of *Comprehensive Therapy,* published by the American Society of Contemporary Medicine and Surgery.

97

acterized medicine as a "social science." He knew that physiological processes are affected profoundly by social factors. Investigating a typhus outbreak in Upper Silesia, Virchow reported that people would not have gotten the disease had they lived in a democratic system and enjoyed more favorable social conditions.[10]

A long-term epidemiological view of mortality and life span across populations suggests that people become more vulnerable to disease when they feel little control over their lives and when they lack nurturing communities and supportive families. Leonard Sagan, in *The Health of Nations*,[11] reports a reduction of mortality and extension of life span when two factors materialize—when community and family supports develop, and a sense of control over one's destiny emerges.

Today we can, at least partially, identify the mechanisms by which psychological and social factors impact biological processes, including the cardiovascular and immune systems. When people have little control in their lives, or when conditions interfere with meeting their basic needs for love or attachment, they become more vulnerable to disease and illness.[12,13] Feeling less in control and unsupported, life events are appraised more negatively giving rise to greater arousal over time of both the sympathetic-adrenal medullary system and hypothalamic-pituitary-adrenal cortical system.[14]

HOW SOCIAL SUPPORT WORKS

After two decades of research, a clearer understanding is emerging of the key features of social support that can help protect people from illness or disease and other effects of excessive stress. Sarason,[15] a pioneer in the field, showed that giving social or tangible "provisions" in the form of information, advice, companionship or money can help a stressed person; however, they are not the critical helping features. The core element, he found, is the person's sense of acceptance, a sense of affirmation and affection he or she feels from others. This is an acquired trait. It becomes part of one's personality and is retained no matter where one goes or what life events are encountered. According to Sarason without a sense of acceptance, a person is vulnerable to illness, disease, and lowered performance.

Marital discord and disruption demonstrate the profound impact that social support can have on health. For example, Somers[16] reports that disruption in a marriage can be the single most powerful sociodemographic predictor of physical and emotional illness. Indeed, poorer immune function has been found in divorced men and women who are lonely and continue to feel drawn to their ex-spouses.[17] Similarly, unhappiness in a marriage, as measured by poor marital quality, is associated with lowered immune functioning.[18] Unhappily married individuals report more illness than either

divorced or happily married persons of the same sex, age, and race.[17] These findings suggest that no simple connection can be inferred between an experience, such as being married, and health or illness. Any outcome will be affected by how an individual evaluates his or her experience and reacts to it.

ILLNESS OR DISEASE?

Whether illness or disease emerges from our reaction to life events is an important variable in the new understanding of why—and how—people get sick. Eisenberg,[9] among others, distinguishes between "disease" and "illness." Physicians think in terms of diseases and conceptualize them as abnormalities in the structure and function of individual body organs and tissues. Patients think in terms of how they feel and function as whole human beings, not as separate parts.[19] Eisenberg[9] describes illnesses as "experiences of disvalued changes in states of being and social function." Illness may occur in the absence of disease, just as disease may occur in the absence of illness. The patient is concerned with subjective signs and symptoms that may signal disease. The doctor looks for objective evidence. If none is found, no disease may be present, but an illness may still exist. Nonetheless, disease and illness are equally real to the patient. Whether the evidence is subjective or objective, psychosocial factors influence both the onset and outcome of the problem.

SUPPORT, CONTROL AND HEART ATTACKS

The influence of perceived control and support can be seen in the alternative outcomes of people who experience a heart attack. The critical life event here is myocardial infarction. Both disease and illness are present. The question is: In a group of people with the same tissue pathology receiving equally good treatment, why do some recover much better and faster than others? And, why does illness persist in some patients even when objective measures of pathology show successful treatment of the disease?

One answer involves the patient's opportunity to participate in his or her own treatment. In one study, a group of hospitalized heart attack patients received explanations about the causes, effects and treatment of myocardial infarctions. They learned how they could join in their own treatment.[20] With access to cardiac monitors, they could obtain an EKG tracing whenever they experienced symptoms. They also were taught mild isometric and foot-pedaling exercises which they did under supervision. Compared with a similar group receiving only routine information and no chance to take part in their own recovery, these patients had shorter hospital stays. Whatever greater sense of control and support the first group acquired may have affected how they continued to view their life event. This in turn would impact their cardiovascular system.

Because the cardiovascular system is particularly influenced by strong emotions, which in turn generate stress chemicals, the heart cannot be regarded simply as a mechanical pump if optimal functioning is desired. Payer[10] has observed that "in the United States the heart is viewed as a pump, and the major cause of heart pathology is considered to be due to a physical blockage in the plumbing serving the pump." She adds that "for Germans the heart is not just a pump, but an organ that has a life of its own, one that pulsates in response to a number of stimuli including the emotions."

Research in the United States and elsewhere shows that acute myocardial infarction and angina pectoris—indicating insufficient blood and oxygen supply to the heart muscle—may occur not only because of congested vessels but also because of spasm in coronary arteries, which are not simply inflexible pipes connected to a mechanical pump.[21] Cognitions can give rise to high levels of catecholamines and testosterone. Consequently, they are a key part of the mechanisms underlying arterial spasms and platelet clumping, both of which can lead to myocardial ischemic.[22] Norepinephrine and epinephrine can also stimulate release of thromboxane A2.[23] Both thromboxane A2 and the catecholamines are potent constrictors of smooth arterial muscle and strong stimulators of platelet aggregation.[24]

Given these factors, how well people recover from a heart attack, or whether they ever will ever encounter such a critical event, might therefore depend on their primary care physician's concept of the heart, a pump or an organ with a life of its own, as well as the prescribed treatment or prevention regimen. On patients' part, an increased perception of control and support plays an important role in the effectiveness of both their treatment and prevention programs.

INFLUENCE OF MEANING AND CONFIDING

The effects of trauma, even severe trauma, such as incest or a Holocaust experience, varies according to the meaning ascribed to the event by the survivors and the amount of support they perceive in their lives. Both Frankl[25] and Dimsdale[26] report how survival in concentration camps was deeply affected by whether the prisoner could find meaning in the experience. Even if meaning was expressed in a vow to live in order to seek revenge or to bear testimony, survival was enhanced and a fatal sense of hopelessness and despair averted. The ability to cling to memories of support from loved ones also was a powerful sustaining influence.

More recently, when a Jewish, Russian "refusnik" was released after 10 years of Soviet confinement, he reported that his strength to endure in prison came from knowing that a community of love supported him from the outside.[15] He maintained a strong sense of support even though he was allowed no contact with his family or the outside world for 10 years. As Sarason[15] has indicated, this political prisoner carried in his head a strong feeling that he was accepted, affirmed and loved by those he had left behind. He never doubted that they were thinking of him and working for his release. His sense of support gave him confidence in dealing with his captors. It lowered his anxiety and facilitated positive coping.

Children who recover with the least damage from years of incest or physical abuse are those who find some loving figure in their lives—a teacher, a neighbor or, in adulthood, an understanding spouse—who will listen to them and support them.[27] The most resilient children also perceived some sense of control by turning to God or becoming absorbed in the mastery of a skill.

People who have close ties to others may also benefit from confiding in them during or after a traumatic experience. In a series of recent studies Pennebaker[28] showed that after traumatic events, both psychological and physiological symptoms are relieved by systematically disclosing one's deepest thoughts and feelings either orally or in writing for 15 minutes on each of 4 consecutive days, repeating the cycle as needed. Where there is no one with whom to share painful memories, writing about one's deep feelings can bring significant benefit.[29]

Spiegel et al.[30] found that women with metastatic breast cancer live twice as long if they participate in group therapy, sharing and expressing feelings, and supporting each other in dealing with their disease. Recent studies at UCLA suggest that when people allow themselves to feel and express grief, immune proliferative response increases over time while repression of feelings and depression are associated with a decrease.[31]

PRENATAL INFLUENCES AND CHILDBIRTH

Happy events, as well as traumatic ones, can be critical in one's life. Their effects on health and illness have been well studied. For example, antibody levels are known to fluctuate with mood and happiness, with high mood being associated with high levels and low mood with low levels.[31] Holmes and Rahe,[32] first to demonstrate a correlation between life experiences and illness, argued that adjustment to change, not an event's undesirability, makes an event stressful.[33] Since then, numerous studies have established this. Events that are perceived as undesirable are more strongly correlated with risk of illness than are desirable experiences.[34] Pregnancy and birth are often viewed as happy events, but the mother may not . . . perceive them in this way. Pregnant women who feel that they have little interpersonal support and little control over life's problems may dread having a baby. These women are at higher risk for bearing low-birth weight babies and babies with complications.[35,36,37] Women under equally high stress, measured by the number of changes occurring in their lives, but who have high social support seem to be protected against these problems.[35]

Maternal attitudes toward a pregnancy and having a child have profound effects on the infant, both at birth and later. Studies in the 1970s in Germany, Austria and the United States confirmed that when a baby is unwanted, complications in pregnancy or at birth are more likely to occur.[36,38,39] High levels of catecholamines have been found in the bloodstreams of pregnant women who feel unsupported, without control or are distressed about the prospects of having a baby.[40] Passing the placental barrier, these chemicals impact the embryo and fetus.[41]

This is not the case for women whose pregnancy is welcomed, and who feel supported. What the unborn child reacts to, not only in the mother but in her environment, has increasingly come under investigation. Verny[41] reports that in the 1920s, a German doctor was told by several of his pregnant patients that they felt they should give up going to concerts because their unborn children reacted so stormily to the music. A half century later, research established that from the 25th week on, a fetus will jump in rhythm to the beat of an orchestra drum.[42] Music by both Vivaldi and Mozart seems to calm the unborn, as measured by fetal heart rate and kicking,[43] whereas music by Beethoven and Brahms has the opposite effect. All forms of rock music tend to create internal storms.[43]

SYMPTOMS AFTER NUCLEAR POWER ACCIDENTS

Pregnancy and birth have been the subject of study and speculation since the dawn of humankind. Two new life events equally as profound, however, are so recent that they have become known only in this century—in fact, only in the last decade. One of these new phenomena comes out of today's technology—the creation of nuclear power plants. The other is acquired immune deficiency syndrome (AIDS). The outcomes of people exposed to a nuclear power plant accident or infected with the AIDS virus are influenced by the individual's sense of support and control.

In March 1979 an accident occurred at the Three Mile Island (TMI) nuclear power station near Harrisburg, Pennsylvania. Although the mishap was less disastrous than the later accident at Chernobyl in the former Soviet Union, it took 11 years until the radioactive wreckage was cleared from the site.[44] Damage to the nuclear reactor produced a continued threat of radiation exposure to thousands of people living in the area. Twenty-eight months following the accident, area residents continued to exhibit higher levels of stress than did people in comparison areas who were less affected by the disaster.[45] Psychological, behavioral and biochemical measurements of 103 subjects were taken at intervals of 17 months, 22 months and 28 months after the accident. Residents with the lowest perceived control in their lives experienced the highest somatic distress and depression.[45]

In another study, heightened symptomatology after the accident was associated with a prior history of poorer social support in 312 young mothers living in the TMI area and 161 nuclear power plant workers.[46]

Compared with natural disasters, such as earthquakes, hurricanes or volcanic eruptions, technological disasters seem to have longer-lasting effects on perceived control. The difference, some researchers suggest, may be that technological disasters reflect a *loss* of control while natural disasters are associated with a *lack* of control.[45] People may accept that they lack control over the forces of nature, but believe that they can control technological power. When something goes wrong as in the case of nuclear accidents, the unexpected loss of control can be more profound. In either case, possessing a sense of control and support in one's life generally demonstrates the importance of faith and/or social affirmation for buffering the effects of stress and protecting against illness.[47,48]

PSYCHOSOCIAL EFFECTS, AIDS, AND CANCER

Control and support have an equally significant influence on patients with AIDS, affecting both the onset and course of the disease. Solomon et al. note that "while the prevalent belief among the general public, among persons with AIDS and even the professional community, is that AIDS is invariably fatal, there is a small but growing number of individuals who are alive and well 3, and even 5 years after diagnosis."[49] In Los Angeles, UCLA researchers are studying a group of men who were diagnosed with AIDS as long as 11 years ago.[50] Other investigators are finding that fatalism among those diagnosed with AIDS significantly compromises the immune system and powerfully predicts survival time.[31] Cognitive-behavioral group therapy, in early results, show improvement in immune functioning for HIV-positive persons.[31]

The San Francisco study found that psychological "hardiness" distinguishes long-term AIDS survivors from those who succumb to the disease.[49] "Hardiness" is measured by how much control, commitment and challenge a person reports.[51] Control, on this measure, means the opposite of a helpless-hopeless attitude toward bad events in life. Commitment is the opposite of alienation. People who score high on this dimension find meaning in their work, values and personal relationships. Challenge describes a person's ability to interpret stressful events as changes to be explored and successfully met rather than threats to be dreaded and feared.

Solomon and colleagues also found that one kind of social support seems to distinguish exceptional AIDS survivors who have *Pneumocystitis carinii pneumonia,* a life-threatening complication of AIDS.[49] Those who followed suggestions or took advice from people in their social network lived longer. The San Francisco researchers caution that the number of subjects in their study was small (N=21) and that their results are preliminary. They note, however, that the results are consistent with findings on the effects of control and support in other diseases. For example, Temoshok, Solomon's associate, has reported that a "Type C" coping style is associated with an unfavorable prognosis for cutaneous malignant melanoma.[52] Type C characteristics include being passive, appeasing, helpless and unexpressing of emotion. The San Francisco research group currently is investigating whether Type C in men infected with the AIDS virus is associated with greater risk of developing Kaposi's sarcoma, another serious complication of immune deficiency.

Because the asymptomatic phase of HIV-1 infection can be as long as 10 to 15 years,[53] helping people remain free of symptoms and slowing down the progression of the disease is a matter of top priority. At the Center for the Biopsychosocial Study of AIDS at the University of Miami, researchers report that aerobic exercise training has improved the immunological functioning and psychological health of a group of both HIV-1 seropositive and seronegative men.[54] They note that the exercising not only seems to have direct physiological benefits, but it also results in a greater sense of control. The researchers also are investigating the effects of a program that includes cognitive restructuring, assertiveness training, mental imagery, social support enrichment and progressive muscle relaxation. Preliminary results seem promising, but need further replication.[55]

Similar psychological intervention has been effective in improving affective state and immune function in a group of postsurgical patients with malignant melanoma.[56,57] Thirty-five patients in a 6-week program received stress management, enhancement of problem-solving skills, relaxation training, and group support. Compared to 26 controls, assessment at a 6-month followup showed significant increases in natural killer cells, NK cytotoxic activity, and percent of large granular lymphocytes. The experimental group also showed significantly less depression, fatigue and mood disturbance. They also used significantly more active-behavioral and active-cognitive coping than did the controls.[56,57]

SUMMARY

What can we conclude from these studies? One fact seems certain: there is no simple connection between life events and illness. Whether we get sick from an infection or a negative life experience depends on more than a germ or stress. All disease is multifactorial, and the resources that help protect us have much to do with our sense of support and control over our lives. What happens in our endocrine system and to our immune response is a function of what is going on inside our heads and hearts—the meanings we give to events and the feelings we have about them.

Skeptics have long doubted these tenets.[7,8] However, emerging evidence increasingly dispels these doubts and has replaced them with a biopsychosocial model based on psychoneuroimmunology (PNI). Indeed, Cousins[50] described PNI as "the new science of medicine." To date, more than a dozen academic medical centers in the United States have PNI research programs and the list is growing.

With expanded scientific study of the mind-body connection, people in general will come to recognize that whether they become ill is not always a matter of chance, but to a considerable extent something under their own control.

REFERENCES

1. Selye H: *The Stress of Life.* New York: McGraw-Hill; 1956.
2. Selye H: A syndrome produced by diverse nocuous agents. *Nature* 1936; 138: 32.
3. Selye H: *Selye's Guide to Stress Research.* New York: Van Nostrand Reinhold; 1980.
4. Selye H: *Stress Without Distress.* New York: Signet; 1975.
5. Lazarus RS: *Psychological Stress and the Coping Process.* New York: McGraw-Hill; 1966.
6. Lazarus RS, Launier R: Stress-related transactions between persons and environment. In: Pervin LA & Lewis M ed. *Perspectives in Interactional Psychology.* New York: Plenum; 1978.
7. Justice B: *Who Gets Sick: How Beliefs, Moods and Thoughts Affect Health.* Los Angeles: Tarcher; 1988.
8. Justice B: *Wer Wird Krank?* (A. Pott, trans.). Hamburg, Germany: Goldmann Verlag; 1991.
9. Eisenberg L: Science in medicine: Too much and too limited in scope? In: White KL ed. *The Task of Medicine.* Menlo Park, CA: Henry J. Kaiser Family Foundation; 1988; 290–217.
10. Payer L: *Medicine & culture.* New York: Henry Holt; 1988.
11. Sagan L: *The Health of Nations: True Causes of Sickness and Well-being.* New York: Basic Books; 1987.
12. Leighton AH: *My Name is Legion.* New York: Basic Books; 1959.

13. Leighton AH: Conceptual perspectives. In: Kaplan RN, Wilson AH and Leighton AH ed. *Further Explorations in Social Psychiatry.* New York: Basic Books; 1976.

14. Rodin J: Managing the stress of aging: The role of control and coping. In: Levine B and Holger U ed. *Coping and Health.* New York: Plenum 1979; 171–202.

15. Sarason IG: Sense of social support. Paper presented at the annual meeting of the American Psychological Association, Atlanta, GA; August 1988.

16. Somers AR: Marital Status, Health, and Use of Health Services. *JAMA* 1979; 241: 1818–1822.

17. Kiecolt-Glaser JK, Kennedy S, Malkoff S, Fisher L, Speicher CE, and Glasser R: Marital discord and immunity in males. *Psychosomatic Med* 1988; 50: 213–229.

18. Kiecolt-Glasser JK, Fisher L, Ogrocki P, Stout JC, Speicher EE, and Glaser R: Martial quality, marital disruption, and immune function. *Psychosomatic Med,* 1987; 49: 13–34.

19. Schwartz MA, Wiggins OP: Scientific and humanistic medicine: A theory of clinical methods. In: White KL ed. *The Task of Medicine.* Menlo Park, CA: Henry J. Kaiser Family Foundation; 1988: 137–171.

20. Cromwell RI, Butterfield EC, Brayfield FM, and Curry JJ: *Acute Myocardial Infarction: Reaction and Recovery.* St. Louis: Mosby; 1977.

21. Ornish D: *Stress, Diet and Your Heart.* New York: Signet; 1982.

22. Oliva PB: Pathophysiology of acute infarction. *Annals of Internal Medicine* 1981: 94: 236–250.

23. Hirsch PD, Hillis LD, Campbell WB, Firth BG, and Willerson JT: Release of prostaglandins and thromboxane into the coronary circulation in patients with ischemic heart disease. *NEJM* 1981; 304: 685–691.

24. Moncada S, Vane JR: Arachidonic acid metabolites and the interactions between Platelet and blood vessel walls. *NEJM* 1979; 300: 1142–1149.

25. Frankl VE: *Man's Search for Meaning.* 3rd ed. New York: Simon & Schuster; 1984.

26. Dimsdale JE: The Coping Behavior of Nazi Concentration Camp Survivors. *American Journal of Psychiatry* 1974; 131(7): 792–797.

27. Mrazek FJ, Mrazek DA: Resilience in child maltreatment victims: A conceptual exploration. *Child Abuse & Neglect* 1987; 11: 357–366.

28. Pennebaker J: *Opening Up: The Healing Powers of Confiding.* New York: Morrow; 1990.

29. Pennebaker J: Writing is healing. Presentation at the Hawthorne Training Conference, Houston, TX; March 1990.

30. Spiegel D, Bloom JR, Kraemer HC, Gottheil E: Effect of psychosocial treatment on survival of patients with metastatic breast cancer. *Lancet* 1989; Oct 14: 1888–891.

31. Kemeny M: Mind, emotions and the immune system. Presentation at annual conference of Institute of Noetic Sciences, Arlington, VA; June 1993.

32. Holmes TH, Rahe RH: The social readjustment rating scale. *J of Psychosomatic Res* 1976; 11: 213–218.

33. Holmes TH, Masuda M: Life Change and Illness Susceptibility. In: Dohrenwend BS Dohrewend BF eds. *Stressful Life Events: Their Nature and Effects.* New York: Wiley; 1974: 9–44.

34. Dohrenwend BB, Dohrenwend BP: Life Stress and Illness. In: Dohrenwend BB and Dohrenwend BP eds. *Stressful Life Events and Their Contexts.* New York, Prodist; 1981: 1–27.

35. Nuckolls KB, Cassel J, Kaplan BH: Psychosocial assets, life crisis, and the prognosis of pregnancy. *Am J Epi,* 1972; 95: 431–441.

36. Morris NM, Udry JR, Chase CL: Reduction of low birth weight birth rates by the prevention of unwanted pregnancies. *Am J Public Health* 1973; 3(11): 935–938.

37. Norbeck JS, Tilden VP: Life stress, social support, and emotional disequilibrium in complications of pregnancy: A prospective, multivariate study. *J of Health and Social Behavior* 1983; 24(3) 30–46.

38. Rottman G: Untersuchungen uber Einstellung zur Schwangerschaft und zur fotalen Entwiklung. In: Graber H ed. *Geist und Psyche* Munchen: Kindler Verlag; 1974.

39. Lukesch M: Psychologie Faktoren der Schwangershaft. Unpublished dissertation, University of Salzburg; 1975.

40. Kruse F: Nos souvenirs du corps maternal, *Psychologie Heute* 1978: 56.

41. Verny T, Kelly J: *The Secret Life of the Unborn Child.* New York: Summit Books; 1981.

42. Liley A: The fetus as a personality. *The Australian and New Zealand Journal of Psychiatry* 1972; 6: 99–105.

43. Clements M: Observations on certain aspects of neonatal behavior in response to auditory stimuli. Paper presented at the Fifth International Congress of Psychosomatic Obstetrics and Gynecology, Rome; 1977.

44. Wald M: After the meltdown, lessons from a clean-up. *New York Times* 1990; April 24: B5–B6.

45. Davidson LM, Baum A, Fleming, Gisriel MM: Toxic Exposure and Chronic Stress at Three Mile Island. In Lebovits AH, Baum A, and Singer JE eds. *Advances in Environmental Psychology.* Hillsdale, NJ: Erlbaum, 1986; 6: 35–46.

46. Bromet EV, Schulberg HC: The Three Mile Island Disaster: A Search for high-risk Groups. In Shore JH ed. *Disaster Stress Studies: New Methods and Findings.* Washington, DC: American Psychiatric Press; 1986: 2–19.

47. Levine JS, Schiller PL: Is there a religious factor in health? *J Religion & Health* 1987; 6: 9–36.
48. King DG: Religion and health relationships: A review. *Journal of Religion and Health* 1990; 29(2): 101–112.
49. Solomon GF, Temoshok L, O'Leary A, Zich J: An Intensive Psychoimmunologic study of long-surviving persons with AIDS. *Annals of the New York Academy of Sciences* 1987; 496: 647–655.
50. Cousins N: New dimensions in healing. Presentation at the Tenneco Distinguished Lecture Series, University of Houston, TX; March 1990.
51. Kobasa SCO, Maddi SR, Puccetti and Zola MA: Effectiveness of hardiness, exercise and social support as resources against illness. *J Psychosomatic Res* 1985; 29(5): 525–533.
52. Temoshok L, Heller BW, Sagebiel RW, Blois MS, Sweet DM, DiClemente RJ, and Gold ML: The relations of psychosocial factors to prognostic indicators in cutaneous malignant melanoma. *J Psychosomatic Med* 1985; 29: 139–153.
53. Munoz A, Wang MC, Good R, Detels H, Ginsberg L, Kingsley J, et al.: Estimation of the AIDS-free times after HIV-1 seroconversion. Paper presented at the Fourth Annual Meeting of the International Conference on AIDS, Stockholm, Sweden, June 1988.
54. Antoni MH, Schneiderman N, Fletcher MA, Goldstein DA: Psychoneuroimmunology and HIV-1. *J Consulting and Clinical Psychology* 1990; 58(1): 38–49.
55. Antoni M: Psychosocial stress management and immune functioning in an HIV-1 risk group. Paper presented at the annual meeting of the American Psychological Association, New Orleans, LA; August 1989.
56. Fawzy FW, Cousins N, Fawzy NW, Kemeny ME, Elashoff R, Morton D: A structured psychiatric intervention for cancer patients; I. Changes over time in methods of coping and affective disturbance. *Arch Gen Psychiatry* 1990; 47: 720–725.
57. Fawzy FI, Kemeny ME, Fawzy NW, Elashoff R, Morton D, Cousins N, et al.: A structured psychiatric intervention for cancer patients; II. Changes over time in immunological measures. *Arch Gen Psychiatry* 1990; 47: 729–735.

the new MIDDLE AGE

MELINDA BECK

A generation verges toward a mass midlife crisis. But wait: it can be a lot better than you think.

The names are culled from driver's license records, credit-card applications, magazine-subscription forms—any place an unsuspecting consumer might have listed his birth date somewhere along the line. They pour into a data-management firm, where they are standardized, merged and purged of duplications. From there, they are assigned one of several different solicitation packets, then bundled and shipped nationwide. It's a point of great pride with the American Association of Retired Persons that on or about their birthdays, roughly 75 percent of the 2.7 million Americans who turned 50 this year received an offer to partake—for just $8!—in all the benefits of membership in the AARP.

Not since the Selective Service Board sent "greetings" to 18-year-old men during the Vietnam War has a birthday salutation been so dreaded by so many. True, the leading edge of the baby boom won't get the official invitations into the quagmire of the 50s for four more years—but these things are always worse in anticipation than in reality. And the icons of the baby boom are already there. Paul McCartney turned 50 this year; so did Aretha Franklin. Bob Dylan is 51, as are Frank Zappa, Paul Simon and Art Garfunkel. Even the heartthrobs have crossed the great divide: Raquel Welch is pinned up at 51, Robert Redford at 55.

Month by month, individually and collectively, the generation that refused to grow up is growing middle aged. The reminders are everywhere—from the gracefully aging Lauren Hutton (49) in the J. Crew catalog to the now ubiquitous prefix *"aging* baby boomers" to the Oval Office itself. Sure, Bill Clinton and Al Gore will breathe new youth into the presidency that has been held for three decades by the PT-109 crowd. But for many in this competitive cohort, their ascension is just one more reminder of time marching on and leaving accomplishment victims in its wake. *See—the president is 46. You're 49. Weren't you supposed to be CEO by now, or at least know what you want to DO with your life?* To be sure, this is hardly the first generation to hit

or anticipate the Big Five-Oh. The baby boomers' group obsession with aging is already sounding, well, old, to everybody else, and, by conventional definitions at least, most boomers have been "middle aged" since they turned 40. But raised with such outsize expectations of life, they may have a tougher time accepting the age of limitations than other generations. "This group was somehow programmed to never get older—that sets us up for a whole series of disappointments," says psychiatrist Harold Bloomfield in Del Mar, Calif. Rice University sociologist Chad Gordon has another take on the angst that is seizing baby boomers. "Let's face it—aging sucks," he says. "It's filled with all those D words—decay, decrepitude, degeneration, dying . . . Then there's balding, paunchiness, losing sex drives and capabilities, back trouble, headaches, cholesterol and high blood pressure—they all go from the far horizon to close up. Then you worry about worrying about those things."

In truth, authorities on aging and ordinary people who've been there say that middle age isn't so bad. "It's the most powerful and glorious segment of a person's life," says Ken Dychtwald, whose company, Age Wave, counsels businesses on how to serve the needs of the aging population. Dychtwald admits, however, that American culture hasn't universally embraced this idea and that most of the soon-to-be-middle-aged themselves haven't gotten into the swing of it yet.

Instead, they are responding with ever more exaggerated forms of foreboding. Bloomfield says he sees an increase in a once rare condition called *dysmorphophobia*—the intense but unfounded fear of looking ugly. In Hollywood, not only do actresses try desperately to disguise their age, but so do agents, scriptwriters and studio executives. "It's hard to age gracefully out here," says Dr. Mel Bircoll, 52, considered the father of the cosmetic pectoral implant, the calf implant and the fat implant (which he layers into face-lifts to add contour and avoid the "overstretched look"). Bircoll says his clients used to start at 55. Now they come to him at about 45.

All of this might have been grist for a great TV series, but when producer Stan Rogow tried it this season, it flopped. Rogow intended "Middle Ages" to be an upbeat portrayal—"pretty hip, pretty life affirming, not angst-ridden. What we tried to do with the show was to say, 'This is OK. It's better than OK'." Critics liked it but viewers never gave it a chance and, in retrospect, Rogow understands why: "The name was a colossal mistake. 'Middle age' is this horrible-sounding thing you've heard throughout your life and hated." As the low ratings piled up, Rogow said to himself: "We have a problem here, and it's called denial."

But the funny thing about denial is that sometimes it works. In the very act of staving off physical aging through exercise, diet and dye, the StairMaster set has actually succeeded in pushing back the boundaries of "middle age." Boomers will look, act and feel younger at 50 than previous generations did. "Fifty will be like 40," says UCLA gerontologist Fernando Torres-Gil, who predicts that this generation won't confront "old age" until well into their 70s. The broad concept of middle age is starting later and lasting longer—and looking better than ever before. "We're seeing that 50 means all kinds of very vibrant, alive, sexy, dynamic people," says June Reinisch, director of the Kinsey Institute for Research in Sex, Gender and Reproduction at Indiana University. "I'm 49 this year. I wear clothes that my mother never would have thought of wearing when she was this age. When skirts went up, my skirts went up." Rogow, 44, says: "I'd really be shocked if I'm wearing plaid golf pants at 60. I suspect I'll be wearing the same ripped jeans I've been wearing for 20 years. They'll be much cooler then."

The new middle age also features more children than ever before, since this generation has delayed marriage and childbearing. Many men are having second families, with even younger children, well into their 50s. Some may be pushing strollers *and* paying college tuition just when psychologists say they should be busting loose and fulfilling themselves. At the same time, today's middle-agers have aging parents who are starting to need care. "For many people, 50 will be just like 20, 30 and 40—tied to providing basic subsistence needs," says University of Texas psychologist David Drum. "They won't see a chance to change, to repattern their lives."

Yet even as they postponed family responsibilities, many people in this fast-track generation reached the peaks of their careers much earlier than their parents did—and are wondering, "Is that all there is?" even in their 30s and 40s. Many of them will top out earlier, too, as record numbers of middle managers chase fewer and fewer promotions. While previous generations worried about sex and marriage, "career crashes are the baby boom's version of midlife crisis," says Barry Glassner, a University of Southern California sociologist. Women, having forged careers of their own in record numbers, may face the same kind of professional crisis traditionally reserved for men—and their incomes will still be needed to make ends meet. "Lose a job—have any piece of the puzzle taken out—and the whole thing falls apart," says Andrea Saveri, a research fellow at the Institute for the Future in Menlo Park, Calif.

The cruel demographic joke is that just as this generation is hitting middle age with unprecedented family responsibilities, corporate America is mustering legions of fiftysomethings out of the work force through early-retirement plans and less compassionate methods. "There is tremendous doubt about the future," says Saveri. "People see their friends getting pink slips. Their M.B.A.s aren't doing them any good now." Retiring earlier—and living longer—will bring a host of financial, emotional and psychological problems in the years ahead. Today's 50-year-olds still have 20 or 30 more years to live. What are they going to do—and how are they going to pay for it? "The 50s are not the beginning of the end—you have an awful long way to go," says University of Chicago gerontologist Bernice Neugarten, now 76. And that may be the most frightening thought of all.

Midway life's journey I was made aware
That I had strayed into a dark forest,
And the right path appeared not anywhere.

Dante was 35 years old and frustrated in his quest for political position in 1300 when he wrote the first lines of "The Inferno"—describing perhaps the first midlife crisis in Western literature. Shakespeare charted similar midlife muddles in "King Lear," "Macbeth," "Hamlet" and "Othello" in the early 1600s, though he barely used the phrase "middle age." Sigmund Freud and Carl Jung studied midlife transitions around the turn of the 20th century. But then "midlife" came much earlier in time. In 1900, average life expectancy in the United States was 47 and only 3 percent of the population lived past 65. Today average life expectancy is 75—and 12 percent of the U.S. population is older than 65.

The longer life gets, the harder it is to plot the midpoint and define when middle age begins and ends. "We've broken the evolutionary code," says Gail Sheehy, author of "Passages" and "The Silent Passage." "In only a century, we've added 30 years to the life cycle." Statistically, the middle of life is now about 37, but what we think of as middle age comes later—anywhere from 40 to 70. As chronological age has less and less meaning, experts are groping for other definitions. When the American Board of Family Practice asked a random sampling of 1,200 Americans when middle age begins, 41 percent said it was when you worry about having enough money for health-care concerns, 42 percent said it was when your last child moves out and 46 percent said it was when you don't recognize the names of music groups on the radio anymore.

However it is defined, middle age remains one of the least studied phases in life. "It's the last uncharted territory in human development," said MacArthur Foundation president Adele Simmons in 1989, announcing a $10 million grant to fund the largest scholarly look ever at the period. Team leader Gilbert Brim and his colleagues at the Research Network on Successful Midlife Development are now partway through their eight-year effort, trying to answer, among other things, why some people hit their

How do I know if what I achieve in life should be called serenity and not surrender?

—JUDITH VIORST, 61

■ Percentage of baby boomers who say they have been through midlife crisis: 27
■ Average age of men who marry for second time: 39.2
■ Average age of women who marry for second time: 34.8

SOURCE: GALLUP, NATIONAL CENTER FOR HEALTH STATISTICS

strides at midlife and others hit the wall. To date, they have concluded that there are no set stages or transition points—that what happens to people is more the result of accident, personal experiences and the historical period in which they live. "Midlife is full of changes, of twists and turns; the path is not fixed," says Brim. "People move in and out of states of success."

In particular, Brim's group debunks the notion of a "midlife crisis." "It's such a mushy concept—not like a clinical diagnosis in the medical field," he says. But, Brim adds, "what a wonderful idea! You could load everything on that—letting people blame something external for what they're feeling." Other scholars agree that very few people suffer full-blown crackups—and that dumping the spouse for a bimbo is more the stuff of fiction—or fantasy— than reality. So is the Gauguin syndrome: running off to Tahiti at 43. People do have affairs and end up with different mates—but that is often after marriages have failed for reasons other than midlife malaise.

Still, the mythology persists. "You ask people if they've had a midlife crisis and some say they have," says sociologist Ronald Kessler at the University of Michigan's Institute for Social Research. "Then you ask them what it was and they'll say that they didn't get to be vice president. So what did they do—try to kill themselves? Buy a sports car? Well no, people come to terms with getting older in a most gradual way." The idea of a crisis sometimes provides an excuse for wild and outrageous behavior, says psychologist Susan Krauss Whitbourne at the University of Massachusetts at Amherst: "It sounds romantic and fun—certainly better than complete boredom." She also suspects it's a class phenomenon: well-educated people with money "have the luxury to reflect on these things."

What does commonly happen, experts say, is a more subtle acceptance of life's limitations. One key task may be to change your self-image. "A lot of the more tangible rewards come in the first half of life, such as good grades, first jobs, early promotions, marriage, first children," says psychologist Robert E. Simmons in Alexandria, Va. After that, "it's harder and harder to rely on external gratifications because there aren't as many. So one is thrown back more on one's internal self-esteem system." That can mean finding new forms of satisfaction—from coaching Little League to taking up the saxophone to tutoring kids in school.

The sooner you accept the idea that life may not turn out as you planned, the easier the transition will be. "It's the person who has just been driving himself and getting burnt out, who is starting to turn 50 and who feels like, 'My God, my life is over'," says Bloomfield. Gail Sheehy agrees: "For those who deny, postpone, elude or fantasize to escape coming to terms with [reality], it comes up again around 50 with a double whammy." Sheehy can see this now, at 54. She barely mentioned life past 50 in "Passages" because she was only 35 at the time and couldn't visualize herself at an older age. Now she says she knows that "you have to work your way up to saying 'I'm not going to go backward. I'm not going to try to stay in the same place. That way lies self-torture and eventually

foolishness. I'm going to have the courage to go forward'."

Contrary to conventional wisdom, many people find that the 50s is actually a period of reduced stress and anxiety. "In terms of mental health, midlife is the best time," says Ronald Kessler. One tantalizing bit of biomedical research has found that between 40 and 60, people actually lose cells in the locus coeruleus, the part of the brain that registers anxiety, which may help explain the "mellowing" many people feel in middle age. Depression does tend to peak in this period, however, which may also be linked to biochemical changes in the aging brain.

Not all mood shifts are biochemical. There are definite life events that can bring about profound changes of heart and direction. The list includes divorce; illness; losing a job; the kids leaving home (or returning); the death of parents, spouses and friends. Those can happen at any point in life, but they begin to mount up in the 50s. Any kind of change is stressful and simply fearing these things can bring tension. "It also happens when mentors retire," says University of North Carolina sociologist Glen Elder. "You have to think about yourself playing that role. It's a major transition, one that is hard to come to terms with."

Professional disappointments weigh especially heavily on men, and they are inevitable even for the most successful, from George Bush to laid-off steelworkers. Being forced out of a job in midlife can be devastating—or liberating, if it brings about a rethinking of what's most important. Men (and increasingly, women) who sacrificed time with their families for their careers in their younger years may be particularly regretful when success proves as empty as the nest. "Men our age have lived such a macho fake life," says Rogers Brackmann, 61, a former advertising executive in Chicago. "When I was in the agency business, I was up at 5 o'clock, home at 7:30. For the first 15 years I worked every Saturday. I didn't make it to my kid's Little League games. When I left that environment I realized how hard and unproductive the work was." Rogers packed it in five years ago and says, "I was so happy to get out I can't describe it." Since then he has turned to other new businesses, including inventing, and now holds five patents—including one for a golf-ball washer that doesn't get your hands wet.

Can I ask you a question? Why do men chase women? . . . I think it's because they fear death.
— Rose (Olympia Dukakis) in "Moonstruck"

Typically, men and women cross paths, psychologically, in middle age. Men become more nurturing and family-oriented. Women become more independent and aggressive. Jung described this as the "contrasexual transition." Northwestern University psychologist David Gutmann found the phenomenon not only in American culture, but also in Navajo, Mayan and Middle Eastern Druze societies he studied for his book "Reclaimed Powers: Toward a New Psychology of Men and Women in Later Life"—suggesting that it is more biological than cultural. Much

---

I live like a monk, almost. A monk with red lips, short dresses and big hair.

—TINA TURNER, 53

■ Percentage of men aged 40 to 49 who say their lives are exciting: 52.4
■ Percentage aged 50 to 59: 43.3
■ Percentage of women aged 40 to 49 who find their lives exciting: 45.6
■ Percentage aged 50 to 59: 40.7

SOURCE: NATIONAL OPINION RESEARCH CENTER

of it has to do with the demands of child rearing, Gutmann explains, in which men provide for the family's physical needs and women do the emotional work, each suppressing the other parts of their personalities. When the children leave home, those submerged forces tend to reassert themselves, Gutmann says.

Ideally, that crossing should be liberating for both halves of the couple and bring them closer together. But often the transition is rocky. "It can be very threatening for men to see their women soar," says counselor Sirah Vettese, Bloomfield's wife. Some men are so unnerved that they do seek out younger, more compliant women, Gutmann says. He thinks Ernest Hemingway is a prime example: devastated after his third wife left him to pursue her own career, the author became increasingly alcoholic. He took another younger wife and killed himself at 61.

It doesn't help that many men wrestling with self-image adjustments in midlife must also accept declining sexual performance. Testosterone levels gradually drop, which can diminish their libido. Erections are less full, less frequent and require more stimulation to achieve. Researchers once attributed that to psychological factors, but increasingly they find that 75 percent of erection dysfunctions stem from physiological problems. "Smoking, diabetes, hypertension, elevated cholesterol—without a doubt, those are the four erection busters," says University of Chicago urologist Laurence A. Levine. Still, psychology does play a role. "If you think you're going to have a problem, suddenly you're going to begin having a problem," says psychologist Jan Sinnott at Towson State University in Baltimore, Md.

Inevitably, pharmaceutical manufacturers have sensed that there's money to be made in the fear of flaccidity. Gynex Pharmaceuticals is researching a daily under-the-tongue testosterone-replacement product called Androtest-SL and already markets an injectable version that is used every two weeks. But there may be considerable side effects. Excessive use of testosterone may lead to testicular atrophy and infertility and spur the growth of some cancers. Too much testosterone can cause some men to grow small breasts, too.

A better remedy for men who find their potency declining is to change the way they think about sex—to take things slower, more romantically and not mourn the seemingly instant erections of their youth. "The midlife male has to finally get the idea that his primary sex organ is not his penis. It's his heart and his brain," says Bloomfield, author of "Love Secrets for a Lasting Relationship." Talking helps, too, though most men are not accustomed to such openness. "It's really important that men and women sit down and say to each other, 'Our lives are changing'," says Vettese.

In many ways, women have it easier in midlife. For all the new willingness to discuss the hot flashes and mood swings some feel during menopause, many women feel a surge of sexual and psychological freedom once their shifting hormones rebalance and they are no longer concerned about getting pregnant. "With each pass-ing generation, women feel sexier and more desire after menopause," says June Reinisch at the Kinsey Institute. Sheehy says that based on studies she has seen, about one third of women have some noticeable diminution of desire after menopause. That can be rectified with hormone supplements or accepted as it is, if the woman doesn't mind.

What many women *do* mind is finding themselves alone and lost in the discouraging midlife singles scene. Zella Case, co-owner of the Someone Special dating service in Dallas, says, "We have hundreds of women who want in, but so few men." The numbers are right there in the census statistics: there are 14 million single women older than 55, and only 4 million single men. Just ask Victoria Anderson, a Dallas private investigator who turned 50 last month. Divorced 13 years, she's been losing confidence and gaining weight and she frets that she'll never fit into the size 3s in her closet again. She despairs of meeting a new mate on the job—"I deal with criminals and jerks," she says. And as far as the bar scene goes, Anderson says ruefully, the typical question now is not "what's your sign, but what's your cholesterol level?"

Women with stable marriages may find other tensions mounting in midlife. With delayed childbirth, kids may be hitting adolescence just when their mothers are in menopause—a volatile combination. Some women desperately fear losing their faces and their figures—especially if those have been the focus of their self-esteem. But the new burst of postmenopausal independence some feel may help to compensate.

Bobbi Altman literally took flight at midlife. "Turning 50 was the best thing that ever happened to me. I could do anything I wanted to," she says. After suffering through a divorce in her early 40s and raising three children, Altman took up aviation, bought an airplane and, at 59, went to aircraft-mechanic school. Last April she graduated and in June she flew cross-country solo. Now 61, she lives in Laguna Beach, Calif., and is involved with a man who finished law school at 70. Altman flies to work every day at the Santa Monica Museum of Flying, where she is helping to restore a World War II P-39. "Aging is not a loss of youth—it's another stage," she says.

I remember now that the toughest birthday I ever faced was my fortieth. It was a big symbol because it said goodbye, goodbye, goodbye to youth. But I think that when one has passed through that age it's like breaking the sound barrier.
    —Writer and director NORMAN CORWIN, 82
    quoted in the 1992 book "The Ageless Spirit"

Baby boomers who dread what will happen to them beyond the age of 50 have only to look at what older people are doing with their lives today. The generation preceding them—the first to enjoy the longevity revolution—are going back to school in record numbers, forging new careers and still making great strides in their old ones. Lydia Bronte, a research fellow at the Phelps Stokes Institute in New York, recently com-

I feel exactly the same as I've always felt: a lightly reined-in voracious beast.

—JACK NICHOLSON, 55

■ Percentage of married men aged 40 to 49 who admit to infidelity: 28.4
■ Percentage aged 50 to 59: 24.3
■ Percentage of married women aged 40 to 49 who admit to infidelity: 15.21
■ Percentage aged 50 to 59: 3.3

SOURCE: NATIONAL OPINION RESEARCH CENTER

pleted a five-year study of the work lives of 150 people 65 to 102, and concludes that "many people are as active as they've ever been during those years . . . The single most important thing was that they found work that they loved." Some of Bronte's subjects switched jobs many times over in their lives. Some found their true calling only in their later years. Julia Child, now 80, learned French cooking after her husband took a job in France and started her TV career in her 50s. The late Millicent Fenwick won her first race for Congress at 65.

Still, the image of elderly people as desperate, frail and unproductive prevails, and that brings an unrealistic fear of growing middle aged and older. "People need to profoundly rethink what aging means, not only for themselves as individuals, but for the whole society," says Harry Moody, deputy director of the Brookdale Center on Aging at Hunter College in New York. By 2030, when the oldest boomers are 84 and the youngest have turned 65, thee will be an estimated 65 million Americans 65 and older—more than twice as many as today.

To find more satisfaction and hope in that future, aging baby boomers need to bust out of the rigid "three boxes of life" mentality that has governed the pattern of American lives for so long. Confining education to youth, work and child rearing to the middle years, and retirement to old age makes less and less sense—and it simply won't fly in an economy that is dismissing people from the work world in their 50s, with an ever-longer stretch of life ahead. "We desperately need some real, contributing roles for people in the third third of life," says New York management consultant Bill Stanley. He argues that the whole concept of "retirement" should be retired.

Some change in the image of aging will come about naturally in the decades ahead. Baby boomers, by sheer force of numbers, have always made their stage in life the hip stage to be in. The generation that thought it could change the world overnight has only a few years left before its members become elders themselves. While some of their frantic efforts to stave off aging may constitute denial, some go hand in hand with forging a healthier, more constructive vision of old age that could last even longer than we now suspect. The boomers will go there, riding Stair-Masters to heaven, and that may be their most lasting legacy of all.

With GINNY CARROLL *in Houston,*
PATRICIA KING *in San Francisco,*
KAREN SPRINGEN *and* TODD BARRETT *in Chicago,*
LUCILLE BEACHY *in New York,* JEANNE GORDON
in Los Angeles and CAROLYN FRIDAY *in Boston*

■ **Total face–lifts in U.S., 1990: 48,743 (91% women)
percentage aged 35 to 50: 27
percentage aged 51 to 64: 58**
■ **Total tummy tucks in U.S., 1990: 20,213 (93% women)
percentage aged 35 to 50: 64
percentage aged 51 to 64: 15**
■ **Total hair transplants in U.S., 1990: 3,188 (100% men)
percentage aged 35 to 50: 57
percentage aged 51 to 64: 10**
■ **Median age of an American using hair–color product: women: 43.14, men: 43.02**

SOURCE: AMERICAN SOCIETY OF PLASTIC
& RECONSTRUCTIVE SURGEONS,
SIMMONS 1992

The Mystery of Suicide

The road to self-destruction starts with depression and ends in the grave. But who chooses to die and why? Is it stress? Brain chemistry? A despair rotting the soul? The answers are as varied as the weapons.

David Gelman

They inhabit a strange pantheon of the suicidal, prowled by brilliant, troubled ghosts. Some came to grief in the nightfall of acclaimed careers, some in the withering, high-noon glare of public adulation. There are Hemingway and Plath, Monroe and Garland, dead by premeditation or by cumulative acts of self-destruction. There are Presley, Morrison, Hendrix and Joplin, all of them fatally overdosed on drugs and fame. Some are noted almost as much for the manner of their deaths as for the impact of their lives. Last summer a depression-prone White House counsel named Vincent Foster burst into unwelcome national prominence with his final act, a self-inflicted gunshot wound to the head. And last week police in Seattle found the bloodied body of Kurt Cobain, leader of the hugely popular group Nirvana, sprawled in his home. He had apparently killed himself at least a day earlier, the police said, with the shotgun they found resting against him.

Once again, the rock world was shaken by the death of one of its gifted young artists, a tragedy that seems endemic to the pop-music scene. To many it was all too predictable. "The whole thing reeks of cliché: 'Pop icon commits suicide'," said Chris Dorr, a 23-year-old Seattle college student. "It makes you wonder if our icons are genetically programmed to self-destruct in their late 20s."

But Cobain's death hit hardest in Seattle. Thousands of grieving callers bombarded local radio stations, prompting the stations to broadcast crisis-hot-line numbers and organize a candlelight vigil for Sunday. Meanwhile, dozens of mourners gathered outside his house, leaving flowers and carting off mementos.

Suicides always take their own portion of mystery with them, as President Bill Clinton suggested after Foster, his close friend and aide, killed himself. For all the recent advances in the study of behavior, there's still much that doctors don't understand about the persistent phenomenon of people taking their own lives. "We can't talk with the person who committed suicide, so we can only piece together the data," says psychiatrist George Murphy, of Washington University in St. Louis. But researchers are making a determined effort to chart the process, and what they're finding, especially on the cutting edge of brain science, may help bring down the annual toll of suicide deaths.

That toll, of course, takes its full measure on those left behind. Suicides don't simply give up on life: they leave a smear of nullity behind them. Their private act of negation attacks our own often tenuous sense of a meaning in existence. It's a kind of desertion, making everyone feel a little less defended against nothingness. "The suicide does not play the game, does not observe the rules," wrote the novelist Joyce Carol Oates in a 1978 meditation on the subject. "He leaves the party too soon, and leaves the other guests painfully uncomfortable."

In life, Cobain was often in pain. Until his death, he was scarcely known outside the youth culture. But his band, most of whose bitter-edged lyrics he wrote and sang, had become the authentic voice of the 20-plus generation. In the few years since its formation, Nirvana helped establish grunge rock as the sound and style of '90s disillusionment. Its 1991 album, "Nevermind," sold nearly 10 million copies, and one of its songs, "Smells Like Teen Spirit," has become a virtual anthem for the rebellious young.

Besieged: Cobain's life began unraveling not long after his band hit the charts, bringing him attention he couldn't seem to handle. He felt besieged by fans and critics. Between bouts of heroin abuse, he was subject to episodes of depression. Yet friends described him as gentle and caring, not really prone to the violence that surrounds much of the rock culture. Small and almost frail-looking, he wrote music that was oddly melodic despite the abrasiveness of its lyrics. But in the end, by some process still unknown, the sadness of life led him to put a shotgun to his head.

In most instances, suicide seems an enormously selfish act. One of the strongest arguments against it is the harm it can do to others, especially the shattering legacy of guilt and grief it bequeaths to the family of the deceased. Many people reacting to Cobain's death expressed concern about what it might do to his 19-month-old daughter, Frances Bean, the only issue of his troubled marriage to singer Courtney Love.

On the other hand, libertarians and others posit a "right" to suicide, especially for the elderly and the ill. Some argue that such suicides, while tragic, may be "rational"—a proposition that Michigan's Dr. Jack Kevorkian is testing in the courts. "There's an honest debate going on, especially on the front of physician-assisted suicides," says clinical psychologist David Jobes, of Catholic University in Washington, D.C. "Should we continue to uphold the principle that suicide is never acceptable? That's the hottest evolving area in the field."

Whatever the ethics of suicide, researchers are digging closer to its roots. The 19th-century French founder of sociology, Emile Durkheim, thought the source lay in the ups and downs of society itself. Modern researchers put more emphasis on genes and neurotransmitters. Nor do all agree with assertions that the primary cause is "life stress." Says Dr. David Clark, director of the Center for Suicide Research and Prevention at Chicago's Rush-Presbyterian-St. Luke's Medical Center: "That's the lay public assumption and that's what drives a lot of suicide-prevention work. And it simply doesn't hold water."

Researchers know, says Clark, that there's as much suicide among the rich as there is among the poor and the middle class. They cite a wide range of potential suicide triggers, from loss of employment or loved ones to aging and physical impairment. But, in almost all cases, they agree there is an underlying psychiatric illness—primarily depression, followed by alcoholism and substance abuse. Clinically depressed people are at a 50 percent greater risk of killing themselves. But the doctors can't agree on whether suicidal depression itself is a state of mind or a result of chemical deficiency.

The good news, if there can be any about suicide, is that it's a relatively rare event: 99.9 percent of Americans don't kill themselves; for better or worse, they stick to the rules—the unspoken "covenant" we all have with each other to affirm life even, perhaps, when there's little left to affirm. The figures tend to climb and fall in waves, but they've remained stable in this country since the end of World War II: at the latest count, around 30,000 people took their own lives in 1991. Gender differences have remained fairly steady as well. Females, by around 3 to 1, attempt suicide more often than males, but males, partly because they employ more violent means, are four times more likely to die. It's estimated there are 20 persons who try suicide for every person who tries successfully.

Violence and despair: The rate for teenagers, after climbing steeply for two decades, began leveling off in the mid-1970s—although it's still not dropping as experts had hoped. The only groups going against the grain are black males and the elderly, especially white men over 65—many of them perhaps victims of the loss of status and income incurred with retirement. The increase among blacks, some demographers guess, might be because suicide is part of the continuum of violence and despair

that surrounds many of them. The old are getting older and healthier; their suicide rate dropped through much of the century after 1933. Yet since about 1980, the rate has begun climbing to higher levels. Yeates Conwell, a geriatric psychiatrist at the University of Rochester, conjectures that as they live longer, people are also growing frailer, more isolated, and harder to find and rescue. The suicide rate for the elderly is higher all over the world than it is for teenagers and young adults, says Conwell. "But it is in the U.S. that we find more elderly men committing suicide."

No profile of likely suicides has emerged. However, there are some typical signs to watch for. According to Clark, for instance, in about two thirds of cases there is usually some form of suicidal communication before the actual attempt. Edwin Shneidman, emeritus professor of thanatology at UCLA, who founded the American Association of Suicidology, was also the leading developer of the "psychological autopsy," aimed, among other things, at finding such patterns. Reviewing several years' worth of postmortems, Shneidman and his colleagues at UCLA found that around 90 percent of the suicides left clear behavioral and verbal clues, such as giving away possessions.

Shneidman, although one of the pioneers in the field, has also become one of its mavericks. He objects, for instance, to the emphasis that mainstream suicide researchers place on psychiatric illness, preferring, he says, the Oxford English Dictionary to psychiatry's diagnostic manual. No one dies of depression, he says. "It's not a tenable entry on the death certificate."

As with much of psychiatry these days, the real cutting edge of suicide research is in biochemistry. In the past few years there have been some exciting advances in studies of serotonin, the

ubiquitous neurotransmitter that modulates the action of other brain chemicals. A variety of violent, impulsive behaviors have been associated with low levels of serotonin. And Dr. Frederick Goodwin, head of the National Institute of Mental Health, reports that 22 of 22 autopsy studies of brains and body fluid have also connected low levels of the chemical with suicide. Since the newer antidepressant medications, like Prozac and Zoloft, are aimed specifically at boosting serotonin, Goodwin says, doctors may eventually have a selective way to treat depressions associated with suicidal behavior.

Greater risk: Lately, researchers studying particular types of serotonin-related suicide have discovered they tend to be the more serious attempts—those characterized by careful planning and greater medical damage. According to psychiatrist J. John Mann, head of the NIMH research center at the University of Pittsburgh School of Medicine, studies in Sweden of hospitalized depressives with low serotonin levels found that about 20 percent committed suicide within the year. In another group with normal levels, between 1 and 2 percent killed themselves. "That's a tenfold greater risk," says Mann. It remains unclear why some people have low serotonin levels. Mann believes the reasons could be genetic, developmental or environmental. Not surprisingly, he notes, men tend to have lower levels than women. That may be one of the reasons why two or three men complete suicides

Suicide Weapon

% OF TOTAL NUMBER OF SUICIDES IN U.S. IN 1990

Firearms	61.0
Hanging & Strangulation	14.5
Gas Poisoning	7.5
Other Poisoning	10.0
Other	7.0

SOURCE: BUREAU OF THE CENSUS

Suicide by Race

RATES PER 100,000 IN 1970

White Male	18.0
Black Male	8.0
White Female	7.1
Black Female	2.6

DEATH RATES IN 1980

White Male	19.9
Black Male	10.3
White Female	5.9
Black Female	2.2

DEATH RATES IN 1990

White Male	22.0
Black Male	12.0
White Female	5.3
Black Female	2.3

SOURCE: BUREAU OF THE CENSUS

compared with women. We don't know if it has any relationship to [unsuccessful] attempts."

What researchers do know, says Mann, is that a person's serotonin level reveals "some sort of vulnerability" to suicide. "This is the biggest leap we've made in terms of identifying people at high risk, as well as offering meaningful intervention." The serotonin connection points the way not only to a potential screening technique, but to treatment. By raising serotonin levels, as the newer antidepressants do, researchers believe they can raise the threshold for acting on suicidal impulses. "It's similar to the way we're treating epilepsy today, by raising the threshold at which seizures occur," says Mann. "In the short term, our hypothesis is that antidepressants may reduce your chances of acting on suicidal thoughts. We believe the anti-suicidal effects occur before the anti-depressant effects kick in."

But some treatment may actually increase the risk of suicide. "When a person is profoundly depressed," says Goodwin, "what protects them is, they can't figure out how to kill themselves. Suicide requires energy, and they don't have it." With treatment, the first thing that comes back is energy and functional capacity. "When they become activated and are still depressed, that is a very dangerous period," he says, "so drugs have to be carefully monitored."

While science tries to piece together the suicide puzzle, other forces seem determined to muddle it. Goodwin is irked by such opportunistic books as the best-selling "Final Exit," a kind of how-to manual for would-be suicides, although the way the book was snatched up suggests many people saw no reason to shun such advice. He thinks, also, that the attention given to Kevorkian's suicide machine "trivializes" suicide and ignores the fact that in Western culture it is not looked on as a normal practice. Rather, he says, "people go to enormous lengths to stay alive, even under the worst possible conditions."

On the whole, we *are* life-affirming, but it's an affirmation that often needs boostering. "Every one . . . is bound to preserve himself," wrote the 17th-century English philosopher John Locke, "and not to quit his station willfully." Locke was talking about an obligation to the Creator, but it's also a duty we owe to ourselves, our families and the society we live in.

With MARY HAGER *and* PAT WINGERT *in Washington,* VICKI QUADE *in Chicago,* TESSA NAMUTH *in New York and* JEANNE GORDON *in Los Angeles*

Relating to Others

People in groups can be seen everywhere: couples in love, parents with their children, teachers and students, gatherings of friends, church groups, theatergoers. People have much influence on one another when they congregate in groups. Groups spend a great deal of time communicating with members and nonmembers. The communication can be intentional and forceful, such as when protesters demonstrate against a totalitarian regime. Or communication can be more subtle, for example, when fraternity brothers reject a prospective brother who refuses to wear the symbols of pledging.

In some groups the reason a leader emerges is clear—perhaps the most skilled individual in the group is elected leader by the group members. In other groups, for example during a spontaneous nightclub fire, the rapidly emerging, perhaps self-appointed, leader's qualities are less apparent. Nonetheless the followers flee unquestioningly in the leader's direction.

Some groups such as corporations issue formal rules in writing; discipline for rule breaking is also formalized. Other groups, like families, possess fewer, less formal rules and disciplinary codes. The rules are learned quickly, nevertheless, and are important to all family members.

Some groups are already large but continually seek more members, such as nationalized labor unions. Other groups seek to keep their groups small and somewhat exclusive, like teenage cliques. There exist groups that are almost completely adversarial with other groups. Conflict between youth gangs is receiving much media attention today. Other groups pride themselves on their ability to remain cooperative, such as neighbors who band together in a community crime watch.

Psychologists are so convinced that interpersonal relationships are important to the human experience that they have intensively studied human relations. There is ample evidence that contact with other people is a necessary part of human existence. Research has shown that most individuals do not like being isolated from other people. In fact, in laboratory experiments where subjects experience total isolation for extended periods, they begin to hallucinate the presence of others. In prisons, solitary confinement is often used as a form of punishment because it is so aversive. Other research has shown that people who must wait under stressful circumstances prefer to wait with others, even if the others are total strangers, rather than wait alone.

The unit begins with two articles on interpersonal relations. The first is about competition. Some individuals are destructively and intensely competitive. In "How Competitive Are You?" Josh Halberstam helps the reader identify his or her own level of competitiveness.

We move next to close relationships between brothers and sisters and between friends. "The Secret World of Siblings" explores how siblings interact with each other and how sibling relations are becoming more important in modern society.

Two articles discuss friendship. In the first, "What Friends Are For," the reasons friendships form are examined. Special friendships, such as those between gays and lesbians, are also investigated by the author, Phillip Lopate. Some friends do not remain friends. Friendships end for a variety of reasons. Caroline Knapp discusses why and how friendships end in the article entitled "When the Bond Breaks."

Paul Gray, in "What Is Love?" attempts to disentangle our notions of love. He looks at several definitions of love and concludes that no matter how it is defined, love is found in every studied society. Sometimes love becomes destructive, such as in domestic violence where spouses batter one another. The final article of this unit relates to these "Patterns of Abuse." Who is abused, who the abuser is, why abuse occurs, and other important matters are disclosed.

Looking Ahead: Challenge Questions

Is competitiveness destructive? Should we stop being so competitive? Explain your answers.

The book examines several close relationships, including siblings, friends, and lovers. For each interpersonal relationship, which factors make the relationship better and which make it worse? Are there other interpersonal relationships and processes besides the ones discussed in this anthology that would be important to study in American society?

Do you think that the same social processes are operative in all close relationships? Are they operative in all societies, or do societies differ greatly?

Do you think adult siblings or childhood siblings bicker more? What causes friction between siblings? How can sibling rivalries be better managed? What positive consequences are there to sibling relationships? Historically, how has the role of siblings changed?

Can opposite-sex friends relate to each other as well as same-sex friends? Have you adopted any strategies for making and keeping friends that you could share with others? Do you think men or women have a harder time making friends? Why?

Why do friendships end? Can a wounded friendship be mended? How?

What is it that happy couples do right? Is it true love that makes couples happy? Do you think it is possible to find happiness by oneself (without an intimate partner)? How so? What are the benefits of an intimate relationship? What are the disadvantages? What do couples need to do to develop positive, friendly relationships?

What types of love are there? How is love defined? Why do people fall in love? Do you think there are sex differences in loving relationships? Do you think love is experienced and expressed the same way in other cultures?

What causes domestic violence? Is any type of person or social class immune to it? Who are the abusers? Who are the victims? What can be done to intervene in abusive relationships?

HOW COMPETITIVE ARE YOU?

*Considering the latest psychological research, it's time to
examine your winning ways*

Josh Halberstam

*Josh Halberstam teaches philosophy at New York University; he
[has also written] about vanity for SELF.*

Divide the players into two teams, give each side "horse-shoes" and begin. Sounds like the start of a rousing competition. But in this children's game on a South Seas island, no one ever wins. After the first side throws horseshoes and gets a certain score, the other side tries to get the same number of hits. Both sides keep tossing until they reach an exact tie. The goal of the game is not to win but to draw. No winners, no losers, just happy kids.

Surprisingly enough, cooperative endeavors like this are common in many societies around the world, including those of the Eskimo, New Guineans and the aboriginal people of South Australia. Such games are alien to most Americans, though; as children we learn combative games like dodgeball, football and hockey. Even musical chairs is a brutal competition—one player wins, and everyone else loses. Our culture inculcates the value of competition in us as toddlers; by the time we're adults, we take it for granted.

Indeed, by almost all cross-cultural measures, the United States is among the most competitive countries in the world. (We win the competition for competitiveness.) We turn practically every activity into a contest, replete with awards, trophies and rankings. The children of the Pacific islands play the games they do because their society values and celebrates cooperation; we play the games we do because we value and celebrate competition. (When soccer was introduced in New Guinea, the games always ended in a draw and it took a long time before the players learned to play to win!)

Competition is a fact of life for most of us. Many of our jobs do pit us against each other. And it is often said that our competitive spirit is precisely what has made this country the economic success that it is. Recent data show, however, that too many people just don't know when to stop, and they carry their competitiveness into everything they do.

To compete means to seek or strive for something (a position, possession or reward) for which others are also contending. Competition always involves a reference to others: If you win, someone else loses. This is a situation we find ourselves in regularly. We contend at work for promotions and status; we battle in the gym to own the most lithe body; we vie at parties for appreciative attention; we strive among our friends for the title of most charming and wise. But our truly wrenching rivalries are those closest to home. The competition between mothers and daughters is a perennial theme for a hundred modern novels. And a third of Americans describe their sibling relationships as lifelong competitions. (Brother-to-brother rivalries tend to be more severe than other sibling relationships, and identical-twin brother relationships are the most intense of all.)

Is all this competition harmful? For the most part, the answer is "yes," according to some surprising recent studies by social scientists, psychologists and philosophers. Granted, in our culture, it would be unrealistic to try to eradicate competition; it can't consistently be escaped. (For one thing, society is full of other competitive people.) But it can be controlled. It helps to examine how competition works in your life. It can be something you enjoy engaging in within a defined arena; something you manage to turn off when it's inappropriate, something you feel is constructive for you. Or it can be all consuming, pervasive, out of control—an obsession masquerading as healthy American sportsmanship.

Most of us are convinced that we play better when we want to win. We make that extra effort to look the sexiest of all at that gala, we spend that extra hour on the proposal to win that account. Competition, we assume, provides the needed edge. In fact, the much-heralded competitive spirit often inhibits us from concentrating on and pursuing our interests, and actually results in underachievement. Instead of focusing on winning, research suggests, we need to learn how to establish realistic personal goals and concentrate on individual performance. Unfortunately, it isn't easy.

The first step is often the hardest: to acknowledge your competitiveness. (Few of us admit to being competitive, although we have little problem attributing competitiveness to others.) Perhaps you're unable to walk into a room without wondering whether you are the prettiest, most engaging, smartest. Or you (secretly) take satisfaction in the fact that a colleague has been criticized by the boss. According to the stereotype, women can be especially competitive with one another—*aka* catty—and there is some hard evidence that women do judge other women in positions of power more harshly than they do men in comparable positions. But paradoxically, women are also very uncomfortable competing with each other. Laura Tracy, author of *The Secret Between Us*, a study of female rivalry, concludes that "their most intense and highly charged relationships existed in the context of competition. . . . But [competition] is a connection that must be kept secret, especially from ourselves."

The result of a life devoted to competition is perpetual uncertainty, exhaustion and not a little bitterness.

If female competitiveness is a secret, it is quickly becoming a secret all around the block. Fifty-six percent of white-collar jobs are now held by women, and those include jobs in the most so-called cutthroat, adversarial professions. The jury is still out on whether the increasing presence of women in top management positions will change the competitive atmosphere of corporate America, but this is no longer a subject women can avoid. Whether at work or at home, the chances are that you are participating in some serious competition. Recognize it.

The second hurdle is the refusal to take responsibility for your competitiveness. It is always a choice. Loretta works at a leading investment house and readily admits to her desire to win. But she doesn't believe it's something she chooses. "Look," she says, "I work in a combat zone. I compete to survive here. The truth is that we all do, everywhere. Competitiveness is a basic, natural human condition."

We hear this message repeatedly: "It's a jungle out there, a dog-eat-dog world where the only rule is the survival of the fittest." We watch nature clips of leopards pouncing on their prey and conclude that that's the way the world works. In fact, it's only a small part of reality. Nature exhibits at least as much evidence of cooperation as competitiveness. And interestingly enough, testosterone, the hormone responsible for aggressiveness, increases at the end of a fight and not at the beginning, suggesting that competition makes us aggressive rather than that natural aggression makes us competitive. As noted naturalist Stephen Jay Gould points out, "The equation of competition with success in natural selection is merely cultural prejudice."

It certainly isn't human nature to be competitive; anthropologists report on societies all over the world in which our style of contending is viewed as exceedingly rude and uncaring. But we aren't naturally cooperative either. Humans can and do cut it both ways. Loretta works in a fiercely competitive environment and has to struggle to succeed. But this isn't true for all our jobs, and even in Loretta's case, she *is* making a choice. So if you are competitive, you can't blame it on your genes.

A third obstacle to controlling the competition in your life is the widespread notion that competition leads to improved performance. *Competition leads to inferior performance; striving for self-mastery produces results.* It isn't really the desire to win that gets you to play extra hard at Scrabble or makes you lunge for those tough returns in your squash games. It's the desire to master a well-defined goal: You want to find a word for that triple and won't, as usual, settle for less, or you're determined to get that backhand finally working well. Internal motivation is, it turns out, a far more effective incentive than exterior motivation.

This seems to be true in all areas of human endeavor, and numerous studies indicate that it is especially true in education and artistic development. In one classic study, reported in *Personality and Social Psychology Bulletin* in 1978, seven-to-11-year-old girls were asked to make "silly" collages, some competing for prizes and some not. A panel of professional artists independently rated their work with the result that "those children who competed for prizes made collages that were significantly less creative than those made by children in the control group." Children in the competitive condition produced works judged to be less spontaneous, less complex and less varied.

The same pattern emerges with adults. In one landmark study, Robert L. Helmreich, Ph.D., professor of psychology at the University of Texas, Austin, examined the publishing records of more than one hundred Ph.D.'s in science. Those who rated high on the scale of interest in work and self-mastery produced significantly more quality work than those who ranked high on the competitive scale. He found the same results with undergraduate students, airline pilots, reservations agents and seven other professions. The most startling finding comes from recent research in business conducted by Janet Spence, Ph.D., professor of psychology, also at the University of Texas, Austin. Dr. Spence found that performance-oriented business executives earned 16 percent more money than those motivated by competition. This result makes sense when you consider that businesspeople locked into a competitive mind-set tend to have a greater fear of failure, are content with just winning and therefore take fewer creative risks and enjoy their work less.

Some of the most intriguing recent studies of competitiveness come, not surprisingly, from sports psychologists. We all grew up hearing slogans such as Vince Lombardi's "Winning isn't everything, it's the only thing" or Leo Durocher's "Show me a good loser and I'll show you a loser." But here again, this research refutes popular assumptions. Athletes who pay attention to personal performance goals—to shoot 70 percent from the free-throw line, say, or run a mile 20 seconds faster than they did the previous month—shoot better and run faster than athletes who just concentrate on beating their opponents.

Other studies indicate that athletes who focus on skill mastery tend to attribute their success more directly to their own efforts and make fewer excuses for poor performance than do athletes who are devoted to being victorious. This also happens elsewhere in our lives—people overly concerned with winning invariably make excuses for losing.

But isn't competition fun? It is, for some—not for most. It has a way of draining the *playfulness* from any activity—sports, music, even conversation. Losing isn't fun, and in most competitions, more than half of the competitors lose—think of beauty-pageant contestants, and the many applicants for a single job.

So what are we to conclude from all this research? That you should avoid all competitive "I win–you lose" interactions? Precisely, says Tufts professor Alfie Kohn in his influential book *No Contest:* " 'Healthy competition' is a contradiction in terms."

But not all experts agree. To some, it's a matter of degree and attitude. Ivan Bresgi, Ph.D., a New York City psychotherapist who is also a competitive swimmer and rugby player, cautions against undervaluing competitiveness: "The problem occurs when you focus *entirely* on winning. For one thing, that always involves an accompanying focus on losing. But the desire to win is helpful in combination with other internal motivations. Your opponent can provide you with strong, clear goals that can inspire you to do even better."

It's helpful to distinguish between constructive and destructive competition, between fair play and dirty tricks. Receiving the "salesperson of the month" prize is a reward for your hard work. But you can't justifiably feel pleased about the award if you won it by surreptitiously sabotaging the efforts of your coworkers.

The key here is to remember that competitiveness is determined by your attitude, not by the activity. For you, the morning jog is about exercise; for Sally, it's a contest to see who has greater stamina. You stay late at work because you need to get your project done; Michael stays late to prove how dedicated he is. You can avoid getting trapped in destructive competitions by keeping a few things in mind:

1. Attend to your own goals, not to beating someone else. When the very best people in any profession talk about their motivation, they always refer to the work itself, rarely about outdoing others. Whether the pursuit is running your business, running the marathon or performing your duties as a daughter or a friend, determine what you want to accomplish and then pursue that goal. Use winning only as a temporary marker to judge your progress, not as an end in itself. In other words, *stop comparing yourself with others*. The end of that road is incessant envy and frustration.

2. Don't tangle with the obsessively competitive. Sure, it's easy to cooperate with cooperative individuals, but what happens when you interact with competitive people? Invariably, you get sucked into their game.

Take Mark, for example. Mark turns every discussion into a competition. He thinks the only interesting conversation is an argument. And even though you're aware of his ploy, you always find yourself trapped in useless debates with him. Or think of your sister. You just want to get Mom a gift for her birthday, but your sister is turning the event into a contest: Who is the more devoted daughter? Somehow, your sister always manages to get you to compete with her.

Decision theorist Thomas Gilovich explains: "Because competitive behavior creates more of a demand for the other person to respond in kind than does cooperation, a competitive person's belief that the world is full of selfish opportunities will always be confirmed, whereas the less gloomy orientation of cooperative individuals will not." In other words, if someone wants to make every interaction a contest, nothing will stop him. But *you* don't have to be a victim and you don't have to engage in the contest. Avoid discussions with the likes of Mark, unless he's willing to have a real talk, not a litigation. It's trickier, of course, with the subtle competitions between family members. But even here, you can lay down the rules: Here's what you're going to do, and your sister can do what she likes. You won't compete.

3. Learn how to manage competition so that it is as cooperative and constructive as possible. The Latin root of the word competition, *competere*, provides a useful clue here. It means "to strive together." When you compete with an ally, there are no losers. Both you and your supportive tennis opponent are really on the same side—you both want to improve your game and have fun. You help pace each other instead of spending your energies calling each others' faults. This is a useful strategy for the workplace as well. Even though only one of you may get the promotion, you can help each other raise the overall quality of your output—and everyone gains in the end.

Most competitions are structured as what economists call zero-sum games—what you win the other person loses (poker is a good example). But keep in mind that much of the best stuff in life is not scarce. There's enough parental love for all children; you can share your friendships, ideas and interests without anyone losing out. The result of a life devoted to competition is perpetual uncertainty, exhaustion and not a little bitterness. So if you're competing more than you think might be good for you, ask yourself what you're trying to prove—and to whom.

The
Secret World
of Siblings

Emotional ambivalence often marks the most enduring relationship in life

They have not been together like this for years, the three of them standing on the close-cropped grass, New England lawns and steeples spread out below the golf course. He is glad to see his older brothers, has always been glad to have "someone to look up to, to do things with." Yet he also knows the silences between them, the places he dares not step, even though they are all grown men now. They move across the greens, trading small talk, joking. But at the 13th hole, he swings at the ball, duffs it and his brothers begin to needle him. "I should be better than this," he thinks. Impatiently, he swings again, misses, then angrily grabs the club and breaks it in half across his knee. Recalling this outburst later, he explains, simply: "They were beating me again."

As an old man, Leo Tolstoy once opined that the simplest relationships in life are those between brother and sister. He must have been delirious at the time. Even lesser mortals, lacking Tolstoy's acute eye and literary skill, recognize the power of the word *sibling* to reduce normally competent, rational human beings to raw bundles of anger, love, hurt, longing and disappointment—often in a matter of minutes. Perhaps they have heard two elderly sisters dig at each other's sore spots with astounding accuracy, much as they did in junior high. Or have seen a woman corner her older brother at a family reunion, finally venting 30 years of pent-up resentment. Or watched remorse and yearning play across a man's face as he speaks of the older brother whose friendship was chased away long ago, amid dinner table taunts of "Porky Pig, Porky Pig, oink, oink, oink!"

Sibling relationships—and 80 percent of Americans have at least one—outlast marriages, survive the death of parents, resurface after quarrels that would sink any friendship. They flourish in a thousand incarnations of closeness and distance, warmth, loyalty and distrust. Asked to describe them, more than a few people stammer and hesitate, tripped up by memory and sudden bursts of unexpected emotion.

Traditionally, experts have viewed siblings as "very minor actors on the stage of human development," says Stephen Bank, Wesleyan University psychologist and co-author of *The Sibling Bond*. But a rapidly expanding body of research is showing that what goes on in the playroom or in the kitchen while dinner is being cooked exerts a profound influence on how children grow, a contribution that approaches, if it may not quite equal, that of parenting. Sibling relationships shape how people feel about themselves, how they understand and feel about others, even how much they achieve. And more often than not, such ties represent the lingering thumbprint of childhood upon adult life, affecting the way people interact with those closest to them, with friends and coworkers, neighbors and spouses—a topic explored by an increasing number of popular books, including *Mom Loved You Best*, the most recent offering by Dr. William and Mada Hapworth and Joan Heilman.

Shifting landscape. In a 1990s world of shifting social realities, of working couples, disintegrating marriages, "blended" households, disappearing grandparents and families spread across a continent, this belated validation of the importance of sibling influences probably comes none too soon. More and more children are stepping in to change diapers, cook meals and help with younger siblings' homework in the hours when parents are still at the office. Baby boomers, edging into middle age, find themselves squaring off once again with brothers and sisters over the care of dying parents or the division of inheritance. And in a generation where late marriages and fewer children are the norm, old age may become for many a time when siblings—not devoted sons and daughters—sit by the bedside.

It is something that happened so long ago, so silly and unimportant now that she is 26 and a researcher at a large, downtown office and her younger brother is her best friend, really, so close that she talks to him at least once a week. Yet as she begins to speak she is suddenly a 5-year-old again on

Christmas morning, running into the living room in her red flannel pajamas, her straight blond hair in a ponytail. He hasn't even wrapped it, the little, yellow-flowered plastic purse. Racing to the tree, he brings it to her, thrusts it at her—"Here's your present, Jenny!"—smiling that stupid, adoring, little brother smile. She takes the purse and hurls it across the room. "I don't want your stupid present," she yells. A small crime, long ago forgiven. Yet she says: "I still feel tremendously guilty about it."

Sigmund Freud, perhaps guided by his own childhood feelings of rivalry, conceived of siblingship as a story of unremitting jealousy and competition. Yet, observational studies of young children, many of them the groundbreaking work of Pennsylvania State University psychologist Judy Dunn and her colleagues, suggest that while rivalry between brothers and sisters is common, to see only hostility in sibling relations is to miss the main show. The arrival of a younger sibling may cause distress to an older child accustomed to parents' exclusive attention, but it also stirs enormous interest, presenting both children with the opportunity to learn crucial social and cognitive skills: how to comfort and empathize with another person, how to make jokes, resolve arguments, even how to irritate.

The lessons in this life tutorial take as many forms as there are children and parents. In some families, a natural attachment seems to form early between older and younger children. Toddlers as young as 14 months miss older siblings when they are absent, and babies separated briefly from their mothers will often accept comfort from an older sibling and go back to playing happily. As the younger child grows, becoming a potential playmate, confidant and sparring partner, older children begin to pay more attention. But even young children monitor their siblings' behavior closely, showing a surprisingly sophisticated grasp of their actions and emotional states.

Parental signals. To some extent, parents set the emotional tone of early sibling interactions. Dunn's work indicates, for example, that children whose mothers encourage them to view a newborn brother or sister as a human being, with needs, wants and feelings, are friendlier to the new arrival over the next year, an affection that is later reciprocated by the younger child. The quality of parents' established relationships with older siblings can also influence how a new younger brother or sister is received. In another of Dunn's studies, first-born daughters who enjoyed a playful, intense relationship with their mothers treated newborn siblings with more hostility, and a year later the younger children were more hostile in return. In contrast, older daughters with more contentious relationships with their mothers greeted the newcomer enthusiastically—perhaps relieved to have an ally. Fourteen months later, these older sisters were more likely to imitate and play with their younger siblings and less apt to hit them or steal their toys.

In troubled homes, where a parent is seriously ill, depressed or emotionally unavailable, siblings often grow closer than they might in a happier environment, offering each other solace and protection. This is not always the case, however. When parents are on the brink of separation or have already divorced and remarried, says University of Virginia psychologist E. Mavis Hetherington, rivalry between brothers and sisters frequently increases, as they struggle to hold on to their parents' affection in the face of the breakup. If anything, it is sisters who are likely to draw together in a divorcing family, while brothers resist forming tighter bonds. Says Hetherington: "Males tend to go it alone and not to use support very well."

Pretend play is never wasted. Toddlers who engage regularly in make-believe activity with older siblings later show a precocious grasp of others' behavior.

Much of what transpires between brothers and sisters, of course, takes place when parents are not around. "Very often the parent doesn't see the subtlety or the full cycle of siblings' interactions," says University of Hartford psychologist Michael Kahn. Left to their own devices, children tease, wrestle and play make-believe. They are the ones eager to help pilot the pirate ship or play storekeeper to their sibling's impatient customer. And none of this pretend play, researchers find, is wasted. Toddlers who engage regularly in make-believe with older siblings later show a precocious grasp of others' behavior. Says Dunn: "They turn out to be the real stars at understanding people."

Obviously, some degree of rivalry and squabbling between siblings is natural. Yet in extreme cases, verbal or physical abuse at the hands of an older brother or sister can leave scars that last well into adulthood. Experts like Wesleyan University's Bank distinguish between hostility that takes the form of humiliation or betrayal and more benign forms of conflict. From the child's perspective, the impact of even normal sibling antagonism may depend in part on who's coming out ahead. In one study, for example, children showed higher self-esteem when they "delivered" more teasing, insults and other negative behaviors to their siblings than they received. Nor is even intense rivalry necessarily destructive. Says University of Texas psychologist Duane Buhrmester: "You may not be happy about a brother or sister who is kind of pushing you along, but you may also get somewhere in life."

They are two sides of an equation written 30 years ago: Michèle, with her raven-black hair, precisely made-up lips, restrained smile; Arin, two years older, her easy laugh filling the restaurant, the sleeves of her gray turtleneck pulled over her hands.

This is what Arin thinks about Michèle: "I have always resented her, and she has always looked up to me. When we were younger, she used to copy me, which would drive me crazy. We have nothing in common except our family history—isn't that terrible? I like her spirit of generosity, her direction and ambition. I dislike her vapid conversation and her idiotic friends. But the reality is that we are very close, and we always will be."

This is what Michèle sees: "Arin was my ideal. I wanted to be like her, to look like her. I think I drove her crazy. Once, I gave her a necklace I thought was very beautiful. I never saw her wear it. I think it wasn't good enough, precious enough. We are so different—I wish that we could be more like friends. But as we get older, we accept each other more."

It is something every brother or sister eventually marvels at, a conundrum that novelists have played upon in a thousand different ways: There are two children. They grow up in the same house, share the same parents, experience many of the same events. Yet they are stubbornly, astonishingly different.

Two children grow up in the same house, share the same parents, experience many of the same events. Yet they are stubbornly, astonishingly different.

A growing number of studies in the relatively new field of behavioral genetics are finding confirmation for this popular observation. Children raised in the same family, such studies find, are only very slightly more similar to each other on a variety of personality dimensions than they are, say, to Bill Clinton or to the neighbor's son. In cognitive abilities, too, siblings appear more different than alike. And the extent to which siblings *do* resemble one another in these traits is largely the result of the genes they share—a conclusion drawn from twin studies, comparisons of biological siblings raised apart and biological children and adopted siblings raised together.

Contrasts. Heredity also contributes to the *differences* between siblings. About 30 percent of the dissimilarity between brothers and sisters on many personality dimensions can be accounted for by differing genetic endowments from parents. But that still leaves 70 percent that *cannot* be attributed to genetic causes, and it is this unexplained portion of contrasting traits that scientists find so intriguing. If two children who grow up in the same family are vastly different, and genetics accounts for only a minor part of these differences, what else is going on?

The answer may be that brothers and sisters don't really share the same family at all. Rather, each child grows up in a unique family, one shaped by the way he perceives other people and events, by the chance happenings he alone experiences, and by how other people—

parents, siblings and teachers—perceive and act toward him. And while for decades experts in child development have focused on the things that children in the same family share—social class, child-rearing attitudes and parents' marital satisfaction, for example—what really seem to matter are those things that are not shared. As Judy Dunn and Pennsylvania State behavioral geneticist Robert Plomin write in *Separate Lives: Why Siblings Are So Different*, "Environmental factors important to development are those that two children in the same family experience differently."

Asked to account for children's disparate experiences, most people invoke the age-old logic of birth order. "I'm the middle child, so I'm cooler headed," they will say, or "Firstborns are high achievers." Scientists, too, beginning with Sir Francis Galton in the 19th century, have sought in birth order a way to characterize how children diverge in personality, IQ or life success. But in recent years, many researchers have backed away from this notion, asserting that when family size, number of siblings and social class are taken into account, the explanatory power of birth ranking becomes negligible. Says one psychologist: "You wouldn't want to make a decision about your child based on it."

At least one researcher, however, argues that birth order does exert a strong influence on development, particularly on attitudes toward authority. Massachusetts Institute of Technology historian Frank Sulloway, who has just completed a 20-year analysis of 4,000 scientists from Copernicus through the 20th century, finds that those with older siblings were significantly more likely to have contributed to or supported radical scientific revolutions, such as Darwin's theory of evolution. Firstborn scientists, in contrast, were more apt to champion conservative scientific ideas. "Later-borns are consistently more open-minded, more intellectually flexible and therefore more radical," says Sulloway, adding that later-borns also tend to be more agreeable and less competitive.

Many people believe in the logic of birth order. "I'm the middle child, so I'm cooler headed," they will say, or "Firstborns are high achievers."

Hearthside inequities. Perhaps most compelling for scientists who study sibling relationships are the ways in which parents treat their children differently and the inequalities children perceive in their parents' behavior. Research suggests that disparate treatment by parents can have a lasting effect, even into adulthood. Children who receive more affection from fathers than their siblings do, for example, appear to aim their sights higher in terms of education and professional goals, according to a study by University of Southern California psychologist

SIMIAN SIBLINGS
Mixed feelings in the treetops

Humans are not alone in having to deal with the ambivalence of sibling relationships. According to a growing body of scientific research simian siblings, too, carry on the subtle dances of cooperation and competition, generosity and animosity well known to any human brother or sister.

Conflict is actually more common—though less intense—among primate siblings than among non-kin, according to Lynn Fairbanks, a University of California at Los Angeles research psychologist and co-editor of the recent book *Juvenile Primates*. "It doesn't get to the Cain and Abel stage," she notes, but juvenile and adolescent brothers and sisters do battle regularly for their mother's attention and then for their own place in society, biting and kicking, interrupting grooming sessions, even pushing a suckling infant off the mother's nipple.

Brother's keeper. In the midst of this conflict, however, primate siblings do cooperate—grooming, sharing food and playing together. In the face of external threats, siblings often protect one another with a direct attack or an alarm call. Becky, a brave Barbary macaque, even threatened a larger male to rescue her 2-month-old brother from danger. Some monkeys have even been known to "adopt" an infant sibling when the mother dies.

Both cooperation and conflict have roots in evolution, say scientists. In the Darwinian jungle, primates (like other animals) struggle ultimately to pass on their genes, about half of which they share with their siblings. With limited resources and constant external threats, they first try to secure their own survival, compromising siblings when necessary. But it also pays to aid brothers and sisters, since a rescuer is indirectly protecting and passing on a shared heredity. "Genes are thicker than water," notes Cornell University anthropologist Meredith Small.

Much like their human counterparts, simian sibs cycle in and out of affection and animosity. Whether on the jungle gym or the jungle floor, says UCLA's Fairbanks, "siblings have the most positive and the most negative relationships."

BY BETSY WAGNER

Laura Baker. Seven year-olds treated by their mothers in a less affectionate, more controlling way than their brothers or sisters are apt to be more anxious and depressed. And adolescents who say their parents favor a sibling over themselves are more likely to report angry and depressed feelings.

Parental favoritism spills into sibling relationships, too, sometimes breeding the hostility made famous by the Smothers Brothers in their classic 1960s routine, "Mom always loved you best." In families where parents are more punitive and restrictive toward one child, for instance that child is more likely to act in an aggressive, rivalrous and unfriendly manner toward a brother or sister, according to work by Hetherington. Surprisingly, it may not matter who is favored. Children in one study were more antagonistic toward siblings even when *they* were the ones receiving preferential treatment.

Many parents, of course, go to great lengths to distribute their love and attention equally. Yet even the most consciously egalitarian parenting may be seen as unequal by children of different ages. A mother may treat her 4-year-old boy with the same care and attention she lavished on her older son when he was 4. But from the 7-year-old's perspective, it may look like his younger brother is getting a better deal. Nor is there much agreement among family members on how evenhandedly love is apportioned: Adolescents report favoritism when their mothers and fathers insist that none exists. Some parents express surprise that their children feel unequally treated, while at the same time they describe how one child is more demanding, another needs more discipline. And siblings almost never agree in their assessments of who, exactly, Mom loves best.

Strong friendships between siblings become less intense after adolescence, diluted by geography, marriage, child-rearing concerns and careers.

Nature vs. nurture. Further complicating the equation is the contribution of heredity to temperament, each child presenting a different challenge from the moment of birth. Plomin, part of a research team led by George Washington University psychiatrist David Reiss that is studying sibling pairs in 700 families nationwide, views the differences between siblings as emerging from a complex interaction of nature and nurture. In this scheme, a more aggressive and active child, for example, might engage in more conflict with parents and later

ONLY CHILDREN
Cracking the myth of the pampered, lonely misfit

Child-rearing experts may have neglected the psychology of sibling ties, but they have never been hesitant to warn parents about the perils of siring a single child. Children unlucky enough to grow up without brothers or sisters, the professional wisdom held, were bound to be self-centered, unhappy, anxious, demanding, pampered and generally maladjusted to the larger social world. "Being an only child is a disease in itself," psychologist G. Stanley Hall concluded at the turn of the century.

Recent research paints a kinder picture of the only child—a welcome revision at a time when single-child families are increasing. The absence of siblings, psychologists find, does not doom children to a life of neurosis or social handicap. Day care, preschool and other modern child-care solutions go far in combatting an only child's isolation and in mitigating the willfulness and self-absorption that might come from being the sole focus of parental attention. And while only children may miss out on some positive aspects of growing up around brothers and sisters, they also escape potentially negative experiences, such as unequal parenting or severe aggression by an older sibling. Says University of Texas at Austin social psychologist Toni Falbo: "The view of only children as selfish and lonely is a gross exaggeration of reality."

Indeed, Falbo goes so far as to argue that only children are often better off—at least in some respects—than those with brothers and sisters. Reviewing over 200 studies conducted since 1925, she and her colleague Denise Polit conclude that only children equal firstborns in intelligence and achievement, and score higher than both firstborns and later-borns with siblings on measures of maturity and leadership. Other researchers dispute these findings, however. Comparing only children with firstborns over their life span, for example, University of California at Berkeley psychologist B. G. Rosenberg found that only children—particularly females—scored lower on intelligence tests than did firstborns with a sibling.

Rosenberg distinguishes between three types of only children. "Normal, well-adjusted" onlies, he says, are assertive, poised and gregarious. "Impulsive, acting out" only children adhere more to the old stereotype, their scores on personality tests indicating they are thin-skinned, self-indulgent and self-dramatizing. The third group resembles the firstborn children of larger families, scoring as dependable, productive and fastidious.

Perhaps the only real disadvantage to being an only child comes not in childhood but much later in life. Faced with the emotional and financial burdens of caring for aging parents, those without siblings have no one to help out. But as Falbo points out, even in large families such burdens are rarely distributed equally.

---

become a problem child at school. A quieter, more timid child might receive gentler parenting and later be deemed an easy student.

In China, long ago, it was just the two of them, making dolls out of straw together in the internment camp, putting on their Sunday clothes to go to church with their mother. She mostly ignored her younger sister, or goaded her relentlessly for being so quiet. By the time they were separated—her sister sailing alone at 13 for the United States—there was already a wall between them, a prelude to the stiff Christmas cards they exchange, the rebuffed phone calls, the impersonal gifts that arrive in the mail.

Now, when the phone rings, she is wishing hard for a guardian angel, for someone to take away the pain that throbs beneath the surgical bandage on her chest, keeping her curled under the blue and white cotton coverlet. She picks up the receiver, recognizes her sister's voice instantly, is surprised, grateful, cautious all at once. How could it be otherwise after so many years? It is the longest they have spoken in 50 years. And across the telephone wire, something is shifting, melting in the small talk about children, the wishes for speedy recovery. "I

think we both realized that life can be very short," she says. Her pain, too, is dulling now, moving away as she listens to her sister's voice. She begins to say a small prayer of thanks.

For a period that seems to stretch forever in the timelessness of childhood, there is only the family, only the others who are unchosen partners, their affection, confidences, attacks and betrayals defining the circumference of a limited world. But eventually, the boundaries expand, friends and schoolmates taking the place of brothers and sisters, highways and airports leading to other lives, to office parties and neighborhood meetings, to other, newer families.

Adult bonds. Rivalry between siblings wanes after adolescence, or at least adults are less apt to admit competitive feelings. Strong friendships also become less intense, diluted by geography, by marriage, by the concerns of raising children and pursuing independent careers. In national polls, 65 percent of Americans say they would like to see their siblings more often than the typical "two or three times a year." And University of Indianapolis psychologist Victoria Bedford finds, in her work, that men and women of child-rearing age often show longing toward siblings, especially those close in age and of the same sex. Yet for some people, the detachment of adulthood brings relief, an escape from bonds that are largely unwanted but never entirely go away. Says one woman about her brothers and sisters: "Our values are different, our politics diametrically opposed. I don't feel very connected, but there's still a pressure to keep up the tie, a kind of guilt that I don't have a deeper sense of kinship."

How closely sibling ties are maintained and nurtured varies with cultural and ethnic expectations. In one survey, for example, 54 percent of low-income blacks reported receiving help from a brother or sister, in comparison with 44 percent of low-income Hispanics and 36 percent of low-income whites. Siblings in large families are also more likely to give and receive support, as are those who live in close geographical proximity to one another. Sex differences are also substantial. In middle and later life, sisters are much more likely than brothers to keep up close relationships.

So important, in fact, is the role that sisters play in cementing family ties that some families all but fall apart without them. They are the ones who often play the major role in caring for aging parents and who make sure family members stay in touch after parents die. And in later life, says Purdue University psychologist Victor Cicirelli, sisters can provide a crucial source of reassurance and emotional security for their male counterparts. In one study, elderly men with sisters reported greater feelings of happiness and less worry about their life circumstances.

Warmth or tolerance? Given the mixed emotions many adults express about sibling ties, it is striking that in national surveys the vast majority—more than 80 percent—deem their relationships with siblings to be "warm and affectionate." Yet this statistic may simply reflect the fact that ambivalence is tolerated more easily at a distance, warmth and affection less difficult to muster for a few days a year than on a daily basis. Nor are drastic breaches between siblings—months or years of silence, with no attempt at rapprochement—unheard of. One man, asked by a researcher about his brother, shouted, "Don't mention that son of a bitch to me!" and slammed the door in the psychologist's face.

Sibling feuds often echo much earlier squabbles and are sparked by similar collisions over shared responsibility or resources—who is doing more for an ailing parent, how inheritance should be divided. Few are long lasting, and those that are probably reflect more severe emotional disturbance. Yet harmonious or antagonistic patterns established in childhood make themselves felt in many adults' lives. Says psychologist Kahn: "This is not just kid stuff that people outgrow." One woman, for example, competes bitterly with a slightly older co-worker, just as she did with an older brother growing up. Another suspects that her sister married a particular man in part to impress her. A scientist realizes that he argues with his wife in exactly the same way he used to spar with an older brother.

For most people, a time comes when it makes sense to rework and reshape such "frozen images" of childhood—to borrow psychologist Bank's term—into designs more accommodating to adult reality, letting go of ancient injuries, repairing damaged fences. In a world of increasingly tenuous family connections, such renegotiation may be well worth the effort. Says author Judith Viorst, who has written of sibling ties: "There is no one else on Earth with whom you share so much personal history."

ERICA E. GOODE

What friends are for

They offer the noblest and most delightful of gifts

Phillip Lopate

Family Therapy Networker

Is there anything left to say about friendship after so many great essayists have picked over the bones of the subject? Aristotle and Cicero, Seneca and Montaigne, Francis Bacon and Samuel Johnson, William Hazlitt, Ralph Waldo Emerson, and Charles Lamb have all taken their cracks at it.

Friendship has been called "love without wings." On the other hand, the Stoic definition of love ("Love is the attempt to form a friendship inspired by beauty") seems to suggest that friendship came first. Certainly a case can be made that the buildup of affection and the yearning for more intimacy, without the release of sexual activity, keeps friends in a state of sweet-sorrowful itchiness that has the romantic quality of a love affair. We know that a falling-out between two old friends can leave a deeper and more perplexing hurt than the ending of a love affair, perhaps because we are more pessimistic about the affair's endurance from the start.

Our first attempted friendships are within the family. It is here we practice the techniques of listening sympathetically and proving that we can be trusted, and learn the sort of kindness we can expect in return.

There is something tainted about these family friendships, however. My sister, in her insecure adolescent phase, told me, "You love me because I'm related to you, but if you were to meet me for the first time at a party, you'd think I was a jerk and not worth being your friend." She had me in a bind: I had no way of testing her hypothesis. I should have argued that even if our bond was not freely chosen, our decision to work on it had been. Still, we are quick to dismiss the partiality of our family members when they tell us we are talented, cute, or lovable; we must go out into the world and seduce others.

It is just a few short years from the promiscuity of the sandbox to the tormented, possessive feelings of a fifth grader who has just learned that his best and only friend is playing at another classmate's house after school. There may be worse betrayals in store, but probably none is more influential than the sudden fickleness of an elementary school friend who has dropped us for someone more popular after all our careful, patient wooing. Often we lose no time inflicting

On a rainy day long ago, a tall, skinny girl with an open smile walked up to me during recess and asked me to play. Her invitation marked the beginning of a friendship that has spanned four states, three marriages, and 30 years. Although we've been separated for most of those years, when we're reunited we can talk for five days straight. Kindred spirits, she called us when we were 11, using our favorite heroine's phrase from *Anne of Green Gables*, and kindred spirits we have remained.

I couldn't have known at 11, of course, how precious this kind of friendship is, and how rarely I would find it in my life. But most people, if they're lucky, will find a kindred spirit or two, and their lives are much richer for it.

Despite the importance of our friendships, we generally take them for granted, giving our best time and attention to family, lovers, and jobs, fitting friends in between the cracks, assuming they'll still be there for us when we need them.

In a tribute then, to friendship, we offer a few reflections on that most overlooked and most vital of relationships.

—L.L.

the same betrayal on someone else, just to ensure that we have got the victimization dynamic right.

What makes friendships in childhood and adolescence so poignant is that we need the chosen comrade to be everything in order to rescue us from the gothic inwardness of family life. Even if we are lucky enough to have several companions, there must be a Best Friend.

I clung to the romance of the Best Friend all through high school, college, and beyond, until my circle of university friends began to disperse. At that point, in my mid-20s, I also acted out the dark, competitive side of friendship that can exist between two young men fighting for a place in life and love by doing the one unforgivable thing: sleeping with my best friend's girl. I was baffled at first that there was no way to repair the damage. I lost this friendship forever, and came away from that debacle much more aware of the amount of

From *Utne Reader,* September/October 1993, pp. 78-84. Originally from *Family Therapy Networker,* September/October 1990. Taken from *Against Joie de Vivre.* © 1989 by Phillip Lopate. Reprinted by permission of Pocket Books, a division of Simon & Schuster, Inc.

injury that friendship can and cannot sustain. Perhaps I needed to prove to myself that friendship was not an all-permissive resilient bond, like a mother's love, but something quite fragile. Precisely because best friendship promotes such a merging of identities, such seeming boundarylessness, the first major transgression of trust can cause the injured party to feel he is fighting for his violated soul against his darkest enemy. There is not much room to maneuver in a best friendship between unlimited intimacy and unlimited mistrust.

Still, it was not until the age of 30 that I reluctantly abandoned the best friend expectation and took up a more pluralistic model. At present, I cherish a dozen friends for their unique personalities, without asking that any one be my soul-twin. Whether this alteration constitutes a movement toward maturity or toward cowardly pragmatism is not for me to say. It may be that, in refusing to depend so much on any one friend, I am opting for self-protection over intimacy. Or it may be that, as we advance into middle age, the life problem becomes less that of establishing a tight dyadic bond and more one of making our way in a broader world, "society." Indeed, since Americans have so indistinct a notion of society, we often try to put a network of friendships in its place.

If a certain intensity is lost in the pluralistic model of friendship, there is also the gain of being able to experience all of one's potential, half-buried selves, through witnessing all the spectacle of the multiple fates of our friends. As it happens, the harem of friends, so tantalizing a notion, often translates into feeling pulled in a dozen different directions, with the guilty sense of having disappointed everyone a little. It is also a risky, contrived enterprise to try to make one's friends behave in a friendly manner toward each other. If the effort fails, one feels obliged to mediate; if it succeeds too well, one is jealous.

Whether friendship is intrinsically singular and exclusive or plural and democratic is a question that has vexed many commentators. Aristotle distinguished three types of friendship: "friendship based on utility," such as businessmen cultivating each other for benefit; "friendship based on pleasure," like young people interested in partying; and "perfect friendship." The first two categories Aristotle calls "qualified and superficial friendships," because they are founded on circumstances that could easily change. The last, which is based on admiration for another's good character, is more permanent, but also rarer, because good men "are few." Cicero, who wrote perhaps the best treatise on friendship, also insisted that what brings true friends together is "a mutual belief in each other's goodness." This insistence on virtue as a precondition for true friendship may strike us as impossibly demanding: Who, after all, feels himself good nowadays? And yet, if I am honest, I must admit that the friendships of mine that have lasted longest have been with those whose integrity, or humanity, or strength to bear their troubles I continue to admire. Conversely, when I lost respect for someone, however winning he or she otherwise remained, the friendship petered away almost immediately. "Remove respect from friendship," said Cicero, "and you have taken away the most splendid ornament it possesses."

Friendship is a long conversation. I suppose I could imagine a nonverbal friendship revolving around shared physical work or sport, but for me, good talk is the point of the thing. Indeed, the ability to generate conversation by the hour is the most promising indication, during the uncertain early stages, that a possible friendship will take hold. In the first few conversations there may be an exaggeration of agreement, as both parties angle for adhesive surfaces. But later on, trust builds through the courage to assert disagreement, through the tactful acceptance that differences of opinion will have to remain.

Some view like-mindedness as both the precondition and the product of friendship. Myself, I distrust it. I have one friend who keeps assuming that we see the world eye-to-eye. She is intent on enrolling us in a flattering aristocracy of taste, on the short "we" list against the ignorant "they." Sometimes I do not have the strength to fight her need for consensus with my own stubborn disbelief in the existence of any such inner circle of privileged, cultivated sensibility. Perhaps I have too much invested in a view of myself as idiosyncratic to be eager to join any coterie, even a coterie of two. What attracts me to friends' conversation is the give and take, not necessarily that we come out at the same point.

"Our tastes and aims and views were identical—and that is where the essence of a friendship must always lie," wrote Cicero. To some extent, perhaps, but then the convergence must be natural, not, as Emerson put it, "a mush of concession. Better be a nettle in the side of your friend than his echo."

Friendship is a school for character, allowing us the chance to study, in great detail and over time, temperaments very different from our own. These charming quirks, these contradictions, these nobilities, these blind spots of our friends we track not out of disinterested curiosity: We must have this information before knowing how far we may relax our guard, how much we may rely on them in crises. The learning curve of friendship involves, to no small extent, filling out this picture of the other's limitations and making peace with the results. Each time I hit up against a friend's inflexibility I am relieved as well as disappointed: I can begin to predict, and arm myself in advance against repeated bruises. I have one friend who is always late, so I bring a book along when I am to meet her. I give her a manuscript to read and she promises to look at it over the weekend. I prepare for a month-long wait.

Though it is often said that with a true friend there is no need to hold anything back ("A friend is a person with whom I may be sincere. Before him I may think aloud," wrote Emerson), I have never found this to be entirely the case. Certain words may be too cruel if they are spoken at the wrong moment—or may fall on deaf ears, for any number of reasons. I also find with all my friends, as they must with me, that some initial resistance, restlessness, some psychic weather must be overcome before that tender ideal attentiveness may be called forth.

I have a good friend, Charlie, who is often very distracted whenever we first get together. If we are

Menfriends

Male friendship and social change

WHY ALL THE FUSS ABOUT MEN'S FRIENDSHIPS? IS IT only about men needing buddies? Or is there also some potential for progressive social change in men's soul searching about friendship?

Discussions of men's friendships traditionally begin with the way men have learned to keep their feelings to themselves as they climb up the hierarchy in a competitive world. Then there's the issue of homophobia. As adults, we don't touch each other, we don't linger too long in an affectionate glance, and we certainly don't get too tearful in male company. Thus our interactions with each other seem dead. And, when we're asked about friends, many of us complain that we don't really have a good friend.

A vicious cycle makes it very difficult for men who want to change. Many of us would like to cross the lines that define and constrict traditional masculinity. It would help to have the support of other men in the crossing. But men are not very good at being close to and supportive of each other. In fact, we tend to distance ourselves from a man who seems unmanly.

Then there is always the risk that, if a man relaxes his guard and displays too much tenderness, or if he is too willing to admit his human foibles, he will be mocked by other men. Men tend to remain silent about their critical concerns. After all, it would not look good if a man who is vying for promotion were to sound off at work about how distasteful he finds men's obsession with their place in hierarchies. So men cultivate the habit of hiding their disdain for traditional male posturing.

Friendship could be the key to breaking this vicious cycle. If men who, as a matter of principle, refuse to take part in traditional manly "fun" were better able to build friendships with like-minded men, the crossing of the lines of traditional masculinity would not be so lonely. Take, for instance, the line at work that divides the loyal company man who stays late from the "less committed" (in other words, unmanly) one who has to get home to be with the kids. The "family man" begins to feel like a failure in comparison. Perhaps he does not get the promotion he coveted, or is laid off. His self-esteem sinks precipitously. Perhaps, merely as a result of the renewed conviction that others love him for the values he holds dear, he can continue to live out his principles.

There might even be a ripple effect, a burgeoning challenge to what many men already believe is wrong with contemporary notions of masculinity. Perhaps, if men begin to know each other better and express feelings and needs more readily to each other, the cycle could be made to work in reverse: Men who are inclined to cross the lines, with the support of like-minded male intimates, could begin to change gender relations in the workplace.

—Terry A. Kupers
TIKKUN

Excerpted from TIKKUN MAGAZINE, A BI-MONTHLY JEWISH CRITIQUE OF POLITICS, CULTURE, AND SOCIETY (March/April 1993). Subscriptions: $31/yr. (6 issues) from TIKKUN, 251 West 100th St., 5th floor, New York, NY 10025.

sitting in a café he will look around constantly for the waiter, or be distracted by a pretty woman or the restaurant's cat. It would be foolish for me to broach an important subject at such moments, so I resign myself to waiting the half hour or however long it takes until his jumpiness subsides. Or else I draw this pattern grumpily to his attention. Once he has settled down, however, I can tell Charlie virtually anything, and he me. But the candor cannot be rushed. It must be built up to with the verbal equivalent of limbering exercises.

The friendship scene—a flow of shared confidences, recognitions, humor, advice, speculation, even wisdom—is one of the key elements of modern friendships. Compared to the rest of life, this ability to lavish one's best energies on an activity utterly divorced from the profit motive and free from the routines of domination and inequality that affect most relations (including, perhaps, the selfsame friendship at other times) seems idyllic. The friendship scene is by its nature not an everyday occurrence. It represents the pinnacle, the fruit of the friendship, potentially ever present but not always arrived at. Both friends' dim yet self-conscious awareness that they are wandering conversationally toward a goal that they have previously accomplished but that may elude them this time around creates a tension, an obligation to communicate as sincerely as possible, like actors in an improvisation exercise struggling to shape their baggy material into some climactic form. This very pressure to achieve "quality" communication may induce a sort of inauthentic epiphany, not unlike what sometimes happens in the last 10 minutes of a psychotherapy session. But a truly achieved friendship scene can be among the best experiences life has to offer.

Contemporary urban life, with its tight schedules and crowded appointment books, has helped to shape modern friendship into something requiring a good deal of intentionality and pursuit. You phone a friend and make a date a week or more in advance; then you set aside an evening, as if for a tryst, during which to squeeze in all your news and advice, confession and opinion. Such intimate compression may add a romantic note to modern friendships, but it also places a strain on the meeting to yield a high quality of meaning and satisfaction, closer to art than life. If I see busy or out-

We are family

Why gays and lesbians build strong bonds

IN HER BOOK *FAMILIES WE CHOOSE* (COLUMBIA UNIversity Press, 1991), anthropologist Kath Weston describes "a conviction widely shared by lesbians and gay men of all ages" that gays and lesbians have closer, more sustaining friendships than heterosexuals. It is common to hear gays and lesbians talk about their "families of choice," by which they mean an intimate circle of close friends, lovers, children, and even former lovers who celebrate holidays and successes together, pitch in during crises, create their own rituals and inside jokes, and enjoy a sense of ease and acceptance they all take for granted.

The most natural explanation for the phenomenon is that gays and lesbians who are alienated or estranged from their families of origin because of homophobia create a substitute family for themselves. Consider Ralph's case: After he came out to his parents and brother when he was 29, they cut him off. Although they relented a few years later and accepted him back into the fold, Ralph says he now feels more loyalty and connection to a close group of friends he has been part of for more than a decade. "There are a group of eight of us—gay and lesbian—who have spent every Thanksgiving, Christmas, and Fourth of July together for the past 11 years," says Ralph, now 44. While he was growing up, he assumed his family would always be more important to him than friends, but when they shunned him he realized that family ties can be broken. Weston points out that this realization is common to nearly every gay and lesbian who ever considers coming out as they anticipate the shock, anger, and rejection of family members that might follow such a revelation.

Ralph says his family of choice is very much like "an ideal family": They borrow money from one another, take care of one another's children, show up for dinner unannounced, look after one another's pets, and cared for two in the group who became sick with AIDS. "We nursed them in their home, supported them when their money ran out, were there when they died, even arranged their funerals," Ralph says. "Their parents were not nearly as [present] as we were in their lives and their deaths."

Contrary to popular belief, however, rejection by one's family of origin may not be the driving force behind these family bonds among friends. If this were the case, Weston says, then one would expect that those who aren't rejected by their families would have no interest in being part of such an intense friendship network—but the networks contain many such "accepted" gays.

More evidence to refute the theory comes from a pilot study comparing 500 straight people to 500 gays and lesbians. Preliminary data from the study, conducted by New York's Ackerman Institute for Family Therapy, seems to show that gays and lesbians aren't estranged from their families any more than straight people are. "These days, most gays and lesbians I know are connected to their original families," says John Patten, codirector of the Gay and Lesbian Families Project and a family therapist in New York City. "The friendships formed by heterosexual men and women in a large urban area like New York are not that [different] from those of gays and lesbians," says Patten. The dislocation of the modern family leaves gaps in straight people's lives, too, causing them to rely heavily on their friends, he says.

Gays and lesbians often differentiate between people in their lives who are just friends and friends who are also family, says Weston. Lesbians, for example, often consider ex-lovers to be family. "It doesn't seem at all strange to me that Diane and I continue to celebrate holidays together, even though we broke up five years ago and have both been in stable relationships since we separated," says Delia, a 43-year-old massage therapist. "We also share custody of our two dogs and talk on the phone regularly. Diane and I know each other more intimately than friends. She's more like a sister."

The intensity and quality of friendship is difficult to measure, but many gays and lesbians say their friendships deepened when they came out. Weston believes there might be a connection between homophobia and straight people's inhibitions about forging bonds with friends of the same sex. "The dominant society tends to suspect you of being a 'fag' or a 'dyke' if you have a close, intimate friendship with someone of the same sex," she points out. "Straights may be intimidated by this and so back off from their same-sex friends, whereas gays and lesbians may be less controlled by that fear."

Disillusionment with the so-called gay and lesbian community may be another factor that led to the rather recent phenomenon of gays and lesbians defining their friendship networks as family, Weston says. "You've never met a gay community, but you imagine it in your head," she says—it's "a fantasy of a connection with others who share this same orientation. But then we realized we were a diverse group and didn't necessarily get along." Chosen families are a smaller community of like-minded people.

"We all need to feel at home somewhere," says Ralph. "My friends are the home of my heart."

—*Laura Markowitz*
Special to *Utne Reader*

Laura Markowitz is an associate editor at Family Therapy Networker *magazine.*

of-town friends only once every six months, we must not only catch up on our lives but also convince ourselves within the allotted two hours together that we still share a special affinity, an inner track to each other's psyches, or the next meeting may be put off for years. Surely there must be another, saner rhythm of friendship in rural areas—or maybe not? I think about "the good old days" when friends would go on walking tours through England together, when Edith Wharton would bundle poor Henry James into her motorcar and they'd drive to the south of France for a month. I'm not sure my friendships could sustain the strain of travel for weeks at a time, and the truth of the matter is that I've gotten used to this urban arrangement of serial friendship "dates," where the pleasure of the rendezvous is enhanced by the knowledge that it will only last, at most, six hours. If the two of us don't happen to mesh that day (always a possibility)—well, it's only a few hours. And if it should go beautifully, one needs an escape hatch from exaltation as well as disenchantment. I am capable of only so much intense, exciting communication before I start to fade; I come to these encounters equipped with a six-hour oxygen tank. Is this an evolutionary pattern of modern friendship, or just a personal limitation?

Perhaps because I conceive of the modern friendship scene as a somewhat theatrical enterprise, a one-act play, I tend to be very much affected by the "set." A restaurant, a museum, a walk in the park through the zoo, even accompanying a friend on shopping errands—I prefer public turf where the stimulation of the city can play a backdrop to our dialogue, feeding it with details when inspiration flags.

I have a number of *chez moi* friends who always invite me to come to their homes while evading offers to visit me. What they view as hospitality I see as a need to control the mise-en-scène of friendship. I am expected to fit in where they are most comfortable, while they play lord of the manor, distracted by the props of decor, the pool, the unexpected phone call, the swirl of children, animals, and neighbors. Indeed, *chez moi* friends often tend to keep a sort of open house, so that in going over to see them—for a tête-à-tête, I had assumed—I will suddenly find their other friends and neighbors, whom they have also invited, dropping in all afternoon. There are only so many Sundays I care to spend hanging out with a friend's entourage before I become impatient for a private audience.

Married friends who own their own homes are apt to try to draw me into their domestic fold, whereas single people are often more sensitive about establishing a discreet space for the friendship to occur. Perhaps the married assume that a bachelor like me is desperate for home cooking and a little family life. I have noticed that it is not an easy matter to pry a married friend away from mate and milieu. For married people, especially those with children, the home often becomes the wellspring of all their nurturing feelings, and the single

friend is invited to partake in the general flow. Maybe there is also a certain tendency on their part to kill two birds with one stone: They don't see enough of their spouse and kids, and they figure they can visit with you at the same time.

From my standpoint, friendship is a jealous goddess. Whenever a friend of mine marries, I have to fight to overcome the feeling that I am being "replaced" by the spouse. I don't mind sharing a friend with his or her family milieu—in fact I like it, up to a point—but eventually I must get the friend alone, or else, as a bachelor at a distinct power disadvantage, I risk becoming a mere spectator of familial rituals instead of a key player in the drama of friendship.

A person who lives alone usually has more energy to give to friendship. The danger is investing too much emotional energy in one's friends. When a single person is going through a romantic dry spell, he or she often tries to extract the missing passion from a circle of friends. This works only up to a point: The frayed nerves of protracted celibacy can lead to hypersensitive imaginings of slights and rejections, and one's platonic friends seem to come particularly into the line of fire.

Today, with the partial decline of the nuclear family and the search for alternatives to it, we also see attempts to substitute the friendship web for intergenerational family life. Since psychoanalysis has alerted us to regard the family as a mine field of unrequited love, manipulation, and ambivalence, it is only natural that people may look to friendship as a more supportive ground for relation. But in our longing for an unequivocally positive bond, we should beware of sentimentalizing friendship, as saccharine "buddy" movies and certain feminist novels do, and of neutering its problematic aspects. Besides, friendship can never substitute for the true meaning of family: If nothing else, it will never be able to duplicate the family's wild capacity for concentrating neurosis.

In short, friends can't be your family, they can't be your lovers, they can't be your psychiatrists. But they can be your friends, which is plenty.

When I think about the qualities that characterize the best friendships I've known, I can identify five: rapport, affection, need, habit, and forgiveness. Rapport and affection can only take you so far; they may leave you at the formal, outer gate of goodwill, which is still not friendship. A persistent need for the other's company, for the person's interest, approval, opinion, will get you inside the gates, especially when it is reciprocated. In the end, however, there are no substitutes for habit and forgiveness. A friendship may travel for years on cozy habit. But it is a melancholy fact that unless you are a saint you are bound to offend every friend deeply at least once in the course of time. The friends I have kept the longest are those who forgave me time and again for wronging them unintentionally, intentionally, or by the plain catastrophe of my personality. There can be no friendship without forgiveness.

When the bond breaks

Do friendships end with a bang or a whimper?

CAROLINE KNAPP · THE BOSTON PHOENIX

Once upon a time, it was easy to have friends, scads of them. In high school and college, you had dozens of friends. You had your primary friends, your soul mates, the people you lived with, ate dinner with, drank and laughed and cried with. You had a tier of secondary friends, people you liked and respected a lot and always wanted to get to know better, but, hey, it didn't really matter because you always ran into them somewhere anyway. And then you had your basic, low-maintenance miscellaneous pals, the people who lived down the hall or always showed up in the same classes or parties, the folks who by dint of proximity or convenience or mutual interest managed to rise above the acquaintance category and become, well, friends.

As you get older, it's different. You're busier, and lives—yours and your friends'—are in flux. On a purely practical level, you don't have time for 30 friends anymore—two or three can be consuming enough. On a less tangible level, you slowly sense that a lot of those old bonds are weakening, the friendships unraveling at the seams. You've changed. Your friends have changed.

As you get older, the forces that once cemented friendships shift.

The forces that cemented relationships—common ground, common circumstances, common needs—have shifted. New forces—competitiveness, envy, events like marriage and children—have emerged. And so it happens. One inevitable day, after a few strained dinners or a string of unsatisfactory phone calls or maybe—but less likely—an all-out blowout, you mutter to yourself, "What am I doing? Why am I talking to this person? This is not worth the energy."

And then you begin a long, slow process for which, strangely, our culture has no rituals: losing a friend.

Sometimes this is not a traumatic event—it's predictable, inevitable, no big deal. According to Sumru Erkut, a psychologist and research scholar at the Wellesley College Center for Research on Women, most people have two types of friends: buddies, with whom the relationship is based on shared activities, and friends, with whom the bond is emotional, and where "mutuality, compatibility, and the quality of time spent together" are what fuel the relationship. Most of us can treat the former pretty casually: You get together when the urge strikes; if six or eight weeks—or even months—lapse between get-togethers, it's understood, and one's stock of buddies can change all the

Given the love and intimacy that develop between really close friends, the phrase "breaking up" may be apt.

time without any profound sense of loss.

In the case of buddies the friendships often just dissolve, having run their natural course. You amass just enough bitterness, or one too many unsatisfying encounters. You quietly cross some threshold, and the break comes to pass almost naturally, as if too much stress has been put on a piece of delicate cloth and, very simply, it tears.

In a few cases you have a last straw, a screaming confrontation. Karen and Ellen, both in their 30s, were "really close friends" for about three years, Karen says, until Ellen had an affair with a guy Karen had had a crush on for years. The affair was short-lived, but Karen was secretly furious. About six months later, she had an affair with the same man. When Ellen found out about it, she called Karen and said she never wanted to see her again. That was that.

And in still others, you make a mutual decision, not unlike a paperless divorce proceeding. One example: Ron and Gary, both in their early 40s, who had something close to an official breakup after Ron went to visit Gary in Florida for Christmas and found a long-simmering set of feelings confirmed. They had grown apart; Ron no longer got any "comfort" out of the relationship. It was time to give it up.

"It was strange," Ron says, describing the slow process of disenchantment that precedes a breakup. "Gary was this wild guy, kind of the social director of our gang. But it slowly became obvious I was having less and less fun in the friendship. Certain characteristics grated on me in a way they didn't when I was younger and drug-addled. Gary was always making scenes, picking up the phone while you were on it and embarrassing you, that kind of thing. I guess normalcy, when you get older, starts to have a certain cachet. And

---

Networking overtime
The difference between "good people" and "good people to know"

YOU CAN ALWAYS USE A FRIEND. UNFORTUNATELY, SOME PEOPLE TAKE this idea a bit too literally. Maybe you can blame it on the '80s, when brute commerce seemed to muscle into every private sphere. Friendship—a traditional value if there ever was one—has increasingly been eroded by that scourge of the go-go era: networking.

Networking, of course, derives from the ancient Anglo-Saxon words "netw" and "orking," which translate to mean "not working." Indeed, the old meaning still rings true: Today's networker most often covets a gig.

Networking has many faces, all of them the same: eager, earnest, and upbeat. If you're an editor, you become a lightning rod for those with hidden (often well-hidden) writing talents. If you're an advertising creative director, every acquaintance seems to have an amazing, untapped visual intuition. If you're working construction, suddenly everyone is a subcontracting son of a gun.

Who among us, in our search for meaningful human contact and meaningless fun, hasn't been detoured by those craving only business contacts? There are few things more annoying than thinking you've found a new pal when you've really just found another amiable hustler on the make, calculating a career move.

Whether you're being grilled over salmon or pumped for info while you're lifting weights, it's disconcerting to feel so blatantly Rolodexed. Not only is this less fun than a real social engagement, it's actually less fun than working.

Sometimes you can see it coming a meal away—particularly at lunch. If you suspect that doing lunch will become an extended infoluncheon, do what they do on those late-night infomercials: Bring along a co-host for diversion. In other words, invite a co-worker. *Your* lunch agenda is escaping your job, but the networker wants the opposite. If you put yourself into the networker's shoes, it's easy to see that he or she would be happy to slip into yours. The networker wants to know three things: How could I freelance for your company? How could I get a job like yours? How could I get *your* job?

To escape a networker at any time, all you have to do is slap your forehead and say, "Geez, I forgot I had a meeting with Johnson—I gotta go." While a pal might get miffed at such cavalier treatment, networkers will take it in stride, and probably admire you for it: They understand the importance of blowing people off for business reasons.

Don't get me wrong, we've all *been* there—and, given today's wobbly economy, we will probably be there again. Everyone concedes, of course, that it's not *what* you know, but who you know (or, in some cases, what you know about who you know). Life is unavoidably full of this sort of squid pro quo, where one hand slimes the other. So if you yourself are a networker, take heed: Networking in and of itself is not the problem. It becomes a problem when you begin to erase the line between recreation and job creation.

As with any other compulsive disorder, networking overtime is probably as difficult for the networker to recognize as it is easy for the long-suffering victim to spot. Networkers, consider these warning signs:

• After work-related chat dwindles, small talk gets microscopic.

• You can no longer distinguish between "good people" and "good people to know."

• You think hobbies are for chumps.

• You wake up in a panic at 4 a.m. and reach for your Filofax.

• You suffer from "laugh run-on," a nervous condition in which you chortle mirthlessly at the weakest imaginable witticisms long after others have snickered politely and moved on.

• When a telemarketer calls you at home during dinner, you ask him how he got his start in the business.

If you recognize any of these warning signs, you probably need help. Normally, I would recommend seeking professional help, but you're already way too fixated on the professional. In your case, I think it would be more appropriate to seek amateur help. Find a *friend* to talk to.

—*Jeff Reid*
Special to *Utne Reader*

Gary was not normal." He was particularly abnormal during the Christmas visit—agitated, argumentative, out of control.

About 48 hours into the visit, Ron thought, "This is it. This is the last time I am ever going to see this guy." They had a fight. Ron left. When he got back to Boston, he found a long, ranting message from Gary on his answering machine. One embattled phone call later, both agreed the friendship was over.

But breaks like that are the exception, not the rule. Most endings are much sloppier. And more passive. As psychologist Erkut puts it, "We tend to pretend that friendships are not as deeply important as the acknowledged lover or family member. This is not a society that honors the place friendships have in our hearts or that sanctions mourning their loss."

Indeed. Though close friends often become like—and feel like—siblings, losing one is not like losing a family member: We tend not to grieve; there is no memorial service for a shattered friendship. Most people don't have screaming blowouts or this-is-the-end discussions or final, definite breaks. They don't seek shoulders to cry on to grieve the loss of friends. They don't go to counselors either to heal the relationship or to cope with the loss. Indeed, despite the apparent premium so many people put on making friends, there is a surprising lack of focus in popular culture on the processes and feelings at work when friendships end. There are no best-sellers or self-help guides, and except for the rather vague and undescriptive term "a falling out," there's not even much of a vocabulary to describe what happens, let alone why. Do you "break up?" That sounds false, too dramatic. Do you have "ex-friends" the way you have ex-spouses or ex-lovers? That sounds harsh, unnecessarily permanent, and artificial.

But given the love and intimacy that develop between really close friends, a phrase like "breaking up" may be more apt than you think.

Friendship breakups can have all the elements of divorce: poor communication; needs, once compatible, that began to conflict; a slow buildup of bitterness and distance on both sides; and, finally, a break.

And yet we do not acknowledge the end of friendship as we do the end of a romantic relationship. Our lack of ritual or closure surrounding this loss doesn't necessarily suggest that people see their friends as more disposable today than they once did, or that friends are more cold-blooded or cavalier with each other. Indeed, it may say more about what happens to feelings of loss when people have no socially sanctioned place to put them. Toward the end of a long discussion about Jill, with whom she had recently ended a 26-year friendship, Diane says, "I really haven't thought about her in a long

Our culture has no rituals for losing a friend.

time." Then she pauses and adds, "I guess I could get really sad if I did. No one, not even my husband, can make me laugh the way Jill could. We used to laugh just hysterically—real pee-in-your-pants hysteria. So inside, I guess there's a little sinking feeling. There's still a part of me that's her."

So does she ever think about mending fences? Well, Diane's preoccupied. She has a husband, a new baby. And anyway, Jill's moving to California. "It seems easier," she says, "to just let it fade away."

Excerpted with permission from The Boston Phoenix *(Jan. 27, 1989). Subscriptions: $52/yr. (52 issues) from 126 Brookline Av., Boston, MA 02215. Back issues available from same address.*

What Is LOVE?

After centuries of ignoring the subject as too vague and mushy, science has undergone a change of heart about the tender passion

By PAUL GRAY

What is this thing called love? What? Is this thing called love? What is this thing called? Love.

HOWEVER PUNCTUATED, COLE Porter's simple question begs an answer. Love's symptoms are familiar enough: a drifting mooniness in thought and behavior, the mad conceit that the entire universe has rolled itself up into the person of the beloved, a conviction that no one on earth has ever felt so torrentially about a fellow creature before. Love is ecstasy and torment, freedom and slavery. Poets and songwriters would be in a fine mess without it. Plus, it makes the world go round.

Until recently, scientists wanted no part of it.

The reason for this avoidance, this reluctance to study what is probably life's most intense emotion, is not difficult to track down. Love is mushy; science is hard. Anger and fear, feelings that have been considerably researched in the field and the lab, can be quantified through measurements: pulse and breathing rates, muscle contractions, a whole spider web of involuntary responses. Love does not register as definitively on the instruments; it leaves a blurred fingerprint that could be mistaken for anything from indigestion to a manic attack. Anger and fear have direct roles—fighting or running—in the survival of the species. Since it is possible (a cynic would say common-

place) for humans to mate and reproduce without love, all the attendant sighing and swooning and sonnet writing have struck many pragmatic investigators as beside the evolutionary point.

So biologists and anthropologists assumed that it would be fruitless, even frivolous, to study love's evolutionary origins, the way it was encoded in our genes or imprinted in our brains. Serious scientists simply assumed that love—and especially Romantic Love—was really all in the head, put there five or six centuries ago when civilized societies first found enough spare time to indulge in flowery prose. The task of writing the book of love was ceded to playwrights, poets and pulp novelists.

But during the past decade, scientists across a broad range of disciplines have had a change of heart about love. The amount of research expended on the tender passion has never been more intense. Explanations for this rise in interest vary. Some cite the spreading threat of AIDS; with casual sex carrying mortal risks, it seems important to know more about a force that binds couples faithfully together. Others point to the growing number of women scientists and suggest that they may be more willing than their male colleagues to take love seriously. Says Elaine Hatfield, the author of *Love, Sex, and Intimacy: Their Psychology, Biology, and History:* "When I was back at Stanford in the 1960s, they said studying love and human relationships was a quick way to ruin my career. Why not go where

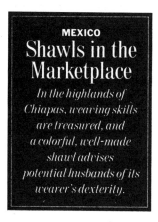

the real work was being done: on how fast rats could run?" Whatever the reasons, science seems to have come around to a view that nearly everyone else has always taken for granted: romance is real. It is not merely a conceit; it is bred into our biology.

Getting to this point logically is harder than it sounds. The love-as-cultural-delusion argument has long seemed unassailable. What actually accounts for the emotion, according to this scenario, is that people long ago made the mistake of taking fanciful literary tropes seriously. Ovid's *Ars Amatoria* is often cited as a major source of misreadings, its instructions followed, its ironies ignored. Other prime suspects include the 12th century troubadours in Provence who more or less invented the Art of Courtly Love, an elaborate, etiolated ritual for idle noblewomen and aspiring swains that would have been broken to bits by any hint of physical consummation.

Ever since then, the injunction to love and to be loved has hummed nonstop through popular culture; it is a dominant theme in music, films, novels, magazines and nearly everything shown on TV. Love is a formidable and thoroughly proved commercial engine; people will buy and do almost anything that promises them a chance at the bliss of romance.

But does all this mean that love is merely a phony emotion that we picked up because our culture celebrates it? Psychologist Lawrence Casler, author of *Is Marriage Necessary?,* forcefully thinks so, at least at first: "I don't believe love is part of human nature, not for a minute. There are social pressures at work." Then falls a shadow over this certainty. "Even if it is a part of human nature, like crime or violence, it's not necessarily desirable."

Well, love either is or is not intrinsic to our species; having it both ways leads nowhere. And the contention that romance is an entirely acquired trait—overly imaginative troubadours' revenge on muddled literalists—has always rested on some teetery premises.

For one thing, there is the chicken/egg dilemma. Which came first, sex or love? If the reproductive imperative was as dominant as Darwinians maintain, sex probably led the way. But why was love hatched in the process, since it was presumably unnecessary to get things started in the first place? Furthermore, what has sustained romance—that odd collection of tics and impulses—over the centuries? Most mass hallucinations, such as the 17th century tulip mania in Holland, flame out fairly rapidly when people realize the absurdity of what they have been doing and, as the common saying goes, come to their senses. When people in love come to their senses, they tend to orbit with added energy around each other and look more helplessly loopy and self-besotted. If romance were purely a figment, unsupported by any rational or sensible evidence, then surely most folks would be immune to it by now. Look around. It hasn't happened. Love is still in the air.

And it may be far more widespread than even romantics imagined. Those who argue that love is a cultural fantasy have tended to do so from a Eurocentric and class-driven point of view. Romance, they say, arose thanks to amenities peculiar to the West: leisure time, a modicum of creature comforts, a certain level of refinement in the arts and letters. When these trappings are absent, so is romance. Peasants mated; aristocrats fell in love.

But last year a study conducted by anthropologists William Jankowiak of the University of Nevada–Las Vegas and Edward Fischer of Tulane University found evidence of romantic love in at least 147 of the 166 cultures they studied. This discovery, if borne out, should pretty well wipe out the idea that love is an invention of the Western mind rather than a biological fact. Says Jankowiak: "It is, instead, a universal phenomenon, a panhuman characteristic that stretches across cultures. Societies like ours have the resources to show love through candy and flowers, but that does not mean that the lack of resources in other cultures indicates the absence of love."

Some scientists are not startled by this contention. One of them is anthropologist Helen Fisher, a research associate at the American Museum of Natural History and the author of *Anatomy of Love: The Natural History of Monogamy, Adultery and Divorce,* a recent book that is making waves among scientists and the general reading public. Says Fisher: "I've never *not* thought that love was a very primitive, basic human emotion, as basic as fear, anger or joy. It is so evident. I guess anthropologists have just been busy doing other things."

Among the things anthropologists—often knobby-kneed gents in safari shorts—tended to do in the past was ask questions about courtship and marriage rituals. This now seems a classic example, as the old song has it, of looking for love in all the wrong places. In many cultures, love and marriage do not go together. Weddings can have all the romance of corporate mergers, signed and sealed for family or territorial interests. This does not mean, Jankowiak insists, that love does not exist in such cultures; it erupts in clandestine forms, "a phenomenon to be dealt with."

Somewhere about this point, the specter of determinism begins once again to flap and cackle. If science is going to probe and prod and then announce that we are all scientifically fated to love—and to love preprogrammed types—by our genes and chemicals, then a lot of people would just as soon not know. If there truly is a biological predisposition to love, as more and more scientists are coming to believe, what follows is a recognition of the amazing diversity in the ways humans have chosen to express the feeling. The cartoon images of cavemen bopping cavewomen over the head and dragging them home by their hair? Love. Helen of Troy, subjecting her adopted city to 10 years of ruinous siege? Love. Romeo and Juliet? Ditto. Joe in Accounting making a fool of himself around the water cooler over Susan in Sales? Love. Like the universe, the more we learn about love, the more preposterous and mysterious it is likely to appear. —*Reported by Hannah Bloch/ New York and Sally B. Donnelly/Los Angeles*

Patterns of Abuse

Two million women are beaten every year, one every 16 seconds. Who's at risk, why does violence escalate—and when should a woman fear for her life?

THE STORIES SPILL OUT FROM BEhind bedroom walls and onto the front pages. Back in 1983, before talk shows dissolved into daily confessionals, actor David Soul offered up the stunning admission that he'd abused his wife, Patti. Two years later, John Fedders, the chief regulator of the Securities and Exchange Commission, resigned after he acknowledged that he'd broken his wife's eardrum, wrenched her neck and left her with black eyes and bruises. In 1988, the nation sat mesmerized by Hedda Nussbaum and her testimony about being systematically beaten by her companion, a brooding New York lawyer named Joel Steinberg, who also struck the blows that killed their adopted daughter, Lisa. Now America is riveted again, this time by the accumulating evidence of O. J. Simpson's brutality against his wife, Nicole. Yet, for all the horror, there is a measure of futility in these tales: one moment, they ignite mass outrage; then the topic fades from the screen.

Americans often shrug off domestic violence as if it were no more harmful than Ralph Kramden hoisting a fist and threatening: "One of these days, Alice . . . Pow! Right in the kisser!" But there's nothing funny about it—and the phenomenon of abuse is just as complicated as it is common. About 1,400 women are killed by their husbands, ex-husbands and boyfriends each year and about 2 million are beaten—on average, one every 16 seconds. Although some research shows women are just as likely as men to start a fight, Justice Department figures released last February reveal that women are the victims 11 times more often than men. Battering is also a problem among gay couples: the National Coalition on Domestic Violence estimates that almost one in three same-sex relationships are abusive, seemingly more than among heterosexual couples. But violence against women is so entrenched that in 1992 the U.S. Surgeon General ranked abuse by husbands and partners as the leading cause of injuries to women aged 15 to 44. Despite more hot lines and shelters and heightened awareness, the number of assaults against women has remained about the same over the last decade.

A disturbing double standard also remains. "If O. J. Simpson had assaulted Al Cowlings nine times and if A.C. called the police, O.J. couldn't have told them, 'This is a family matter'," says Mariah Burton Nelson, author of the book "The Stronger Women Get the More Men Love Football." "Hertz and NBC would have dropped him and said, 'This man has a terrible problem.' But family violence is accepted as no big deal." New York University law professor Holly Maguigan says wife-beating was actually once sanctioned by the so-called Rule of Thumb—English common law, first cited in America in an 1824 Mississippi Supreme Court decision, that said a man could physically chastise his wife as long as the stick he used was no wider than his thumb. Even now, Maguigan says, "we're not very far removed from a time when the criminal-justice system saw its task as setting limits on the amount of force a man could use, instead of saying that using force against your wife is a crime."

Changing attitudes is difficult. Although advocacy groups are already claiming that Nicole Simpson's case can do for spousal abuse what Rock Hudson did for AIDS and Anita Hill did for sexual harassment, that may be more rhetoric than reality; there is great ambivalence about family violence. Americans cling to a "zone of privacy"—the unwritten code that a man's home is his castle and what happens inside should stay there. It helps explain why, in some states, a man who strikes his wife is guilty only of a misdemeanor, but if he attacks a stranger, it's a felony. It helps explain why a woman can walk away from a friend who says she got her black eye walking into a door. And it helps explain why men retreat when a buddy dismisses brutality as the ups and downs that "all" marriages go through.

So many look away because they don't know what constitutes domestic violence. Who's a victim? Who's an abuser? Most people believe that, unless a woman looks as pathetic as Hedda Nussbaum did—her nose flattened, her face swollen—she couldn't possibly be a victim. And despite highly publicized cases of abuse, celebrity still bestows credibility. What's more, it's hard for many to comprehend how anything short of daily brutality can be wife-beating. Even Nicole's sister fell into the trap. "My definition of a battered woman is somebody who gets beat up all the time," Denise Brown told The New York Times last week. "I don't want people to think it was like that. I know Nicole. She was a very strong-willed person. If she was beaten up, she wouldn't have stayed with him. That wasn't her." Or was it? The patterns of abuse—who's likely to be at risk, why women take action and when battering turns deadly—can often be surprising, as paradoxical as the fact that love can coexist with violence.

MICHELE INGRASSIA AND MELINDA BECK, WITH
REPORTING BY GINNY CARROLL, NINA ARCHER BIDDLE,
KAREN SPRINGEN, PATRICK ROGERS, JOHN MCCORMICK,
JEANNE GORDON, ALLISON SAMUELS AND MARY HAGER.

WHO IS MOST AT RISK

EXPERTS USED TO THINK THAT BATTERED WOMEN WERE "asking for it"—somehow masochistically provoking abuse from their men. Mercifully, that idea has now been discredited. But researchers do say that women who are less educated, unemployed, young and poor may be more likely to have abusive relationships than others. Pregnant women seem to make particular targets: according to one survey, approximately one in six is abused; another survey cites one in three. There are other common characteristics: "Look for low self-esteem, a background in an abusive family, alcohol and drug abuse, passivity in relationships, dependency, isolation and a high need for approval, attention and affection," says psychologist Robert Geffner, president of the Family Violence and Sexual Assault Institute in Tyler, Texas. "The more risk factors a woman has, the more likely she is to become a candidate."

But not all women fit that profile: statistically, one woman in four will be physically assaulted by a partner or ex-partner during her lifetime, so it's not surprising that abuse cuts across racial, ethnic, religious and socioeconomic lines. "I'm treating physicians, attorneys, a judge and professors who are, or were, battered women," says Geffner. "Intelligent people let this happen, too. What goes on inside the home does not relate to what's outside."

And what's outside is often deceiving. Dazzling blond Nicole Simpson didn't look like someone who could have low self-esteem. But she met O.J. when she was just 18, and devoted herself to being his wife. In her 1992 divorce papers, she claimed that O.J. forced her to quit junior college and be with him all the time. She

Ten Risk Factors

Previous domestic violence is the highest risk factor for future abuse. Homes with two of these others show twice as much violence as those with none. In those with seven or more factors, the violence rate is 40 times higher.

- **Male unemployed**
- **Male uses illicit drugs at least once each year**
- **Male and female have different religious backgrounds**
- **Male saw father hit mother**
- **Male and female cohabit and are not married**
- **Male has blue-collar occupation, if employed**
- **Male did not graduate from high school**
- **Male is between 18 and 30 years of age**
- **Male or female use severe violence toward children in home**
- **Total family income is below the poverty line**

SOURCE: RISK-MARKERS OF MEN WHO BATTER, A 1994 ANALYSIS BY RICHARD J. GELLES, REGINA LACKNER AND GLENN D. WOLFNER

Striking a wife can be a misdemeanor while hitting a stranger is a felony

said she'd do anything to keep him from being angry: "I've always told O.J. what he wants to hear. I've always let him . . . it's hard to explain." For all their jet-setting, she was isolated—and reluctant to discuss what was happening at home, even though some friends say they had known. "She would wear unsuitable clothing to cover the bruises, or sunglasses to hide another shiner," says one. "She was trapped. She didn't have any training to do anything, and he knew that and he used it."

But even feisty women with their own careers can get involved with violent men. Earlier this month, Lisa (Left Eye) Lopes, a singer with the hip-hop group TLC, allegedly burned down the $800,000 home of her boyfriend, Atlanta Falcons' wide receiver Andre Rison. Police say the barely 5-foot, 100-pound Lopes appeared bruised and beaten when they arrived on the scene; friends say it was an open secret that she was abused. (Rison denies the allegations.) Curiously, the lyrics of Lopes's debut album are peppered with references about standing up to men: "I have my own control/I can't be bought or sold/ And I never have to do what I'm told . . ." Was that just a tough act to mask insecurity? Jacquelyn Campbell, a researcher in domestic violence at Johns Hopkins University, concludes that a woman's risk of being battered "has little to do with her and everything to do with who she marries or dates."

WHO BECOMES AN ABUSER

WHAT KIND OF MAN HEAPS PHYSICAL AND EMOTIONAL abuse on his wife? It's only in the last decade that researchers have begun asking. But one thing they agree on is the abuser's need to control. "There is no better way of making people compliant than beating them up on an intermittent basis," says Richard Gelles, director of the Family Violence Research Program at the University of Rhode Island. Although Gelles says men who have less education and are living close to the poverty line are more likely to be abusers, many white-collar men—doctors, lawyers and accountants—also beat their partners.

"Amy," a 50-year-old Colorado woman, spent 23 years married to one of them. Her husband was an attorney, well heeled, well groomed, a pillar of the community. She says he hit her, threw her down the stairs, tried to run her over. "One night in Vail, when he had one of his insane fits, the police came and put him in handcuffs," says Amy, who asked that her real name not be used. "My arms were still red from where he'd trapped them in the car window, but somehow, he talked his way out of it." Lenore Walker, director of the Domestic Violence Institute in Denver, sees the pattern all the time. "It's like Jekyll and Hyde—wonderful one minute, dark and terrifying the next."

Indiana University psychologist Amy Holtzworth-Munroe divides abusers into three behavioral types. The majority of men who hit their wives do so infrequently and their violence doesn't escalate. They look ordinary, and they're most likely to feel remorse after an attack. "When they use violence, it reflects some lack of communication skills, combined with a dependence on the wife," she says.

A second group of men are intensely jealous of their wives and fear abandonment. Most likely, they grew up with psychological and sexual abuse. Like those in the first group, these men's dependence on their wives is as important as their need to control them — if she even talks to another man, "he thinks she's leaving or sleeping around," says Holtzworth-Munroe. The smallest — and most dangerous — group encompasses men with an antisocial personality disorder. Their battering fits into a larger pattern of violence and getting in trouble with the law. Neil S. Jacobson, a marital therapist at the University of Washington, likens such men to serial murderers. Rather than becoming more agitated during an attack, he says, they become calmer, their heart rates drop. "They're like cobras. They're just like criminals who beat up anybody else when they're not getting what they want."

For women aged 15 to 44, domestic abuse is the leading cause of injury

Men who batter share something else: they deny what they've done, minimize their attacks and always blame the victims. Evan Stark, codirector of the Domestic Violence Training Project in New Haven, Conn., was intrigued by Simpson's so-called suicide note. "He never takes responsibility for the abuse. These are just marital squabbles. Then he blames her — 'I felt like a battered husband'." Twenty-nine-year-old "Fidel" once felt the same way. When he began getting counseling in Houston's Pivot Project, he blamed everyone else for his violence — especially his new wife, who, he discovered, was pregnant by another man. "When I came here, I couldn't believe I had a problem," he says. "I always thought of myself as a well-mannered person."

Avoiding Abuse

Battered women use a range of desperate methods to discourage partners from injuring them, from running away to fighting back.

STRATEGIES USED BY WOMEN TO END SEVERE SPOUSAL VIOLENCE

Avoid him or avoid certain topics	69%
Talking him out of it	59
Get him to promise no more violence	57
Threaten to get a divorce	54
Physically fight back	52
Hide or go away	37
Threaten to call the police	36
Leave home for two or more days	32

SOURCE: INTIMATE VIOLENCE, BY RICHARD J. GELLES AND MURRAY A. STRAUS (DATA FROM A 1985 STUDY)

WHY WOMEN STAY

IT LOOKS SO SIMPLE FROM THE OUTSIDE. MANY WOMEN THINK that if a mate ever hit them, they'd pack up and leave immediately. But women who have been in abusive relationships say it isn't that easy. The violence starts slowly, doesn't happen every day and by the time a pattern has emerged there may be children, and financial and emotional bonds that are difficult to break. "I know when I took my marriage vows, I meant 'for better or for worse'," G. L. Bundow, a South Carolina physician, wrote in The Journal of the American Medical Association, describing her own abusive relationship. "But when 'until death do us part' suddenly became a frightening reality, I was faced with some terrifying decisions."

With more women working and greater availability of shelters, financial dependence is less of a factor than it used to be. The emotional dependence is often stronger. "Women are trained to think that we can save these men, that they can change," says Angela Caputi, a professor of American Studies at the University of New Mexico. That mythology, she notes, is on full display in "Beauty and the Beast": the monster smashing furniture will turn into a prince if only the woman he's trapped will love him.

Many abusers *can* be charming — and abused women often fall for their softer side. Denver's Lenore Walker says there are three parts to the abuse cycle that are repeat over and over — a phase where tension is building and the woman tries desperately to keep the man calm; an explosion with acute battering, and then a period where the batterer is loving and contrite. "During this last phase, they listen to the woman, pay attention, buy her flowers — they become the ideal guy," Walker says. Geffner adds that in this part of the relationship, "they make love, the sex is good. And that also keeps them going."

Eventually, however, the repeated cycles wear women down until some are so physically and mentally exhausted that leaving is almost impossible. The man gradually takes control of the woman's psyche and destroys her ability to think clearly. Even the memory of past abuse keeps the woman in fear and in check. "You can't underestimate the terror and brainwashing that takes place in battering relationships," says psychiatrist Elaine Carmen of the Solomon Carter Fuller Mental Health Center in Boston. "She really comes to believe that she deserves the abuse and is incompetent."

WHEN WOMEN TAKE ACTION

THE TURNING POINT MAY COME WHEN A WOMAN CAN NO longer hide the scars and bruises. Or when her own financial resources improve, when the kids grow up — or when she begins to fear for their safety. Sometimes, neighbors hear screaming and call police — or a doctor challenges a woman's made-up story about how she got those broken ribs. "There are different moments of truth," says psychiatrist Carmen. "Acting on them partly depends on how safe it is to get up and leave." Walker says that women decide to get help when the pain of staying in a relationship outweighs the emotional, sexual or financial benefits.

For "Emma," a bank teller, the final straw came the day she returned from work to find that her husband hadn't mowed the lawn as she asked. "You promised me you'd mow the lawn," she said, then dropped the issue. Later they were seated calmly on the couch, when suddenly he was standing on the coffee table, coming down on her with his fists. He beat her into the wall until plaster fell down. "I was dragged through the house by my hair. At some point I began thinking I don't want to live anymore. If it hadn't been for this tiny voice in the background saying, 'Mama, please don't die,' I would have surrendered." Emma finally crawled to the car but couldn't see to drive, so her grandmother took her to the emergency room, where the doctor didn't believe her story about being mugged. "He said, 'You're not fine. You're bleeding internally. You've got a concussion.' He got a mirror and showed me my face. I looked like a monster in a horror movie. It was the first time I recognized how bad things had gotten." For a while, though, life got even harder. "When I arrived in Chicago, I had two children, two suitcases and $1,500 in my pocket to start a new life." She found it running a coalition that provides shelter for more than 700 battered women.

When women do take action, it can run the gamut from calling a hot line, seeking counseling, filing for divorce or seeking a court order of protection. Often those measures soothe the abuser—but only temporarily. "They think he's changed. Then it starts three months later," says Chicago divorce attorney David Mattenson. Some women weaken, too: they may lock the doors, check the shadows—but still let him have the keys to the house. Emma herself briefly returned to her husband when he begged and pleaded. "The same week I went back, he was beating me again."

WHEN COPS AND COURTS STEP IN

BLUNTLY PUT, COPS HATE DOMESTIC CALLS—IN PART BEcause they are so unpredictable. A neighbor may simply report a disturbance and cops have no idea what they will find on the scene. The parties may have cooled down and be sitting in stony silence. Or one may be holding the other hostage, or the kids. Sometimes, warring spouses even turn on cops—which is why many police forces send them in pairs and tell them to maintain eye contact with each other at all times. But dangerous as family combat is, many cops still don't see such calls as real police work, says Jerome Storch, a professor of law and police science at John Jay College of Criminal Justice in New York. "There's this thing in the back of the [cops'] mind that it's a domestic matter, not criminal activity."

Many cities have started training programs to make police take domestic-violence calls more sensitively—and seriously. For several years, the San Diego Police Department has even used details of O. J. Simpson's 1989 arrest for spousal battery as an example to recruits not to be intimidated by a famous name or face. Laws requiring police to make arrests in domestic cases are on the books in 15 states. But compliance is another matter. Since 1979, New York City has had a mandatory-arrest law, which also requires cops to report every domestic call. Yet a 1993 study found that reports were filed in only 30 percent of approximately 200,000 annual domestic-violence calls, and arrests were made in only 7 percent of the cases. Many cops insist they need to be able to use their own judgment. "If there's a minor assault, are you going to make an arrest just because it's 'a domestic crime'?" asks Storch. "Then if you take it to court and the judge says, 'This is minor,' it's dismissed. If you place mandates on the police, you must place them on the courts."

Prosecutors are just as frustrated. Testimony is often his word against hers; defense attorneys scare off victims with repeated delays and many victims decline to cooperate or press charges. "When women call the police, they don't call because they want to prosecute," says Mimi Rose, chief of the Family Violence and Assault Unit at the Philadelphia District Attorney's Office. "They are scared and want the violence to stop. Ten days later when they get the subpoena to appear in court, the situation has changed. The idea of putting someone you live with in jail becomes impossible." Pressing charges is just the first step. The victim is faced with a range of potential legal remedies: orders of protection, criminal prosecution, family-court prosecution, divorce, a child-custody agreement. Each step is complex and time-consuming, requiring frequent court appearances by the victim—and the abuser, if he'll show up.

Courts around the country have made an effort to streamline the procedures; more than 500 bills on domestic violence were introduced in state legislatures last year, and 100 of them became law. In California alone, new bills are pending that would impose mandatory minimum jail sentences and long-term counseling for abusers, set up computer registries for restraining orders, ban abusers from carrying firearms, mandate training for judges—and even raise the "domestic-violence surcharge" on marriage licenses by $4 to be used

STOPPING ABUSE: WHAT WORKS

Can a man who batters his partner learn to stop? Can psychotherapy turn an abuser into a respectful companion? Specialized treatment programs have proliferated in recent years, most of them aimed at teaching wife-beaters to manage their anger. But abusive men tend to resist treatment, and there are no proven formulas for reforming them. "We don't have any research that tells us any particular intervention is effective in a particular situation," says Eve Lipchik, a private therapist in Milwaukee. "We have nothing to go on."

Some abusers are less treatable than others. Researchers have identified a hard core, perhaps 10 to 20 percent, who seem beyond the reach of therapy. Experts differ on how best to handle the rest, but they agree that abusers shouldn't be coddled, even if they have grown up as victims themselves. "These men need to be confronted," says New York psychologist Matthew Campbell, who runs a treatment program in Suffolk County. "Giving them TLC just endangers women. The man has to take full responsibility. He has to learn to say, 'I can leave. I can express upset. But I cannot be abusive'."

Some therapists favor counseling abusers and victims as couples, provided the beating has stopped and the relationship has a healthy dimension to build on. But couples therapy is controversial, especially among feminists. In fact, several states have outlawed it. "Couples therapy says to the victim, 'If you change, this won't happen'," says Campbell. "That's dangerous."

To avoid that message, most clinics deal exclusively with abusers, often having them confront each other in groups. During a typical session at Houston's Pivot Project, a private, not-for-profit counseling agency, batterers take

for shelter services. On the national level, women's groups are pushing for the $1.8 million Violence Against Women act that would set up a national hot line, provide police training, toughen penalties and aid shelters and prevention programs. But those in the field say the question is whether the justice system can solve a highly complex social problem. "We need to rethink what we're doing," says Rose. "Prosecution isn't a panacea. It's like a tourniquet. We put it on when there is an emergency and we keep it on as long as necessary. But the question is, then what?"

WHEN ABUSE TURNS DEADLY

AFTER YEARS OF ABUSE, LEAVING IS OFTEN THE MOST dangerous thing a woman can do. Probably the first thing a battered wife learns in counseling is that orders of protection aren't bulletproof. Severing ties signals the abuser that he's no longer in control, and he often responds in the only way he knows how—by escalating the violence. Husbands threaten to "hunt them down and kill them," says Margaret Byrne, who directs the Illinois Clemency Project for Battered Women. One man, she recalled, told his wife he would find her shelter and burn it down, with her in it. "It's this male sense of entitlement—'If I can't have her, no one can'," says University of Illinois sociologist Pauline Bart. Friends claim O.J. made similar threats to Nicole.

Although conventional wisdom has it that women are most vulnerable in the first two years after they separate, researcher Campbell is suspicious of limiting danger to a particular time. Typically, she says, women report they're harassed for about a year after a breakup, "but we think the really obsessed guys remain that way much longer." In the last 16 years, the rate of homicides in domestic-abuse cases has actually gone down slightly—particularly for black women—according to an analysis of FBI data by James Fox, dean of

turns recounting the past week's conflicts. (As a reminder that women aren't property, the participants must refer to their partners by name. Anyone using the phrase "my wife" has to hold a stuffed donkey.) As each man testifies, his peers offer criticism. Therapist Toby Myers says one client recently boasted that he had avoided punching his wife by ramming his fist through a wall. Instead of praising him, a counselor asked the other participants what message the gesture had sent to the man's wife. A group member's reply: "It says she better be careful or she's next."

There's no question that such exercises can change men's behavior. At the Domestic Abuse Project in Minneapolis, follow-up studies suggest that two out of three clients haven't battered their partners 18 months after finishing treatment. Unfortunately, few abusers get that far. Only half of the men who register at the Abuse Project show up, even though most are under court or-

ders. And only half of those who start treatment see it through.

Drug treatment may someday provide another tool. Preliminary findings suggest that Prozac-style antidepressants, which enhance a brain chemical called serotonin, help curb some men's aggressiveness. Neither counseling nor drug treatment is a cure-all. "We need psychological services," says Campbell, the New York psychologist. "But services mean nothing without sanctions. Men need to know that if they don't change, they'll go to jail."

Not every abuser is sensitive to that threat. Dr. Roland Maiuro, director of the Harborview Anger Management and Domestic Violence Program in Seattle, notes that some men simply become more bitter—and more dangerous—after they're arrested. But until treatment becomes a surer science, keeping those men behind bars may be the best way to keep their victims alive.

GEOFFREY COWLEY *with* GINNY CARROLL *in Houston and bureau reports*

murders her husband is squashed, terrified by, 'You're never going to get away from me, I'm going to take the kids.' There's nothing left for her. To protect herself or her kids, she ends up killing the batterer."

the College of Criminal Justice at Northeastern University. Fox is not certain why. "More and more women are apparently getting out of a relationship before it's too late."

Or perhaps women are getting to the family gun first. While studying some 22,000 Chicago murders since 1965, researcher Carolyn Block of the Illinois Criminal Justice Information Authority discovered that among black couples, women were more likely to kill men in domestic-abuse situations than the other way round. In white relationships, by contrast, only about 25 percent of the victims were male. Nationwide, about one third of the women in prison for homicide have killed an intimate, according to the Bureau of Justice Statistics. While judges and juries are increasingly sympathetic to "Burning Bed" tales of longtime abuse, the vast majority don't get off.

Whatever the numbers, men and women kill their partners for very different reasons. For men, it's usually an escalation of violence. For women, killing is often the last resort. "The woman who is feisty and strong would have left," says Geffner. "The one who

One third of women in prison for homicide have killed an intimate

WHAT HAPPENS TO THE KIDS

THE CHILDREN OF O.J. AND NICOLE SIMPSON WERE REPORTEDLY with their maternal grandparents in Orange County, Calif., last week, riding their bikes and playing with cousins on the beach. Sydney, 9, and Justin, 5, know their mother is dead, but they reportedly have not been told that their father has been charged in her murder. Even if their family unplugs the TV and hides the newspapers, the scars may already be too deep.

"The worst thing that can happen to kids is to grow up in an abusive family," says Gelles. Research has shown that children reared amid violence risk more problems in school and an increased likelihood of drug and alcohol abuse. And, of course, they risk repeating the pattern when they become parents. Former surgeon general C. Everett Koop says domestic violence is often three-generational: in families in which a grandparent is abused, the most likely assailant is the daughter—who's likely to be married to a man who abuses her. Together, they abuse their children. "If you are going to break the chain," Koop says, "you have to break it at the child level."

The effects of violence can play out in many ways. Some boys get angry when they watch their father beat their mother, as Bill Clinton did as a teenager. Other children rebel and withdraw from attachment. All of them, says Northwestern University child psychiatrist David Zinn, suffer by trying to hide their family's dirty little secret. As a result, they feel isolated and unlike other kids. Sadly, it's a good bet the Simpsons' children will never again feel like everyone else. "The worst of all tragedies is to become social orphans—they lost their mother through a horrific crime and now their father has been turned into Mephistopheles," says Gelles. It's difficult enough for any child to overcome the legacy of domestic violence; having it play out on a national stage may make it all but impossible.

Dynamics of Personal Adjustment: The Individual and Society

The passing of each decade brings changes to society. Some historians have suggested that changes are occurring more rapidly. In other words, history appears to take less time to happen. How has American society changed historically? The inventory is long. Technological advances can be found everywhere. A decade ago few people knew what "user-friendly" or "60MB RAM" signified. Today these terms are readily identified with the quickly expanding computer industry. Fifteen years ago Americans felt fortunate to own a thirteen-inch television that received three local stations. Now people feel deprived if they cannot select from 100 different worldwide channels on their big, rear-screen sets. Today we can "fax" a message to the other side of the world just as quickly as we can propel a missile to the same place.

In the Middle Ages, Londoners worried about the bubonic plague. Before vaccines were available, people feared polio and other diseases. Today much concern is focused on the transmission and cure of AIDS, the discovery of more carcinogenic substances, and the greenhouse effect. In terms of mental health, psychologists see few hysterics, the type of patient seen by Sigmund Freud in the 1800s. Depression, psychosomatic ulcers, and alcohol and drug addiction are more common today. Similarly, issues about the changing American family continue to grab headlines. Nearly every popular magazine carries a story or two bemoaning the passing of the traditional, nuclear family and declining "family values." And if these spontaneous or unplanned changes are not enough to cope with, some individuals are purposely trying to change the world. Witness the continuing and dramatic changes in Eastern Europe and the Middle East, for example.

This list of societal transformations, while not exhaustive, reflects society's continual demands for adaptation by each of its members. However, it is not just society at large that places stress on us. Smaller units within society, such as our work group or our family, also demand constant adaptation by individuals. Families change as children leave the proverbial nest, as parents divorce, and as new babies are born. Work groups expand and contract with every economic fluctuation. Even when group size remains stable, new members come and go as turnover takes place; hence, changes in the dynamics of the group occur in response to the new personalities. Each of these changes, welcome or not, places stress on the individual who then needs to adjust or cope with the change.

This unit of the book addresses the interplay between the individual and society in producing the problems each creates for the other. The first article discusses how the good of society is often pitted against the cost to individuals. Specifically, Natalie Glance and Bernardo Huberman, describe social dilemmas and their effects. In most social dilemmas, individual gain is pitted against collective gain in a win-lose battle.

In the second article, social signs are discussed in detail. In "Trying to Decipher Those Inscrutable Signs of Our Times," Richard Wolkomir introduces the reader to semiotics, the science of studying and interpreting signs and symbols.

The next three articles feature ideas about the big "isms" in American society: racism and sexism. In "Crossing the Divide," the author believes that, through education and other antiprejudice programs, we can overcome racial prejudice in the United States. Then, in contrast, "The Ruses of Racism" highlights explanations for the return of violent racism in our society. This is followed by an article on sexual harassment. While it is true that men can be harassed by women, most sexual harassment happens to women. In "Flirting with Disaster," Joshua Halberstam suggests that sexual harassment looms large as an issue because more and more women are entering the workplace.

The final article in this unit examines the problem of violence in the media. The medium about which many psychologists are most concerned is, of course, television. In "Media, Violence, Youth, and Society," Ray Surette describes the relationship between violence in a culture and its portrayal on that culture's televisions. He concludes that television is not singularly responsible for violence in our streets; there are other causes. The real

issue then becomes how we can reduce violence, given these multiple causes.

Looking Ahead: Challenge Questions

Is society today more stressful than it was a century ago? How so? Are there changes from the previous decade that make our living easier? More difficult?

What is a social dilemma? Can you give some specific examples of social dilemmas from the article "The Dynamics of Social Dilemmas"? From your own life? How do social dilemmas relate to an individual's adjustment?

What is the science of semiotics? What signs and symbols can be used to assess and interpret what is going on in society? Give some specific examples.

Do you think men's and women's roles have changed in the last few years? How so? What is it about American society that perpetuates the "isms" (racism, sexism, and other prejudices)? How can we eliminate or overcome racism, sexism, and sexual harassment?

Name some positive uses for television. Name some negative uses that have been developed for television. Should we censor or restrict certain types of television? Why and for whom? Should networks voluntarily make programming changes, or should such changes be legislated?

Do you think televised violence has caused the epidemic of street violence in the United States? If so, what can we do to reduce violence on television? If not, what else has caused violence to increase over the last decade?

The Dynamics
of Social Dilemmas

*Individuals in groups must often choose between acting selfishly
or cooperating for the common good. Social models explain how group
cooperation arises—and why that behavior can suddenly change*

Natalie S. Glance
Bernardo A. Huberman

Imagine that you and a group of friends are dining at a fine restaurant with an unspoken agreement to divide the check evenly. What do you order? Do you choose the modest chicken entrée or the pricey lamb chops? The house wine or the Cabernet Sauvignon 1983? If you are extravagant, you could enjoy a superlative dinner at a bargain price. But if everyone in the party reasons as you do, the group will end up with a hefty bill to pay. And why should others settle for pasta primavera when someone is having grilled pheasant at their expense?

This lighthearted situation, which we call the Unscrupulous Diner's Dilemma, typifies a class of serious, difficult problems that pervade society. Sociologists, economists and political scientists find that this class of social dilemma is central to a wide range of issues,

NATALIE S. GLANCE and BERNARDO A. HUBERMAN explore their joint interest in the dynamics of social systems at the Xerox Palo Alto Research Center. For several years, Glance has studied the role of expectations and beliefs in systems of intentional agents. She received her Ph.D. in physics from Stanford University. Huberman is a Xerox Research Fellow and has been a visiting professor at the University of Paris and the University of Copenhagen. He received his physics degree from the University of Pennsylvania and has worked in condensed matter physics, statistical mechanics and chaotic dynamics. He is a co-recipient of the 1990 Prize of the Conference on Economics and Artificial Intelligence.

such as protecting the environment, conserving natural resources, eliciting donations to charity, slowing military arms races and containing the population explosion. All these issues involve goals that demand collective effort and cooperation. The challenge is to induce individuals to contribute to common causes when selfish actions would be more immediately and personally beneficial. Studies of these problems cast light on the nature of interactions among individuals and the emergence of social compacts. Moreover, they explain how personal choices give rise to social phenomena.

Social dilemmas have often been studied using groups of people who are given choices that present a conflict between the general good and the costs to an individual. Such experiments confirmed the hypothesis, first made by the economist Mancur L. Olson in the 1950s, that small groups are more likely to secure voluntary cooperation than are larger ones. They also revealed that repeated iterations of a situation tend to promote cooperative attitudes. The amount of cooperation further increases when communication among the participants is permitted.

More recently, powerful computers have been drafted for simulations of the social behavior of groups. The computer experiments gloss over the complexities of human nature, but we believe they can help elucidate some of the principles that govern interactions involving many participants. For the past three years, we have investigated social cooperation using both analytical techniques and computer simulations. We have tried to look not just at

the outcomes of the dilemmas but also at the dynamics of the interactions and the ways in which those outcomes evolve in various groups.

Our mathematical theory of social dilemmas indicates that overall cooperation cannot generally be sustained in groups that exceed a critical size. That size depends on how long individuals expect to remain part of the group as well as on the amount of information available to them. Moreover, both general cooperation and defection can appear suddenly and unexpectedly. These results can serve as aids for interpreting historical trends and as guidelines for constructively reorganizing corporations, trade unions, governments and other group enterprises.

Mathematical theories of social dilemmas have traditionally been formulated within the framework of game theory. The mathematician John von Neumann and the economist Oskar Morgenstern developed that discipline in the mid-1940s to model the behavior of individuals in economic and adversarial situations. An individual's choices are ranked according to some payoff function, which assigns a numerical worth—in dollars or apples or some other commodity—to the consequences of each choice. Within game theory, individuals behave rationally: they choose the action that yields the highest payoff. (Real people may not be consistently rational, but they do behave that way when presented with simple choices and straightforward situations.)

Social dilemmas can readily be mapped into game settings. In general

From *Scientific American*, March 1994, pp. 76-81. © 1994 by Scientific American, Inc. All rights reserved. Reprinted by permission.

terms, a social dilemma involves a group of people attempting to provide themselves with a common good in the absence of central authority. In the Unscrupulous Diner scenario, for instance,

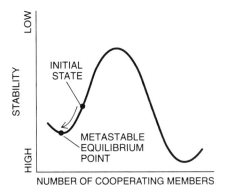

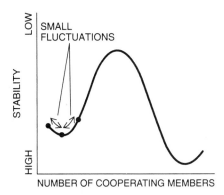

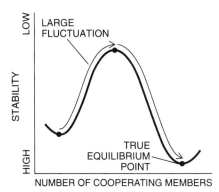

STABILITY FUNCTION explains the dynamics of groups confronting social dilemmas. No matter what a group's initial state may be, it quickly shifts into a state of relative equilibrium, in which either many or few people are cooperating (*top*). Small fluctuations around this equilibrium point are routine (*middle*). Large fluctuations, however, which are rare, can carry the group over a stability barrier. The group will then very rapidly advance to a lower true equilibrium state (*bottom*). In the long run, a group will always settle into the lowest equilibrium state.

the common good is achieved by minimizing the amount of the check. The individuals are said to cooperate if they choose a less expensive meal; they defect if they spare no expense (for the group, that is!). Of course, the game is only an idealized mathematical model—how well can one quantify intangibles such as the enjoyment of the meal or guilt over saddling friends with a large bill? Nevertheless, the dynamics of the game are still instructive.

Each individual can choose either to contribute to the common good or to shirk and "free ride" on the sacrifices of others. All individuals share equally in the common good, regardless of their actions. Each person who cooperates therefore increases the common good by a fixed amount but receives back only some fraction of that added value. (The return is diminished by free riders who benefit without contributing.)

When an individual realizes that the costs of cooperating exceed her share of the added benefit, she will rationally choose to defect and become a free rider. Because every individual faces the same choice, all the members of a group will defect. Thus, the individually rational strategy of weighing costs against benefits has an inferior outcome: no common good is produced, and all the members of the group are less well off than they could be.

The situation changes, however, if the players know they will repeat the game with the same group. Each individual must consider the repercussions of a decision to cooperate or defect. The issue of expectations then comes to the fore. Individuals do not simply react to their perceptions of the world; they choose among alternatives based on their plans, goals and beliefs.

Of what do these expectations and beliefs consist? First, an individual has a sense of how long a particular social interaction will last, and that estimate affects her decision. A diner who goes out with a group once is more likely to splurge at the expense of others than is one who goes out with the same friends frequently. We call the expected duration of a game the horizon length. A short horizon reflects a player's belief that the game will end soon, whereas a long one means the player believes the game will repeat far into the future.

Second, each player has beliefs about how her actions will influence the rest of the group's future behavior. A diner may reject the option of an expensive meal out of fear that it would prompt

others to order lavishly at the next gathering. The size of the group bears directly on this thinking. In a large crowd, a player can reasonably expect that the effect of her action, cooperative or not, will be diluted. (Ten dollars more or less on the group's bill matters less when it is divided among 30 diners rather than five.) The player will reason that her actions become less influential as the size of the group increases.

For groups beyond some size, overall cooperation becomes unsustainable. The likelihood of bad consequences from an individual's defection becomes so small, whereas the potential gain stays so large, that the disincentive to defect vanishes. As our experiments have determined, this critical size depends on the horizon length: the longer that players expect the game to continue, the more likely they are to cooperate. That conclusion reinforces the commonsense notion that cooperation is most likely in small groups with lengthy interactions.

The smallest possible social group, consisting of only two players, raises the special limiting case widely known as the Prisoner's Dilemma. It is so named because of one common way in which it is framed: a prisoner is given the choice of betraying a fellow prisoner (defecting) and going free or keeping silent (cooperating) and thereby risking a harsh punishment if the other prisoner betrays him. Because the psychology of the interactions is unique, certain strategies that work well for individuals in the Prisoner's Dilemma fail in larger groups. The highly successful one known as tit-for-tat depends on retaliation and forgiveness. A player initially cooperates and thereafter does whatever the other player last did. Tit-for-tat works because it allows each player to recognize that the other's actions are in direct response to her own. In groups of more than two, however, it is impossible for one player to punish or reward another specifically because any modification of her own actions affects the entire group.

In larger groups, an individual caught in a social dilemma forms a strategy for conditional cooperation from a calculation of the expected payoffs: she will cooperate if at least some critical fraction of the group is also cooperating. When enough of the others are cooperating, she expects that her future gains will compensate for present losses. If the number of cooperating individuals falls below that threshold, then her expected losses rule out cooperation, and she will defect. The strategies, expectations and thresholds of the individuals determine whether cooperation within a group is sustainable.

Quite aside from the question of whether a group can achieve cooperation is the equally important matter of how cooperation or defection emerges in a social setting. Imagine that the hypothetical diners, after many consecutive budget-busting meals, decide to split into smaller groups, hoping that the limited size of the resulting tables will aid cooperation. How long does it take for the small groups of defectors to switch? Is the process smoothly evolutionary or sudden?

To study the evolution of social cooperation, we borrowed methods from statistical thermodynamics. This branch of physics attempts to derive the macroscopic properties of matter from the interactions of its constituent molecules. We adapted the approach to study the aggregate behavior of individuals confronted with social choices.

Our method relies on the mathematical construction of a curve called a stability function. This curve describes the relative stability of a group's behavior in terms of the amount of cooperation present. The values of the curve derive from a knowledge of the costs, benefits and individual expectations associated with a given social dilemma. The stability function generally has two minima, or troughs, which represent the most stable states of the group: widespread defection and widespread cooperation. They are separated by a high barrier, which is the least stable state. The relative heights of these features depend on the size of the group and the amount of information available to its members. From this function, one can predict the possible outcomes of the dilemma and how long the group will stay in a particular state.

Like a ball rolling downhill, the group's behavior will always gravitate from its initial state toward the closest trough. Once in a trough, however, the system does not become static. Instead it jiggles back and forth randomly, just as a small ball would be moved by vibrations. These random perturbations are caused by the uncertainty that individuals have about the behavior of others. If an individual misperceives the level of cooperation in the group, she may erroneously defect and thereby briefly move the system away from equilibrium. The more uncertainty there is in the system, the more likely there will be fluctuations around an equilibrium state.

These perturbations are usually small, so in the short run the system

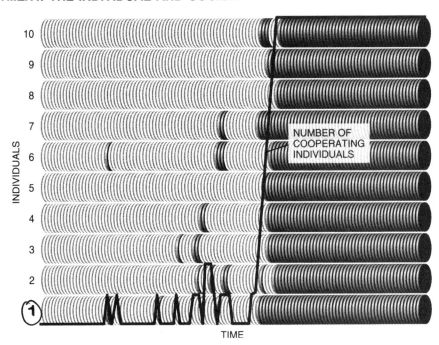

OUTBREAKS OF COOPERATION can be simulated using computer agents that act like individuals. In a homogeneous group of agents that are all initially defectors (*light gray***), the shift to widespread cooperation (***dark gray***) is sudden and rapid.**

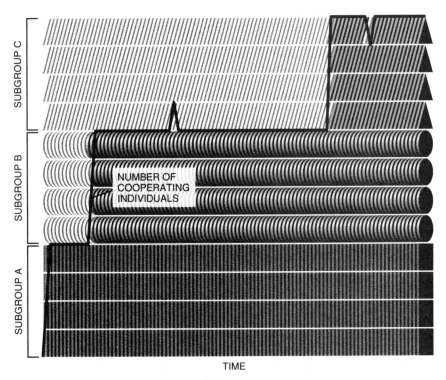

HETEROGENEOUS GROUPS evolve stepwise toward overall cooperation, with each subgroup experiencing a distinct transition on its own.

stays near one minimum. Over the long run, however, large fluctuations become important. Such fluctuations, caused by many individuals switching from defection to cooperation, or vice versa, can push the group over the barrier between the minima. Consequently, given

sufficient time, a group will always end up in the more stable of the two equilibrium states, even if it initially moves into the other, metastable one.

Huge random fluctuations are extremely rare—on average, they occur over periods proportional to the exponential of the size of the group. Once the transition from the local minimum to the maximum of the function takes place, however, the system slides down to the global minimum very quickly—in a period proportional to the logarithm of the group size. Thus, the theory predicts that although the general behavior of a group in a dilemma stays the same for long periods, when it does change, it does so very fast.

Computer experiments demonstrate those predictions. A society of computational agents, or programs acting like individuals, can be presented with a social dilemma. The agents intermittently and asynchronously reevaluate their options and decide whether to cooperate or to defect. They base their decisions on information, which may be imperfect and delayed, about how many of the others are cooperating. The sum of all the agents' actions reveals the degree of cooperation or defection in the group. The experimenter can compile statistics on the level of cooperation over time.

One typical experiment features a group of 10 agents, all of which are initially defecting. If one agent misjudges how many others are cooperating and switches its behavior, that change might lead the rest of the group to make a similar shift. The group therefore stays at or near its initial metastable state of mutual defection for a long time, until a sudden and abrupt transition carries the group to mutual cooperation.

That abrupt appearance of cooperation in a computer simulation well describes certain real social phenomena, such as the recent upsurge in environmental awareness and activism. In many parts of the U.S. and Europe, voluntary recycling has become a normal part of daily life. A decade ago that was not the case. Recycling poses a social dilemma for the consumer: the environmental benefits are great if most of the population recycles but marginal if only a few do, and the individual's invested effort in bringing bottles and newspapers to the recycling center is the same in either case. Our theory may help explain why the population, after a long period of relative apathy, has so quickly embraced recycling, emissions controls and other environmental protection measures.

In the hypothetical social dilemmas we have described so far, all the individuals evaluate their payoffs the same way and share the same expectations about the outcomes of their actions. In any real group of humans, however, individuals have largely disparate beliefs. We have therefore looked at how diversity affects the dynamics of social dilemmas.

A heterogeneous group can display two different types of diversity: variation around a common average or segregation into factions. The first involves a simple spread in opinion or concern among individuals who are fundamentally the same. For example, some unscrupulous diners may anticipate and value more future meals than others. If the typical diner looks about 10 meals into the future, then individuals will have horizons that vary but cluster around that average.

Although models of social dilemmas that include this type of diversity are more complicated than ones for homogeneous groups, their dynamics still follow a clear pattern. Basically the diversity acts as an additional form of uncertainty, instigating fluctuations in the state of the group. If most individuals are defecting, the first to decide to cooperate will probably be the one who has the longest horizon. That decision might then convince others who have longer-than-average horizons to cooperate, too. Those transitions can trigger a cascade of further cooperation, until the whole group is cooperating.

The events that led to the mass protests in Leipzig and Berlin and to the subsequent downfall of the East German government in November 1989 vividly illustrate the impact of such diversity on the resolution of social dilemmas. Earlier that year Mikhail S. Gorbachev, then president of the Soviet Union, stopped backing the Eastern European governments with the force of the Soviet military. His new policy reopened the issue of whether the Eastern European population would still subscribe to the existing social compact. The citizens of Leipzig who desired a change of government faced a dilemma. They could stay home in safety or demonstrate against the government and risk arrest—knowing that as the number of demonstrators rose, the risk declined and the potential for overthrowing the regime increased.

A conservative person would demonstrate against the government only if thousands were already committed; a revolutionary might join at the slightest sign of unrest. That variation in threshold is one form of diversity. People also differed in their estimates of the duration of a demonstration as well as in the amount of risk they were willing to take. Bernhard Prosch and Martin Abraham, two sociologists from Erlangen University who studied the Leipzig demonstrations, claim that the diversity in thresholds was important in triggering the mass demonstrations. They also documented that over just six weeks the number of demonstrators grew from a handful of individuals to more than 500,000.

A second type of diversity within a social group describes differences that do not range around an average value. It is found in groups composed of several distinct factions, each characterized by a distinct set of beliefs. Among the diners, for example, might be a mix of students and professionals. Students on a tight budget have concerns different from those of well-off professionals. On the whole, the variation among the students' preferences would be small as compared with the average differences between the two subgroups.

When a large group containing several factions changes from overall defection to cooperation, it does so through progressive transitions. The subgroup with the greatest tendency to cooperate (for example, the one with the longest horizon in its average expectations or the one with the lowest average costs for cooperation) will usually be the first to cross over. The other groups will then follow in turn, probably in the order of their willingness to cooperate.

Relationships among subgroups may powerfully influence the evolution of cooperation, a fact that is notably important in large hierarchical organizations. The weight that an individual in one division gives to the actions of others depends on those persons' placement in the hierarchy. Hierarchies are therefore very different from level groups.

Functional hierarchies often hide in informal settings. Air pollution is a problem that the whole world faces and must solve collectively. Yet each person is usually bothered more by a neighbor burning a compost pile than by someone across town doing the same. The dilution of environmental impact with distance can be represented as a hierarchy of layered interactions between neighborhoods, towns, counties, states, countries and continents. The effect of someone else's actions on your own choices will depend on how many layers distant she is from you.

The effective size of the hierarchy is therefore much smaller than the number of its constituents. Suppose that in its effect on your decisions, the action of your nearby neighbor counts as much as the summed actions of an entire distant neighborhood. Then the effective number of people influencing your decision is much smaller than the total population of your town. We can say that the hierarchy has been rescaled, because the whole is smaller than the sum of its parts.

Computer experiments show how cooperation can spread in large hierarchical organizations. Transitions from defection to cooperation (or the other way around) tend to originate within the smallest units, which usually occupy the lowest level of the hierarchy. Cooperation can then progressively spread to higher levels. The switching trend can even terminate if the cooperative influence of distant units is too attenuated to be felt. In such a case, the organization may contain some branches that cooperate and others that defect for long periods.

These results suggest practical ways to restructure organizations to secure cooperation among members faced with a social dilemma. Corporations benefit, for example, when managers share their knowledge with one another. Yet managers may withhold information they fear their colleagues can use for their own advancement. To volunteer information, a person needs to feel secure that others will, too. Setting up a network of smaller groups of managers could overcome the dilemma by promoting that sense of security. Moreover, restructuring a large corporation into smaller units may encourage the appearance of pockets of collaboration that might spread rapidly.

Conversely, when organizations grow without a major reorganization, the tendency to ride for free grows and lowers efficiency. The act of reorganizing does not guarantee instant improvement: the switch to collective cooperation may still take a long time. That time can be shortened by increasing the benefits for individuals who cooperate and by dispersing the most cooperative managers among small core groups throughout the organization.

The study of social dilemmas provides insight into a central issue of behavior: how global cooperation among individuals confronted with conflicting choices can be secured. These recent advances show that cooperative behavior can indeed arise spontaneously in social settings, provided that the groups are small and diverse in composition and that their constituents have long outlooks. Even more significantly, when cooperation does appear, it does so suddenly and unpredictably after a long period of stasis.

The world still echoes with the thunderous political and social events marking the past few years. The fall of the Berlin Wall, leading to a unified Germany, and the breakdown of the centralized Soviet Union into many autonomous republics are examples of abrupt global defections from prevailing social compacts. The member countries of the European Union currently face their own social dilemma as they try to secure supranational cooperation. The pressing issue is whether or not those countries can build a beneficial cooperative superstructure while each one remains autonomous. If our predictions are accurate, these restructurings will not proceed smoothly. Rather they will always be punctuated by unexpected outbreaks of cooperation.

FURTHER READING

THE LOGIC OF COLLECTIVE ACTION: PUBLIC GOODS AND THE THEORY OF GROUP. Mancur Olson, Jr. Harvard University Press, 1965.

THE TRAGEDY OF THE COMMONS. Garrett Hardin in *Science,* Vol. 162, pages 1243–1248; December 13, 1968.

COLLECTIVE ACTION. Russell Hardin. Johns Hopkins University Press, 1982.

INSTITUTIONAL STRUCTURE AND THE LOGIC OF ONGOING COLLECTIVE ACTION. Jonathan Bendor and Dilip Mookherjee in *American Political Science Review,* Vol. 81, No. 1, pages 129–154; March 1987.

THE OUTBREAK OF COOPERATION. N. S. Glance and B. A. Huberman in *Journal of Mathematical Sociology,* Vol. 17, Issue 4, pages 281–302; April 1993.

SOCIAL DILEMMAS AND FLUID ORGANIZATIONS. N. S. Glance and B. A. Huberman in *Computational Organization Theory.* Edited by K. M. Carley and M. J. Prietula. Lawrence Erlbaum Associates (in press).

Trying to decipher those inscrutable signs of our times

*Semiotician Marshall Blonsky can look at
a coffee cup–or Vanna White–and arrive
at conclusions that are, well, astounding*

Richard Wolkomir

*Richard Wolkomir remembers the pre-semiotic
era when signs conveyed simpler messages,
such as "Burma Shave," "Yield" and "Stop!"*

Marshall Blonsky is about to "read" my suit. I asked him to do it. He is a leading semiotician, skilled at deciphering the underlying messages in things. But I suspect my suit's underlying message is "Hick!"

"Read your own jacket first," I say, as we talk in the restaurant of a Manhattan hotel, where the elevator chitchat is about million-dollar deals and skiing in the Andes.

Marshall stands to display his jacket. To me, it appears merely black and droopy. But couture is not my strong point–when I left home to catch the plane to New York this morning, two moose were wading in the bog behind my mailbox. My own "look" is *Northern Exposure.*

"This is a mélange of Giorgio Armani's old and new styles," says Marshall, a semiotics professor at both New York University and the New School for Social Research who counterpoints baldness on top with an emphatic mustache. "The jacket has bone-crusher shoulders, and a long line that gives it . . . *gravitas,* seriousness . . . and feel the fabric!" I feel the fabric.

"It is crepe, the fabric of serious mourning," Marshall tells me. "Actually, Armani wants it even more droopy–I've had it tailored away from that because the real meaning of this jacket is penitence, regret for the excesses of the 1980s–the greenmail, the hostile takeovers–and I personally have no interest in the idea of penitence because I never made any money in the 1980s anyway." Who would have thought a sport jacket could be so loquacious? I am already learning about the semiotic view of the world.

But for a signwise top gun like Marshall Blonsky, an Armani suit is merely the stuff of target practice. His latest book, *American Mythologies,* gives the "new world cultural order" a semiotic trouncing. To write it, he spent four years hanging out with international glitterati like newscaster Ted Koppel, Russian poet Yevgeny Yevtushenko, horror novelist Stephen King, *Wheel of Fortune*'s Vanna White, and her creator, game-show producer Merv Griffin. I have come to New York to find out what he learned from these notables, whom I visualize as wearing trousers that actually match their jackets. That thought occurs to me because Marshall is now "reading" the nubby tweed of my own jacket and the telltale fact that my tie, as usual, has twisted around.

"The tweed, the slight riskiness of the striped tie with the checked jacket, the oxford button-down collar–it all says 'working journalist,' as opposed to the decadence and outrageous luxuriousness of what I'm wearing," Marshall says. Is he just being kind to a visitor from moose country? Even so, I am now amiably disposed toward semiotics. I point out that every man in the hotel lobby, except us, is wearing essentially the same squarish suit, in varying shades of dark gray or dark blue.

"It's the standard business suit, which originated in the 19th century," Marshall explains. "Its message is the immobilization of the body, declaring that the wearer is a *brain* person, who no longer does country work."

To semioticians, the world is a broth of such signs and signals. "We live in the semiosphere," says Marshall. Cars send messages about their owners: "I'm a sophisticate who drives a precision automobile crafted in Bavaria" or "I'm an outdoor macho guy who needs power to all four wheels." Italian designer jackets beam out messages. So do book jackets (Marshall's is hot pink, with Marilyn Monroe peeking out). So do telephones you carry in your briefcase, Presidential haircuts and Arnold Schwarzenegger's biceps. And semioticians like Marshall Blonsky read these invisible memos.

For instance, he says, a man standing on a street corner looking at his watch is not really interested in the time. He is actually transmitting a message to passers-by, who, he imagines, wonder why he is loitering on the corner. He is signaling: "I am not a bum—I have an appointment."

"All life is like that—a grand theater of communication," Marshall tells me. "Semiotics is the attempt to understand these seemingly disparate signs, from the shapes of new coffeepots to the underlying messages in the waiflike emaciation of some high-fashion models."

A semiotic news flash: the jury is still out on coffeepots, but Marshall relates the neurasthenic, prepubescent look of today's hottest models to the designers' "tapping into the collective unconsciousness" for a vision of a world "stalked by AIDS and ecological disaster." He says it evokes Sophocles' tragedy *Oedipus Rex*, which begins with calamity upon the land. "The cattle and fruit are sickened," he says, "and a blight is on the women." And I thought it was just that the models dieted too much!

"Did I mention that my friends call me Dr. Sign?" Marshall asks, and he proceeds to "read" our restaurant table. "The small coffee cup, the fluted shape—it's declaring elegance with an English touch . . . and the lobby's chesterfield sofas, a carnation on the table, the restraint . . ."

In the 1980s, he says, designer Ralph Lauren created multipage advertisements showing his clothes on models in settings that featured country estates and prep schools. This hotel's lobby decor derives in part from those advertisements, he reasons. "Ralph Lauren created an image of the American ruling class based on the British, so we're dealing with a text, which is the Laurenesque reading of imperial pseudo-Britain."

Who would have thought? But Marshall's reading of the hotel goes further: a feature of the international culture now taking shape is that most of it is ersatz, just as this hotel is merely a simulacrum of upper-class Britain. People who turn up their noses at jogging outfit themselves in running shoes and sweatsuits. And we flock to theme parks like Epcot Center to experience faux Europe: generally, image replaces substance. A Japanese government economist told Marshall that the Suzuki Corporation flopped marketing its new motorbikes in Europe until advertisements began presenting the motorized bicycles as aluminum ponies, steeds for urban Euro-cowboys.

That is just the sort of thing I came to New York to hear, even if I don't actually understand every word. I'd been seeing ever more frequent mention of semiotics in rarefied intellectual journals. And many university literature courses are now taught from the semiotic point of view, looking for "codes" hidden in the relationships between words. Even the *New York Times* reported on the April 1993 Vancouver summit meeting by zeroing in on the "perennial semiotic summit issue of 'who blinks first.'" The reporter analyzed such key semiotic points as

Bill Clinton's haircut versus Boris Yeltsin's. And she noted that President Clinton trumped President Yeltsin's "*nyet*" to an umbrella to ward off the Pacific drizzle by doing without both an umbrella and a coat. Meanwhile, semiotic buzzwords, like "deconstruction," regularly pop up in trendy fashion magazines, semiotics being currently hip.

Actually, semiotics is old. The word itself, from the Greek term for "sign," appeared in early discourses on theology and medicine. But in the 1600s the British philosopher John Locke recoined "semiotics" to mean a science of signs. In the late 1800s the U.S. polymath Charles Sanders Peirce (philosopher, mathematician, scientist) developed semiotics as an aspect of logic. Linguists and, later, anthropologists adapted semiotics to their own scientific disciplines. But after World War II European intellectuals widened the spectrum, applying semiotics more systematically to philosophy and literature. To these thinkers, like Marshall Blonsky, society and everything in it—from novels to tablecloths to skyscrapers—became a "text," bristling with embedded signs and codes. The semiotician's work is to "read" these codes.

One tool is "deconstruction," which involves the tweaking apart of any "text," whether it is a dictator's oratory or a wallpaper pattern, into its constituent intellectual nuts and bolts. (The point being to reveal that nothing is as simple as it is being made to look.) "The aim is to 'destabilize' the message, so that the codes no longer control us," says Blonsky. "It checks the totalitarian impulse." But he says the discipline sometimes wanders from its roots. "It's possible to cut away semiotics' ethical dimension and use it to sell soap," he says. "I recently received a telephone call—they said, 'We're an advertising agency and we need a semiotician.'" And he points out that the long-running-Energizer-battery commercial, in which a seemingly legitimate advertisement for, say, laundry detergent is abruptly "destabilized" by the unexpected appearance of the battery-powered Energizer bunny, insanely beating its drum, is an example of deconstruction.

"Deconstruction": the word buzzes with aggression. Trained semioticians, no doubt, wield this intellectual scalpel with precision. But in the hands of a fellow from moose country . . . ? Still, it is irresistible.

Let us now have a go at deconstructing Marshall Blonsky.

We see the erudite professor, with his swank Italian jacket and his mustache and his way of compacting ideas and counterideas and ramifications of those ideas into sentences that writhe with clauses. But is there, perhaps, an underlying subtext?

We know this: he grew up in Kansas City. His father was a banker and his mother sold real estate. His younger brother is a geriatric-center administrator, but Marshall's career took a more exotic turn, starting at age 7, when his mother took him to a concert. "Little Marshall got up and imitated the conductor, and then imitated the violin soloist," he says. "My mother immediately decided that I was destined to be a violinist, and from the age of 7 to 17

I fiddled away." He was, he says, so committed to becoming a concert violinist that he had only one other interest. "I studied the Talmud," he says. Music and religious law–preparation, perhaps, for semiotics.

Ultimately, he jettisoned the musical career when he studied with a leading violin teacher, who pronounced him lacking spark. "Let him go off to Yale and join the ruling class," the great master commanded. And Marshall went off to Yale. He mournfully played his "terrific French violin" with his "terrific English bow" in a campus building whose acoustics he liked. Once he told some classmates: "I don't have to study esthetics–I *am* esthetics!" "Actually, I was a little monster," he admits. Even so, he majored in English and graduated magna cum laude in 1959. His aim was show business, to become a producer.

He went to work for a Broadway and TV impresario, doing a variety of chores, from reading scripts to serving as a gofer for writer Buck Henry on the TV show *That Was The Week That Was.* Meanwhile, he was working on advanced degrees. In 1970, at the urging of his professors, he intensively studied the proceedings of a 1966 conference at Johns Hopkins University, which was the introduction of European semiotic thinking to the United States. "I didn't know what they were saying, but it wiped me out," he recalls. "My girlfriend and I went to Avignon to study with the great ones, riding around in her red VW Beetle convertible, and for me, who'd never been abroad before, semiotics got sensualized in the South of France–but what really hooked me was the realization that *everything* around us could be signs."

Marshall went on to professoring and authoring erudite articles and books on semiotics. But he got to "feeling dusty and moth-eaten," and decided to hit the road. He aimed at becoming "an intellectual in action," sort of a Jack Kerouac with a silk tie. For several years he jetted around America, Europe and Asia, carrying his semiotics concealed, so to speak, in a shoulder holster, inveigling multinational moguls and media stars to tell his tape recorder what they were up to.

The result is his latest book, *American Mythologies*, in which he shows how American myths–mass-processed into images and beamed around the world by the media–are creating the "semiosphere" in which we currently live, up to our hairlines in signs and signals. The imagemakers he interviewed, he says, are the global equivalent of the "high school fast crowd" who decide what is "in" and "out." "President Bush talked about the new world order–I'm giving you a glimpse at what it really is," he told me.

"What is it?" I asked. For one thing, it is the "Vanna Factor," which TV newscaster Ted Koppel revealed is one secret of his success. Blonsky spent three weeks hanging around the ABC studio in Washington where Koppel relentlessly grills politicians and statesmen for *Nightline*, listening in on conference calls until Koppel got him to stop, sharing pre-show pizzas and take-out Chinese din-

ners. And Koppel explained his theory about game-show hostess Vanna White, who has become famous, although, says Blonsky, in the early years she never spoke and appeared on *Wheel of Fortune* solely to turn over letters.

"Vanna leaves an intellectual vacuum, which can be filled by whatever the predisposition of the viewer happens to be," Koppel told Blonsky. And Koppel said that he, too, has the Vanna Factor: "In theory, I am equally tough on everyone: therefore viewers can project on me their own politics, their own views, their own predispositions. That makes me the beneficiary of a certain public acceptance that I would not have if I were, let's say, a commentator who expressed his own views on subjects."

Making Vanna whatever they want

Blonsky later put in time at the *Wheel of Fortune* studio in Burbank, where he told Vanna White what Ted Koppel had said, as she was having her hair done. He asked her if she agreed. "Absolutely," she said. "I like that. I like that a lot." She thought about it. "Because of the fact I don't speak on television, people are able to make me whatever they want me to be. It's almost like being a puppet up there. You can make the puppet say or do anything."

And what about those game shows that millions of us watch every day? I myself, for instance, usually manage to fit in a half-hour of *Jeopardy* (between writing sonnets and studying up on Kant's metaphysics, of course). Blonsky checked it out at the source, with game-show entrepreneur Merv Griffin, who said that *Jeopardy* slakes a thirst for knowledge among people "who didn't go to college, couldn't go to college." As Marshall puts it: watching the show, you get a simulacrum of education.

Wheel of Fortune has a different semiotic subtext. It is based on piecing together phrases that are part of everyday conversation, like "Boy Scout leader" or "in the public interest." It verifies watchers as Middle Americans, sharers of certain values. But Marshall discovered a Dantesque dimension to the show: "Vanna is Beatrice taking you through the circles of ignorance, encouraging and applauding you every time you decipher one of the riddles of the Universe." Merv Griffin told Blonsky that one secret of certain game shows is that they are designed so that viewers at home can get the answer before the contestants in the studio. "You are a hero in the living room," Griffin said. "The son-in-law they always thought was a dork . . . suddenly they will look at him in the living room and he gets it before the contestant." Game shows, says Blonsky, give you the illusion of power. And the Vanna Factor, in his reading, is a sign of a Postmodern hallmark: image over content, surface over substance.

He pressed on. From the chairman of Fiat USA, Furio Colombo, he learned that serious international moguls now pick wardrobes that combine "something European and also something American." Taking time out from marketing strategies, Colombo waxed semiotically eloquent on the multinational executive shoe: "Shoes still tend to be Italian, but whereas they used to be glove leather, perfect and smooth–the Gucci style–now they recall American shoes, which are harsher, larger, more manly, with an element of remembering New England boats and walking on the beach." Yet, those shoes are too fine and soft–"too tender"–to be strictly American. And so they signify Americanness, while also evoking the "softer, sweeter, more complacent life of Europe."

That left me looking at my own running sneakers, which are developing interesting rips across the toe area, while puzzling over what the Fiat executive's explication of shoe styles might mean. Marshall told me it means that international popular culture, formerly driven by American imagery, is increasingly heterogeneous. American myths, such as the perennially popular cowboy, may still dominate, but with modifications from other countries. Now Pecos Bill wears "tender" Italian shoes.

Speed is another characteristic of the new world order, as the semiotician reads it. Now messages and images flash around the world at photon speed. Madonna probably has fans just about everywhere. Blonsky asked an adviser to French president François Mitterrand, economist Jacques Attali, about America's influence on the world. According to Attali, America's chief influence is on the culture of daily life, with everything speeded up. "You change your cars, you change your ideas, you change your wife, you change your friends quicker and quicker," he said. "America is going faster and faster on the route where everybody is going in terms of increasing the speed of amortization of ideas, signs and goods."

Stephen King: himself a semiotician

When Blonsky visited horror novelist Stephen King, he made a happy discovery: "King is actually a wild semiotician himself!" King's macabre tales, he says, teach millions to view the emerging world culture with semiotic skepticism. For instance, King discussed his book *The Talisman*, about American hustlers discovering a parallel planet that is untouched–as yet. "The message is the Postmodern urge to 'commodify' every person and every parcel of space in the world," says Blonsky.

Blonsky didn't just talk with the glitterati. He also went to the opposite extreme and visited homeless people living in the New York City subway tunnels, which turned out to be "an underground socioeconomic nation" with its own codes of behavior. In "Subwayland," says Blonsky, "if a man is seated on the stairway, we don't ask him to remove himself; we simply sidestep him." In fact, the subways–home to the homeless–send a semiotic message, a modern image of hell. And after getting friendly with citizens of Subwayland, who sleep in the tunnels and live on coins they harvest in Styrofoam cups from denizens of the upper world, Blonsky concluded that the underground homeless are a living form of deconstruction: the homeless, he says, are "an invitation to question a fundamental myth, that of progress."

Meanwhile, aboveground, in Blonsky's semiotic reading, New Yorkers are "barnacled" with in-your-briefcase telephones, laptop fax-computers, Walkmans, credit cards and ATM cards that provide instant money. The message is speed and mobility. And the result is a new sort of "urban nomad," with allegiance to no particular country or company or ideology. Maybe that will reduce destructive nationalism, Blonsky says. But he is pessimistic: as we become "encrusted" with signs and attitudes generated by the imagemakers, we may lose the ability to see the human beings underneath. Semiotics, Blonsky believes, is an antidote.

But after a few days with Marshall Blonsky, I need an antidote for the antidote. I am over my head in messages. I discover that Marshall is an avid baseball fan–solid ground at last! But he says "baseball's the master way in which regional and ethnic frictions are mediated and mythically resolved." Back into the semiotic soup.

He shows me a new Times Square hotel where podlike elevators shoot up and down unnervingly fast, stopping so briefly it is hard to get in or out. "Postmodernism," Marshall pronounces. Speed! Denial of the individual! Appearance over substance!

In the hotel's vast atrium, 30-odd stories high, is a 4-story tower of girders. Inside is a huge mechanical pocket watch, spinning just fast enough to make the giant face impossible to read clearly. It stops Marshall in his tracks, like David first glimpsing Goliath. We have finally reached the danger point, I realize. Semiotic overload is imminent.

"Look! The tower encysts the simulacrum of modernity!" Marshall cries, pointing.

"The clock is revolving," he goes on, "deconstructing the reading of time, and it is enclosed in its little house, modernity imprisoned by Postmodernity!"

I flew home. Now I look at the bog behind the mailbox, where the moose wade. I am thinking of declaring this a "semiotics-free zone."

But I can't. I would have to erect a sign.

Crossing the Divide

How we can solve America's racial problem

Leonard Pitts Jr.

Leonard Pitts is The Herald's pop music critic.

"All life is interrelated. We are caught in an inescapable network of mutuality, tied in a single garment of destiny."
—**Martin Luther King Jr.**

In a speech I delivered to the American Civil Liberties Union in December (and reprinted as a Viewpoint essay on Jan. 3 [1993]), I spoke of rap music, of how it has "become a voice of rage and despair for those who feel they have no other way to be heard." The essay urged readers to "take a good, hard listen" and promised that they would be stunned by the depth of rage, the sense of complete isolation from society's mores. Rap, it said, is the sound of racism, of inner-city decay. It is the beat of disaffection, a sound beyond hopelessness.

The response to that piece was swift and fierce—the kind of feedback a writer usually doesn't see outside his day-dreams, including an invitation to meet with members of the Dade County School Board and separately with Miami Mayor Xavier Suarez and members of his staff.

But in the midst of all that overwhelmingly positive feedback, a sizable minority of people also took me to task for not offering concrete solutions beyond a few feel-good paragraphs about making real the promises of the Constitution. What would you propose? demanded one anguished writer. The folks at the School Board also asked. And Mayor Suarez fixed me with a hard, interested look, and asked simply, so what can we do?

Gulp.

OK, allow me a mea culpa. And a caveat.

The original speech took 20 minutes to outline the problem. It would have taken at least that long to deal in any depth with possible solutions.

That said, let me also say this: It's no great mystery what needs to be done. No rocket scientists need apply here. Because what we're lacking isn't the knowledge—it's the will.

Some folks will say it's also the money, but I don't necessarily buy that. We almost always find a way to pay for the things we deem important.

For instance, Washington has been crying broke for more years than I can remember, but when greed and mismanagement ran many of the nation's savings and loans into the ground, the government magically found the money to fund a bail-out that the Resolution Trust Corp. estimates will cost at least $110 billion. This because, of course, the collapse of the nation's S&Ls represented a clear and present danger.

And there's the problem in a nutshell. For some reason, we haven't yet decided that the cancer of racism, the decay of our cities, the loss of generation after generation of young people, constitutes that same sort of danger.

I happen to believe our children come first. Black children are important. *All* our children are important. We must decide that once and for all, and decide also that anything that endangers their future threatens us all.

And in so doing we must also rid our minds of the notion that all the problems that plague us can be solved in a minute or a month or a year by a single piece of legislation or an innovative new program.

We tend to think that we as a society have been wrestling with this decay and disaffection and racism forever and that it's not gotten any better. In historical terms at least, that's demonstrably untrue.

Former Herald Staff Writer Dave Von Drehle, in a powerful 1991 essay in Tropic magazine, made an observation that refutes that perception—an observation that surprised me, even though it shouldn't have. We are living, Von Drehle wrote, in the *first* generation "even to attempt to erase America's color barriers." The first.

So you see, we *haven't* been dealing with this forever. We've only just begun. And our lack of patience is more troubling than our lack of progress. Consider: It took 246 years and a ferocious war for most Americans to decide that slavery was a bad idea. We fooled around with Jim Crow segregation for another century before finally junking that, too. And yet the Great Society programs that were instituted in the '60s to address the horrendous inequities caused by those racist years got maybe a 15-year trial before Mr. Reagan and Mr. Bush came to office and began dismantling them.

Solving the anguish of the hip-hop nation (the larger movement of which rap is a part) requires commitment—a long-term investment of time and energy. What kinds of things can we do? Most of what I would suggest can be summed up in three words: Educate. Educate. Educate. Because if you buy the notion that ignorance breeds the fear, poverty, racism, distrust and crime that plague us, then the solution seems clear. Eliminate ignorance.

Educate. And not just at the public-school level, nor even just in college. But rather, society-wide. Here are a few more specific suggestions:

SCHOOL FUNDING
PAY TEACHERS WELL, AND EXPECT PERFORMANCE

• *We need to fully fund our schools instead of making beggars of our educators.* What does it say about our priorities when Madonna and Michael Jordan are multimillionaires, yet we hand teachers a paycheck they can just about cash on a city bus? We need to pay what it takes to attract and keep the best, most inventive teachers, and then give them well-maintained classrooms containing a manageable number of students. We need to do this because we need to be able to expect a great deal from them.

HISTORY
PUT IT IN CONTEXT, AND INCLUDE EVERYONE

• Teach history—not as a meaningless compendium of dusty names and dates, but as a living and vivid thing that provides context to our daily struggle. And in the teaching, resist tokenism and the urge to marginalize the achievements—or the oppression—of Africans, women, Asians, Jews—all those different peoples who make up the American pastiche. And carry that philosophy to all the subjects on the educational calendar. I resent the English teachers who drilled me on John Milton, yet told me nothing of Langston Hughes. It bothers me that I had to get out of school to learn that Lincoln, while he abhorred slavery just as I'd always been taught, also had a white supremacist streak a mile wide. Quit lying and denying by omission. Teach the truth. The whole truth. And let the chips fall.

SCHOOL DESEGREGATION
IT'S A CRUCIAL PART OF ENDING IGNORANCE

• Desegregate our schools. I don't care if it takes busing, tax incentives or magnet schools. Let's agree that it's important and let's do it. Desegregating our schools is a crucial part of ending ignorance. Because as things now stand, our kids—white kids especially—are raised in dangerous isolation. They often know nothing about African Americans that they don't pick up on The Fresh Prince of Bel Air. I remember going to school at the University of Southern California with white kids who asked if they could touch my hair because they were curious about its texture. One guy demanded I get rid of the Afro pick I carried in those days and get myself a "normal" comb.

While we work on desegregating the schools, let us institute an exchange program between predominantly black and white schools—perhaps some sort of weekly swap between specific classes

that would bring each group of kids into the others' environs. They say familiarity breeds contempt, but in this case it can also work to breed understanding and common ground.

NON-BLACK AMERICANS
CLEAR UP MISCONCEPTIONS ON STEREOTYPES, CRIME

• Educate non-black Americans. By which I mean those who are beyond school age. Use the power of the media in much the way Nancy Reagan used it to campaign against drugs. Large corporations might sponsor seminars like the ones given by Osage, Iowa-based Jane Elliot, who teaches about the insidiousness, the ingrained nature, of racism and racial attitudes.

It's like the joke I heard once: six black guys walking down the street wearing backward caps and holding bats, six white guys on the other side of the street wearing and holding the same.

Which one's the baseball team?

Meaning that, where there isn't overt racism, there is often a great deal of insensitivity and racially-biased misperceptions that are traceable to simple ignorance.

One of the worst and most persistent of these has to do with black crime. Meaning the perception that there is some innate, inherent criminality in black men and that whites are almost always their victims of choice. And yet, the notion of the hulking black rapist/robber/murderer slavering for an innocent white person to victimize is another demonstrable lie.

According to the U.S. Department of Justice, over 70 percent of all crimes of violence (including rape) committed against white persons between 1985 and 1988 were done by white offenders. Approximately 80 percent of the black crime victims suffered at the hands of black criminals.

In simple robbery, the statistics are closer but still show a distinct racial disparity. Fifty-two percent of the white robbery victims lost their property to a white thief; 29 percent of the time, the robber was black. Black victims in the same age group were robbed by blacks 83 percent of the time.

In murder, the numbers are downright startling. According to the Uniform Crime Report for 1990, 93 percent of the blacks slain in that year were murdered by other blacks. Eighty-six percent of whites were killed by other whites.

Clearly, crime is segregated to a degree David Duke would admire. Just as clearly, there are pernicious myths at work out there, comfortable fictions that give aid and comfort to our basest racism.

BLACK AMERICANS
QUIT COMPLAINING AND GET DOWN TO WORK

• Educate black Americans—and again, I'm talking about something that goes beyond the schoolyard. Enlist black and mainstream media, the schools, the churches, the grass-roots organizations and the venerable old civil rights groups in this cause.

Because all these years of oppression have produced a victim mentality in many African Americans. I remember, for instance, my son telling me about a friend, a 14-year-old kid, who complained about the white man holding him down.

I wish I could've found that kid. I'd have told him to get off his butt and quit complaining. I'd have told him to study harder, to set a goal, to make a plan and to go for it. Quit whining. Quit giving himself excuses to fail. It is more difficult for him to make it—much more so—but it is not impossible.

And let me emphasize that none of this is to minimize the part white American racism has played in the plight of blacks. That racism is indisputably the one thing that, more than any other, put blacks down and works overtime to keep them there. And because of that, white Americans owe a debt of conscience they have scarcely even begun to repay.

But, that said, what are African Americans going to do in the meantime? Defer their individual dreams and goals, decline to aspire, until our white American brethren see the light? That's foolish.

I'm reminded of something mama used to say: God helps those who help themselves.

Seems to me that many of us as African Americans have forgotten a lot of things we learned at mama and grandmama's knees. Lessons about thrift. And pride. And dignity. And integrity. And about perseverance, holding on stubbornly, stupidly, blindly . . . nobly to our ideals and forcing their vindication.

Most of all, we've forgotten about taking care of our own. If our children are lost, let us be in the forefront in finding them. If a man is illiterate, teach him to read. If a boy on the block is growing up fatherless, let another man take him aside and teach him the things he should know. Reject the self-loathing that says substandard is just fine, and "good" hair is better than bad, and "nigger" be thy name.

Because, it is not.

THE MEDIA
HOLD IT RESPONSIBLE WITH CALLS AND LETTERS

• *Hold the media responsible.* Write letters, make phone calls, complain. For myself, if I hear WINZ Newsradio (940 AM) gratuitously identify a suspect as black one more time, I am going to do violence to my car radio. It's that same old myth of black criminality again. I mean, if race is one component in a general description of someone the police are hunting for, fine and dandy. But this stuff where stories begin, "A black man is being held in the rape and torture murder of so and so," is tiresome and borderline racist. I *never* hear, "A white man is being held . . ." or "A Jewish arsonist is in custody . . ." Similarly, why is it that the multitude of white junkies, addicts, prostitutes, murderers and other assorted low-lifes so seldom show up on the evening news, ducking *their* faces in shame as they are being led to the squad cars?

And while you're badgering the news media, don't forget the entertainment media, which have done yeoman's work to marginalize blacks. The Los Angeles Times quoted a People magazine editor some years back as saying blacks seldom make the cover of that magazine because they are always poor sellers. The editor said his magazine wouldn't consider most black celebrities coverworthy unless there was some other hot angle to go along with it—such as if

Diana Ross were found to have anorexia nervosa.

The Times ran a separate piece a few years later in which filmmakers rationalized their snubbing of blacks as lead characters. The story, which ran before the recent black film boom got under way, postulated that whites simply aren't interested in black stories or culture.

Let me see . . . the top mini-series of all time (*Roots*) dealt with the history of a black family, the top TV series of the '80s (*Cosby*) was about the daily life of a black family, the top recording artist of the '80s was a black man (Michael Jackson), the top sports stars of the '80s were black athletes (Magic Johnson and Michael Jordan), one of the top box-office draws of the decade was a black comic (Eddie Murphy). But whites aren't interested in black stories or culture?!?

I think white people, like any other people, are interested in seeing that which is good and entertaining, period. And I think Hollywood sells them short.

AFFIRMATIVE ACTION
AN IMPERFECT SOLUTION, BUT THE BEST SO FAR

• *Reconsider Affirmative Action.* Not because it's a perfect solution, but because it's the best we've come up with so far—the only one that addresses not just historical inequities, but also deals with the ongoing unwillingness of many employers to hire African-American applicants.

Like I said, it's imperfect. A white job hopeful loses out to a less qualified black applicant, and he or she is justifiably resentful. A black employee hired under such a program must deal with the lingering suspicion from co-workers that he is second best for the job.

And yet. . . .

For some people, such a program might offer the only opportunity for advancement. For some employers, it might be the only thing that forces them to open their doors to black applicants.

An imperfect solution. But the best we've come up with so far.

I realize it's all a wish list—every bit as fanciful as the Christmas lists I used to hand to my mother every year. And if I'm to be truthful, then I'm forced to admit that I don't expect to see the vast majority of these things happen in my lifetime. Or my children's.

And so, like most of us, I content myself with small victories.

We are too lacking in will for big ones. We are too wedded to the quick and the easy, have too little patience for the long and the hard. I think of that 14-year-old who says the white man is keeping him down, or of those college kids who wanted to touch my hair, and I wonder where they are or will be in 20 years. The white kid will probably be hiring workers at a company somewhere. The black kid will be selling himself short and making excuses for it.

I have hope—not despair. And yet, it's harder some days than others.

I think I understand the frustration many white Americans of good will feel. The frustration of having come through the '60s, come through the fire, having seen the blood flow and the heroes fall and the laws passed and the hopes raised and the battle won . . . and then to see it all come to this, this place of bitterness and polarization.

I can only ask them what I ask of myself: to swallow the frustration, bend your shoulder to the task anew, and dare to dream on. And think about it: If it feels that crushingly overwhelming over on that side for people like you, what must it feel like over here . . . for people like me?

The ruses of racism

Racist violence has recently resurfaced. What conditions encourage its growth?

Michel Wieviorka

MICHEL WIEVIORKA, a French sociologist, is a lecturer at the University of Paris-Dauphine and assistant director of the Centre d'Analyse et d'Intervention Sociologiques in Paris. His published works include *Terrorisme à la une* (with Dominique Wolton, 1987) and *Sociétés et Terrorisme* (1988).

RACISM is not always overtly, brutally violent—it does not always kill. Racial discrimination, expressions of prejudice and racist tracts can all carry ominous overtones of violence, but they cannot be ranked alongside the physical violence perpetrated in pogroms, lynchings, immigrant-bashing, murders and other types of assault, which is what I wish to discuss.

What is more, the most violent forms of racism do not necessarily grow out of other varieties of racism. Contrary to popular belief, prejudice does not invariably and inevitably lead on to acts of violence. Deep-seated racism may be widespread in societies where there is no outward sign of naked violence.

For racist violence to erupt, a certain set of conditions must exist. One conditioning factor is the attitude of those in authority: what they are willing and able to do in order to deal with those who engage in racist acts. When a government is weak or remote, or even tinged with racism itself, it encourages political groups and forces wishing to turn their message of hatred, contempt, subordination and rejection into deeds. It may even become actively racist itself or manipulate racist violence, as happened in the Russian Empire at the turn of the century, where the Czarist regime was largely instrumental in setting off the pogroms.

But there are other factors. Some institutions—particularly the legal system and the police—may use methods which, although not deliberately or explicitly racist in themselves, nevertheless contribute to the spread of serious outbreaks of violence. Many official enquiries have found that when police behaviour has exacerbated ethnic and social tensions instead of defusing them, it has often led to an escalation of violence in which racism occupies a prominent place.

Yet another factor is the existence of political forces capable of providing racist violence with an organized structure and an ideological foundation. As long as such forces do not exist or are relegated to the sidelines of society, violence is always possible and sometimes erupts, but it crops up in the form of sudden outbursts and short-lived explosions, in other words of acts which, numerous though they may be, are not linked by any apparent unifying principle.

Reprinted by courtesy of *The UNESCO Courier,* February 1993, pp. 13-15.

When such forces do gain a political foot-hold, however, the violence for which they provide a structure, even if it is not directly organized by them, nonetheless becomes more cold-blooded, methodical, and active. It becomes a matter of schemes and strategies; it channels popular feelings of hatred and hostility towards the group marked out as a racial target, but does not allow them to be expressed spontaneously. It may even prevent them from being expressed at all, on the political grounds that any act of violence should be consistent with the aims and thinking of the party or organization.

This is why the emergence of a political force with a racist ideology and plans does not necessarily mean that there will be an immediate increase in violence, for violence may actually be detrimental to its attempts to achieve legitimate political status. Violence may create an image of disorder and accordingly be played down until the movement achieves power, when it will be able to indulge in violence in its most extreme forms. Conversely, there may be an increase in violence when the power of a racist force or party is on the wane, because some of its members may take a harder line if they feel they have no political future. The end of apartheid in South Africa is providing scope not for more racism but for more racial violence.

Since the beginning of the modern era, racism has been linked to patterns of domination, especially those of colonialism set against the background of empire-building. But it has also informed trends in thinking which, from the nineteenth century onwards, influenced aspects of physical anthropology and other doctrinaire intellectual movements. When the term "racism" emerged in the period between the two World Wars, some of the theories from the past were refurbished. Above all, racist attitudes spread all over the world in the wake of the social upheavals that are at the root of various forms of racial violence.

Racial violence is no longer only the crude expression of colonial-type domination. It may also stem from an economic crisis, in which a deprived group, threatened with a decline in social status or exclusion from the mainstream, turns against another group in an attempt to oust it, on racial grounds, from a shrinking job market. The racism of the poor whites, which led to the lynching of blacks in the southern United States at the end of the nineteenth century and to race riots in the big cities of the northern United States in the first half of the twentieth century, came about when the whites saw their black neighbours as dangerous competitors on the industrial job market.

But racial violence may also occur among more affluent classes, which want to maintain the gap separating them from the less privileged. The method they use is a combination of social and racial segregation, which may in fact lead to more cold-blooded and calculated forms of violence. At the beginning of the century, well-to-do white citizens in the southern United States organized lynching parties to punish black men accused of raping white women or of theft.

However, racist violence does not always stem solely or directly from social factors. It may originate in a real or imagined threat to the identity of a group, or it may accompany the expansion of a state or religion, sometimes claiming to represent universal values, as often happened during the colonial period.

The urge to uphold a particular identity can lead to unlimited violence, fuelled either by an obsessive fear of "racial intermingling" or by reference to an absolute difference that prohibits all social intercourse and all contact between races except in war. Such forms of racism are intended to keep others at bay, to ensure that they are segregated or even expelled or destroyed. The aim is not so much to establish the inferior status of a given group on the grounds of its physical attributes as to ensure that a community remains homogeneous or a nation remains pure, or to justify their unimpeded expansion.

Identity-related racism and the violence that goes with it can have three quite distinct motivations.

In some cases, this form of racism is founded on the affirmation of an identity that claims to be universal and seeks to crush everything that opposes it. The history of colonization contains many instances of this phenomenon. Conversely, it may be based on the resistance of a nation or community to the modern world, in which case the chosen target is a group that is seen as the incarnation of evil, intrusion, or the corruption of culture or traditional values. The Jews have long been denounced and attacked as representives of a hated modernity. The explosive violence of the pogroms and the more methodical violence of the gas chambers largely grew out of criticisms, phantasms and rumours that reproached the

Jews on the grounds of their cosmopolitanism, wealth, political power and influence in the media.

Thirdly, this identity-related racism may flare up as a result of a clash between two or more communities within the same political entity or a multiracial or multicultural society. In such cases, violence results from strained relations between communities, from a process of interaction in which one group's real or imagined attempt to assert itself prompts reactions from other groups and triggers off a spiralling power struggle that may end in an outburst of violence and political chaos. The civil war in Lebanon and the breakup of Yugoslavia are recent examples of conflicts where overt or implied references to race can be sensed behind rhetorical appeals to the nation or to the cultural, confessional and historical community.

When violence is associated with racism, therefore, it is governed by various conditions that dictate the course it takes and is rooted in a wide range of social and identity-related fac-tors. But the important thing about violence is that it compresses into a single action factors that may be not only different but contradictory. Perpetrators of racist violence may wish, for example, to exclude a specific group from their society, and also assign it an inferior position in society so as to exploit it. This happens frequently in industrialized countries, where immigrants are employed to do low-grade jobs and rejected on account of their culture. Or to take another case, in Czarist Russia and central Europe at the beginning of the present century, it was the rich, assimilated Jew, symbol of modernity, who was regarded as an intolerable threat, yet the victims of the pogroms were the culturally conspicuous and poverty-stricken Jewish masses.

This is the paradox of violence: not only is it unembarrassed by its inherent contradictions, it also creates its own logic and its own dynamics, so that in the end it alters the conditions that allowed it to emerge in the first place.

flirting

with disaster

You and your coworker are attracted to each other. Is a little sexual innuendo at work okay? Or have sexual harassment laws abolished flirtation forever?

Joshua Halberstam

Let's begin with her lips. Wonderful, sensual lips. Terrific smile, too, which she flashes in my direction much too infrequently. But when she does, I cast a smile back and then comes that delightful surge of (shall I presume?) shared arousal. But she and I work together. We're professionals and respect each other as such. And, mind you, I don't take the smile as a come-on. She's got a boyfriend, happily so, monogamously so. I'm not especially up for an affair with her, either. This is just fleeting, flirtatious fun.

There are moments, however, when I have the urge to *tell* her that she has wonderful, sensual lips. But I don't dare. I worry that I'll be misunderstood. I worry that flirting with her could be flirting with a pink slip.

Coquettish behavior in the workplace isn't simple—not with the laws of sexual harassment buzzing in the background. Not with women still vulnerable to the injuries of sexism. And not with the usual male insecurities that make it hard for him to tell whether his flirting is appreciated or perceived as obnoxious. Women flirt too, of course. But because they are more often the victims, not the perpetrators, of sexual harassment, this flirting business is not so tricky for them—or at least it hasn't been so far.

My point is that consciousness of sexual harassment is a good thing, but the inhibiting atmosphere this creates at the workplace isn't. It's very difficult for the decent guy to know how to behave, especially if he doesn't believe we should, or even could, eradicate every hint of our sexuality from the workplace.

I'm just your average friendly, properly evolved guy. I like women. I like the idea of women liking me. I like

flirting. I don't want to offend. And I really don't want to be associated with the lingering Neanderthals who advise their female employees that the vertical movement of their career depends on a horizontal recline on the sofa. Those guys give all the rest of us a bad name.

Indeed, a 1985 study cited by the American Psychological Association found that in the work environment, men are four times more likely than women to think that the people they flirt with will be flattered by their sexual overtures and four times less likely to predict that the object of their flirting will be insulted or put off. Men undoubtedly misstep often.

"What does a woman want?" Sigmund Freud asked the now clichéd question in a letter to a colleague, but never could answer it to anyone's satisfaction. Today, my question is: "What do women feel is appropriate?" Even the most enlightened men aren't sure what is acceptable behavior at the watercooler, in a meeting, across the desk. Is the sexual innuendo okay? Where does gallantry leave off and sexism begin? Does a woman want to be included when we repeat a dirty joke or would she prefer that we wait until she leaves the room?

"Don't worry," you assure me and the men for whom I speak. "Be natural, be respectful, and no one will mistake you for one of the sleazeballs." But it's just not that simple. What's intended may not be what's perceived. Flirting is, like beauty, in the eye of the beholder. And there's also the matter of power. Behavior that seems appropriate with a peer might be inappropriate with someone who is junior or even senior.

We've lost sight of the fun of flirting at work—it's become so tangled up in a web of legal, moral and personal issues. Perhaps there's a way to sift out flirting as a social art form from sexual harassment, so that men

This article was originally published in *Self*, March 1994, pp. 152-155. © 1994 by Professor Joshua Halberstam, New York University, Department of Philosophy. Reprinted by permission of the author.

and women can rediscover the little teasing exchange and the fleeting rush. Shouldn't we be free to deliver a compliment—and perhaps, joy of joys, get one back?

The goal of flirting isn't always a sexual liaison. People flirt at the office for all sorts of reasons. Some flirt for fun, for attention, even just for something to do. Others flirt because it's good business. Carla is a high-achieving salesperson who uses her wiles to close deals. She deliberately continues to look into her customer's eyes longer than is routine. She knows he notices, just as she knows he notices the hint of thigh she's showing. But she has no interest in spending the night with this man—in fact, she'd rather watch reruns of old movies on cable. What Carla desires is to close the deal on favorable terms; so she'll charm the customer and flirt with him to get the job done.

The way matters now stand, I can tell a colleague that she looks elegant in her new dress but not that she looks sexy.

No matter the purpose, all flirting is sexual and creates an immediate aura of arousal between two consenting people. This is one of the chief pleasures of flirting. Indeed, biologists have recently discovered that the chemistry between a flirting couple is more than a metaphor. Flirting triggers a series of hormonal and neural changes that typically accompany pleasureable sexual activities.

Flirting's other great satisfaction lies in its inherent subtlety. If he asks her to go to bed with him, that's a proposition, not a flirtation. If she runs her hand gently across his cheek, that's a gesture of seduction, not a flirtation. When we flirt, our messages are always ambiguous; we can interpret the signals in more ways than one. Are you just imagining that when she handed you the pen, she stroked your palm ever so delicately? Is he spending so much time on the layouts because he enjoys looking at your design work, or because he enjoys looking at you? Social psychologists Maury Silber and John Sabini, in their book *Moralities of Everyday Life*, explain that when you flirt you experience " . . . the pleasure in carrying off just the right move, of exercising strategic talents, or of deciphering the mysteries of your partner's motives."

And that is my problem. Our problem. Uncertainty is fun only when the consequences of making a mistake aren't painful. That's why flirting in a bar or at the Christmas party is so easy, so fluid—you don't get crucified for inadvertently stepping over the line. Since flirtation is by necessity highly ambiguous, it hasn't been easy for managers and legal scholars to outline and reinforce proper conduct. How many seconds of eye contact constitute flirting? How many inches from a person should you

stand? Did they cover this sort of thing in the Antioch College Rules for Dating?

In 1980, the Equal Employment Opportunity Commission first issued guidelines that deemed sexual harassment a violation of Title VII of the Civil Rights Act of 1964. Sexual harassment was now a federal offense. Employers would be liable for failing to take reasonable steps to prevent harassment or for failure to take steps to remedy it.

Harassment could take two forms. One was "quid pro quo" exploitation. That's where your superior makes it clear that if you want to advance in your job, or not lose it altogether, you have to date him or sleep with him (or her, for that matter). The second type of harassment was more general, and referred to the presence of a "hostile working environment": when derogatory sexual comments, sexual innuendos or unwanted touching impede your job performance, or drive you to despair.

The law is no longer so simple. Last November, in *Harris v. Forklift Systems, Inc.*, the Supreme Court decided, with what *The New York Times* called "surprising speed and unanimity," on a much broader definition of sexual harassment. No longer do you have to prove that the harassment interferes with your work, or drives you batty. All you need to demonstrate is "an environment that a reasonable person would find hostile or abusive." For example, some courts have deemed that pinups on walls contribute to a hostile environment; even nudes in reproductions of classical paintings have figured in harassment proceedings.

Does this affect the way men and women flirt in the workplace? You bet it does. Sexual harassment no longer requires that a specific person be harassed. My friend Eric was called on the carpet for exchanging some sexual banter with a member of his staff. "But, she didn't complain, she didn't mind at all," Eric explained. "In fact, she initiated the exchange and traded with me line for line." The corporate voice of authority was not appeased. "It doesn't matter how she felt. Your remarks contributed to what some might perceive as an abusive environment, and that's cause for serious concern."

Your behavior can be construed as contributing to a hostile environment even when you are flirting "laterally"—with colleagues at the same level. But the fact that Eric was flirting with someone in a subordinate position invited stronger censure. This continues to be a bigger problem for men than for women; statistically, men still predominate in positions of power. No doubt, it will become more of a problem for women as they increasingly command more power and fill higher posts in their fields.

Unquestionably, a code of conduct guarding against sexual harassment is much needed. But will that, along with concerns about male chauvinism, spell the end of flirting at work? I'd say it's neither possible nor desirable.

One of the most significant cultural developments in American life during this past century is the massive entry of women into the workplace. And all Americans, men and women, are putting in longer and longer workdays. (We now work an average 160 hours more a year—a full month—than we did two decades ago.) The upshot is that men and women are spending most of their waking hours together at the office, and the division between life at work and life on the outside is blurring. While the sociology might be new, the biology is not. Put that many men and women in the same environment for that many hours, and you will get lots of sexual tension and lots of flirting. Sure, the workplace isn't the bedroom, but we certainly do not leave our bodies at home for the day. To deny our sexuality in the workplace is to deny who we really are—human beings with a sense of humor and a sense of play.

To deny even a small part of our sexuality in the workplace is to deny who we really are.

In fact, the workplace is increasingly a place in which to meet one's mate. Intraoffice romances are undeniably a flourishing phenomenon. A recent Gallup poll shows that a majority of Americans consider dating between coworkers acceptable, and so do most corporations. They have adopted an attitude of "benign neglect" toward intraoffice dating; one survey of 1,500 personnel managers found that 92 percent have no policy prohibiting it. That's hardly surprising when you consider how many couples work together—at AT&T, for example, there are

8,000 couples out of 260,000 U.S. employees. Presumably, all of these relationships began with some form of flirting.

Naomi Weinstein, a vice president at The Equitable Life Assurance Society in Secaucus, New Jersey, agrees that it's foolhardy to try to eradicate flirting by decree. "Flirting is a fact of office life. It goes on at all levels, although there's still more of it between male superiors and the women who work for them than the other way around. I'll step in only when someone crosses the line between the harmless and the offensive. If some guy's got nude photos on his desk, or a woman comes to work dressed half-naked, or someone is constantly on the make, I'll let them know that his or her behavior is inappropriate. Usually the problem can be resolved with an honest conversation, well before I need to threaten anyone with corporate sanctions."

The end of flirting is hardly desirable, either. It certainly means a loss of spontaneity. The corporate atmosphere has a new grayish tinge, a Calvinist tone to it. Yes, the climate is safer. But I wonder what we're missing out on. Doesn't the casual, impulsive banter contribute something to our creative efforts at work? Don't most of us feel, men *and* women, that our wings are clipped?

The way matters now stand, I can tell a colleague that she looks elegant in her new dress but not that she looks sexy. Perhaps that's not so bad. Some guys may accept this state of affairs and give up flirting altogether. But I—and a fair number of men, I'd venture to say—aren't ready to quit just yet; there are enough barriers between men and women. So, heeding my own advice, I did mention those terrific lips to my coworker. And hey, it went over just fine. Those lips don't bite, except ever so gently in my fantasy world—which she never needs to know about.

MEDIA, VIOLENCE, YOUTH, AND SOCIETY

Ray Surette

Ray Surette is professor of criminal justice in the School of Public Affairs and Services, Florida International University, North Miami, and author of Media, Crime and Criminal Justice: Images and Realities.

It is guns, it is poverty, it is overcrowding, and it is the uniquely American problem of a culture that is infatuated with violence. We love it, we glamorize it, we teach it to our children.[1]

The above testimony by Dr. Deborah Prothrow-Stith on gangs and youth violence presented before the U.S. Senate contains two important points concerning the mass media and youth violence. First, it does not mention the media as a factor in violence, lending support to the view that the media are not crucial agents in youth violence. Second, it does cite an American culture that is infatuated with violence, and the glamorization and teaching of violence to our children, as problems. Culture, glamorization, and instruction, however, are areas where the media have been shown to play important social roles. The above statement simultaneously provides support for the position that the media are indeed important players in the production of youth violence and yet paradoxically also supports the position that they are not contributors. The relative validity of these two dichotomous positions, the media as unimportant and the media as central in fostering youth violence, has dominated the public discussion, resulting in much confusion about this issue and public posturing by various groups and individuals. The actual relationship of the media to youth violence lies somewhere between these two extremes.

Research interest in the relationship of the mass media to social violence has been elevated for most of this century. Over the twentieth century, the issue of the media as a source of violence has moved into and out of the public consciousness in predictable ten-to twenty-year cycles. If a consensus has emerged from the research and public interest, it is that the sources of violence are complex and tied to our most basic nature as well as the social world we have created and that the media's particular relationship to social violence is extremely complicated. (See the discussion in this author's *Media, Crime, and Criminal Justice* [1992] and in *Crime and Human Nature* [1985] by J. Wilson and R. Herrnstein.)

Therefore, when discussing the nature of the relationship between the media and violence, it is important not to be myopic. Social violence is embedded in historical, social forces and phenomena, while the media are components of a larger information system that creates and distributes knowledge about the world. The media and social violence must both be approached as parts of phenomena that have numerous interconnections and paths of influence between them. Too narrow a perspective on youth violence or the media's role in its generation oversimplifies both the problem and the solutions we pursue. Nowhere is this more apparent than in the current concern about media, youth, and violence.

STATISTICS ON YOUTH VIOLENCE

The source of this concern is revealed by a brief review of the statistics of youth violence.[2] Youth violence, and particularly violent crime committed by youth, has recently increased dramatically. Today about 5 out of

every 20 robbery arrests and 3 of every 20 murder, rape, and aggravated assault arrests are of juveniles. In raw numbers, this translates into 3,000 murder, 6,000 forcible rape, 41,000 robbery, and 65,000 aggravated assault arrests of youths annually.

The surge in youth criminal violence is concentrated within the past five years. During the first part of the 1980s, there was a general decline in youth arrests for both violent and property crimes. In the latter half of the 1980s, however, youth arrests increased at a pace greater than that of adults for violent crimes. Youth arrests increased substantially between 1981 and 1990 for nonaggravated assault (72 percent), murder and nonnegligent manslaughter (60 percent), aggravated assault (57 percent), weapons violations (41 percent), and forcible rape (28 percent). Looking over a generational time span from 1965 to 1989, the arrest rate for violent crimes by youths grew between the mid-1960s and the mid-1970s but then leveled off and remained relatively constant until the late 1980s. At that time, the rate again began to increase, reaching its highest recorded level in the most recent years.

Thus, while the proportion of youth in the general population has declined as the baby-boom generation has aged, the rate of violence from our youth has increased significantly. We have fewer youth proportionately, but they are more violent and account for increased proportions of our violent crime. Attempts to comprehend and explain this change have led invariably to the mass media as prime suspects, but deciphering the media's role has not been a simple or straightforward task.

This difficulty in deciphering the media's role is due to the fact that the relationship of media to violence is complex, and the media's influence can be both

■ The Trojan priest Laocoon and his twin sons, Antiphas and Thymbraeus, being attacked by Apollo's sea serpents. A Roman copy, c. 100 B.C.

direct and indirect. Research on their relationship (reported, for example, in George Comstock's 1980 study *Television in America*) has revealed that media effects that appear when large groups are examined are not predictable at the individual subject level. The media are also related to social violence in ways not usually considered in the public debate, such as their effects on public policies and general social attitudes toward violence.

Adding to the complexity of the media's relationship, there are many other sources of violence that either interact with the media or work alone to produce violence. These sources range from individual biology to characteristics of our history and culture. The importance of nonmedia factors such as neighborhood and family conditions, individual psychological and genetic traits, and our social structure, race relations, and economic conditions for the generation of violence are commonly acknowledged and analyzed, as in Jeffrey Goldstein's 1986 study *Aggression and Crimes of Violence*. The role of the mass media is confounded with these other sources, and its significance is often either lost or exaggerated. One task of this essay is thus to dispel the two popular but polarizing notions that have dominated the public debate. The first is that the media

are the primary cause of violence in society. The second is that the media have no, or a very limited, effect on social violence.

The former view of the media as the source of primary effects is often advanced along with draconian policy demands such as extensive government intervention or direct censorship of the media. The counterargument to this position is supported by a number of points. The most basic is that we were a violent nation before we had mass media, and there is no evidence that the removal of violent media would make us nonviolent.[3] Some research into copy-cat crime additionally provides no evidence of a criminalization effect from the media as a cause.[4] The media alone cannot turn a law-abiding individual into a criminal one nor a nonviolent youth into a violent one. In sum, individual and national violence cannot be blamed primarily on the media, and violence-reducing policies directed only at the media will have little effect.

The latter argument, that the media have limited to no effect on levels of social violence, is structured both in posture and approach to the tobacco industry's response to research linking smoking to lung cancer and it rings just as hollow. The argument's basic approach is to ex-

pound inherent weaknesses in the various methodologies of the media-violence research and to trumpet the lack of evidence of strong, direct effects, while ignoring the persistent pattern of positive findings. Proponents of the nil effect point out that laboratory experiments are biased toward finding an effect. To isolate the effect of a single factor, in this case the media, and observe a rare social behavior, namely violence, experiments must exaggerate the link between media and aggression and create a setting that will elicit violent behavior. They therefore argue that all laboratory research on the issue is irrelevant. They continue, however, to dismiss the nonlaboratory research because of a lack of strict variable controls and designs that leave open noncausal interpretations of the results. "No effects" proponents lastly argue that while society reinforces some behaviors shown in the media such as that found in commercials, it does not condone or reinforce violence and, therefore, a violence-enhancing effect should not be expected (a view discussed in "Smoking Out the Critics," a 1984 *Society* article [21:36–40] by A. Wurtzel and G. Lometti).

In reality, the research shows persistent behavioral effects from violent media under diverse situations for differing groups.[5] Regarding the strong behavioral effects apparent in fashion and fad, effects that Madison Avenue touts, the argument of a behavioral effect only on sanctioned behavior but not on unsanctioned violence is specious. The media industry claim of

If a consensus has emerged from the research and public interest, it is that the media's particular relationship to social violence is extremely complicated.

having only positive behavioral effects is as valid as the tobacco industry claiming that their ads do not encourage new smokers but only persuade brand switching among established smokers. First, violence is sometimes socially sanctioned, particularly within the U.S. youth and hypermasculine culture that is the target audience of the most prominently violent media. And although the media cannot criminalize someone not having criminal predispositions, media-generated, copycat crime is a significant criminal phenomenon with ample anecdotal and case evidence providing a form for criminality to take.[6] The recurring mimicking of dangerous film stunts belies the argument of the media having only positive behavioral effects. It is apparent that while the media alone cannot make someone a criminal, it can change the criminal behavior of a predisposed offender.

CONFLICTING CAUSAL CLAIMS

The two arguments of primary cause and negligible cause compete for public support. These models not only posit differing causal relations between the media and violence but imply vastly different public policies regarding the media as well. The primary-cause model (fig. 1) is that of a significant, direct linear relationship between violent media and violent behavior. In this model, violent media, independent of other factors, directly cause violent behavior. If valid, it indicates that strong intervention is necessary in the content, distribution, and creation of violent media.

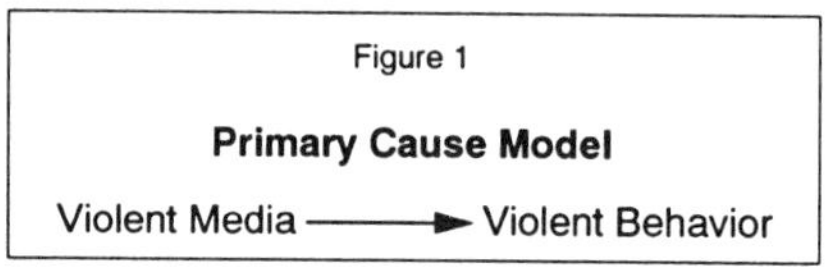

Figure 1

Primary Cause Model

Violent Media ⟶ Violent Behavior

The negligible-cause model (fig. 2) concedes a statistical association between the media and violent behavior but poses the connection as due not to a causal relationship but to persons predisposed to violence simultaneously seeking out violent media and more often behaving violently. As the relationship is associative and not causal in this model, policies targeted at the media will have no effects on violent behavior and the media can be safely ignored.

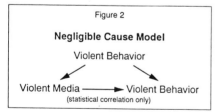

Figure 2

Negligible Cause Model

Violent Behavior

Violent Media ⟶ Violent Behavior
(statistical correlation only)

Both models inaccurately describe the media-violence relationship. The actual relationship between the factors is felt to be bidirectional and cyclical (fig. 3). In addition to violently predisposed people seeking out violent media and violent media causing violent behavior, violent media play a role in the generation of violently predisposed people through their effects on attitudes. And as the made-for-

The view of the media as the source of primary effects is often advanced along with draconian policy demands such as extensive government intervention or direct censorship of the media.

TV movie industry reflects, violent behavior sometimes results in the creation of more violent media. Finally, by providing live models of violence and creating community and home environments that are more inured to and tolerant of violence, violent behavior helps to create more violently predisposed youth in society. Therefore, while the direct effect of media on violence may not be initially large, its influence cycles through the model and accumulates.

An area of research that provides an example of the bidirectional model is the relationship of pornography to sexual violence; a recent (1993) overview of such research can be found in *Pornography,* by D. Linz and N. Malamuth. On one hand, the research establishes that depictions of sexual violence, specifically those that link sex with physical violence toward women, foster antisocial attitudes toward women and lenient perceptions of the

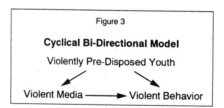

Figure 3

Cyclical Bi-Directional Model

Violently Pre-Disposed Youth

Violent Media ⟶ Violent Behavior

crime of rape. Aberrant perceptions, such as increased belief in the "rape myth" (that women unconsciously want to be raped or somehow enjoy being raped), have been reported. Virtually none of the research, however, reveals strong direct effects from pornography, and even sexually violent media do not appear to negatively affect all male viewers. Many cultural and individual factors appear to mediate the effects and to foster the predisposition to sexually violent media and sexual violence. Researchers in this area have concluded that the media are one of many social forces that affect the development of intervening variables, such as thought patterns, sexual arousal patterns, motivations, and personality characteristics that are associated with tolerance for

sexual violence and perhaps an increase in sexually violent behavior in society.[7] As in other areas of media-violence research, sexually violent media emerge as neither a primary engine nor an innocuous social factor.

THE KEY TO MEDIA EFFECTS

The key to media effects occurring in any particular instance, then, are the intermediate, interactive factors. In terms of the media, there are numerous interactive factors that have been identified as conducive to generating aggressive effects. Among the many delineated in the research, a sample includes: reward or lack of punishment for the perpetrator, portrayal of violence as justified, portrayal of the consequences of violence in a way that does not stir distaste, portrayal of violence without critical commentary, the presence of live peer models of violence, and the presence of sanctioning adults (all discussed in Comstock's *Television in America*). Only unambiguous linking of violent behavior with undesirable consequences or motives by the media appears capable of inhibiting subsequent aggression in groups of viewers.

A list of nonmedia factors deemed significant in the development of crime and the number of violently predisposed individuals can be culled from *Crime and Human Nature* by J. Wilson and R. Herrnstein. The authors list constitutional, developmental, and social-context factors including gender, age, intelligence, personality, psychopathology, broken and abusive families, schools, community, labor markets, alcohol and heroin, and finally history and culture. As can be seen, most aspects of modern life are implicated, and only tangential factors like diet and climate (which other researchers would have included) are left out. With such a large number of factors coming into play, the levels of interactions and complexity of relationships are obviously enormous.

The research on violence suggests that certain factors are basic to violent crime, as detailed by Wilson and Herrnstein. None of these factors dominates, but none are without significant effects.

Accordingly, the research (contained in this author's 1992 study *Media, Crime and Criminal Justice*) clearly signifies the media as only some of many factors in the generation of youth violence and that media depictions of violence do not affect all persons in the same way. The media contribute to violence in combination with other social and psychological factors. Whether or not a particular media depiction will cause a particular viewer to act more aggressively is not a straightforward issue. The emergence of an effect depends on the interaction between each individual viewer, the content of the portrayal, and the setting in which exposure to the media occurs. This gives the media significant aggregate effects but makes these effects difficult to predict for individuals. There is no doubt, however, that violent children, including those who come to have significant criminal records, spend more time exposed to violent media than do less violent children. The issue is not the existence of a media effect but the magnitude or importance of the effect.

Media violence correlates as strongly with and is as causally related to the magnitude of violent behavior as any other social behavioral variable that has been studied. This reflects both the media's impact and our lack of knowledge about the etiology of violence. Because of the many individual and social factors that come into play in producing any social behavior, one should not expect to find more than a modest direct relationship between the media and violence. Following their review of the research, Thomas Cook and his colleagues conclude:

> No effects emerge that are so large as to hit one between the eyes, but early measure of viewing violence adds to the predictability of later aggression over and above the predictability afforded by earlier measures of aggression. These lagged effects are consistently positive, but not large, and they are rarely statistically significant, although no reliable lagged negative effects have been reported. . . . But is the association causal? If we were forced to render a judgment, probably yes. . . . There is strong evidence of causation in the wrong setting (the lab) with the right population (normal children) and in the right setting (outside the lab) with the wrong population (abnormal adults).[8]

MEDIA AMONG MANY FACTORS

In summation, despite the fact that the media are among many factors, they should not be ignored, regardless of the level of their direct impact. Because social violence is a pressing problem, even those factors that only modestly contribute to it are important. Small effects of the media accumulate and appear to have significant long-term social effects.[9] The

research strongly indicates that we are a more violent society because of our mass media. Exactly how and to what extent the media cause long-term changes in violent behavior remains unknown, but the fact that it plays an important, but not independent, role is generally conceded.

What public policies are suggested by the knowledge we now possess about media and violence? Not all of the factors discussed above are good candidates for public intervention strategies, but there are three sources of youth violence that government policy can influence. In order of importance, they are: extreme differences in economic conditions and the concentration of wealth in America; the American gun culture; and, exacerbating the problems created by the first two, the media's violence-enhancing messages. Family, neighborhood, and personality factors may be more important for generating violence in absolute magnitude, but they are not easily influenced by public actions.

The magnitude of economic disparity and the concentration of wealth in the United States is greater than in comparable (and, not surprisingly, less violent) societies. Our richest citizens not only earn vastly more than our poorest, but, more important, the wealth in the country is increasingly concentrated in fewer and fewer hands. The trend during this century, which accelerated during the 1980s, is for an ever-shrinking percentage of the richest Americans to control greater proportions of the country's wealth, while the poorest have access to increasingly smaller proportions. The burden of this economic disenfranchisement, both psychologically and fiscally, falls heavily on the young, and especially on the young who are urban poor minorities, as is shown in Elliott Currie's 1985 study *Confronting Crime*. In a consumerism-saturated society like the United States, hopelessness, bitterness, and disregard for moral values and law are heightened by this growing economic disparity.

And as the economic polarization and violent crime have grown, we also became nationally fixated on heightening and extending our punishment capacities in an attempt to suppress violent behavior, evidenced by Diana Gordon's 1991 study *The Justice Juggernaut*. Since 1975, we have increased the rate of juvenile incarceration steadily. Today we hold in custody approximately one hundred thousand juveniles every year. Despite our strengthened capacity to punish, however, youth violence has not abated.

■ Marsyas being flayed alive by Apollo after losing a musical contest to him, c. 200 B.C.

This result should have been expected because two social mechanisms are needed to reduce violence—punishing violent criminal behavior and rewarding law-abiding, nonviolent behavior. Societies that are more successful in balancing the two mechanisms are less violent, as shown in *Crime and Control in Comparative Perspective*, by H. Heiland and L. Shelley (1992). While punishment of violent behavior is certainly necessary and justified, its emphasis, coupled with the concentration of wealth in America, has resulted in the degrading of the equally important social capacity to reward law-abiding behavior. By emphasizing one, we have lamed and discredited the other. Nonmaterial rewards like social status, an esteemed reputation, and a clear conscience have been losing their legitimacy

A Brief History of Television and Youth Violence Research

The logic of science requires that in order to establish the causal effect of a variable, one must be able to examine a situation without the variable's effect. In terms of television and violence, this requirement means that a group of subjects (a control group) who have not been exposed to violent television is necessary for comparison with a violent television-exposed group. Television, however, is ubiquitous and an integral part of a modern matrix of influences on social behaviors. Therefore, when the interest is in the effects of television on mainstream citizens in Western industrialized and urbanized nations, finding nontelevision-exposed controls is essentially impossible. In response, artificial laboratory situations are created, or statistical controls and large data sets are employed. Thus, while social sciences abound with research reporting variables that are correlated with one another, research firmly establishing causal relationships is rare. Unlike the content of television, there are few smoking guns in social science. Rather than conclusively proven, cause is more often inferred in a trial-like decision from the predominance of evidence. Such is the case with television and violence.

In a traditional laboratory experiment, two sets of matched, usually randomly assigned, subjects are placed in identical situations except for a single factor of interest. Early research in the television-violence quest were in this vein, with the seminal ones conducted in the 1960s by researchers Bandura, Ross, and Ross.[1] These laboratory studies basically consisted of exposing groups of young children to either a short film containing violence (frequently an adult beating up an inflated Bobo doll) or a similar but nonviolent film. The two groups of children were then placed in playrooms and observed. Children who watched the film where a doll was attacked would significantly more often attack a similar doll if given the opportunity shortly after viewing their film than children who had observed a nonviolent film. These and other studies established the existence of an "observational imitation" effect from visual violence; in short, children will imitate violence they see in the media. It was concluded by many that television violence must therefore be a cause of youth violence.

However, critics of this conclusion argued that because laboratory situations are purposely artificial and contrived to isolate the influence of a single variable, the social processes producing aggression in the laboratory are not equal to those found in the real world. In summary, one cannot assume that behavior and variable relationships observed in the lab are occurring in the home or street.

In addition to the laboratory studies, at about the same time a number of survey studies were reporting positive correlations between youth aggression and viewing violent television.[2] Efforts to extend the laboratory findings and determine if the correlational studies reflected real-world causal relationships led to two types of research: natural field experiments[3] and longitudinal panel studies.

The better known and most discussed research efforts came from longitudinal panel studies conducted in the 1970s and early '80s. Expensive and time consuming, in panel studies a large number of subjects are selected and followed for a number of years. Three such studies are particularly important due to their renown, similarities in approach, and differences in conclusions.

The first study (called the Rip van Winkle study) by L. Rowell Huesmann, Leonard Eron, and their colleagues used a cross-lag panel design (that is, comparison over time and with different populations) in which television habits at grade three (approximately age eight) were correlated with aggression in grade three and with television viewing and aggression ten years later for a sample of 211 boys.[4] The researchers collected their data in rural New York State from students in the third, eighth, and "thirteenth" grades (one year after graduation). Favorite television programs were rated based on their violent content, and frequency of viewing was obtained from the children's mothers in grade three and from the subjects in grades eight and thirteen. The measure of aggression was a peer-nominated rating obtained from responses to questions such as, "Who starts fights over nothing?" The most significant finding

---

1. See, for example, A. Bandura, D. Ross, and S. A. Ross, "Transmission of Aggression through Imitation of Aggressive Models," *Journal of Abnormal and Social Psychology* 63 (1961), 575–82; and "Imitation of film-mediated aggressive models" *Journal of Abnormal and Social Psychology* 66 (1963), 3–11.

2. See G. Comstock, et al., *Television and Human Behavior* (New York: Columbia University Press, 1978) for a review.

3. Natural field experiments typically take advantage of a planned introduction of television to a previously unexposed population. This allows both a pretelevision and posttelevision comparison of the new television group and comparisons with similar but still unexposed other groups. Although rare because of the unique circumstances necessary and by definition confined to nonmainstream populations, these studies report significant increases in aggressive behavior for children who watched a lot of television in the new-television populations. See, for example, G. Granzberg, "The Introduction of Television into a Northern Manitoba Cree Community" in G. Granzberg and J. Steinberg, eds. *Television and the Canadian Indian* (Winnipeg, Manitoba; University of Winnipeg Press, 1980); and T. Williams, ed., *The Impact of Television: A Natural Experiment in Three Communities* (New York: Academic Press, 1985).

4. M. Lefkowitz, et al., "Television Violence and Child Aggression: A Follow-up Study" in G. A. Comstock and E. A. Rubinstein, eds. *Television and Social Behavior*, vol 3 *Television and Adolescent Aggressiveness* (Washington, D.C.: U.S. Government Printing Office, 1971).

reported was a strong, positive association between violent television viewing at grade three and aggression at grade thirteen. However, this study was criticized for a number of reasons. For example, the measure of aggression used in grade thirteen was poorly worded and phrased in the past tense (i.e., "Who started fights over nothing?") and thus the answers were ambiguous in that the grade thirteen subjects may have been referring to general reputations rather than current behaviors. In addition, cross-lagged correlation analysis has a built-in bias toward finding relationships where none exist. Despite the study's weaknesses, Huesmann and Eron concluded that a causal relationship between television violence and aggression existed. This study had a strong public impact.

A second longitudinal panel study was conducted by Ronald Milavsky and his colleagues in the early 1970s that had an opposite conclusion. This study was based on surveys of about 2,400 elementary students age seven to twelve, and 403 male teenagers age twelve to sixteen in Minneapolis, Minnesota, and Fort Worth, Texas.[5] The subjects were surveyed five to six times over nineteen months. This study also used peer-nominated aggression measures for the younger group and four self-reported measures of aggression for the teenagers.[6] Unlike the "van Winkle" study, which used the children's mothers' selection of favorite programs, this study measured exposure to violent programming based on the subjects' own reports. Their analysis further controlled for earlier levels of aggression and exposure to television violence, in effect searching for evidence of significant incremental increases in youth aggression that could be attributed to past exposure to television violence after taking into account past levels of aggressive behavior.

Huesmann and Eron report meaningful lagged associations between later aggression and a number of prior conditions such as earlier aggression in a child's classroom, father's use of physical punishment, family conflict, and violent environments—but not for prior exposure to violent television. Although some significant positive relationships were found between exposure to television violence and later aggression, the overall pattern and number of findings regarding television were interpreted as inconsistent. These researchers conclude that chance, not cause, is the best explanation for their findings regarding television and aggression.

Partly in response to the Milavsky study and criticisms of their earlier methodology, Huesmann, Eron, and their colleagues conducted a third panel study (the Chicago Circle study) in the late 1970s using first and third graders in Chicago public and parochial schools as subjects.[7] Six hundred seventy-two students were initially sampled and tested for three consecutive years in two groups. One group was followed from first through third grades, the second from third through fifth grades. Aggression was measured once more by a peer-generated scale in which each child designated other children on fifteen descriptive statements, ten of which dealt with aggression. (An example is, "Who pushes and shoves other children?") Exposure to violent television was measured by asking each child to select the show most often watched and frequency of watching from eight different ten-program lists. Each list contained a mix of violent and nonviolent programs.

The study was simultaneously conducted in the United States, Australia, Finland, Israel, the Netherlands, and Poland. Their analysis of the U.S. data showed a significant general effect for television violence on girls but not for boys. However, the interaction of viewing violent television and identification with aggressive television characters was a significant predictor of male aggression. Huesmann and Eron conclude that the relationship between television violence and viewer aggression is causal and significant but bidirectional.

At this time, most reviewers of these studies and the subsequent research that followed conclude that a modest but genuine causal association does exist between media violence and aggression.[8] The fact is that, once introduced, the effect of television on a society or an individual can never be fully extricated from all the other forces that may contribute to violence. Television's influence is so intertwined with these parallel forces that searches for strong direct causal effects are not likely to be fruitful. But similar to smoking/lung cancer research, evidence of a real causal connection of some sort has been established beyond a reasonable doubt for most people.

—*R.S.*

---

5. J. Milavsky, et al., *Television and Aggression: A Panel Study* (New York: Academic Press, 1982).

6. Personal aggression toward others, aggression against a teacher (rudeness or unruliness), property aggression (theft and vandalism), and delinquency (serious or criminal behaviors).

7. See Rowell Huesmann and Leonard Eron, "Television Violence and Aggressive Behavior" in D. Pearl, L. Bouthilet, and J. Lazar, eds. *Television and Behavior: Ten Years of Scientific Progress and Implications for the 80's* (Washington, D.C., 1982); and "Factors Influencing the Effect of Television Violence on Children" in Michael Howe, ed., *Learning from Television: Psychological and Educational Research* (New York: Academic Press, 1983).

8. See, for example, L. Heath, L. Bresolin, and R. Rinaldi, "Effects of Media Violence on Children: A Review of the Literature," *Archives of General Psychiatry* 46 (1989), 376–79.

The fear and loathing we feel toward criminals—youthful, violent, or not—is tied to our media-generated image of criminality.

with the young, while material rewards for law-abiding life-styles such as careers, comfortable incomes and affordable goods are less generally available to our poorest and, not surprisingly most crime-prone and violent citizens.

We have chosen to emphasize the mechanism, punishment, that is actually the weaker of the two in actually influencing behavior. As operant conditioning theory would predict, punishment, if severe enough, can suppress one type of violent crime. But the suppression of one behavior gives no push toward a desirable replacement activity, and a substitute violent crime will likely emerge. So "smash and grab" robberies give way to "bump and rob" holdups. Shaping behavior requires a credible reward system. In social terms, youth must see law-abiding behavior as credible and potentially rewarding as well as seeing violent behavior as potentially resulting in punishment.

The second area that government policy can immediately address is the gun culture in America. Our culture of violence, referred to in the opening quote, is made immeasurably more deadly by the enfolded gun culture. The availability of guns as cheap killing mechanisms is simply a national insanity. The mass production of these killing "toys" and the easy access to them must be addressed. The most recent statistics show that one out of every ten high school students report that they carry a handgun. Gun buy-back programs should be supported, and production and availability must be reduced if a positive net effect is to be expected. Irrespective of the difficulty of controlling the sources of individual violent behavior, the implements of fatal violence should not be ignored.

The third area of policy concern, the mass media, exacerbates the gun culture by portraying guns as glamorous, effective, omnipotent devices. The mass media also heighten the negative effects of economic disparities through their consumer messages in advertising and entertainment. Although both of these effects that add to the problem of youth violence are

sometimes discussed, the debate about the media remains tightly focused on measuring and reviewing violent media content. Within this focus, the emphasis has been on counting violent acts rather than on exploring the context of its portrayal. Deciphering the media's moral and value messages about violence has been mostly ignored.

EFFECTS ON CRIMINAL JUSTICE

A closer examination of the context of violence in the media would tell us that we should not try to purge the media of violence, for violent media can be good when programs teach that violence is bad. Our goal should be to reduce graphic, gratuitous, and glorified violence; to portray it not as a problem solver but as a reluctant, distasteful, last resort with tragic, unanticipated consequences. Violence shown consistently as a generator of pain and suffering, not as a personal or social panacea, would be positive media violence. Too often, violence in the media is shown as an effective solution, and, too often, it is simply met by increased counterviolence. But, despite the recurring interest and current debate about media violence, there is little direction for the media industry regarding the context of violence and its effects. A goal should be to provide better information to the industry that details the various contexts and messages of violence and their effects.

Perhaps the most significant social effect of media violence is, however, not the direct generation of social violence but its impact on our criminal justice policy. The fear and loathing we feel toward crimi-

nals—youthful, violent, or not—is tied to our media-generated image of criminality. The media portray criminals as typically animalistic, vicious predators. This media image translates into a more violent society by influencing the way we react to all crime in America. We imprison at a much greater rate and make reentry into law-abiding society, even for our nonviolent offenders, more difficult than other advanced (and, not coincidentally, less violent) nations. The predator-criminal image results in policy based on the worst-case criminal and a constant ratcheting up of punishments for all offenders. In its cumulative effect, the media both provide violent models for our youth to emulate and justify a myopic, harshly punitive public reaction to all offenders.

Currently, the debate concerning both the media and youth violence has evolved into "circles of blame" in which one group ascribes blame for the problem to someone else in the circle. Thus, in the media circle, the public blames the networks and studios, which blame the producers and writers, who blame the advertisers, who blame the public. In the violence circle, the government blames the youth, who blame the community, which blames the schools, which blame the parents, who blame the government. A more sensible, productive process would be a shift to a "ring of responsibility," with the groups addressing their individual contributions to the problem and arriving at cooperative policies. We can't selectively reduce one aspect of violence in a violent society and expect real results. Youth violence will not be seriously reduced without violence in other aspects of our culture being addressed. In the same vein, modifying media violence alone will

■ **A Lapith woman fighting the brutal grip of a centaur.**
From the west pediment of the temple at Olympia, c. 460
B.C.

not have much effect but to ignore it will make efforts on other fronts less successful. Ironically, despite the fact that the media have limited independent effects on youth violence, we need to expand the

---

Youth violence will not be seriously reduced without violence in other aspects of our culture being addressed.

---

focus on them. This should incorporate other social institutions, such as the media industry itself, and the social norms and values reflected in the media. We could then derive more general models of media effects and social violence.

Violence is a cultural product. The media are reflections of the culture and engines in the production process. Although they are not the only or even the most powerful causes, they are tied into the other violence-generating engines, and youth pay particular attention to them. The aggregate result of all of these forces in the United States is a national character that is individualistic, materialistic, and violence prone. If we wish to change our national character regarding violence, we cannot take on only some aspects of its genesis. We must address everything we can, such as economic inequities, the gun culture, and the glamorization of violence. And, by a slow, painful, generational process of moral leadership and example, we

must work to modify the individual, family, and neighborhood factors that violently predispose youth.

In conclusion, our youth will be violent as long as our culture is violent. The local social conditions in which they are raised and the larger cultural and economic environments that they will enter generate great numbers of violently predisposed individuals. As we have experienced, violently predisposed youth, particularly among our poor, will fully develop their potential and come to prey upon us. Faced with frightful predators, we subsequently and justly punish them, but the use of punishment alone will not solve the problem. The role that the media play in the above scenario versus their potential role in deglorifying violence and showing our youth that armed aggression is not an American cultural right, will determine the media's ultimate relationship to youthful violence in society.

NOTES

1. Dr. Deborah Prothrow-Stith testifying before the Senate Subcommittee on Juvenile Justice, November 26, 1991.

2. Sources of the statistics cited in this essay are drawn from "Arrests of Youth 1990," January 1992, *Office of Juvenile Justice and Delinquency Prevention Update on Statistics; and Sourcebook of Criminal Justice Statistics—1992,* Bureau of Justice Statistics, U.S. Department of Justice, 1993.

3. Hugh Davis Graham and Ted Robert Gurr, eds., *Violence in America* (Beverly Hills, CA: Sage, 1979).

4. See S. Milgram and R. Shotland, *Television and Antisocial Behavior: Field Experiments* (New York: Academic Press, 1973) and A.

Schmid and J. de Graaf, *Violence as Communication* (Newbury Park, CA: Sage, 1982).

5. T. Cook, D. Kendzierski, and S. Thomas, "The Implicit Assumptions of Television Research," *Public Opinion Quarterly* 47: 161–201.

6. For a listing of examples see S. Pease and C. Love, "The Copy-Cat Crime Phenomenon," in *Justice and the Media* by R. Surette (Springfield IL: Charles C. Thomas, 1984), 199–211; and A. Schmid and J. de Graaf, *Violence as Communication* (Newbury Park, CA: Sage, 1982).

7. N. Malamuth and J. Briere (1986), Sexual Violence in the Media: Indirect Effects on Aggression against Women," *Journal of Social Issues 42,* 89.

8. T. Cook, D. Kendzierski, and S. Thomas (1993), "The Implicit Assumptions of Television Research," *Public Opinion Quarterly* 47: 191–92.

9. R. Rosenthal (1986), "Media Violence, Anti-Social Behavior, and the Social Consequences of Small Effects," *Journal of Social Issues* 42: 141–54.

ADDITIONAL READING

George Comstock, *Television in America,* Sage, Newbury Park, Calif., 1980.

Elliott Currie, *Confronting Crime,* Pantheon, New York, 1985.

Jeffrey Goldstein, *Aggression and Crimes of Violence,* Oxford University Press, New York, 1986.

Diana Gordon, *The Justice Juggernaut,* Rutgers University Press, New Brunswick, N.J., 1991.

Joshua Meyrowitz, *No Sense of Place,* Oxford University Press, New York, 1985.

Ray Surette, *Media, Crime, and Criminal Justice,* Brooks/Cole, Pacific Grove, Calif., 1992.

James Q. Wilson and Richard Herrnstein, *Crime and Human Nature,* Simon & Schuster, New York, 1985.

Enhancing Human Adjustment: Learning to Cope Effectively

On each college and university campus a handful of students experiences overwhelming stress and life-shattering crises. One student learns that her mother, living in a distant city, has terminal cancer and two months to live. Another receives the sad news that his parents are divorcing. Those students may descend into a deep depression that may lower their grades. A sorority blackballs a young woman whose heart was set on becoming their sister. She commits suicide. The sorority sisters now experience a weighty sense of responsibility. Fortunately almost every campus houses a counseling center for students. Some universities also offer assistance to employees. At the counseling service, trained professionals such as psychologists are available to offer aid and therapy to troubled members of the campus community.

Many individuals cope on their own. They are able to adapt to life's vagaries, even to life's disasters. Other individuals flounder. They simply do not know how to adjust to change and cope with negative, or even positive, life events. These individuals sometimes seek professional assistance from a therapist or counselor. For these professionals the first difficulty may not be *how* to intervene but *when* to intervene.

There are as many definitions of maladjustment as there are mental health professionals. Some practitioners define maladjustment or mental illness as "whatever society cannot tolerate." Others define maladjustment in terms of statistics: "If a majority do not behave that way, then the behavior signals maladjustment." Some professionals suggest that an inadequate self-concept is the cause of maladjustment, while others cite a lack of contact with reality as an indicator of mental illness. A few psychologists claim that mental disorder is a fiction: to call one individual ill suggests that the rest are healthy by contrast, when, in fact, there may be few real distinctions between people.

Because maladjustment is difficult to define, it is sometimes difficult to treat. For each definition, each theorist develops a different treatment strategy. Psychoanalysts press clients to recall their dreams, their childhoods, and their intrapsychic conflicts in order to empty and analyze the contents of the unconscious. Humanists encourage clients to explore all of the facets of their lives in order for the clients to become less defensive and more open to experience. Behaviorists are usually not concerned with the psyche but rather with observable and, therefore, treatable symptoms or behaviors. For behaviorists, no underlying causes such as intrapsychic conflict are postulated to be the roots of adjustment problems. Other therapists, namely psychiatrists, who are physicians by training, may utilize these therapies and add somatotherapies such as drugs and psychosurgery.

This brief list of interventions raises further questions. For instance, is one form of therapy more effective, less expensive, or longer-lasting than another? Should a particular diagnosis be treated by one form of therapy while another diagnosis is more amenable to another treatment? Who should make the diagnosis? If two experts disagree on the diagnosis and treatment, who is correct? Should psychologists be allowed to prescribe psychoactive drugs? These questions are being debated now.

Some psychologists question whether professional intervention is necessary at all. In one well-publicized but highly criticized study, researcher Hans Eysenck was able to show that spontaneous remission rates were as high as therapeutic "cure" rates. You may be wondering whether professional help is always necessary. Can people be their own healers? Is support from friends as productive as professional treatment?

The first three articles are general guides to interventions commonly offered to individuals who are having a difficult time adjusting and coping. In "What You Can Change and What You Cannot Change," noted psychologist Martin Seligman discusses what can be realistically managed in terms of self-improvement. He emphasizes diets and various psychological disorders. In the second article, Frank Pittman, writing in *Psychology Today*, offers advice on what types of therapies and therapists seem to produce successful change. Finally, Susan Baxter chastises individuals associated with self-help groups. Baxter discloses that some self-help groups can be downright dangerous, a situation made worse by the fact that these groups are fairly unregulated compared to professionals in the mental health field.

The next two articles concern themselves with "knowing thyself." In "The Importance of Solitude," Rae André prods us to consider how important time for oneself is. Solitude provides us time for self-reflection and introspection. In the second article, "How to Master Your Moods," Melvin Kinder provides examples of four different mood styles. Knowing one's style is the first step in managing moods.

The next six articles address individual problems of adjustment: stress, depression, obesity, sexual-desire disorders, alcoholism, and high anxiety. In "Unload Stress for '94," John Butterfield elaborates upon what causes stress, how to avoid stress, and how to manage stress once it strikes. The article includes some interesting self-assessment tests.

If stress is not the plague of today, depression surely is. Millions of Americans suffer from depression each day. What causes depression and how to intervene in its downward momentum are important features of the next article.

Many Americans are on perpetual diets. They find that they are riding on a diet roller coaster, losing weight in June and gaining in January. A *Consumer Reports* article provides an accurate assessment of various weight loss strategies.

Sexual-desire disorders, for example, feeling no need for sex, are also endemic today. Many Americans come home exhausted from work and are too tired to enjoy themselves. In "Sexual Desire," descriptions of several disorders and their treatments are disclosed. Alcohol contributes to some sex disorders as well as to some of the other problems of adjustment. "Alcohol in Perspective" provides a good overview of what alcoholism is and how it can be treated. Finally, the article "High Anxiety" details various drug treatments available for more serious disorders, such as clinical depression and panic attacks. Pharmaceutical interventions are used as a last resort when the individual cannot cope alone and when other professional assistance does not seem to be effective.

Looking Ahead: Challenge Questions

There are a myriad of definitions for maladjustment. Catalog and discuss the pros and cons of each one. Is it possible that maladjustment is a fiction created by society to repress the few who are differently adjusted? Is mental health the absence of mental illness?

What does Martin Seligman suggest can be changed by self-determination or with professional assistance? What problems seem immune to change?

Do you think most individuals can successfully cope with everyday difficulties? When do you believe professional intervention is necessary?

What are the various types of psychotherapy that are available? Does one form seem better than another? Which type of therapy suits you best and why?

How can you discriminate between effective and ineffective therapists? What about effective and ineffective therapies?

People often feel distressed at home or on the job, miss deadlines, feel moody, and gain weight. What are other signs and symptoms of other everyday adjustments? How do most people cope with these situations?

What are self-help groups? Why are they proliferating?

Why is solitude so important? Why do some people have so much trouble accepting solitary figures?

What are the four mood styles identified in the article "How to Master Your Moods"? Which mood style seems to describe you? Are you happy with this style? Can you change it?

What are some common causes of stress? Why is stress so problematic for many people? What can people do to eliminate or manage stress in their lives?

What is a sexual-desire disorder? How common are such disorders? What can be done about sexual-desire disorders?

What are the major symptoms of and forms of treatment for depression and alcoholism? What seems to cause or exacerbate each problem?

What is anxiety? Why does it interfere with our performance, our happiness, and our lives? Can anxiety ever be beneficial? How can we manage anxiety?

What You Can Change & What You Cannot Change

There are things we can change about ourselves and things we cannot. Concentrate your energy on what is possible—too much time has been wasted.

Martin E. P. Seligman, Ph.D.

This is the age of psychotherapy and the age of self-improvement. Millions are struggling to change: We diet, we jog, we meditate. We adopt new modes of thought to counteract our depressions. We practice relaxation to curtail stress. We exercise to expand our memory and to quadruple our reading speed. We adopt draconian regimens to give up smoking. We raise our little boys and girls to androgyny. We come out of the closet or we try to become heterosexual. We seek to lose our taste for alcohol. We seek more meaning in life. We try to extend our life span.

Sometimes it works. But distressingly often, self-improvement and psychotherapy fail. The cost is enormous. We think we are worthless. We feel guilty and ashamed. We believe we have no willpower and that we are failures. We give up trying to change.

On the other hand, this is not only the age of self-improvement and therapy, but also the age of biological psychiatry. The human genome will be nearly mapped before the millennium is over. The brain systems underlying sex, hearing, memory, left-handedness, and sadness are now known. Psychoactive drugs quiet our fears, relieve our blues, bring us bliss, dampen our mania, and dissolve our delusions more effectively than we can on our own.

Our very personality—our intelligence and musical talent, even our religiousness, our conscience (or its absence), our politics, and our exuberance—turns out to be more the product of our genes than almost anyone would have believed a decade ago. The underlying message of the age of biological psychiatry is that our biology frequently makes changing, in spite of all our efforts, impossible.

But the view that all is genetic and biochemical and therefore unchangeable is also very often wrong. Many people surpass their IQs, fail to "respond" to drugs, make sweeping changes in their lives, live on when their cancer is "terminal," or defy the hormones and brain circuitry that "dictate" lust, femininity, or memory loss.

The ideologies of biological psychiatry and self-improvement are obviously colliding. Nevertheless, a resolution is apparent. There are some things about ourselves that can be changed, others that cannot, and some that can be changed only with extreme difficulty.

What can we succeed in changing about ourselves? What can we not? When can we overcome our biology? And when is our biology our destiny?

I want to provide an understanding of what you can and what you can't change about yourself so that you can concentrate your limited time and energy on what is possible. So much time has been wasted. So much needless frustration has been endured. So much of therapy, so much of child rearing, so much of self-improving, and even some of the great social movements in our century have come to nothing because they tried to change the unchangeable. Too often we have wrongly thought we were weak-willed failures, when the changes we wanted to make in ourselves were just not possible. But all this effort was necessary: Because there have been so many failures, we are now able to see the boundaries of the unchangeable; this in turn allows us to see clearly for the first time the boundaries of what *is* changeable.

With this knowledge, we can use our precious time to make the many rewarding changes that are possible. We can live with less self-reproach and less remorse. We can live with greater confidence. This knowledge is a new understanding of who we are and where we are going.

CATASTROPHIC THINKING: PANIC

S. J. Rachman, one of the world's leading clinical researchers and one of the founders of behavior therapy, was on the phone. He was proposing that I be the "discussant" at a conference about panic disorder sponsored by the National Institute of Mental Health (NIMH).

"Why even bother, Jack?" I responded. "Everyone knows that panic is biological and that the only thing that works is drugs."

"Don't refuse so quickly, Marty. There is a breakthrough you haven't yet heard about."

Breakthrough was a word I had never heard Jack use before.

"What's the breakthrough?" I asked.

"If you come, you can find out."

So I went.

I had known about and seen panic patients for many years, and had read the literature with mounting excitement during

From *Psychology Today*, May/June 1994, pp. 34-41, 70, 72-74, 84. Excerpted from *What You Can Change and What You Can't* by Martin E. P. Seligman. © 1993 by Martin E. P. Seligman. Reprinted by permission of Alfred A. Knopf, Inc.

So much child rearing, therapy, and self-improvement have come to nothing.

the 1980s. I knew that panic disorder is a frightening condition that consists of recurrent attacks, each much worse than anything experienced before. Without prior warning, you feel as if you are going to die. Here is a typical case history:

The first time Celia had a panic attack, she was working at McDonald's. It was two days before her 20th birthday. As she was handing a customer a Big Mac, she had the worst experience of her life. The earth seemed to open up beneath her. Her heart began to pound, she felt she was smothering, and she was sure she was going to have a heart attack and die. After about 20 minutes of terror, the panic subsided. Trembling, she got in her car, raced home, and barely left the house for the next three months.

Since then, Celia has had about three attacks a month. She does not know when they are coming. She always thinks she is going to die.

Panic attacks are not subtle, and you need no quiz to find out if you or someone you love has them. As many as five percent of American adults probably do. The defining feature of the disorder is simple: recurrent awful attacks of panic that come out of the blue, last for a few minutes, and then subside. The attacks consist of chest pains, sweating, nausea, dizziness, choking, smothering, or trembling. They are accompanied by feelings of overwhelming dread and thoughts that you are having a heart attack, that you are losing control, or that you are going crazy.

The Biology of Panic

There are four questions that bear on whether a mental problem is primarily "biological" as opposed to "psychological":

- Can it be induced biologically?
- Is it genetically heritable?
- Are specific brain functions involved?
- Does a drug relieve it?

Inducing panic. Panic attacks can be created by a biological agent. For example, patients who have a history of panic attacks are hooked up to an intravenous line. Sodium lactate, a chemical that nor-

mally produces rapid, shallow breathing and heart palpitations, is slowly infused into their bloodstream. Within a few minutes, about 60 to 90 percent of these patients have a panic attack. Normal controls—subjects with no history of panic—rarely have attacks when infused with lactate.

Genetics of panic. There may be some heritability of panic. If one of two identical twins has panic attacks, 31 percent of the cotwins also have them. But if one of two fraternal twins has panic attacks, none of the cotwins are so afflicted.

Panic and the brain. The brains of people with panic disorders look somewhat unusual upon close scrutiny. Their neurochemistry shows abnormalities in the system that turns on, then dampens, fear. In addition, the PET scan (positron-emission tomography), a technique that looks at how much blood and oxygen different parts of the brain use, shows that patients who panic from the infusion of lactate have higher blood flow and oxygen use in relevant parts of their brain than patients who don't panic.

Drugs. Two kinds of drugs relieve panic: tricyclic antidepressants and the antianxiety drug Xanax, and both work better than placebos. Panic attacks are dampened, and sometimes even eliminated. General anxiety and depression also decrease.

Since these four questions had already been answered "yes" when Jack Rachman called, I thought the issue had already been settled. Panic disorder was simply a biological illness, a disease of the body that could be relieved only by drugs.

A few months later I was in Bethesda, Maryland, listening once again to the same four lines of biological evidence. An inconspicuous figure in a brown suit sat hunched over the table. At the first break, Jack introduced me to him—David Clark, a young psychologist from Oxford. Soon after, Clark began his address.

"Consider, if you will, an alternative theory, a cognitive theory." He reminded all of us that almost all panickers believe that they are going to die during an attack. Most commonly, they believe that they are having heart attacks. Perhaps, Clark suggested, this is more than just a mere symptom. Perhaps it is the root cause. Panic may simply be the *catastrophic misinterpretation of bodily sensations.*

For example, when you panic, your heart starts to race. You notice this, and you see it as a possible heart attack. This makes you very anxious, which means

your heart pounds more. You now notice that your heart is *really* pounding. You are now *sure* it's a heart attack. This terrifies you, and you break into a sweat, feel nauseated, short of breath—all symptoms of terror, but for you, they're confirmation of a heart attack. A full-blown panic attack is under way, and at the root of it is your misinterpretation of the symptoms of anxiety as symptoms of impending death.

We are now able to see the boundaries of the unchangeable.

What Can We Change?

When we survey all the problems, personality types, patterns of behavior, and the weak influence of childhood on adult life, we see a puzzling array of how much change occurs. From the things that are easiest to those that are the most difficult, this rough array emerges:

Panic	Curable
Specific Phobias	Almost Curable
Sexual Dysfunctions	Marked Relief
Social Phobia	Moderate Relief
Agoraphobia	Moderate Relief
Depression	Moderate Relief
Sex Role Change	Moderate
Obsessive–Compulsive Disorder	Moderate Mild Relief
Sexual Preferences	Moderate Mild Change
Anger	Mild, Moderate Relief
Everyday Anxiety	Mild Moderate Relief
Alcoholism	Mild Relief
Overweight	Temporary Change
Posttraumatic Stress Disorder (PTSD)	Marginal Relief
Sexual Orientation	Probably Unchangeable
Sexual Identity	Unchangeable

I was listening closely now as Clark argued that an obvious sign of a disorder, easily dismissed as a symptom, is the disorder itself. If he was right, this was a historic occasion. All Clark had done so far, however, was to show that the four lines of evidence for a biological view of panic could fit equally well with a misinterpretation view. But Clark soon told us about a series of experiments he and his colleague Paul Salkovskis had done at Oxford.

First, they compared panic patients with patients who had other anxiety disorders and with normals. All the subjects read the following sentences aloud, but the last word was presented blurred. For example:

dying

If I had palpitations, I could be
excited

choking

If I were breathless, I could be
unfit

When the sentences were about bodily sensations, the panic patients, but no one else, saw the catastrophic endings fastest. This showed that panic patients possess the habit of thinking Clark had postulated.

Next, Clark and his colleagues asked if activating this habit with words would induce panic. All the subjects read a series of word pairs aloud. When panic patients got to "breathlessness-suffocation: and "palpitations-dying," 75 percent suffered a full-blown panic attack right there in the laboratory. No normal people had panic attacks, no recovered panic patients (I'll tell you more in a moment about how they got better) had attacks, and only 17 percent of other anxious patients had attacks.

The final thing Clark told us was the "breakthrough" that Rachman had promised.

"We have developed and tested a rather novel therapy for panic," Clark continued in his understated, disarming way. He explained that if catastrophic misinterpretations of bodily sensation are the cause of a panic attack, then changing the tendency to misinterpret should cure the disorder. His new therapy was straightforward and brief:

Patients are told that panic results when they mistake normal symptoms of mounting anxiety for symptoms of heart attack, going crazy, or dying. Anxiety itself, they are informed, produces shortness of breath, chest pain, and sweating. Once

Issues of the soul can barely be changed by psychotherapy or drugs.

they misinterpret these normal bodily sensations as an imminent heart attack, their symptoms become even more pronounced because the misinterpretation changes their anxiety into terror. A vicious circle culminates in a full-blown panic attack.

Patients are taught to reinterpret the symptoms realistically as mere anxiety symptoms. Then they are given practice right in the office, breathing rapidly into a paper bag. This causes a buildup of carbon dioxide and shortness of breath, mimicking the sensations that provoke a panic attack. The therapist points out that the symptoms the patient is experiencing— shortness of breath and heart racing—are harmless, simply the result of overbreathing, not a sign of a heart attack. The patient learns to interpret the symptoms correctly.

"This simple therapy appears to be a cure," Clark told us. "Ninety to 100 percent of the patients are panic free at the end of therapy. One year later, only one person had had another panic attack."

This, indeed, was a breakthrough: a simple, brief psychotherapy with no side effects showing a 90-percent cure rate of a disorder that a decade ago was thought to be incurable. In a controlled study of 64 patients comparing cognitive therapy to drugs to relaxation to no treatment, Clark and his colleagues found that cognitive therapy is markedly better than drugs or relaxation, both of which are better than

Self-Analysis Questionnaire
Is your life dominated by anxiety? Read each statement and then mark the appropriate number to indicate *how you generally feel.* There are no right or wrong answers.

1. I am a steady person.

Almost never	Sometimes	Often	Almost always
4	3	2	1

2. I am satisfied with myself.

Almost never	Sometimes	Often	Almost always
4	3	2	1

3. I feel nervous and restless.

Almost never	Sometimes	Often	Almost always
1	2	3	4

4. I wish I could be as happy as others seem to be.

Almost never	Sometimes	Often	Almost always
1	2	3	4

5. I feel like a failure.

Almost never	Sometimes	Often	Almost always
1	2	3	4

6. I get in a state of tension and turmoil as I think over my recent concerns and interests.

Almost never	Sometimes	Often	Almost always
1	2	3	4

7. I feel secure.

Almost never	Sometimes	Often	Almost always
4	3	2	1

nothing. Such a high cure rate is unprecedented.

How does cognitive therapy for panic compare with drugs? It is more effective and less dangerous. Both the antidepressants and Xanax produce marked reduction in panic in most patients, but drugs must be taken forever; once the drug is stopped, panic rebounds to where it was before therapy began for perhaps half the patients. The drugs also sometimes have severe side effects, including drowsiness, lethargy, pregnancy complications, and addictions.

After this bombshell, my own "discussion" was an anticlimax. I did make one point that Clark took to heart. "Creating a cognitive therapy that works, even one that works as well as this apparently does, is not enough to show that the *cause* of panic is cognitive." I was niggling. "The biological theory doesn't deny that some other therapy might work well on panic. It merely claims that panic is caused at the bottom by some biochemical problem."

Two years later, Clark carried out a crucial experiment that tested the biological theory against the cognitive theory. He gave the usual lactate infusion to 10 panic patients, and nine of them panicked. He did the same thing with another 10 patients, but added special instructions to allay the misinterpretation of the sensations. He simply told them: "Lactate is a natural bodily substance that produces sensations similar to exercise or alcohol. It is normal to experience intense sensations during infusion, but these do not indicate an adverse reaction." Only three out of the 10 panicked. This confirmed the theory crucially.

The therapy works every well, as it did for Celia, whose story has a happy ending. She first tried Xanax, which reduced the intensity and the frequency of her panic attacks. But she was too drowsy to work, and she was still having about one attack every six weeks. She was then referred to Audry, a cognitive therapist who explained that Celia was misinterpreting her heart racing and shortness of breath as symptoms of a heart attack, that they were actually just symptoms of mounting anxiety, nothing more harmful. Audrey taught Celia progressive relaxation, and then she demonstrated the harmlessness of Celia's symptoms of overbreathing. Celia then relaxed in the presence of the symptoms and found that they gradually subsided. After several more practice sessions, therapy terminated. Celia has gone two years without another panic attack.

EVERYDAY ANXIETY

Attend to your tongue—right now. What is it doing? Mine is swishing around near my lower right molars. It has just found a minute fragment of last night's popcorn (debris from *Terminator 2*). Like a dog at a bone, it is worrying the firmly wedged flake.

Attend to your hand—right now. What's it up to? My left hand is boring in on an itch it discovered under my earlobe.

Your tongue and your hands have, for the most part, a life of their own. You can bring them under voluntary control by consciously calling them out of their "default" mode to carry out your commands:

---

8. I have self-confidence.

Almost never	Sometimes	Often	Almost always
4	3	2	1

9. I feel inadequate.

Almost never	Sometimes	Often	Almost always
1	2	3	4

10. I worry too much over something that does not matter.

Almost never	Sometimes	Often	Almost always
1	2	3	4

To score, simply add up the numbers under your answers. Notice that some of the rows of numbers go up and others go down. The higher your total, the more the trait of anxiety dominates your life. If your score was:

10–11, you are in the lowest 10 percent of anxiety.

13–14, you are in the lowest quarter.

16–17, your anxiety level is about average.

19–20, your anxiety level is around the 75th percentile.

22–24 (and you are male) your anxiety level is around the 90th percentile.

24–26 (and you are female) your anxiety level is around the 90th percentile.

25 (and you are male) your anxiety level is at the 95th percentile.

27 (and you are female) your anxiety level is at the 95th percentile.

Should you try to change your anxiety level? Here are my rules of thumb:

• If your score is at the 90th percentile or above, you can probably improve the quality of your life by lowering your general anxiety level—regardless of paralysis and irrationality.

• If your score is at the 75th percentile or above, and you feel that anxiety is either paralyzing you or that it is unfounded, you should probably try to lower your general anxiety level.

• If your score is 18 or above, and you feel that anxiety is unfounded and paralyzing, you should probably try to lower your general anxiety level.

Anxiety scans your life for imperfections. When it finds one, it won't let go.

"Pick up the phone" or "Stop picking that pimple." But most of the time they are on their own. They are seeking out small imperfections. They scan your entire mouth and skin surface, probing for anything going wrong. They are marvelous, nonstop grooming devices. They, not the more fashionable immune system, are your first line of defense against invaders.

Anxiety is your mental tongue. Its default mode is to search for what may be about to go wrong. It continually, and without your conscious consent, scans your life—yes, even when you are asleep, in dreams and nightmares. It reviews your work, your love, your play—until it finds an imperfection. When it finds one, it worries it. It tries to pull it out from its hiding place, where it is wedged inconspicuously under some rock. It will not let go. If the imperfection is threatening enough, anxiety calls your attention to it by making you uncomfortable. If you do not act, it yells more insistently—disturbing your sleep and your appetite.

You can reduce daily, mild anxiety. You can numb it with alcohol, Valium, or marijuana. You can take the edge off with meditation or progressive relaxation. You can beat it down by becoming more conscious of the automatic thoughts of danger that trigger anxiety and then disputing them effectively.

But do not overlook what your anxiety is trying to do for you. In return for the pain it brings, it prevents larger ordeals by making you aware of their possibility and goading you into planning for and forestalling them. It may even help you avoid them altogether. Think of your anxiety as the "low oil" light flashing on the dashboard of your car. Disconnect it and you will be less distracted and more comfortable for a while. But this may cost you a burned-up engine. Our *dysphoria,* or bad feeling, should, some of the time, be tolerated, attended to, even cherished.

GUIDELINES FOR WHEN TO TRY TO CHANGE ANXIETY

Some of our everyday anxiety, depression, and anger go beyond their useful function. Most adaptive traits fall along a normal spectrum of distribution, and the capacity for internal bad weather for everyone some of the time means that some of us may have terrible weather all of the time. In general, when the hurt is pointless and recurrent—when, for example, anxiety insists we formulate a plan but no plan will work—it is time to take action to relieve the hurt. There are three hallmarks indicating that anxiety has become a burden that wants relieving:

First, is it *irrational?*

We must calibrate our bad weather inside against the real weather outside. Is what you are anxious about out of proportion to the reality of the danger? Here are some examples that may help you answer this question. All of the following are not irrational:

• A fire fighter trying to smother a raging oil well burning in Kuwait repeatedly wakes up at four in the morning because of flaming terror dreams.

• A mother of three smells perfume on her husband's shirts and, consumed by jealousy, broods about his infidelity, reviewing the list of possible women over and over.

• A student who had failed two of his midterm exams finds, as finals approach, that he can't get to sleep for worrying. He has diarrhea most of the time.

The only good thing that can be said about such fears is that they are well-founded.

In contrast, all of the following are irrational, out of proportion to the danger:

• An elderly man, having been in a fender bender, broods about travel and will no longer take cars, trains, or airplanes.

• An eight-year-old child, his parents having been through an ugly divorce, wets his bed at night. He is haunted with visions of his bedroom ceiling collapsing on him.

• A housewife who has an MBA and who accumulated a decade of experience as a financial vice president before her twins were born is sure her job search will be fruitless. She delays preparing her résumés for a month.

The second hallmark of anxiety out of control is *paralysis.* Anxiety intends action: Plan, rehearse, look into shadows for lurking dangers, change your life. When anxiety becomes strong, it is unproductive; no problem-solving occurs. And when anxiety is extreme, it paralyzes you. Has your anxiety crossed this line? Some examples:

• A woman finds herself housebound because she fears that if she goes out, she will be bitten by a cat.

• A salesman broods about the next customer hanging up on him and makes no more cold calls.

• A writer, afraid of the next rejection slip, stops writing.

The final hallmark is *intensity.* Is your life dominated by anxiety? Dr. Charles Spielberger, one of the world's foremost

> ## 'Dieting below your natural weight is a necessary condition for bulimia. Returning to your natural weight will cure it.'

testers of emotion, has developed well-validated scales for calibrating how severe anxiety is. To find out how anxious *you* are, use the self-analysis questionnaire.

LOWERING YOUR EVERYDAY ANXIETY

Everyday anxiety level is not a category to which psychologists have devoted a great deal of attention. Enough research has been done, however, for me to recommend two techniques that quite reliably lower everyday anxiety levels. Both techniques are cumulative, rather than one-shot fixes. They require 20 to 40 minutes a day of your valuable time.

The first is *progressive relaxation,* done once or, better, twice a day for at least 10 minutes. In this technique, you tighten and then turn off each of the major muscle groups of your body until you are wholly flaccid. It is not easy to be highly anxious when your body feels like Jell-O. More formally, relaxation engages a response system that competes with anxious arousal.

The second technique is regular *meditation.* Transcendental meditation ™ is one useful, widely available version of this. You can ignore the cosmology in which it is packaged if you wish, and treat it simply as the beneficial technique it is. Twice a day for 20 minutes, in a quiet setting, you close your eyes and repeat a *mantra* (a syllable whose "sonic properties are known") to yourself. Meditation works by blocking thoughts that produce anxiety. It complements relaxation, which blocks the motor components of anxiety but leaves the anxious thoughts untouched.

Done regularly, meditation usually induces a peaceful state of mind. Anxiety at other times of the day wanes, and hyperarousal from bad events is dampened. Done religiously, TM probably works better than relaxation alone.

There's also a quick fix. The minor tranquilizers—Valium, Dalmane, Librium, and their cousins—relieve everyday anxiety. So does alcohol. The advantage of all these is that they work within minutes and require no discipline to use. Their disadvantages outweigh their advantages, however. The minor tranquilizers make you fuzzy and somewhat uncoordinated as they work (a not uncommon side effect is an automobile accident). Tranquilizers soon lose their effect when taken regularly, and they are habit-forming—probably addictive. Alcohol, in addition, produces gross cognitive and motor disability in lockstep with its anxiety relief. Taken regularly over long periods, deadly damage to liver and brain ensue.

If you crave quick and temporary relief from acute anxiety, either alcohol or minor tranquilizers, taken in small amounts and only occasionally, will do the job. They are, however, a distant second-best to progressive relaxation and meditation, which are each worth trying before you seek out psychotherapy or in conjunction with therapy. Unlike tranquilizers and alcohol, neither of these techniques is likely to do you any harm.

Weigh your everyday anxiety. If it is not intense, or if it is moderate and not irrational or paralyzing, act now to reduce it. In spite of its deep evolutionary roots, intense everyday anxiety is often changeable. Meditation and progressive relaxation practiced regularly can change it forever.

DIETING: A WAIST IS A TERRIBLE THING TO MIND

I have been watching my weight and restricting my intake—except for an occasional binge like this—since I was 20. I weighed about 175 pounds then, maybe 15 pounds over my official "ideal" weight. I weigh 199 pounds now, 30 years later, about 25 pounds over the ideal. I have tried about a dozen regimes—fasting, the Beverly Hills Diet, no carbohydrates, Metrecal for lunch, 1,200 calories a day, low fat, no lunch, no starches, skipping every other dinner. I lost 10 or 15 pounds on each in about a month. The pounds always came back, though, and I have gained a net of about a pound a year—inexorably.

This is the most consistent failure in my life. It's also a failure I can't just put out of mind. I have spent the last few years reading the scientific literature, not the parade of best-selling diet books or the flood of women's magazine articles on the latest way to slim down. The scientific findings look clear to me, but there is not yet a consensus. I am going to go out on a limb, because I see so many signs all pointing in one direction. What I have concluded will, I believe, soon be the consensus of the scientists. The conclusions surprise me. They

will probably surprise you, too, and they may change your life.

Here is what the picture looks like to me:

• Dieting doesn't work.
• Dieting may make overweight worse, not better.
• Dieting may be bad for health.
• Dieting may cause eating disorders—including bulimia and anorexia.

ARE YOU OVERWEIGHT?

Are you above the ideal weight for your sex, height, and age? If so, you are "overweight." What does this really mean? Ideal weight is arrived at simply. Four million people, now dead, who were insured by the major American life-insurance companies, were once weighed and had their height measured. At what weight on average do people of a given height turn out to live longest? That weight is called ideal. Anything wrong with that?

You bet. The real use of a weight table, and the reason your doctor takes it seriously, is that an ideal weight implies that, on average, if you slim down to yours, you will live longer. This is the crucial claim. Lighter people indeed live longer, on average, than heavier people, but how much longer is hotly debated.

But the crucial claim is unsound because weight (at any given height) has a normal distribution, *normal* both in a statistical sense and in the biological sense. In the biological sense, couch potatoes who overeat and never exercise can legitimately be called overweight, but the buxom, "heavy-boned" slow people deemed overweight by the ideal table are at their natural and healthiest weight. If you are a 155-pound woman and 64 inches in height, for example, you are "overweight" by around 15 pounds. This means nothing more than that the average 140-pound, 64-inch-tall woman lives somewhat longer than the average 155-pound woman of your height. It does not follow that if you slim down to 125 pounds, *you* will stand any better chance of living longer.

In spite of the insouciance with which dieting advice is dispensed, no one has properly investigated the question of whether slimming down to "ideal" weight produces longer life. The proper study would compare the longevity of people who are at their ideal weight without dieting to people who achieve their ideal weight by dieting. Without this study the common medical advice to diet down to your ideal weight is simply unfounded.

This is not a quibble; there is evidence

that dieting damages your health and that this damage may shorten your life.

MYTHS OF OVERWEIGHT

The advice to diet down to your ideal weight to live longer is one myth of overweight. Here are some others:

• *Overweight people overeat.* Wrong. Nineteen out of 20 studies show that obese people consume no more calories each day than nonobese people. Telling a fat person that if she would change her eating habits and eat "normally" she would lose weight is a lie. To lose weight and stay there, she will need to eat excruciatingly less than a normal person, probably for the rest of her life.

• *Overweight people have an overweight personality.* Wrong. Extensive research on personality and fatness has proved little. Obese people do not differ in any major personality style from nonobese people.

• *Physical inactivity is a major cause of obesity.* Probably not. Fat people are indeed less active than thin people, but the inactivity is probably caused more by the fatness than the other way around.

• *Overweight shows a lack of willpower.* This is the granddaddy of all the myths. Fatness is seen as shameful because we hold people responsible for their weight. Being overweight equates with being a weak-willed slob. We believe this primarily because we have seen people decide to lose weight and do so in a matter of weeks.

But almost everyone returns to the old weight after shedding pounds. Your body has a natural weight that it defends vigorously against dieting. The more diets tried, the harder the body works to defeat the next diet. Weight is in large part genetic. All this gives the lie to the "weak-willed" interpretations of overweight. More accurately, dieting is the conscious will of the individual against a more vigilant opponent: the species' biological defense against starvation. The body can't tell the difference between self-imposed starvation and actual famine, so it defends its weight by refusing to release fat, by lowering its metabolism, and by demanding food. The harder the creature tries not to eat, the more vigorous the defenses become.

BULIMIA AND NATURAL WEIGHT

A concept that makes sense of your body's vigorous defense against weight loss is *natural weight*. When your body screams "I'm hungry," makes you lethargic, stores fat, craves sweets and renders them more delicious than ever, and makes you obsessed with food, what it is defending is your natural weight. It is signaling that you have dropped into a range it will not accept. Natural weight prevents you from gaining too much weight or losing too much. When you eat too much for too long, the opposite defenses are activated and make long-term weight gain difficult.

There is also a strong genetic contribution to your natural weight. Identical twins reared apart weigh almost the same throughout their lives. When identical twins are overfed, they gain weight and add fat in lockstep and in the same places. The fatness or thinness of adopted children resembles their biological parents—particularly their mother—very closely but does not at all resemble their adoptive parents. This suggests that you have a genetically given natural weight that your body wants to maintain.

The idea of natural weight may help cure the new disorder that is sweeping young America. Hundreds of thousands of young women have contracted it. It consists of bouts of binge eating and purging alternating with days of undereating. These young women are usually normal in weight or a bit on the thin side, but they are terrified of becoming fat. So they diet. They exercise. They take laxatives by the cup. They gorge. Then they vomit and take more laxatives. This malady is called *bulimia nervosa* (bulimia, for short).

Therapists are puzzled by bulimia, its causes, and treatment. Debate rages about whether it is an equivalent of depression, or an expression of a thwarted desire for control, or a symbolic rejection of the feminine role. Almost every psychotherapy has been tried. Antidepressants and other drugs have been administered with some effect but little success has been reported.

I don't think that bulimia is mysterious, and I think that it will be curable. I believe that bulimia is caused by dieting. The bulimic goes on a diet, and her body attempts to defend its natural weight. With repeated dieting, this defense becomes more vigorous. Her body is in massive revolt—insistently demanding food, storing fat, craving sweets, and lowering metabolism. Periodically, these biological defenses will overcome her extraordinary willpower (and extraordinary it must be to even approach an ideal weight, say, 20 pounds lighter than her natural weight). She will then binge. Horrified by what this will do to her figure, she vomits and takes laxatives to purge calories. Thus, bulimia is a natural consequence of self-starvation to lose weight in the midst of abundant food.

The therapist's task is to get the patient to stop dieting and become comfortable with her natural weight. He should first convince the patient that her binge eating is caused by her body's reaction to her diet. Then he must confront her with a question: Which is more important, staying thin or getting rid of bulimia? By stopping the diet, he will tell her, she can get rid of the uncontrollable binge–purge cycle. Her body will now settle at her natural weight, and she need not worry that she will balloon beyond that point. For some patients, therapy will end there because they would rather be bulimic than "loathsomely fat." For these patients, the central issue—ideal weight versus natural weight—can now at least become the focus of therapy. For others, defying the social and sexual pressure to be thin will be possible, dieting will be abandoned, weight will be gained, and bulimia should end quickly.

These are the central moves of the cognitive-behavioral treatment of bulimia. There are more than a dozen outcome studies of this approach, and the results are good. There is about 60 percent reduction in binging and purging (about the same as with antidepressant drugs). But unlike drugs, there is little relapse after treatment. Attitudes toward weight and shape relax, and dieting withers.

Of course, the dieting theory cannot fully explain bulimia. Many people who diet don't become bulimic; some can avoid it because their natural weight is close to their ideal weight, and therefore the diet they adopt does not starve them. In addition, bulimics are often depressed, since binging-purging leads to self-loathing. Depression may worsen bulimia by making it easier to give in to temptation. Further, dieting may just be another symptom of bulimia, not a cause. Other factors aside, I can speculate that dieting below your natural weight is a necessary condition for bulimia, and that returning to your natural weight and accepting that weight will cure bulimia.

OVERWEIGHT VS. DIETING: THE HEALTH DAMAGE

Being heavy carries some health risk. There is no definite answer to how much, because there is a swamp of inconsistent findings. But even if you could just wish pounds away, never to return, it is not certain you should. Being somewhat above your "ideal" weight may actually be your healthiest natural condition, best for your particular constitution and your particular metabolism. Of course you can diet, but

the odds are overwhelming that most of the weight will return, and that you will have to diet again and again. From a health and mortality perspective, should you? *There is, probably, a serious health risk from losing weight and regaining it.*

In one study, more than five thousand men and women from Framingham, Massachusetts, were observed for 32 years. People whose weight fluctuated over the years had 30 to 100 percent greater risk of death from heart disease than people whose weight was stable. When corrected for smoking, exercise, cholesterol level, and blood pressure, the findings became more convincing, suggesting that weight fluctuation (the primary cause of which is presumably dieting) may itself increase the risk of heart disease.

If this result is replicated, and if dieting is shown to be the primary cause of weight cycling, it will convince me that you should not diet to reduce your risk of heart disease.

DEPRESSION AND DIETING

Depression is yet another cost of dieting, because two root causes of depression are failure and helplessness. Dieting sets you up for failure. Because the goal of slimming down to your ideal weight pits your fallible willpower against untiring biological defenses, you will often fail. At first you will lose weight and feel pretty good about it. Any depression you had about your figure will disappear. Ultimately, however, you will probably not reach your goal; and then you will be dismayed as the pounds return. Every time you look in the mirror or vacillate over a white chocolate mousse, you will be reminded of your failure, which in turn brings depression.

On the other hand, if you are one of the fortunate few who can keep the weight from coming back, you will probably have to stay on an unsatisfying low-calorie diet for the rest of your life. A side effect of prolonged malnutrition is depression. Either way, you are more vulnerable to it.

If you scan the list of cultures that have a thin ideal for women, you will be struck by something fascinating. All thin-ideal cultures also have eating disorders. They also have roughly twice as much depression in women as in men. (Women diet twice as much as men. The best estimate is that 13 percent of adult men and 25 percent of adult women are now on a diet.) The cultures without the thin ideal have no eating disorders, and the amount of depression in women and men in these cultures is the same. This suggests that around the world, the thin ideal and dieting not only cause eating disorders, but they may also cause women to be more depressed than men.

THE BOTTOM LINE

I have been dieting off and on for 30 years because I want to be more attractive, healthier, and more in control. How do these goals stack up against the facts?

Attractiveness. If your attractiveness is a high-enough priority to convince you to diet, keep three drawbacks in mind. First, the attractiveness you gain will be temporary. All the weight you lose and maybe more will likely come back in a few years. This will depress you. Then you will have to lose it again and it will be harder the second time. Or you will have to resign yourself to being less attractive. Second, when women choose the silhouette figure they want to achieve, it turns out to be thinner than the silhouette that men label most attractive. Third, you may well become bulimic particularly if your natural weight is substantially more than your ideal weight. On balance, if short-term attractiveness is your overriding goal, diet. But be prepared for the costs.

Health. No one has ever shown that losing weight will increase my longevity. On balance, the health goal does not warrant dieting.

Control. For many people, getting to an ideal weight and staying there is just as biologically impossible as going with much less sleep. This fact tells me not to diet, and defuses my feeling of shame. My bottom line is clear: I am not going to diet anymore.

DEPTH AND CHANGE: THE THEORY

Clearly, we have not yet developed drugs or psychotherapies that can change all the problems, personality types, and patterns of behavior in adult life. But I believe that success and failure stems from something other than inadequate treatment. Rather, it stems from the depth of the problem.

We all have experience of psychological states of different depths. For example, if you ask someone, out of the blue, to answer quickly, "Who are you?" they will usually tell you—roughly in this order—their name, their sex, their profession. whether they have children, and their religion or race. Underlying this is a continuum of depth from surface to soul—with all manner of psychic material in between.

I believe that issues of the soul can barely be changed by psychotherapy or by drugs. Problems and behavior patterns somewhere between soul and surface can be changed somewhat. Surface problems can be changed easily, even cured. What is changeable, by therapy or drugs, I speculate, varies with the depth of the problem.

My theory says that it does not matter *when* problems, habits, and personality are acquired; their depth derives only from their biology, their evidence, and their power. Some childhood traits, for example, are deep and unchangeable but not because they were learned early and therefore have a privileged place.

Rather, those traits that resist change do so either because they are evolutionarily prepared or because they acquire great power by virtue of becoming the framework around which later learning crystallizes. In this way, the theory of depth carries the optimistic message that we are not prisoners of our past.

When you have understood this message, you will never look at your life in the same way again. Right now there are a number of things that you do not like about yourself and that you want to change: your short fuse, your waistline, your shyness, your drinking, your glumness. You have decided to change, but you do not know what you should work on first. Formerly you would have probably selected the one that hurts the most. Now you will also ask yourself which attempt is most likely to repay your efforts and which is most likely to lead to further frustration. Now you know your shyness and your anger are much more likely to change than your drinking, which you now know is more likely to change than your waistline.

Some of what does change is under your control, and some is not. You can best prepare yourself to change by learning as much as you can about what you can change and how to make those changes. Like all true education, learning about change is not easy; harder yet is surrendering some of our hopes. It is certainly not my purpose to destroy your optimism about change. But it is also not my purpose to assure everybody they can change in every way. My purpose is to instill a new, warranted optimism about the parts of your life you can change and so help you focus your limited time, money, and effort on making actual what is truly within your reach.

Life is a long period of change. What you have been able to change and what has resisted your highest resolve might seem chaotic to you: for some of what you are never changes no matter how hard you try, and other aspects change readily. My hope is that this essay has been the beginning of wisdom about the difference.

—*Excerpted from the book* What You Can Change and What You Can't *(Alfred A. Knopf) by Martin E. P. Seligman. Copyright © 1993 by Martin E. P. Seligman.*

A Buyer's Guide to
Psychotherapy

How does a consumer, shopping for answers to life's dilemmas, know whose wisdom to buy? Hire a therapist who leads a life that seems desirable to you, insists psychiatrist Frank Pittman III, M.D.

For 33 years as a psychotherapist, I've sold myself by the hour. People pay to talk to me about themselves. They come singly, in pairs, and in small groups. Some of them ask me to help them figure out what they could do differently to make their life and relationships work better. Other just bitch and moan and demand pity.

I sell them my time and whatever wisdom I have developed. If they expect their insurance to pay for it, I may apply a psychiatric diagnosis to them as well. If their brain chemistry is too messed up for them to think through their situation and to do whatever needs to be done, I sometimes prescribe medicine to fix the problem in their brain so they can then go on to fix the problems in their life. I also give them my humor; I try to make an hour with me entertaining as well as enlightening. I feel honored that they have brought their pain to me. The least I can do is make the removal of their pain as painless as possible.

I used to be proud of what I did. That has changed. Perhaps it was the unsettling experience of trying to explain to friends from abroad—for whom American psychotherapy is a foreign culture—how perennial psychotherapy customer Woody Allen could have undergone therapy for most of his life and still not have seen anything incestuous in his sexual relationship with his de facto stepdaughter, the sister of his children. When asked about his analyst's reaction, Allen is rumored to have said, "It didn't come up. It wasn't a relevant issue for my therapy."

Most humiliating for a respectable psychotherapist is the recently popular application of the format and jargon of psychotherapy to people's search for a victim identity. The victim identity is like a doctor's excuse from a gym class or history exam, only it is an excuse from life itself. People who want to be victims may nurture their inner child, may style themselves as adult children of imperfect parenting, or may announce that they are survivors of real or imagined unpleasant experiences. Either way, they resign from the adult world, eschew responsibility for their conduct in relationships, and whimper that the world owes them a life.

Values and Psychotherapy

There *is* such a thing as mental illness. It is real and it is horrible, whether it occurs as schizophrenia or mania or depression. Treating real mental illness may be the major professional expertise of mental health professionals, but it is a minor activity of psychotherapists. Most psychotherapy is about values—about the value dilemmas of sane and ordinary people trying to lead a life amidst great personal, familial, and cultural confusion. The therapists who do psychotherapy effectively do so because they understand value conflicts and they convey, without having to preach about it, values that work.

Psychotherapy is a process in which people in pain and/or turmoil purchase the time and expertise of a therapist who helps them: 1) define the problem; 2) figure out what normal people might do under these circumstances; 3) expose the misinformation, the misplaced loyalty, or the uncomfortable emotion that keeps the customer from doing the sensible thing; and 4) provide the customer with the courage (or fear of the therapist's disapproval) to change—that is, to do what needs to be done.

Psychotherapists vary widely in the rapidity with which they provide their customers with answers to the questions being raised, and the degree to which they take credit for providing the answers. Some will simply tell people what to do; others will make the customer guess for a few years before subtly signaling they've finally gotten it right.

Most therapists work hard at trying to get people to do what we think is right and to take credit for it themselves. The trick is to keep pushing and hinting without seeming so bossy, controlling, or disapproving that we run them out of therapy before they have changed their behavior or solved their problems. It's not an easy job and, while it doesn't require brilliance or magic or even a loving nature, it takes both talent and skill—the talent to keep the customer in therapy long enough for it to work and the skill to define the problems and solutions to the dilemmas of human existence.

Psychotherapy ordinarily offers a safe and accepting format for helping people come to grips with their emotions and then go ahead and do sensible things with their lives, whether they feel like it or not. It's a process by which people identify and talk about what they feel,

Choosing A Therapist to Hire

Before you turn your life over to a therapist, you need to know what manner of person that therapist is. Find out. If you can, hire a therapist who has worked effectively with people you know. Find out what sort of person the therapist is and hire a therapist who leads a life that seems desirable to you. Read anything he or she has written. Ask questions, even personal ones about whatever you consider relevant. The therapist being interviewed may not want to answer personal questions and may treat your asking them as if it were pathological, but don't be daunted by that. You have a right to know.

Even if the therapy you're considering is classical psychoanalysis (where the analyst just sits there silently treating everything you do as neurotic), you should insist on a couple of sessions at the beginning in which you ask all the questions you can think of about the therapy being proposed: how long it takes; how much it costs; and what happens if you want to drop out.

It is certainly appropriate to ask about a therapist's training and experience. In addition, go ahead and ask a therapist about his or her marital status and children, experiences with therapy, and personal experience with the issues (including grieving, divorce, infidelity, substance abuse, sexual orientation, depression, etc.) being addressed in the therapy. The therapist doesn't have to answer, of course, but should not object to being asked. I worry a bit about therapists who play it too close to the chest and fear revealing very much of themselves. It would be grossly inappropriate for a therapist to share a personal secret with a patient, but it seems almost paranoid to withhold the parts of a therapist's life that are common knowledge.

From time to time, prospective customers will call and ask if I am a "Christian psychiatrist." Some of them want reassurance that I do not seduce customers or conduct satanic rituals in my office. Some of them want to know that I will try to hold or bring families together rather than seeing

mental health as an escape from responsibilities and relationships. Some of them want to know that I am committed to preserving patriarchy and protecting women from the burdens of gender equality and men from feminism. As I answer their questions, I realize that very few are concerned with whether I might be Baptist, Jewish, Hindu, or atheist. Religious affiliation is not a reliable gauge of people's values, or lack thereof.

You can't interview the therapist about only his or her life. You have to tell the therapist about you and your life, and then assess the response; a therapist's values are in his or her responses to you and your dilemmas.

As the therapy proceeds, you should expect responses from the therapist. Unless you have agreed to go into classical psychoanalysis, you should expect the therapist to talk to you and to demonstrate understanding and good sense. Don't go back to a therapist who passively listens to your story and has nothing enlightening or intelligent to say. You can't demand magical solutions, but don't assume the therapist is thinking sensible thoughts if they are not voiced.

A therapist should treat you with respect. Don't go back to a therapist who makes a sexual pass at you or hits on you. It might be nice if the therapist hugs you, or laughs at you, or tells you you've screwed up. But if you don't like being hugged, or laughed at, or told you've screwed up, say so—but expect your reticence to be explored rather than simply respected. The therapist must be able to move in close and to help you laugh at life and at yourself.

If you convince your therapist you are dangerously fragile, you may be able to control the therapy so totally that you will be treated just as you want to be treated—and no therapy will take place. Do not expect the therapy sessions to make you feel good. Worry instead if the therapy sessions fail to provoke any thoughts at all, and you don't think about them between sessions.

Be a demanding consumer, although you probably will be labeled

difficult. Challenge the therapist when his or her values seem to conflict with your own or when he or she has a different take on reality than you have. The therapist may be offering you the wisdom that will save your life, but not until you thoroughly examine and understand it. You don't need a therapist to agree with you; you need a therapist to disagree with you and the way you have handled things, and then to explain at least one alternative way of looking at your dilemma and handling it.

Don't be in too big a hurry. Brief therapy can bring about magical fixes in some situations, such as phobias or family conflicts. But the social and psychological learning that makes psychotherapy transformative takes time, as all aspects of the customer's value system are challenged by the value system of the therapist—and vice versa.

There are a lot of therapists you can hire to listen to you if you are feeling lost and lonely, but there are not many therapists worth hiring for you to listen to. There are plenty of therapists out there eager to save you or protect you, which may be bad for you. There are some out there ready and able to fix you, which may be good for you. But try to find one who wants to help you understand how to take responsibility for your life, and how to live it.

Therapy is a highly personal process and the match between a therapist and a customer is highly personal. Good therapy may be rare, but it is well worth seeking, purchasing, savoring.

Most important, if a therapist is gentle and soothing and makes you feel that your life is not your fault, run for your life. Choose the therapist who pisses you off by insisting that you take more than your share of the responsibility for your life and your relationships. Hire the one who cuts through your defenses, your projections, and your rationalizations; one who makes you feel like a fool for continuing to screw up your life in the same old way, and offers optimism that he or she finds life worth living, so you can come to feel that way too.

rather than act on their emotions and do what they feel like doing. In the process, there may be a transfer of sanity and reality testing from therapist to patient. The therapist's calm may soothe the frantic patient. Sometimes the therapist is the one who must get frantic in order to alarm an inappropriately calm patient who fails to see the dangers in his or her actions.

Either way, psychotherapy involves applying the value system of the therapist to the dilemmas of the clients. The most important work of psychotherapy takes place inside the therapist's head as he or she thinks through the patient's snag points in dealing with this latest bump along the road of life.

When you go to a psychiatrist for medication or shock treatment, or to a psychologist for psychological testing, it may not matter very much what sort of person the professional is. But if you're choosing to bring a psychotherapist into your life as a consultant, his or her value system is more important to you than training, credentials, or even a professional degree.

The Myth of
Therapeutic Neutrality

Whatever psychotherapy is, it is not about therapeutic neutrality. Therapeutic neutrality is a stance inherited from classical psychoanalysis, in which the silent, passive analyst refuses to react or comment on what the patient is saying or doing, thus encouraging the patient to regress into a "transference neurosis" on the analyst. Needless to say, such

unresponsiveness brings forth all manner of crazy emotional responses. Except in classical psychoanalysis, neutrality is not only rude and inappropriate, it also makes you crazy.

Even is a therapist *could* be neutral about the issues at hand—impossible!—that neutrality would at best bring the therapy to a limping halt and at worst seem to be an endorsement of the client's persistence to barrel the wrong way down a one-way street. (For a therapist to feign neutrality about someone racing for disaster is not neutral; it is sadistic.)

Yet therapists try to make themselves less threatening by pretending to be neutral about anything that borders on a moral issue. We therapists are trained to pretend to have no value systems at all

---

The Mental Health Professionals

How does a consumer, shopping for answers to life's dilemmas, know whose wisdom to buy? There are several recognized professions of mental health experts. I can make a few generalizations about them, but like all generalizations, they are often false and frequently inapplicable.

• **Psychiatrists** are medical doctors who go all the way through medical school with the surgeons, pediatricians, and dermatologists, learning to take responsibility for people's lives. They then spend four or more years in a psychiatric residency, learning a fair amount about how the brain works, a lot more about how medicine works, and even more about how to make diagnoses according to an ever changing manual put out by the American Psychiatric Association. Psychiatrists used to learn how to do psychotherapy according to the model designed by Freud. Classical Freudian psychoanalysis seems too inefficient and expensive to be applied generally these days, so current psychiatric residents are more likely to learn various modifications that make it more practical and more applicable to more kinds of patients.

Psychiatrists used to learn how to do family therapy and group therapy, too. Some still do. The psychoanalytic preoccupation in the training of psychiatrists has given way to psychopharmacological preoccupation in recent years, so older psychiatrists are more likely to be well-trained psychotherapists than are younger psychiatrists.

Many psychiatrists have become little more than pill pushers for nonmedical psychotherapists. Some psychiatrists seem not to know how to treat people who are upset without first locking them up in an expensive and unwieldy psychiatric hospital, which is rarely necessary.

• **Psychologists**, who may have a degree of Doctor of Philosophy (Ph.D.) or Doctor of Psychology (Psy.D.), don't go to medical school, are not licensed to prescribe medicine, and generally don't hospitalize patients (there are exceptions in some places). They have traditionally gotten more academic training with far more emphasis on behavioral and psychological research, on the process of learning and education, and on objective psychological testing and diagnosis. Psychologists are likely to spend more actual years (if not more hours) learning to do psychotherapy, and are likely to devote most of their training to people with less severe problems, i.e., with neurotic rather than psychotic people.

Family therapy and concern with systems came late to psychology, and many older psychologists are stuck with an individual perspective with which they try to protect individuals from their relationships. A therapist oriented toward only individuals can permit clients to retain a single-minded preoccupation with themselves, with their own wants and needs, slights and dissatisfactions, and may inadvertently encourage customers to become increasingly dependent on the therapist and detached from the real people in their lives.

• **Social workers** have a master's degree, and while they have fewer years of training than doctors of either psychology or psychiatry, their training is quite practical. They may get more continuing supervision of their therapy than either psychiatrists or psychologists. Social workers get less training in the brain chemistry of severe mental illness, less training in the more intricate details of people's mental functioning, and more training in the things that are happening in the society to affect people's relationships and security. Social workers are likely to be well-grounded in family theory and family therapy.

M.S.W.s have been especially active in developing feminist therapies, and while this brings an awareness of societal and historic context to people's lives, it may also infect social workers with political correctness, which blames just about everything on social

and no sense of direction about the client's life, except for such benign virtues as unlimited patience, accurate empathy, steady optimism, nonpossessive warmth, and unconditional positive regard for whoever has rented the couch for that hour. Some therapists are opinionated people, with clearly established values, but they try to maintain their cramped neutral stances by detaching from patients and their dilemmas.

THE BLAMING BLIGHT

One of the horrors of psychotherapy is the affirmation clients may feel from their seemingly neutral therapists that they are "okay" even when they are doing terrible things to themselves and their loved ones. Some therapists listen without comment to tales of violence, substance abuse, infi-

delity, even incest. Their silence is tacit approval. Some therapists do worse than silently accept whatever the customer says or does; some actively affirm that the customer is always right. Therapists, as they ingratiate themselves to their customers, may actually provide "interpretations" to relieve clients of the guilt they need in order to keep them from hurting others and bringing disaster upon themselves.

Therapists may actually encourage customers to feel better about themselves by blaming their lives on other people, on the nature of human existence, or on the peculiar mores of the society around them. Repeatedly, men who are being unfaithful or violent are told by therapists that they are working out their anger at their mothers, while women who are being dishonest or mean are told they are battling patri-

archy. Everyone gets distracted from the impact of the betrayal or the power play upon the marriage.

It used to be stylish for therapists to help people blame their lives on their mothers or on their wives—whoever loved them too possessively. Lately, the style has been to blame everything on fathers, husbands, or men in general—whoever failed to love them enough. There are therapists who are expert at finding errors made by parents and grant the now-grown children the right to consider themselves adult children of imperfect parenting. People who center their lives around blaming their parents aren't free to be adults and parents themselves. This blaming of others may relieve pain briefly, but it is not therapeutic; it does not lead to empowerment or control over one's life and behavior.

forces. (There are psychologists and psychiatrists infected with political correctness as well, of course.) Political correctness is incompatible with therapeutic correctness, which empowers people to get control of their lives in an unfair, imperfect, and rapidly changing world. A therapist can't easily turn a patient into an innocent victim of social inequities and then help the patient take responsibility for his or her own life.

• **Marriage and family therapists** (MFTs) are also masters-level professionals. Like M.S.W.s, their training has centered more on practical supervision than on academic theorizing. Theirs is a new profession, and they are especially well trained to deal with systemic issues, intergenerational conflicts, and marriage problems. Many marriage and family therapists got their training before the new profession was designated, and they may have masters degrees in psychology (M.A.) or in educational counseling (M.Ed.) with many years of supervision and experience. Like M.S.W.s, MFTs are likely to be cheaper than psychiatrists and psychologists, but insurance may not cover masters-level therapists. MFTs also may not have much training in brain chemistry or individual psychology.

There are lots of other people who call themselves **counselors** and who have various kinds of training of various quality. Some are officially educa-

tional counselors, others are pastoral counselors, and still others are trained to counsel people with specific problems like grief and mourning, drug and alcohol abuse, or posttraumatic stress. States vary in their licensing requirements, some counselors have only a bachelor's degree, most have a master's, and some have a doctorate. Some of the therapists I respect most have an M.Ed. or Ed.D., a master's, or doctorate in educational counseling. The designation "counselor" does not tell me much about a person's training, but I do know that the profession and the training of a psychotherapist are far less important than what type of person the therapist is.

I am not at all convinced that the training of psychotherapists determines how they will practice after they have gotten some experience under their belt. They tend to get away from their training and to do the things that they find workable in their practices. Almost all psychotherapists, however dutifully purist they may be at the beginning of their careers, become eclectic or "integrative" before long. The training serves the crucial function of grounding fresh therapists, of providing a road map through the morass of all that pain and all that dependency and all those emotions. The seasoned therapist can improvise creatively and personally after he or she is safely and comfortably on familiar territory. After a few years, some

therapists are a great deal better than they were trained to be.

Sad to say, some therapists get a great deal worse—having forgotten or rejected what they were trained to do, or having so few successes in their own lives or the lives of their clients, that they haven't learned anything new to take its place. Some therapists are nuts, and get nuttier the longer they try to absorb the pain of their clients that they can't relieve. I remember Timothy Leary-like therapists who got increasingly drug-soaked in the Sixties and took a lot of people with them on their trip out of reality. A life without crisis or pain is not helpful for a therapist; a clear head is.

It may be that the therapists who spent the most years in training and in personal therapy are better grounded and more secure. They should certainly have had the most opportunity to deal with themselves as therapists, to discover their own sensitivities, prejudices, and blind spots. It is clearly better to deal with one's personal weaknesses while still in training and supervision than to stumble across them later. Still, some of the worst therapists I've encountered were among the best trained and had undergone the most personal psychotherapy. All the training and supervision and psychotherapy in the world is not going to make a good therapist out of someone who is not naturally therapeutic.

If people can't remember being victimized, some therapists specialize in uncovering forgotten abuse of various sorts. Forgotten incest is especially popular. I don't know whether it does more harm to forget abuse or to remember it, but I'm sure that much of the incest gradually remembered in therapy or under hypnosis is a dutiful fabrication of dependent people trying to please a victimizing therapist.

THERAPY IS AN ADVERSARIAL PROCESS

Therapists should of course help people step out of their crippling state of victimhood. Good therapy is not a chaste love affair between buyer and seller of psychotherapeutic services. The therapist and the customer don't even have to like one another. The therapy may be working best when you don't like your therapist, when you get the firm impression that your therapist doesn't like you very much either, and when you are being told that you have to do something you don't want to do if you are ever to feel good about yourself.

In fact, the therapist is hired to scrutinize you sharply and find something about you that is unlikable and unworkable, and then to help you isolate and discard the offending behavior. If the therapist sees everything the way you do, the therapist would be in the same fix you're in. And if the therapist thinks you're wonderful the way you are and just wants you to realize it, the love affair that results is different from therapy. Therapy is an inherently adversarial process, not an alliance to buffer innocent victims against a world that isn't gentle enough.

THE WORLD TURNS

We are all given faulty instruction books by our parents. For the past 200 years, the old patriarchal system of gender role assignments has been eroding, too slowly of course, but still with disorienting speed. Each generation faces a new world in which girls have more options and more challenges in life and boys have less deference and less expectation that they will automatically sacrifice their lives for the masculine mystique.

While this is liberating for both men and women, it is also disorienting. Each generation of boys and girls must redefine for themselves and for one another what it expects of men and women. Boys and girls, to become men and women in a new world, must challenge, reject, and selectively rebel against their parents' values,

which is frightening and can feel painfully disloyal.

Boys and girls don't have to fix their parents and don't have to cut off from them. They make the best use of their parents' values when they study their parents closely and question them about how they came to hold the values they hold, as well as how they find them to be working.

There are other aspects of us besides gender that are affected by the rapid changes in society. Social, cultural, and economic expectations change. We are now in a period of economic reversal. In many families the younger generation won't have it as cushy as their parents did, and may remain dependent on them.

Most younger people have moved part or all the way from their patriarchal roots and are enjoying greater range in their gender expression. Yet even the most progressive and open-minded of men and women may still carry within them, unchallenged, some of the models of marriage from their parents' or great-great-grandparents' generation, with the responsibilities, expectations, and privileges of a "head of the household" and his little "helpmate." Gender equality in marriage, championed by most (but not all) marriage therapists, may feel foreign operationally to many men and women. Those who recoil from equality may seek out a patriarchal therapist, perhaps a fundamentalist Christian counselor, who will try to protect them from having to challenge the model they learned growing up. Intellectually, they may want an equal relationship, but they feel deprived if they don't also have the loving domesticity of an idealized old-fashioned mother or the imperturbable strength of an idealized old-fashioned father. They just want the world to slow down until they can catch up.

THUS COME THE THERAPISTS

The world is changing so rapidly that people don't have to be mentally ill to be out of their minds some of the time, behaving inappropriately much of the time and a little bit disoriented all of the time. Therapists claim to have expertise in dealing with mental illness but also in dealing with the problems of living, in finding happiness and security in a rapidly changing world. Therapists, in effect, claim to have wisdom about human existence.

Actually, some probably do and some definitely don't. Therapists don't come into the business with any more wisdom than anyone else, though an inordinate number of them come from messed-up families

that have made them wiser and more alert than those who slide into adulthood without enough trauma to trigger development of an armamentarium of coping skills.

But after meddling intimately in a few lives, the therapist changes. If the therapist is paying close attention to what is going on inside the client and inside the therapist, and having success in understanding people and in helping them change, the experience of doing therapy should make the therapist increasingly aware of various layers of emotional, interpersonal, and social reality. The therapist must either get callous, get depressed, or get wise. The most experienced therapist is not necessarily the best, but the happiest experienced therapists are undoubtedly the wisest, since the therapy they do works and the wisdom they get from doing therapy helps them shape values that work in their own lives.

THINKING LIKE A THERAPIST

I know as a therapist I don't have to have all the right answers to life's questions. But I do have to have some. I'm likely to have better answers than the people who are stuck. If I don't, at least I have different ones, which may be just as good in moving someone out of the fix they're stuck in. It takes only a little wisdom to provide hope that there are other ways to do things.

I try to explain to therapists who are overwhelmed by what they see in their offices that there are no techniques and no solutions that will solve these problems. But there are ways in which the therapist can think about the issues, ways in which the therapist can reframe the problem, that permits it to be either accepted or solved, not perhaps in the way that anyone would *want* to solve it, but at least in a way that permits life to go on. I try to teach therapists how to think about human dilemmas in a way that is therapeutic.

THE DANGERS OF EMOTION WORSHIP

Some therapists can't think therapeutically because they let feelings take priority, as if all actions must be emotionally coherent. These therapists assume that when people follow their feelings purely and clearly, they will get to the desired destination. In his book, *Another Roadside Attraction*, Tom Robbins says "Living from your feelings is like nailing a chiffon pie to the wall."

When therapists give their primary attention in therapy to how people feel, they convey the notion that feelings are the most important determinant of action.

They distract customers from their exercises in reality testing, their efforts to explore and observe, and to understand the workings of the world around them. Instead, they turn their patients' attention inward, as if they were doping them up on hallucinogens. Such therapists seem to believe that the secrets of the universe, the true and accurate instruction book of life, are inside the increasingly muddled heads of their customers.

This might have made some sense back in Freud's day, when people were not accustomed to thinking, much less talking, about how they felt. But no one has an inner emotional life any more, since any feeling, before it is fully formed, is spilled out to the world on Sally, Oprah, or Phil. Introspectiveness does not lead to workable relationships because romantics spend their time thinking about how they want the people around them to be in order to make their dreams come true, rather than attempting to understand what their loved ones are like and why they are like that. Unceasing introspectiveness leads to narcissism and ultimately to loneliness and very few invitations to dinner with others.

If your therapist seems to give a great deal more weight to your feelings than to the feelings of the people who share your life, you may have to keep your attention focused on how you might be affecting them rather than just on how they are affecting you. You may even need to remind your therapist that acting on your impulses may not necessarily be good for your loved ones.

The most dangerous extreme of emotion worship is romanticism. Romantics are eager to sacrifice their lives, or the lives of their loved ones, in pursuit of emotional coherence. For romantics, life is inherently tragic. Romantic therapists may encourage the notion that following your emotions will give you the power to overcome reality, time, or gravity. Married people in affairs may think that, if they love each other enough, they can leave their mates and children and, after stepping over their bodies in their walk down the aisle, live happily ever after.

BEWARE OF CONSPIRATORIAL THERAPISTS

A few years ago, I wrote a book about the disruptive effect of infidelity and secrets, and found myself attacked by prominent marriage therapists. They explained that infidelity was normal behavior but too

emotionally provocative to bring up in therapy, especially since it was no doubt the fault of the marriage partner who was being betrayed, and who could thus not be told about it. My male colleagues explained that women who had been betrayed would just get "stirred up" and ruin the therapy with a lot of anger. My female colleagues explained that men shouldn't be told bad news since they would just get violent. Both explained that it was necessary to lie to people of other genders. Those therapists who were still speaking to me after the book came out offered to teach me their techniques for keeping the cuckold so disoriented about what was going on in the marriage and in therapy that the infidelity wouldn't have to be dealt with at all, and could continue untouched by the therapy.

To me it is arrogant of therapists to conspire with one member of a family or a couple to keep others in the family disoriented about matters that are crucial to their orientation and understanding of their life. Infidelity scares therapists. Couples therapists who conspire to keep sexual secrets are showing tremendous disrespect for the cuckold who is being betrayed, first by a spouse and then by the therapist.

Men have come in, referred by their divorce attorneys, asking for a course of ersatz marriage counseling that will look good in the divorce case and distract their wives from realizing that there is a secret affair going on. They hope that I can sufficiently confuse and disorient the wife, and make her think she is in some way responsible for the failure of the marriage. Then they can get by with a less expensive divorce settlement. Most therapists would refuse such a mission, but some enjoy the chance to champion a client against enemies.

A buyer of psychotherapy should not use a therapist as an instrument for inflicting harm on loved ones, for dispensing misinformation or concealing information that will drive his or her partner too crazy to understand what's going on. A therapist is not supposed to be your champion, but your critic. A therapist is not like a lawyer. The lawyer is out to prove you innocent of any wrongdoing; thereby the lawyer saves your skin. The therapist is out to show you how you screwed up and brought disaster upon yourself; thereby the therapist saves your life. Your therapist, in pleading your case to the people in your life, will emphasize your guilt, not your innocence. Your lawyer wants to confuse the judge and the jury so you will never have to deal with those people again. The therapist wants to reveal the truth and enlighten the people in

your life, so you can honestly and intimately deal with those people forever after.

As a therapy consumer, you may be tempted to see the therapist as a judge rather than as a defense attorney, and ask the therapist to take your side and declare you to be right. That would be a misunderstanding of the function of the therapist, which is to understand the ways in which you are wrong.

Foolish therapy customers have been known to hit their relatives with actual extracted or invented quotes from the therapist that are critical of the relatives and defensive of the patient. This can effectively sabotage couples or family therapy, where the therapist knows the relatives being criticized. When the relatives are criticized in absentia by a therapist, they understandably go on the defensive and will actively undercut the therapy. What a waste of a therapist!

WHAT'S YOUR THERAPIST'S VIEW OF MARRIAGE?

Some therapists believe in marriage so strongly they see singlehood as a state of emotional deprivation that is the cause of all the pain in the life of single people. Such therapists may rush people into ill-advised marriages, some of which work and some of which won't.

Other therapists distrust marriage so totally they see it as a dangerously oppressive state of exploitation and impending doom. They assume that any pain a married person suffers is brought on by the marriage. These therapists likely experienced disappointment in their marriages or their parents' marriages.

In between are therapists who idealize marriage, and give full support to perfect

> # Most psychotherapy is not about mental illness but about values—about the value dilemmas of sane and ordinary people trying to lead a life amidst great personal, familial, and cultural confusion.

What Makes A Good Therapist?

1. A good therapist has got to like doing therapy. A wise old therapist friend acknowledged that those of us who become psychotherapists are people who need more hours of therapy each day than we can afford to buy for ourselves. I don't mean that therapists have more mental illness than other people, but that they get more out of therapy. Good therapists are good patients, people who enjoy swimming in emotions without drowning in them. They feel refreshed after an emotional workout.

2. Good therapists have got to be optimistic, believing that life is a comedy, not a tragedy, even if you can't get out of it alive. They can't be afraid of failures and embarrassment and pain, or even of tragedies. Good therapists aren't protective of their clients. Therapists can't do good therapy when they are afraid of losing their customers, of having customers commit suicide or sue them.

3. Good therapists have got to be eager detectives and explorers, people who like to solve mysteries and figure out how life works. They have a homing device that leads them quickly and directly to the aspects of the situation that don't make sense. Sherlock Holmes and Sigmund Freud had more in common than cocaine. Good therapists don't take things at face value, they don't assume they understand everything from the beginning, and they certainly don't assume that everyone is alike and that one solution fits all. They have to be eager to understand the intricacies of a new situation. Good therapists are excited by each new client, and learn something new from each.

4. Good therapists certainly have to be warm—they may not be especially loving or nurturing, but they delight in intimacy. They must be able to understand and share experiences: their own, those of their customers, and those of the people whose lives are touched by their customers. Good therapists are not quite like good parents, who are massively invested in those they would raise—that position is inevitably too possessive. They are more like aunts and uncles, offering an alternate view of reality while invested in the outcome, but not so possessive that their own identity is at stake.

5. Good therapists have got to have a sense of humor. Without it, they may try to protect their customers from the cruelties of life—those unpleasant but necessary experiences that give people chances to expand consciousness and build character. Of course, good patients have to have a good sense of humor too. Good therapy is fun, and spoils both therapist and patient for the sort of cautious, polite interaction that takes place at social occasions.

6. Above all, good therapists have got to be fairly sane—not rigidly, anxiously, cautiously sane, but able to see fairly clearly how the world works. It also helps if therapists are happy people, not stuck in happiness like manics or TV weather forecasters, but able to experience a full range of human emotions.

marriages and short shrift to those with problems. Some therapists, especially those who didn't come in from the Sixties in time, still believe that mental health comes from running away from home, and if people are too old to run away from their parents, they can run away from their marriage.

They don't understand that the struggle of marriage is second only to the raising of children as the central maturing experience of life. As with the combat of war, you win the important victory, the one over yourself and your fears, simply by not running away.

Married people would do well to stick with therapists who believe in marriage. But such therapists must believe in divorce too, not as a path to happiness and a more perfect partner next time (second marriages have an even higher divorce rate than first ones, and third marriages are probably uninsurable), but as an escape from the unendurable, like recurrent violence, chronic alcoholism, or philandering. Therapists should make customers contemplating divorce aware of the devastating impact on the children and the shock waves that will continue for generations.

A therapist who endorses divorce too glibly or dismisses marriage too offhandedly is dangerous. But so is a therapist who does not empower you to leave a truly abusive marital situation. Knowing you can leave, and convincing your abusive partner that you can leave, perhaps by actually leaving for a time, may be more helpful than divorce. The point of therapy should not be to protect you from unpleasantness and disappointment, but to empower you to take charge of your life and your marriage. You must realize your marriage is not the property of your partner, but is yours. And you have a say in how it goes and whether it goes. You must not be bullied into it. Or out of it.

The Last Self-Help Article You'll Ever Need

There must be something wrong with you if you don't know there's something wrong with you.

Susan Baxter

Blame the primordial ooze. If it hadn't woken up one day from its nice warm bed of volcanic rock, looked around at all the *Sturm und Drang,* and complained, "I don't like this. Why don't I go out and seek some greater personal fulfillment?", none of this would have happened. But primordial ooze went on to become hydrogen, and, ever since, the Earth has simply teemed with self-improvement schemes. Of course, in those days, transforming oneself didn't involve group hugs and confessions, no one stood up and said, "Hi, I'm Molten Lava and I suffer from dreadful hot flashes." That came later, with civilization.

I first came across the notion of self-help in 1982, with Werner Erhardt's "est" promising self-awareness ("Know myself? If I knew myself I'd run away," said Goethe), fulfillment, and how to get everything you wanted, or "noblesse without the oblige" as one writer called it. Tired of the evangelical zeal adherents displayed (and the nonsense they spouted), I actually met with a bunch of esties (esters?) with a tape recorder cunningly hidden in my bag and a misguided notion of writing the Ultimate Exposé as visions of Pultizers danced in my head. (The article never got written, but that's another story.) The conversation was totally unremarkable; all I remember is one chap earnestly telling me that, with est, I would learn how to separate from "my act"—look at "my act," stand back and change "my act." I couldn't help myself: "then can I take it on the road?" I inquired. Which was when I discovered that those who embark on the road to

Self-help now includes every permutation of pop-psychology. Even the buzzwords changed: Now, to err is dysfunctional; to forgive, codependent.

inner peace have absolutely no sense of humor.

Much has changed in 10 years; alas, the "humor thing" has not, and today's self-helpers are just as dreary today as they were then. Self-help has grown to include every permutation of pop-psychology possible, from positive thinking to family systems (est, incidentally, is now the kinder, gentler "Forum"); as well as encompassing mainstream medicine with every disease, disorder, condition, or illness ever known (or imagined). Even the buzzwords have changed: Now, to err is dysfunctional; to forgive, co-dependent.

Self-help is warmer and fuzzier than it used to be, says one critic, but the focus is still *self, self, self.* . . .

Self-help began truly proliferating in the 1980s with what humorist Fran Lebowitz called "a rate of speed traditionally associated with the more unpleasant amoebic disorders"—going from some 300 groups in 1963 to more than 500,000 in 1992. The reason, say the authors of *Self-Help Concepts and Applications* (from Charles Press; 1992), lies in our stars—namely, Oprah, Geraldo, Phil, and Ann Landers; also *New Woman,*

Cosmopolitan, and other magazines; plus prime-time TV dramas, which refer, with increasing frequency, to self-help groups. These bastions of popular culture no doubt appreciate that self-help fills a need in a fragmented society, where many traditional sources of support—such as the extended family—no longer exist. They also realize that misery is, well, endlessly fascinating.

I had pretty much decided to ignore self-help after the est debacle, but soon it became difficult. Not only was the language permeating everything I read, from articles on the economy and politics to features in women's magazines; but no less an authority than former Surgeon General C. Everett Koop organized a workshop on self-help and proclaimed that "the future of health care in these troubled times requires cooperation between organized medicine and self-help groups." Koop also said that "a partnership between professional traditional care and the self-help movement can provide a superior service."

Various self-help groups became politically active, lobbying governments for funding and recognition. I started to get peeved. Then people came out of the woodwork with bizarre phrases like "dysfunctional family" (redundant?) and "I'm feeling my feelings." finally, when a (former) friend insisted to me that I was abused as a child (because my parents had expressed disapproval when I declared—at 16, after appearing in two school plays—that I was going to study acting), I had had enough. What next? The vet suggesting my cat read *Nurturing Your Inner Kitten*? A 12-step program for conquering chronic nail-biting? A self-help group for adult children (an oxymoron?) of absent-minded parents? Orwell, I feared, had been right—with the demise of language would come chaos.

Soon, whoever you were, whatever you had, might have, there was a group you could join, and just in case you didn't know there was a name for some of these things, much less support groups, "disease-of-the-week" movies told you in graphic detail. "It matters little whether the threat comes from some modern technology, from heart surgery or hemodialysis, whether it's a threat based on reaction to stress, or whether it is due to an addiction, to violent behavior, or to trauma," says Leonard D. Borman, Ph.D., former executive director of the Self-Help Center in Illinois and master of the run-on sentence. (Pardon? Cancer equals heart transplant equals hives-equals PMS equals an unfortunate tendency to shop till you drop?)

We are obsessed with the recognition, praise, and, if necessary, the manufacture of victims these days, writes Robert Huges in *Time*. The range of victims has expanded to include "every permutation of the halt, the blind, and the short, or, to put it correctly, the vertically challenged."(!) As one who is vertically challenged, naturally I know that tall people are out to oppress short ones (hey, you try looking through a peephole designed for the Jolly Green Giant), but I would be too polite to say so. But when everyone is equally a victim—of their physiology, their background, their race, their sex, their quirks—then personal responsibility goes out the door. "Whatever our folly, venality, or outright thuggishness, we are not to be blamed," suggests Hughes, since we are all victims.

It may not be perfect, say proponents huffily, but self-help provides bang for the buck. For people with a common problem, groups provide support, information, an opportunity to network, and a focus on emotional, social, and spiritual dimensions—something traditional medicine does not often provide. I have no quibble with self-help groups for serious, life-threatening, chronic illness, where state of mind can improve the prognosis. A host of studies demonstrate that this holistic approach has, for a fraction of the cost, immense value.

For example, David Spiegel, a Stanford University psychiatrist, tired of the touchy-feely claims of therapy, decided to prove, once and for all, that emotional support was useless. He went back to a 1984 study in which 50 of 86 women undergoing conventional cancer therapy also attended a support group, where he found, to his astonishment, that those receiving emotional support not only felt less depressed and in less pain—they lived nearly twice as long (an average of 37 months versus 19) as the women not attending the group. "Believe me," he told *Health* magazine in 1992, "if we'd seen these results with a new drug it would be in every cancer hospital in the country."

Where the self-help argument breaks down is in extending this model to include *everything,* from fairly benign (although admittedly unpleasant) conditions such as migraine, PMS, or irritable bowel, to otherwise healthy people going through a normal life passage such as menopause or the death of a parent. Even more problematic is the vast, uncharted sea of the "worried well" into which the John Bradshaw & Co. domain of 12 steps, addiction, and recovery would fall. (If this were an ancient map, at this point it would read: "here Be Dragons.")

As a migraine, er, survivor (self-help disapproves of words like "victim" or "sufferer")—actually, as one who survives migraines on a fairly regular basis—I would seriously question the efficacy of self-help in the benign-illness context. Pain or discomfort, while "real," is nevertheless more than simple physiology, and is irrevocably tied with mood, stress levels, fatigue, even expectation (as Melzack and Wall and countless pain clinics have proved). Oliver Sachs (of *Awakenings* fame) in his book *Migraine,* writes that not only will an expected migraine rise nobly to the occasion, but migraines can actually come in *handy* at times! With some skepticism, I tested Sachs' point—and I'll be goshdarned if it didn't work. The more I focus on migraine, define myself as a person with migraines, expect migraines, the more it backfires. Which of course makes me wonder: How many migraines did I get simply because I thought I would? Or because I was overextended and it gave me an acceptable excuse to go lie down?

I can't see how self-help would be anything but counterproductive with migraines, unless short-term and informational—i.e., to exchange tips, find out what other people do to prevent/shorten

a migraine, get moral support, and complain about all those people who've never had a migraine and tell one airily to take an aspirin. ("I personally think we developed language because of our deep need to complain," said Lily Tomlin.) but self-help's emphasis on experiential learning and tendency to reject professional input makes me a little nervous. Call me paranoid, but I would prefer to have someone leading a group that knew what they were doing, not just a fellow-traveler who could pass on whatever nonsense they liked.

Now if migraine, which is relatively cut-and-dried, is prone to psychological mismanagement, what about something with less obvious symptoms, like PMS or chronic fatigue, where membership in the club can be as nebulous as feeling anxious or exhausted? It stands to reason that if you can get a migraine when you expect one, you can also get premenstrual symptoms. Where does one draw the line between life and disease?

We may no longer live lies of quiet desperation, but we do live in nervous times, and quite a lot of people are feeling threatened by quite a lot of problems: pollution, acid rain, HDL (or LDL, who can remember?) cholesterol. Emissions from ubiquitous, humming machines like microwaves and computer monitors. Crime. Unemployment. A dizzying rate of change, and, most ominous of all, the chilling workplace message: Perform or perish. Adapt or "become redundant."

"All of a sudden someone comes along and says it isn't really what you know anymore, it's how quickly you can *learn,*" says Carol Kinsey Goman, Ph.D., once a clinical psychologist and now a consultant and keynote speaker on the "human side of organizational change. Today it's impossible to lay out your career or your life in those predetermined paths that were so set [before]." Add to that the fact that most of us are working harder and earning less, and one has to concede that things really are getting more stressful. Get used to it. "Stress control has got to become a way in the '90s," says Goman flatly.

Ably preying on what *Newsweek* calls our "self-doubt and self-deprecation" are the pundits of gloom and purveyors of the quick fix. And whatever the problem, there's somebody out there ready and willing to sell us something to cure it. Woman alone? Worried about crime? Get a car phone so you can call for help faster. Feeling a little tubby compared to all those sleek people in advertisements? Try this powdered-meal substitute. Not happy? Having problems with relationships, anxiety? Have we got a book/tape/group/seminar for you!

And the largest consumers of these claims, be they cosmetics or cosmetic surgery? *Women.* "Women are brought up to believe that they are inadequate and insufficient and that to be complete [they must] seek fulfillment outside themselves," said Ari Kiev. Women flock to self-help in droves, to improve everything from their sex lives and their relationships to their careers. Why? Because, writes Carol Tavris in her brilliant analysis of the second sex, *The Mismeasure of Woman,* "Despite women's gains . . . the fundamental belief in the *normalcy of men and the corresponding abnormality of women* has remained virtually untouched" (italics mine). Everything from women's management style (cooperative) to their behavior in relationships (conciliatory) is suspect, wrong. So, there are countless books, groups, seminars directing attention to every alleged female flaw—whether it's "fear of independence, fear of codependency, fear of success, fear of failure, or fear of fear."

If a woman—or a man—is lucky enough, through some combination of adequate nurturing, okay genes, reasonable health, enough money, encouragement, and opportunity, to be all right, thank you very much; the latest pop-psychology self-help fad has generously widened its admission criteria so that virtually anyone can join in the rousing chorus of "Nobody knows the trouble I've seen." Because there is, by all accounts, not one "functional" family in the universe. David Rieff, in a controversial 1991 *Harper's* article, "Victims All? Recovery, codependency, and the art of blaming somebody else" writes: "It is hard to see how, given the way (recovery guru) Dr. Whitfield (*Healing the Child Within*) has defined childhood trauma, any reader could feel exempt. Questions range from relatively benign queries like 'Do you seek approval and affirmation?' through the more ominous 'Do you respond with anxiety to authority figures and angry people?' (here one wants to ask, 'With or without a firearm in their hands?') to the . . . old standby, 'Do you find it difficult to express your emo-

tions?' " It turns out that the whole thing is rigged anyway, says Rieff, since even one answer of "occasionally" means that the respondent needs his or her inner child attended to.

I don't really want to pick on the recovery movement per se, however much I agree with Rieff and, more recently, Wendy Kaminer's well-written indictment of recovery, *I'm Dysfunctional, You're Dysfunctional.* For one thing, the "True Confessions" style of people like Melody Beattie make them sitting ducks—albeit rich, famous ducks. (Beattie cites her own background as proof that 12 steps work. Reading some of those stories one suspects that Thorazine would too.) Neither do I want to belittle the accounts of those who have experienced genuine childhood trauma such as physical or sexual abuse. But this total focus on experiential proof added to the lack of professional involvement gives me the heeby-jeebies.

"There's no screening in terms of who attends [these groups]," says registered clinical counsellor Jessica Easton, M.A. "Let's say someone had just got out of a psychiatric unit and was on heavy medication. They could attend a 12-step program, they could attend Context, they could attend any group and react quite strongly—or get to a point where they might not be able to function." Furthermore, there is an enormous potential for abuse in this sort of uncontrolled free-for-all pop-psych messing with your head. Easton and a colleague held a free public meeting last December for victims—are you ready for this?—of self-help groups! One of the things they did, said Easton, was distribute a sheet delineating "client's rights."

"I would say that 50 percent of the people sitting there didn't even know they had rights," Easton says indignantly. With many groups, she points out, the assumption or premise is that "process is everything." And woe betide the person who questions it. They can be ridiculed, belittled, damaged.

Why hasn't anyone—the American Psychological Association, to name the most likely candidate—initiated some sort of public-education program, some process to help people not become victims of self-help, as well as give legitimate groups some backup, such as a *Good Housekeeping* Seal of Approval? The APA spokesman I talked to rather sheepishly admitted that

"there is no official position" on self-help; that some 10 years ago there had been a "task force," but that there was some "difficulty in finding a consensus" and a position was "never adopted." Gerald Rosen, Ph.D., a Seattle clinical psychologist who had headed the 1978 Task Force, said he is critical of the APA's "failure to set a standard or provide a direction" for the profession.

The Task Force wasn't *against* self-help; they wrote that self-help has "tremendous potential to help individuals understand themselves and others and to promote human welfare. But they also warned that the promotional claims and titles that accompany these programs are increasingly exaggerated and sensationalized," promising total cures and professing to eliminate the need for any outside professional help. They recommended that the APA take some steps, for instance publish an informational pamphlet on self-help.

Psychology shares some of self-help's aims. Humanistic psychology has long concentrated on improving the human condition—a lofty, if ambiguous, aim. (Improving it for whom? By whose standards?) Neither have individual clinicians been immune to the self-help trends, from Rational-Emotive Therapy to Bradshaw. But at least they recognize the pitfalls. "I encourage people to use self-help," says Rosen, "but I encourage them to use it with accurate expectancies."

Humanism's notion of developing human potential is one thing; but when everything, including life itself (which, let's face it, is enough to give anyone a migraine) is dangerous and threatening and everyone's a victim, then the solution has become part of the problem.

Some years ago I reviewed a book about adoption, in which the writer painstakingly and painfully described the price she had had to pay for being adopted: an alienated adolescence, "knowing" as a child that she felt "different"; insecurities, fears, and moments of anxiety as an adult. I could have sworn, on reading this book that I was adopted. As a child I frequently thought I must be a foundling. I was, like most teenagers, alienated. As an adult, I even felt anxious or fearful at times. Aha!

Suppose that book (as so many now) had instead ascribed those all-too-common feelings to codependency, addiction, or a dysfunctional family? What if the topic were not finding one's birth mother but one's inner child? I could have believed it. I could then spend the rest of my life with a handy label that would explain everything that ever went wrong. I could find a rationale for every failing, every insecurity, every mistake. I could corner people at parties! I could be a bore! I could write a book . . . get rich! *Hmmmmm.*

It's tempting—to believe that there is one answer and one person, like the Wizard of Oz, who has the formula. (Believe those who are seeking the truth, said Andre Gide, but doubt those who find it.) Unfortunately, wizards are only too often muddled individuals hiding behind a lot of smoke and mirrors; their only genius a knack for pointing out the obvious, which, if we'd only stopped to think for a moment, we could have figured out. Twelve steps (or five or 20) are only one way of reducing complexity in a world we all occasionally feel a little overwhelmed by. But, like it or not, life (unlike surgery—which "robodocs" can do—or drywalling) just can't be reduced to a series of cosmic or karmic how-to's.

But the parable has a long and honorable tradition in our collective unconscious, be it religion, myth, science, or advertising (like The Parable of the Lost Traveler's Checks). It's powerfully didactic. As you journey through life, says the parable, there will be problems; here's how they are solved. The assumption is that (1) there is a problem, and (2) every problem can be solved. Since Darwin and Freud we've steered away from divine intervention and religious determinism, only to replace it with the same old dogma couched in less apocalyptic terms. But the subtext remains perennial: determinism. We are powerless, doomed to live out the dictates of our nature, our childhood, original sin, unless we find salvation through a higher power, holistic medicine, positive thinking, psychoanalysis, est . . . or something else.

There's something very bleak about this obsession with what's lacking—the realization that misery is, well, endlessly fascinating.

There's something very bleak with this endless fascination with what's wrong, what's lacking. "Self-help usually focuses on the negative quadrant of your life," says Goman, "the thing that isn't working. And the more you define yourself by that narrow little piece that's out of whack, the greater the chances that you're going to stay out of whack." But then maybe there's something restful in being "out of whack" in a world that demands high-powered efficiency, endless flexibility, and, for most of us, a wish for a 29-hour day. It's a lot easier to bleat that it's not my fault.

Newsweek used to run a long letter to the editor every week, a forum for individuals to air their views on everything from baseball to taxes. I remember vividly a piece written by a woman who wrote that she had been physically abused as a child. She was now a mother, and seriously resented the implication that abused [people] have to grow up to become abusers themselves. This woman argued that she was far less likely to be abusive with her children because she knew what it felt like (similar to the piece in *Psychology Today* written from prison last issue). She had, quite bluntly, chosen to exercise her free will by breaking free of the pattern.

The truth is that we *do* have free will, provided, like this woman, we choose to exercise it. We can take the lessons of the past and learn from them, not be controlled by them. Use them as a springboard for growth, not as an excuse. We can be overwhelmed by what we lack—or work from a position of strength—maybe even try to help those worse-off than ourselves.

"Low grumbles, high grumbles, and meta-grumbles" was what humanist Abe Maslow (originator of the phrase "self-actualization") called this pessimistic tendency we have to focus on our deficits, deficiencies, and problems. Why not, he asked, radically, "shake free of this cultural relativism, which stresses passivity, plasticity, and shapelessness?" Why not, instead realize our potential by concentrating on autonomy and growth. Why not think about the "maturation of inner forces?"

Or, as Disney put it, why not look on the bright side?

The Importance Of Solitude

Dr. Rae André
Northeastern University

Many Americans admire the rugged individualists in novels and films who take on the system or overcome adversity single-handedly.

Yet, we don't feel comfortable with those who keep to themselves. We tend to distrust contemplation and view solitary people and pursuits with suspicion.

Opportunity: We would be better off if we engaged in *positive solitude*—time alone that is used thoughtfully to benefit mind and soul. Positive solitude is an important element of self-discovery and growth.

Solitude provides the opportunity to identify your most cherished goals and develop ways of achieving them. Regular reflection contributes to a sense of inner peace...and makes you feel more in control of your life.

THE PROBLEMS OF BEING ALONE

Positive solitude takes conscious effort, whether you live with others or alone.

●**People who live with others** are often so caught up in the demands of family life that they don't take time for self-reflection. Time alone feels like an expendable luxury to them. Thus, they're in danger of defining themselves through others.

These people need to make private time a priority and be creative about ways of finding it.

Examples: Evaluate work and community responsibilities, and determine which are essential—and which can be cut back. Join a babysitting co-op so someone else can look after your children one or two days a week. Plan a solitary retreat to a quiet place for a few days to reflect on what's really important to you.

●**People who live alone** may feel left out in a world of couples and families. They may *fight* solitude by compulsively seeking company, filling their days with "busyness" that isn't very satisfying...and missing a wonderful opportunity for self-discovery and growth.

They need to challenge the belief that having a family is the only way to be happy...look for ways to nurture themselves instead of waiting for a partner to make life satisfying...and take advantage of the chance to learn more about their own values and perceptions.

I believe that living alone doesn't have to be lonely—nor should it be viewed as a way station on the path to "coupledom." Living alone can be a deeply rewarding lifestyle in its own right.

Positive solitude actually enhances relationships when people do come together. People who are not afraid of solitude can meet as strong wholes instead of incomplete halves that are desperate for fulfillment.

TURN OFF THE TV

One of the biggest threats to positive solitude is television. It's the easiest, but possibly least-satisfying, way to fill up your time.

Watching television does not put you in contact with other people *or* yourself.

Bottom Line/Personal interviewed Rae André, PhD, associate professor of management psychology at Northeastern University. A consultant, lecturer and workshop leader, she is the author of *Positive Solitude: A Practical Program for Mastering Loneliness and Achieving Self-Fulfillment*. HarperCollins, 10 E. 53 St., New York 10022. $10.

Instead, it bombards you with the agenda and values of the TV programmers and advertisers.

Spending a lot of time in front of the TV feeds loneliness. It encourages us to let someone else decide what's interesting, discourages us from looking inward and takes up time that could be spent developing original ideas or actively challenging or supporting the ideas of others.

WAYS TO USE PRIVATE TIME

In solitude, we can explore what's most meaningful to us—free from other people's expectations. We can begin to develop a personal philosophy or life plan.

This isn't an easy task, but it's an exciting one. *Key:* Ask yourself the kinds of questions that don't have simple answers…and be prepared to return to them again and again. *Examples…*

What contribution do I want to make to the world? Focus on what's significant to you—not to your parents, spouse or boss. *Possibilities:* Create a new variety of rose…raise healthy, loving children…comfort people in distress…make music…gather and analyze information about nature or politics.

What are the gaps in my life? Are there things you'd like to understand better or have more control over? Goals you've abandoned out of fear—but still wonder about? What are some ways to address these gaps?

Tools that can help in your exploration include a journal…walking…meditation…quiet time in a natural environment. *Exercises:*

• Write for 15 minutes about a topic of your choice, *without stopping or censoring yourself.* You'll be surprised at the ideas that come up.

• Write about a dream you had recently, the emotions it stirred and the messages it might have. Dreams often introduce important themes we haven't yet faced consciously.

MOVING OUTWARD

Quietly thinking and writing aren't the only ways to discover meaning. In fact, planning and taking part in challenging activities can be an outgrowth of positive solitude. We can try activities that reveal new aspects of ourselves—physical, intellectual and spiritual. The key is to identify and follow those pursuits that engage *you*—not to please friends or family or because you've always done them. *Exercises:*

• Write down 10 or 20 activities that you used to love but haven't done for a long time. What did you most enjoy as a child or adolescent? Try some of these activities again.

• Make a list of activities you always wanted to try but never got around to. Pick one—and do it.

Planning is essential for this stage. If we don't plan, then the *easiest* things will happen, not the most fulfilling. We'll come home and switch on the TV instead of going to a concert or arranging a kayaking trip.

Make activity dates for yourself…pencil them into your calendar…and make sure you keep them.

BE PATIENT

Don't be surprised if this self-analysis feels uncomfortable at first—or if you don't make dramatic discoveries right away.

Getting to know yourself takes some time. Challenging and reexamining your assumptions do not happen in a day. But the effort will bring satisfying rewards…including a deeper understanding of your values and needs…increased confidence in your capabilities…a richer enjoyment of life…and a greater receptivity to others.

How to Master Your Moods

Recognize your emotion style and make it work for you.

Do you often feel apprehensive but can't pinpoint any reason for your anxiety? Do you tend to experience intense feelings and think you're going to explode unless you express them immediately? Or are you the kind of person who secretly wonders why you're so restless, so quickly bored with jobs or romances?

Melvin Kinder, Ph.D.

If you're like most people, you may find that your moods are sometimes baffling. While everything we read tells us we should be able to *control* our emotions, we just can't seem to do it. The gap between what we feel and what we're told we *should* feel is a constant condemnation. What is wrong with us? The answer may be surprising.

As a therapist, I have always been intrigued by the psychological myths that give us misleading information and unrealistic expectations about ourselves. I believe that the core dilemma behind our problems in our relationships, our work, and our sense of self is that we have neglected the emotional cornerstone of who we are. Under the layers of "shoulds" and "should nots" about our feelings is the source of our true, **instinctive emotional response**—what I call the natural self.

The exciting news is that our emotions may be largely biochemical—not a product of childhood traumas, moral deficiencies, the wrong husband, the wrong job, and so forth. But we're still operating on old ideas and outdated theories about why we feel the way we do. As a result, we're left confused and disheartened by the puzzling and enigmatic nature of our emotions. The new findings point to their true source:

- **Our emotions have biological origins.**
- **Each of us is born with an emotional temperament.**
- **Who we are and how we react to the world around us is determined more by these inborn traits than by environment or our upbringing.**

The answer then to the question of "what's wrong with me" may well be a combination of false expectations and **denying your natural self.**

Indisputably, life experiences shape us in many ways, but they are not the most important determinants. Our natural temperament will give the signature, the definitive mark, to who we are, how we navigate through the world. And, when you understand this, you will find that it is *liberating* rather than imprisoning— you will know exactly why you feel the way you do and what you need to do in order to feel better.

And you'll feel more at ease with those around you.

The Four Temperament Types

As my observations crystallized over the years, I eventually identified distinct similarities and differences between my clients. Four emotional types emerged:

1. The Sensor—prone to be extra sensitive to outer stimulation; sometimes wonderfully sensitive, other times overly anxious and fearful.

2. The Seeker—craves sensation and is emotionally satisfied with its quest; can also be inclined to unhappy cravings and unsettling restlessness and boredom.

3. The Discharger—vents his or her feelings; can be spontaneous, expressive, and passionate, but is also prone to anger and easily set off by frustrations.

4. The Focuser—prone to excessive awareness of inner feelings or lack of them; can be delicately aware and inwardly focused, but is also prone to worry and sadness.

The Sensor is perceptive, empathetic, even soulful and sensual. Sensors are aware of every nuance of mood in people around them but often feel too much and become overwhelmed. They are predisposed to anxiety; life can be too intense, too painful—there are far too many ups and downs. People inclined to emotional sensitivity often feel touchy, high-strung, tense, nervous. Many sensors ignore their fears and lead, risk, socialize, and compete with the most thick-skinned and outgoing of the pack. They are very likely to rush into that which they fear.

Digest Synopsis: Each of us is born with a particular emotional style that, to some extent, dictates our emotions. By working within our style, we can be less vulnerable to unpleasant moods.

These are broad groups, and there are individual differences within each group, but the similarities outweigh the differences. Each temperament type has a biochemical base that dictates emotional patterns and responses in any situation. In addition, each temperament has an emotional *comfort zone*—a range of experiences, intensity, and stimulation—that each of us finds tolerable. When we're pushed outside our comfort zone, we're vulnerable to unpleasant emotions and moods.

Our goal, therefore, is to expand our emotional comfort zone so that we are less vulnerable to bad feelings, and more comfortable with a broader range of experience. I believe it is possible to become educated about your temperament and to work within that context to achieve a more genuine sense of self as well as emotional self-confidence.

Sensors: From Anxiety to Courage

Sherry, a marketing executive, loves and hates her work at the same time. At 33, she already felt burned out, mentally exhausted, and fearful that she would fall behind and no longer be considered a player in her industry.

In childhood she had been shy, hypersensitive, and timid in new situations. Her parents had pushed her to be more outgoing; consequently, Sherry forced herself to act confident in spite of her feelings. As an adult, she still feels nervous and secretly views herself as scared rather than courageous.

Profile
• **In relationships:** Your emotional sensitivity and ability to empathize can cause serious problems in a marriage. The danger is that you can be so afraid to displease your mate that you compromise your own goals and values.

• **Friendships:** You typically establish friendships in a slower and more cautious manner than others. Wary of possible threats, you implicitly require that others prove their trustworthiness. Yet when trust is established, you may be more steadfast and loyal.

• **As a parent:** You're likely to be caring and attentive, building your life around home and family. You may, however, find that you're oversensitive to your children's needs and need to encourage autonomy and independence in them.

• **At work:** You work best in a secure atmosphere where there is little turnover. You are most comfortable with a defined work role, and with the right combination of prodding and reassurance, you work creatively and confidently.

The Sensor's Task
The key to enlarging your comfort zone is to stop avoiding and start facing threats. "Systematic desensitization" means

---

Myths About Emotions

1. The Myth of Uniformity: We are all alike in our emotional makeup. All "normal" and "healthy" people should feel and respond in the same ways.

2. The Myth of Good and Bad: Feelings are either good or bad; unpleasant feelings are bad and should be eliminated.

3. The Myth of Control: We can and should strive to control our emotions.

4. The Myth of Perfectibility: We can and should strive for psychological perfection.

5. The Myth of Emotional Illness: Emotional distress is a sign of mental illness.

6. The Myth of Positive Thinking: We create what we feel by what we think. We believe "it's all in our minds" and willpower can change our emotions.

gradual exposure to feared situations. In time, less anxiety is aroused by employing mental imagery and visualization. For example, the more you rehearse a speech in your mind, the less anxious you may feel giving it.

1. First become aware of your body and its signals of arousal, including breathing, sweating, jitters, lack of concentration, fearful thoughts. Begin looking at these as natural and commonplace. Start reminding yourself that they won't kill you. Awareness defuses the power of these signals.

2. Rehearse in your mind situations that trigger your arousal. Close your eyes and think about that scary date, the talk you have to give, or a boss criticizing you. Now focus solely, coolly, and deliberately on what you feel in your body. Some desensitization will occur. Arousal will tend to decrease as you are now raising your threshold.

3. Next, do the last step in real life. Pick out a scary situation. Maybe it's a phone call you've been avoiding. Let arousal wash over you as you deliberately face the anxiety-provoking situation. You'll find you're not overwhelmed.

4. Inventory the situations and people that overstimulated you and take them on. But don't expect to have lost your temperament entirely.

> *Seekers live in a perpetual state of craving. Classic extroverts—gregarious and assertive—they are driven to reach goals they set for themselves. In a society that values achievement and action, they are often held in high regard. Their relentless drive often translates into success. Yet for every entrepreneur or sportsperson or dynamo, there is probably a seeker who is a compulsive gambler, romance addict, or alcoholic. There are also seekers who have never found their niche in life—people with big ideas and too little luck or opportunity.*

PARTNERS

Potentially Problematic Pairings

The Focuser/Sensor Couple

While the focuser tends to criticize and make demands, the sensor is predisposed to feeling anxious. And the no-win battle is engaged. As the sensor withdraws, the focuser worries and becomes more critical. The bruised sensor withdraws even more. Bad chemistry.

The Focuser/Seeker Couple

The focuser is threatened by the seeker. Focusers are biochemically "allergic" to any threat of loss. The seeker's elusiveness, noncommitment, and inevitable abandonment can throw the focuser into a depression. The focuser can be easily shattered by a love affair with a seeker.

The Sensor/Sensor Couple

The cautious sensor often marries a sensor who denies their own temperament and blindly reaches far beyond their comfort zone. They may empathize with each other's anxiety and feel understood. But they may encounter contagious anxiety. When they sense the other's apprehension, they may pull away. One reads the other's withdrawal as rejection, and apprehension doubles.

The Sensor/Seeker Couple

The sensor is easily threatened, but intimidation is often overpowered by fascination with the courageous, charismatic seeker. Chemistry pops and crackles when the timid sensor feels a contact high of boldness and confidence in connecting with the seeker.

The Discharger/Sensor Couple

It's not uncommon for the male sensor to be with a woman who seems loud, overbearing, and overcontrolling. One may cringe and think this woman will push him over the edge. But it doesn't happen. If they've been together long enough, he feels secure in her love for him, even though others may not see it. Security can override a confrontational style.

Seekers: From Craving to Contentment

Janet often wondered, "What's wrong with me that I feel so bored and empty when I'm doing everything right? I thought I had grown out of that phase." Feeling ashamed and morally defective for secretly missing the drama and excitement of her past, she was unaware that her innate emotional biochemistry had set up her craving for adventure and sensation.

Profile

• **In relationships:** You can be a challenge as a husband or wife. Your intense emotional hunger sends out powerful messages that you cannot be satisfied by one person for long. Your mate can easily fear that you will abandon him or her.

• **Friendships:** You gather friends effortlessly, looking for others who are engaging and enlivening. But if the relationship becomes dull or routine, you may easily tire of it.

• **As a parent:** You are both dynamically engaging and a bit of a burden because you have little time for quietude and patience—the hallmarks of good parenting. Yet by providing intensity and stimulation, you can also be an interesting parent.

• **At work:** You prove outstanding in career situations that are goal and results oriented. You prefer to work in situations where your energy remains unfettered; you do well in leadership roles.

The Seeker's Task

When you are not in motion, you feel underaroused—and you loathe this dead feeling. Your innate tendency to escape is to seek external stimuli. Your task therefore is to learn to tolerate periods of calm and relaxation, and to alternate these with constructive, challenging activities that will satisfy your needs.

1. Search for behaviors that will provide a counterbalance to sensation seeking. Alternate between moderate sensation and calm. Balance is the key for the seeker—not sitting on the middle ground but somewhere between calm and sensation.

2. Find calmness on a daily basis. When you are *overly* intense, your thermostat becomes conditioned to register only high-level sensations or emotions. You can gradually reset your emotional thermostat so that you feel satisfied more often.

3. Find a variety of sources for your excitement. With several diverse focuses—work, love, sports, community—you don't deplete individual parts of your life.

Dischargers: From Anger to Release

Ellen's friends describe her as vivacious, charming—and fiery: "the most loyal person I know, but at the drop of a hat, she gets hurt and angry." Ever since she was a child, Ellen had been excitable and temperamental. Secretly, she felt uncomfortable with her emotional reactivity. Whenever she had an outburst, she felt ashamed afterward.

Profile

• **In relationships:** Often, you will find a passive partner who admires you and won't challenge your authority—a classic dominant/submissive role split. You can have the satisfac-

> *Dischargers are demonstrative, quick to react to others, not afraid of interpersonal clash. Containing their emotions is foreign to them—intense feelings must be expressed. But they are also easily frustrated and likely to vent on anyone who happens to be handy, often feeling ashamed after expressing their anger.*

tion of venting your feelings without being suppressed or punished for doing so.

• **Friendships:** You often feel frustrated, disappointed, hurt, or ignored by the people around you. And you find creative ways to tell them off or put them in their place.

• **As a parent:** You may be seen as overbearing, but you are not mean or bad. You are expressive, and your children may be fearful at times, but will still feel loved. Indeed, your children will always know where they stand.

• **At work:** Often one of two people—a dynamic leader or a source of problems for yourself and those around you. When you get into emotional difficulty, it is usually because you have not harnessed your energy in adaptive and positive ways.

The Discharger's Task

Simple or brief expression of your anger will do the job, but you need to shift attention away from the target and back onto the arousal. Such catharsis has an inherent appeal for the discharger, for release is partly what is needed. Express your emotion in a way that does no harm to others or yourself: Don't hit people or things, don't insult others, and don't tell off your boss or your best friend. These are all self-defeating strategies. Venting anger briefly while you are alone is sufficient to air your arousal.

What the discharger needs to realize is that the majority of the time when they are aroused, the arousal comes from within. It often has no meaning or purpose, but is a biological phenomenon.

1. Identify the triggers in your life. Most are familiar and need no analysis: your spouse, a boss, a friend, a family feud, even a political figure. The spark may be internally generated with no apparent trigger.

2. Don't stifle your anger. It only builds up because your arousal will build, but don't just let it blow. Follow the next step.

3. Allow yourself some release or catharsis. Move away from the target—leave the room, go for a walk. As you walk, clench your muscles, breathe deeply, expel your anger with your breath, yell, walk vigorously, and swing your arms. You have to do something with the energy or it loops back into your arousal. Benign release raises your threshold and the arousal-caused anger drops.

4. Distract your thoughts from the target. You may have to analyze the situation later, but focusing on the target will typically make you angrier.

Focusers: From Moody to Alive

For years, Willis worked long hours. Both his wife and his cardiologist were concerned. His symptoms ranged from a sense of agitation, to exhaustion, to an inner "hollowness"—he felt that life was meaningless. Yet it was obvious that whenever he spoke about his work, he came alive. It was at home that he most often found himself feeling blue. "Am I exhausted and depressed because I'm a workaholic?" he asked.

> *Focusers' strengths include a heightened ability to concentrate on, analyze, and devise solutions to intricate issues or projects. Their vulnerabilities are boredom, sadness, and worry, especially when they're not busy. In times of quiet, they may work themselves into anxious, unsettled moods, imagining worst-case scenarios.*

THERAPY

How to Reset Your Emotional Thermostat

We cannot change the biological determinants of our feelings. What we can do is change the way we relate to our emotions and modify the ways we respond to them.

1. Accept the Unchangeable

Any desire to alter our psychological existence starts at the moment of acceptance, when we automatically alter how we experience our feelings.

2. Embrace Your Temperament

Acceptance is an active process. It is not passive, nor is it resignation. Enlarge your comfort zones if you choose to. But I have found that many people are satisfied by simply understanding why they feel the way they do and have no need and/or discipline to systematically modulate their emotions.

3. Be Patient

I cannot overemphasize the importance of pure understanding. So often in therapy, patients get, well, impatient. As I explain my ideas or observations, they will say, "Yeah, okay. I get it. Now what do I do?"

This happens in any therapy. What the patient is saying is, "I don't care about *theory,* I don't want to *analyze* and all that. I only want to fix things fast, and get rid of whatever it is I'm feeling." Some patients don't realize that any strategies or processes built on self-deception or self-rejection are doomed to fail—that denial is the very core of their problem.

4. Accept Your Limitations

As you assess your own ebbing and flowing of emotions and arousal, whether at work or in your personal life, it is your choice to do what you need to do. You can learn to design your own comfort zone through awareness of your response patterns.

Realize that your emotional style is innate and unchangeable. With enlightened acceptance, you can begin to carve out new goals, new strategies for feeling better—for truly *mastering* your emotional life.

Profile

• **In relationships:** You are usually drawn to people who excite you. The quest for love and for someone who will change everything—to save you from your moodiness or boredom—is likely to be the solution to your internal lack of arousal.

• **Friendships:** You are certainly a good friend, but you may have difficulty trusting people. The fear that you are not getting enough back from your friends may trouble you.

• **As a parent:** You probably worry a lot more than other parents. The good news is you are also very conscientious and consistent in your loving and protectiveness.

• **At work:** You can be an outstanding employee—analytical, precise, and attentive to details. Yet you may also get bogged down in details, become overanalytical, and may lose time fixating on problems.

The Focuser's Task

Find an ideal balance between attentiveness and distraction. Many of us shift between the two instinctively. If we become too worried, we'll get up, take a walk, return a phone call. By using distraction, the focuser finds emotional relief.

1. First, have faith. You often end up feeling very pessimistic. You may have withdrawn from the very activities in your life that would prove to be distracters because you feel sad or worried. You are ashamed of your emotions: you feel weak, vulnerable. You shame yourself into solitary confinement, where you can work your way deeper into a rut.

2. Deliberately focus, then distract. Deal with your emotions head on, without fear, and then take action to embrace distracters. This becomes a learning chain, by which you break the linkage between arousal and reflexive self-focusing.

3. Develop a repertoire of distracters: friends, sports activities, workout videos, movies, shopping. Even when distracters are only momentary, they can be effective, for they create room to break the fixation on self-focusing behavior and direct your attention elsewhere.

4. Take action. In the case of actual losses and real worries, for example, the appropriate action is to jump right in and find substitutes. If a romance ends, don't sit home and sink into sadness. If you suffer a career setback, don't work yourself into feeling worthless. Get busy facing the problem.

Unload Stress for '94

Difficult? Yes. Do-able? Absolutely. Here are four anti-stress strategies prescribed for USA WEEKEND readers. Do one, feel better. Do all, feel great!

John Butterfield

About 90 percent of American adults feel "high levels of stress" at least once a week. Now, as millions of freshly broken New Year's resolutions litter the country's psychic landscape, stress definitely is the "disease" of the day.

Paul J. Rosch, head of The American Institute of Stress, defines the word that makes us sick as "the sense or feeling of being out of control." Stress can thicken your waistline, increase your susceptibility to the common cold and heart attacks, skew your cholesterol count, lower your test scores and destroy your peace of mind. Those research findings are just the tip of the iceberg: More than 200 stress-related studies were detailed in scientific journals in the past three years. In 1994, . . . results from the largest national sampling ever, the University of Michigan's National Survey of Health and Stress [are expected].

But you needn't wait for more bad news before sorting out *your* stress. This special issue is designed to help you find real solutions for real stress—today.

We began our reporting by asking our readers to volunteer questions about stress. Hundreds of you responded with money worries, strained relationships, health mysteries and tales of too little time and too many responsibilities. We selected several readers and matched them with experts in the most current, scientifically valid stress-busting tactics.

In this issue, you'll find practical, specific advice for beating stress while using your choice of four different strategies:

- Relaxation
- Exercise and diet
- Medical/psychological help
- Organizing and setting priorities

Review the advice—it might be the first step toward creating a new balance and ease in your life.

HOW TO USE THIS SPECIAL ISSUE

Sample all the advice. Our four experts focus on their specialities in medicine or organization. As you review the different approaches, think of them as individual courses of a balanced meal. In order to achieve a healthy stress-busting diet, you should vary the menu. "Just as stress is different for all of us," Paul Rosch says, "there is no stress-reduction program that is a panacea for all of us."

It's up to you and your physician to determine what combination will work best for you.

Talk to your physician. Stress-busting is a serious business. Again and again, our experts emphasized that "self-help" programs, while appealing in their simplicity, cannot cover all of the stress-busting bases.

Physicians are more attuned than ever to the stress-related concerns of their patients. "Most good doctors have a level of suspicion about the role of stress even before the patient brings it up," says our psychological expert,. David Spiegel. "It's so common, it's almost the rule, not the exception." So make your doctor "part of the whole care," says Herbert Benson, our relaxation expert. "Don't try to keep separate books. Make sure whoever you're dealing with knows what's going on."

But don't rely solely on your doctor. Remember that you're the one who has the power over your body. "We tend to think of advances in medicine as being a new drug or a new surgical procedure, or something high-tech," says Dean Ornish, the headline-making physician who is our diet and exercise expert. "But what we are learning is that simple choices we make—what we eat, how we respond to stress, whether or not we smoke, how much exercise we get, the quality of our social relationships—are much more powerful determinants of most people's health and well-being than whatever a doctor could provide."

Avoid quacks. Keeping your doctor well-informed also may quench your desire for a quack's quick fix. Hundreds of programs and stress-busting gurus promise you peace of mind in exchange for a little (or large) chunk of your bank account.

Some of it might work. "If you have a great deal of faith in any [technique for reducing stress] you pursue, whether it's running, meditation, religion, sitting under a

From *USA Weekend*, December 31, 1993–January 2, 1994, pp. 4-5, 7-8, 10-11, 14, 16, 19-20, 22. © 1994 by USA Weekend, a division of Gannett Company, Inc. Reprinted by permission.

Stress is a factor in more than two-thirds of visits to primary-care doctors

pyramid or putting magnets on, that in itself is going to have some restorative value," says Rosch, of The American Institute of Stress. The fabulous experience of the believer will be touted in glossy advertising brochures, but *your* experience will not necessarily be the same. Your best defense is to be alert to advances in stress therapy, but to sort out the charlatans from the healers by looking for hard scientific research.

Science has brought some unconventional anti-stress techniques into the medical mainstream. For instance, biofeedback—the use of electronic monitoring to train subjects to modify their physical and mental responses to stress—has become an accepted treatment for some stress problems. Yet even a biofeedback expert like Erik Olesen, the author of *Twelve Steps to Mastering the Winds of Change* (Rawson Associates, $20), often advises patients to try more conventional techniques before hooking up to a machine. "I'm someone who's open to alternative approaches," he says. "But I've got to see research showing they work." So should you.

· ·

DON'T GET STRESSED OUT, BUT... The country's most stressful jobs (in descending order of stress): 1. Inner-city high school teacher 2. Police officer 3. Miner 4. Air-traffic controller 5. Medical intern 6. Stockbroker 7. Journalist 8. Customer service or complaint worker 9. Waiter/waitress 10. Secretary
SOURCE: THE AMERICAN INSTITUTE OF STRESS

And keep things in perspective. Stress keeps us up at night, brings on headaches and makes us sick. But it also energizes us, forces us to achieve and helps us expand our boundaries. You cannot escape from stress completely, nor should you want to. It's an indispensable part of life. "Without stress," Rosch says, "There would *be* no life."

HOW STRESSED ARE YOU?

Find out in this quick quiz. Use the results to choose a stress-busting strategy.

INSTRUCTIONS

Rate how closely you agree with each of the following statements by filling in the blank with a number from 1 to 10.

Strongly disagree	Agree somewhat	Strongly agree
1 2 3	4 5 6	7 8 9 10

1. I can't honestly say what I really think or get things off my chest at work, school or home. _____

2. I seem to have lots of responsibilities but little authority. _____

3. I seldom receive adequate acknowledgment or appreciation when I do a good job. _____

4. I have the impression that I am repeatedly picked on or discriminated against. _____

5. I feel I am unable to use my talents effectively or to their full potential. _____

6. I tend to argue frequently with co-workers, customers, teachers or other people. _____

7. I don't have enough time for family and social obligations or personal needs. _____

8. Most of the time I have little control over my life at work, school or home. _____

9. I rarely have enough time to do a good job or accomplish what I want to. _____

10. In general, I'm not particularly proud of or satisfied with what I do. _____

Add your replies for your total stress score. _____

IF YOU SCORED BETWEEN:

10 AND 30: *You have little stress and handle it well. Still, the advice in this issue can give you fresh ideas.*

40 AND 60: *You have moderate stress and handle it OK. You easily* can improve by implementing tactics described in this issue. **70 AND 100:** *You are overstressed and may encounter problems that need to be resolved. Reading this issue closely could be the first step.*

Quiz developed by The American Institute of Stress, a non-profit clearinghouse for information about stress.

There are some stresses you can do something about and some you can't," he says. "The wisdom is in being able to distinguish between the two, so you aren't constantly frustrated, like Don Quixote tilting at windmills. Instead, use your time and talents effectively, where they can make a difference."

PART I
Decide your priorities

Stephen Covey

Stephen R. Covey follows his best seller The Seven Habits of Highly Effective People *with the new* First Things First: A Principle-Centered Approach to Time-Life Management *($22, Simon & Schuster).*

I've gone back to school, starting a two-year evening program for a master's degree in business—while working full time, plus two to four hours of overtime a week. We live far from any relatives who might help my wife with the children. I am frustrated, because I would like to be able to spend more time with my wife and kids, as well as give my wife time for herself. But with work, classes and studying, I have not been able to do so. I admit I am a "Type A" personality. How can I deal with each demand without becoming overwhelmed?

**—Bret Woolley, 30, of Durham, N.C.,
systems analyst with GTE**

Bret Woolley wants to do the right thing for his job, wife, kids and himself. But he has more than seven days' responsibility each week. At work, he wrestles with the computer, supervises employees and works overtime. He takes master's degree classes three nights a week at a college 45 minutes from work, and books spare moments for studying. He feels guilty about neglecting his wife, Julie; daughter Brittany, age 20 months; and newborn son Taylor, and although he realizes the dangers of that neglect, he expects the next two years to be short on time, long on stress.

They needn't be, says Stephen R. Covey, our expert on managing stress through organization. Stress isn't the problem, just the symptom. What matters is how you deal with it. The best way is to have a "purpose larger than one's own situation, a contribution to be made, some value to be added." If Woolley develops that, his course will be clear.

ESTABLISH YOUR LONG-TERM GOAL

The quick fix is less important than the long look.

Take New Year's resolutions. A goal of, say, giving up smoking may be desirable in itself. But without a thorough underpinning—a full sense of why quitting is important, what it will add to life—the effort is likely to fail. Then, integrity and self-confidence drop, and we become more oriented to the way others feel about us, rather than how we feel about ourselves. The result is stress.

There's a better way. Covey recommends that Woolley sit with his wife and discuss not just what they want to *accomplish* but also the type of people they want to *be.* They should write a mission statement about what their life is about. This is the hardest step—and, Covey says, the most important.

THINK THROUGH EACH OF YOUR ROLES

Parent, provider, spouse, student. Set goals for each role and plan to meet them. But never break down your plans into anything smaller than week-long blocks. "If you're buried in daily planning, all you are doing is prioritizing crises." Write down when you'll achieve each goal. But don't watch the clock; look at your internal "compass." "A compass says which way is north—what are the principles that are going to govern my life." Keep scheduling soft, "so if something comes up, it doesn't frustrate you."

STICK TO YOUR GUNS

By focusing on what's truly important and saying no to the rest, you may find that your stress level drops. As Goethe said, " 'That which matters most must never be at the mercy of things which matter least,' " Covey says.

TRY THESE EFFICIENCY TIPS

In his career, Woolley should:
1. Add "reading time" by listening to audio books in the car.

2. Touch business papers only once. "Throw it away, file it, delegate it or handle it."
3. Role-play how to say no pleasantly.
4. Plan *for* meetings, not *at* meetings.

At home, the Woolleys should:
1. Find help for Julie. Perhaps they could trade baby sitting or alternate grocery shopping with another couple.
2. Think creatively. Stress can break us out of the box of self-imposed limits. Too busy? That's like being too busy sawing to sharpen a saw that you use every day. "If you've got three minutes," Covey says, "use one to plan the other two."

PART II

A case for your doctor

David Spiegel

David Spiegel is a professor of psychiatry and behavioral sciences at Stanford University. His current book is Living Beyond Limits: New Hope and Help for Facing Life-Threatening Illness.

> I have a high-pressure job and a big family, but I don't consider myself overly stressed. A salesman visiting a construction site I was supervising offered me a popular cola drink. Within 30 minutes of drinking it, I became so depressed that life itself seemed unimportant. This stressed-out feeling lasted for nearly an hour. Since then, I have drunk other drinks that contain caffeine and have experienced the same depressed feelings. Drinks with no caffeine have no effect on me, except to quench my thirst. Why did caffeine cause me to feel so stressed out?
>
> **—Keith Welch, 39, of South Weber, Utah, construction consultant and supervisor**

As Keith Welch, a construction consultant and dad of seven, can testify, stress doesn't weigh just on the mind. It also gets snarled in the body chemistry, diseases we may catch and the activities around us. It's physical.

It's a complex, often contradictory puzzle—one that David Spiegel, a professor at Stanford University, has been deciphering through a landmark study showing that terminally ill patients live longer if they're given emotional support, which helps to reduce their stress.

Stress alone may not be a problem. We all react differently to stressful situations. (For instance, having seven children under age 16 might be super-stressful for some, yet Welch finds wrestling on the floor with his brood a stress buster.) But when combined with a preexisting

YOUR TO-DO LIST
- ☑ Find your triggers — and avoid them
- ☑ Talk to your doctor
- ☑ Examine your feelings
- ☑ Keep counseling as an option

medical condition, stress can become serious. Welch's caffeine jag from hell is a perfect illustration.

Welch spends each workday on-site, away from the office. For relaxation, he inputs data on his computer. He remembers that he wasn't under undue stress when the first attack occurred. The depressed state recurred a half-dozen times before Welch made the connection with caffeinated soft drinks.

Enter Spiegel, medical detective, who picked up on the data-entry clue: "Welch views as recreation something the rest of us would view as tedious work. He strikes me as someone who's a hardworking guy, but doesn't make life easy for himself." Spiegel theorizes that Welch's stress level was high enough so that caffeine, a stimulant, caused his nerves to shoot off their supply of chemical arousers. Result: anxiety and depression. (Similarly, hyperactive children are given the stimulant Ritalin to *calm* them.)

'Part of good stress management is recognizing your vulnerabilities'

It's vital to recognize when stress is interacting negatively with other medical or environmental factors. "It is common for a man having a [first] heart attack to think it is *just* stress or indigestion and not get the appropriate treatment," Spiegel says. "I've known doctors who died of heart attacks because they ignored the symptoms."

FIND YOUR TRIGGERS

First, identify the things that aggravate your basic stress levels. As with Welch, many people may find themselves in the middle of a stressful situation without realizing what is happening. They may have a vague feeling of unease, or a panicky response to innocuous situations.

Second, look for patterns. For Welch, the pattern became clear: Have caffeine, get depressed. Once he established the connection, he could determine a response.

Third, develop a strategy for coping. For Welch, it was simple: Avoid caffeine.

TAKE THE INFORMATION TO A DOCTOR

If you recognize your pattern but not its cause, then it's time for a physician's diagnosis.

Pinpointing patterns can save your life. Say you feel tightness in your chest, shortness of breath and queasiness. If these attacks occur "when your boss just yelled at you or your mother-in-law said you're no good, that would tend to [indicate] stress," Spiegel says. "If it tends to happen when you lift heavy loads or walk up stairs, that might tell you that . . . your heart muscles aren't getting enough oxygen." He advises keeping a log of your stress symptoms, noting what activities coincided with them. (*See list of symptoms.*)

Stress alone won't kill you. But it can conspire with preexisting conditions or diseases to lower your resistance. Listen to your body; pay attention to the way it responds to the stress. Most doctors today accept the mind-body connection. They need to hear whether you are worried, to be told what triggers you have observed and how your body has reacted to the stress. The solution might be deeply hidden. Or it might be very obvious, as in the case of the now caffeine-free Welch—though, he says, "you get tired of root beer and Sprite."

EXAMINE YOUR FEELINGS

Stress can have psychological causes when we pressure ourselves and respond badly to external forces. Consider counseling if you see these signs:
- "When the stress begins to generalize—when it goes from 'I feel lousy when I'm in this situation' or 'I feel terrible about something I did' to 'I'm a worthless person.' " That's a sign that, psychiatrically, the stress is getting out of hand.
- The tendency to blame all pressures and setbacks to the outside world, without acknowledging your own part. "The kind of person who is self-righteous, saying, 'I did not do anything wrong at all; it's all his fault'—that kind of rigidity is usually a sign that they are setting up interactions that tend to result in an increase in stress."

ACCEPT HELP

Of course, a person who blames others might be unable to recognize that as a problem. That's where friends and relatives can play an important role, Spiegel says.

Get help for your loved one if he or she:
- Is chronically distressed, unhappy, anxious or frightened. "If it is dragging on, that is a sign to get help."
- Becomes dysfunctional—what ordinarily is no problem (getting a full night's sleep or completing a project at the office) becomes impossible.

Need help finding mental health experts? The best sources: the nearest major hospital or the local United Way. All you have to lose is your stress.

DON'T GET STRESSED OUT, BUT . . .

- **Stress-related disabilities reported to one major insurer more than doubled from 1982 to 1990. "Stress-related disabilities" refers to diagnoses of anxiety, ulcers, depression, colitis, hypertension and headaches.**

YEAR	PERCENTAGE OF DISABILITY CASES THAT WERE RELATED TO STRESS*
1982	6%
1984	10%
1986	12%
1988	13%
1990	13%

SOURCE: NORTHWESTERN NATIONAL LIFE, 1991

*Based on the number of disabilities managed in Northwestern National Life rehabilitation services

Help at your library

For in-depth information about stress, Paul J. Rosch, the head of The American Institute of Stress, suggests:
- *The Doctor's Guide to Instant Stress Relief*, Ronald G. Nathan, T. E. Statts and Paul J. Rosch (BALLANTINE, $5.99)
- *Stress Management*, Dorothy H. Cotton (BRUNNER/MAZEL, $31.95)
- *A Clinical Guide to the Treatment of the Human Stress Response*, G. S. Everly Jr. (PLENUM PRESS, $32.50)
- *Mind Body Medicine*, Daniel Goleman and Joel Gurin (CONSUMER REPORTS BOOKS, $24.95)
- *Principles and Practices of Stress Management*, Robert L. Woolfolk and Paul M. Lehrer (GUILFORD PRESS, $35)
- *Comprehensive Stress Management*, Jerrold S. Greenburg (WILLIAM C. BROWN COMMUNICATIONS, $29)

PART III

Countdown to relaxation

Herbert Bensen

Herbert Benson, an expert on techniques for relieving stress through relaxation, is founding president and associate professor of medicine at the Mind/Body Medical Institute in Boston.

> How do I deal with the excessive gastric juices, the overchurning of my mind and the sleepless nights before pay day, when I realize that no matter how I revamp my budget or how much overtime I've worked, my paycheck isn't enough? Inflation, recession—whatever you call it, it seems as if half is for me and the other half is for the government.
>
> —Anna L. S. Battle, 42, of Trenton, N.J., a head nurse at Ewing Residential Treatment Center for troubled youths

YOUR TO-DO LIST

☑ Find a mental focus

☑ Get comfortable

☑ Consciously relax

☑ Practice daily

Anna Battle has had it up to *here.* She is continually under stress from her work with tough youngsters. She worries that budget cuts soon will have her doing more work for less pay. What's more, cold winter weather keeps her from fishing, her favorite stress buster. She's a prime candidate for relaxation therapy, says Herbert Benson, who literally wrote the book on the subject (*The Relaxation Response*).

Battle is battling her body's natural, physiological response to stress, according to Benson. It's called the "fight-or-flight response." When the body is exposed to stress, it naturally brews a hormonal soup that increases heart rate, blood pressure, metabolism and blood flow to the muscles; temporarily shuts down some body functions; and depresses the immune system. The high-octane mixture prepares one either to make a stand and aggressively confront the source of stress, or make like a jack rabbit and high-tail it out of harm's way.

Those responses served our prehistoric ancestors well when they faced a saber-toothed tiger prospecting for lunch. But today's stress agents are more likely to be an angry boss at work, a bully at school or financial worries. We can't kill them; we can't run away and hide. So the hormonal soup bubbles inside us without release, triggering many of the symptoms that plague Battle: insomnia, racing thoughts, worry, headaches and indigestion.

Because Battle cannot eliminate her problems without eliminating her job, Benson says, she must deal with the symptoms. And "that's where the relaxation response comes in." (*See description, below.*)

"Get into the discipline," Benson advises. "Within several weeks, most people start seeing very real changes, based on the physiology but reflected in the way they deal with problems, and the feelings of control they have."

Warning: This is no substitute for a doctor's care. "First, make sure there's nothing [wrong] that isn't better treated with our marvelous modern medicine," Benson says. "It would be tragic and totally inappropriate . . . to start with this." Doctors are clued in: Even such a bastion of orthodoxy as Harvard Medical School has established a chaired professorship in mind/body medicine.

"Here's something that shifts care to people themselves in a responsible way," Benson says. "It's therapeutic, preventative and cost-effective at the same time."

So, Anna, take a deep breath and *relax.*

BENSON'S RELAXATION RESPONSE

1. Pick a mental focusing device. A word or phrase, religious or secular. Most of Benson's patients choose something religious: "Hail, Mary, full of grace"; "Allah be praised"; "*Sh'ma Yisroel.*" The specific words are unimportant.

2. Assume a comfortable position or activity. You may sit quietly or listen to music; others might prefer to exercise.

3. Close your eyes, to help you focus.

4. Relax muscles, to counter physical tightness.

5. Breathe slowly and naturally, and repeat your focus

Check your symptoms

Stress symptoms can mimic the symptoms of diseases and other medical conditions. That's why experts emphasize that stress-busting activities be supervised by a health professional. If you notice any of the following common warnings signs of stress, you may want to circle the symptoms and take the list to your doctor:

PHYSICAL SYMPTOMS
- Headaches / Indigestion / Stomachaches / Sweaty palms
- Sleep difficulties / Dizziness / Back pain / Racing heart
- Tightness in neck and/or shoulders
- Tiredness
- Ringing in the ears
- Restlessness

BEHAVIORAL CHANGES
- Excess smoking
- Bossiness
- Compulsive gum chewing / Attitude critical of others
- Grinding of teeth at night / Inability to get things done

- Overuse of alcohol
- Compulsive eating

EMOTIONAL SIGNS
- Crying / Edginess (ready to explode)
- Boredom (no meaning to things)
- Nervousness, anxiety / Feeling powerless to change things / Loneliness
- Overwhelming sense of pressure
- Anger / Easily upset / Unhappiness for no reason

THOUGHT SYMPTOMS
- Forgetfulness
- Trouble thinking clearly / Lack of creativity / Inability to make decisions
- Memory loss
- Thoughts of running away
- Constant worry
- Loss of sense of humor

Source: *The Wellness Book*

20 STRESS-BUSTING TIPS FROM THE PROS

Our stress experts have given you the big picture on reducing stress in your life. Here are 20 other concrete steps you can take, culled from stress clinics, employee assistance programs, stress specialists and research organizations, to help you keep your cool:

1. Take a warm bath.
2. Write a nasty letter to whoever is stressing you out—then tear it up.
3. Play with a pet.
4. Make decisions based as much on your heart as on your head.
5. Don't eat unless you're hungry.
6. Volunteer to do good. You'll feel better about what you've done and who you are.
7. If your company's employee assistance program offers a stress reduction program, sign up for it.
8. Cultivate a sense of humor, and smile.
9. Unplug the phone, send the family to a movie and listen, uninterrupted, to your favorite music.
10. Remember: While you can't control the timing of stressful events, you're in complete control of the way you react to them.
11. Don't be afraid to say no. You are in charge of your time.
12. Reduce your sugar consumption. Excess sugar can heighten your stress response.
13. Set a comfortable, steady pace at work, then focus totally on the task at hand to improve productivity.
14. Eat lots of fiber and starches; carbohydrates tend to calm you down.
15. Eat breakfast, so you start the day on a full tank. And avoid big meals late at night; they can disrupt your sleep and cause stress.
16. Don't be afraid of your tears. Sometimes a good cry is called for—it releases anxiety.
17. Schedule time for fun. It's as vital as work.
18. Leave the job at work. Leave family pressures at home.
19. Remember that some things don't have to be done perfectly.
20. Lighten up! Once you have examined a perceived failing from the past, let it go and focus on the future.

word or phrase, replacing the fight-or-flight response with a calm-down attitude.

6. Assume a passive attitude. This may be the hardest step, because we're keyed to "doing something." Don't be discouraged if outside thoughts intrude. Just say, "Oh, well," and return to your discipline. Why get stressed over stress-busting?

7. Continue for 10–20 minutes. Make the time—think how much time you waste worrying.

8. Practice once or twice a day.

DON'T GET STRESSED OUT, BUT...

● More men younger than age 35 now are willing to report feeling depressed because of stress. But overall, more women (60 percent) than men (54 percent) admit to it. ● Job stress costs U.S. industry more than $200 billion a year; 550 million work days each year are lost to absenteeism. A Blue Cross-Blue Shield report found that five out of six workers felt job stress played a major factor in their illnesses. ● Teenage girls and boys face similar amounts of stress, but girls report greater personal distress. Reason: Girls tend to dwell on their feelings.

PART IV
Rig an easy exercise plan

Dean Ornish

Dean Ornish is a physician who directs the Preventive Medicine Research Institute in Sausalito, Calif. His current best seller is Eat More, Weigh Less *(HarperCollins, $25).*

I'm responsible for transporting $200,000+ worth of equipment and product safely and on time. Working out in a truck stop parking lot brought stares and jeers from truckers, and because I'm shy, that caused me stress. Add to that the problem of finding healthy food on a truck stop menu, no regular sleep time, never getting home and payroll screwing up my paycheck. I do some floor exercises and stretch in the truck's bed sleeper berth every day, but I'm getting fatter. My back hurts! Please answer my letter.

—**Johannah Blum, 39, of Muldrow, Okla., a long-distance trucker who drives as a team with her husband, Donald Greenway, 46**

This trucker's life is an exaggerated version of what millions of workers face daily: separation from family and stability; the pressure of an unyielding schedule; and sedentary work with too little a window for exercise. That formula leads to stress that feeds on itself, says Dean Ornish, our expert on beating stress through diet and exercise.

"When you're overweight, that creates back problems, which makes it more difficult to exercise, which makes it harder to sit and drive a truck, which makes her more stressed, which makes her back hurt more, which makes her want to overeat, which makes her more overweight."

Breaking Blum's stress spiral calls for an overhaul of her lifestyle, not just another short-term diet. A recent government study found that a year after dieting, 66 percent of people had regained the weight; after five years, 97 percent.

Here's Ornish's solution:

YOUR TO-DO LIST
- ☑ **Overhaul habits**
- ☑ **Eat less fat**
- ☑ **Exercise moderately**
- ☑ **Stretch gently**
- ☑ **Meditate**

CUT THE FAT

Go ahead: Eat all the carbohydrates and lean proteins you want—just keep fat to 10 percent of daily calories, Ornish says. To accomplish this, you need to know a few nutrition basics: 1 gram of fat has 9 calories; 1 gram of other food has 4 calories. So, if you need 2,000 calories a day, fat intake shouldn't exceed 200 calories ($2,000 \times 0.10 = 200$) or 22 grams of fat ($200/9 = 22$). Most Americans eat 60 or more fat grams a day.

For Blum, that means no more chicken-fried steak at the truck-stop counter. But even there, Ornish says, "you can find foods that are low in fat that are familiar. You don't have to go to a health food restaurant." In place of bacon and eggs for breakfast, have *all* of this: shredded wheat with skim milk and a banana, whole-wheat toast with jam (not butter or margarine), and orange juice and tea or decaffeinated coffee.

Blum may need to bring non-fat salad dressing to a restaurant, or ask for her fish to be broiled instead of breaded and fried. But it's not a major project: Just tell the

Turn your boss into mulch. Cut up your credit cards. Switch off the television.

Those are just three of the thought-provoking, stress-busting tips sent in by USA WEEKEND readers.

Instead of trying to suppress my negative thoughts or feelings, I allow them to be expressed in the peace and quietude of my mind and body while I meditate. My problems seem to lose some of their velocity.
RICK JOHNSTON *Hopatcong, N.J.*

At work, request that all information and materials be given to you early in the day, so that you have as much of the day as possible to complete it. At home, cut down on repetitions that wear you out. Require that all family members pick up after themselves, clear their places at the table and put away their belongings.
BETSYE A. HEGGINS *Humble, Texas*

It is very tension-relieving to reduce a pile of branches to wonderful, ecologically compatible mulch for my garden. I pretend the branches are what I am angry about—boss, work, etc.
ELAINE SPENCER *Fort Collins, Colo.*

Have complete confidence in eternal life and all of the ramifications that it entails. Enjoy situations that develop spontaneously.
JOE KELLEY *Freeport, Ill.*

Lying down for a half-hour with my feet resting on something above my head works wonders.
DOROTHY L. HILL *Salem, Ore.*

1. Leave work at the office.

2. Reduce life to the essentials. Organize. Make a list and delete all of those things you don't really need.

3. Pay cash. But keep one credit card, for emergencies only.

4. Have two or more hobbies, one of which involves exercise. (I build balsawood airplanes and tap-dance.)

5. Sleep often. If you're tired, nap.

6. Treat yourself to one fun (and inexpensive) outing each week.

7. Eat regular meals. Don't be obsessed about calories.

8. Get a pet. (Dogs are good.)

9. Speak to God regularly. Emphasize your good fortune rather than your problems.
BEN HERRIN *Falls Church, Va.*

When my neck and back muscles tense and my forehead constricts, I find a private spot and walk like an elephant. I lean over from the waist as far as I can and pretend my dangling arms are the trunk of an elephant. I relax my neck muscles. Then I breathe deeply, slowly swinging my "trunk" from left to right. Ten swings does it.
BEVERLY CONEY HEIRICH *Franklin, Tenn.*

Even though I am only 16, I've figured out a way to relieve stress temporarily. I have studied martial arts for almost four years now and have seen adults come to our studio who are stressed to the limit. After just a few months' training, they come out totally stress-free.
ANTHONY DE MARCO *Holmdel, N.J.*

Spend some time alone. Avoid unnecessary debt. Serve others with your talents; it is a cure for depression. Respect your husband. Quickly forgive one who has hurt you. Think positive, noble thoughts about situations and people.
SUSAN HAUSER *Thomasville, N.C.*

Take a walk and get some fresh air. Take a warm bath or shower. A sympathetic person sometimes can help you think of practical solutions. Sometimes you feel like screaming; count to 10. Sip a cup of herbal tea—slowly.
TRUDY PURCELL *Mount Vernon, N.Y.*

Slow down. Use common sense. Spend more time at home. Turn off the TV and visit with your neighbors. Get rid of fast food (learn to cook from scratch), and have family dinners.
E. A. MATTINGLY *Cumberland, Md.*

Have a full-body massage twice a month, or arrange for people to come to your office and give massages. As you sit clothed in a special chair, they work your neck and back muscles.
WALTER EDGE *Holmes Beach, Fla.*

Living and striving for triumph should provoke some stress. There is no trick to beating stress. It is a worthy opponent, a challenge to be deciphered and tolerated. Don't become dejected. Nothing is wrong with you.
MAUREEN FEEHAN *Marshfield, Mass.*

waiter or waitress you're on a special diet and would like, say, spaghetti without oil or butter.

And don't feel guilty if you slip up. "It's not all or nothing," Ornish says. "Change a little, get lesser results; change a lot, and the difference in how you feel is dramatic."

EXERCISE REGULARLY

Non-competitive exercise is an amazingly effective stress reliever. "Your body is designed to be exercised. It does well when you use it." Moderate exercise—20–30 minutes a day, or an hour three times a week—provides almost all the cardiovascular benefits of strenuous exercise but minimizes the risk of injury. That means Blum can break tension without breaking anything else. She tried jumping rope, but fellow truckers' jeers embarrassed her.

Right idea, wrong exercise, Ornish says. Try a brisk walk. "Nobody will make fun of somebody walking."

STRETCH GENTLY AND OFTEN

Blum worries about her weak back and wonders if she should lift weights. Light hand weights can help increase Blum's aerobic conditioning while walking, but Ornish thinks heavy lifting would make her sore back worse. The problem isn't weakness; it's tension. Instead, try yoga. Blum can stretch slowly and gently in her truck's sleeper compartment or seated next to the driver. (Readers with Blum's concerns but not her occupation can stretch at a desk or in a bedroom.) Simple meditation aids relaxation, and again, it's portable, low-tech and free. Just what we all need on the road of life.

DON'T GET STRESSED OUT, BUT... ● Yo-yo dieting increases stress, which in turn can lead to irregular eating habits, which can lead to weight gain, which can lead to ... yo-yo dieting. Try to lose weight slowly and permanently, through a combination of exercise and a nutritious diet low in fat. ● The body's supply of HDL cholesterol (the "good" kind) decreases because of hormones released by "Type A" people under stress from high-pressure living. ● Stress can thicken women's waists. It causes fat cells to be deposited in the torso, putting stressed-out sufferers in greater danger of a heart attack.

Send for free stress busters

■ For a two-page guide from the **National Institute of Mental Health** on handling stress, write to: Consumer Information Center, Dept. 563Z, Pueblo, Colo. 81009.

■ For information about certified biofeedback professionals, send a letter and self-addressed, stamped envelope to: **Biofeedback Certification Institute of America,** 10200 W. 44th Ave., Suite 304, Wheat Ridge, Colo. 80033.

■ For information about stress from **The American Institute of Stress,** write a letter explaining your sources of stress (family, job, etc.) to: American Institute of Stress, Dept. U, 124 Park Ave., Yonkers, N.Y. 10703. You will receive articles and sources of help.

■ For brochures telling how to handle tension and depression, call **The National Mental Health Association** in Alexandria, Va., toll-free, 1-800-969-6642.

DEFEATING

Depression

An array of new treatments combats the "common cold of mental illness"

Nancy Wartik

Nancy Wartik is a Contributing Editor at AMERICAN HEALTH.

For Charles Kennedy* of Princeton, N.J., the overwhelming sensation was a leaden slowness, as if a heavy weight were bearing down on him. Just beginning a competitive retraining program, the 51-year-old banker needed all his wits about him. Instead Kennedy found it harder and harder to function.

"Usually a challenge triggers my adrenaline," he says. "This time I found it difficult to respond. I couldn't understand the course assignments, much less complete them, which made me feel helpless and hopeless. Everything became very slow." At night Kennedy tossed and turned. He plodded through days in a pall of indifference. "The feeling was, 'Oh yeah, a bus is coming right at me. Should I move or not?' " he says. It was not until a therapist suggested he try an antidepressant drug that Kennedy found relief. "I could sleep better, proceed with initiative," he says. "My indifference disappeared. I became much more of a player again."

Everyone falls into the doldrums at times, or luxuriates in a bit of self-pity or melancholy. But depression is different. A mind-warping, energy-sapping malady, it unbalances the normal rhythms of the body and turns the psychic landscape bleak, robbing a person of vigor and hope. For someone afflicted with clinical (also called unipolar) depression, the sensations of sadness and loss, familiar to everyone on occasion, stretch into weeks or months. Nor does there seem to be an end in sight: Perhaps depression's worst torment is the conviction that things will never change. The depressed feel they will be mired in numbing despair forever.

The trappings of good fortune—wealth, talent or power—confer no immunity. "I am now the most miserable man living," wrote Abraham Lincoln. "If what I feel were equally distributed to the whole human family, there would not be one cheerful face on earth." Sir Winston Churchill, writer Sylvia Plath and actress Jean Seberg were similarly visited with bouts of despair. More recently, TV journalist Mike Wallace, author William Styron and talk show host Dick Cavett went public about their struggles with depression. Last summer, White House aide Vincent Foster committed suicide in the throes of depression apparently triggered by the Capitol Hill pressure cooker. Like Foster, 15% of those suffering from the more severe form of the disorder, which doctors call major depression, will ultimately take their own lives.

Not so long ago, the prevailing belief was that depressed people simply needed to pull themselves together and snap out of it. But an explosion of new research in recent decades has shown depression to be a real disorder that can be diagnosed and successfully treated. "Depression used to be viewed as some sort of moral weakness or personal failure," says Dr. Ewald Horwath, director of the intensive care unit at the New York State Psychiatric Institute in New York City. "Now there's more of a tendency to think of it as a disease, and that's a big improvement."

Most scientists think depression results from an interaction of biochemical, genetic and psychological factors, often, although not always, combined with a change in life circumstances—from the failure of a relationship to the loss of a job. In other words, depression is like many other diseases. "The factors that cause a physical illness such as coronary artery disease include diet, genetics and the way people who have a Type A personality put pressure on themselves," says Horwath. "Cultural factors influence who gets it, how frequent it is in each sex, and how prevalent it is in different epochs. It's the same kind of thing with depression."

Treatments for depression have expanded along with knowledge of its origins. There are now more than 20 antidepressants on the market, many of them "cleaner" drugs with fewer side effects than their predecessors. The most popular is the much-ballyhooed Prozac, already prescribed to more than 5 million Americans. Not that pills are the only antidote to depression: Cognitive psychotherapy, developed specifically to attack the disorder, teaches people how to correct the thought patterns that generate black moods. There's now evidence that regular exercise can alleviate more moderate cases of depression, perhaps because it increases levels of certain brain chemicals that mediate mood,

From *American Health,* December 1993, pp. 38-45, 86. © 1993 by Nancy Wartik. Reprinted by permission.

and has arousing effects on body metabolism and energy. Victims of seasonal affective disorder, whose despondency comes and goes as the seasons change, often benefit from light therapy. And in some extreme cases of depression, electroconvulsive therapy, a much refined and milder form of the "shock therapy" first used here in the 1940s, can help when other treatments fail or would take too long—as when there is a likelihood of suicide. Through one or more of these treatments, the National Institute of Mental Health estimates that 80% to 90% of the depressed can find relief. As researchers sometimes say jokingly, today is the best time in history to feel miserable.

That's fortunate, because huge numbers of Americans do. More than 9 million people endure major depression yearly in this country, and about one in 20 will face the struggle at some point in his or her life. So ubiquitous is depression that researchers now refer to it as the "common cold of mental illness." And millions more are affected by other mood-related disorders. Victims of dysthymia, a recently identified form of chronic, milder depression, may battle gloom for years at a time (see "Long-Term Blues"). People with manic depression (also called bipolar disorder) veer dizzyingly between protracted emotional heights and depths, and cyclothymics go through less intense but more frequent ups and downs (see "Manic Depression: Not for Artists Only").

Many more women than men experience depression. Puberty is the dividing line: Before it, young boys and girls feel gloomy in almost equal numbers, but at adolescence, girls' depression rates begin to soar. At least twice as many women as men will fall prey to the disorder over the course of a lifetime, most studies have shown. Recent research by Johns Hopkins University psychiatrist Alan Romanoski paints an even more alarming picture: Although women and men have a similar risk of major depression, women suffer from more moderate depressions at *10 times* the rate men do. Researchers hotly debating the reason for this disparity have focused on three areas: physiological causes, such as genetic factors or hormonal imbalances; psychological factors, including differences in how men and women learn to deal with emotions; and social issues, from women's greater susceptibility to sexual abuse and battering to their lower economic status.

Sadly, the greatest obstacles to eliminating depression are ignorance and lack of understanding. For all its prevalence, and despite the many therapies available, two-thirds of those who have it don't get the help they need, often because they don't want to admit the problem or don't recognize its signs. "Many people who have major depression wouldn't even call themselves depressed," says psychiatrist A. John Rush of the University of Texas Southwestern Medical Center in Dallas. "If you ask them, 'Do you know you have clinical depression?'—depression serious enough to need treatment—they say, 'I don't know what that is.' " Trying to intervene in more cases, the Department of Health and Human Services (HHS) this year issued guidelines to alert general practitioners and other primary-care physicians to depression's warning signs.

As yet, there's no physical test to pinpoint the disease. Instead doctors look for a constellation of symptoms that persist for longer than two weeks (see "Are You Depressed?"). These include deep sadness or numbing apathy, a

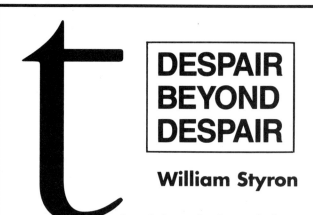

DESPAIR BEYOND DESPAIR

William Stryron

The pain is unrelenting, and what makes the condition intolerable is the foreknowledge that no remedy will come—not in a day, an hour, a month or a minute. If there is mild relief, one knows that it is only temporary; more pain will follow. It is hopelessness even more than pain that crushes the soul. So the decision-making of daily life involves not, as in normal affairs, shifting from one annoying situation to another less annoying—or from discomfort to relative comfort, or from boredom to activity—but moving from pain to pain. One does not abandon, even briefly, one's bed of nails, but is attached to it wherever one goes. And this results in a striking experience—one which I have called, borrowing military terminology, the situation of the walking wounded. For in virtually any other serious sickness, a patient who felt similar devastation would be lying flat in bed, possibly sedated and hooked up to the tubes and wires of life-support systems, but at the very least in a posture of repose and in an isolated setting. His invalidism would be necessary, unquestioned and honorably attained. The sufferer from depression has no option and therefore finds himself, like a walking casualty of war, thrust into the most intolerable social situations. There he must, despite the anguish devouring his brain, present a face approximating the one that is associated with ordinary events and companionship. He must try to utter small talk, and be responsive to questions, and knowingly nod and frown and, God help him, even smile. But it is a fierce trial attempting to speak a few simple words.

That December evening, for example, I could have remained in bed as usual during those worst hours, or agreed to the dinner party my wife had arranged downstairs. But the very idea of a decision was academic. Either course was torture, and I chose the dinner not out of any particular merit but through indifference to what I knew would be indistinguishable ordeals of fogbound horror. At dinner I was barely able to speak, but the quartet of guests, who were all good friends, were aware of my condition and politely ignored my catatonic muteness. Then, after dinner, sitting in the living room, I experienced a curious inner convulsion that I can describe only as despair beyond despair. It came out of the cold night; I did not think such anguish possible.

Excerpted from Darkness Visible: A Memoir of Madness, © *1990 by William Styron. Reprinted by permission of* Random House.

Manic Depression: Not for Artists Only

at age 22, Susan Dime-Meenan started her own court reporting company. By 27, she nearly bankrupted it. During one two-month period, she traveled to Los Angeles from Chicago more than 30 times, just for lunch. There was the time she charged $27,000 in clothing purchases on a corporate credit card. Then the 4'10" Dime-Meenan stopped eating and dropped down to 68 pounds. But it wasn't until she told her husband the FBI was trailing her that her family finally took action.

The night they committed her to a psychiatric ward was among the worst of Dime-Meenan's life, but it marked the start of her recovery from an illness that had long gone undiagnosed. "At first I didn't take it very well when they told me I was manic-depressive," says Dime-Meenan, now 38 and executive director of the Chicago-based National Depressive and Manic-Depressive Association. "But the head of the nursing staff showed me a description of manic depression in a medical dictionary, and when I read it, I knew immediately that I was a textbook case."

Some 2 to 3 million Americans, equal numbers of men and women, have the mood disorder known as manic depression, or bipolar illness. The disorder tends to strike early in life: Many manic-depressives first experience symptoms in adolescence. Manic depression manifests itself in different forms: Some patients, like Dime-Meenan, endure manic (high-energy) episodes mostly, others experience mostly depressions, and still others career equally between the two extremes. Many people have symptoms of both mania and depression at the same time.

In a manic state, people feel either intensely irritable or euphoric. They may experience racing thoughts and speech, poor judgment, feelings of grandeur, less need for sleep or a sense of boundless energy; at its extremes, mania can produce hallucinations and delusions. Untreated, mania lasts an average of one to three months, while periods of depression last six to nine months. Cyclothymia resembles a milder form of bipolar disorder, marked by brief, less drastic mood swings over a period of at least two years. A significant number of cyclothymics later become manic-depressives.

While the depressive phase of bipolar illness looks the same as major depression, researchers still don't understand the underlying link between the two. Genetic influences figure much more strongly in manic than in ordinary depression, and an intensive effort is now under way to find the gene responsible for bipolar disorder. The disease clearly runs in families: Like his father, Ernest Hemingway was a manic-depressive (and, like his father, he committed suicide). One of the writer's sons also has the disorder.

That Hemingway's talent coexisted with his illness was probably no coincidence. A number of studies link manic depression to creativity. In her book *Touched With Fire: Manic-Depressive Illness and the Artistic Temperament*, Johns Hopkins psychologist Kay Redfield Jamison estimates that rates of manic depresson and cyclothymia are 10 to 40 times higher among artists than the general public. "People with manic depression have faster, most fluid thinking, high energy levels and a wide range of emotional experience to draw on, from elation to despair," says Dr. Jamison. "Artists have to go where others won't, emotionally speaking, and manic-depressives do that automatically." Writer Virginia Woolf had bipolar illness: "I can't fight [this terrible disease] any longer," she wrote before drowning herself at age 59. Mark Twain, probably a cyclothymic, referred to his "periodical and sudden changes in mood." Jamison adds that there's some evidence bipolar disorders occur at elevated rates among movers and shakers: Broadcasting magnate Ted Turner is among those who've spoken about battling mood disorders.

Today, two-thirds of manic-depressives go untreated, but if ignored, says Jamison, the disease tends to worsen. Many manic-depressives develop substance abuse problems and an estimated 15% to 20% eventually commit suicide. With ongoing treatment—in particular the drug lithium and certain anticonvulsants—up to 80% of those with manic depression significantly improve.

Treatment turned Dime-Meenan's life around: "I've never had a day without medication in 10 years," she says, "and some days are still better than others. Some days the illness wins. But only for a day. The disease isn't controlling my life anymore. I won't let it."

lack of interest in things that once brought pleasure—from sex to socializing—and at least four of seven other markers: appetite disturbances, sleep problems, fatigue, difficulty concentrating, undue restlessness or lethargy, feelings of worthlessness, or suicidal thoughts. (Someone mourning a death may have one or more of these symptoms for several months without necessarily being clinically depressed.) Many depressed people are also afflicted with vague physi-

Exercise can alleviate moderate cases.

cal symptoms or complaints. "They come into the doctor's office with stomachaches or joint pain, or they feel blah," says Dr. Rush. "Many of these patients turn out to have major depression." Untreated, the disorder typically lasts for six months or longer.

Researchers now know several risk factors that raise a person's vulnerability to depression, including a family history of the disorder. Research with twins has provided evidence that depression's roots are at least partially inherited. A 1992 study of more than 1,000 pairs of female twins showed that if one identical twin (who shares all of her sister's genes) suffered major depression, the other's risk was 66% higher than that of someone from the general population. If a fraternal twin was depressed, however, her twin (who is no more genetically similar to her than any other sibling) had a risk only 27% higher. While such statistics suggest genetics play a significant role in depression, Medical College of Virginia psychiatrist Kenneth Kendler, who conducted the study, notes that "depression isn't something you inherit 100%, as you do eye color or height. It's probably about 40% influenced by your genes."

Inheritance may also influence certain personality traits that can make a person depression-prone. Some researchers now argue for the existence of a syndrome—at least partially innate—known as depressive personality disorder, which predisposes those who have it to depression problems. People with this disorder, explains psychiatrist Robert Hirschfeld of the University of Texas Medical Branch in Galveston, tend to be pessimistic and brooding, critical of themselves and others. The probability that such individuals will develop clinical depression is correspondingly higher than the average person's.

Genetics or personality structure may prime a person for depression, but life's travails often play a marked role in pushing someone over the brink. Although some people fall into depressions with no apparent cause, the experience of Angela Wolf* is more typical. A vice president at a Manhattan marketing firm, she plunged into paralyzing despair after she discovered that her husband of 16 years was cheating on her. She was unable to work efficiently or sleep soundly; she cried often and paced restlessly. Not until a friend referred her to a cognitive therapist did Wolf realize what was happening to her. "It was a relief when he told me I was depressed," she says. "I could say, 'No wonder! So there's a reason I feel this way.'"

A growing body of research supports the idea that major depressions are often triggered by stressful events of the kind Wolf experienced. A study of 680 pairs of female

twins, published this year in *The American Journal of Psychiatry*, ranked the importance of nine risk factors for serious depression, including recent upsetting events, genetics, lack of social support, traumas suffered over a lifetime (for example, rape or sexual abuse), and childhood loss of a parent. Of all the variables, recent stress—divorce, illness, legal troubles, bereavement—was the best predictor of a depressive episode. A family history of the disorder ranked second. Similarly, Dr. Romanoski's study, based on data gathered from 800 Baltimore residents, found that 86% of major depressions were precipitated by a real-life event or situation. This research contradicts a prevailing belief that depressions triggered by an identifiable event aren't really illnesses and don't need professional treatment. "Just because we can understand why a person is depressed doesn't mean we shouldn't treat the problem seriously," says psychiatrist Sidney Zisook of the University of California at San Diego. "Depression can develop a life of its own, and once it does, it needs to be addressed, because it's still associated with decreased functioning and suicide."

Painful experiences in early life can also sow the seeds of future gloom. A 1991 Stanford University study attributed up to 35% of the discrepancy between male and female depression rates to sexual abuse of women in childhood. Other research suggests that growing up in the wake of a divorce may also predispose a person to depression. Such trauma may literally be etched into a young brain, some scientists speculate. "Life experiences might create enduring changes in the central nervous system," says Horwath, "and that might alter neurochemistry and place the person at higher risk for depression. The environmental factor ultimately has a biological effect."

Studies have long linked alcoholism and depression, but it's not always clear which is cause and which is effect. Logic would suggest that people in pain drink to ease their sorrow. Yet many studies show that people who are already alcoholic—men in particular—go on to develop major depression, perhaps because high levels of prolonged intoxication eventually unbalance brain chemistry. For women, the cause-and-effect pattern tends to go the other way, although researchers aren't sure why as yet.

No matter what its origins are, the neurochemistry of despair is the same. Imbalances of certain mood-regulating neurotransmitters—chemical messengers that transmit electrochemical signals between brain cells—are thought to underlie depression at its most fundamental level. Among possible scenarios of what goes awry in the brain: Levels of the neurotransmitters that control mood may be abnormally low, or the neural receptors that normally intercept neurotransmitters as they pass from cell to cell may malfunction.

Scientists have so far identified about 100 of the brain's many neurotransmitters. Two of these, norepinephrine and serotonin, appear to be most closely tied to depression. Says psychiatrist Elliott Richelson, director of research at a branch of the Mayo Clinic in Jacksonville, Fla., "It could be that changes in norepinephrine or serotonin levels affect some other neurotransmitter more directly involved in depression. There are probably at least 100 neurotransmitters we haven't even identified yet, so it's highly possible we still have to find the one that's absolutely key in regulating depression."

Antidepressants, which correct brain chemistry imbalances, have been on the market for over 30 years. Some early ones—specifically the tricyclic drugs, such as imipramine—affect neurochemicals other than serotonin and norepinephrine, causing a wide range of potential side effects, including dry mouth, weight gain and drowsiness. Other early antidepressants, the so-called monoamine oxidase (MAO) inhibitors, are inconvenient to take: Patients must avoid cheese, wine and a long list of other foods containing a chemical that reacts with the drug and can send blood pressure soaring. More targeted medications that act solely on mood-regulating neurotransmitters are generally easier on patients' systems. For example, Prozac and another relatively new drug, Zoloft, act only on serotonin. Fewer side effects combined with tales of miracle cures have made these new drugs more popular than the previous generations of antidepressants, which may nonetheless work as well or better in some people.

Researchers estimate that about 75% of those suffering from major depression can benefit from one of these medications. "In the last decade, there's been a shift toward using antidepressants, and I think that's good," says Brown University psychologist Tracie Shea. "They can be extremely helpful when depression has started to affect functioning. Pills don't solve life's problems, but they can put people in a better position to solve the problems themselves. They give people the energy to look at issues going on in their lives, and that gives them more choice and control."

This sort of talk alarms some mental health professionals, who worry that antidepressants are turning into the latest pharmaceutical fad, used in ever milder cases of the blues, rather than for the severe disorders they were developed to treat. "I'm not saying they should never be used," says Dr. Roger Greenberg, a psychologist at the State University of New York Health Science Center in Syracuse, "but I'm concerned at the promise being held out for drugs. I think people should be more cautious about taking them than they have

Are You Depressed?

	0-Not at all	1-Somewhat	2-Moderately	3-A lot
Sadness: Have you been feeling sad or down in the dumps?				
Discouragement: Does the future look hopeless?				
Low self-esteem: Do you feel worthless or think of yourself as a failure?				
Inferiority: Do you feel inadequate or inferior to others?				
Guilt: Do you get self-critical and blame yourself for everything?				
Indecisiveness: Do you have trouble making up your mind about things?				
Irritability and frustration: Have you been feeling resentful and angry a good deal of the time?				
Loss of interest in life: Have you lost interest in your career, your hobbies, your family or your friends?				
Loss of motivation: Do you feel overwhelmed and have to push yourself hard to do things?				
Poor self-image: Do you think you're looking old or unattractive?				
Appetite changes: Have you lost your appetite, or do you overeat or binge compulsively?				
Sleep changes: Do you suffer from insomnia and find it hard to get a good night's sleep, or are you excessively tired and sleeping too much?				
Loss of libido: Have you lost your interest in sex?				
Hypochondriasis: Do you worry a great deal about your health?				
Suicidal impulses*: Do you have thoughts that life is not worth living or think you might be better off dead?				

After you have completed the test, add up your total score. It will be somewhere between 0 and 45. Use the key at right to interpret your score.

*Anyone with suicidal urges should seek immediate consultation with a qualified psychiatrist or psychologist.

From *The Feeling Good Handbook,* © 1989 by David D. Burns, M.D. Reprinted by permission of William Morrow.

Total score	Degree of depression
0-4	Minimal or none
5-10	Borderline
11-20	Mild
21-30	Moderate
31-45	Severe

About 75% can benefit from medication.

been up to now. We want quick and easy solutions for complex and difficult problems—it's a fast-food kind of mentality. Drugs have a natural appeal, they help people say, 'I'm not responsible for my actions, it's my body chemistry.' "

Psychiatrist Peter Kramer, author of the best-selling book *Listening to Prozac,* views drug treatment differently. "There's an idea that there's a moral price to be paid if you're on medication, and that it's better to do things by other means. Is it more comfortable and easier to believe that disorders can be treated through honesty and hard work? Yes. But if you have someone in front of you who's suffering, you have to be realistic about choosing the best way to alleviate their pain."

Patients who've benefited from antidepressants tend to agree with Dr. Kramer. Charlotte Goldberg*, 30, of New York City was plagued by depression after she separated from her husband and switched careers. Yet she had reservations about trying an antidepressant. "I was very hesitant," she recalls. "I was afraid I'd become falsely happy, that it wouldn't really be me. It bothered me to think of being chemically altered." But after she began taking Zoloft, Goldberg changed her mind: "I feel good but not in a stupid, high way," she says. "I can think more clearly, I'm calmer, not as anxious. Being less moody and having more energy has helped me to work through my problems better."

In sum, antidepressants can often restore emotional and physical equilibrium, but they don't make people euphoric or eliminate life stresses. After reviewing more than 400 clinical trials of antidepressants, a panel of distinguished researchers who developed the HHS depression treatment guidelines concluded that "no one antidepressant is clearly more effective than another. No single medication results in remission for all patients." Only 50% to 60% of patients respond to the first drug they try; the rest need to experiment until they find a drug that works for them. Moreover, for reasons researchers still don't understand, it usually takes four to six weeks before patients begin to feel the medication's full effects.

When the HHS guidelines were issued, the American Psychological Association, whose members specialize in talk therapy, issued a press release disassociating the organization from the guidelines on the grounds that they "do not encourage sufficient collaboration with mental health specialists and appear to be biased toward medication." In fact, says Rush of Texas Southwestern Medical Center, who chaired the government panel, 60% of antidepressants are now distributed by primary-care doctors, meaning that many people already take the drugs without accompanying psychotherapy. Some experts see no problem with that. "For the severely depressed patient, I don't think talk therapy is helpful," says the Mayo Clinic's Richelson. "The folks I see are really ill, and they're not going to be helped by the addition of a 50-minute hour."

Still, when the HHS panel compared the efficacy of talk therapy *and* medication with drug treatment alone, they found the combination treatment to be somewhat more ef-

Long-Term Blues

a milder form of depression known as dysthymia can dog a sufferer for years on end. "It's like a low-grade infection people just can't get rid of," says psychologist James McCullough, director of the Unipolar Mood Disorders Institute at Virginia Commonwealth University in Richmond. "They're not taken out of the work force or the home—they just feel bad most of the time. They don't know why, but they've felt that way for as long as they can remember."

An estimated 3% to 4% of Americans—two out of three of them women—experience dysthymia during their lifetime. Like victims of major depression, they may have sleep, appetite, energy and concentration problems. The disorder often strikes early in life: Dr. James Kocsis, a dysthymia expert at Cornell Medical Center in New York City, says his average patient has been despondent for 20 years, usually beginning in childhood or adolescence. Only about 10% to 15% of cases clear up on their own. Not surprisingly, dysthymics tend to have interpersonal problems, poor self-esteem and difficulty asserting themselves. They're also at significantly increased risk of major depression: Those who experience a severe slump are said to have "double depression."

Prior to 1980, when the disorder was first identified, dysthymics were typically dismissed as dark, gloomy people. Now mental health practitioners increasingly treat dysthymia like depression, with promising results. A 1988 study by Kocsis published in the *Archives of General Psychiatry* showed that six out of 10 dysthymics respond to antidepressants. "Patients say, 'This is the first time in my life I've ever felt normal,' " says Kocsis. "Their occupational underachievement and social problems tend to improve rapidly. One of the outcomes of treating dysthymia is that you start receiving wedding invitations. Patients get married and invite their psychiatrists to their weddings."

Unfortunately, even after a year of drug treatment, 60% to 70% of patients who discontinue medication will relapse. So far, there have been no controlled clinical trials of psychotherapy's effectiveness against the disorder. But Dr. McCullough, who has treated some 150 dysthymics with a combination of cognitive and behavioral therapy, says he's encouraged by the outcome. Of 20 therapy patients on whom he's kept systematic records, 70% were still depression-free after two years. "If their basic thought and behavior patterns don't change, dysthymics will stay depressed no matter what good things happen to them," notes McCullough. "These are issues that therapy can address."

fective. And a number of studies show that in less severe depressions psychotherapy by itself may work just as well as antidepressants. "My hunch is that whatever drugs are doing to brain chemistry, effective therapy can do also," notes Vanderbilt University clinical psychologist Steven Hollon, a specialist in cognitive therapy. "You're changing an attitude and that changes biology—just as biology changes attitude. I think the two are interactive processes."

A 1989 National Institute of Mental Health study of people with mild to moderate depressions found therapy to be as successful as medication in helping patients recover over a 16-week period. Overall, research suggests that some 50% of the depressed can alleviate the symptoms of depression with either cognitive therapy or other types.

Cognitive therapy was developed in the '60s by psychiatrist Aaron Beck, now at the University of Pennsylvania. Its premise is that thoughts create feelings: Change destructive ideas, Beck said, and unhappy emotions will change too. One such destructive pattern is a tendency to blame oneself exclusively when something goes wrong. Explains Dr. Hollon, "Someone who loses his job and says, 'I'm not good enough,' is more likely to get depressed than someone who says, 'It's a lousy economy and Bill Clinton is to blame.' "

The inclination to brood rather than act on difficulties is another pattern believed to be self-defeating and one that might help explain some of the male-female disparity in depression rates. When Stanford University psychologist Susan Nolen-Hoeksema reviewed the literature, she was struck by the fact that "women generally seem to stay with negative emotions, like depression or anxiety, more than men do. It's often talked of as a woman's strength to be able to acknowledge negative emotions, but I started looking at how it works against them."

Dr. Nolen-Hoeksema concluded that people who obsessively ponder a problem and its negative implications can find themselves sucked into a vicious circle of gloom. Those who distract themselves with sports or other enjoyable activities—as many men seem to do instinctively—emerge from unhappy moods faster and in a better state to tackle problems. Why do women tend to be brooders and men doers? "One of our guesses is that young boys aren't allowed to ruminate," says Nolen-Hoeksema. "They're taught to be active from an early age. Research on preschoolers seems to show that one thing parents will not tolerate is emotionality in boys. It's also possible that the things girls worry about actually are harder to deal with than the things boys worry about. Girls think a lot more about interpersonal relationships than boys do, and those are hard to control."

The logic behind cognitive therapy may sound simplistic, but it boasts many enthusiastic converts. Angela Wolf, the woman whose depression was triggered by her husband's infidelities, says cognitive therapy saved her life. " I was assaulted by automatic negative thoughts and my therapist would have me try to prove them to myself, the way you would to a jury. I'd think, 'If I leave this marriage, no man will ever be attracted to me.' Then I'd have to write down why I thought that statement was true, and also why I thought it wasn't. Inevitably, I'd wind up proving it *wasn't* true." Now divorced, Wolf says, "I'm infinitely happier today."

One particularly controversial issue among scientists who debate the merits of psychological vs. drug treatments is recurrence: At least 50% of those who suffer an attack will experience another. "Our whole concept of the disorder is shifting from thinking of it as time-limited to recognizing that it's much more chronic than we thought," says Brown's Dr. Shea. "For many people, depression won't be a one-shot deal." She adds that a few months of treatment with drugs or therapy, until fairly recently considered standard, often aren't enough to keep a patient well: "People shouldn't think of depression as something that can necessarily be cured in 16 weeks."

Therapy proponents argue that patients have a better chance of staying depression-free over time if they learn psychological techniques to help ward off relapses. "Pharmacology [drug therapy] is marvelous," says Hollon, "but it mostly suppresses symptoms. It's like taking aspirin. If you want to take it every day, it will do a very good job of stopping your headache. But if you learn to meditate and you reduce your overall stress level, maybe you won't get headaches to begin with. In that sense, cognitive therapy may be analogous to learning to meditate."

In a recent study published in the *Archives of General Psychiatry,* Hollon and colleague Mark Evans, a University of Minnesota psychologist, found that about 75% of depressed people in each of two groups treated either with medication or cognitive therapy felt well enough to stop treatment after three months. But over the next two years, 50% of those treated with medication relapsed into depressions, while only 20% of those treated with therapy did.

A growing number of doctors, however, are dealing with the threat of recurrence by keeping patients on medication for much longer periods of time—in some instances, many years beyond the six to nine months typically allotted for treating an episode of depression. Some 90% of those who stay on antidepressants remain symptom-free, but it has yet to be seen if prolonged antidepressant use carries undiscovered risks. "I'm a little nervous about the amount of time people are kept on drugs these days," says Hollon. "There probably aren't any really nasty complications lurking out there, but we're mucking around with complex physiology. You always wonder about the risk of side effects."

Clearly, there are complex questions remaining about depression that can only be answered through years of research. One point, however, is clear: Today, no one need stoically endure the lethargy and sense of futility that descend with an episode of depression. "I don't think long-term suffering is very therapeutic," sums up Dr. Zisook of UC-San Diego. "It doesn't help someone become a better person. And it's not something that people need to go through when we have treatments for it."

For more information on mood disorders, contact the following organizations: D/ART (Depression Awareness, Recognition, and Treatment), 800-421-4211; the National Depressive and Manic-Depressive Association, 800-826-3632; and the Depression and Related Affective Disorders Association, 410-955-4647.

LOSING WEIGHT

WHAT WORKS.
WHAT DOESN'T.

In the first large-scale survey of the major weight-loss programs, we found that no program is very effective. Here's why diets usually don't work, and how you can manage your weight more wisely.

Fifty million Americans are dieting at any given time, and these days, most of them are thoroughly confused. After decades in which medical authorities, the fashion industry, and most ordinary people agreed that the pursuit of thinness was an unmitigated good, the wisdom of dieting has come into question. Researchers have found that yo-yo dieting, the common cycle of repeatedly losing and regaining weight, may be as bad for you as weighing too much in the first place. Sobered by that research—and by the realization that many dieters become yo-yo dieters—members of a growing antidiet movement have urged people to throw away their calorie counters and eat whenever they're hungry.

Despite those developments, it is still possible and worthwhile for some people to lose weight. But a review of the scientific literature, interviews with experts in the field, and CU's own research show that a major shift in thinking about weight loss is in order. For the typical American dieter, the benefits of weight loss are no longer certain—and the difficulty of losing weight permanently has become all too clear.

Medical researchers have suspected for years that most diets end in failure; studies done at weight-loss clinics in medical centers showed that people almost always regained the weight they lost. But it was never clear whether people at those clinics had an unusually poor success rate because they were "hard cases" who needed special help.

Now CU has undertaken the first large-scale survey of people on ordinary diet programs and shown that they, too, usually fail at losing weight in the long term. We collected information from 95,000 readers who had done something to lose weight over the previous three years, including some 19,000 who had used a commerical diet program. . . . our survey showed that people do lose weight on these programs—but the great majority of them gain back most of that weight within two years.

Although different weight-loss programs use different diets and strategies, none have been able to overcome this basic pattern. The problem is that losing weight is much more than a matter of willpower: It's a process that pits the dieter against his or her own physiology.

Why people get fat

A small number of people have struggled with obesity since childhood and are massively overweight as adults. A greater number are not overweight when they enter adulthood, but become so as they gain 10, 20, or 30 pounds over the course of two or three decades. And about three-quarters of American adults are not overweight at all.

What makes for the difference? Primarily, it's the genes. An individual's body size, studies have conclusively shown, is genetically coded as surely as the shape of a nose. Inheritance overwhelms other factors in determining an individual's normal range of weight, which may be rela-

tively high for one person, low for another. While diet and exercise certainly play a role, they do so within limits set by heredity.

Over and over again, researchers have observed the human body's remarkable resistance to major weight change. Dr. Rudolph Leibel, an obesity researcher at Rockefeller University in New York City, describes how extremely obese people repeatedly enter the university's weight-loss clinic, lose dozens of pounds, go home, and return six months later having regained precisely the amount of weight they lost. Other clinicians have reported similar, if less dramatic, results.

What's less widely known is that the body resists major weight *gain* as much as it resists a major loss. In a classic study conducted in the 1960s by Dr. Ethan Allen Sims of the University of Vermont, a group of 20 prisoners of normal weight volunteered to gain as much weight as possible. Only by forcing themselves to overeat—some by thousands of extra calories a day—were the men able to add 20 percent to their weight and keep it on. Once the study ended, almost everyone returned quickly to his starting weight.

No one knows just how the body keeps weight within a fairly narrow range; researchers posit the existence of some sort of biochemical control system, but they haven't found it. Whatever the mechanism is, however, it allows weight to drift slowly upward as people get older. Two major changes take place with age. People tend to become less physi-

The first modern diet book
In 1863, the Englishman William Banting published his "Letter on Corpulence Addressed to the Public." His advice: Cut back on carbohydrates.

cally active. And, partly as a result of inactivity, people lose lean muscle mass, which burns calories more rapidly than fatty tissue.

No wonder, then, that the prime time for dieting is the mid-40s. "That's when people start to look fat or study a height-weight table and say to themselves, 'Gee, I've crossed over a line,'" says David Williamson, an epidemiologist who studies weight patterns for the Centers for Disease Control and Prevention.

Weight and health

Even if some people are genetically programmed to be fatter than others, their natural body size may not necessarily be a healthy one. Researchers are now struggling with a difficult question: At what point do the risks of overweight make the effort to lose weight worthwhile?

To begin to answer that question, scientists have used a measure called the body mass index, or BMI, which incorporates both height and weight to assess a person's level of fatness. You can find your own BMI by following the instructions on the opposite page. Scientists consider a BMI of 25 or less to be desirable for most people. A BMI between 25 and 30—mild or moderate overweight—carries a slightly increased risk of weight-related health problems such as high blood pressure, high blood cholesterol, heart disease, and Type II (adult-onset) diabetes. At a BMI of 30 or more—considered truly overweight—the risk of developing those conditions and others rises sharply.

There is little doubt that people with a *lifelong* BMI of 25 or less have the lowest risk of disease and premature death (except for cigarette smokers, who are both lean and suffer high rates of cancer, chronic lung disease, and cardiovascular disease). But the benefits of thinness may be greatest for people who have always been thin. Someone who starts out overweight and then slims down is still worse off than someone who never was overweight at all.

The people with the hardest decision to make about their weight are those who are mildly to moderately overweight, with a BMI between 25 and 30. If they have diabetes or cardiovascular risk factors, such as high blood cholesterol or high blood pressure, they may have a medical reason to try to reduce; if not, they may be relatively safe.

Age also affects the risk for this middle group. Americans' median weight rises steadily between the

A clash of ideals The woman on the right—5-foot-4 and 130 pounds—has an ideal body type from a health standpoint. But many women her size long to attain a thinner ideal: the super-svelte body, shown in the mirror, that only a tiny fraction of the population can ever match.

ages of 20 and 55, and a number of studies indicate that isn't necessarily dangerous. The overall risk of moderate overweight apparently diminishes, or even disappears altogether, with advancing age. The reason is not entirely clear, and the data have been the subject of much debate. However, most researchers now accept the phenomenon as fact, as does the U.S. Government. Since 1990, the Government has published weight guidelines for Americans that give different ranges for older and younger adults.

One other critical variable has emerged in the last several years: the waist-to-hip ratio, calculated as the measure of a person's waist at its smallest point divided by the circumference of the hips at their widest point. This ratio distinguishes "apples"—that is, people who carry excess weight above their waist—

from "pears," whose extra fat settles around the hips and buttocks. The higher the waist-to-hip ratio, the more apple-shaped the figure. Most men are apples, with the classic beer belly; most women are pears, although there is a significant minority of female apples.

The correlation between the waist-to-hip ratio and cardiovascular disease has been investigated in at least a half-dozen long-term studies, with consistent results: The higher the ratio, the greater the risk of disease, especially among people who are at least moderately overweight. Many scientists even believe that the waist-to-hip ratio predicts cardiovascular disease better than the degree of overweight. For men, the risk seems to rise above a waist-to-hip ratio of 0.95; for women, the cutoff point is 0.80. Paradoxically, surveys show that overweight men, most of whom are apples, are much less likely to try to lose weight than women, whose fat distribution is more benign.

Scientists think that abdominal fat does its damage because it is more metabolically active than below-the-waist fat. It's also associated with increased insulin resistance (a precursor to diabetes) and may be a cause of hypertension.

Why diets don't work

Even the most optimistic weight-control professionals admit that traditional dieting—cutting calories to lose weight—rarely works in the long term. Clinicians have tried everything to make diets more effective. They've devised ultra-low-calorie regimens that produce fast, large weight losses. They've brought patients in for months, even years, of behavior modification to help them deal with "impulse" eating and distract themselves from hunger pangs. The results are unvarying: When treatment stops, weight gain begins.

IS YOUR WEIGHT BAD FOR YOUR HEALTH?

While being overweight can raise the risk of disease, especially cardiovascular disease, your risk is only partially determined by the number you see on the scale. By completing this worksheet, you can get a fuller picture of how your weight is likely to affect your health. The approach used here is largely adapted from work by Dr. George Bray of the Pennington Biomedical Research Center at Louisiana State University and psychologist Thomas A. Wadden of Syracuse University. To begin, you need to calculate your body mass index (BMI) and your waist-to-hip ratio.

Finding your BMI

Using a calculator, you can calculate your BMI as follows: Multiply your weight in pounds by 700, divide by your height in inches, then divide by your height again.
BMI _____

Finding your waist-to-hip ratio

Using a tape measure, find the circumference of your waist at its narrowest point when your stomach is relaxed.
Waist: _____ in.
Next, measure the circumference of your hips at their widest (where your buttocks protrude the most).
Hips: _____ in.
Finally, divide your waist measurement by your hip measurement.
Waist/hip = _____ Waist-to-hip ratio

Determining your risk

Long-term studies show that the overall risk of developing heart disease is generally related to BMI as follows:

BMI of 25 or less—Risk is very low to low.
BMI between 25 and 30—Risk is low to moderate.
BMI of 30 or more—Risk is moderate to very high.

The BMI determines your likely range of risk. But where you fall within that range depends on the factors at right. The more items you have in the "High-Risk Factors" column, the higher your risk; the more you have in the "Low-Risk Factors" column, the lower your risk. Bear in mind that these factors give you only an approximation of your risk; your physician can give you more precise advice. (It's also possible for someone with a large number of high-risk factors to have a high risk of heart disease at any weight.)

HIGH-RISK FACTORS

- Being male
- Under age 40 with BMI above 25
- Waist-to-hip ratio greater than 0.80 for women or 0.95 for men
- Sedentary life-style
- Smoking
- High blood pressure
- Blood cholesterol of more than 200 mg/dl
- HDL less than 35
- Heart disease or Type II (adult-onset) diabetes—personal or in family history

LOW-RISK FACTORS

- Being female
- Waist-to-hip ratio of less than 0.80 for women or 0.95 for men
- Regular exercise
- Normal blood pressure
- Blood cholesterol of less than 200 mg/dl
- HDL more than 45
- No personal or family history of heart disease or diabetes

Scientists can't yet fully explain this nearly inevitable pattern, but the explanation may lie in our prehistoric roots. According to one hypothesis, humans evolved under the constant threat of famine. As a result, the human body is programmed by evolution to respond to caloric restriction as if starvation were at hand. After a few weeks on a low-calorie diet, the body goes on a sort of protective red alert. The basal metabolic rate—the speed at which the body burns calories when at rest—begins to decline. In addition, the body uses lean muscle mass as fuel in an effort to preserve fat, which is the major long-term source of energy. Both changes mean that the body burns fewer calories, making it more difficult to maintain a weight loss.

Finally, hunger—true, physiological hunger—increases. And, faced with hunger, "people are not able to keep up with the food restrictions required to maintain a lower weight," says David Schlundt, a psychologist at Vanderbilt University who specializes in obesity. Although the folklore of dieting says that hunger can be overcome by anyone with a decent amount of willpower, this basic biological drive is exceedingly difficult to ignore.

Most obesity researchers now believe that stringent dieting is actually a major trigger for binge eating. This connection was shown vividly in an experiment conducted during World War II by University of Minnesota physiologist Ancel Keys with a group of young, healthy men. Keys put the men on a balanced diet that provided about half their usual caloric intake—a regimen that he called "semistarvation" but that was remarkably similar to the diets prescribed by today's commercial weight-loss programs. When the men were released from the diet after six months, they went on massive eating binges, eating up to five meals and 5000 calories a day until they had returned to their normal weight. The lesson: "Going back to eating after a period of starvation is as natural as taking a breath," says Susan Wooley, a University of Cincinnati psychologist who specializes in obesity and eating disorders.

Is weight loss safe?

In addition to the high physical and emotional cost of dieting, new epidemiological evidence suggests that the practice may actually carry a greater health risk than staying overweight for some people.

For years everyone assumed that if overweight damaged a person's health, losing weight would improve it. That assumption seemed to be well-founded: Many studies have shown that as soon as dieters start to lose weight, their blood cholesterol levels and blood pressure drop and their insulin resistance declines.

Surprisingly, however, not a single long-term epidemiological study has ever proven that losing weight extends life. And over the past year, two important studies have provided evidence to the contrary.

One, headed by Elsie Pamuk of the Centers for Disease Control and Prevention, used the results of the First National Health and Nutrition Examination Survey, a Government survey of the health status of thousands of Americans. When they entered that study in the early 1970s, participants were given a complete checkup that, among other things, recorded what they weighed then and what was the most they had ever weighed. A decade later, the Government scientists tracked the participants to see who had died, and of what causes.

Recently, the CDC team analyzed the records of 5000 men and women who had been between the ages of 45 and 74 when they entered the Government study. The goal was to see whether those who had once been overweight but had lost weight lived longer than peers who had stayed fat. The team eliminated from the analysis anyone who had died within five years of starting the study, to make sure a pre-existing disease had not made them thin. They also adjusted their data to account for the effects of smoking, age, and gender.

The analysis did confirm one piece of conventional wisdom: Maintaining a stable adult weight and avoiding severe overweight is the best possible course. The data also supported the view that moderate overweight is not necessarily detrimental in middle age: Over the period of the study, men and women with a stable BMI between 25 and 30 had death rates as low as those with a stable BMI of 25 or less.

But when the CDC analysts looked at the effect of weight loss, what they found upset all their expectations:

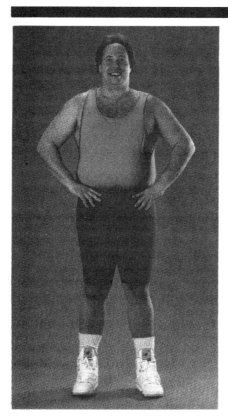

Same weight, different physique Weight is only one determinant of physical health. The man at left is 6 feet tall and weighs 240 pounds; the man at right is almost identical in height and weight, at 6-foot-1 and 230. But the man on the left is a classic "apple," with a high risk of heart disease, while the man on the right is muscular and at low risk.

Instead of improving health, losing weight seemed to do the opposite. Women who lost *any* amount of weight had a higher death rate than those who didn't; the more weight they lost, the higher their risk. Among the fattest group of men, who began with a BMI of 30 or above, those who had a moderate weight loss had a slightly lower than average death rate. But those who lost 15 percent or more had a higher death rate—unless, surprisingly, they were so fat that their weight loss still left them overweight.

The second study was even larger: It included 11,703 middle-aged and elderly Harvard alumni whose weight was recorded in the early 1960s and again in 1977. Like the CDC study, the Harvard study controlled for pre-existing disease.

In 1988, the researchers checked alumni records to see who had died. The men whose weight changed least between the 1960s and 1977 had the lowest death rates, whether the researchers looked at deaths from all causes, deaths from cancer, or, especially, deaths from cardiovascular disease. Any significant weight change, whether up *or* down, markedly increased the risk of dying from cardiovascular disease.

Researchers are hard-pressed to explain the findings of the CDC and Harvard studies. The most likely explanation, however, is that people whose weight changed the most over time were more likely to have had cycles of yo-yo dieting in between—especially if they were overweight. Since our culture stigmatizes fatness, anyone who has been overweight for more than a few years has very likely gone through at least one cycle of significant weight loss and regain. Of the 95,000 respondents to our diet survey, 40 percent had had two or more weight-loss cycles within the previous five years; in that survey, overweight people cycled more often than people of normal weight.

Other studies have suggested that repeatedly losing and gaining weight is hazardous to health. One recent analysis used data from the Framingham Heart Study, a long-term study of some 5000 residents of a Boston suburb that began in 1948. Compared with subjects whose weight remained the most stable, those whose weight fluctuated frequently or by many pounds had a 50 percent higher risk of heart disease.

Weighing your options

Studies like those will animate seminars at scientific meetings for years to come. But they're confusing to people who must decide right now what, if anything, to do about their weight.

For some groups, the decision is relatively clear-cut. People who are not already overweight should place top priority on avoiding weight gain through a combination of moderate eating habits and exercise. Most seriously overweight people—those with a BMI of 30 or more—should attempt to lose some weight; for them, the evidence favoring weight loss is greater than the evidence against it. Most adult-onset diabetics should also reduce, since blood-sugar control usually improves with even relatively small amounts of weight loss. Given the possibility that large losses and regains may be hazardous, however, the best strategy is to stay away from quick weight-loss diets and aim instead for slow, modest, but permanent weight loss using the approaches we'll describe below.

The choice for nondiabetic, moderately overweight adults is not so clear. They should do what they can to avoid gaining more weight. But it is not certain that losing weight in and of itself will reduce their risk—especially if they gain it back again.

Fortunately, there is an approach to losing weight through diet and exercise that doesn't involve low-calorie quick-weight-loss plans. It's safer than conventional dieting; it's more likely to be effective; and it can lessen the risk of cardiovascular disease dramatically, even if it doesn't result in a large weight loss.

The importance of exercise

Apart from the risk of developing shinsplints or being chased by a dog, there's almost nothing bad to be said about regular, moderate physical exercise. And a number of studies now show that exercise can be very effective in weight control.

In one recent study, Stanford University researchers put 71 moderately overweight men and women on a low-fat diet for a year, and another, matched group of 71 on a diet with the same kinds of foods—plus a three-day-a-week program of aerobic exercise. After a year, the diet-plus-exercise group had lost more weight overall and more pounds of fat, even though they actually ate more calories per day than the diet-only group. Other studies have shown that exercise can help people lose weight even if they don't change their regular diet at all.

The explanation lies in the nature of human metabolism. More than half the calories we take in are burned up by what's called basal metabolism—the energy expended just to stay alive. In addition to increasing the number of calories burned in activity, exercise increases the basal metabolic rate, so the body burns more calories even at rest. Studies have shown that the basal metabolic rate is closely linked to the amount of muscle on the body, which is built up through exercise.

For most people, exercise alone will be enough to prevent future weight gain; for many, it will enable them to lose weight effectively and safely. In addition, even if exercise doesn't help you lose pounds, it may help you become thinner. A pound of muscle takes up less space than a pound of fat. So as you build muscle and lose fat, you can lose inches even without actually losing any weight.

Exercise plays a critical role not only in burning fat, but in keeping weight off. That was shown dramatically in a study of 184 mildly overweight Massachusetts policemen and civil servants. All were put on a low-calorie diet, and half were also put through three 90-minute exercise sessions per week. After eight weeks, everyone had lost weight. But when the men were re-examined three years later, those who had never exercised—or who had stopped once the study ended—promptly regained all or most of the weight they had lost. In contrast, exercisers who kept at it maintained virtually all their initial weight loss.

The rationale for exercise goes well beyond becoming thinner. "A lot of the health benefits that people are seeking from weight loss can be achieved by exercise, even in the absence of any weight loss," says Steven Blair, director of epidemiology at the Institute for Aerobics Research in Dallas.

In 1970, scientists at that institute began keeping records on more than 13,000 then-healthy middle-aged men and women to determine the effects of physical fitness on cardiovascular risk. The results are now coming in: Exercise seems to protect against disease and death even in people whose risk factors would otherwise put them in danger. Physically fit men in the study who had high blood pressure, insulin resistance, a high BMI, or an unfavorable family history were less likely to die than unfit men with none of those risk factors. Overall, the fittest men in the study had a death rate less than one-third that of the least fit; for women, there was a five-fold differ-

Trading pounds for lung cancer? Smoking tends to make people thinner, and cigarette manufacturers once promoted their products as if they were diet aids. In 1928, the American Tobacco Company introduced the slogan, "Reach for a Lucky instead of a sweet."

ence. The rates for cardiovascular disease were even more dramatically affected by fitness.

This study has now been followed up by a number of others showing that, among people with almost any known cardiovascular risk factor, exercisers do better than nonexercisers. In addition, exercisers develop adult-onset diabetes about 40 percent less often than nonexercisers, according to a study of 21,000 male American doctors.

It may even be that lack of exercise, rather than excess body fat itself, is the true culprit behind many of the ill effects of obesity. Since inactivity often leads to weight gain, overweight may turn out to be more a result of an unhealthful life-style than a cause of ill health.

Despite the evident benefits of exercise, most people with a weight problem still choose dieting instead. One reason has been the exercise community's historic fixation on high-intensity aerobic exercise, with its intimidating target-heart-rate charts and elaborate workout schedules. Most people simply won't attempt such demanding, time-consuming regimens—especially not the sedentary, overweight people who have the greatest need to exercise.

But intense exercise may not be necessary. Blair's study at the Institute for Aerobics Research suggests that the chief benefits of exercise come when people go from a sedentary life-style to moderate activity—not when they move from moderate exercise to intense athletics. In that study, men in the moderate-fitness group had a death rate from all causes nearly 60 percent lower than that of the sedentary group. In contrast, the very fittest men had a death rate only 23 percent lower than that of the moderately fit group. (Moderate exercise was defined as the equivalent of 30 to 60 minutes a day of brisk walking, either in small spurts or all at once.)

Influenced by these findings, Blair has become a prominent advocate of what might be called opportunistic exercise, which is essentially the art of devising an activity plan that can mesh with any schedule, no matter how frenetic. Blair, like many fitness experts, recommends looking for exercise everywhere you can. Park at the far edge of the mall lot instead of next to the front door; get off a bus one stop early and walk the rest of the way; pace the floor while you're on the phone; use an old-fashioned reel-type mower instead of a gasoline-powered one; take the stairs

instead of the elevator. Any kind of exercise, however mundane, has potential benefits.

Eat less fat, lose fat

In addition to exercise, changing the kinds of food you eat—even without changing the caloric content—can improve both weight and health. Despite the decades-old wisdom that a calorie is a calorie is a calorie, some recent studies have suggested that calories from fat follow a straighter trajectory to the hips or the belly than calories from other sources. The body can store fat very efficiently. But the body's ability to store carbohydrates is limited, so when people eat more than their bodies can use, the excess is burned.

For that reason, researchers have found that the composition of the diet may be more important than the number of calories in determining who gains and who loses weight. The percentage of fat in the diet was the single strongest predictor of subsequent weight gain, for example, among 294 adults monitored for three years by Memphis State University investigators. By contrast, the total calorie consumption they reported had only a weak relationship to weight gain for women, and none at all for men.

If a high-fat diet can add pounds, a low-fat diet may help take them off. Researchers at the University of Illinois at Chicago switched 18 women volunteers from a diet that derived 37 percent of calories from fat—roughly the fat content of the average American's diet—to a diet that was only 20 percent fat. Over the 20-week experiment, the women lost four to five pounds, even though they increased their caloric intake.

One way to reduce fat intake without feeling chronically hungry is to fill up on something else, namely fruits, vegetables, and whole grains. Those foods are all high in carbohydrates, and a diet rich in fruits and vegetables seems to lower the risk of cancer and cardiovascular disease.

Some high-fat foods are easier to give up than others, as scientists at Seattle's Fred Hutchinson Cancer Research Center found in a study of the relationship between dietary fat and breast cancer. They taught a large group of women simple ways to reduce their fat consumption, and tracked down some of the participants after a year to see if they'd kept up their low-fat habits. The easiest changes to sustain turned out to be those that were least noticeable from a sensory standpoint: switching to

SAME CALORIES, DIFFERENT FOODS

When you switch from high-fat to low-fat foods, you can actually eat more food for the same number of calories—as the examples shown below demonstrate.

180 calories

1 oz. mixed nuts, 17 g fat

2 oz. unbuttered microwave popcorn, 2 g fat

370 calories

Fried shrimp with tartar sauce, 27 g fat

Boiled shrimp with cocktail sauce, 3 g fat

500 calories

Fettucine Alfredo, 28 g fat

Fettucine with marinara sauce, 10 g fat

250 calories

Strawberry premium ice cream, 15 g fat

Strawberry sorbet, 0 g fat

low-fat milk, mayonnaise, margarine, and salad dressing; trimming fat from meats and skin from chicken; having occasional vegetarian meals. Hardest to give up were the foods for which fat was an integral part of the food's appeal: pastries and ice cream, butter, hamburgers, lunch meats, and cheese.

Fortunately, the fat-reducing strategies that are easiest to follow can yield a significant decrease in total fat consumption. A group from Pennsylvania State University calculated the effect of such changes on an average woman's diet. They determined that by substituting skim milk for whole, switching to lower-fat meats and fish (such as skinless chicken and water-packed tuna), and using low-fat dressings and spreads, a woman could cut the fat in her diet from 37 percent of calories to 23 percent.

Your natural weight

Exercising and eating less fat are healthful changes that can benefit anyone, and may lead to weight loss as a bonus. But for many people,
especially those who have been overweight all their lives, even faithful adherence to healthful habits won't slim the body to the thin ideal our culture holds dear.

Janet Polivy, an obesity researcher at the University of Toronto, believes that people should learn to be comfortable with their "natural weight"—the body size and shape that results after a person adopts a healthful diet and gets a reasonable amount of exercise. Similarly, Kelly Brownell, a Yale University psychologist who has done extensive research on behavioral obesity treatments, speaks of a "reasonable weight" as an attainable goal. "It's the weight that individuals making reasonable changes in their diet and exercise patterns can seek and maintain over a period of time," he explains. Brownell suggests that people who want to lose weight should start by losing a moderate amount, 10 pounds or so, and should then see how comfortably they can maintain that lower weight before trying to lose a bit more, stabilizing again, and so on.

Accepting the goal of a "natural" or "reasonable" weight may involve giving up long-held fantasies of a slim, youthfully athletic body, and being content with the realities of a middle-aged shape instead. It means accepting a slower rate of weight loss, or none at all. For long-term dieters, many of whom have spent years monitoring everything they put into their mouths and suppressing hunger pangs, it also means learning anew how to eat normally—eating when hungry and stopping when full.

Nevertheless, we believe this moderate approach to weight control is the only one worth trying for most people. It makes sense whether you are trying to maintain your current weight, reverse middle-age spread, or deal with a weight problem that's plagued you all your life. If you change your eating and exercise patterns gradually, and maintain the changes over time, you will almost certainly look and feel better, have more energy, and reduce your risk of cardiovascular disease, whether or not you lose much weight.

SEXUAL DESIRE

Whether it's dull appetite or ravenous hunger, millions of Americans are unhappy with their intimate lives

She won't look at him. Keeps staring out the window, even though there's nothing to see but the black Minnesota night and a car speeding past, headlights sliding along the glass. "I thought it would just go away," the petite woman says finally, in a small, tired voice. "That it was just a phase I was going through. I would make excuses."

The muffled thuds and shouts of playing children drift from the basement. Her wiry husband, seated on the Early American sofa, is a machinist in his late 30s. She is a homemaker. And all that matters now is that they haven't had sex in eight months. "He'd start a little foreplay. I'd say 'No. Just leave me alone!'"

"Boy, would that put me away," says her husband, his bearded face stony above a red T-shirt. "I was already feeling hurt. I'd roll over and go to sleep."

"Sometimes, every three to four months, I'd force myself," she confesses. "Grit my teeth and get through it."

Neither partner looks at the other, and a hesitant hush hovers over the room. Finally, the husband turns to psychologist Eli Coleman, who runs a sex-therapy clinic in nearby Minneapolis. "There's just one thing I want to know," he says, frowning. "Is this a common situation?"

Common? Try epidemic. The problem under discussion is sexual desire, an instinct that should flow as freely and unself-consciously between two loving humans as the urge for a fine meal or a good night's sleep. This is a story about what happens when desire goes askew. It is a tale of people who typically are articulate, competent and to all appearances quite ordinary, yet they cannot enjoy one of humankind's most basic pleasures. Madonna may be falling out of her bustier on MTV, Prince may be singing the joys of masturbation on FM and the latest sex-and-gore thriller may be packing them in at the Cineplex, but in the bedroom, an estimated 1 in 5 Americans—some 38 million adults—don't want sex at all. As many as 9 million more, meanwhile, suffer almost uncontrollable sexual desire, compulsively masturbating or prowling a surreal landscape of massage parlors and rumpled beds in a frenzied quest for loveless sex.

To be sure, sexual-desire disorders date back a lot further than "The Devil and Miss Jones," or even Don Juan. What's new is that such complaints now constitute the No. 1 problem bringing clients to sex therapists.

Women without orgasms and men who ejaculated prematurely once dominated the practice; now—because of the pioneering research of Dr. William Masters and Virginia Johnson in the 1960s—people with such common conditions seek do-it-yourself solutions. "The simpler cases can go out and get self-help books," says Dr. Constance Moore, head of the Human Sexuality Program at Houston's Baylor College of Medicine. "Today, sex therapists are seeing the more complicated problems."

No one is sure whether the onslaught of Americans seeking help reflects a real rise in desire disorders or whether such problems are simply more visible. In the 1960s, public expectations of sex began to shift in profound ways. Thanks to the birth-control pill, women could for the first time in history separate sex from the fear of pregnancy. Suddenly, it was not only OK for women to enjoy sex—it was *de rigueur*. The 1953 Kinsey report that as many as 29 percent of single women were sexually unresponsive now seemed as old-fashioned as stiff petticoats and white gloves.

At the same time, new cultural messages glorified casual sex. More than 80 percent of women and 90 percent of men now engage in premarital intercourse, compared with 50 percent of women and 80 percent of men in the 1920s. And from seductive Calvin Klein–jeans ads to the estimated 176 monthly sex scenes on prime-time TV, free sex has emerged as the presumptive symbol of the good life. Sexual health has become a right.

And so they come for help: A man who, after pursuing his bride-to-be for months, shuts down sexually on his wedding night in their $200-a-day bridal suite. A school administrator with five boyfriends who sandwiches frenzied appointments for sex between dashes to office and supermarket. They are farmers and salesmen, consultants and lawyers, homemakers and clerks. In the sanitized confines of therapists' offices, they haltingly reveal their secrets—it's hard, after all, to confess even to a best friend that one masturbates five times a day or hasn't slept with one's spouse in a year. Eyes downcast, voices leaden, they evoke the anguish of abusive fathers, of religiously suffocating mothers, of families where sex, if discussed at all, was shameful and dirty and where dad sometimes slipped into bed with the kids.

What unites them is fear. As children, they learned that caring too much for others was risky. As adults, they found they could control their fear by controlling sex. Instead of an intimate and loving act, sex became a tool to manipulate those who might get too close. And while no one can properly distinguish why some people channel childhood anxieties into food or booze while others fasten on sex, it may be that what eating disorders were to the '80s, desire disorders will be in the '90s: the designer disease of the decade, the newest symptom of American loneliness and alienation. "Sex isn't just sex," explains Raul C. Schiavi, head of the Human Sexuality Program at Mount Sinai Medical Center. "It's an avenue to express many more needs: intimacy, support, self-esteem or whatever."

Given that baggage, it's no wonder that the treatments for sex problems are neither identical nor tidy. In the past three years, researchers have discovered that antidepressants like Prozac can markedly improve symptoms in sexual compulsives. But for victims of low desire, the results are sketchier. The quest for an aphrodisiac, of course, is ancient: King Tut gulped licorice root before romancing his queen, and other love potions, from powdered rhinoceros horn to bees' wings, have proved just as disappointing. But for most cases, treatment involves counseling and therapy, beginning with an attempt to define when things went wrong.

WHAT IS NORMAL?

At first it was fun: feverish kisses in his red Chevy, giggly nights of passion in the apartment. But then came marriage, two kids, and suddenly her husband's hands on her flesh felt like tentacles, and the sight of him approaching made her body stiffen with revulsion. Then the disagreements began, hurtful scenes ending with each of them lying wedged against opposite sides of the bed, praying for sleep. "I didn't know what to do—look in the yellow pages?" recalls Karen, 35, a clerk-cashier in suburban Minneapolis. Her husband didn't know, either. "We finally got a phone number from our family doctor," he says. "It was three more months before we called."*

It wasn't so long ago that low sexual desire was considered a good thing—at least in women. Madame Bovary scandalized 19th-century France with her extramarital fling in Gustave Flaubert's novel. And no one ever said that the remote Estella of Dickens's "Great Expectations" had a low-desire problem. Indeed, from Eve's seduction of Adam, women's sexuality outside of procreation was often considered evil, and early Christian thinkers were just as unsparing toward men—a philosophy that found particularly fertile ground in the New World. As recently as 1907, Dr. John Harvey Kellogg developed his popular corn flakes in an unsuccessful effort to curb desire.

Nor were men and women always physically able to enjoy sex. In late 17th-century England, for instance,

*Like many desire disorder victims quoted here, Karen is a client of the University of Minnesota's Program in Human Sexuality. All names and identifications have been changed.

people suffered from long bouts of crippling illness, not to mention bad breath from poor dentistry, running sores, ulcers and skin diseases. Without antibiotics, women endured repeated vaginal and urinary tract infections that made sex painful.

Then came marriage, two children, and suddenly her husband's hands felt like tentacles. His approach made her stiffen with revulsion.

In fact, the idea of "normal" sexual appetite is such a 20th-century artifice that few experts are comfortable defining it. Clinically, hypoactive sexual desire means having sexual urges, fantasies and/or activity less than twice a month. But even that is the loosest of definitions, since if both partners are happy, once a month may be as "proper" as once a day. "I make the diagnosis [of HSD] if there's been a definite change in desire," says sexologist Moore, "and if it's causing the patient some distress." In Karen's case, the distress was acute: Each night she huddled on her side of the bed, tormenting herself with guilt and dread that her marriage was slipping away.

More typically, though, it's the patient's *partner* who is in distress. Consider Tom, 35, a Midwestern advertising executive whose wife has HSD. "I would try to ignore it as long as I could," he says. "Then she'd give in [and have sex]. But she'd lie limp, waiting for me to get it over with. She could have been downtown. I felt terrible afterward, very guilty."

Prodded by their mates, victims of desire disorders often show up for therapy complaining of impotence or lack of orgasm. But in the mid-1970s, therapists began to notice that the real problem was often that, as in Karen's case, they didn't truly *want* to have sex. In her groundbreaking 1979 work, "Disorders of Sexual Desire," Dr. Helen Singer Kaplan found that unlike sexual arousal, desire exists primarily in the mind. As a result, Kaplan concluded, HSD stems not from a lack of ability to perform but from a lack of motivation. Even so, the fact that HSD may be "all in your mind" doesn't make living with it any easier. "The most important part of sex," Kaplan says, "is the emotional, subjective part. Without that, mechanical function is not gratifying."

Therapists have found that HSD appears to be about twice as prevalent in women as in men. While no national samples are available, one 1978 study of 100 nonclinical American couples found that 35 percent of the women reported lack of sexual interest, compared with 16 percent of the men. But despite this gap, the causes of HSD for both men and women are the same, and the problem usually begins with the emotions.

CAUSES OF LOW DESIRE

The memories started coming after two years in therapy: gauzy, not quite distinct, yet so haunting that tears slowly squeezed from her eyes right in front of the therapist. Jeanine was 8 years old, lying in bed in her Wisconsin home, watching the door creak open. Suddenly, her father was silently over her, breathing heavily. She never told anybody. How could she? There were crucifixes in every room of the house, and her father led the family in the rosary nightly during Lent. Her mother once lectured her on how little girls who "touched themselves" must confess to the priest. Years later, after she got married, Jeanine never had an orgasm with her husband, Tom. Later, she shut down altogether. She and Tom last had sex 4 ¹/₂ years ago.

The roots of desire disorders often lie between the "Sesame Street" years and junior high. Some adults, like Jeanine, report having been sexually abused as children; for others, the abuse was more emotional. John Money, who has pioneered treatments for deviate sexuality at Johns Hopkins University, says children raised in homes where sex is viewed as evil and harmless activities like "playing doctor" are cruelly punished are likely to grow up with warped sexual identities. "In girls, often you extinguish the lust completely, so that they can never have an orgasm, and marriage becomes a dreary business where you put up with sex to serve the maternal instinct," says Money. "In boys, sex gets redirected into abnormal channels."

Jeanine was 8 years old, lying in bed, watching the door creak open. Suddenly, her father was silently on her, breathing heavily.

Not surprisingly, women like Jeanine, who learn as children not to trust those closest to them, often have trouble melding passion and intimacy. Although victims of low desire may be drawn to hit-and-run encounters with strangers, when they get close to a partner, it's too dangerous to let themselves go sexually. Many men suffer from Freud's famous "Madonna-whore complex," whereby a man endows his partner with the "Madonna-like" qualities of his mother. "You find a sudden cessation of interest in sex right after the wedding, even on the night the engagement was announced," says Harold Lief, professor emeritus of psychiatry at the University of Pennsylvania. "These men can't lust after someone they love, or vice versa."

Then there are the tangled cases, where the core problem is not so much historical as personal: The husband and wife detest each other. Marital difficulties, say Lief and other therapists, underlie as many as half of desire disorder cases. Often the problem stems from suppressed anger. "If a couple comes into my office," says Kaplan, "and they fight about where they're gonna sit, and the

only question is who's gonna complain about the other more, I know why they're not having sex."

Childbirth, stress and depression can also precipitate low sexual desire. But only in a minority of cases—roughly 15 percent—are the causes medical, such as hormone deficiencies or diseases like diabetes. Some antidepressants and antihypertensives can also squelch desire. The good news is that such problems usually have a medical solution, sparing patients lengthy hours on an analyst's couch. But the story is not so simple for most HSD sufferers.

TREATMENT FOR HSD

"I just can't do this," Karen announced, midway through the first "homework" session. The kids were asleep in the next room, and the suburban Minneapolis woman and her husband, Bruce, lay naked on the bed. For 15 minutes, according to their therapist, Bruce was to gently explore her breasts and genitals, while she told him what felt good. But as she guided his hand across her rigid body, it might have been made of marble: She felt nothing. Devastated she thought: "This is a waste of time. Nothing's going to change." Later, she told Bruce, "I don't want to go back to therapy." He replied: "We have no choice. We've got to go back."

Reversing low desire takes time. "I went into therapy thinking I'd get an instant fix," says Karen, who has seen a psychologist for a year but still has not had intercourse with her husband. Many therapists estimate the cure rate for low desire is 50 percent at best, and can take months or years of therapy. Nor do desire disorders lend themselves to any standard formula. "It's not a cookbook," says Kaplan. "We work out a different program for each."

Take Jeanine, the Wisconsin woman who was abused by her father. At first, her therapist assigned a set of widely used "homework" exercises based on the work of Masters and Johnson. The program aims to demystify the sex act by having couples practice mutual, noncoital "pleasuring" at first. Therapists emphasize that the practice is not strictly mechanical—a loving atmosphere is considered crucial. In Jeanine's case, the exercises helped her experience the first orgasm of her life by masturbating. And while sex with her husband hasn't yet improved, she has begun in therapy to deal with long-suppressed memories of childhood sexual abuse.

It would be a lot simpler, of course, if scientists could somehow find that elusive "sex pill"—a notion that might not be as farfetched as it seems. Researchers know desire is triggered in the brain by the male hormone testosterone, with the help of chemicals like dopamine that act as "messengers" between nerve cells in the brain. In recent years, doctors have begun using testosterone to stimulate desire in menopausal women, as well as in men with low hormone levels. And the pharmaceutical giant Eli Lilly & Co. has had promising preliminary results with drugs that affect dopamine; the results of a full-scale study are due out next year. But for now, drugs hold far more promise for treating people who have too much desire, not too little.

WHEN SEX BECOMES COMPULSIVE

Gary's pattern was always the same: first, the unbearable anxiety, never feeling good enough to handle the latest stress at his architect's job. Then, the familiar response—a furtive scanning of newspaper ads, a drive to a strip show, two straight Scotches to catch a buzz, and finally a massage parlor. He would park about a block away, slip off his wedding ring and dart through the door, where $100 bought a massage, sex and momentary relief. Afterward, he'd sit naked on the edge of the bed, his thoughts roiling in disgust: "I must be sick . . . I can't change." But a few days later, the anxiety would begin again and he'd pore over the ads.

Too *much* sex? For many Americans, especially young men, the notion sounds like an oxymoron. In fact, the downside of sexual compulsiveness has been largely overshadowed throughout history by a romanticized view of the rake, from Casanova to basketball legend Wilt Chamberlain, with his claims of 20,000 affairs. Compulsive sexual behavior is perhaps easiest to define by what it is not: It does not include someone who masturbates occasionally, periodically rents an X-rated video or engages in a limited period of promiscuity following the breakup of a relationship. As best therapists can tell, those prey to CSB alternate between profound anxiety and all-embracing self-loathing.

But these are not perverts in raincoats. Gary, the architect described above, wears a well-cut tweed sports jacket and speaks in measured tones. "I was two different people," he says quietly, seated in a psychologist's office in Minneapolis. "Most people who knew my wife and me would say we were a good couple. But when I was home I wasn't really there. I felt like a dirty person, rotten." Indeed, one hallmark of compulsive sexual behavior is secrecy: Gary's wife didn't find out about his clandestine visits to porn shops and prostitutes until she discovered a phone bill listing multiple calls to a "900" sex line.

After $100 bought a massage, sex and momentary relief, he'd sit naked on the bed, his thoughts roiling in disgust: "I must be sick."

So secret are their escapades that CSB victims have never even been counted, and experts' figures—they estimate roughly 5 percent of the adult American population—are the merest guess. But if the figures are flimsy, the portrait is precise. To the sexual compulsive, sex is not about love or intimacy or even pleasure. It is mainly about relief. "These are highly anxious people who respond to

stress by attempting to 'medicate' their pain through sex," says Eli Coleman, director of the University of Minnesota's Program in Human Sexuality, and a pioneer in treating CSB. Just as the obsessive compulsive washes his hands 100 times in a row, the sexual compulsive turns to a vast erotic menu that might include compulsive masturbation, feverish cruising and anonymous sex, frenzied multiple affairs or insatiable demands within a relationship.

A small proportion of CSB victims cross the criminal divide into hard-core deviations: voyeurism, obscene phone calls, pedophilia, exhibitionism and others. But the majority prefer ordinary sex—taken to an extreme. What they share is an overwhelming sense of powerlessness. Like the alcoholic, the sexual compulsive is so intent on diverting his pain that he often doesn't even *see* a choice. "If I saw a prostitute on the street, that was it," says Jeff, 36, a public-relations executive from St. Paul, Minn. "It was impossible to not do it."

THE CAUSES OF CSB

His parents were strict Catholics who said the rosary every night and sent their 11 kids to parochial school. The messages about sex began early. Once, at age 12, Jeff overheard his 19-year-old sister tell his father. "Sex is fun." His father shouted. "Don't you ever say that!" Jeff's mother didn't even like hugging and protested loudly on the rare occasions that her husband kissed her in front of the children. As for the nuns, Sister Frances told Jeff's third-grade class: "One should never be naked for longer than necessary." The little boy worried that he had condemned his soul to hell by dawdling in the bathroom. "The message was: 'Lord I am not worthy,' " says Jeff, who became hooked as an adult on compulsive phone sex, masturbation and prostitutes. "I took all of it to heart."

Though he has never cheated on his wife, Karl has spent much of his adult life obsessing about sex: fantasizing, masturbating, demanding sex.

Certainly most people survive strict religious upbringing without becoming "Fantasy Hotline" junkies. Yet over and over, as CSB victims have recounted their stories, therapists have seen a disturbing pattern: As children, these men and women learned that sex was anything but a loving, natural experience. Their parents were rarely able to nurture them or allow them to express feelings in healthy ways. In some cases, they simply neglected the kids: Jeff remembers going weeks without a bath and wearing his clothes to bed. Other parents expected their kids to toe some unattainable line of perfection. "My dad yelled at me, taunted me," says Kevin, 32, a professional from the Midwest who started cruising for anonymous sex in public bathrooms at 16. "Sometimes, he would shake me or choke me. He called me Sissie, told me I was worthless, a mess."

In recent years, family therapist Patrick Carnes—author of the 1983 book "Out of the Shadows"—has gained thousands of followers for his claim that CSB is not an anxiety-based disorder but an addiction, much like alcoholism. It is a spiritual disease, he believes, as well as an emotional and physical one, and his plan for recovery involves belief in a higher power. But while the addiction model has spawned four popular nationwide AA-style support groups, many researchers are skeptical, maintaining that it's impossible to be "addicted" to sex since there is no addictive substance involved. Both the chemical and spiritual explanations, they maintain, grossly oversimplify a complex phenomenon. "It's also sex-negative and moralistic," argues Howard Ruppel of the Society for the Scientific Study of Sex. "They confuse normal activity like masturbating with addiction."

TREATMENT OF CSB

Karl is a Wisconsin farmer, a beefy guy of 42 with sharp blue eyes and hands as big as pie plates. "If I went into town here and told them I was a sexual compulsive," he says, "they'd probably shoot me dead." Instead, he went once a week for group therapy. Though he has never cheated on his wife, Karl has spent months obsessing about sex: fantasizing, masturbating, demanding sex two or three times a day. When he eventually sought help, his therapist prescribed the antidepressant Prozac, which immediately "seemed to take the edge off" his craving. The deeper work came in therapy, where Karl found it was safe to talk—even laugh—about his "problem"; no one condemned or ridiculed him, the way his father had. The turning point came when a group member agreed to role-play Karl's dad and Karl shouted back, finally venting his rage at the way his father always put him down. When his dad died, Karl sat by the coffin at the funeral home and told him haltingly that he knew he'd done the best he could. And then he wept.

"It is so inspiring watching people recover—because they *do*," says Minneapolis psychologist Anne J. McBean. "I can see someone in my office who's an utter wreck, depressed, anxious, and I know that two years later, the same person is going to be sitting here saying, 'I can't believe it—I've got my life back.' "

For years, psychiatrists treated sex offenders with anti-androgens, compounds that partly block the action of the male sex hormones. But because such drugs have potential side effects and are not government-approved for treating CSB, therapists considered them unsuitable for widespread use. In 1989, when Judith L. Rapoport published groundbreaking studies on obsessive compulsive disorders, researchers who had been attempting to link sexual compulsivity with OCD got a boost. Rapoport and others found that drugs that affect the brain chemical serotonin seem to help many people reduce their obsessive-compulsive behaviors, such as constant hand washing.

Sexologists like Coleman have applied the same principle to CSB. In small studies and clinical trials, they tested the effects of both lithium carbonate, which is also used to treat manic depression, and Prozac, which enhances serotonin activity in the brain. Both drugs, they found had some success interrupting the compulsive sexual cycle.

But drugs are only half of the answer. By the time CSB victims seek help, they need therapy as well. Typically, sexual compulsives are largely disconnected from the childhood loneliness and shame that drive their behavior. After Karl, the farmer, saw his farm sold at auction a few years ago, he began obsessing about sex constantly—even driving his pickup or feeding the hogs. In fact, one of the first aims of therapy—once medication had relieved his compulsive symptoms—was to bring back for Karl memories of his father's intolerance, so that he could begin to release them. Within two years of entering therapy, Karl was virtually cured.

Ultimately, the problem with treating both extremes of sexual desire is that researchers still struggle with their own ignorance. The most comprehensive national survey of American sexual behavior is still the Kinsey report, completed nearly 40 years ago. Such studies are expensive and inevitably controversial. Just in the past year, for instance, the Bush administration, under pressure from conservatives, has derailed two planned surveys of American sexual practices. Yet in the absence of such research, knowledge about HSD and CSB is based largely on privately funded studies requiring heroic extrapolations from small samples. Key research—studying the areas of the brain that control sexual behavior or the effects of drugs on desire—awaits funding. "We have almost no information about how people form their sexual habits," says psychologist Elizabeth Allgeier, co-author of "Sexual Interactions," a widely used college text. "If we don't know how it develops, we can't change it."

Still, for millions of Americans it is reassuring to know that no one is doomed to a life of torment by sex. At the very least, educating and encouraging adults to have more enlightened sexual attitudes might enable children to grow up with healthier feelings toward sex. Psychologist John Money says that sexually repressive attitudes now force "at least 50 percent of the nation [to] get 57 cents to the dollar on their sex lives." When Americans are less imprisoned by public expectations and a private sense of sexual shame, perhaps more couples will earn their full satisfaction.

The American Academy of Clinical Sexologists (202-462-2122) and the American Association of Sex Educators, Counselors and Therapists (send an SASE with $2 to 435 North Michigan Ave., Suite 1717, Chicago, IL 60611) will provide names of qualified local sex therapists.

Lynn Rosellini

Alcohol in perspective

True or false?

1. An ounce-and-a-half of 80-proof vodka or whiskey contains more alcohol than a 12-ounce can of beer.
2. A woman gets more intoxicated than a man from the same amount of alcohol.
3. Most Americans drink little or no alcohol.
4. Fatalities caused by alcohol-impaired driving are declining.
5. Measured in real dollars, the cost of alcoholic beverages has risen steadily during the last 40 years.

Answers

1. False. They contain the same amount. So does a five-ounce glass of wine.
2. True. The box on page 5 explains why.
3. True. Abstainers account for about 35% of the adult population, and light drinkers another 35%. Light drinkers, in the official definition, are those consuming two drinks a week or less. Moderate drinkers, who average one-half to two drinks a day, account for another 22%. Heavier drinkers—8% of us—consume more than two drinks a day.
4. True. The percentage of road crashes involving alcohol declined from 57% to 49% over the past decade. And the greatest decline was among teens and young adults. This is attributed to new laws setting the minimum drinking age at 21 in all states and to widespread educational efforts.
5. False. It cost less (in inflation-adjusted dollars) to drink in 1992 than it did in 1951. That's not a good thing—see below.

Double messages

Alcohol, a natural product of fermentation, is probably the most widely used of all drugs. It has been a part of human culture since history began and part of American life since Europeans settled on this continent. "The good creature of God," colonial Americans called it—as well as "demon rum." At one time, beer or whiskey may have been safer to drink than well water, but there have always been many other reasons for drinking: the sociability of drinking, the brief but vivid sense of relaxation alcohol can bring, and the wish to celebrate or participate in religious and family rituals where alcohol is served. In some cultures, abstention is the rule. In others, the occasional use of alcohol is regarded as pleasurable and necessary—but such use is carefully controlled and intoxication frowned upon. Tradition and attitude play a powerful role in the use of this drug.

Some people, unfortunately, drink because of depression and/or addiction to alcohol. Apart from such needs, powerful social and economic forces encourage people to drink. For starters, alcoholic beverages are everywhere—from planes and trains to restaurants and county fairs. Also, drink is cheap. The relative cost of alcohol has declined in the last decades. Since 1967 the cost of soft drinks and milk has quadrupled, and the cost of all consumer goods has tripled, but the cost of alcohol has not even doubled. This is because the excise tax on alcohol is not indexed to inflation. Congress has raised the federal tax on beer and wine only once in 40 years (in 1990). The tax on hard liquor has been increased only twice—small raises in 1985 and 1990. Opinion polls have shown that the public is in favor of raising federal excise taxes on alcohol, but the alcohol industry successfully fights increases. Furthermore, about 20% of all alcohol is sold for business entertainment and is thus tax deductible, making it that much less costly to whoever pays the bar bill.

Finally, the alcohol, advertising, and entertainment industries tirelessly promote the idea that it's normal, desirable, smart, sophisticated, and sexy to drink. In print, on television, and at the movies, we see beautiful, healthy people drinking. Beer ads associate the product with sports events, fast cars, camaraderie, and sex. Hollywood's stars have always imbibed plentifully, on and off camera: "Here's looking at you, kid," echoes down the ages. Among modern American male writers, alcoholism has been a badge of the trade: Hemingway, Fitzgerald, and Faulkner were all alcoholics. In *The Thirsty Muse*, literary historian Tom Dardis cites the deadly effect of alcohol on male American writers, many of whom made a credo of heavy drinking.

Considering all these pro-drinking forces, it is amazing that 35% of us over 18 never drink, and another 35% drink lightly and only occasionally. It's equally amazing that our drinking levels have been declining for the past 10 years. But it's estimated that only 8% of us consume more than half of all the alcohol. Still, out-and-out alcoholism is only one factor in the grief caused by drinking, and alcohol problems are not a simple matter of the drunk versus the rest of us.

Alcohol's toll

It's a rare person in our society whose life goes untouched by alcohol. Alcohol causes, or is associated with, over 100,000 deaths every year, often among the young. In 1990, alcohol-related traffic crashes killed more than 22,000 people—almost the same number as homicides. Half the pedestrians killed by cars have elevated blood alcohol levels. At some time in their lives, 40% of all Americans will be involved in an alcohol-related traffic crash. Alcoholism creates unhealthy family dynamics, contributing to domestic violence and child abuse. Fetal alcohol syndrome, caused by drinking during pregnancy, is the leading known cause of mental retardation. After tobacco, alcohol is the leading cause of premature death in America. The total cost of alcohol use in America has been estimated at $86 billion annually, a figure so huge as to lose its meaning. But money is a feeble method for measuring the human suffering.

In a free society, banning alcohol is neither desirable nor acceptable. But government, schools, and other institutions could do more than they do to protect the public health, teach the young about the dangers of alcohol, and treat alcoholics. As individuals and as citizens, we could all contribute to reducing the toll alcohol exacts on American life.

Alcohol and the body: short-term effects

Five ounces of wine, 12 ounces of beer, and 1.5 ounces of 80-proof spirits—all average servings—put the same amount of pure alcohol (about 1/2 to 2/3 ounce) into the bloodstream. But how fast it gets into the blood depends on many things. Some alcohol is absorbed through the stomach lining, enabling it to reach the bloodstream very quickly. If the stomach is empty, absorption is even faster: food slows it down. Aspirin in the stomach can hasten alcohol absorption. Since the alcohol in beer and wine is less concentrated, it tends to be absorbed more slowly than straight whiskey (and presumably you drink beer and wine more slowly than a shot of whiskey). But downing two beers in an hour raises blood alcohol concentration (BAC) more than one drink of whisky sipped for an hour. It's the alcohol that counts. A BAC of 0.10 is defined as legal intoxication in most states (0.08 in California, Maine, Oregon, Utah, and Vermont). It's hard to predict BAC accurately, since so many factors affect it. But a 150-pound man typically reaches a BAC of 0.10 if he has two or three beers in an hour. Any BAC impairs driving ability.

It takes the body about two hours to burn half an ounce of pure alcohol (the amount in about one drink) in the bloodstream. Once the alcohol is there, you can't hurry up the process of metabolizing it. You can't run it off, swim it off, or erase the effects with coffee. Leaner, larger people will be less affected by a given amount of alcohol than smaller ones with more fatty tissue—women, for instance. The effects of a given BAC are also greater in older people than in younger.

Every cell in the body can absorb alcohol from the blood. Of the short-term effects, none is more dramatic than those on the central nervous system. At first the drinker gets a feeling of ease and exhilaration, usually short-lived. But as BAC rises, judgment, memory, and sensory perception are all progressively impaired. Thoughts become jumbled; concentration and insight are dulled. Depression usually sets in. Some people get angry or violent. Alcohol induces drowsiness but at the same time disrupts normal patterns of sleeping and dreaming. It also adversely affects sexual performance.

The most unpleasant physical after-effect of too much alcohol is a hangover: dry mouth, sour stomach, headache, depression, and fatigue. Its cause is over-indulgence—not, as some believe, "mixing" drinks or drinking "cheap booze." No remedy has ever been found for hangovers.

The heart effect: worth drinking for?

Much recent research shows that moderate drinkers have a lower risk of developing heart disease. Supposedly, this beneficial effect comes from alcohol's ability to raise HDL cholesterol, the "good" type that protects against atherosclerosis. Some researchers have suggested that only one kind of beverage—for example, red wine—is protective. But it's more likely to be alcohol itself. Still, it's only moderate drinking that's helpful, and some people can't stick to moderation, while others (pregnant women) shouldn't drink at all. Few doctors suggest that nondrinkers begin drinking to protect their hearts.

Different for a woman

The alcohol industry has tried for some time to hitch a ride on women's quest for equality. Liquor ads promote the idea that if a woman can work like a man, she can, and indeed should, drink like a man. Nothing could be further from the truth.

Today 55% of women drink alcoholic beverages, and 3% of all women consume more than two drinks a day. But the ads don't tell a woman that she'll get more intoxicated than a man from the same amount of alcohol. Alcohol is distributed through body water, and is more soluble in water than in fat. Since women tend to be smaller than men and have proportionately more fatty tissue and less body water than men, the blood alcohol concentration resulting from a given intake will be higher for a woman than for a man of the same size. Recent research also shows that the stomach enzyme that breaks down alcohol before it reaches the bloodstream is less active in women than in men.

This may explain why excessive drinking seems to have more serious long-term consequences for women. They develop cirrhosis (liver disease) at lower levels of alcohol intake than men, for instance, and alcohol also puts them at increased risk for osteoporosis.

Finally, pregnant women who drink heavily risk having babies with fetal alcohol syndrome—characterized by mental retardation, structural defects of the face and limbs, hyperactivity, and heart defects. Because no level of alcohol consumption during pregnancy is known to be safe, pregnant women (as well as women planning pregnancy or having unprotected intercourse) are advised not to drink and to continue to abstain while breastfeeding. The amount of alcohol that passes into breast milk is smaller than the amount that crosses the placenta during pregnancy, but recent studies suggest that even a small amount can inhibit motor development in an infant. The idea that drinking beer promotes milk supply and benefits the baby is a myth.

Heavy drinking: long-term effects

Chronic, excessive use of alcohol can seriously damage nearly every organ and function of the body. When alcohol is burned in the body it produces another, even more toxic substance, acetaldehyde, which contributes to the damage. Alcohol is a stomach irritant. It adversely affects the way the small intestine transports and absorbs nutrients, especially vitamins and minerals. Added to the usually poor diet of heavy drinkers, this often results in severe malnutrition. Furthermore, alcohol can produce pancreatic disorders. It causes fatty deposits to accumulate in the liver. Cirrhosis of the liver, an often fatal illness, may be the ultimate result. Though alcohol is not a food, it does have calories and can contribute to obesity.

The effects of heavy drinking on the cardiovascular system are no less horrific. For many years doctors have observed that hypertension and excessive alcohol use go together, and according to a number of recent studies, heavy drinkers are more likely to have high blood pressure than teetotalers. Heavy alcohol consumption damages healthy heart muscle and puts extra strain on already damaged heart muscle. And it can damage other muscles besides the heart.

Some of the worst effects of alcohol are directly on the brain. The most life-threatening is an acute condition leading to psychosis, confusion, or unconsciousness. Heavy drinkers also tend to be heavy smokers and are also more likely to take and abuse other drugs, such as tranquilizers. Excessive drinking, particularly in combination with tobacco, increases the chance of cancers of the mouth, larynx, and throat. Alcohol appears to play a role in stomach, colorectal, and esophageal cancers, as well as possibly liver cancer.

What causes alcoholism?

Alcoholism is a complex disorder: the official definition, recently devised by a 23-member committee of experts, is "a primary, chronic disease with genetic, psychosocial, and environmental factors influencing its development and manifestations. The disease is often progressive and fatal. It is characterized by impaired control over drinking, preoccupation with the drug alcohol, use of alcohol despite adverse consequences, and distortions in thinking, most notably denial."

Alcohol use, by itself, is not sufficient to cause alcoholism. Medical science cannot yet explain why one person abstains or drinks rarely, while another drinks to excess—or why some heavy drinkers are able to stop drinking, while others continue until they die of cirrhosis. One area currently under intensive investigation is heredity. Are children of heavy drinkers more likely to fall victim to alcohol than others?

The answer is yes, but not just because these children were raised in an adverse environment. Studies have shown that, even when raised in nonalcoholic households, a significant number of children of alcoholic parents become alcoholics. This suggests that the ability to handle alcohol may be in part genetically determined. Not long ago, researchers claimed to have located an alcoholism gene, setting off a bitter controversy and raising the possibility of testing children, job applicants, and even fetuses for latent alcoholism. But if there are alcoholism genes, they remain to be identified, and a test for potential alcoholism is a long way off. Researchers point to differences in blood enzymes among alcoholics and non-users—but do not know whether the difference is responsible for the alcoholism or the result of it. Perhaps the chemistry of the body will prove to be the key to whether a person can drink moderately or not. Though most investigators believe that alcoholism has genetic, as well as environmental, causes, this does not mean that any individual is "doomed" to be an alcoholic. Alcoholic parents don't always produce alcoholic children. And many alcoholics come from families where no one ever drank.

Alcoholism is treatable

One problem in treating alcoholism is that it is hard to recognize. A person who is chronically drunk in public is obviously an alcoholic. But not all alcoholics display their problem by falling down in the street, losing their jobs, causing traffic crashes, or getting arrested. Many drink secretly or only on weekends, only in the evening, or even only once a month. Some may drink from depression, while others are sensation-seekers. They may successfully hold down a job or practice a profession. Yet at some point, whatever their drinking patterns, they have lost their ability to control their use of alcohol.

Many of the serious physical and personal consequences of alcoholism can be halted or reversed if drinking is discontinued soon enough. There are many different approaches to alcoholism: Alcoholics Anonymous and similar 12-step programs, individual or group psychotherapy, hospitalization and detoxification, and other methods. No single system will work for everyone. For some people, a combination of methods can help. Others may do as well with individual counseling. Family therapy may help others. The families of alcoholics also need therapy and other forms of social support. Scientific data about treatment are inconclusive. The crucial factor, most experts agree, is for the drinker to recognize that a problem exists and to seek the kind of treatment he or she needs.

HIGH ANXIETY

The most widely used tranquilizer in America is more addictive than Valium—and is often less effective than nondrug treatments for anxiety.

The woman we'll call Rachel G.—now age 31—had experienced attacks of anxiety since she was a child. But those occasional incidents did not prevent her from marrying and taking a responsible job at an East Coast biotechnology company. Then, in late 1990 and early 1991, her life took a stressful turn. There was turmoil at the lab where she worked, her mother fell seriously ill, her grandmother committed suicide, and her marriage deteriorated. In early April of 1991, after a confrontation with her boss, she had a full-blown panic attack.

"I broke into a cold sweat," she recalls. "My heart was palpitating. I swore I was having a heart attack. I was scared that I was dying . . . . I couldn't walk. I couldn't even move." The attacks went on for two days.

Rachel G. went to a psychologist for help, and simultaneously asked her regular internist for a pill to ease her suffering. Her physician prescribed *Xanax* (alprazolam). That was no surprise. In 1990, *Xanax* had become the only drug ever approved by the U.S. Food and Drug Administration for the treatment of panic disorder—repeated, intense bouts of anxiety that can make life almost unbearable.

The drug gave her some relief, but she felt it wasn't really solving her problem. After about three months on *Xanax*, she tried to cut her dose in half. Within 48 hours, she recalls, "I couldn't sleep. My heart was racing, and I was getting dizzy spells." Only going back up to an intermediate dose would suppress the withdrawal symptoms.

In February 1992, Rachel G. began having frightening thoughts of killing herself. She visited a psychiatrist, who prescribed *Tofranil* (imipramine), an antidepressant that also works against panic. Today, she is doing well, still taking imipramine—and also *Xanax*. Though she feels the *Xanax* is no longer helping her, she can't bring herself to try to quit. "I know I'm going to have to experience the withdrawal symptoms," she says, "and those are the exact symptoms that I went on it to escape from in the first place."

Rachel G.'s problem is far from unusual. *Xanax* is not only the most common treatment for panic attacks, but also the drug most often prescribed for run-of-the-mill anxiety—the kind that anyone might experience during a rough period in life. It is now the nation's largest-selling psychiatric drug; more than that, it is the fifth most frequently prescribed drug in the U. S.

Even if you've never taken *Xanax* yourself, you almost certainly know someone who has. Yet the risks are significant. Anyone who takes *Xanax* for an extended period—even as little as a few weeks—risks developing a stubborn dependency on the drug.

Xanax is just the latest in a long line of tranquilizers that have promised to deliver psychiatry's holy grail: relief from anxiety with no significant side effects. And like the pills that came before it, *Xanax* has fallen short. As psychiatrists and their patients are discovering, *Xanax* does have some serious drawbacks—even more than the drugs it was supposed to improve on.

Like the sleeping pill *Halcion* (triazolam), its closest chemical relative, *Xanax* demonstrates that no pill can deliver peace of mind without a price. It also raises a troubling question: How did such a flawed drug become a pharmacological superstar?

The selling of *Xanax* has been fueled by a vigorous promotional campaign. The drug's manufacturer, the Upjohn Co., has made *Xanax* highly visible in the medical community by promoting it as a uniquely effective drug for panic disorder. But *Xanax* does not represent a remarkable treatment advance so much as a marketing coup. In fact, it is little different from other, related tranquilizers—members of the drug fam-

Anxious and blue? This ad suggests Xanax is especially useful for anxious people who are also depressed. While the FDA has approved this claim, many clinicians take issue with it.

Reprinted with permission from *Consumer Reports*, January 1993, pp. 19-24. © 1993 by Consumers Union of U.S., Inc., Yonkers, NY 10703-1057.

ily known as benzodiazepines, which have held an uneasy place in American culture for three decades.

Beyond Valium

Though the word "benzodiazepine" is meaningless to most people, the trade names of the drugs in this family are almost as familiar as *Kleenex* or *NutraSweet*. The first drug in this category, *Librium* (chlordiazepoxide), came on the market in 1960; *Valium* (diazepam) came along three years later.

In 1979, a survey showed that 11 percent of Americans were taking antianxiety drugs, mostly benzodiazepines. The figure has dropped only slightly since then.

That was also the year the hazards of these drugs gained national attention through hearings held by Senator Edward Kennedy. As the hearings made clear, *Valium* and similar drugs caused two major problems: Physical dependency and sedation. People on benzodiazepines often found that they couldn't stop taking the drugs, and that they couldn't function well while they were on them. The drugs accumulated in the body; over time, they made the user more and more sluggish, drowsy, and forgetful.

Ironically, while the Kennedy hearings offered frightening testimony on *Valium*, they also set the stage for the arrival of its successor, *Xanax*. Introduced in 1981, *Xanax* was hailed as the first of a new chemical class

The more things change . . . A 1967 CU report on Xanax's predecessor, Valium, pointed out that it didn't work much better than an inactive placebo in soothing the symptoms of anxiety.

of benzodiazepines that were completely eliminated from the body in less than half a day. Since *Xanax* didn't accumulate, the hope was that it wouldn't make people increasingly drowsy or slow them down as they continued to take it.

In addition to this chemical advantage, *Xanax* gave Upjohn a marketing edge. The patent on *Valium* expired in 1984, just as sales of *Xanax* were beginning to build. As generic competitors undercut *Valium's* sales, the drug's manufacturer promoted it less actively, and sales of *Valium* dropped further. Upjohn took advantage of the opportunity. By 1986, *Xanax* had overtaken *Valium* as the most widely prescribed benzodiazepine. By 1987, it reached fourth place on the national sales list of all prescription drugs. And in 1991, *Xanax* accounted for almost one-fifth of Upjohn's worldwide sales.

The trouble is, *Xanax* has now turned out to be more addictive than *Valium* itself.

Stuck on Xanax

All benzodiazepines produce physical dependency if you take them long enough. Over time, it seems, the brain "learns" to expect a certain level of the drug. If the drug is removed, the brain reacts with agitation, sleeplessness, and anxiety—the symptoms that led people to take the drug in the first place. Frequently, these symptoms are worse than the original ones, a phenomenon known

as the "rebound" effect. In addition, abrupt withdrawal from the drugs can cause muscle cramps and twitches, impaired concentration, and occasionally even seizures.

Unlike people who are addicted to cocaine and heroin, users of benzodiazepines don't develop a psychological craving for the drugs, or escalate the doses they take over time. But they do have a true physical dependency, and their withdrawal symptoms make the benzodiazepines extremely difficult to kick.

A number of clinical studies have found that *Xanax* and other benzodiazepines that are eliminated rapidly from the body produce a quicker, more severe rebound effect than drugs like *Valium* that are eliminated more slowly. Some people who take *Xanax* three times a day, a standard schedule for panic disorder, find that they even have symptoms as the drug wears off between one dose and the next.

In one major study, Dr. Karl Rickels and his colleagues at the University of Pennsylvania took 47 anxious patients who had been on benzodiazepines for a year or more and tried to take them off their medication. Fully 57 percent of the patients on *Xanax* and similar drugs simply could not stop taking them— but only 27 percent of the people on drugs like *Valium* were that physically dependent.

Other studies have produced similar results. A Yale study of patients

---

ALL-PURPOSE PRESCRIPTIONS

WHO TAKES XANAX, AND WHY?

Xanax presents a paradox: It is a powerful psychiatric drug, but it is most often prescribed for people who have no psychiatric diagnosis at all. While many of those people may be suffering from a serious problem with anxiety that is never recorded on a diagnostic chart, others may simply be people who ask their doctors for some relief from stress.

We analyzed data from the 1990 National Ambulatory Medical Care Survey, a representative sample of doctor's visits conducted periodically by the U.S. Government. Our analysis shows that the drug is prescribed by a wide range of different kinds of doctors, for people with a wide range of conditions—a situation that increases the odds of misuse.

Xanax is usually prescribed by physicians in general practice. In the 1990 study, only 30 percent of *Xanax* prescriptions were written by psychiatrists, whereas nearly half were written by family, general, and internal-medicine practitioners. (Various other specialists wrote the rest.)

Of all *Xanax* prescriptions, only 28 percent were written for people who were diagnosed with clinical anxiety or panic attacks.

Another 21 percent were for people diagnosed with depression, a condition for which the use of *Xanax* is still controversial. The rest were generally written for people who had no diagnosed psychiatric problem at all, although they did have a variety of medical diagnoses, the most frequent being high blood pressure. The statistics are similar to those obtained in another large national survey: IMS America, a private organization that monitors drug sales, found that only about one-fourth of all benzodiazepines prescribed in 1989 were given for anxiety-related conditions.

Many of those *Xanax* prescriptions may have been written appropriately for people suffering from short-term anxiety triggered by a medical problem. But the data, combined with the huge sales volume of *Xanax*, suggest that the drug may often be prescribed as an all-purpose stress reliever. The FDA-approved package insert (which can be requested from the pharmacist) states specifically that *Xanax* should not be given simply to help people deal with the "stress of everyday life," and that the drug should be given only as a short-term treatment for clear symptoms of anxiety, or as a treatment for full-blown anxiety or panic disorders.

who had taken *Xanax* in a four-month treatment program for panic attacks found that most of those who were still using the drug two years later had shifted to a lower dose—but only 30 percent had been able to quit the drug entirely. Similarly, a study of long-term *Xanax* users done at Toronto's Addiction Research Foundation found that two-thirds had tried to stop using the drug and failed.

The experience of individual doctors underscores the problem. In 1988, researchers at the Johns Hopkins School of Medicine interviewed 31 American physicians who specialized in helping people withdraw from the benzodiazepines. Asked which drugs were especially hard for patients to give up, 84 percent of the doctors specifically mentioned *Xanax,* while only 29 percent cited *Valium.* Even under the best of circumstances, clinicians have found that, to get people off *Xanax,* they must reduce the dose in tiny steps—a process that often takes months.

An 'eraser' for the mind?

The fact that so many people try so hard to quit *Xanax*—as difficult as that is to do—shows that it is not an entirely pleasant drug to take. One woman we spoke with, a 41-year-old technical writer in San Francisco, started taking *Xanax* to deal with bouts of anxiety that made her feel "like I was going headlong toward some frightening and dangerous unknown." After taking *Xanax* for 14 months, she decided to stop because, as she puts it, "It made me too stupid. I just couldn't function professionally. People would say things to me, and I'd be in a sort of fog and not be able to respond appropriately." (She ultimately succeeded in quitting, but had to go through a very difficult withdrawal process—even though she was taking a low dose, one her psychiatrist told her would not cause dependency.)

A 1990 report by the American Psychiatric Association backs up this woman's experience. It found that the benzodiazepines tend to impair memory; a person on one of these drugs may have difficulty retaining new information.

Clinicians report the same problem. "One patient of mine, a physician who took *Xanax,* described it as 'a big eraser.' It sort of wipes out people's attention to things," says Dr. Robert J. Gladstone, a psychiatrist in Carlisle, Mass. "I think all benzodi-

azepines cause memory lapses, especially in the elderly," says Dr. Stuart Yudofsky, chairman of the Department of Psychiatry at Baylor College of Medicine in Houston.

Yudofsky also refers to evidence that the drugs impair coordination. And in his own experience, he says, patients who have used benzodiazepines for years have often suffered falls and head injuries.

Xanax can also have the paradoxical effect of causing rage and hostility rather than tranquility. While this is relatively rare, it's another reason for caution in using a drug that many people will be all but unable to quit.

Despite the risks, benzodiazepines have one clear use: They can be helpful for people in crisis who need short-term anxiety relief. "They're appropriate for what are called adjustment reactions," says Dr. Peter Tyrer, a professor of psychiatry at St. Mary's Hospital Medical School in London and a longtime benzodiazepine researcher. "For example, if someone has been in a car accident and is nervous afterward when he goes out into the street, he could take *Xanax* for a short time after that."

The problem, though, is that many people who start taking tranquilizers for the short term end up staying on them over the long haul. "For anxiety, in general, these medications tend to be used much too long and in too high doses," says Dr. Yudofsky. "People get put on a drug, the reason for taking it passes, but they're maintained on it week after week, year after year. That's misuse." Even Upjohn, in its own labeling for *Xanax,* cautions that the drug has never been established as effective for use over more than four months.

Pushing the panic button

The people most at risk for becoming dependent on *Xanax* are those with panic disorder, because they are prescribed high doses of the drug for an extended period of time to deal with their chronic panic attacks. Since they suffer from severe or disabling anxiety, they might find dependency an acceptable price to pay for effective relief. But even though Upjohn built *Xanax's* reputation on studies of people with panic attacks, it's not at all clear how much they were really helped.

A panic attack is intense anxiety in a concentrated dose. Victims with a severe case may suffer several full-scale attacks a day, during which

their hearts race and they hyperventilate, sweat, tremble, and feel a profound sense of terror. According to the largest, most thorough survey of psychiatric problems, conducted in the 1980s by the National Institute of Mental Health (NIMH), between 4 and 7 percent of Americans have panic attacks that are frequent enough to be considered a panic disorder. The majority of people with panic disorder also have a related condition, agoraphobia—a term now used to describe a fear of ordinary activities, such as driving a car or shopping at the supermarket, that can leave the sufferer housebound.

By the early 1980s, researchers had begun to recognize that at least some types of benzodiazepines, in addition to easing ordinary anxiety, could also stop panic attacks. Upjohn proceeded to spend lavishly on studies to see whether *Xanax* could be used to treat panic disorder, and enlisted highly respected consultants in the effort. "The most senior psychiatrists in the world were . . . flooded with offers of consultancies [from Upjohn]," recalls Dr. Isaac Marks, a professor of experimental psychopharmacology at the University of London's Institute of Psychiatry.

In fact, the research could just as well have been done with another benzodiazepine—one called lorazepam (*Ativan*)—that is also cleared from the body quickly, and has also been shown to stop panic attacks. But this drug has not been under patent protection for years—and since it has not had the profit potential that *Xanax* has, it has not been aggressively tested and promoted. Today, a bottle of 100 one-milligram *Xanax* tablets costs $72.55, according to the Red Book, a standard drug price guide. The same amount of generic lorazepam in a therapeutically equivalent dose costs as little as $3.75.

Upjohn's major study on panic was a two-phase project called the Cross-National Panic Study. Phase One, conducted in the U.S., Canada, and Australia, involved more than 500 subjects with severe panic attacks; half received *Xanax* and half, a look-alike placebo. Phase Two, conducted in North and South America and Europe, enrolled 1122 subjects to compare *Xanax* not only with a placebo, but also with imipramine, an antidepressant from a different chemical class that also blocks panic attacks (even though it has never received formal FDA approval for

Street abuse Drug abusers traffic in Xanax because of an unusual property: When combined with methadone, Xanax produces a 'high' much like heroin, the drug methadone is meant to replace.

this use). At the time, the two studies were among the largest ever done on psychiatric drugs.

Well before the results were published, Upjohn used the research to promote its drug. The company sponsored conferences and symposiums on drug treatment for panic and anxiety, and then invited its consultants to speak at them—a strategy now used by many large pharmaceutical companies (see "Pushing Drugs to Doctors," CONSUMER REPORTS, February 1992). Many of those meetings were then written up in Upjohn-sponsored supplements to scientific journals, sent to thousands of psychiatrists in the U.S. and abroad.

When the Phase One results were finally published, they made a huge splash: Four articles on the study consumed the better part of the May 1988 issue of the *Archives of General Psychiatry*, the most prestigious psychiatric journal in the U.S. By that time, however, the international psychiatric community had already been hearing about *Xanax* as a treatment for panic for several years. Upjohn's publicity had made psychiatrists—and, later, general-practice physicians—more aware of *Xanax* than they were of other, similar drugs. It

HIGH NOTORIETY

HALCION AND PROZAC

Though *Xanax* is the best-selling psychiatric drug in the U.S., it's not the most notorious. Vying for that distinction are *Prozac,* a drug for depression, and *Halcion,* a benzodiazepine sold as a sleeping pill.

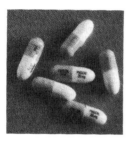

Both *Halcion* and *Prozac* have been reported to induce irrational behavior, including outbursts of murderous violence and suicide attempts. (*Halcion* was even blamed by some observers for President Bush's illness on his trip to Japan.) Lawsuits have been brought against their manufacturers, seeking damages for cases of suicide and assault committed by people taking the drugs. The accusations against both drugs prompted the U.S. Food and Drug Administration to ask expert committees to look at them more closely. Here's an update.

Prozac (fluoxetine)

Introduced in 1987 by the Eli Lilly Co., *Prozac* rocketed up the pharmaceutical bestseller list on the strength of Lilly's strenuous promotional efforts, its evident effectiveness against mild depression, and its relative absence of side effects. Overlooked in the initial enthusiasm for the drug, however, was the lack of evidence that *Prozac* worked well against *major* depression, a prolonged, serious psychiatric disorder that puts victims at high risk of suicide.

In any event, *Prozac*'s honeymoon ended three years ago, when a psychiatrist published a report on six chronically depressed patients who developed obsessive, violent suicidal thoughts after starting on the drug. The psychiatrist did emphasize that these six patients had unusually severe cases of depression; they had not responded to any other treatments, and five had had suicidal thoughts, though less severe ones, before they ever took *Prozac.* But those distinctions disappeared in the uproar that followed.

The FDA review panel, convened late in 1991, concluded that people taking *Prozac* did not seem to have any more suicidal or violent thoughts than patients on other antidepressants (though the panel recommended further monitoring of the drug, just in case). In the panel's view, the suicidal thinking some patients experienced was caused by the depression itself, not the drug.

Psychiatrists point out that patients can react "paradoxically" to almost any powerful drug, including *Prozac,* and therefore should be monitored closely—especially early in treatment, when they're getting used to the new drug. Meanwhile, *Prozac* remains the nation's best-selling antidepressant.

Halcion (triazolam)

Though marketed as a sleeping pill, not an antianxiety drug, *Halcion* is actually *Xanax*'s close chemical cousin. Like *Xanax, Halcion* is a benzodiazepine that's eliminated from the body very rapidly, meaning you can take it to get to sleep at night without being drowsy the next day. Upjohn started marketing *Halcion* in 1982; by 1987, the peak of its popularity, it was the 18th largest-selling prescription drug and the largest-selling sleeping pill in the U.S.

The disadvantages of *Halcion* eventually made themselves known. People who used it for any length of time found that, when they tried to stop, they experienced "rebound" insomnia worse than the original. There were also reports that *Halcion* seemed to make some people hostile or paranoid. The FDA was worried, and analyzed the thousands of voluntary reports of adverse reactions to *Halcion* the agency had received from doctors. *Halcion* indeed was linked to more hostility reactions than any other sleeping pill, relative to the numbers prescribed.

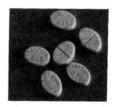

Another troublesome side effect also emerged: Some people who took even small doses experienced a bizarre reaction called anterograde amnesia. The day after they took *Halcion* to get to sleep they were up and about, apparently functioning normally. But later, they would have absolutely no memory of their actions. In 1991, *Halcion* was banned in the United Kingdom.

An FDA advisory committee decided, in May of 1992, to let *Halcion* stay on the U.S. market. But the panel agreed that the original recommended dose of 0.5 milligrams a day was too high, especially for elderly people; a lower dose of 0.25 milligrams was less likely to cause side effects (though it could also make the drug less effective). The committee also recommended strengthening the package insert's warnings on rebound insomnia and hostility reactions.

While the controversy over *Prozac* didn't seem to affect its upward sales trajectory, *Halcion*'s sales have suffered. By 1991 it had fallen to 38th place. And last November, in a widely publicized case, a Dallas jury decided *Halcion* had been partly responsible for driving a man to murder—a decision that may damage the drug's reputation even more.

almost certainly was responsible for the rapid growth of *Xanax* as a drug for all sorts of anxiety problems, not just panic disorder.

"The Cross-National Study was the best advertising ever done," says Dr. Rickels of the University of Pennsylvania. "Upjohn sold millions of doses of this drug before they even got it approved for panic."

No panacea for panic

Since receiving FDA approval to market *Xanax* for panic disorder, Upjohn has been using data from Phase One of the Cross-National Study in ads for the drug—including ads in journals for general-practice physicians. These doctors are likely to be unfamiliar with the actual results of the study, and to take Upjohn's word for what it showed. But despite the ads' claims, the study produced highly ambiguous results.

In the first four weeks of the eight-week study, *Xanax* looked much better than placebo treatment. By the fourth week, 50 percent of patients taking *Xanax* were completely free of panic attacks, versus 28 percent of those on an inactive placebo.

Many of Upjohn's ads for *Xanax* quote results from this midpoint of the study. But the drug's effectiveness was much less clear by the study's end. A look at the people who stayed in the study for the full eight weeks shows a remarkable picture: At the end of the study, there was no significant difference in the average number of panic attacks—or in functioning in work, home, and social life—between the people who had been taking *Xanax* and those who were taking placebos.

In addition, the Phase One study showed clearly how severe the "rebound" effect of *Xanax* withdrawal is. At the two study locations in Canada, 109 patients who had completed the eight weeks of treatment were observed as the dose of the drug (or placebo) was tapered down over a month's time. The *Xanax* group had averaged only 1.7 panic attacks a week—and the placebo group, 2.1 attacks a week—at the end of the eight-week treatment phase. But just two weeks after they stopped medication entirely, patients in the *Xanax* group were back up to 6.8 attacks a week—slightly worse off than they had been at the beginning of the study. By contrast, two weeks after the patients on placebo discontinued their "drug," they averaged only 1.8 panic attacks a week.

The findings are complicated by the Phase One study's greatest flaw:

About 10 percent of the people on *Xanax*, and half of those on placebo, dropped out between the fourth and the eighth week. At the time they left the study, the dropouts from the placebo group had more symptoms than people taking *Xanax*—a fact that would suggest the drug was doing some good. But many people on placebo may have been suffering from withdrawal symptoms, since many had been taking benzodiazepines just *before* they entered the study. There's also no way to tell whether they would have felt better by the end of the eight-week study if they had stuck it out, as other people in the group taking placebos did.

The findings of the Phase Two study were similar to Phase One's, except they also demonstrated that the antidepressant drug imipramine worked as well as *Xanax*. At the end of the eight weeks, 78 percent of people taking *Xanax* were panic-free, compared with 81 percent of those on imipramine and 75 percent of the people on placebo—virtually identical numbers.

Upjohn researchers and their supporters believe *Xanax* came out the clear winner in the studies. They point out that it acts much more quickly than imipramine and is easier to take. Imipramine is one of a class of antidepressants that can cause a range of unpleasant side effects, including sedation, dry mouth, severe constipation, blurred vision, weight gain, and impotence.

But other psychiatrists focus on the fact that people taking placebos did nearly as well as those on *Xanax* by the end of the study—and avoided the rebound effect that plagued people on the real drug. That suggests that for many people, the mere act of visiting a doctor might have been reassuring enough to produce a measurable decrease in symptoms. It also suggests that nondrug treatment could help many other panic sufferers learn how to control their symptoms.

The same may be true for people who have more generalized anxiety—a form of chronic, excessive worrying, combined with physical and emotional symptoms, that affects about 4 percent of Americans, according to NIMH estimates. *Xanax* itself, surprisingly, has never been tested as a long-term treatment for such chronic anxiety disorders. But Dr. David Barlow, a clinical psychologist who directs the Center for Stress and Anxiety Disorders of the State University of New York at Albany, points out that the benzodi-

azepines in general have not proved effective for treating these problems—except to offer temporary relief of symptoms.

Barlow reviewed two decades' worth of studies that used benzodiazepines to treat chronic anxiety. He observed that patients in the "control" groups for these studies—that is, patients who received inactive placebo pills—generally improved over time. In many cases, their anxiety decreased as much as that of the people who were on the real drugs. This suggests that chronic anxiety waxes and wanes over time, and that drugs may have little effect after their initial benefit.

Recommendations

If anxiety is an inevitable part of the human condition, then the wish for a magic potion to banish anxiety is probably a timeless human desire. In our own time, drug companies have marketed one tranquilizer after another, each one supposedly safer and more effective than the one before. But tranquilizers—in particular, the benzodiazepines—are still powerful, potentially dangerous drugs, subject to abuse and misuse.

Given the hazards and their widespread use, we still know surprisingly little about the risks and benefits of long-term benzodiazepine use—and too little in particular about *Xanax*, now the leader of the pack.

No one knows how many people are physically dependent on *Xanax* and how they may be affected by it. But there are some warning signs. A recent FDA analysis of reports of adverse reactions to drugs, which physicians send to the agency voluntarily, showed a number of cases in which the drug seemed to cause bouts of rage and hostility. Those side effects were rare, and were much less common with *Xanax* than with *Halcion*. But they were six times more common with *Xanax* than with *Ativan*, relative to each drug's sales. And *Ativan's* suspected side effects have been cited in a pending British class-action lawsuit against its manufacturer.

Consumers Union believes that more information is necessary to determine the frequency of side effects from *Xanax*—not only its effects on mood, but its potential for impairing memory and causing other cognitive problems. Careful surveillance of the drug's clinical use could do much to resolve these questions.

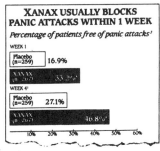

As time goes by A 1991 Upjohn ad ran the chart below showing that nearly half of Xanax patients were panic-free after four weeks of treatment, versus just one in four people on placebo. What the ad didn't show: By the eighth week, placebo patients who finished the study were panic-free almost as often as patients on Xanax were.

XANAX USUALLY BLOCKS PANIC ATTACKS WITHIN 1 WEEK
Percentage of patients free of panic attacks

WEEK 1
Placebo (n=259) — 16.9%
XANAX (n=203) — 33.2%

WEEK 4
Placebo (n=259) — 27.1%
XANAX (n=203) — 46.8%

In the meantime, if you or a loved one has a serious problem with anxiety, you need to understand your options clearly.

If you're not normally an anxious person, but are going through a particularly difficult time—a divorce or the death of a parent, for instance—you may be able to handle your anxiety with no professional help, or perhaps with a few visits to a psychotherapist to talk about the immediate stress. According to Dr. Yudofsky of Baylor, exercise, dietary changes (such as giving up caffeine), and other lifestyle changes can also help keep anxiety in check.

It can also be useful, and appropriate, to take *Xanax* or another benzodiazepine to cope with acute stress—as long as you take the drug carefully. If your doctor prescribes one of these drugs, take it at the lowest dose possible and for the shortest time possible. Remember that even a few weeks of daily *Xanax* use can lead to dependency.

If you're suffering from panic disorder, agoraphobia, or chronic anxiety, you have a serious problem that requires professional evaluation and treatment by a psychiatrist or psychologist. It's not clear, however, that drug treatment should be your first option. CU's medical consultants recommend seeing a mental-health professional who is familiar with cognitive-behavioral therapy (described below) before resorting to tranquilizers. Our consultants who have experience in both drug and nondrug therapy generally try the nondrug approaches first.

Whatever your problem is, you should avoid *Xanax* and its chemical cousins if you have any history of alcohol abuse or previous problems with other benzodiazepines. Those factors in your personal history make it more likely that you will become dependent on the drug. Alternative forms of drug therapy may be less risky. Antidepressants like imipramine can block panic attacks as effectively as *Xanax* can. For people with chronic anxiety who do not have panic attacks, a drug called *BuSpar* (buspirone) can frequently reduce anxiety and does not cause the sedation or physical dependency produced by the benzodiazepines.

Finally, if your physician does prescribe *Xanax* or another benzodiazepine, question him or her closely about how long you are expected to take the medication and exactly how you are to withdraw from it. While on the medication, use extreme caution when driving, since these drugs can impair coordination. Do not exceed the prescribed dose, and do not drink alcohol while on the drug. (The interaction can be disastrous; at the least, it can worsen the slurred speech, poor coordination, drowsiness, and mental slowness that often stem from use of benzodiazepines.) Inform your doctor immediately of any unexpected side effects, such as feelings of rage or agitation. And seriously consider trying some sort of psychotherapy to gain insight into your problem.

> **Long-term users** Among people who use benzodiazepines for a year or more, about 70 percent are older than 50; about 60 percent are women.

SHORT-TERM PSYCHOTHERAPY

RELIEF WITHOUT DRUGS

People with serious anxiety—including those with panic attacks—don't need to choose between a life on tranquilizers and a life under severe stress. The past decade has seen the development of a new type of nondrug treatment called cognitive-behavioral therapy. While it doesn't give the immediate relief of a drug like *Xanax*, it does produce results quickly—and may be the most helpful approach over the long term.

Cognitive-behavioral therapists believe that many people, perhaps even most, have panic symptoms at one time or another—a stressful situation, for example, may trigger a racing heartbeat or rapid breathing. These symptoms usually pass quickly, and most people never give them a second thought. But a few people overreact intensely when they experience panic symptoms; they misinterpret them as symptoms of impending insanity or death.

"They tend to catastrophize their symptoms," explains Dr. Robert Liberman, who treats panic-attack patients at the UCLA Neuropsychiatric Institute. "Anyone might feel dizzy getting suddenly out of a chair. A person vulnerable to panic might exaggerate that feeling, leading to sustained feelings of panic."

Cognitive-behavioral therapy works by teaching panic victims a new way of thinking about their physical symptoms. "The therapies consciously induce panic sensations—spinning patients on a chair to get dizzy, or having them run up and down stairs to get out of breath," Liberman says. "Even when their heart is pounding, and they're short of breath and dizzy, they learn that nothing terrible happens and that these sensations naturally subside."

This technique and variations on it have been studied at a number of centers, with consistent results: After an average of a dozen weekly sessions, patients have few or no panic symptoms. More important, they maintain their improvement for a year or more.

Dr. David Barlow and his colleagues at the Center for Stress and Anxiety Disorders in Albany conducted one such study, comparing cognitive-behavioral therapy with *Xanax* and placebo over 15 weeks. The *Xanax* and behavior-therapy groups experienced roughly equivalent declines in general anxiety. But two weeks after the study ended, 87 percent of the behavior-therapy patients were completely free of panic attacks, while half of those in the *Xanax* group were still having attacks, even though almost all were still on the drug. Late in 1991, cognitive-behavioral therapy was endorsed by an expert panel convened by the National Institutes of Health to evaluate treatments for panic disorder.

Short-term therapy for depression had similarly positive results in a study conducted over the past decade by the National Institute of Mental Health. For people with mild to moderate depression, both cognitive therapy and a form of short-term treatment called interpersonal psychotherapy worked as well as drug treatment (in this case, imipramine). For patients with severe depression, drug treatment worked slightly better than either kind of therapy.

Despite the evident advantages of cognitive-behavioral therapy, it is still less accessible to most people than drug treatments. Relatively few psychologists and psychiatrists are trained in this form of therapy. Most health-insurance plans reimburse poorly for psychotherapy. And without the kind of expensive publicity that the drug companies can put behind their products, nondrug approaches have received less attention than they deserve.

Not everyone is a good candidate for cognitive-behavioral therapy. "You have to have someone who is highly motivated, and some people having prolonged and frequent panic attacks are just not able to endure the pain," says Dr. John Pecknold, a McGill University psychiatrist who participated in Upjohn's *Xanax* study.

Nevertheless, CU's medical consultants believe psychiatrists and their patients should more frequently consider this kind of short-term therapy as a treatment for anxiety and other psychological problems. These focused, effective methods entail less risk and offer better long-term results than drug therapy generally produces. They may also have the potential to be highly cost-effective. One recent study, for example, found even a single therapy session helped many people with panic attacks to overcome the problem.

This glossary of psychology terms is included to provide you with a convenient and ready reference as you encounter general terms in your study of personal growth and behavior that are unfamiliar or require a review. It is not intended to be comprehensive, but, taken together with the many definitions included in the articles themselves, it should prove to be quite useful.

Abnormal Irregular, deviating from the norm or average. Abnormal implies the presence of a mental disorder that leads to behavior that society labels as deviant. There is a continuum between normal and abnormal. These are relative terms in that they imply a social judgment. See Normal.

Accommodation Process in cognitive development; involves altering or reorganizing the mental picture to make room for a new experience or idea.

Acetylcholine A neurotransmitter involved in memory.

Achievement Drive The need to attain self-esteem, success, or status. Society's expectations strongly influence the achievement motive.

ACTH (Adrenocorticotropic Hormone) The part of the brain called the hypothalamus activates the release of the hormone ACTH from the pituitary gland when a stressful condition exists. ACTH in turn activates the release of adrenal corticoids from the cortex of the adrenal gland.

Action Therapy A general classification of therapy (as opposed to insight therapy) in which the therapist focuses on symptoms rather than on underlying emotional states. Treatment aims at teaching new behavioral patterns rather than at self-understanding. See Insight Therapy.

Actor-Observer Attribution The tendency to attribute the behavior of other people to internal causes and the behavior of yourself to external causes.

Adaptation The process of responding to changes in the environment by altering one's responses to keep one's behavior appropriate to environmental demands.

Addiction Physical dependence on a drug. When a drug causes biochemical changes that are uncomfortable when the drug is discontinued, when one must take ever larger doses to maintain the intensity of the drug's effects, and when desire to continue the drug is strong, one is said to be addicted.

Adjustment How we react to stress; some change that we make in response to the demands placed upon us.

Adrenal Glands Endocrine glands involved in stress and energy regulation.

Affective Disorder Affect means feeling or emotion. An affective disorder is mental illness marked by a disturbance of mood (e.g., manic depression.)

Afferent Neuron (Sensory) A neuron that carries messages from the sense organs toward the central nervous system.

Aggression Any act that causes pain or suffering to another. Some psychologists believe that aggressive behavior is instinctual to all species, including man, while others believe that it is learned through the processes of observation and imitation.

Alienation Indifference to or loss of personal relationships. An individual may feel estranged from family members, or, on a broader scale, from society.

All-or-None Law The principle that states that a neuron only fires when a stimulus is above a certain minimum strength (threshold), and that when it fires, it does so at full strength.

Altered State of Consciousness (ASC) A mental state qualitatively different from a person's normal, alert, waking consciousness.

Altruism Behavior motivated by a desire to benefit another person. Altruistic behavior is aided by empathy and is usually motivated internally, not by observable threats or rewards.

Amphetamine A psychoactive drug that is a stimulant. Although used in treating mild depressions or, in children, hyperactivity, its medical uses are doubtful, and amphetamines are often abused. See Psychoactive Drug.

Anal Stage Psychosexual stage, during which, according to Freud, the child experiences the first restrictions on his impulses.

Antisocial Personality Disorder Personality disorder in which individuals who engaged in antisocial behavior experience no guilt or anxiety about their actions; sometimes called sociopathy or psychopathy.

Anxiety An important term that has different meanings for different theories (psychoanalysis, behavior theory); a feeling state of apprehension, dread, or uneasiness. The state may be aroused by an objectively dangerous situation or by a situation that is not objectively dangerous. It may be mild or severe.

Anxiety Disorder Fairly long-lasting disruptions of the person's ability to deal with stress; often accompanied by feelings of fear and apprehension.

Applied Psychology The area of psychology that is most immediately concerned with helping to solve practical problems; includes clinical and counseling psychology, and industrial, environmental, and legal psychology.

Aptitude Tests Tests which are designed to predict what can be accomplished by a person in the future with the proper training.

Arousal A measure of responsiveness or activity; a state of excitement or wakefulness ranging from deepest coma to intense excitement.

Aspiration Level The level of achievement a person strives for. Studies suggest that people can use internal or external standards of performance.

Assertiveness Training Training which helps individuals stand up for their rights while not denying rights of other people.

Assimilation Process in cognitive development; occurs when something new is taken into the child's mental picture of the world.

Association Has separate meanings for different branches of psychology. Theory in cognitive psychology suggests that we organize information so that we can find our memories systematically, that one idea will bring another to mind. In psychoanalysis, the patient is asked to free associate (speak aloud all consecutive thoughts until random associations tend of themselves to form a meaningful whole). See Cognitive Psychology; Psychoanalysis.

Association Neurons Neurons that connect with other neurons.

Associationism A theory of learning suggesting that once two stimuli are presented together, one of them will remind a person of the other. Ideas are learned by association with sensory experiences and are not innate. Among the principles of associationism are contiguity (stimuli that occur close together are more likely to be associated than stimuli far apart), and repetition (the more frequently stimuli occur together, the more strongly they become associated).

Attachment Process in which the individual shows behaviors that promote the proximity or contact with a specific object or person.

Attention The tendency to focus activity in a particular direction and to select certain stimuli for further analysis while ignoring or possibly storing for further analysis all other inputs.

Attitude An overall tendency to respond positively or negatively to particular people or objects in a way that is learned through experience and that is made up of feelings (affects), thoughts (evaluations), and actions (conation).

Attribution The process of determining the causes of behavior in a given individual.

Autism A personality disorder in which a child does not respond socially to people.

Autonomic Nervous System The part of the nervous system (the other part is the central nervous system) that is for emergency functions and release of large amounts of energy (sympathetic division) and regulating functions such as digestion and sleep (parasympathetic division). See Biofeedback.

Aversion Therapy A counterconditioning therapy in which unwanted responses are paired with unpleasant consequences.

Avoidance Conditioning Situation in which a subject learns to avoid an aversive stimulus by responding appropriately before it begins.

Barbiturates Sedative-hypnotic, psychoactive drugs widely used to induce sleep and to reduce tension. Overuse can lead to addiction. See Addiction.

Behavior Any observable activity of an organism, including mental processes.

Behavior Therapy The use of conditioning processes to treat mental disorders. Various techniques may be used, including positive reinforcement in which rewards (verbal or tangible) are given to the patient for appropriate behavior, modeling in which patients unlearn fears by watching models exhibit fearlessness, and systematic desensitization in which the patient is taught to relax and visualize anxiety-producing items at the same time. See Insight Therapy; Systematic Desensitization.

Behaviorism A school of psychology stressing an objective approach to psychological questions, proposing that psychology be limited to observable behavior and that the subjectiveness of consciousness places it beyond the limits of scientific psychology.

Biofeedback The voluntary control of physiological processes by receiving information about those processes as they occur, through instruments that pick up these changes and display them to the subject in the form of a signal. Blood pressure, skin temperature, etc. can be controlled.

Biological (Primary) Motives Motives that have a physiological basis; include hunger, thirst, body temperature regulation, avoidance of pain, and sex.

Biological Response System System of the body that is particularly important in behavioral responding; includes the senses, endocrines, muscles, and the nervous system.

Biological Therapy Treatment of behavior problems through biological techniques; major biological therapies include drug therapy, psychosurgery, and electronconvulsive therapy.

Bipolar Disorder Affective disorder that is characterized by extreme mood swings from sad depression to joyful mania; sometimes called manic-depression.

Body Language Communication through position and movement of the body.

Brain Mapping A procedure for identifying the function of various areas of the brain; the surgeon gives tiny electrical stimulation to a specific area and notes patient's reaction.

Brain Stimulation The introduction of chemical or electrical stimuli directly into the brain.

Brain Waves Electrical responses produced by brain activity that can be recorded directly from any portion of the brain or from the scalp with special electrodes. Brain waves are measured by an electroencephalograph (EEG). Alpha waves occur during relaxed wakefulness and beta waves during active behavior. Theta waves are associated with drowsiness and vivid visual imagery, delta waves with deep sleep.

Cannon-Bard Theory of Emotion Theory of emotion that states that the emotional feeling and the physiological arousal occur at the same time.

Causal Attribution Process of determining whether a person's behavior is due to internal or external motives.

Cautious Shift Research suggests that the decisions of a group will be more conservative than that of the average individual member when dealing with areas for which there are widely held values favoring caution (e.g., physical danger or family responsibility). See Risky Shift.

Central Nervous System The part of the human nervous system that interprets and stores messages from the sense organs, decides what behavior to exhibit, and sends appropriate messages to the muscles and glands; includes the brain and spinal cord.

Central Tendency In statistics, measures of central tendency give a number that represents the entire group or sample.

Cerebellum The part of the brain responsible for muscle and movement control and coordination of eye-body movement.

Cerebral Cortex The part of the brain consisting of the outer layer of cerebral cells. The cortex can be divided into specific regions: sensory, motor, and associative.

Chaining Behavior theory suggests that behavior patterns are built up of component parts by stringing together a number of simpler responses.

Character Disorder (or Personality Disorder) A classification of psychological disorders (as distinguished from neurosis or psychosis). The disorder has become part of the individual's personality and does not cause him or her discomfort, making that disorder more difficult to treat psychotherapeutically.

Chromosome See Gene.

Chunking The tendency to code memories so that there are fewer bits to store.

Classical Conditioning See Pavlovian Conditioning.

Client-Centered Therapy A nondirective form of psychotherapy developed by Carl Rogers in which the counselor attempts to create an atmosphere in which the client can freely explore herself or himself and her or his problems. The client-centered therapist reflects what the client says back to him, usually without interpreting it.

Clinical Psychology The branch of psychology concerned with testing, diagnosing, interviewing, conducting research and treating (often by psychotherapy) mental disorders and personality problems.

Codependency The relationship of one person to a second person who is often a substance abuser. The codependent assists or enables the abuser to continue the drug dependency or problem behavior. The codependent becomes as addicted to the enabling life-style as the abuser is to the problem behavior or substance.

Cognitive Appraisal Intellectual evaluation of situations or stimuli. Experiments suggest that emotional arousal is produced not simply by a stimulus but by how one evaluates and interprets the arousal. The appropriate physical response follows this cognitive appraisal.

Cognitive Behavior Therapy A form of behavior therapy that identifies self-defeating attitudes and thoughts in a subject, and then helps the subject to replace these with positive, supportive thoughts.

Cognitive Dissonance People are very uncomfortable if they perceive that their beliefs, feelings, or acts are not consistent with one another, and they will try to reduce the discomfort of this dissonance.

Cognitive Psychology The study of how individuals gain knowledge of their environments. Cognitive psychologists believe that the organism actively participates in constructing the meaningful stimuli that it selectively organizes and to which it selectively responds.

Comparative Psychology The study of similarities and differences in the behavior of different species.

Compulsive Personality Personality disorder in which an individual is preoccupied with details and rules.

Concept Learning The acquisition of the ability to identify and use the qualities that objects or situations have in common. A class concept refers to any quality that breaks objects or situations into separate groupings.

Concrete-Operational Stage A stage in intellectual development, according to Piaget. The child at approximately seven years begins to apply logic. His or her thinking is less egocentric, reversible, and the child develops conservation abilities and the ability to classify.

Conditioned Reinforcer Reinforcement that is effective because it has been associated with other reinforcers. Conditioned reinforcers are involved in higher order conditioning.

Conditioned Response (CR) The response or behavior that occurs when the conditioned stimulus is presented (after the conditioned stimulus has been associated with the unconditioned stimulus).

Conditioned Stimulus (CS) An originally neutral stimulus that is associated with an unconditioned stimulus and takes on its capability of eliciting a particular reaction.

Conditioned Taste Aversion (CTA) Learning an aversion to particular tastes by associating them with stomach distress; usually considered a unique form of classical conditioning because of the extremely long interstimulus intervals involved.

Conduction The ability of a neuron to carry a message (an electrical stimulus) along its length.

Conflict Situation that occurs when we experience incompatible demands or desires.

Conformity The tendency of an individual to act like others regardless of personal belief.

Conscience A person's sense of the moral rightness or wrongness of behavior.

Consciousness Awareness of experienced sensations, thoughts, and feelings at any given point in time.

Consensus In causal attribution, the extent to which other people react the same way the subject does in a particular situation.

Consistency In causal attribution, the extent to which the subject always behaves in the same way in a particular situation.

Consolidation The biological neural process of making memories permanent; possibly short-term memory is electrically coded and long-term memory is chemically coded.

Continuum of Preparedness Seligman's proposal that animals are biologically prepared to learn certain responses more readily than others.

Control Group A group used for comparison with an experimental group. All conditions must be identical for each group with the exception of the one variable (independent) that is manipulated. See Experimental Group.

Convergence Binocular depth cue in which we detect distance by interpreting the kinesthetic sensations produced by the muscles of the eyeballs.

Convergent Thinking The kind of thinking that is used to solve problems having only one correct answer. See Divergent Thinking.

Conversion Disorder Somatoform disorder in which a person displays obvious disturbance in the nervous system, however, a medical examination reveals no physical basis for the problem; often includes paralysis, loss of sensation, or blindness.

Corpus Callosum Nerve fibers that connect the two halves of the brain in humans. If cut, the halves continue to function although some functions are affected.

Correlation A measurement in which two or more sets of variables are compared and the extent to which they are related is calculated.

Correlation Coefficient The measure, in number form, of how two variables vary together. They extend from -1 (perfect negative correlation) to a $+1$ (perfect positive correlation).

Counterconditioning A behavior therapy in which an unwanted response is replaced by conditioning a new response that is incompatible with it.

Creativity The ability to discover or produce new solutions to problems, new inventions, or new works of art. Creativity is an ability independent of IQ and is opened-ended in that solutions are not predefined in their scope or appropriateness. See Problem Solving.

Critical Period A specific stage in an organism's development during which the acquisition of a particular type of behavior depends on exposure to a particular type of stimulation.

Cross-Sectional Study A research technique that focuses on a factor in a group of subjects as they are at one time, as in a study of fantasy play in subjects of three different age groups. See Longitudinal Study.

Culture-Bound The idea that a test's usefulness is limited to the culture in which it was written and utilized.

Curiosity Motive Motive that causes the individual to seek out a certain amount of novelty.

Cutaneous Sensitivity The skin senses: touch, pain, pressure and temperature. Skin receptors respond in different ways and with varying degrees of sensitivity.

Decay Theory of forgetting in which sensory impressions leave memory traces that fade away with time.

Defense Mechanism A way of reducing anxiety that does not directly cope with the threat. There are many types, denial, repression, etc., all of which are used in normal functioning. Only when use is habitual or they impede effective solutions are they considered pathological.

Delusion A false belief that persists despite evidence showing it to be irrational. Delusions are often symptoms of mental illness.

Dependent Variable Those conditions that an experimenter observes and measures. Called "dependent" because they depend on the experimental manipulations.

Depersonalization Disorder Dissociative disorder in which individuals escape from their own personalities by believing that they don't exist or that their environment is not real.

Depression A temporary emotional state that normal individuals experience or a persistent state that may be considered a psychological disorder. Characterized by sadness and low self-esteem. *See* Self-Esteem.

Descriptive Statistics Techniques that help summarize large amounts of data information.

Developmental Norms The average time at which developmental changes occur in the normal individual.

Developmental Psychology The study of changes in behavior and thinking as the organism grows from the prenatal stage to death.

Deviation, Standard and Average Average deviation is determined by measuring the deviation of each score in a distribution from the mean and calculating the average of the deviations. The standard deviation is used to determine how representative the mean of a distribution is. *See* Mean.

Diagnostic and Statistical Manual of Mental Disorders (DSM) DSM-III was published in 1980 by the American Psychiatric Association.

Diffusion of Responsibility As the number of witnesses to a help-requiring situation—and thus the degree of anonymity—increases, the amount of helping decreases and the amount of time before help is offered increases.

Discrimination The ability to tell whether stimuli are different when presented together or that one situation is different from a past one.

Displacement The process by which an emotion originally attached to a particular person, object, or situation is transferred to something else.

Dissociative Disorders Disorders in which individuals forget who they are.

Distal Stimuli Physical events in the environment that affect perception. *See* Proximal Stimuli.

Distinctiveness In causal attribution, the extent to which the subject reacts the same way in other situations.

Divergent Thinking The kind of thinking that characterizes creativity (as contrasted with convergent thinking) and involves the development of novel resolutions of a task or the generation of totally new ideas. *See* Convergent Thinking.

DNA *See* Gene.

Double Bind A situation in which a person is subjected to two conflicting, contradictory demands at the same time.

Down's Syndrome Form of mental retardation caused by having three number 21 chromosomes (trisomy 21).

Dreams The thoughts, images, and emotions that occur during sleep. Dreams occur periodically during the sleep cycle and are usually marked by rapid movements of the eyes (REM sleep). The content of dreams tends to reflect emotions (sexual feelings, according to Freud) and experiences of the previous day. Nightmares are qualitatively different from other dreams, often occurring during deep or Stage 4 sleep.

Drive A need or urge that motivates behavior. Some drives may be explained as responses to bodily needs, such as hunger or sex. Others derive from social pressures and complex forms of learning, for example, competition, curiosity, achievement, *See* Motivation.

Drive Reduction Theory Theory of motivation that states that the individual is pushed by inner forces toward reducing the drive and restoring homeostasis.

Drug Dependence A state of mental or physical dependence on a drug, or both. Psychoactive drugs are capable of creating psychological dependence (anxiety when the drug is unavailable), although the relationship of some, such as marijuana and LSD, to physical dependence or addiction is still under study. *See* Psychoactive Drug; Addiction.

Drug Tolerance A state produced by certain psychoactive drugs in which increasing amounts of the substance are required to produce the desired effect. Some drugs produce tolerance but not withdrawal symptoms, and these drugs are not regarded as physically addicting.

Effectance Motive The striving for effectiveness in dealing with the environment. The effectance motive differs from the need for achievement in that effectance depends on internal feelings of satisfaction while the need for achievement is geared more to meeting others' standards.

Efferent Neuron (Motor) A neuron that carries messages from the central nervous system to the muscles and glands.

Ego A construct to account for the organization in a person's life and for making the person's behavior correspond to physical and social realities. According to Freud, the ego is the "reality principle" that is responsible for holding the id or "pleasure principle" in check. *See* Id.

Egocentrism Seeing things from only one's own point of view; also, the quality of a child's thought that prevents her or him from understanding that different people perceive the world differently. Egocentrism is characteristic of a stage that all children go through.

Electra Complex The libidinal feelings of a child toward a parent of the opposite sex. *See also* Oedipus Complex

Electroshock Therapy A form of therapy used to relieve severe depression. The patient receives electric current across the forehead, loses consciousness, and undergoes a short convulsion. When the patient regains consciousness, his or her mood is lifted.

Emotion A complex feeling-state that involves physiological arousal; a subjective feeling which might involve a cognitive appraisal of the situation and overt behavior in response to a stimulus.

Empathy The ability to appreciate how someone else feels by putting yourself in her or his position and experiencing her or his feelings. Empathy is acquired normally by children during intellectual growth.

Empiricism The view that behavior is learned through experience.

Encounter Groups Groups of individuals who meet to change their personal lives by confronting each other, discussing personal problems, and talking more honestly and openly than in everyday life.

Endocrine Glands Ductless glands that secrete chemicals called hormones into the blood stream.

Equilibration According to Piaget, the child constructs an understanding of the world through equilibration. Equilibration consists of the interaction of two complementary processes, assimilation (taking in input within the existing structures of the mind, e.g., putting it into mental categories that already exist) with accommodation (the changing of mental categories to fit new input that cannot be taken into existing categories) and is the process by which knowing occurs. One's developmental stage affects how one equilibrates.

Ethnocentrism The belief that one's own ethnic or racial group is superior to others.

Experiment Procedures executed under a controlled situation in order to test a hypothesis and discover relationships between independent and dependent variables.

Experimental Control The predetermined conditions, procedures, and checks built into the design of an experiment to ensure scientific control; as opposed to "control" in common usage, which implies manipulation.

Experimental Group In a scientific experiment, the group of subjects that is usually treated specially, as opposed to the control group, in order to isolate just the variable under investigation. *See* Control Group.

Experimental Psychology The branch of psychology concerned with the laboratory study of basic psychological laws and principles as demonstrated in the behavior of animals.

Experimenter Bias How the expectations of the person running an experiment can influence what comes out of the experiment. Experimenter bias can affect the way the experimenter sees the subjects' behavior, causing distortions of fact, and can also affect the way the experimenter reads data, also leading to distortions.

Extinction The elimination of behavior by, in classical conditioning, the withholding of the unconditional stimulus, and in operant conditioning, the withholding of the reinforcement.

Extrasensory Perception (ESP) The range of perceptions that are "paranormal," (such as the ability to predict events, reproduce drawings sealed in envelopes, etc.).

Fixed Interval (FI) Schedule Schedule of reinforcement in which the subject receives reinforcement for the first correct response given after a specified time interval.

Fixed Ratio (FR) Schedule Schedule of reinforcement in which the subject is reinforced after a certain number of responses.

Fixed-Action Pattern Movement that is characteristic of a species and does not have to be learned.

Forgetting The process by which material that once was available is no longer available. Theory exists that forgetting occurs because memories interfere with one another, either retroactively (new memories block old) or proactively (old memories block new); that forgetting occurs when the cues necessary to recall the information are not supplied, or when memories are too unpleasant to remain in consciousness. *See* Repression.

Formal Operational Stage According to Piaget, the stage at which the child develops adult powers of reasoning, abstraction, and symbolizing. The child can grasp scientific, religious, and political concepts and deduce their consequences as well as reason hypothetically ("what if . . .").

Frustration A feeling of discomfort or insecurity aroused by a blocking of gratification or by unresolved problems. Several theories hold that frustration arouses aggression. *See* Aggression.

Functionalism An early school of psychology stressing the ways behavior helps one adapt to the environment and the role that learning plays in this adaptive process.

Gene The unit of heredity that determines particular characteristics; a part of a molecule of DNA. DNA (dioxyribonucleic acid) is found mainly in the nucleus of living cells where it occurs in threadlike structures called chromosomes. Within the chromosomes, each DNA molecule is organized into specific units that carry the genetic information necessary for the development of a particular trait. These units are the genes. A gene can reproduce itself exactly, and this is how traits are carried between generations. The genotype is the entire structure of genes that are inherited by an organism from its parents. The environment interacts with this genotype to determine how the genetic potential will develop.

General Adaptation Syndrome (GAS) The way the body responds to stress, as described by Hans Selye. In the first stage, an alarm reaction, a person responds by efforts at self-control and shows signs of nervous depression (defense mechanisms, fear, anger, etc.) followed by a release of ACTH. In stage 2, the subject shows increased resistance to the specific source of stress and less resistance to other sources. Defense mechanisms may become neurotic. With stage 3 comes exhaustion, stupor, even death.

Generalization The process by which learning in one situation is transferred to another, similar situation. It is a key term in behavioral modification and classical conditioning. *See* Pavlovian Conditioning.

Generalized Anxiety Disorder Disorder in which the individual lives in a state of constant severe tension; continuous fear and apprehension experienced by an individual.

Genetics The study of the transfer of the inheritance of characteristics from one generation to another.

Genotype The underlying genetic structure that an individual has inherited and will send on to descendants. The actual appearance of a trait (phenotype) is due to the interaction of the genotype and the environment.

Gestalt Psychology A movement in psychology begun in the 1920s, stressing the wholeness of a person's experience and proposing that perceiving is an active, dynamic process that takes into account the entire pattern of ("gestalt") of the perpetual field. *See* Behaviorism; Associationism.

Glia Cells in the central nervous system that regulate the chemical environment of the nerve cells. RNA is stored in glial cells.

Grammar The set of rules for combining units of a language.

Group Therapy A form of psychotherapy aimed at treating mental disorders in which interaction among group members is the main therapeutic mode. Group therapy takes many forms but essentially requires a sense of community, support, increased personal responsibility, and a professionally trained leader.

Growth The normal quantitative changes that occur in the physical and psychological aspects of a healthy child with the passage of time.

Gustation The sense of taste. Theory suggests that the transmission of sense information from tongue to brain occurs through patterns of cell activity and not just the firing of single nerve fibers. Also, it is believed that specific spatial patterns or places on the tongue correspond to taste qualities.

Habit Formation The tendency to make a response to a stimulus less variable, especially if it produced successful adaptation.

Hallucination A sensory impression reported by a person when no external stimulus exists to justify the report. Hallucinations are serious symptoms and may be produced by psychoses. *See* Psychosis.

Hallucinogen A substance that produces hallucinations, such as LSD, mescaline, etc.

Hierarchy of Needs Maslow's list of motives in humans, arranged from the biological to the uniquely human.

Higher Order Conditioning Learning to make associations with stimuli that have been previously learned (CSs).

Hippocampus Part of the cortex of the brain governing memory storage, smell, and visceral functions.

Homeostasis A set of processes maintaining the constancy of the body's internal state, a series of dynamic compensations of the nervous system. Many processes such as appetite, body temperature, water balance, and heart rate are controlled by homeostasis.

Hormones Chemical secretions of the endocrine glands that regulate various body processes (e.g., growth, sexual traits, reproductive processes, etc.).

Humanism Branch of psychology dealing with those qualities distinguishing humans from other animals.

Hypnosis A trancelike state marked by heightened suggestibility and a narrowing of attention that can be induced in a number of ways. Debate exists over whether hypnosis is a true altered state of consciousness and to what extent strong motivating instructions can duplicate so-called hypnosis.

Hypothalamus A part of the brain that acts as a channel that carries information from the cortex and the thalamus to the spinal cord and ultimately to the motor nerves or to the autonomic nervous system, where it is transmitted to specific target organs. These target organs release into the bloodstream specific hormones that alter bodily functions. *See* Autonomic Nervous System.

Hypothesis A hypothesis can be called an educated guess, similar to a hunch. When a hunch is stated in a way that allows for further testing, it becomes a hypothesis.

Iconic Memory A visual memory. Experiments suggest that in order to be remembered and included in long-term memory, information must pass through a brief sensory stage. Theory further suggests that verbal information is subject to forgetting but that memorized sensory images are relatively permanent.

Id According to Freud, a component of the psyche present at birth that is the storehouse of psychosexual energy called *libido,* and also of primitive urges to fight, dominate, destroy.

Identification The taking on of attributes that one sees in another person. Children tend to identify with their parents or other important adults and thereby take on certain traits that are important to their development.

Illusion A mistaken perception of an actual stimulus.

Imitation The copying of another's behavior; learned through the process of observation. *See* Modeling.

Impression Formation The process of developing an evaluation of another person from your perceptions; first, or initial, impressions are often very important.

Imprinting The rapid, permanent acquisition by an organism of a strong attachment to an object (usually the parent). Imprinting occurs shortly after birth.

Independent Variable The condition in an experiment that is controlled and manipulated by the experimenter; it is a stimulus that will cause a response.

Inferential Statistics Techniques that help researchers make generalizations about a finding based on a limited number of subjects.

Inhibition Restraint of an impulse, desire, activity, or drive. People are taught to inhibit full expression of many drives (for example, aggression or sexuality) and to apply checks either consciously or unconsciously. In Freudian terminology, an inhibition is an unconsciously motivated blocking of sexual energy. In Pavlovian conditioning, inhibition is the theoretical process that operates during extinction, acting to block a conditioned response. *See* Pavlovian Conditioning.

Insight A sudden perception of useful or proper relations among objects necessary to solve the problem.

Insight Therapy A general classification of therapy in which the therapist focuses on the patient's underlying feelings and motivations and devotes most effort to increasing the patient's self-awareness or insight into his or her behavior. The other major class of therapy is action therapy. *See* Action Therapy.

Instinct An inborn pattern of behavior, relatively independent of environmental influence. An instinct may need to be triggered by a particular stimulus in the environment, but then it proceeds in a fixed pattern. The combination of taxis (orienting movement in response to a particular stimulus) and fixed-action pattern (inherited coordination) is the basis for instinctual activity. *See* Fixed-Action Pattern.

Instrumental Learning *See* Operant Conditioning.

Intelligence A capacity for knowledge about the world. This is an enormous and controversial field of study, and there is no agreement on a precise definition. However, intelligence has come to refer to higher-level abstract processes and may be said to comprise the ability to deal effectively with abstract concepts, the ability to learn, and the ability to adapt and deal with new situations. Piaget defines intelligence as the construction of an understanding. Both biological inheritance and environmental factors contribute to general intelligence. Children proceed through a sequence of identifiable stages in the development of conceptual thinking (Piaget). The degree to which factors such as race, sex, and social class affect intelligence is not known.

Intelligence Quotient (IQ) A measurement of intelligence originally based on tests devised by Binet and now widely applied. Genetic inheritance and environment affect IQ, although their relative contributions are not known. IQ can be defined in different ways; classically it is defined as a relation between chronological and mental ages.

Interference Theory of forgetting in which information that was learned before (proactive interference) or after (retroactive interference) the material of interest causes the learner to be unable to remember the material.

Interstimulus Interval The time between the start of the conditioned stimulus and the start of the unconditioned stimulus in Pavlovian conditioning. *See* Pavlovian Conditioning.

Intrauterine Environment The environment in the uterus during pregnancy can affect the physical development of the organism and its behavior after birth. Factors such as the mother's nutrition, emotional, and physical state significantly influence offspring. The mother's diseases, medications, hormones, and stress level all affect the pre- and postnatal development of her young.

Intrinsic Motivation Motivation inside of the individual; we do something because we receive satisfaction from it.

Introspection Reporting one's internal, subjective mental contents for the purpose of further study and analysis.

James-Lange Theory of Emotion Theory of emotion that states that the physiological arousal and behavior come before the subjective experience of an emotion.

Labeling-of-Arousal Experiments suggest that an individual experiencing physical arousal that she or he cannot explain will interpret her or his feelings in terms of the situation she or he is in and will use environmental and contextual cues.

Language A set of abstract symbols used to communicate meaning. Language includes vocalized sounds or semantic units (words, usually) and rules for combining the units (grammar). There is some inborn basis for language acquisition, and there are identifiable stages in its development that are universal.

Language Acquisition Linguists debate how children acquire language. Some believe in environmental shaping, a gradual system of reward and punishment. Others emphasize the unfolding of capacities inborn in the brain that are relatively independent of the environment and its rewards.

Latency Period According to Freud, the psychosexual stage of development during which sexual interest has been repressed and thus is low or "latent" (dormant).

Law of Effect Thorndike's proposal that when a response produces satisfaction, it will be repeated; reinforcement.

Leadership The quality of exerting more influence than other group members. Research suggests that certain characteristics are generally considered essential to leadership: consideration, sensitivity, ability to initiate and structure, and emphasis on production. However, environmental factors may thrust authority on a person without regard to personal characteristics.

Learned Helplessness Theory suggests that living in an environment of uncontrolled stress reduces the ability to cope with future stress that *is* controllable.

Learned Social Motives Motives in the human that are learned, including achievement, affiliation, and autonomy.

Learning The establishment of connections between stimulus and response, resulting from observation, special training, or previous activity. Learning is relatively permanent.

Life Span Span of time from conception to death; in developmental psychology, a life span approach looks at development throughout an individual's life.

Linguistic Relativity Hypothesis Proposal by Whorf that the perception of reality differs according to the language of the observer.

Linguistics The study of language, its nature, structure, and components.

Locus of Control The perceived place from which come determining forces in one's life. A person who feels that he or she has some control over his or her fate and tends to feel more likely to succeed has an internal locus of control. A person with an external locus of control feels that it is outside himself or herself and therefore that his or her attempts to control his or her fate are less assured.

Longitudinal Study A research method that involves following subjects over a considerable period of time (as compared with a cross-sectional approach); as in a study of fantasy play in children observed several times at intervals of two years. *See* Cross-Sectional Study.

Love Affectionate behavior between people, often in combination with interpersonal attraction. The mother-infant love relationship strongly influences the later capacity for developing satisfying love relationships.

Manic-Depressive Reaction A form of mental illness marked by alternations of extreme phases of elation (manic phase) and depression.

Maternalism Refers to the mother's reaction to her young. It is believed that the female is biologically determined to exhibit behavior more favorable to the care and feeding of the young than the male, although in humans maternalism is probably determined as much by cultural factors as by biological predisposition.

Maturation The genetically-controlled process of physical and physiological growth.

Mean The measure of central tendency, or mathematical average, computed by adding all scores in a set and dividing by the number of scores.

Meaning The concept or idea conveyed to the mind, by any method. In reference to memory, meaningful terms are easier to learn than less meaningful, unconnected, or nonsense terms. Meaningfulness is not the same as the word's meaning.

Median In a set of scores, the median is that middle score that divides the set into equal halves.

Memory Involves the encoding, storing of information in the brain, and its retrieval. Several theories exist to explain memory. One proposes that we have both a short-term (STM) and a long-term memory (LTM) and that information must pass briefly through the STM to be stored in the LTM. Also suggested is that verbal information is subject to forgetting, while memorized sensory images are relatively permanent. Others see memory as a function of association—information processed systematically and the meaningfulness of the items. Debate exists over whether memory retrieval is actually a process of reappearance or reconstruction.

Mental Disorder A mental condition that deviates from what society considers to be normal.

Minnesota Multiphasic Personality Inventory (MMPI) An objective personality test that was originally devised to identify personality disorders.

Mode In a set of scores, the measurement at which the largest number of subjects fall.

Modeling The imitation or copying of another's behavior. As an important process in personality development, modeling may be based on parents. In therapy, the therapist may serve as a model for the patient.

Morality The standards of right and wrong of a society and their adoption by members of that society. Some researchers believe that morality develops in successive stages, with each stage representing a specific level of moral thinking (Kohlberg). Others see morality as the result of experiences in which the child learns through punishment and reward from models such as parents and teachers.

Motivation All factors that cause and regulate behavior that is directed toward achieving goals and satisfying needs. Motivation is what moves an organism to action.

Narcissism A strong tendency to glorify the self at the expense of other people or other more mentally healthy tendencies. The concept relates primarily to physical attractiveness but can also mean any strong self-glorification.

Narcotic A drug that relieves pain. Heroin, morphine, and opium are narcotics. Narcotics are often addicting.

Naturalistic Observation Research method in which behavior of people or animals in the normal environment is accurately recorded.

Nature vs. Nurture A controversy in psychology that centers on whether behaviors and traits are biologically determined (e.g., genes) or environmentally determined (e.g., learned).

Negative Reinforcement Any event that upon termination, strengthens the preceding behavior; taking from subject something bad will increase the probability that the preceding behavior will be repeated. Involves aversive stimulus.

Neuron A nerve cell. There are billions of neurons in the brain and spinal cord. Neurons interact at synapses or points of contact. Information passage between neurons is electrical and biochemical. It takes the activity of many neurons to produce a behavior.

Neurosis Any one of a wide range of psychological difficulties, accompanied by excessive anxiety (as contrasted with psychosis). Psychoanalytic theory states that neurosis is an expression of unresolved conflicts in the form of tension and impaired functioning. Most neurotics are in much closer contact with reality than most psychotics. Term has been largely eliminated from DSM-III.

Nonverbal Behaviors Gestures, facial expressions, and other body movements. They are important because they tend to convey emotion. Debate exists over whether they are inborn or learned.

Norm An empirically set pattern of belief or behavior. Social norm refers to widely accepted social or cultural behavior to which a person tends to or is expected to conform.

Normal Sane, or free from mental disorder. Normal behavior is the behavior typical of most people in a given group, and "normality" implies a social judgment.

Normal Curve When scores of a large number of random cases are plotted on a graph, they often fall into a bell-shaped curve; there are as many cases above the mean as below on the curve.

Object Permanence According to Piaget, the stage in cognitive development when a child begins to conceive of objects as having an existence even when out of sight or touch and to conceive of space as extending beyond his or her own perception.

Oedipus Complex The conflicts of a child in triangular relationship with his mother and father. According to Freud, a boy must resolve his unconscious sexual desire for his mother and the accompanying wish to kill his father and fear of his father's revenge in order that he proceed in his moral development. The analogous problem for girls is called the Electra complex.

Olfaction The sense of smell. No general agreement exists on how olfaction works, though theories exist to explain it. One suggests that the size and shape of molecules of what is smelled is a crucial cue. The brain processes involved in smell are located in a different and evolutionarily older part of the brain than the other senses.

Operant Conditioning The process of changing, maintaining, or eliminating voluntary behavior through the consequences of that behavior. Operant conditioning uses many of the techniques of Pavlovian conditioning but differs in that it deals with voluntary rather than reflex behaviors. The frequency with which a behavior is emitted can be increased if it is rewarded (reinforced) and decreased if it is not reinforced, or punished. Some psychologists believe that all behavior is learned through conditioning while others believe that intellectual and motivational processes play a crucial role. *See* Pavlovian Conditioning.

Operational Definitions If an event is not directly observable, then the variables must be defined by the operations by which they will be measured. These definitions are called operational definitions.

Organism Any living animal, human or subhuman.

Orienting Response A relatively automatic, "what's that?" response that puts the organism in a better position to attend to and deal with a new stimulus. When a stimulus attracts our attention, our body responds with movements of head and body toward the stimulus, changes in muscle tone, heart rate, blood flow, breathing, and changes in the brain's electrical activity.

Pavlovian Conditioning Also called classical conditioning, Pavlovian conditioning can be demonstrated as follows: In the first step, an *unconditioned stimulus* (UCS) such as food, loud sounds, or pain is paired with a neutral *conditioned stimulus* (CS) that causes no direct effect, such as a click, tone, or a dim light. The response elicited by the UCS is called the *unconditioned response* (UCR) and is a biological reflex of the nervous system (for example, eyeblinks or salivation). The combination of the neutral CS, the response-causing UCS, and the unlearned UCR is usually presented to the subject several times during conditioning. Eventually, the UCS is dropped from the sequence in the second step of the process, and the previously neutral CS comes to elicit a response. When conditioning is complete, presentation of the CS alone will result in a *conditioned response* (CR) similar but not always the same as the UCR.

Perception The field of psychology studying ways in which the experience of objects in the world is based upon stimulation of the sense organs. In psychology, the field of perception studies what determines sensory impressions, such as size, shape, distance, direction, etc. Physical events in the environment are called distal stimuli while the activity at the sense organ itself is called a proximal stimulus. The study of perceiving tries to determine how an organism knows what distal stimuli are like since proximal stimuli are its only source of information. Perception of objects remains more or less constant despite changes in distal stimuli and is therefore believed to depend on relationships within stimuli (size *and* distance, for example). Perceptual processes are able to adjust and adapt to changes in the perceptual field.

Performance The actual behavior of an individual that is observed. We often infer learning from observing performance.

Peripheral Nervous System The part of the human nervous system that receives messages from the sense organs and carries messages to the muscles and glands; everything outside of the brain and spinal cord.

Personal Space The area around the body that people feel is their own space. When interacting with others, we maintain a distance sufficient to protect our personal space or personal "bubble."

Persuasion The process of changing a person's attitudes, beliefs, or actions. A person's susceptibility to persuasion depends on the persuader's credibility, subtlety, and whether both sides of an argument are presented.

Phenotype The physical features or behavior patterns by which we recognize an organism. Phenotype is the result of interaction between genotype (total of inherited genes) and environment. *See* Genotype.

Phobia A neurosis consisting of an irrationally intense fear of specific persons, objects, or situations and a wish to avoid them. A phobic person feels intense and incapacitating anxiety. The person may be aware that the fear is irrational, but this knowledge does not help.

Pituitary Gland Is located in of the brain and controls secretion of several hormones: the antidiuretic hormone that maintains water balance, oxytocin that controls blood pressure and milk production, and ACTH that is produced in response to stress, etc. *See* ACTH.

Placebo A substance that in and of itself has no real effect but which may produce an effect in a subject because the subject expects or believes that it will.

Positive Reinforcement Any event that, upon presentation, strengthens the preceding behavior; giving a subject something good will increase the probability that the preceding behavior will be repeated.

Prejudice An attitude in which one holds a negative belief about members of a group to which he or she does not belong. Prejudice is often directed at minority ethnic or racial groups and may be reduced by contact with these perceived "others."

Premack Principle Principle that states that of any two responses, the one that is more likely to occur can be used to reinforce the response that is less likely to occur.

Prenatal Development Development from conception to birth. It includes the physical development of the fetus as well as certain of its intellectual and emotional processes.

Primary Reinforcement Reinforcement that is effective without having been associated with other reinforcers; sometimes called unconditioned reinforcement.

Probability (p) In inferential statistics, the likelihood that the difference between the experimental and control groups is due to the independent variable.

Problem Solving A self-directed activity in which an individual uses information to develop answers to problems, to generate new problems, and sometimes to transform the process by creating a unique, new system. Problem solving involves learning, insight and creativity.

Projective Test A type of test in which people respond to ambiguous, loosely structured stimuli. It is assumed that people will reveal themselves by putting themselves into the stimuli they see. The validity of these tests for diagnosis and personality assessment is still at issue.

Propaganda Information deliberately spread to aid a cause. Propaganda's main function is persuasion.

Prosocial Behavior Behavior that is directed toward helping others.

Proximal Stimulus Activity at the sense organ.

Psychoactive Drug A substance that affects mental activities, perceptions, consciousness, or mood. This type of drug has its effects through strictly physical effects and through expectations.

Psychoanalysis There are two meanings to this word: it is a theory of personality development based on Freud and a method of treatment also based on Freud. Psychoanalytic therapy uses techniques of free association, dream analysis, and analysis of the patient's relationship (the "transference") to the analyst. Psychoanalytic theory maintains that the personality develops through a series of psychosexual stages and that the personality consists of specific components energized by the life and death instincts.

Psychogenic Pain Disorder Somatoform disorder in which the person complains of severe, long-lasting pain for which there is no organic cause.

Psycholinguistics The study of the process of language acquisition as part of psychological development and of language as an aspect of behavior. Thinking may obviously depend on language, but their precise relationship still puzzles psycholinguists, and several different views exist.

Psychological Dependence Situation when a person craves a drug even though it is not biologically necessary for his or her body.

Psychophysiological Disorders Real medical problems (such as ulcers, migraine headaches, and high blood pressure) that are caused or aggravated by psychological stress.

Psychosexual Stages According to Freud, an individual's personality develops through several stages. Each stage is associated with a particular bodily source of gratification (pleasure). First comes the oral stage when most pleasures come from the mouth. Then comes the anal stage when the infant derives pleasure from holding and releasing while learning bowel control. The phallic stage brings pleasure from the genitals, and a crisis (Oedipal) occurs in which the child gradually suppresses sexual desire for the opposite-sex parent, identifies with the same-sex parent and begins to be interested in the outside world. This latency period lasts until puberty, after which the genital stage begins and mature sexual relationships develop. There is no strict timetable, but, according to Freudians, the stages do come in a definite order. Conflicts experienced and not adequately dealt with remain with the individual.

Psychosis The most severe of mental disorders, distinguished by a person being seriously out of touch with objective reality. Psychoses may result from physical factors (organic) or may have no known physical cause (functional). Psychoses take many forms, of which the most common are schizophrenia and psychotic depressive reactions, but all are marked by personality disorganization and a severely reduced ability to perceive reality. Both biological and environmental factors are believed to influence the development of psychosis, although the precise effect of each is not presently known. *See* Neurosis.

Psychosomatic Disorders A variety of body reactions that are closely related to psychological events. Stress, for example, brings on many physical changes and can result in illness or even death if prolonged and severe. Psychosomatic disorders can affect any part of the body.

Psychotherapy Treatment involving interpersonal contacts between a trained therapist and a patient in which the therapist tries to produce beneficial changes in the patient's emotional state, attitudes, and behavior.

Punishment Any event that decreases the probability of the preceding behavior being repeated. You can give something bad (positive punishment) to decrease the preceding behavior.

Rational-Emotive Therapy A cognitive behavior modification technique in which a person is taught to identify irrational, self-defeating beliefs and then to overcome them.

Rationalization Defense mechanism in which individuals make up logical excuses to justify their behavior rather than exposing their true motives.

Reaction Formation Defense mechanism in which a person masks an unconsciously distressing or unacceptable trait by assuming an opposite attitude or behavior pattern.

Reality Therapy A form of treatment of mental disorders pioneered by William Glasser in which the origins of the patient's problems are considered irrelevant and emphasis is on a close, judgmental bond between patient and therapist aimed to improve the patient's present and future life.

Reflex An automatic movement that occurs in direct response to a stimulus.

Rehearsal The repeating of an item to oneself and the means by which information is stored in the short-term memory (STM). Theory suggests that rehearsal is necessary for remembering and storage in the long-term memory (LTM).

Reinforcement The process of affecting the frequency with which a behavior is emitted. A reinforcer can reward and thus increase the behavior or punish and thus decrease its frequency. Reinforcers can also be primary, satisfying basic needs such as hunger or thirst, or secondary, satisfying learned and indirect values, such as money.

Reliability Consistency of measurement. A test is reliable if it repeatedly gives the same results. A person should get nearly the same score if the test is taken on two different occasions.

REM (Rapid-Eye Movement) Type of sleep in which the eyes are rapidly moving around; dreaming occurs in REM sleep.

Repression A defense mechanism in which a person forgets or pushes into the unconscious something that arouses anxiety. See Defense Mechanism; Anxiety.

Reticular Formation A system of nerve fibers leading from the spinal column to the cerebral cortex that functions to arouse, alert, and make an organism sensitive to changes in the environment. See Cerebral Cortex.

Retina The inside coating of the eye, containing two kinds of cells that react to light: the rods that are sensitive only to dim light and the cones that are sensitive to color and form in brighter light. There are three kinds of cones, each responsive to particular colors in the visible spectrum (range of colors).

Risky Shift Research suggests that decisions made by groups will involve considerably more risk than individuals in the group would be willing to take. This shift in group decision depends heavily on cultural values. See Cautious Shift.

Rod Part of the retina involved in seeing in dim light. See Retina.

RNA (Ribonucleic Acid) A chemical substance that occurs in chromosomes and that functions in genetic coding. During task-learning, RNA changes occur in the brain.

Role Playing Adopting the role of another person and experiencing the world in a way one is not accustomed to.

Role Taking The ability to imagine oneself in another's place or to understand the consequences of one's actions for another person.

Schachter-Singer Theory of Emotion Theory of emotion that states that we interpret our arousal according to our environment and label our emotions accordingly.

Schizoid Personality Personality disorder characterized by having great trouble developing social relationships.

Schizophrenia The most common and serious form of psychosis in which there exists an imbalance between emotional reactions and the thoughts associated with these feelings. It may be a disorder of the process of thinking. See Psychosis.

Scientific Method The process used by psychologists to determine principles of behavior that exist independently of individual experience and that are untouched by unconscious bias. It is based on a prearranged agreement that criteria, external to the individual and communicable to others, must be established for each set of observations referred to as fact.

Secondary Reinforcement Reinforcement that is only effective after it has been associated with a primary reinforcer.

Self-Actualization A term used by humanistic psychologists to describe what they see as a basic human motivation: the development of all aspects of an individual into productive harmony.

Self-Esteem A person's evaluation of oneself. If someone has confidence and satisfaction in oneself, self-esteem is considered high.

Self-Fulfilling Prophecy A preconceived expectation or belief about a situation that evokes behavior resulting in a situation consistent with the preconception.

Senses An organism's physical means of receiving and detecting physical changes in the environment. Sensing is analyzed in terms of reception of the physical stimulus by specialized nerve cells in the sense organs, transduction or converting the stimulus' energy into nerve impulses that the brain can interpret, and transmission of those nerve impulses from the sense organ to the part of the brain that can interpret the information they convey.

Sensitivity Training Aims at helping people to function more effectively in their jobs by increasing their awareness of their own and others' feelings and exchanging "feedback" about styles of interacting. Sensitivity groups are unlike therapy groups in that they are meant to enrich the participants' lives. Participants are not considered patients or ill. Also called T-groups.

Sensorimotor Stage According to Piaget, the stage of development beginning at birth during which perceptions are tied to objects that the child manipulates. Gradually the child learns that objects have permanence even if they are out of sight or touch.

Sensory Adaptation Tendency of the sense organs to adjust to continuous, unchanging stimulation by reducing their functioning; a stimulus that once caused sensation no longer does.

Sensory Deprivation The blocking out of all outside stimulation for a period of time. As studied experimentally, it can produce hallucinations, psychological disturbances, and temporary disorders of the nervous system of the subject.

Sex Role The attitudes, activities, and expectations considered specific to being male or female, determined by both biological and cultural factors.

Shaping A technique of behavior shaping in which behavior is acquired through the reinforcement of successive approximations of the desired behavior.

Sibling Rivalry A (somewhat psychoanalytic) concept which suggests that we compete with our brothers and sisters for our parents' attention and for other rewards.

Sleep A periodic state of consciousness marked by four brain-wave patterns. Dreams occur during REM sleep. Sleep is a basic need without which one may suffer physical or psychological distress. See Brain Waves; Dreams.

Social Comparison Theory proposed by Festinger that states that we have a tendency to compare our behavior to others to ensure that we are conforming.

Social Facilitation Phenomenon in which the presence of others increases dominant behavior patterns in an individual; Zajonc's theory of social facilitation states that the presence of others enhances the emission of the dominant response of the individual.

Social Influence The process by which people form and change the attitudes, opinions, and behavior of others.

Social Learning Learning acquired through observation and imitation of others.

Social Psychology The study of individuals as affected by others and of the interaction of individuals in groups.

Socialization A process by which a child learns the various patterns of behavior expected and accepted by society. Parents are the chief agents of a child's socialization. Many factors have a bearing on the socialization process, such as the child's sex, religion, social class, and parental attitudes.

Sociobiology The study of the genetic basis of social behavior.

Sociophobias Excessive irrational fears and embarrassment when interacting with other people.

Somatic Nervous System The part of the peripheral nervous system that carries messages from the sense organs and relays information that directs the voluntary movements of the skeletal muscles.

Somatoform Disorders Disorders characterized by physical symptoms for which there are no obvious physical causes.

Somesthetic Senses Skin senses; includes pressure, pain, cold, and warmth.

Species-Typical Behavior Behavior patterns common to members of a species. Ethologists state that each species inherits some patterns of behavior (e.g., birdsongs).

Stanford-Binet Intelligence Scale Tests that measure intelligence from two years of age through adult level. The tests determine one's intelligence quotient by establishing one's chronological and mental ages. See Intelligence Quotient.

State-Dependent Learning Situation in which what is learned in one state can only be remembered when the person is in that state.

Statistically Significant In inferential statistics, a finding that the independent variable did influence greatly the outcome of the experimental and control group.

Stereotype The assignment of characteristics to a person mainly on the basis of the group, class, or category to which he or she belongs. The tendency to categorize and generalize is a basic human way of organizing information. Stereotyping, however, can reinforce misinformation and prejudice. See Prejudice.

Stimulus A unit of the environment that causes a response in an individual; more specifically, a physical or chemical agent acting on an appropriate sense receptor.

Stimulus Discrimination Limiting responses to relevant stimuli.

Stimulus Generalization Responses to stimuli similar to the stimulus that had caused the response.

Stress Pressure that puts unusual demands on an organism. Stress may be caused by physical conditions but eventually will involve both. Stimuli that cause stress are called stressors, and an organism's response is the stress reaction. A three-stage general adaptation syndrome is hypothesized involving both emotional and physical changes. *See* General Adaptation Syndrome.

Sublimation Defense mechanism in which a person redirects his socially undesirable urges into socially acceptable behavior.

Subliminal Stimuli Stimuli that do not receive conscious attention because they are below sensory thresholds. They may influence behavior, but research is not conclusive on this matter.

Substance-Induced Organic Mental Disorders Organic mental disorders caused by exposure to harmful environmental substances.

Suggestibility The extent to which a person responds to persuasion. Hypnotic susceptibility refers to the degree of suggestibility observed after an attempt to induce hypnosis has been made. *See* Hypnosis; Persuasion.

Superego According to Freud, the superego corresponds roughly to conscience. The superego places restrictions on both ego and id and represents the internalized restrictions and ideals that the child learns from parents and culture. *See* Conscience; Ego; Id.

Sympathetic Nervous System The branch of the autonomic nervous system that is more active in emergencies; it causes a general arousal, increasing breathing, heart rate, and blood pressure.

Synapse A "gap" where individual nerve cells (neurons) come together and across which chemical information is passed.

Syndrome A group of symptoms that occur together and mark a particular abnormal pattern.

Systematic Desensitization A technique used in behavior therapy to eliminate a phobia. The symptoms of the phobia are seen as conditioned responses of fear, and the procedure attempts to decondition the fearful response until the patient gradually is able to face the feared situation. *See* Phobia.

TAT (Thematic Apperception Test) Personality and motivation test that requires the subject to devise stories about pictures.

Theory A very general statement that is more useful in generating hypotheses than in generating research. *See* Hypothesis.

Therapeutic Community The organization of a hospital setting so that patients have to take responsibility for helping one another in an attempt to prevent patients from getting worse by being in the hospital.

Token Economy A system for organizing a treatment setting according to behavioristic principles. Patients are encouraged to take greater responsibility for their adjustment by receiving tokens for acceptable behavior and fines for unacceptable behavior. The theory of token economy grew out of operant conditioning techniques. *See* Operant Conditioning.

Traits Distinctive and stable attributes that can be found in all people.

Tranquilizers Psychoactive drugs that reduce anxiety. *See* Psychoactive Drug.

Trial and Error Learning Trying various behaviors in a situation until the solution is hit upon; past experiences lead us to try different responses until we are successful.

Unconditioned Response (UR) An automatic reaction elicited by a stimulus.

Unconditioned Stimulus (US) Any stimulus that elicits an automatic or reflexive reaction in an individual; it does not have to be learned in the present situation.

Unconscious In Freudian terminology, a concept (not a place) of the mind. The unconscious encompasses certain inborn impulses that never rise into consciousness (awareness) as well as memories and wishes that have been repressed. The chief aim of psychoanalytic therapy is to free repressed material from the unconscious in order to make it susceptible to conscious thought and direction. Behavior-

ists describe the unconscious as an inability to verbalize. *See* Repression.

Undifferentiated Schizophrenia Type of schizophrenia that does not fit into any particular category, or fits into more than one category.

Validity The extent to which a test actually measures what it is designed to measure.

Variability In statistics, measures of variability communicate how spread out the scores are; the tendency to vary the response to a stimulus, particularly if the response fails to help in adaptation.

Variable Any property of a person, object, or event that can change or take on more than one mathematical value.

Wechsler Adult Intelligence Scale (WAIS) An individually administered test designed to measure adults' intelligence, devised by David Wechsler. The WAIS consists of eleven subtests, of which six measure verbal and five measure performance aspects of intelligence. *See* Wechsler Intelligence Scale for Children.

Wechsler Intelligence Scale for Children (WISC) Similar to the Wechsler Adult Intelligence Scale, except that it is designed for people under fifteen. Wechsler tests can determine strong and weak areas of overall intelligence. *See* Wechsler Adult Intelligence Scale (WAIS).

Withdrawal Social or emotional detachment; the removal of oneself from a painful or frustrating situation.

Yerkes-Dodson Law Prediction that the optimum motivation level decreases as the difficulty level of a task increases.

Source for the Glossary:

The majority of terms in this glossary are reprinted from *The Study of Psychology,* Joseph Rubinstein. © by The Dushkin Publishing Group, Inc., Guilford, CT 06437.

The remaining terms were developed by the Annual Editions staff.

abortion, teens and, 90, 93–94
accessory olfactory bulb, 50, 52
Adolescent Family Life Act, 91, 94
adoption, teens and, 94
adversarial process, therapy as, 180
affirmative action, 151
agreeableness, personality and, 20
AIDS, 88; illness and, 100–101
alcoholism, 110, 208, 224–226; anxiety and, 172–173; effect of, on children, 64–69
Allen, Laura, 31
Allen, Woody, 74, 76
Allgeier, Elizabeth, 223
amygdala, 37
anorexia, 173
anxiety, 171–173, 227–232
apple-shaped people, waist-to-hip ratio of, 213–214
athletes, competition and, 115–116
Ativan, 231
attributional style, optimism and, 57

baby boomers, middle age and, 104–108
Baker, Laura, 119–120
Bank, Stephen, 117, 118
Barlow, David, 231, 232
basal metabolism, 216
behavioral changes, stress and, 201
behaviorism, 7–8, 9, 19
Benson, Herbert, 195, 200–201
Berliner, David, 49–50, 51, 53
bipolar depression. See manic depression
biological psychiatry, 168
birth order, importance of, 119
blacks, racism and, 149–151, 152–154
blame: psychotherapy and, 179–180; self-help and, 183
Blonsky, Marshall, semiotics and, 145–148
blood alcohol concentration (BAC), 225
body mass index (BMI), 213, 214, 215, 216
Bradshaw, John, 184, 185
brain: dreams and, 15–18; gender differences and, 29–33; mapping the, 37–41; panic and, 169; of Phineas Gage, 42–45
Brim, Gilbert, 105–106
Bronte, Lydia, 107–108
bulimia, 173–174
Buspar, 232

cancer, illness and, 100–101
castration anxiety, 12
CAT (computer-assisted tomography) scan, 37
catastrophic thinking, panic and, 168–171
catecholamines, 100
change, possibility of, 168–175
character, temperament and, 20–21
children: effect of daycare on, 70–73; effect of prenatal substance abuse on, 64–69; prejudice and, 82–86; self-esteem and, 11; sexual abuse of, 74–78; siblings and, 117–122
cholinergic chemicals, 16, 17
Chomsky, Noam, 27
Christian psychiatry, 177
Cicero, 124
circles of blame, 165
Clark, David, 110, 169–171
clinical depression, 205
Cloninger, C. Robert, 20–21
Cobain, Kurt, suicide of, 109

cognitive therapy, for anxiety, 232; for bulimia, 174; for depression, 205, 208, 211; for panic disorder, 169–171
Coleman, Eli, 219, 222, 223
communication, semiotics as, 145–148
competition, vs. cooperation, 114–116
Comstock, George, 159, 161
conjugation, 32
conscientiousness, personality and, 20
consciousness, dreams and, 15–18
conspiratorial therapists, 181
contrasexual transition, 106
control, myth of emotional, 190
convergence zones, 41
cooperation: character and, 20; group behavior and, 140–144; vs. competition, 114–116
corpus callosum, 31, 37
cortisol, 97
Cosmides, Leda, 28, 30
Costa, Paul T., 20, 22
counselors, 179
courtly love, 132
comprehensive human psychology, Maslow's theory of, 6–9
compulsive sexual behavior (CSB), 222–223
Crick, Francis, 46, 47
criminal justice, violence and, 164–165
criminality, heredity and, 26–28
Crosby, Elizabeth, 50, 51
cross-lag panel design, 162
cyclical bi-directional model, of violent behavior, 160
cyclothymia, 207

Damasio, Antonio, 39, 41
day care, benefits of, 70–73
deconstruction, 146
defensive pessimism, 57
depression, 12, 19, 20, 110, 176, 205–211, 221, 228; dieting and, 174–175
desegregation, school, 150
Diagnosis and Statistical Manual of Mental Disorders, 19–21
dieting, 173–175, 212–218
discharger, emotional style of, 189–194
disease, vs. illness, 98
domestic violence, 133–137
dopamine, 221
dreams, analysis of, 12, 14, 15–18
drugs, effect of prenatal exposure to, 64–69
Dunn, Judy, 118, 119
Durkheim, Emile, 27–28, 109
dysmorphophobia, 104
dysphoria, 172
dysthymia, 206, 210

education: gender bias in, 79–81; racism and, 149–150
efficiency, intelligence and, 39
ego, 12
emotion, 52; gender differences and, 30; stress and, 201
emotion worship, psychotherapy and, 180–181
emotional style, moods and, 189–194
epinephrine, 97, 99
Erhardt, Werner, 11, 183
Erikson, Erik, 22
Erkut, Sumru, 128, 130
Eron, Leonard, 162, 163

estrogen, 30
exercise: stress and, 202–204; weight loss and, 216, 217
extroversion, personality and, 20

false memory, child abuse and, 74–78
fathers, teen, 95
fetal alcohol syndrome, 225
fight-or-flight response, 200
five-factor model, of personality, 19, 20
flirting, in the workplace, 155–157
focuser, emotional style of, 189–194
Fox, James, 136–137
Freud, Sigmund, 26, 105, 118, 155, 181, 221; criticism of, 12–14
friendship, 123–127, 128–130; emotional styles of, 189–194

Gage, Phineas, 42–45
gangs, youth, 158
gays, friendship and, 126
Geffner, Robert, 134, 135
Gelles, Richard, 134, 137
gender bias, in education, 79–81
gender differences, brain and, 29–33
genes, influence of, 26–28, 34–36, 119, 168, 169, 174
genetic research, 46–48
goals, stress and, 197
Goman, Carol Kinsey, 184, 186
good and bad, myth of emotional, 190
Goodwin, Frederick K., 12, 110, 111
Gould, Stephen Jay, 115
Gorski, Roger, 31
group behavior, cooperation and, 140–144
"growing tip" statistics, 9
gun culture, American, violence and, 164
Gutmann, David, 106–107

Halcion, 227, 230
handicapism, 82
Harris v. Forklift Systems, Inc., 156
Hatfield, Elaine, 131–132
heart attacks, stress and, 98–99
heredity. See genes
Herrnstein, Richard, 26, 27, 158, 161
Hetherington, E. Mavis, 118, 120
hierarchies, group behavior and, 143–144
Hines, Melissa, 29, 30
history, racism and, 150
Hobson, Allan, 15–16
Holtzworth-Munroe, Amy, 134–135
homosexuality, heredity and, 26–28, 30–31, 34–36
homunculus theory, 47
Horwath, Ewald, 205, 208
hostility, mind-body connection and, 60–61
Huesmann, L. Rowell, 162, 163
Human Genome Project, 47, 48
humanistic psychology, 185
hypoactive sexual desire, 220

id, 12
identity crisis, 22
illness, stress and, 97–104
intelligence, heredity and, 26–28
intensity, anxiety and, 172, 173
irrational, anxiety as, 172, 173

Jafek, Bruce, 50–51
James, William, 13, 22

Jews, racism and, 153–154
Johnson, Virginia, 219
Jung, Carol Gustav, 13, 105, 106

Kahn, Michael, 118, 122
Kaplan, Helen Singer, 220, 221
Koop, C. Everett, 137, 183
Kramer, Peter, 14, 210

language, 27, 40; gender differences in, 32
learning, effect of prenatal substance abuse on, 64–69
lesbians, friendship and, 126
Levay, Simon, 30, 35
Librium, 228
limbic system, 52
Locke, John, 111, 146
LOT (Life Orientation Test), 54–55
love, 131–132; friendship and, 123

Madonna-whore complex, 221
mandated reporting, of child abuse, 75
manic depression, 176, 206, 207
Mann, J. John, 110–111
marriage and family therapists, 179
Maslow, Abraham, 11, 186; interview with, 6–9
Masters, William, 219
McCral, Robert R., 20, 22
Mead, Margaret, 30
media: racism and, 151; and violence and youth, 158–165
meditation, for anxiety, 172, 173
memory, 39; false, child abuse and, 74–78; repressed, 12
men, friendship and, 125
menarche, 88
Mendel, Gregor, 46–47
menopause, 107
mesomorphs, 27
metamotivation, 8
middle age, 104–108
mind-body connection, 59–61
Mitchell, Anne, 71–72
Money, John, 221
Monti-Bloch, Luis, 49, 52
moods, emotional style and, 189–194
Moran, David, 50–51, 52
MRI (magnetic resonance imaging), 41
Murray, Charles, 26

natural self, 189
natural weight, 173–174, 218
nature, vs. nurture, 26–28, 34–36, 119, 120. See also heredity
negligible cause model, of violent behavior, 160
networking, 129
Neugarten, Bernice, 105
neural pruning, 39–40
neurochemicals, 97
neuroticism, personality and, 20
neurosis, 13, 20
neurotransmitters, 208
neutrality, myth of therapeutic, 178–179
nicotine, effect of prenatal exposure to, 64–69
norepinephrine, 97, 99, 208, 209
nuclear power accidents, illness and, 100

Oedipus complex, 12

Olson, Mancur L., 140
only children, 121
optimism, 54–58
organization, stress and, 197
Ornish, Dean, 195–196, 202
Ovid, 132

panic attacks, 168–171, 228, 229, 232
paralysis, anxiety and, 172, 173
parents: emotional styles of, 189–194; siblings and, 118–119, 120
parthenogenesis, 33
peak experiences, 8
pear-shaped people, waist-to-hip ratio of, 213–214
penis envy, 12
perception, gender differences in, 31
perfectibility, myth of emotional, 190
personality, 168; brain and, 42–45; Diagnosis and Statistical Manual of Mental Disorders and, 19–21; stability of, 22–23
PET (positron emission tomography) scan, 37, 39, 40, 169
phallic symbols, 12
phenylketonuria (PKU), 47–48
pheromones, human, 49–53
physical symptoms, of stress, 201
Pillard, Richard, 35
Plomin, Robert, 119, 120
pontine-geniculate-occipital (PGO) waves, 16, 17
pornography, violence and, 160
positive solitude, 187
positive thinking: power of, 54–58; myth of, 190
postmodernism, 148
posttraumatic stress disorder, 75
pregnancy, teenage, 87–96
prejudice, children and, 82–86
prenatal influences, illness and, 99–100
prenatal substance abuse, effect of, on children, 64–69
primary cause model, of violent behavior, 160
primates, siblings and, 120
Prisoner's Dilemma, 141
progressive relaxation, for anxiety, 172, 173
Prozac, 205, 209, 210, 230
psychiatrists, 178
psychoanalysis, Freudian, 12–14, 177
psychologists, 178
psychoneuroimmunology, 97
psychosocial effects, of illness, 100–101
psychotherapy, buyer's guide to, 176–182

race, intelligence and, 26–27
Rachman, S. J., 168, 169
racism, 82, 149–151, 152–154
rap music, 149
rape myth, 160
Rapoport, Judith L., 223
Ravitch, Diane, 81
Reinisch, June, 31, 33, 105, 107
relationships, emotional styles in, 189–194
relaxation, stress and, 200–201
Richelson, Elliot, 208, 210
Rip van Winkle study, of youth violence, 162–163
Rogers, Carl, 11
Rogow, Stan, 104–105
Romanoski, Alan, 206, 208

romantic love, 131
romanticism, emotion worship and, 181
Rosch, Paul J., 195, 196
Rule of Thumb, 133
Rush, A. John, 206, 208

Sachs, Oliver, 184
satanic ritual abuse (SRA), 76
Schiavi, Raul C., 220
schizophrenia, 12, 15, 19, 26, 176
seasonal affective disorder, 206
seeker, emotional style of, 189–194
self-actualization, 6, 8, 186
self-directedness, character and, 20
self-efficacy, optimism and, 57
self-esteem, 10–11
self-help movement, 183–186
self-transcendence, character and, 20
Selye, Hans, 97
semiotics, 145–148
sensor, emotional style of, 189–194
serotonin, 110–111, 208, 209
sex: evolution of, 32, 33; pheromones and, 49–53
sex education, for teens, 91–92, 95
sexual abuse, of children, 74–78
sexual desire disorders, 219–223
sexual harassment, in the workplace, 155–157
Shea, Tracie, 209, 211
Sheehy, Gail, 105, 106, 107
sibling relationships, 117–122
Simpson, O. J., 134, 135, 136
Skinner, B. F., 88
sleep, dreams and, 15–18
slips of the tongue, 12, 13
smell, sense of, pheromones and, 49–53
smoking, effect of prenatal, 64–69
social dilemmas, dynamics of, 140–144
social support, stress and, 98, 100
social workers, 178–179
sociobiology, 27
solitude, importance of, 187–188
Spiegel, David, 184, 195, 198
SQUID (superconducting quantum interference device) scan, 37, 39, 41
stability function, 141
Stensaas, Larry, 51, 52
stress, 208, 221; coping with, 195–204; illness and, 97–104; mind-body connection and, 59–60
Styron, William, on depression, 206
suggestibility, and child abuse cases, 74–78
suicide, 109–110
Sulloway, Frank, 14, 119
Sumner, William Graham, 9
superego, 12
synergy, 9

Tavris, Carol, 185
teens: pregnancy and, 87–96; and violence and media, 158–165
television, youth violence and, 162–163
temperament, personality and, 20–21, 189, 193
Terman, Lewis, 9
testosterone, 29, 30, 31, 107, 221
Thorndike, Edward L., 8
thought symptoms, stress and, 201
thromboxane A2, 99
Tofranil, 227

Tolstoy, Leo, 117
Tooby, John, 28, 32
Torres-Gil, Fernando, 105
tranquilizers, for anxiety, 172–173, 227–232
transgenics, 48
Type A behavior, 60, 197, 205
Type C behavior, 101

unconditional positive regard, 11
unconscious, 12, 14
uniformity, myth of emotional, 190
unipolar depression, 205
Unscrupulous Diner's Dilemma, 140, 141
urban nomad, 148

Valium, 172, 228
values, psychotherapy and, 176, 177, 178
violence: domestic, 133–137; racist, 152–154; youth, 158–165
Virchow, Rudolph, 97–98
vomeronasal organ (VMO), 49–53
Vorenberg, Elizabeth, 75–76

waist-to-hip ratio, body weight and, 213–214
Watson, James, 37, 46, 47
Watson, John B., 7–8
weight-loss programs, effectiveness of, 212–218
Wertheimer, Max, 9

Whitehead, Alfred North, 9
Widiger, Thomas A., 19, 20, 21
Wilson, James, 27, 158, 161
winning, competition and, 114–116
Wittgenstein, Ludwig, 12
workplace, emotional styles in, 189–194; sexual harassment in, 155–157
Wysocki, Charles, 51, 53

Xanax, 169, 171, 227, 228–229, 230

yo-yo dieters, 212

Zoloft, 209

Credits/ Acknowledgments

Cover Design by Charles Vitelli

1. Becoming a Person
Facing overview—Dushkin Publishing Group, Inc., photo by Pamela Carley.

2. Determinants of Behavior
Facing overview—WHO photo by Jean Mohr. 38—Illustration by Lewis E. Calver. 39—(top right) Hank Morgan—Rainbow; (middle left and bottom right) Buchsbaum; (middle right) Dan McCoy—Rainbow; (bottom left) Howard Sochurek. 6-7—WHO photos by Zafar.

3. Problems Influencing Personal Growth
Facing overview—Photo by EPA-Documerica.

4. Relating to Others
Facing overview—Photo by Louis P. Raucci.

5. Dynamics of Personal Adjustment
Facing overview—United Nations photo. 141-142—Graphics by Jared Schneidman Design.

6. Enhancing Human Adjustment
Facing overview—United Nations photo by Margot Granitsas.

ANNUAL EDITIONS ARTICLE REVIEW FORM

■ NAME: _____ DATE: _____

■ TITLE AND NUMBER OF ARTICLE: _____

■ BRIEFLY STATE THE MAIN IDEA OF THIS ARTICLE: _____

_____

_____

_____

_____

■ LIST THREE IMPORTANT FACTS THAT THE AUTHOR USES TO SUPPORT THE MAIN IDEA:

_____

_____

_____

_____

_____

_____

■ WHAT INFORMATION OR IDEAS DISCUSSED IN THIS ARTICLE ARE ALSO DISCUSSED IN YOUR TEXTBOOK OR OTHER READING YOU HAVE DONE? LIST THE TEXTBOOK CHAPTERS AND PAGE NUMBERS:

_____

_____

_____

_____

_____

_____

_____

■ LIST ANY EXAMPLES OF BIAS OR FAULTY REASONING THAT YOU FOUND IN THE ARTICLE:

_____

_____

_____

_____

_____

■ LIST ANY NEW TERMS/CONCEPTS THAT WERE DISCUSSED IN THE ARTICLE AND WRITE A SHORT DEFINITION:

_____

_____

_____

_____

_____

_____

*Your instructor may require you to use this Annual Editions Article Review Form in any number of ways: for articles that are assigned, for extra credit, as a tool to assist in developing assigned papers, or simply for your own reference. Even if it is not required, we encourage you to photocopy and use this page; you'll find that reflecting on the articles will greatly enhance the information from your text.

ANNUAL EDITIONS:
PERSONAL GROWTH AND BEHAVIOR 95/96
Article Rating Form

Here is an opportunity for you to have direct input into the next revision of this volume. We would like you to rate each of the 47 articles listed below, using the following scale:

1. **Excellent: should definitely be retained**
2. **Above average: should probably be retained**
3. **Below average: should probably be deleted**
4. **Poor: should definitely be deleted**

Your ratings will play a vital part in the next revision. So please mail this prepaid form to us just as soon as you complete it.
Thanks for your help!

Rating	Article	Rating	Article
	1. The Last Interview of Abraham Maslow		23. The New Middle Age
	2. Self-Esteem: The Keystone to Happiness		24. The Mystery of Suicide
	3. The Assault on Freud		25. How Competitive Are You?
	4. Clues to the Irrational Nature of Dreams		26. The Secret World of Siblings
	5. Piecing Together Personality		27. What Friends Are For
	6. Personality: Major Traits Found Stable Through Life		28. When the Bond Breaks
	7. Nature or Nurture? Old Chestnut, New Thoughts		29. What Is Love?
	8. Sizing Up the Sexes		30. Patterns of Abuse
	9. Born Gay?		31. The Dynamics of Social Dilemmas
	10. Mapping the Brain		32. Trying to Decipher Those Inscrutable Signs of Our Times
	11. The Return of Phineas Gage: Clues About the Brain from the Skull of a Famous Patient		33. Crossing the Divide
			34. The Ruses of Racism
	12. Understanding the Genetics Age		35. Flirting with Disaster
	13. The Sniff of Legend		36. Media, Violence, Youth, and Society
	14. On the Power of Positive Thinking: The Benefits of Being Optimistic		37. What You Can Change and What You Cannot Change
	15. The Mind and the Body		38. A Buyer's Guide to Psychotherapy
	16. Clipped Wings		39. The Last Self-Help Article You'll Ever Need
	17. How Kids Benefit from Child Care		
	18. Rush to Judgment		40. The Importance of Solitude
	19. Why Schools Must Tell Girls: "You're Smart, You Can Do It"		41. How to Master Your Moods
			42. Unload Stress for '94
	20. Teaching Young Children to Resist Bias: What Parents Can Do		43. Defeating Depression
			44. Losing Weight: What Works, What Doesn't
	21. Adolescent Childbearing: Whose Problem? What Can We Do?		45. Sexual Desire
			46. Alcohol in Perspective
	22. Critical Life Events and the Onset of Illness		47. High Anxiety

(continued on back)

ABOUT YOU

Name_____ Date_____

Are you a teacher? ☐   Or student? ☐

Your School Name _____

Department _____

Address _____

City _____ State _____ Zip _____

School Telephone #_____

YOUR COMMENTS ARE IMPORTANT TO US!

Please fill in the following information:

For which course did you use this book? _____

Did you use a text with this Annual Edition?   ☐ yes   ☐ no

The title of the text? _____

What are your general reactions to the Annual Editions concept?

Have you read any particular articles recently that you think should be included in the next edition?

Are there any articles you feel should be replaced in the next edition? Why?

Are there other areas that you feel would utilize an Annual Edition?

May we contact you for editorial input?

May we quote you from above?

ANNUAL EDITIONS: PERSONAL GROWTH AND BEHAVIOR 95/96

BUSINESS REPLY MAIL

First Class   Permit No. 84   Guilford, CT

Postage will be paid by addressee

The Dushkin Publishing Group, Inc.
Sluice Dock
DPG **Guilford, Connecticut 06437**

No Postage
Necessary
if Mailed
in the
United States